The Mismeasure of Wealth

Historical Materialism Book Series

The Historical Materialism Book Series is a major publishing initiative of the radical left. The capitalist crisis of the twenty-first century has been met by a resurgence of interest in critical Marxist theory. At the same time, the publishing institutions committed to Marxism have contracted markedly since the high point of the 1970s. The Historical Materialism Book Series is dedicated to addressing this situation by making available important works of Marxist theory. The aim of the series is to publish important theoretical contributions as the basis for vigorous intellectual debate and exchange on the left.

The peer-reviewed series publishes original monographs, translated texts, and reprints of classics across the bounds of academic disciplinary agendas and across the divisions of the left. The series is particularly concerned to encourage the internationalization of Marxist debate and aims to translate significant studies from beyond the English-speaking world.

For a full list of titles in the Historical Materialism Book Series available in paperback from Haymarket Books, visit:
https://www.haymarketbooks.org/series_collections/1-historical-materialism

The Mismeasure of Wealth

Essays on Marx and Social Form

Patrick Murray

Haymarket Books
Chicago, IL

First published in 2016 by Brill Academic Publishers, The Netherlands

Published in paperback in 2017 by
Haymarket Books
P.O. Box 180165
Chicago, IL 60618
773-583-7884
www.haymarketbooks.org

ISBN: 978-1-60846-822-5

Trade distribution:
In the US, Consortium Book Sales, www.cbsd.com
In Canada, Publishers Group Canada, www.pgcbooks.ca
In the UK, Turnaround Publisher Services, www.turnaround-uk.com
All other countries, Ingram Publisher Services International, ips_intlsales@ingramcontent.com

Cover design by Jamie Kerry of Belle Étoile Studios and Ragina Johnson.

This book was published with the generous support of Lannan Foundation and the Wallace Action Fund.

Library of Congress Cataloging-in-Publication data is available.

For Jeanne

Contents

Preface

The Mismeasure of Wealth: Essays on Marx and Social Form brings together in a single volume most of what I have written on Marx and Marxian theory since the publication of my *Marx's Theory of Scientific Knowledge* in 1988. All but the introduction and 'The Grammar of Value: A Close Look at Marx's Critique of Samuel Bailey' have been previously published. Most of the chapters started out as papers written for the annual working conferences of the interdisciplinary research group the International Symposium on Marxian Theory (ISMT).[1] The essays, which focus on Marx as a theorist of specific social forms – in particular, capitalist ones – appear here in a rough conceptual order rather than in order of publication. There are several writings that primarily respond to the ideas of other interpreters of Marx: Chris Arthur; Enrique Dussell; James Furner; Geert Reuten and several proponents of the Temporal Single System Interpretation (TSSI), namely Alan Freeman, Andrew Kliman, Maya Gonzalez and Michael Posner. I have collected these under the heading 'Critical Engagements' at the end of the book.[2]

---

1 A few have been translated: 'Marx's "Truly Social" Labour Theory of Value: Part I, Abstract Labour in Marxian Value Theory' has been translated into Spanish by Mario L. Robles Baez as 'La dialectica de la conceptualizacion de la abstraccion del trabajo', in *Dialectica y Capital: Elementos para una reconstruccion de la critica de la economia politica*, edited by Mario L. Robles Baez (Mexico City: Universidad Autonoma Metropolitana, 2005), pp. 59–95. 'The Necessity of Money: How Hegel Helped Marx Surpass Ricardo's Theory of Value' has been translated into Spanish by Mario L. Robles Baez as 'La necesidad del dinero: como Hegel ayudo a Marx a superar la teoria del valor de Ricardo' in *Dialectica y Capital*, pp. 143–70. 'Redoubled Empiricism: The Place of Social Form and Formal Causality in Marxian Theory' has been translated into the Italian by Tommaso Redolfi Riva as '"Empirismo raddoppiato": Il posto della forma sociale e della causalita formale nella terorea marxiana', in *Marx in questione: Il dibattito 'aperto' dell'International Symposium on Marxian Theory*, edited by Riccardo Bellofiore and Roberto Fineschi (Naples: La Citta del Sole: 2009), pp. 119–50. 'The Place of "The Results of the Immediate Production Process" in *Capital*', has been translated into Chinese as part of a translation of *Re-reading Marx: New Perspectives after the Critical Edition*, edited by Riccardo Bellofiore and Roberto Fineschi, Basingstoke, Hampshire: Palgrave Macmillan, 2009.

2 Parts I and II of 'Marx's "Truly Social" Labour Theory of Value' are, among other things, a reply to Reuten 1993 and 'Unavoidable Crises: Reflections on Backhaus and the Development of Marx's Value-Form Theory in the *Grundrisse*' is in part a reply to Hans-Georg Backhaus's 'On the Dialectics of the Value-Form', but I include all three with the essays in the first part of the present volume as Chapters Four, Five and Seven, respectively.

Several terms have been put forward to characterise various streams in the renewal of research into Marx and Marxian theory beginning in the late 1960s and the 1970s. They include 'Hegelian Marxism', 'systematic dialectics', 'new dialectics' and 'value-form theory'. In his reinterpretation of Marx's critical theory, Moishe Postone criticises 'Traditional Marxism' for adopting the classical labour theory of value, which treats the categories of value and of the labour that produces value as applicable across history rather than being specific to capitalist societies.[3] 'New dialectics' and 'systematic dialectics' are more recent phrases; they focus on method in contrast to the older, broader rubric of 'Hegelian Marxism'.[4] These three terms encompass interpreters with divergent views on Hegel, Marx's criticisms of Hegel and the actual relationships between Hegel and Marx.[5] In an exchange with Geert Reuten, I argue for the distinctiveness of Marx's experientially based systematic dialectics, which departs from the 'presuppositionlessness' of Hegelian systematic dialectics.[6] As for 'value-form' theory, I argue that its proponents diverge. Michael Eldred and Marnie Hanlon go one way; in their view, value is constituted solely in the exchange of commodities for money. Value-form theory is sometimes mistaken for this one-sided view. The other direction, which I attribute to Marx and defend, sees value as being co-constituted across production and exchange.[7]

My work can be associated with all these labels, but, with the subtitle 'essays on Marx and social form', I want to emphasise a broader consideration, that of attending to historically specific social forms, a subject matter that characterises the best recent work in Marxian theory. I agree with Chris Arthur, who coined the term 'new dialectics':

> While the mainstream position in Marxist theory has read concepts such as value, socially necessary labour time and abstract labour, largely in a technical sense, I adhere to the growing minority that centralises the idea of *social form*, insisting that all such categories have to be explicated

---

3 Postone 1993. I mention only those streams most closely related to the interpretative approach taken in the present essays. There are others, including Analytical Marxism, Sraffian or neo-Ricardian Marxism, Althusserian Marxism, postmodern Marxism and post-Marxism.

4 See the introductions to Arthur 2002a and to Albritton and Simoulidis 2003.

5 For some assessments see Burns and Fraser (eds.) 2000 and Moseley and Smith (eds.) 2014.

6 See Murray 2000a, 2000b and 2002c, included in the present volume as Chapters Four, Five and Eighteen, respectively, and Reuten 2000.

7 See 'Avoiding Bad Abstractions: A Defence of Co-constitutive Value-Form Theory', included as Chapter 15 in the present volume.

> within an account of specifically capitalist social forms of production and exchange.[8]

What Arthur refers to as 'the mainstream position in Marxist theory' matches what Postone criticises as 'Traditional Marxism'. It is Marx's attention to historically specific social forms – in particular the constitutive forms of the capitalist mode of production, the 'value forms' – that separates Marx and Marxian theory from traditional Marxism.[9] Here, in his investigation into the commodity, value, money, surplus value, wage labour and capital, lies the heart of *Capital* and the basis of Marx's singular relevance for critical social theory today.[10] These social forms make up the grammar of commercial societies, but, today, where do we look to learn this grammar? Its topics lie outside the horizons of mainstream social theories, whether in social philosophy or social science, for they pay no heed to the specific social forms constitutive of the capitalist mode of production.

---

8 Arthur 2002a, p. 39. The topic of abstract labour is complex and controversial.

9 'The value-form of the product of labour is the most abstract, but also the most universal form of the bourgeois mode of production; by that fact it stamps the bourgeois mode of production as a particular kind of social production of a historical and transitory character. If then we make the mistake of treating it as the eternal natural form of social production, we necessarily overlook the specificity of the value-form, and consequently of the commodity-form together with its further developments, the money form, the capital form, etc.' (Marx 1976a, p. 174, n. 33).

10 I intend to explore the scope of Marx's significance for social theory in a future book, *Capital's Reach: How Capital Shapes and Subsumes*.

Acknowledgements

In the fall of 1990 a thick letter-sized envelope showed up in my office mailbox. The sender was Fred Moseley, a member of the Economics Department at Mount Holyoke College. The letter was an invitation to participate in a week-long conference on Marx's method in *Capital*. It would be a working conference with eight participants: three other philosophers, Chris Arthur, Paul Mattick Jr and Tony Smith, along with three economists, Martha Campbell, Guglielmo (Mino) Carchedi and Geert Reuten, in addition to Fred Moseley. What was originally intended as a one-off event became an annual one as the International Symposium on Marxian Theory (ISMT) took off. Over the years, a couple of people left and several people joined the group; Riccardo Bellofiore joined early on and then Roberto Fineschi, Nicola Taylor, Andrew Brown and Guido Starosta. The remarkable collaboration that I have had a share in as member of this interdisciplinary research group made this book possible. I want to thank all the members of the ISMT for their generosity, warmth, critical-mindedness and dedication to the work. I have learned so much from them. Thank you Fred, Tony, Martha, Chris, Geert, Riccardo, Roberto, Andrew, Guido, Paul, Mino, and Nicky.

Nine books collecting papers from ISMT conferences have been published. All nine of my essays from those books are included in the present volume. I want to thank all the editors of those books for their work. Riccardo Bellofiore and Roberto Fineschi edited a book of articles by ISMT authors that had been translated into Italian. Essays by Chris Arthur, Geert Reuten and me were translated into Spanish by Mario L. Baez Robles and included in a book that he edited. *Re-reading Marx: New Perspectives after the Critical Edition*, edited by Riccardo Bellofiore and Roberto Fineschi, Basingstoke, Hampshire: Palgrave Macmillan (2009) has been translated into Chinese. I thank all the translators and editors who worked on these books.

Many other researchers on Marx and Marxian theory have participated in ISMT conferences or contributed to books based on a conference. The former group, the participants, include Juan Iñigo Carrera, Jean Cartelier, Enrique Dussel, Howard Engelskirchen, Roberto Finelli, Duncan Foley, Claus Germer, Joseph Halevi, Makoto Itoh, Michael A. Lebowitz, Iren Levina, Pitchit Likitkijsomboon, Mark Meaney, Abelardo Medina, Anitra Nelson, Mario Baez Robles, Regina Roth, Jeanne Schuler, Peter Thomas, Massimiliano (Max) Tomba, John Weeks, Amy Wendling, and Michael Williams. The latter group includes Gastón Caligaris, Suzanne de Brunhoff, Igor Hanzel, Rolf Hecker, Michael Heinrich and Costas Lapavitsas. I want to thank all these contributors as well.

Several of my teachers have had such a lasting influence on me that I want to recognise them for helping to make this book possible. James Collins (deceased) supervised my dissertation and taught me much about working as a historian of modern philosophy; his presence is enduring. Paul Piccone (deceased), with whom I studied Marx's *Grundrisse* when the full English translation appeared (Dan Dahlstrom and Jeanne Schuler were also in that class), brought the journal *Telos* to St. Louis, which opened up new worlds. Paul encouraged and helped me to study in Frankfurt. In Frankfurt I took advantage of the opportunity to learn from many teachers; I would like to thank Rüdiger Bubner for his kindness to me as a foreign student and for all he taught me in his two-semester course on Hegel's *Science of Logic*.

Five philosophers whom I came to know in St. Louis took the kind of interest in my work that has been a great resource and support over decades. Albert William Levi (deceased), who directed my wife Jeanne Schuler's dissertation on Hegel at Washington University, was gracious in opening up his home and his broad mind to us. Peter Fuss let me sit in on his course at University of Missouri, St. Louis, on Hegel's *Phenomenology of Spirit* in the early 1970s, where I was first exposed to his and (later) John Dobbins' translation of the *Phenomenology*. We just kept talking about Hegel, Kant, Rousseau, Arendt, Marx and more. James Marsh was a reader of my dissertation, and we were in a Marx study group together in St. Louis while he was teaching at St. Louis University. Since he moved to Fordham University, I have continued to learn from his phenomenological approach to critical theory, and I am thankful for his interest in my thinking. Tom Jeannot, who wrote his dissertation on Marx under Marsh's supervision and has kept up his research on Marx, has taken an interest in my work since our days as graduate students at St. Louis University; I am grateful for Tom's exuberant intelligence. The Reverend John F. Kavanaugh, S.J., who, sadly, died before this book project was completed, was an inspiration and an unfailing advocate for my work as well as the work that Jeanne Schuler and I have done together. He is sorely missed.

Taking up research into Marx in the mid-1970s, I was greatly aided by what had already been written by researchers including Hans-Georg Backhaus, Lucio Colletti, Hans-Jürgen Krahl, Helmut Reichelt, Roman Rosdolsky, I.I. Rubin and Zindrich Zelený. I am indebted to their work.

Over the decades during which this book has been taking shape, I have benefitted from various interactions at conferences and elsewhere with other researchers into Hegel, Marx and critical social theory; among them, I want to acknowledge and thank Christine Achinger, Rob Albritton, Pete Amato, Kevin B. Anderson, Dennis Badeen, Jacques Bidet, George Caffentzis, Andrew Chitty, John Clegg, Daniel Dahlstrom, Gareth Dale, Fred Evans, Norm Fischer,

Joseph Fracchia, Peter Hudis, Andrew Kliman, Michael R. Krätke, Bill Martin, Joe McCarney (deceased), George McCarthy, Tom McCarthy, Martin McIvor, David McNally, John Milios, Bertell Ollman, Nicole Pepperell, Anne Pomeroy, Will Roberts, Alfredo Saad-Filho, Sean Sayers and Gil Skillman. I have also gained from conversations over the years with members of the St. Louis community I once lived in: Mary Beth Gallagher, Michael Bartz, Mark Neilsen, Judy Gallagher, Cathy Nolan, Michael Goeke, Trish Curtis, Sharon McMullen, and Julie Kerksick, as well as from ongoing conversations with friends John Duggan, Wolfgang Richter-Girard and Dan Semrad.

As I was completing this book, thanks to a generous invitation from Hohai University in Nanjing, China, I had the opportunity to present and discuss some key ideas from this book with students and faculty at Hohai University. I want to thank Hohai's Vice-President Tang Hongwu and faculty members of Hohai University's Institute of Marxism Yu Dahaui, Wu Jing and Zheng Libing for the exchange of ideas and their gracious hospitality. While in Nanjing, I was given the opportunity to meet Zhang Yibing and colleagues in the Nanjing University Department of Philosophy and the Nanjing University Marxist Research Centre and to make a presentation followed by a discussion. I am grateful to Nanjing University and to Zhang Yibing and his colleagues for that opportunity.

It has been my good fortune to work in a diverse, supportive and intellectually alive philosophy department. I am grateful to my Creighton colleagues in philosophy: J.J. Abrams, Michael Brown, Elizabeth Cooke, Randolph Feezell, Patricia Fleming (now Provost at St. Mary's College), Kevin Graham, Jeffrey Hause, Anne Ozar, Chris Pliatska, the Reverend M. Ross Romero, S.J., Jeanne Schuler, Eugene Selk, William O. Stephens, Amy Wendling, Richard White and Jinmei Yuan. My colleague Jack Carlson died suddenly before this book was completed. I miss him and our conversations. For most of the years that this book was in the making, Margaret (Peggy) Troy was office manager for the department; I am grateful for her attention to detail, from which I learned much. I would like to thank two Creighton colleagues outside the department for their interest, ideas and support, Fidel Fajardo-Acosta, of the English Department, and Marong Jiang, director of Asian World Centre.

To the Creighton College of Arts and Sciences, I am grateful for sabbaticals, funding for travel and for hosting two ISMT conferences at Creighton University. In particular, I want to thank the Deans and Associate Deans who have generously helped: the Rev. Michael Proterra, S.J. (deceased); the Rev. Albert Agresti, S.J. (deceased), Dr Patricia Fleming, Dr Timothy Austin; Dr Robert Kennedy (deceased), and Ms Rose Hill.

I am grateful to Creighton University Graduate School and to Dr Gail Jensen, Dean of the Graduate School, for a grant to support the preparation of the present book. Thank you to Barb Bittner and Amy Berendzen for expert technical assistance.

Editors of the journal *Historical Materialism* took an interest in my work when the journal was in formation. I am very grateful for their interest and for all the encouragement they have continued to provide. I especially want to thank editors Sebastian Budgen, Peter Thomas, Alberto Toscano, Guido Starosta, Jim Kincaid, Sam Ashman and Martin McIvor. I owe special thanks to Peter Thomas and Sebastian Budgen for the encouragement they have given me to bring this book to press. Thank you Peter and Sebastian. In copy-editing and preparing this book for publication, Danny Hayward has been patient and immensely helpful; thank you, Danny.

In the fall of 1975, I met Moishe Postone at the Goethe University in Frankfurt, (West) Germany. We began a conversation on Hegel, Marx, critical theory, social movements and history that we have pursued ever since. I am thankful to have gained much from his knowledge and force of mind, and from the depth of his vision.

This book would not have been possible without years of love and support that I received from my family, first of all, my step-father, George Stehney, my mother, Muriel Stehney (both deceased), and my in-laws, Mary Schuler and Ted Schuler (both deceased). My three sisters, Cathy, Sue and Joyce, along with their husbands, Scott, Paul and Kevin, have been loyal, loving and generous. I am lucky to have such sisters. Our children John Patrick (JP), David and Savita have grown up through the years that this book was being written; they have brought excitement and joy into our life. To my wife and philosophy colleague, Jeanne Schuler, I am thankful that she chose to live her life with me, to form a family, and to think together. All of the chapters in this book are better because of her close reading and her ideas. She keeps teaching me to think and to realise why thinking well is so important. I dedicate this book to her.

Notes on Chapters

Part 1: The Essays

1. 'Value, Money and Capital in Hegel and Marx', in *Karl Marx and Contemporary Philosophy*, edited by Andrew Chitty and Martin McIvor (Basingstoke, Hampshire: Palgrave Macmillan, 2009), pp. 174–87, with the kind permission of Palgrave Macmillan.

2. 'Redoubled Empiricism: The Place of Social Form and Formal Causality in Marxian Theory', in *New Investigations of Marx's Method*, edited by Fred Moseley and Martha Campbell (Atlantic Highlands, N.J.: Humanities Press, 1997), pp. 38–65, with the kind permission of Humanity Books.

3. 'Things Fall Apart: Historical and Systematic Dialectics and the Critique of Political Economy', in *New Dialectics and Political Economy*, edited by Rob Albritton and John Simoulidis (Basingstoke, Hampshire: Palgrave Macmillan, 2002), pp. 150–72, with the kind permission of Palgrave Macmillan.

4. 'Marx's "Truly Social" Labour Theory of Value: Part I, Abstract Labour in Marxian Value Theory', *Historical Materialism*, Number 6 (Summer 2000), pp. 27–65. Geert Reuten's reply, 'The Interconnection of Systematic Dialectics and Historical Materialism', appears in *Historical Materialism*, Number 7 (Winter 2000), pp. 137–65.

5. 'Marx's "Truly Social" Labour Theory of Value: Part II, How is Labour that Is Under the Sway of Capital *Actually* Abstract?,' *Historical Materialism*, Number 7 (Winter 2000), pp. 99–136.

6. 'The Grammar of Value: A Close Look at Marx's Critique of Samuel Bailey', previously unpublished manuscript.

7. 'Unavoidable Crises: Reflections on Backhaus and the Development of Marx's Value-Form Theory in the *Grundrisse*', in *Marx's Laboratory. Critical Interpretations of the 'Grundrisse'*, edited by Riccardo Bellofiore, Peter Thomas, and Guido Starosta (Leiden/Boston: Brill, 2013).

8. 'The Necessity of Money: How Hegel Helped Marx Surpass Ricardo's Theory of Value', in *Marx's Method in 'Capital'*, edited by Fred Moseley (Atlan-

tic Highlands, N.J.: Humanities Press, 1993), pp. 37–61, with the kind permission of Humanity Books.

9. 'Money as Displaced Social Form: Why Value cannot be Independent of Price', in *Marx's Theory of Money: Modern Appraisals*, edited by Fred Moseley (Basingstoke, Hampshire: Palgrave Macmillan, 2005), pp. 50–64, with the kind permission of Palgrave Macmillan.

10. 'The Social and Material Transformation of Production by Capital: Formal and Real Subsumption in *Capital*, Volume I', in *The Constitution of Capital: Essays on Volume I of Marx's 'Capital'*, edited by Riccardo Bellofiore and Nicola Taylor (Basingstoke, Hampshire: Palgrave Macmillan, 2004), pp. 243–73, with the kind permission of Palgrave Macmillan.

11. 'The Place of "The Results of the Immediate Production Process" in *Capital*', in *Re-reading Marx: New Perspectives after the Critical Edition*, edited by Riccardo Bellofiore and Roberto Fineschi (Basingstoke, Hampshire: Palgrave Macmillan, 2009), pp. 163–77, with the kind permission of Palgrave Macmillan.

12. 'Beyond the "Commerce and Industry" Picture of Capital', in *The Circulation of Capital: Essays on Volume Two of Marx's 'Capital,'* edited by Chris Arthur and Geert Reuten (London: Macmillan, 1998), pp. 33–66, with the kind permission of Palgrave Macmillan.

13. 'The Secret of Capital's Self-Valorisation "Laid Bare": How Hegel Helped Marx to Overturn Ricardo's Theory of Profit', in *Marx's 'Capital' and Hegel's 'Logic'*, edited by Fred Moseley and Tony Smith (Leiden/Boston: Brill, 2014).

14. 'The Illusion of the Economic: The Trinity Formula and the "religion of everyday life"', in *The Culmination of Capital: Essays on Volume III of Marx's 'Capital'*, edited by Martha Campbell and Geert Reuten (Basingstoke, Hampshire: Palgrave, 2002), pp. 246–72, with the kind permission of Palgrave Macmillan.

Part 2: Critical Engagements

15. 'Avoiding Bad Abstractions: A Defence of Co-constitutive Value-Form Theory', a response to three essays by Alan Freeman, Andrew Kliman, and Maya Gonzalez and Michael Posner, *Critique of Political Economy*, Volume 1 (2011), pp. 217–48, with the kind permission of the primarily online journal *Critique of Political Economy*.

16. 'The New Giant's Staircase', a review essay and contribution to a symposium on Christopher J. Arthur's book *The New Dialectic and Marx's 'Capital'*, *Historical Materialism*, 13.2 (2005), pp. 61–83.

17. 'In Defence of the "Third Thing Argument": A Reply to James Furner's "Marx's Critique of Samuel Bailey"', in *Historical Materialism*, Volume 14, Issue 2 (2006), pp. 149–68.

18. 'Reply to Geert Reuten', *Historical Materialism*, Volume 10, Issue 1 (2002), pp. 155–76.

19. 'The Trouble with Ricardian Marxism: Comments on "The Four Drafts of *Capital*: Towards a New Interpretation of the Dialectical Thought of Marx", by Enrique Dussel', *Rethinking Marxism*, Volume 14, Number 3 (2002), pp. 114–22, with the kind permission of the journal *Rethinking Marxism*.

Introduction: Putting the Spotlight on Social Form and Purpose

The distinctive features of the present essays arise from understanding Marx as an investigator of historically specific social forms, as a historical materialist. Already in the *German Ideology*, Marx and Engels emphasise that a mode of production involves a distinctive way of life:

> This mode of production [*Weise der Produktion*] must not be considered simply as being the reproduction of the physical existence of the individuals. Rather it is a definite form of activity of these individuals, a definite form of expressing their life, a definite *mode of life* [*Lebensweise*] on their part.[1]

This is the simple, profound lesson of historical materialism: there is no production in general; production always has a specific social form and purpose, and the form and purpose of production matter in many ways.[2] A particular way of life possesses a particular moral character. Morality for Marx is like the weather, the question is not will we have any but what will it be. In the opening remarks of the *Grundrisse*, Marx encapsulates the insight of historical materialism: 'All production is appropriation of nature by an individual within and through a particular form of society'.[3] This general insight of historical materialism guides *Capital*, where Marx immediately calls attention to the specific social character of wealth and production in capitalism and keeps it in focus throughout the book.

---

1 Marx and Engels 1976b, p. 31. Production, then, always has a double character: '[t]he production of life, both of one's own in labour and of fresh life in procreation, now appears as a twofold relation: on the one hand as a natural, on the other as a social relation – social in the sense that it denotes the co-operation of several individuals, no matter under what conditions, in what manner and to what end' (Marx and Engels 1976b, p. 43).

2 Martha Campbell observes, 'property relations are relations for the collective use of both the elements and results of production. This collective use assumes different forms, each with its own goal ... Marx's case ... against economics ... is that satisfying needs is the means for realizing the goal of a particular way of life' (Campbell 1993b, p. 146). 'Economics' assumes either that its object is a general way of life or else that the specific forms and goals of different ways of life are insignificant. Neither assumption is tenable.

3 Marx 1973, p. 86.

When Marx subtitles *Capital* 'a critique of political economy', he points to political economy's failure to make specific social forms ingredient to its basic concepts. The opening sentence of *Capital* is a reproach to Adam Smith: 'The wealth of societies in which the capitalist mode of production prevails appears as an "immense collection of commodities"; the individual commodity appears as its elementary form'.[4] Later in *Capital*, in discussing the division of labour, one of Smith's signature topics, Marx makes his criticism more explicit, quoting Smith's celebrated title. He points out that the division of labour in manufacture is merely a method of 'augmenting the self-valorization of capital – usually described as social wealth, "wealth of nations", etc.'[5] Smith reduces the socially specific phenomenon of accumulated capital to 'wealth', which is like treating a magnet as a mere piece of metal. Marx's critique of political economy observes that, since there is no production in general – there are only historically and socially specific modes of production – there is no economics in general.[6]

When thought to be a generally applicable social science, the enterprise of economics is misconceived from the start. John Stuart Mill recognises that production is a social phenomenon and that diverse human pursuits affect it, but he sets aside all motives other than the pursuit of 'wealth' in defining political economy as 'The science which traces the laws of such of the phenomena of society as arise from the combined operations of mankind for the production of wealth, in so far as those phenomena are not modified by the pursuit of any other object'.[7] The 'wealth' that humans pursue always has a definite social form, as does the manner in which they combine to produce that wealth, but these topics lie beyond the horizon of Mill's thinking. Lionel Robbins's neoclassical definition of economics, unlike Mill's, does not specify its subject as a social phenomenon and does not select from among human motivations: 'Economics is the science which studies human behavior as a relationship between ends and scarce means which have alternative uses'.[8] A social theory, whether philosophical or scientific, whose fundamental concepts omit the social forms constitutive of a particular mode of production – and way of life – falsifies its subject matter from the first.

---

4 Marx 1976a, p. 125.

5 Marx 1967a, p. 486.

6 'Political economy has to do with the specific social forms of wealth or rather of the production of wealth' (Marx 1973, p. 852).

7 Mill 1994, p. 54.

8 Robbins 1994, p. 85.

Where Smith's *Wealth of Nations* presents itself as applicable to all nations and times, regardless of the social form or purpose of their wealth, Marx makes it clear from the start that his investigation concerns a historically specific mode of production, the capitalist. This mode produces not 'wealth', not wealth in general, but wealth in a specific social form, the commodity. As the argument of *Capital* unfolds, the commodity proves to be commodity capital, that is, a commodity carrying surplus-value, which reveals that profit is the specific purpose of capitalist production. The commodity is fraught with momentous consequences for the way of life in those societies where the capitalist mode of production dominates.[9] As a fetish, a bearer of purchasing power, that peculiarly abstract social power, the commodity 'is a very strange thing, abounding in metaphysical subtleties and theological niceties'.[10] Because it assumes that the commodity owner is a free and equal person, the commodity-form possesses a revolutionary egalitarian power, a power that continues to exert itself.[11] The commodity is ominously crisis-laden: by splitting exchange into independent acts of buying and selling, the commodity lays the basis for commercial crises. Commodities are in love with money, but Marx reminds us, 'the course of true love never did run smooth'.[12] Where overproduction leaves commodities unsold, the romance between commodities and money goes to the rocks. Marx points to Ricardo's failure to figure in the forms characteristic of capitalist production in explaining why Ricardo mistakenly denies the possibility of general overproduction: 'In order to prove that capitalist production cannot lead to general crises, all its conditions and distinct forms, all its principles and specific features – in short *capitalist production* itself – are denied'.[13] The first of those

9 Georg Lukács wrote in the opening paragraph of his seminal essay 'Reification and the Consciousness of the Proletariat', 'At this stage in the history of mankind there is no problem that does not ultimately lead back to that question and there is no solution that could not be found in the solution to the riddle of commodity-*structure*' (Lukács 1971, p. 83).

10 Marx 1976a, p. 163.

11 In presupposing the social roles of buyer and seller, the commodity form presupposes the moral and legal category of the person: 'In order that these objects may enter into relation with each other as commodities, their guardians must place themselves in relation to one another as persons whose will resides in those objects, and must behave in such a way that each does not appropriate the commodity of the other, and alienate his own, except through an act to which both parties consent' (Marx 1976a, p. 178).

12 Marx 1976a, p. 202.

13 Marx 1968b, p. 501. Marx later comments, '[t]his fiction arises entirely from the inability to grasp the specific form of bourgeois production and this inability in turn arises from the obsession that bourgeois production is production as such, just like a man who believes

features is that wealth is produced in the commodity-form. These conceptual failures of political economy are, as Marx repeatedly observes, indicative of a faulty way of thinking.

1 Beyond the 'Bourgeois Horizon': Concepts of a Different Kind

As Francis Bacon observed, 'things in themselves new will yet be apprehended with reference to what is old'.[14] Marx is widely misunderstood because most of us not only lack the needed concepts but also the philosophical mind-set needed to grasp them. Bertell Ollman began his study of Marx's concept of alienation with the observation: 'the most formidable hurdle facing all readers of Marx is his "peculiar" use of words'.[15] Ollman recalled Vilfredo Pareto's remark that Marx's words are like bats: they can be taken for birds or mice. However, the difficulty in coming to grips with Marx's terms lies, generally, not in their ambiguity or instability; the difficulty is that his concepts are of a kind that lies beyond the horizons of many interpreters. Ollman quotes Engels as saying:

> It is self-evident that where things and their interrelations are conceived, not as fixed, but as changing, their mental images, the ideas, are likewise subject to change and transformation, and they are not encapsulated in rigid definitions, but are developed in their historical or logical process of formulation.[16]

Engels lends more credence to Pareto's remark than it deserves. Engels slurs the differences between change and development and between historical and 'logical' (conceptual) development. Developing (or transforming) a concept is not the same as switching it for an improved one. A definition that has developed is not 'rigid', but its development makes explicit what is already implicit in it. When Marx develops (or transforms) concepts, as he does throughout *Capital*, he is not being shifty; he is demonstrating what is presup-

in a particular religion and sees it as *the* religion, and everything outside of it only as *false* religions' (Marx 1968b, p. 529). 'The illusion of the economic', the misconception that there is an economy in general – and that capitalism is this economy – seals off the concepts needed to grasp capitalist crises.

14 Bacon 1994, p. 52.

15 Ollman 1971, p. 3.

16 Ollman 1971, p. 4. See Arthur 1997 for a criticism of Engels' conflation of the logical and historical orders.

posed by initial concepts that are devised for development. As he develops concepts in *Capital*, Marx does not retract his initial definitions; he takes advantage of their openness to development.[17] Over and over, Marx cites the failure of the political economists to develop concepts – which he attributes to the horizon of their thinking – as resulting in their incapacity to comprehend properly the workings of the capitalist mode of production. One such failure is political economy's inability to work out the conceptual difference between surplus value and profit and the necessity of the transformation of surplus value into profit: 'This whole BLUNDER of Ricardo's ... spring[s] from his failure to distinguish between *surplus-value* and *profit*; and in general his treatment of *definitions of form* is crude and uncomprehending, just as that of the other economists'.[18] Marx's way of thinking about concepts, though perplexing to many interpreters, is responsible for his advances over the tradition of political economy.

Marx challenges the 'bourgeois horizon', which he identifies as the philosophical orientation that structures political economy, much of modern philosophy and many forms of socialism.[19] Marx's critique of the 'bourgeois horizon' renews Hegel's criticism of the mind-set of the 'reflective understanding' [*Verstand*].[20] In the patterns of bourgeois thinking, Marx finds a series of bifurc-

---

17 I do not say that there are no changes in Marx's terminology or concepts; there are. But these are ordinary consequences of working out an original scientific conception. See also Dussell 2001, especially p. 16. One troublesome example is that, in earlier works (including *A Contribution to the Critique of Political Economy*), Marx does not make the terminological distinction between exchange-value and value that he draws first in the second edition of *Capital* (Marx 1976a, pp. 125–7). In earlier texts Marx uses only the term 'exchange-value', even where he has in play the two concepts that he distinguishes in *Capital* as exchange-value and value. See the editors' note 4 on pp. 455–6 of Marx 1988a.

18 Marx 1989, p. 439. On this topic, see the chapter 'The Secret of Capital's Self-Valorisation "Laid Bare"', included in the present volume as Chapter 13.

19 Marx identifies Locke as '"the philosopher" *par excellence*' of the later political economy (Marx 1976a, p. 513) and with the bourgeois manner of thinking generally: 'John Locke ... championed the new bourgeoisie in every way – he took the side of the manufacturers against the working classes and the paupers, the merchants against the old-fashioned usurers, the financial aristocracy against governments that were in debt; he even demonstrated in a separate work [*An Essay on Human Understanding*] that the bourgeois way of thinking is the normal human way of thinking' (Marx 1970a, p. 77). Of Ricardo, Marx observes that '[a]lthough encompassed by this bourgeois horizon [*Obgleich umfangen von diesem bürgerlichen Horizont*], Ricardo analyses bourgeois economy, whose deeper layers differ essentially from its surface appearance, with such theoretical acumen that Lord Brougham could say of him: "Mr. Ricardo seemed as if he had dropped from another planet"' (Marx 1970a, pp. 60–1).

20 One indication of Marx's sweeping criticism of the 'bourgeois horizon' is his enthusiasm,

ations: mind versus world, subjective versus objective, form versus content, concept versus object, passive versus active and immediate versus mediated.[21] The factoring philosophy – characteristic of the bourgeois mind-set – which rashly treats as separable whatever can be distinguished in thought, trades in these dualisms.[22] Marx's first thesis on Feuerbach shows that the target of his criticism is not so much German idealism or the previous materialism as it is the purist split that yields the two:

> The chief defect of all previous materialism (that of Feuerbach included) is that things [*Gegenstand*], reality, sensuousness are conceived only in the form of the *object, or of contemplation* [*Anschauung*], but not as *sensuous human activity, practice* [*Praxis*], not subjectively. Hence, in contradistinction to materialism, the *active* side was set forth abstractly by idealism – which, of course, does not know real, sensuous activity as such.[23]

---

which he shared with Hegel, for Aristotle, that 'giant of thinking' [*Denkriese*] (Marx 1976a, p. 175, n. 35). See Meikle 1985 and McCarthy 1990 and 1994. Thinkers functioning within the 'bourgeois horizon' generally are hostile to Aristotle.

21 The bifurcation between form and content is one of many that Hegel rejects: 'Form and content are a pair of determinations that are frequently employed by the reflective understanding, and, moreover, mainly in such a way that the content is considered as what is essential and independent, while the form, on the contrary, is inessential and dependent. Against this, however, it must be remarked that in fact both of them are equally essential' (Hegel 1991b, §133, addition, p. 202). Marx employs this thought over and over in criticising the political economists.

22 What David Hume calls a 'distinction of reason' describes what can be separated for the purpose of analysis but cannot exist separately. Borrowing from George Berkeley's critique of abstract ideas, Hume explains a 'distinction of reason' in relation to colour and shape: '[a]fter a little more practice ... we begin to distinguish the figure from the colour by a *distinction of reason*; that is, we consider the figure and colour together, since they are in effect the same and indistinguishable; but still view them in different aspects, according to the resemblances, of which they are susceptible' (Hume 1978, p. 25). Identifying a 'distinction of reason' requires a phenomenological judgment of necessity, in this case that figure and colour are inseparable. The factoring philosophy is heedlessly analytic, drawing distinctions but overlooking the phenomenological inquiry needed to distinguish between what is actually separable and what is only conceptually distinguishable. Jeanne Schuler and I develop the idea of the factoring philosophy in our book manuscript *False Moves: Basic Problems with Philosophy* (in progress).

23 Marx, 1976c, p. 3. I take the term 'purist split' from Collins 1972, pp. 14–22. In a remarkable anticipation of his mature conception of capital, Marx includes Hegel in this criticism of idealism, and he develops this line of thought in the final Paris manuscript, on the critique

Marx puts the accent on 'actual, sensuous activity' (praxis) precisely because action is worldly; action repels the dualisms that characterise the 'bourgeois horizon'.[24] Whether in philosophy or political economy, Marx presses his criticism of purist – as opposed to 'real, sensuous' – conceptions of human activity.[25] In his 1844 critique of Hegel's philosophy in general, Marx finds a purist conception of human activity in Hegel: 'The rich, living, sensuous, concrete activity of self-objectification is therefore reduced to its mere abstraction, *absolute negativity* – an abstraction which is again fixed as such and considered as an independent activity – as sheer activity [*Tätigkeit schlechthin*]'.[26] Late in life, Marx charges the first plank of the socialist *Gotha Programme*, that 'labour is the source of all wealth', with trading in 'bourgeois phrases'. He points out: 'Labour is *not the source* of all wealth. *Nature* is just as much the source of use values (and it is surely of such that material wealth consists!) as is labour'. To claim that labour is the source of all wealth is to follow the bifurcating bour-

of Hegel's philosophy as a whole. Though Marx stuck with this critical interpretation, Hegel's joint criticism of 'subjective idealism' and 'so-called realism' closely matches Marx's first thesis: 'It is just as one-sided to represent analysis as though there were nothing in the subject matter that was not *imported* into it, as it is one-sided to suppose that the resulting determinations are merely *extracted* from it. The former view, as everyone knows, is enunciated by subjective idealism, which takes the activity of cognition in analysis to be merely a one-sided *positing*, beyond which the thing-in-itself remains concealed; the other view belongs to so-called realism which comprehends the subjective Notion as an empty identity that *receives* the thought determinations into itself *from outside*' (Hegel 1969, p. 788). I believe that Marx's precocious identification of Hegel's absolute idealism with the logic of capital is one factor that led him to persist in a caricature of Hegel's philosophy.

24 Opposing the bifurcating way of thinking that characterises the 'bourgeois horizon' with a phenomenology of actuality is one of the most important ways that Marx, like Hegel, retrieves the legacy of Aristotle's philosophy from its modern critics. Aristotle comments on splitting soul from body or matter from form: 'That is why we can dismiss as unnecessary the question whether the soul and the body are one: it is as though we were to ask whether the wax and its shape are one, or generally the matter of a thing and that of which it is the matter. Unity has many senses … but the proper one is that of actuality' (from *De Anima* II.1, 412b6–9; cf. II.1, 413a3–7, and II.2, 414a19–28, as quoted in Lear 1988). In his youth, Marx translated Aristotle's *De Anima* into German, but the manuscript is lost.

25 Purist thinking – the notion that something is purely subjective (say, an intention or a value judgment), or purely objective (say, what is given immediately), or else a mixture of the purely subjective and purely objective – underlies factoring philosophy. The factoring philosophy, which always looks to factor out the purely subjective from the purely objective, and the purist thinking it presupposes, establishes the bourgeois horizon.

26 Marx 1964a, p. 189.

geois train of thought by 'fancifully ascribing *supernatural creative power* to labour'.[27] Purist conceptions of thought and action, wherever they turn up, belong to the 'bourgeois horizon' that Marx's worldly philosophy of praxis aims to overcome.

Marx uses the term 'bourgeois horizon' in criticising Proudhon, who conjoined political economy, idealist philosophy and socialism in his book *The Philosophy of Poverty*, to which Marx replied with *The Poverty of Philosophy*. Marx writes to Annenkov that Proudhon 'does not rise above the bourgeois horizon'.[28] Throughout his lifelong engagement with classical political economy, Marx points out the ways that being confined to the 'bourgeois horizon' incapacitates that political economy. For example:

> Yet even its best representatives remained more or less trapped in the world of illusion their criticism had dissolved, and nothing else is possible from the bourgeois standpoint; they all fell therefore more or less into inconsistencies, half-truths and unresolved contradictions.[29]

In his preface to the English edition of *Capital* Volume I, Engels points up the self-imposed confinement of political economy:

> Every new aspect of a science involves a revolution in the technical terms of that science ... Political economy has generally been content to take, just as they were, the terms of commercial and industrial life, and to operate with them, entirely failing to see that by so doing it confined itself within the narrow circle of ideas expressed by those terms ... It is, however, self-evident that a theory which views modern capitalist production as a mere passing stage in the economic history of mankind, must make use of terms different from those habitual to writers who look upon that form of production as imperishable and final.[30]

In his last observation Engels perceptively connects historical materialism with the need for a new kind of concept. Paul Mattick Jr, puts the point this way, 'Marx's critique – his "scientific revolution" – therefore involved not merely a reworking of economic categories but the construction of another set of

---

27 Marx 1966a, p. 3.

28 Marx 1963a, p. 190.

29 Marx 1981, p. 969.

30 Engels 1976, p. 111. Ollman cites this passage (Ollman 1971, pp. 3–4).

concepts, explicitly social and historical ones'.[31] Marx is often misinterpreted or misused because his ideas are forced into conceptual moulds that he set out to break.

Not all of Marx's concepts are 'explicitly social and historical' in nature, however.[32] Marx has a place for generally applicable concepts, such as use value or the labour process, but there is no actual production in general:

> All epochs of production have certain common traits, common characteristics. *Production in general* is an abstraction, but a rational abstraction in so far as it really brings out and fixes the common element ... If there is no production in general, then there is also no general production.[33]

We can make some generally applicable observations about production – for example, every labour process involves a place, objects of production, some means of production and living labour – but there is no production in general.[34] Production always has a specific social form and purpose, and production always has a specific useful object as its end – 'there is also no general production'. Use value and the labour process are among the generally applicable categories in *Capital*, whereas all the value categories, i.e. commodity, exchange value, value, money, capital, surplus value (as opposed to surplus product, a generally applicable category), wages, and more, are explicitly social and historical. All of the latter are proper to the capitalist mode of production, though they have often been mistaken for transhistorical abstractions, not only in classical and neoclassical economics but also by Marxists.[35] Fixing in mind that

---

31 Mattick Jr 1993, p. 124. Likewise, Martha Campbell draws the consequence 'there are no counterparts to Marx's economic concepts in either classical or utility theory' (Campbell 1993b, p. 152).

32 On the difference between general and determinate abstractions, see Murray 1988, Chapter Ten.

33 Marx 1973, pp. 85–6. 'It is entirely certain that human production possesses definite *laws* or *relations* which remain the same in all forms of production. These identical characteristics are quite simple and can be summarised in a very small number of commonplace phrases' (Marx 1994, p. 236). Obviously, no such summary would count as a science.

34 Marx considers the labour process in a general way in the first part of Chapter Seven of *Capital* Volume 1, The Labour Process and the Valorization Process (Marx 1976a, pp. 283–91). Marx observes, 'the labour process ... is the everlasting nature-imposed condition of human existence, and it is therefore ... common to all forms of society in which human beings live' (Marx 1976a, p. 290).

35 Tony Smith states clearly Marx's observation that commercial forms predate capitalism but take on a new reality in capitalism: 'Commodities, money, profits, and so on, can all

there is no production in general and then carefully distinguishing between generally applicable categories and socially specific ones are among Marx's singular achievements.

Here are two examples of how Marx's 'explicitly social and historical' concepts differ from those of mainstream social science; both examples concern value. First, the common distinction between 'descriptive' and 'prescriptive' will not fit Marx's value categories. Allen Wood's description of Marx's law of value is misleading: 'The law of value is a proposition of economic science, employed to explain what actually happens in capitalism'.[36] Wood claims that Marx's ideas about value are purely descriptive – 'not in any sense normative or "evaluative" ideas'.[37] But value, for Marx, is far from a purely descriptive category. Rather, value is a historically specific reality bound up with capitalist liberty, equality and self-regard as well as with capitalist alienation, fetishism, domination, exploitation and crisis tendencies. On the one hand, Marx describes the sphere of simple commodity circulation, in which value is realised and circulates, as 'a very Eden of the innate rights of man. It is the exclusive realm of Freedom, Equality, Property and Bentham'.[38] On the other hand, Marx explicitly links value with domination: the fact that labour 'is expressed in the magnitude of the value of the product ... [is] the unmistakable stamp belonging to a social formation in which the process of production has mastery over man, instead of the opposite'.[39] Marx argues in *Capital* that, inasmuch as the

---

be found in precapitalist societies. One of Marx's fundamental insights is that these were not the same social forms as commodities, money, and profits in capitalism, although we use the same words. In *Capital*, Marx examines these social forms insofar as they are moments of a social order whose organizing principle is the self-valorisation of value (or, equivalently, the systematic reproduction of the exploitative capital/wage-labour relation). This was not the organizing principle of precapitalist societies, nor is it the organizing principle of democratic socialism. Commodities, money, and 'profits' (in one sense of the term, at least) may be found in the latter. But these are not the same as the commodities, money, and profits of capitalism, although, here too, we use the same words' (Smith 1990, p. 336).

36 Wood 1981, p. 225. Wood is right that Marx is not claiming that labour is the only valuable thing or that Marx is offering a theory of just price or that people have a right to the value of their commodities or that commodities ought to be exchanged at their values. Marx's theory of value is of profound moral significance, but its significance does not lie in any of those claims.

37 Ibid.

38 Marx 1976a, p. 280.

39 Marx 1976a, pp. 174–5. Marx's statement seems tame compared to the young Hegel's observation: 'Need and labour, elevated into this universality, then form on their own account

sphere of simple commodity circulation presupposes the circulation of capital, value presupposes surplus-value, hence exploitation. The liberating powers of capitalist freedom and equality and the exploitation of wage-labourers that makes surplus-value possible – as well as the domination of all by the insatiable demands of capital accumulation – all belong to the fabric of social relations that make a moral reality of value. Marx's theory of value represents his mature theory of alienated labour. Marx's revolutionary aim is not to redistribute value but rather to do away with it.[40]

Second, in Marx's theory of value and price, value is not the independent variable that explains the dependent variable, price, as in political economy. In the equation force equals mass times acceleration (F = ma), force is taken to be the independent variable that determines the acceleration of a body, the dependent variable, and force is understood to exist whether or not it causes any body to accelerate. In Marx's dialectical theory, value does not exist independently of price. Price is the necessary form of appearance of a commodity's value without simply being that value itself, in line with Hegel's complex logic of essence, according to which essence must appear as something other than itself.[41] Hegel thinks his way beyond the bourgeois, bifurcating conception of the categories of essence and appearance as 'products of the reflecting understanding, which both assumes the distinctions as *independent* and at the same time posits their relationality *as well* ... [I]t does not bring these thoughts together'.[42] Just as Hegel recognises that essence and appearance are inseparable, Marx argues in his theory of the value form that money is value's necessary form of appearance. Marx complained of political economy: 'It is one of the chief failings of classical political economy that it has never succeeded, by means of its analysis of commodities, and in particular of their value, in discovering the form of value which in fact turns value into exchange-value'. The classical political economists, he continued, fail precisely because they take value and the expression of value to be independent of one another: 'Even its best representatives, Adam Smith and Ricardo, treat the form of value as something of indifference, something external to the nature of the commodity

---

a monstrous system of community and mutual interdependence in a great people; a life of the dead body, that moves itself within itself, one which ebbs and flows in its motion blindly, like the elements, and which requires continual strict dominance and taming like a wild beast' (Hegel 1979, p. 249).

40 That should be clear from his polemics against Proudhonism and Left Ricardianism.

41 More broadly, Marx's systematic dialectics involves a conceptual structure of mutual presupposition.

42 Hegel 1991b, § 114, p. 179.

itself'.[43] Not only is their concept of value wrong, it is the wrong kind of concept for the task. The fact that Marx's dialectical theory of the value form, which is integral to his theory of value, has been so widely ignored indicates that many of Marx's interpreters have lacked the kind of concepts and the mind-set needed to understand him. Instead, they have imposed the 'bourgeois horizon' on the ideas that Marx devised to overcome it.[44]

2 Subsumption and Specific Social Forms

Marx's ideas about the subsumption of labour under capital went largely unrecognised until recent decades. When noticed, they have often been misunderstood, and they still remain on the margins of Marxian theory and studies of Marx.[45] There are conceptual and textual reasons why this is the case. The conceptual reason is that Marx's rubric of subsumption forces the topic of specific social forms into the open, since subsumption refers to subsumption under specific social forms. Because Marx was widely interpreted, by friend and foe, as a radical political economist rather than a radical critic of political economy, the topic of social form was not on the radar. Marx's disclosure of political economy's failure to make specific social forms ingredients of its concepts was,

43 Marx 1976a, p. 174, n. 33.

44 See Murray and Schuler 2008.

45 Ernest Mandel, in his introduction to the first English translation of the *Results of the Immediate Production Process*, makes the common mistake of identifying the real subsumption of labour with large-scale industry: 'Formal subsumption is characteristic of the period of manufacture; real subsumption is characteristic of the modern factory' (Mandel 1976, p. 944). But all the capitalist strategies for increasing the productive power of labour, including simple cooperation and the division of labour and manufacture, are forms of real subsumption, as indicated by their being included under the heading of relative surplus-value (Part Four of *Capital* Volume 1). Jon Elster writes in the same vein as Mandel, 'Real subsumption occurs when capitalism is fully developed in the factory system' (Elster 1985, p. 128). Likewise, James D. White writes, 'It was only with large-scale industry that specifically capitalist forms of production appeared. This made possible the real Subsumption of labour under capital' (White 1994, p. 95). This identification of real subsumption with the factory system wrongly implies that various forms of production identified as 'post-industrial' constitute shifts away from real subsumption rather than constituting new forms of it. For Marxian responses to the 'post-industrial' shift toward 'flexible' production, see Postone 1999 and Smith 2000. For a defence of the relevance of the law of value against those who hold that 'immaterial labour' or 'cognitive capitalism' spells its end, see Starosta 2012.

with a few exceptions, missed. The key failure concerns Marx's theory of value, which has generally been identified with the classical labour theory of value, especially as articulated by David Ricardo. Though indebted to Ricardo, Marx moved the labour theory of value onto entirely new conceptual foundations: Marx identifies value as a strange, suprasensible and strictly social objectivity that is the consequence of a specific social form of labour, namely, commodity-producing labour.[46] Since Marx conceives of capital as value that is valorised (increased in value), the failure to recognise value as a specific social form carries over to capital. If capital is not conceived of as a specific social form, in fact the mainspring of capitalist modernity, then the very idea of subsuming labour under capital makes no sense.[47] There is a mismatch between Marx's rubric

---

46 Marx's transformation of the classical (Ricardian) labour theory of value is a good example of what James Collins calls the 'basal acts' of the modern philosophers. These acts 'are basic for constituting the tradition of master works in modern philosophy' (Collins 1972, p. 50). Not that *Capital* is everywhere regarded as a masterwork. In the first edition of *Philosophy and Myth in Karl Marx*, Robert Tucker, in the thick of praise for Marx's *Paris Manuscripts*, wrote, '*Capital*, the product of twenty years of hard labour to which, as he said, he sacrificed his health, his happiness in life and his family, is an intellectual museum-piece for us now, whereas the sixteen-page manuscript of 1844 on the future as aesthetics, which he probably wrote in a day and never even saw fit to publish, contains much that is still significant' (Tucker 1961, p. 235). (Tucker withdrew this passage in the second edition.) With the renewal of investigations into Marx that began in the late 1960s, however, Marx's 'basal act' has begun to be recognised: in some quarters, *Capital* has come to be esteemed as a masterwork, and a Marxian tradition (as opposed to a Marxist tradition bound to the conceptual horizons of political economy) has sprung up. Moishe Postone's *Time, Labour, and Social Domination: A Reinterpretation of Marx's Critical Theory*, a watershed in this renewal, sprang from his reading of the *Grundrisse* (first available in English in 1973), his knowledge of European history, and his reflection on the international emergence and decline of the New Left. Responsive to all three, Postone's reinterpretation of Marx bears out Collins's hypothesis of the co-factors in the historical understanding of modern thinkers: 1. the insistent sources, 2. the historical questions and 3. the interpreting present.

47 'Just as it is convenient for the apologists of capital to confuse it with the use value in which it exists, and to call use value as such capital, in order to present capital as an eternal factor of production, as a relation independent of all social forms, immanent in every labour process, hence immanent in the labour process in general, so equally does it happen that it suits Messieurs the economists when reasoning away some of the phenomena which belong peculiarly to the capitalist mode of production to forget the essential feature of capital, namely that it is value positing itself as value, hence not only self-preserving but at the same time self-multiplying value' (Marx 1988a, p. 33). The failure to recognise capital as a specific, and exceptionally potent, social form is one of the most common blunders

of subsumption and the conceptual horizons of political economy, to which Marx's thought has been wrongly confined.

The textual reason for the neglect of Marx's subsumption concepts was that the only extended discussions of Marx's primary subsumption concepts, formal and real subsumption, occur in two writings that have become available comparatively recently, the *Results of the Immediate Production Process* (the so-called unpublished 'sixth chapter' of *Capital* Volume I) and the huge *Economic Manuscript of 1861–3*.[48] As these texts have become available, what James Collins calls 'the insistency of modern sources' has gathered momentum.[49] Once Marx's concepts of subsumption come into view, certain questions cannot be ignored: subsumption of what under what? Such questions bring the topic of specific social form out of the shadows because the only answer to the latter question is that subsumption brings something, say labour, under the sway of some particular social form, say capital.

When labour power is purchased and formally subsumed under capital, the wage labourer is not simply put to work but rather is brought under a specific social form, namely capital, which structures the social relation between the capitalist and the wage labourer.[50] In his account of the valorisation process in *Capital* Volume I, Marx points out two features of the formal subsumption

---

committed in social science and philosophy. This stubborn conceptual failure explains the mushrooming in scientific and public discourse of supposed kinds of capital: human capital, social capital, intellectual capital, conceptual capital, natural capital and more. But the conceptual breakdown occurs already with the concept of value: 'It is naturally still more convenient to understand by value nothing at all. Then one can without difficulty subsume everything under this category' (Marx 1976a, p. 677, n. 6).

48 See Marx 1976b, pp. 1,019–38 (also Marx 1994, pp. 355–466) and Marx 1994, pp. 93–121. On the *Results*, see Chapter 11 in the present volume. The *Economic Manuscript of 1861–3* has been published in the new MEGA and, in a complete English translation, in *Karl Marx, Frederick Engels, Collected Works*, Volumes 30–4. To my knowledge, Marx uses the terms 'formal subsumption' and 'real subsumption' exactly once in *Capital* Volume I, on p. 645. However, in the *Results of the Immediate Production Process*, Marx identifies formal and real subsumption with absolute and relative surplus value, respectively, two of the central categories of *Capital* Volume I (see Parts Three, Four and Five): 'If the production of absolute surplus-value was the material expression of the formal subsumption of labour under capital, then the production of relative surplus-value may be viewed as its real subsumption' (Marx 1976b, pp. 1,024–5).

49 See Chapter II, 'The Insistency of Modern Sources', in Collins 1972, where he emphasises the power of research that opens itself to new textual sources, breaks with preconceived schemes and renews the interpretation of major historical figures.

50 Marx's interest in the social character of wage-labour and the relationship between wage labourer and capitalist goes back at least to his reflections on the topic in his notes

of labour under capital: (i) the capitalist is in charge of the labour process simply by virtue of paying wages and (ii) with the purchase of labour power, the capitalist becomes the rightful owner of the resulting products.[51]

In the *Results*, Marx calls attention to further features of labour's formal subsumption under capital. Because the relationship between capitalist and wage labourer is an impersonal, '*purely financial*' one, 'the process of exploitation is stripped of every patriarchal, political or even religious cloak'.[52] Unlike a slave, 'the free worker ... is impelled by his wants. The consciousness (or better: the *idea*) of free self-determination, of liberty, makes a much better worker of the one than of the other, as does the related feeling (sense) of *responsibility*'.[53] This sense of responsibility is related to payment in the form of money, the wage: 'he must pay his own way; he is responsible to himself for the way he spends his wages. *He learns to control himself, in contrast to the slave*, who needs a master'.[54] Another facet of working for a wage is that the wage-labourer becomes 'indifferent towards the *content* of his labour and hence his own particular form of activity'.[55] This indifference, in tandem with the diversification of products characteristic of capitalist society, induces versatility, a 'perfect indifference towards the particular content of work and the free transition from one branch of industry to the next'.[56] Capital, which presupposes labour in the social form of wage-labour, is not simply a thing, whether means of production, a product or money; capital is a specific social form of wealth that profoundly shapes social life and human interactions with nature.

I.I. Rubin observed, 'The basic error of the majority of Marx's critics consists of ... their complete failure to grasp the qualitative sociological side of Marx's theory of value'.[57] Not only Marx's critics have failed in this regard; Marxists

---

on James Mill's *Elements of Political Economy* (Marx 1967b, Marx 1975a) and his 1844 manuscript on alienated labour (in Marx 1975c).

51 Marx 1976a, pp. 291–2.

52 Marx 1976b, p. 1,027. For the peasant, however, this liberation from age-old forms of personal domination comes at the price of 'the loss of an earlier *independence* in the process of production' (Marx 1976b, p. 1,029).

53 Marx 1976b, p. 1,031.

54 Marx 1976b, p. 1,033.

55 Ibid.

56 Marx 1976b, p. 1,034.

57 I.I. Rubin 1972, pp. 73–4. Hans-Georg Backhaus picks up on this point of Rubin: 'The "economistic one-sidedness" chastised by Marx consists in the fact that economics operates as a separate branch of the scientific division of labour on the plane of pre-constituted economic objects' (Backhaus 1980, p. 107). These objects of 'economic' inquiry are 'preconstituted' to exclude specific social forms.

who picture Marx operating within the horizons of political economy likewise close off this 'qualitative sociological side' of his value categories. This aspect of Marx's theory of value encompasses matters of fundamental social and moral significance. By bringing attention to the topic of specific social forms of needs, wealth and labour, Marxian subsumption concepts disclose the socially, morally and politically qualitative dimensions of Marx's thought. The scope and power of Marx's grasp of the social forms specific to capitalism – at the heart of which is self-valorising value – is only beginning to be recognised and developed by contemporary Marxian theorists.

3 In Defence of Marx's Labour Theory of Value

What is value? This is perhaps the most urgent, yet neglected, question of contemporary social theory. Despite the proliferating talk about 'adding value', little thought is given to what is being added. As Marx sarcastically commented, 'It is naturally still more convenient to understand by value nothing at all. Then one can without difficulty subsume everything under this category'.[58] The word 'value', of course, is used widely and diversely. The value in question here is the kind that money represents and measures in its roundabout way.[59] This value is an abstract sort of social objectivity that requires expression in money. The value of my house depends not on how much my family is attached to it but on what the market will offer in exchange for it. A real-estate appraiser can form a reasonable idea of what that value is at a given time. What happens to value in a financial crisis is one of the strangest phenomena of capitalist societies; it caught Marx's attention early on. Consider the U.S. financial crisis of 2007–8. Households in the United States lost 12–13 trillion dollars, reducing the net assets of middle-class households by about 40 percent. Carl B. Weinberg, chief economist at High Frequency Economic, referred to this massive devaluation as 'the dramatic destruction of wealth'.[60] But what is so perplexing about this sudden loss of value is that it occurred without any 'dramatic destruction of wealth' in the ordinary sense. No war or natural catastrophe destroyed homes

58 Marx 1976a, p. 677, n. 6.

59 As value's necessary form of appearance, money is the external, observable measure of value; labour time, which Marx identifies as the magnitude of value, is the immanent but – due to the qualification 'socially necessary' labour time – non-observable measure of value.

60 Alderman and Thomas 2012, p. B1. Much of the value lost can be attributed to the bursting of the real estate bubble of the years leading up to the financial crisis.

or businesses, wiping out their usefulness along with their value. This unnatural financial disaster destroyed value without destroying the useful things that Marx caustically refers to as value's 'carriers'.[61] The puzzling nature of this phenomenon, with its wild discrepancy between value and wealth as ordinarily understood, calls for inquiry into value – but the call goes largely unanswered.[62]

One of Marx's preeminent virtues, then, is that he thinks deeply about value and arrives at a unique, poorly understood yet (nevertheless) widely rejected theory of value.[63] One reason for this widespread rejection of Marx's labour theory of value is that it is identified with the classical labour theory, which is untenable. Though it arises out of the classical labour theory, which reaches back to William Petty and Adam Smith, and was refined by David Ricardo, Marx's theory of value is cut from different cloth. The classical, or Ricardian, labour theory of value considers any labour that produces useful

---

61 Marx, 1976a, p. 126. The destruction of value in a crisis generally results in losses in terms of usefulness as foreclosed homes and bankrupted businesses deteriorate with disuse.

62 This discrepancy between value and wealth in the ordinary sense also affects surplus value (and more particularly the rate of profit). David Ricardo forecast that the rate of profit would fall because population growth would lower the productive power of agricultural labour – thereby increasing the price of food and driving up wages – by forcing the cultivation of poorer land. Marx argued, on the contrary, that the rate of profit tends to fall because the productive power of labour increases, revealing that the use value and value dimensions of capital's accumulation process are working at cross purposes.

63 It is common to be critical, often dismissive, of Marx's theory of value, even among Marxists or others sympathetic to Marx's work. For example, John Cassidy, in his surprising two-part *New Yorker* magazine tribute to Karl Marx as 'the next' great social thinker, discards Marx's theory of value in a sentence or two (Cassidy 1997). Allen Wood suggests that Marx dismissed his own argument for a labour theory of value in Chapter One of *Capital* Volume I: 'Despite its prominent place in *Capital*, Marx's "proof" of the law of value is not taken seriously as such by its author. I think it is best regarded as an expository device, part of Marx's avowed attempt to "popularize" his discussion of value in *Capital*' (Wood 2004, p. 236). Despite this startling claim, Wood admits in a footnote (n. 53, p. 291) that Marx accepted the argument and its key premise. For a litany of scorn, we may turn to the sub-headings under the index entry for 'labour theory of value' in Jon Elster's *Making Sense of Marx*: 'ill-defined because of heterogeneity of labour, plays no role in the determination of equilibrium prices and rate of profit, cannot explain the possibility of exchange and profit, does not provide a criterion for the socially desirable choice of technique, does not explain the actual choice of technique under capitalism, ill-suited to the analysis of balanced economic growth, inconsistent with the Marxist theory of class, constitutes a weakness in the theory of exploitation, vitiates the theory of fetishism, vitiates the critique of vulgar economy, rests on obscure Hegelian foundations' (Elster 1985, p. 554).

things to be the source and substance of value. Since useful labour is found in all human societies, value, as the classical political economists conceived of it, is a category applicable to all human societies. For Marx, by contrast, value is a consequence not of just any labour but of labour of a peculiar social kind, namely, the labour that produces commodities in those societies where the commodity is the form that wealth generally takes.[64] With Marx, value is entirely a consequence of the peculiar social form of the labour that produces value; it is 'purely social'.[65]

In saying that value is 'purely social', Marx is claiming that value is wholly a consequence of the particular social form of labour in capitalism. If the production and distribution of use values were organised in a different way and to a different end – if production and distribution had a different measure – value could be eliminated, not redistributed. That is Marx's expectation for communism. Marx recognises that, though it is 'purely social' in this sense, value presupposes use value and value-producing labour presupposes concrete labour aimed at the production of specific useful things: 'nothing can be a value without being a useful object. If the thing is useless, so is the labour contained in it; the labour does not count as labour, and therefore creates no value'.[66] And Marx states emphatically that use value is not 'purely social': '*Nature* is just as much the source of use values (and it is surely of such that material wealth consists!) as is labour'.[67] Value, then, is a historically specific category proper to the capitalist mode of production.[68] This is the first of two ways in which Marx radically reconceives the labour theory of value.

Due to their asocial conception of value, the classical political economists fail to recognise that money is value's necessary form of expression. Yet

---

64 Marx states this contrast plainly in the *Critique*: 'labour is a natural condition of human existence, a condition of material interchange between man and nature, quite independent of the form of society. On the other hand, the labour which posits exchange-value [value, in the terminology of *Capital*] is a specific social form of labour' (Marx 1970a, p. 36). Marx goes on in *Capital* to argue that, where that social form of labour prevails, production is undertaken on a capitalist basis, which presupposes that labour takes the form of free wage labour.

65 Marx 1976a, p. 139.

66 Marx 1976a, p. 131, translation amended.

67 Marx 1966a, p. 3.

68 Marx singles out Sir James Steuart as the sole prior analyst who recognised that 'labour which creates exchange-value [value] is a specifically bourgeois feature'. Marx adds, 'His clear differentiation between specifically social labour which manifests itself in exchange-value and concrete labour which yields use-values distinguishes Steuart from his predecessors and his successors' (Marx 1970a, p. 58).

money is not simply value. Samuel Bailey, whom Marx names as one of the few authors 'who have concerned themselves with the analysis of the form of value', makes this mistake of confusing 'the form of value [exchange-value] with value itself'.[69] Of course, if the value of a commodity just is its exchange-value, a thing external to a commodity, then value cannot be intrinsic to a commodity – the point that Bailey pressed against Ricardo. By drawing in Hegel's insight that essence must appear as something other than itself, Marx unifies a socially specific labour theory of value with a theory of the value form according to which exchange value (price) is the necessary form of appearance of value. Value, Marx argues against Bailey's criticism of Ricardo, is intrinsic to the commodity because – arguing in this regard against Ricardo – value belongs to the specific social form of the commodity, and wealth is inseparable from its social form. The expression of a commodity's value is necessarily a polar one. As the product of privately undertaken labour, the commodity has yet to be socially validated; the labour expended to produce it may prove to be wasted. We put a price on a commodity hoping that it sells. Money, by contrast, is already socially validated. A commodity, then, gains social validation only by being sold. The inseparability of money (price) and value has its source in and signals the historical specificity of value and of the social kind of labour that necessarily gives rise to it.

Marx agreed with several conventional objections against the classical labour theory of value.[70] In order to defend his own theory against these objections, Marx has to reconceive the classical theory in a second fundamental way: he transforms it from a theory directed at individual commodities to one that holds only for the 'heap' of commodities and the total capital (and for their aliquot parts). At the end of the first chapter of his *A Contribution to the Critique of Political Economy* (1859), Marx identifies four fundamental problems with the classical theory of value.[71] The first two concerned the failure of the

69 Marx 1976a, p. 141, n. 17.

70 With a back-handed compliment, Marx commends Samuel Bailey for identifying major problems in Ricardian theory: 'despite the narrowness of his own outlook, he was able to put his finger on some serious defects in the Ricardian theory' (Marx 1976a, p. 155, n. 25).

71 There are other big problems. For example, Marx observes, 'The great economists such as Smith, Ricardo, etc. focused their attention on the basic form of capital, capital as industrial capital ... They were therefore perplexed by commercial capital as a special variety of its own. The principles about value formation, profit, etc. derived straight from the examination of industrial capital cannot be applied directly to commercial capital. They therefore entirely ignored the latter. They only refer to it as a kind of industrial capital' (Marx 1981, pp. 441–2). Then there is interest-bearing capital and the credit system:

classical theory to distinguish between labour power and labour, which kept it from developing proper concepts of the wage, surplus value and capital. (i) The classical theory, because it lacked a clear distinction between labour power (the commodity that wage labourers sell) and labour (which is the use of labour-power), mixed up the value that labourers add in the labour process with the value of their own labour power. Consequently, no coherent theory of the determination of wages was available.[72] (ii) Lacking the distinction between labour and labour power, the classical theorists could not distinguish between the value added by wage labourers in production and the value of the labour power they sell to capitalists. Hence, they were unable to explain surplus-value – as Marx explains it – by the margin between the value of labour power and the new value added by living labour.

(iii) The third objection is one that Samuel Bailey pressed against Ricardo. This objection points up the impossibility of reconciling the tendency toward an average rate of profit with the facts that capitalist firms have different organic compositions of value – roughly, differences in how labour intensive firms are – and have different turnover times. As a consequence, prices will, as a rule, diverge from 'individual values'.[73]

> The exchange value of commodities is, *consequently*, determined not by the labour-time contained in them, but by the relation of demand and supply. In fact, this strange conclusion only raises the question of how on the basis of exchange-value a market-price differing from this exchange-value asserts itself only in its antithesis. This problem is solved in the theory of competition.[74]

Marx's solution to this problem comes in *Capital* Volume III with his account of how competition forms an average rate of profit and of prices of production. That solution, of course, has been a neuralgic point in the interpretation of *Capital* since Böhm-Bawerk complained of a blatant contradiction between

---

'the credit system is, in Marx's view, so essential that no presentation of capital would be complete without it' (Campbell 2002, p. 212).

72 One indicator of this problem was the widespread use of the phrase 'the value of labour', which Marx shows to be nonsensical. See Chapter 19, on wages, in Marx 1976a, especially p. 679.

73 The rubric of 'individual value' is a fiction useful to Marx in developing a tenable labour theory of value. Since value is 'purely social', the notion of actual individual values is misbegotten.

74 Marx 1970a, p. 62.

what he took to be an account in terms of individual values in *Capital* Volume I and the account of prices of production in *Capital* Volume III. This belief that *Capital* Volume I offered a theory of individual values that had to be retracted in *Capital* Volume III (a) creates the 'transformation problem', the problem of consistently transforming individual values into prices of production and (b) lends support to understanding the method of *Capital* in terms of 'successive approximations'.[75]

(iv) 'The last and apparently the decisive objection ... is this: if exchange-value [value, in the terminology of *Capital*] is nothing but the labour-time contained in a commodity, how does it come about that commodities which contain no labour possess exchange-value [price]?'[76] Marx answers, 'this problem is solved in the theory of rent'. Nonetheless, this fourth objection continues to be a sore point in the reception of the first chapter of *Capital*: how can Marx say that (abstract) labour is the substance of value when commodities such as undeveloped land are not products of labour yet have a price? Chris Arthur points to the problem that this creates for Marx's argument in Chapter One of *Capital* that abstract labour is the substance of value: 'the argument that there is indeed a content to the value form in labour cannot be correct as far as the pure form of exchange is concerned because many non-products are coherently inscribed within the form'.[77] How can abstract labour be the substance of value when not all commodities are products of labour?

I argue that, since Marx was aware of objections (iii) and (iv) well before *Capital* Volume I appeared – unbeknown to Böhm-Bawerk, the manuscripts of *Capital* Volume III (1864–5) were drafted before the first publication of *Capital* Volume I (1867) – Marx did not start off *Capital* with a couple of howling contradictions.[78] But how could he avoid them?

What is said of commodities in *Capital* Volume I (and the first two parts of *Capital* Volume II and Parts One and Three of *Capital* Volume III) is true not of commodities taken individually but only of the aggregation of all commodities, hence, of any aliquot or representative part of that aggregation. Long before

---

75 For the 'successive approximations' interpretation, which, I argue, the systematic dialectical reading of *Capital* supersedes, see Grossman 1992, Dobb 1968 and Sweezy 1942.

76 Marx 1970a, p. 62.

77 Arthur 2002a, p. 157.

78 In *Capital* Volume III, Marx observes of the third objection, 'The theory of value thus appears incompatible with the actual movement, incompatible with the actual phenomena of production, and it might seem that we must abandon all hope of understanding these phenomena' (Marx 1981, p. 252).

publishing *Capital* Volume I, Marx knew that the classical labour theory of value fails as a theory of commodities taken individually: (i) it is impossible to reconcile the tendency toward the formation of a general rate of profit with the facts that capitalist firms have different organic compositions of value and different turnover times and (ii) some commodities are not products of labour. In *Capital* Volume I Marx calls attention to the fact that the price form subsumes useful things that are not products of labour:

> The price-form ... may also harbour a qualitative contradiction, with the result that price ceases altogether to express value, despite the fact that money is nothing but the value-form of commodities ... Hence a thing can, formally speaking, have a price without having a value.[79]

The labour theory of value, then, does not hold at the level of the individual commodity; it is defensible only with reference to the aggregate of commodities and to aliquot parts of that aggregate. Likewise, the identification of an individual firm's profit with the individual surplus-value that it extracts is untenable.

Marx had to overthrow the individualistic classical labour theory of value in order to reconcile his labour theory of value with the formation of a general rate of profit. Marx replaces the failed classical labour theory of value, which explains individual prices in terms of individual values and individual profits in terms of individual surplus values, with a labour theory of value that holds at the aggregate level (the level of total capital) and explains subordinate phenomena on that basis. Marx explains:

> Every section of the *aggregate capital* [*Gesamtkapital*] would in accordance with its magnitude participate in the aggregate surplus-value and draw a corresponding part [*aliquot Teil*] of it ... But in plain language this just means that the capitalists strive (and this striving is competition) to divide among themselves the quantity of unpaid labour – or the products of this quantity of labour – which they squeeze out of the working class, not according to the surplus-labour produced directly by a particular capital, but corresponding *firstly* to the relative portion [*aliquoten Teil*] of the aggregate capital which a particular capital represents and *secondly* according to the amount of surplus-labour produced by the aggregate capital. The capitalists, like hostile brothers, divide among themselves the

79 Marx 1976a, p. 197.

> loot of other people's labour which they have appropriated so that on an average one receives the same amount of unpaid labour as another.[80]

Individual prices do not track individual values; neither do individual profits track individual surplus values.[81] But the labour theory of value holds at the aggregate level and explains individual phenomena with transformed value categories: 'The sum of the profits for all the different spheres of production must accordingly be equal to the sum of surplus-values, and the sum of prices of production for the total social product must be equal to the sum of its values'.[82] Prices of production explain individual prices no longer in terms of individual values but rather on the basis of cost price plus profit, as determined by the average rate of profit, which is determined by the ratio of the aggregate surplus-value (= aggregate profit), that is, the ΔM of the total social capital to the total original investment (M). Individual profits are no longer explained by individual surplus values but by the transformed forms of surplus value and rate of surplus value, namely profit and rate of profit.[83]

Once we recognise how Marx revolutionises the classical labour theory of value by making the aliquot or representative commodity the object of inquiry, we see how Marx answers the objection that not all commodities are products of human labour. The 'heap' of commodities will include both produced and non-produced commodities, while the total social capital will include industrial, merchant and interest-bearing capitals. The only way that a representative part of the 'heap' would not be a product of labour would be if no commodities were products of labour. Since we are assuming that wealth generally takes the commodity-form, this amounts to saying that a society's wealth could be renewed with no labour. Likewise, the only way that a representative part of the total social capital would not involve labour would be if no capital employed labour. Since Marx assumes that labour is required to meet human needs, he assumes that a representative commodity

80 Marx 1968b, pp. 29–30.

81 Like individual values, individual surplus values are a useful fiction.

82 Marx 1981, p. 273.

83 As previously noted, there are other serious issues that come up in *Capital* Volume III (Parts Four, Five and Six) that provide fresh reasons why the labour theory of value cannot work at the level of individual commodities. These new difficulties, of which Marx was well aware before the publication of *Capital* Volume I, stem from the fact that the total surplus value is divided not only among industrial capitalists but is also shared out to commercial capitalists, to capitalists engaged in money dealing and lending at interest and to land and real estate owners, who collect rent.

will be a product of labour and that a representative capital will employ labour. Understood in this way, Marx's claims are neither false nor gratuitous.

It is often overlooked that Marx argues first for a theory of value, reasoning that there must be some homogeneous 'third thing' common to all commodities that is expressed by their exchange-values (their prices). Only after establishing that there must be a 'third thing', which he calls value, does he argue that its substance must be abstract labour. Marx explains why he follows this order:

> we must, first of all, consider the value-relation quite independently of its quantitative aspect. The usual mode of procedure is the precise opposite of this: nothing is seen in the value-relation but the proportion in which definite quantities of two sorts of commodity count as equal to each other. It is overlooked that the magnitudes of different things only become comparable in qualitative terms when they have been reduced to the same unit. Only as expressions of the same unit do they have a common denominator, and are therefore commensurable magnitudes.[84]

Marx takes the 'third thing' argument in earnest.

I defend Marx's two-step argument for his unique labour theory of value: (i) the argument to the 'third thing' (called value), which does not mention labour; and (ii) the argument that abstract labour is the substance of value. Marx employs the reasoning of the 'third thing' argument to criticise proponents of the classical labour theory of value for failing to recognise that only human labour in the abstract is homogeneous enough to be the substance of value: 'it does not occur to the economists that a purely quantitative distinction between the kinds of labour presupposes their qualitative unity or equality, and therefore their reduction to abstract human labour'.[85] Regarding (1), James Furner criticises Marx's argument to the 'third thing' for begging the question, concluding, 'It would therefore be surprising if Marxists were to continue to give much positive weight to the "third thing argument"'.[86] Regarding (ii), Jon Elster, for example, criticises Marx as follows: 'First, labour is not necessarily a component of all goods; secondly, there may be other common features that in fact explain the exchange'. Of course, the other possible common feature that Marx supposedly neglects turns out to be 'the potential for human want satisfaction,

84 Marx 1976a, pp. 140–1.

85 Marx 1976a, p. 73, n. 33. See also, Marx 1970a, pp. 29–30.

86 Furner 2004, p. 108. See 'Avoiding Bad Abstractions: A Defence of Co-constitutive Value-Form Theory', included in the present volume as Chapter 15.

or utility or use-value'.[87] Elster's first objection reinforces the second because a utility theory of value can address the phenomenon of commodities that are not products of labour, whereas the labour-theory appears unable to.

Utility, however, is no candidate for being the substance of value. Marx early on rejected the very idea of utility (as opposed to usefulness).[88] Marx developed his theory of value prior to the 'marginalist revolution' of the late nineteenth century that brought utility and subjectivist theories of value to prominence; however, in his engagement with Samuel Bailey and elsewhere, Marx criticised utility and subjectivist theories of value. Utility, unlike usefulness, regards all useful things as commensurable and abstracts from all particular useful qualities of a useful thing. Consequently, I take Marx's point on the second page of *Capital* to be a flat rejection of the very idea of utility:

> The usefulness of a thing makes it a use-value. But this usefulness does not dangle in mid-air. It is conditioned by the physical properties of the commodity, and has no existence apart from the latter.[89]

---

87 Elster 1985, p. 140. As noted above, Marx was well aware of the objection that there are things that have prices but no value, notably, undeveloped land. As Marx indicates in the *Critique*, however, his answer to this objection lies in his theory of rent, which he develops in the latter part of *Capital* Volume III. But, in a different sense, his answer lies in his reinvention of the labour theory of value not as one that explains individual prices on the basis of individual values – which is the presupposition of the objection – but rather as a theory of the total capital or, equivalently, of its aliquot parts.

88 In *The German Ideology*, Marx and Engels dismiss utility and point to capitalist commerce as its source: 'The apparent absurdity of merging all the manifold relationships of people in the one relation of utility [*Brauchbarkeit*], this apparently metaphysical abstraction arises from the fact that in modern bourgeois society all relations are subordinated in practice to the one abstract monetary-commercial relation' (Marx and Engels 1976b, p. 409).

89 Marx 1976a, p. 126. Marx's derivation of value as the 'third thing' that commodities have in common may look as though it is leading to the concept of utility, but that is only if we forget that Marx's argument begins with commodities, useful things that all have (valid) prices. Only by starting with a specific social form of wealth, the commodity form, does Marx arrive at the 'third thing' (value). Any similarity to a deduction of utility from quantitative comparisons of useful things is an illusion created by superimposing the commensurability of commodities onto useful things of whatever social sort. As Bernard Williams points out, it is precisely this illusion that gives utility whatever currency it has: 'Utilitarianism is unsurprisingly the value system for a society in which economic values are supreme; and also, at the theoretical level, because quantification in money is the only obvious form of what utilitarianism insists upon, the commensurability of values' (Williams 1972, p. 89). Money, unlike utility, is actual.

If the usefulness of a thing is conditioned by its physical properties, then, when I abstract away all those properties, its usefulness is simply gone; no residue, no usefulness-in-the-abstract, is left over.

Marx points out where the legitimate category of abstract human labour differs from the oxymoron of abstract use-value, 'dangling in mid-air'. He writes:

> With the disappearance of the useful character of the products of labour, the useful character of the kinds of labour embodied in them also disappears; this in turn entails the disappearance of the different concrete forms of labour. They can no longer be distinguished, but are all together reduced to the same kind of labour, human labour in the abstract.[90]

The case of the commodity and the case of the concretely purposive human labour that produces it are not the same; Marx's argument turns on the difference. If I abstract from all useful features of the commodity, I do not arrive at abstract usefulness: nothing is left of usefulness once all the useful properties of a thing are gone. Usefulness disappears. However, the same is not true of useful human labour:

> If I leave aside the determinate quality of productive activity, and therefore the useful character of the labour, what remains is its quality of being an expenditure of human labour-power ... a productive expenditure of human brains, muscles, nerves, hands etc.[91]

The difference in the two cases enables Marx to argue to eliminate utility and argue that the substance of value must be congealed abstract human labour.

That abstract human labour is the substance of value is critical to Marx's explanation of the 'value treadmill', which explains why capitalism is inherently technologically dynamic and sets up Marx's theory of relative surplus value. The 'value treadmill' refers to the fact that, as increases in the productive power of labour are generalised across a branch of production, more use values are produced per hour but no more value is created, leading to a cheapening of products. The reason for this is that abstract labour is the substance of value and productive power is a concrete feature of labour: 'as productive power [*Produktivkraft*] is an attribute of labour in its concrete useful form, it naturally ceases to have any bearing on that labour as soon as we abstract from its

---

90 Marx 1976a, p. 128.

91 Marx 1976a, p. 134.

concrete useful form'.[92] The 'value treadmill' expresses the mismatch between use value and value; it is the basis of what Moishe Postone calls capitalism's 'shearing pressures'.[93]

Marx states repeatedly that it is *human* labour in the abstract, the expenditure of human 'brains, muscles, nerves, hands', that forms the substance of value. Why? The fact that human labour forms the substance of value reminds us that value is 'purely social'. Value is not the embodiment of 'physiological' labour. Labour in any human setting can be viewed in 'physiological' terms; moreover, 'physiological' labour can just as well be the exertions of non-human animals.[94] Value, for Marx, is all about the way that capitalist societies recognise human labour. Human labour in the abstract is the substance of value where human labour is 'practically abstract', that is, wherever human labour is socially validated as human labour in the abstract, as happens through the circulation of commodities and money. Because human labour is recognised in the abstract, such a society, a capitalist society, is, in its roots, egalitarian. Marx's account of surplus value, hence of capital, depends on human labour in the abstract forming the substance of value. Human labour can create surplus value because humans can create more new value than the value of their labour power.

For there to be surplus value, there must be a class of wage labourers, workers who own their own labour power, so that they can sell it to members of the capitalist class at a price that is lower than the value they add when put to work.[95] If workers did not own their own labour power in the first instance, they would not be able to sell it, so there would be no wages; capitalists would own everything and all commercial transactions would take place within the capitalist class. However, the argument of Chapter Five of *Capital* Volume I is that surplus value (the ΔM that accrues not to individual capitalists but to the

---

92 Marx 1976a, p. 137, translation amended.

93 Postone 1993.

94 On the significance of Marx's studies of physiology for his thinking about labour, see Wendling 2009.

95 As Tony Smith points out, Marx's idea of the 'capitalist class' is a placeholder. Capital's functions may be carried out in a variety of ways: 'Marx's critique is of capital, not capitalists. The latter are relevant to his theory only insofar as they function as personifications of the former. In principle, it is possible for a society without capitalists to still be subject to the alien logic of capital. A society of nationalized firms subject to the valorization imperative would remain under the alien logic of capital, even if there were no capitalist owners of those firms' (Smith, 2006, p. 333).

capitalist class) cannot be explained on that basis.[96] Conversely, if non-human animals owned their own labour power, and thus could sell it, we humans would be in the sort of social relations with them such that they could create value and surplus value.

Utility, then, is a pseudo-concept, but even if it were not, it would not be a candidate to answer the question: what is the substance of value? Utility presents itself as a transhistorical (generally applicable) category, whereas value is a historically specific social reality. Consequently, utility is the wrong kind of category to explain value. A related reason why utility could not be the substance of value is because there is no basis in the concept of utility for generating the polarity of the value form.[97] In his account of the value-form, Marx argues that money is the necessary form of appearance of value: price and value are inseparable. But there is no basis on which to generate the necessity for utility to be expressed as money.[98] Value must be expressed in money; money is in what Marx calls the 'equivalent form' of value. As such, money is *per se* socially validated. Money is directly exchangeable for commodities, whereas commodities, which are in the 'relative form' of value, have to be socially validated by being exchanged for money. The fact that these basic points are missed when critics complain that Marx overlooked utility shows how little his theory of value has been understood.

96 Chapter Five makes it clear that the ΔM that Marx is trying to explain is the net surplus value that goes to the capitalist class taken as a whole.

97 One of the main criticisms that Marx makes of Samuel Bailey, a forerunner of neoclassical economics, is that, while he is one of the few to recognise the necessity of value being expressed in an exchange relation, he fails to recognise the necessary polarity of that expression of value. As a consequence, he thought that any commodity might be regarded as money and that we could speak of prices measured in barrels of oil or bottles of wine just as well as in ounces of gold. Bailey's claim, which is echoed in neoclassical accounts of money, amounts to a flat denial of the polarity of the value form.

98 By contrast, with Marx's labour theory of value, there is a reason why value must be expressed in money: the social kind of labour that produces commodities, that is, privately undertaken production for use by unknown others, requires some mechanism of social validation of that labour. The sale of commodities, their conversion into money, is that mechanism.

4 Defending the 'Purely Social' and 'Suprasensible' Objectivity of Value

One of the most audacious and confounding claims of Marx's theory of value – one easily lost sight of in the usual debates over the labour theory – is that value is objective.[99] Strangely, its objectivity is 'purely social' and 'suprasensible'.[100] Marx describes this 'phantom-like objectivity' of value:

> not an atom of matter enters into the objectivity of commodities as values [*Wertgegenständlichkeit*]; in this it is the direct opposite of the coarsely sensuous objectivity of commodities as physical objects. We may twist and turn a single commodity as we wish; it remains impossible to grasp it as a thing possessing value.[101]

This 'purely social' and 'suprasensible' objectivity of value makes fetishes of the commodity, money and capital.[102] As values they are possessed of a peculiar

99 The subjectivist turn in economics toward neoclassical theory – a shift within the 'bourgeois horizon' – scoffs at the objectivity of value. Carl Menger, a founder of neoclassical economics, assures us: 'value does not exist outside the consciousness of men' (Menger 1950, pp. 6–7). This turn was anticipated by Samuel Bailey: 'Value, in its ultimate sense, appears to mean the esteem in which any object is held. It denotes, strictly speaking, an effect produced on the mind' (Bailey 1967, p. 1). Robert Torrens elegantly dismissed the objectivity of value: 'When we say that any article of utility possesses exchangeable value, the expression is figurative, and, in its precise and real import, does not predicate any quality, or attribute, as inhering in this article; but merely implies, that there are two persons able and willing to give other articles of utility instead of it. The phrase, exchangeable value, has a reference to the power and inclinations of those persons who possess articles of utility, and not to any thing actually belonging and essential to those articles themselves' (Torrens 1821, pp. 10–11). Bailey and Torrens do their best to make the ordinary import of the everyday expression 'value of corn' go away. See 'The Grammar of Value: A Close Look at Marx's Critique of Bailey', included in the present volume as Chapter 6. In criticising both neoclassical economics and the institutionalist economics of Geoffrey M. Hodgson, Martha Campbell forcefully defends the objectivity of value (Campbell 2004).

100 'Since the exchange-value [value] of commodities is indeed nothing but a mutual relation between various kinds of labour of individuals regarded as equal and universal labour, i.e., nothing but a material expression of a specific social form of labour, it is a tautology to say that labour is the *only* source of exchange-value [value]' (Marx 1970a, p. 35).

101 Marx 1976a, pp. 138–9. Marx adds that this objectivity of value is 'purely social' [*rein gesellschaftlich*].

102 'The products of labour become commodities, sensuous things which are at the same time

social power – to provide access to the wealth and labour of others – a power that is qualitatively the same regardless of the physical properties of the valuable goods.[103] As Marx quotes 'old Barbon': 'One hundred pounds [Sterling] worth of lead or iron, is of as great a value as one hundred pounds [Sterling] worth of silver and gold'.[104] Each wields the same social clout.

Marx highlights the difference between this abstract generality of a commodity's social power as a value and the particularity of a commodity as a use value:

> The commodity, as a use-value, satisfies a particular need and forms a particular element of material wealth. But the value of a commodity measures the degree of its attractiveness [*Grad ihrer Attraktionskraft*] for all other elements of material wealth, and therefore measures the social wealth of its owner.[105]

In talking of value's power to attract, Marx imagines value as magnetic force. Like the value of a commodity, the attractive power of a magnet is suprasensible – occult.[106] Mimicking Marx's description of value, we might say that a magnet is a riddle: twist and turn it as we wish, it remains impossible to grasp

---

suprasensible or social' (Marx 1976a, p. 165). 'In the expression of value of the linen the coat represents a supra-natural property; their value, which is something purely social' (Marx 1976a, p. 149). These are not expressions of Ricardian value theory; they represent a basic rethinking of value.

103 We call the social clout of value 'purchasing power'. Purchasing power is one of Samuel Bailey's definitions of value, which he finds also in Adam Smith: 'the definition of Adam Smith, therefore, that the value of an object "expresses the power of purchasing other goods, which the possession of that object conveys", is substantially correct' (Bailey 1967, p. 4). But value cannot be defined as purchasing power, for that definition overlooks the polarity of the expression of value.

104 Nicholas Barbon, as quoted in Marx 1976a, p. 128.

105 Marx 1976a, p. 230.

106 Magnetism has the air of magic. Imagine a child watching a junkyard crane levitate a car with a huge electromagnet. Now, switch off the electromagnet. Gravity is another occult power of attraction to which Marx compares value: 'in the midst of the accidental and ever-fluctuating exchange relations between the products, the labour-time socially necessary to produce them asserts itself like a law of nature. In the same way, the law of gravity asserts itself when a person's house collapses on top of him' (Marx 1976a, p. 168). Gravity is not as suitable a metaphor for value, however, because, unlike magnetic force, polarity is not involved.

it as a thing possessing magnetic force.[107] Yet, like value, magnetism has measurable sensible effects.

In *Capital*, Marx frequently – and, it appears, systematically – associates value with phenomena of magnetism and electricity; these include (i) polarity, (ii) attraction and repulsion, (iii) alternation, (iv) crystallization and (v) circuits.[108]

(i) Marx begins his examination of the value-form with the simple form of value (x commodity A = y commodity B), stating, 'The whole mystery of the form of value lies hidden in this simple form'.[109] Immediately, he identifies a feature of the expression of value missed by previous investigators – its polarity.[110] Commodities A and B play different roles in the expression of value; A, whose value is being expressed, is in the relative value form, while B, in which A's value is expressed, is in the equivalent value form. Of the two forms, Marx writes, 'The relative form of value and the equivalent form are two inseparable moments, which belong to and mutually condition each other; but, at the same time, they are mutually exclusive or opposed extremes, i.e. poles of the expression of value'.[111] The polarity of the expression of value is implicit in the double character of the commodity; it is externalised through the process of exchange, which establishes money as the universal equivalent: 'Exchange, however, produces a differentiation of the commodity into two elements, commodity and money, an external opposition which expresses the opposition between use-value and value which is inherent in it'.[112] Exchange works like a centrifuge to separate use value and value into the polar opposites, commodities and money, respectively. We can no more understand a commodity or money without the concept of polarity than we can understand a magnet without it. This polarity extends

107 Of value, Marx writes, 'Value, therefore, does not have its description branded on its forehead; it rather transforms every product of labour into a social hieroglyphic' (Marx 1976a, p. 167).

108 Because they spin and have electrical charge, electrons are mini-magnets. An electrical current creates a magnetic field; conversely, the movement of a conductor in a magnetic field creates an electrical current. These principles make possible electromagnets, electric motors and electric generators. With the equations that bear his name, James Clerk Maxwell (1831–79) identified the basic laws of electricity and magnetism.

109 Marx 1976a, p. 139.

110 When the difficult Section Three of Chapter One of *Capital* is skipped, this critical concept of the polarity of value can be overlooked.

111 Marx 1976a, pp. 139–40. Marx writes: 'money and commodities always come into physical confrontation with each other, one at the positive pole of purchase, the other at the negative pole of sale' (Marx 1976a, p. 213).

112 Marx 1976a, p. 199.

to the social roles of buyer and seller: one brings money to the market, the other brings commodities. 'Sale and purchase are one identical act, considered as the alternating relation between two persons who are in polar opposition to each other, the commodity-owner and the money-owner'.[113] Purchasing and selling – as opposed to exchanging use values – manifest the polarity of value: they involve money. One buys with money; one sells for money. In barter there is exchange but neither purchase nor sale:

> The commodity is divested of its original form through its sale, i.e. the moment its use-value actually attracts the gold [money], which previously had a merely imaginary existence in its price ... This single process is two-sided: from one pole, that of the commodity-owner, it is a sale, from the other pole, that of the money owner, it is a purchase. In other words, a sale is a purchase, C-M is also M-C.[114]

What circulates in the market are not bare use values – there are none – but commodities and money polarised by the social magnetism of value.

(ii) We already saw that Marx conceives of value as a power of attraction: 'the value of a commodity measures the degree of its attractiveness for all other elements of material wealth'.[115] Marx plays with the notion of attraction, invoking the animal magnetism of romance. To price a commodity is to flirt with money: 'the prices, those wooing glances cast at money by commodities'.[116] In articulating the several forms and functions of money in Chapter Three of *Capital* Volume I, Marx identifies a further polarization – they keep coming – between commodity circulation proper, where money functions in the roles of measure of value, standard of price and means of circulation, and money that collects in hoards. In hoards, money functions 'as money', that is, as value incarnate, a store of value – like a value capacitor. Marx depicts the relationship between the money functioning as means of circulation ('coin') and money lying in hoards ('money') in terms of circulation attracting and repelling money: 'the quantity of money in circulation unceasingly ebbs and flows. This quantity must therefore be capable of expansion and contraction. At one time money must be attracted as coin, at another time coin must be repelled as money'.[117]

113 Marx 1976a, p. 208.
114 Marx 1976a, p. 203.
115 Marx 1976a, p. 230.
116 Marx 1976a, p. 205.
117 Marx 1976a, p. 231.

Where there is no money, as in barter, this polarization, which requires the value storage (capacitation) function, has no place.[118]

(iii) The sphere of commodity circulation is one of constant alternations between buying and selling, whether it is the wage labourer selling labour power in instalments in order to purchase the commodities to support daily life or it is the capitalist constantly buying (investing) in order to sell (at a profit):

> commodities as use-values confront money as exchange-value. On the other hand, both sides of this opposition are commodities, hence themselves unities of use-value and value. But this unity of differences is expressed at two opposite poles, and at each pole in an opposite way. This is the alternating relation between the two poles: the commodity is in reality a use-value; its existence as a value appears only ideally, in its price, through which it is related to the real embodiment of its value, the gold which confronts it as its opposite ... These antagonistic [*gegensätzlichen*] forms of the commodities are the real forms of motion of the process of exchange.[119]

The sphere of simple commodity circulation is one of constant alternation, from one of its polarised 'real forms' to another: M-C-M-C-M-C-M.

(iv) Marx repeatedly associates crystallization with commodities, value and money. Reflecting on his argument that the substance of value must be already expended abstract labour leads Marx to imagine value in these terms:

> Let us now look at the residue of the products of labour. There is nothing left of them in each case but the same phantom-like objectivity; they are merely congealed quantities of homogeneous human labour, i.e. of human labour-power expended without regard to the form of its expenditure ... As crystals of this social substance, which is common to them all, they are values – commodity values.[120]

Marx's analysis of the expression of value, the value form, concludes that value must appear as money. The 'money crystal' is the commodity (or a symbol of

118 On hoards in Marx's account of money, see Campbell 1997 and Campbell 2002.

119 Marx 1976a, p. 199.

120 Marx 1976a, p. 128. Marx made this association already in the *Critique*: 'As objectification [*Materiatur*] of social labour, all commodities are crystallisations of the same substance [*Einheit*]' (Marx 1970a, p. 29).

that commodity – not a symbol of value) that, through the exchange process, establishes itself alone in the equivalent value form:

> We have already seen, from the simplest expression of value ... that the thing in which the value of another thing is represented appears to have the equivalent form independently of this relation, as a social property inherent in its nature. We followed the process by which this false semblance became firmly established, a process which was completed when the universal equivalent form became identified with the natural form of a particular commodity [gold], and thus crystallized into the money-form.[121]

The polarising of the commodity into commodity and money makes it seem as though money's social power inheres in it naturally. Money, then, appears to be a commercial lodestone, naturally endowed with purchasing power.[122] Crystallisation and crystals are images of value that serve Marx's expository purposes well: crystals are homogeneous solids, sometimes clear or translucent, that are associated with electrical and magnetic forces.[123] As in the cases of a crystal ball or crystal charm, crystals are often attributed occult powers. In 'The New Giant's Staircase' I associate the crystallization of abstract labour into value and money with Dante's image of ice at the bottom of the inferno, since value is indifferent to the particularities of use values and concrete labours, and, for Dante, nothing is more satanic than indifference.[124]

(v) The creation of value in capitalism is not like that of static electricity (an image more suitable to the haphazard commerce of pre-capitalist societies): value in capitalism is created as a sustained current. Just as an electrical current requires a circuit to sustain itself, the valorisation of value 'takes place only within this constantly renewed movement' of commodity circulation's alternation between commodities and money.[125] With the introduction of the value-creating commodity labour power, Marx shows how this alternation, which would seem to go nowhere in value terms, can generate surplus value. In introducing the formula for capital in Chapter Four, Marx begins: 'The circulation of

121 Marx 1976a, p. 187.

122 A lodestone is a piece of magnetite, a crystal that is a naturally occurring magnet.

123 It is illuminating to see what Hegel writes about crystals in his *Philosophy of Nature*, Part Two of his *Encyclopaedia*.

124 See Murray 2005b, included in the present volume as Chapter 16. In his novel *Hard Times*, Charles Dickens focuses on this satanic indifference of capital (Dickens 1990).

125 Marx 1976a, p. 253.

commodities is the starting-point of capital'.[126] In the previous chapter, he says of the circulation of commodities:

> This movement of commodities [C-M-C] is therefore a circuit. On the other hand, the form of this movement excludes money from the circuit. The result of the movement is not the return of the money, but its continued removal further and further away from its starting-point.[127]

But the circuit of capital, M-C-M', begins and ends with money, closing the circuit of monetary flow. In the circuit of capital, 'money, commodity and elements of production are only alternating forms of the capital value in process ... in which the past magnitude of the value is compared with the present, changed value of the capital'.[128] The circuit of capital keeps the power of value flowing and even increasing.

Keeping in mind that the objectivity of value is not natural but rather strictly social, I propose this analogy between value and electromagnetic power: value is like an electrical current created by a magnet spinning inside a coil of wire or vice versa.[129] Compare buying and selling, the constant alternation between the two poles of the value-form – commodity-money-commodity-money-commodity-money – which keeps the rotor of commerce spinning and value surging, to a generator that creates electrical power.[130] The value that surges through circulation supplies the juice needed to make the motors of capitalist production turn. When the magnet's spinning slows or stops, we have a brownout or a blackout, analogous to a recession or depression that occurs when commercial transactions slow, circuits of capital fail to close and cap-

126 Marx 1976a, p. 247.

127 Marx 1976a, p. 210.

128 Marx 1978a, pp. 185–6.

129 'The commodity-form, and the value-relation of the products of labour within which it appears, have absolutely no connection with the physical nature of the commodity and the material [*dinglich*] relations arising out of this. It is nothing but the definite social relation between men themselves which assumes here, for them, the fantastic form of a relation between things' (Marx 1976a, p. 165).

130 One of the points the analogy brings home is basic to Marx's value-form theory of value, namely: the circulation of commodities and money – the transformation of commodities into money – is co-constitutive, along with the expenditure of human labour, of value. Marx further associates the workings of the market with occult powers by framing market transactions in alchemical terms: 'Circulation becomes the great social retort into which everything is thrown, to come out again as the money crystal' (Marx 1976a, p. 229). Stuff in, money out.

ital accumulation suffers a loss of power.[131] Just as putting out electrical power requires special physical arrangements – the spinning of magnets arranged within coiled wire – generating value requires a special social set-up. The special set-up required for the generation of value is production for the market (or its analogue), where value, polarised into commodities and money, can circulate. As Marx points out in Section Four of Chapter One, when we look at noncapitalist social arrangements, value – with its inescapable fetish character – is absent.[132] The movements of such societies resemble neither the workings of a generator – they do not put out the homogeneous, suprasensible objectivity of value – nor does production resemble an electric motor propelled by a single kind of power.

Let us briefly consider several features of that peculiar kind of social power that value involves. Some of its features have grown so obvious as to become virtually imperceptible, yet these features offer a glimpse of what Rubin called the neglected 'qualitative sociological side of Marx's theory of value'. Analysis of the peculiar powers of value points up the loss for social theory involved in the autonomisation of economics.[133] (i) Value's power is homogeneous; it is unrelated to the particular characteristics of commodities or money or to the particularities of sellers or buyers. (ii) Value's homogeneity derives from the market's practice of treating human labour as qualitatively equal: 'The labour of every individual in so far as it manifests itself in exchange-values possesses this social character of equality'.[134] (iii) Value is a 'radical leveller': anyone can produce value and anyone can be a buyer or seller. Value's power is available (in principle) to anyone.[135] (iv) As a leveller, the abstract power of value threatens the social and moral bonds of noncapitalist societies and institutions: value is a social solvent. Martha Campbell writes, 'because, as value, social interdependence is abstract and embodied as money, atomism is the way people relate to each other'.[136] Just as indifference is an attitude, not

131 Disruptions of the flow of commerce often lead to or result from breakdowns in the financial sector.

132 See also Marx 1970a, pp. 33–4.

133 See Clarke 1982, Sandel 1996 and Fine and Milonakis 2009.

134 Marx 1970a, p. 32.

135 A popular bumper sticker in the United States is simply an equals sign, '='.

136 Campbell 2004, pp. 83–4. Against the naturalisation of atomism in neoclassical economics, she observes, 'Atomism, in other words, is a social relation that combines the contradictory aspects of the "exclusively individual" and the "exclusively social"' (Campbell 2004, p. 80). Marx maintains that, once money becomes the 'incarnation of all human labour', people are 'related to each other ... in a purely atomistic way' (Marx 1976a, p. 187).

the lack of one, atomism is not the absence of sociality – as in neoclassical theory, where 'there is no society' (Margaret Thatcher) – but rather a seemingly asocial, abstract kind of sociality. (v) Value's social power is privately held and generally directed to private ends; any relation to the common good is contingent. (vi) Value's power is borne by things; here lies the primary meaning of the fetish character of the commodity and of money. (vii) Value's power is, ordinarily, transferable: on a given day, Fiat may buy Chrysler or Warren Buffett may hand billions over to the Gates Foundation.[137] (viii) The exercise of value's power cannot be one-sided and preemptive; it requires the voluntary – if constrained – cooperation of other property holders. That includes wage labourers, who, in capitalist societies, are recognised as the rightful owners of their own labour power. (ix) As 'purely social', value is subject to revaluations, notably to drastic devaluations in periods of crisis.[138] Value's power, then, is insecure, subject to impersonal, non-natural forces, as well as to natural ones (since destruction of use-value results in loss of value). (x) Value appears to be natural, not social: 'it is a characteristic feature of labour which posits exchange-value [value] that it causes the social relations of individuals to appear in the perverted form of a social relationship between things'.[139] While it is a type of fetishism to treat this 'perverted form' as natural, the truth is that 'the social relations between their private labours appear as what they are, i.e. they do not appear as direct social relations between persons in their work, but rather as material [*dinglich*] relations between persons and social relations between things'.[140] Value's fetish character is for real.

In the following passage, Marx pulls together a number of features of value's social power as expressed in money:

> Just as in money every qualitative difference between commodities is extinguished, so too for its part, as a radical leveler, it extinguishes all distinctions. But money is itself a commodity, an external object capable of becoming the private property of any individual. Thus the social power becomes the private power of private persons. Ancient society therefore denounced it as tending to destroy the economic and moral order. Mod-

137 This transferability of value makes possible the centralization (as opposed to concentration) of capital through mergers and acquisition, an important dimension of capital's accumulation process.

138 The feature film *Margin Call* provides a close-up view from inside a New York investment firm of the severe devaluations of the 2007–8 financial crisis.

139 Marx 1970a, p. 34.

140 Marx 1976a, p. 166.

> ern society ... greets gold as its Holy Grail, as the glittering incarnation of its innermost principle of life.[141]

That innermost principle is a refined avarice;[142] as Marx puts it, the capitalist is the 'rational miser'. Marx observes of the power of value, 'the power that each individual exercises over the activity of others or over social wealth exists in him as the owner of *exchange values*, of *money*. He carries his social power, as also his connection with society in his pocket'.[143] In Arthur Miller's play *Death of a Salesman*, Willy Loman's neighbour Charley says to him, 'Who liked J.P. Morgan? Was he impressive? In a Turkish bath he'd look like a butcher. But with his pockets on he was very well liked'.[144] With his description of money as a fetish, Marx assumes an outsider's perspective in order to wake up his readers and get them to see how very strange money, as value's incarnation, really is.[145]

Because commodities and money bear the power of value that makes them fetishes, participants in capitalist societies live under the domination of powers of their own creation. To understand this fetish character of the commodity, Marx brings in religion:

---

141 Marx 1976a, pp. 229–30. Martha Campbell draws the connections between money, the social form of production and the objectivity of value: 'The objectivity of value stems from the indirectly social (in other words, simultaneously private and social) character of production. The entire significance of money as universal equivalent is that it mediates (allows the existence of) this contradiction but does not remove it' (Campbell 2002, p. 224). Even barter tends to dissolve the economic and moral bonds of a non-commercial society: 'This is where barter begins and moves thence into the interior of the community, exerting a disintegrating influence upon it' (Marx 1970a, p. 50). This reflects the difference between barter and what Marcel Maus identified as gift exchange, which serves to bind people together (Maus 1990).

142 'The capitalist does not share the hoarder's superstitions. The forms in which exchange value [value] appears, commodity or money, are indifferent to him, they are impermanent forms, because all real wealth is for him in fact merely exchange value [value] in its different embodiments' (Marx 1991, p. 79).

143 Marx 1986, p. 94. Commercial transactions are levelling not only because they posit the social roles of buyer and seller, lender and borrower, which are in principle open to all members of a commercial society, but also because commerce treats all human labour as equal.

144 Miller 1977, p. 97.

145 Paul Mattick Jr portrays Marx as a kind of anthropologist of his own social world in Mattick Jr 1986.

> In order, therefore, to find an analogy, we must take flight into the misty realm of religion. There the products of the human brain appear as autonomous figures endowed with a life of their own, which enter into relations both with each other and with the human race. So it is in the world of commodities with the products of men's hands.[146]

Marx's theme of the fetishism involved with value represents his judgment that the Enlightenment's attack on religion as superstition backfires, resulting in capitalism's secularised fetishism, where abstract powers of our own making lord it over us.[147]

In saying that the commodity, money and capital are fetishes, Marx is not saying – as Samuel Bailey did in criticising Ricardo's claim that value is intrinsic to the products of labour – that we are fools to attribute occult powers to them.[148] No, the powers are real: where Superman leaps over tall buildings in a bound, Donald Trump builds towers with a big check. Value is strangely objective.[149] The trouble lies not with our thinking – at least not in the first place – but deeper, in the makeup of those societies that produce wealth in the commodity form.

The primary meaning of fetishism concerns the objectivity of value, not how we think about commodities and money or what attitude we take toward them. It is about fetishes and their power, not about individual subjective attitudes or 'insights'. Of course, since value is at the same time objective and 'purely social', the fetish character of the commodity and money says much about us and the social relations that are responsible for value and the fetishism that comes with it. But that fact is hidden by the peculiarity that value appears to be natural rather than social. The commodity in the equivalent form of value,

---

146 Marx 1976a, p. 165.

147 *Capital*, then, is Marx's response to Hegel's account of the Enlightenment in *The Phenomenology of Spirit*: where, in Hegel's account, the Enlightenment culminates in an empty concept of utility that topples over into absolute freedom and then the Terror, Marx arrives at value and capital as the concepts key to understanding the Enlightenment.

148 See Kliman 2000.

149 In the *Critique* (1859) Marx writes, 'Money is not a symbol, just as the existence of a use-value in the form of a commodity is no symbol. A social relation of production appears as something existing apart from individual human beings, and the distinctive relations into which they enter in the course of production in society appear as the specific properties of a thing – it is this perverted [*verkehrte*] appearance, this prosaically real, and by no means imaginary, mystification that is characteristic of all social forms of labour positing exchange-value [value]' (Marx 1970a, p. 49).

which becomes fixed in money, 'seems to be endowed with its equivalent form, its property of direct exchangeability, by nature, just as much as its property of being heavy or its ability to keep us warm'.[150] Money is inscrutable as the social form of wealth in the commodity form.

Though the fetish character of the commodity, money and capital refers to social powers that they possess, these powers appear to be their natural characteristics.[151] Such appearances support a way of thinking about the commodity, money and capital that is fetishistic, not because it attributes occult social powers to them, but rather because it mistakes those powers as being natural rather than social.[152] Marx concludes the first chapter of *Capital* Volume I by mocking those topsy-turvy economists who regard value as a natural property of commodities yet think that use-value is independent of a commodity's physical properties:

> So far no chemist has ever discovered exchange-value either in a pearl or a diamond. The economists who have discovered this chemical substance, and who lay special claim to critical acumen, nevertheless find that the

150 Marx 1976a, p. 149.

151 Indeed, the deep problem with classical political economy (and economics generally) is that it naturalises the capitalist mode of production, along with all its value forms: 'The value-form of the product of labour is the most abstract, but also the most universal form of the bourgeois mode of production; by that fact it stamps the bourgeois mode of production as a particular kind of social production of a historical and transitory character. If then we make the mistake of treating it as the eternal natural form of social production, we necessarily overlook the specificity of the value-form, and consequently of the commodity-form together with its further developments, the money form, the capital form, etc.' (Marx 1976a, p. 174, n. 33).

152 Marx calls this naturalisation of social realities, 'fetishism': 'The adherents of the Monetary System did not see gold and silver as representing money as a social relation of production, but in the form of natural objects with peculiar social properties ... And what of modern political economy, which looks down so disdainfully on the Monetary System? Does not its fetishism become quite palpable when it deals with capital? How long is it since the disappearance of the Physiocratic illusion that ground rent grows out of the soil, not out of society?' (Marx 1976a, p. 176) In *Capital* Volume II, Marx comments on the way that political economy had mixed up the distinction between constant and variable capital with that between fixed and circulating capital, 'What is also brought to fulfillment here is the fetishism peculiar to bourgeois economics, which transforms the social, economic character that things are stamped with in the process of social production into a natural character arising from the material nature of these things' (Marx 1978a, p. 303).

use-value of material objects belongs to them independently of their material properties, while their value, on the other hand, forms a part of them as objects.[153]

Thinking that value is a natural property of products is fetishistic because value is 'purely social'; by the same token, thinking that natural or material factors play value-producing roles in producing useful things is fetishistic. Marx praises MacCulloch because he 'stands above the fetishism of German "thinkers" who assert that "material" and half a dozen similar irrelevancies are elements of value'.[154]

So, Marx does identify certain ways of thinking about value as fetishistic. But Marx's concepts of fetish and fetishism – the first refers to the social power possessed by commodities and money and the second refers to ways of thinking about value – are widely mistaken for more popular notions that have to do with our attitudes toward commodities and money. The commodity fetish is popularly identified with one's attitude: having a measureless craving for costly commodities makes one a fetishist. The root of this popular conception lies in what Thorstein Veblen calls 'conspicuous consumption'.

Veblen explains 'conspicuous consumption' on the basis of the possession of wealth becoming the ordinary basis of esteem (including self-esteem). In Veblen's account of 'predatory societies' that have evolved into commercial and industrial ones, wealth becomes an honour fetish: 'The possession of wealth, which was at the outset valued simply as an evidence of [predatory] efficiency, becomes, in popular apprehension, itself a meritorious act. Wealth is now itself intrinsically honourable and confers honour on its possessor'.[155] Veblen's conception of wealth as an honour fetish resembles Marx's conception of the fetish character of the commodity, with which it is frequently confused, but they are not the same. Veblen saw that the connection between possessing wealth and doing deeds that merit being honoured has worn away, and that this makes continued regard for wealth a fetish. This resembles Marx's point that value's kind of social power is disconnected from the useful properties of commodities. In both cases there is a kind of heedless objectivity: wealth *per se* confers honour, and value conveys purchasing power. Both are kinds of

153 Marx 1976a, p. 177. Once again, Marx mocks the subjectivist theory of usefulness, which, for its part, regards Marx's common sense view of usefulness as its own brand of fetishism.

154 Marx 1970a, p. 35. See also, Marx 1976a, p. 176. This tells us how Marx would have regarded neoclassical ideas of the marginal productivity of capital (meaning produced means of production) and land.

155 Veblen 1997, p. 322.

social power, but two different types. Not only are the two powers different, their sources differ as well; conferring honour depends on cultural factors in ways that adding value does not.[156]

The commodity fetish, money fetish and capital fetish all refer to the peculiar objectivity of value, which is strictly social and suprasensible. Marx exposes the source of the fetish character of the commodity, writing, 'this fetishism of the world of commodities arises from the peculiar social character of the labour which produces them'.[157] The denial of the objectivity of value – and with it the denial of the fetish character of the commodity, money and capital – goes hand in hand with the denial of the social specificity of value and value-producing labour. Since the topic of the specific social form of labour lies outside the horizons of economics (classical and neoclassical), it is in no position to recognise the source of the fetishism. Marx argues that value is intrinsic to commodities but, contra the classical labour theory of value, not simply because they are products of human labour. Value is intrinsic to commodities because social form is intrinsic to human wealth, and value belongs to the peculiar asocial social form of labour and wealth in capitalist societies. To deny the objectivity of value is to treat the wealth of a capitalist society as if it had no social form at all. That is to fall victim to 'the illusion of the economic'. The objectivity of value, however, will not go away because we fail to acknowledge it.

5 Capital: The Mismeasure of Wealth

Marx's approach to the measure of wealth has roots reaching back to Plato, and, especially, to Aristotle. Plato's thinking about measure takes shape in the midst of the disorienting encounter of Athenians with foreign gods and the imperious god of commerce, money.[158] Plato's *Republic* is set in the port of Athens, the Piraeus, at the home of the wealthy foreigner Cephalus and his son Polemarchus; the occasion is the festival for a new goddess. The issue of justice arises quickly in Book I, and Socrates argues against definitions proposed by Cephalus and then Polemarchus. Both definitions are of the sort that one would expect to be proposed by moneymakers. The Sophist Thrasymachus, portrayed as a wild beast, introduces what may represent to Plato the epitome of the moneymaker's idea of justice, the advantage of the stronger.[159] As the conversa-

156 For an ingenious synthesis of Marx, Veblen and Weber, see Baudrillard 1997.

157 Marx 1976a, p. 165.

158 I draw here on the introduction to the chapter on Plato in Murray 1997b, pp. 39–41.

159 In first responding to Thrasymachus, Socrates states that when searching for justice we are

tion between Socrates and Thrasymachus unfolds, this definition morphs into the assertion that justice is tyranny. But tyranny is not recognizable as justice. So Thrasymachus is forced to relent and describe the tyrant as the unjust, but most advantaged, man, 'the man who has the ability to overreach on a large scale'.[160] Socrates presses him on the extent of the tyrant's overreaching, and Thrasymachus agrees that 'the unjust man will overreach' not only 'the just man and the just action' but 'also both the unjust man and the unjust action'.[161] The unjust man or tyrant is thus revealed as a man without measure – in Socrates' words, 'an ignoramus'.[162] The association of moneymaking with boundlessness, then, reaches back to Plato.

Aristotle, to whom Marx appeals, looks to the purpose of a thing for its measure. The theory of virtue that Aristotle works up in his *Nicomachean Ethics* is tailored to his conception of the purpose of a human life. Aristotle develops his thinking about practical virtue further in his *Politics*, where he begins with an inquiry into the art of acquiring wealth, whether for the management of the household or the polity. The purpose of acquiring wealth is to bring about human excellence: 'Thus it is clear that household management attends more to men than to the acquisition of inanimate things, and to human excellence more than to the excellence of property which we call wealth'.[163] Aristotle endorses the use of money as a suitable means of exchanging goods, C-M-C, but he finds using money to make money, M-C-M' (where M' = M + ΔM), to be blameworthy, for it is in its very nature measureless. He observes, 'for the end is always the limit, so, too, in this art of wealth-getting there is no limit of the end, which is riches of the spurious kind, and the acquisition of wealth'.[164] Greed, or *pleonexia*, is native to this 'chrematistical' form of circulation, M-C-M', where money is endlessly spun into more money.

Thomas Aquinas concurs with Aristotle that purposes set limits and that virtue is the proper end and measure of wealth:

> Now, things directed to an end, must take their measure from the exigency of the end. Wherefore riches are good forasmuch as they serve the

searching for something 'more precious than much fine gold', indicating that he is looking for an alternative to money as a measure (as quoted in Murray 1997b, p. 51).

160 As quoted in Murray 1997b, p. 58.

161 As quoted in Murray 1997b, p. 63.

162 As quoted in Murray 1997b, p. 64.

163 As quoted in Murray 1997b, p. 77.

164 As quoted in Murray 1997b, p. 75.

> use of virtue: and if this measure be exceeded, so that they hinder the practice of virtue, they are no longer to be reckoned as a good but as an evil.[165]

Virtue establishes a determinate purpose capable of directing action in a way that an unqualified pursuit of wealth cannot. In his approach to using money to make money, however, Aquinas is more permissive than Aristotle, who flatly condemns its boundlessness. While insisting that virtue is wealth's measure and rejecting boundless moneymaking, Aquinas accepts, conditionally, the use of money to make money: 'the gain itself may be lawfully intended not as a last end, but for the sake of some other end which is necessary or virtuous'.[166] On the one hand, this implies that Aquinas would find the purpose of the capitalist as defined by Marx morally unacceptable, since

> the objective content of the circulation we have been discussing – the valorization of value – is his subjective purpose, and it is only in so far as the appropriation of ever more wealth in the abstract is the sole driving force behind his operations that he functions as a capitalist.[167]

On the other hand, it means that Aquinas sees no necessity for those who engage in the M-C-M' circuit to function as capitalists in Marx's sense. Rather, Aquinas conceives of moneymaking as subordinated to the acceptable circuit C-M-C.[168] For Marx, the competitive conditions of modern capitalism make

---

165 As quoted in Murray 1997b, p. 90. On the influence of Aristotle and Scholastic philosophy on Marx, see Meikle 1985 and 2009.

166 As quoted in Murray 1997b, p. 101. Aquinas addresses Aristotle on this point: Aristotle, Aquinas writes, regards chrematistics as 'justly deserving of blame, because, considered in itself, it satisfies the greed for gain, which knows no limit and tends to infinity. Hence trading, considered in itself, has a certain debasement attaining thereto [*sic*], in so far as, by its very nature, it does not imply a virtuous or necessary end. Nevertheless gain which is the end of trading, though not implying, by its nature, anything virtuous or necessary, does not, in itself, connote anything sinful or contrary to virtue: wherefore nothing prevents gain from being directed to some necessary or even virtuous end, and thus trading becomes lawful' (ibid.).

167 Marx 1976a, p. 254.

168 We might say that Aquinas sees no obstacle to money being used to make money indefinitely in the form that Max Weber calls 'traditional capitalism', which is not animated by the grasping 'spirit of capitalism'. Frank Capra's film *It's a Wonderful Life* pits the 'traditional capitalism' of the Bailey Savings and Loan against the 'spirit of capitalism' driving Mr Potter's bank.

unrealistic the notion that the circuit M-C-M' can be subordinated to C-M-C, such that use value aimed at virtue, rather than the measureless accumulation of capital (value), could be the goal of capitalist production.

Marx adopts the Aristotelian conception that the measure of wealth derives from wealth's specific social form and purpose.[169] Historical materialism tells us that the social production process is purposive and that not all production processes are organised around the same purpose. We look to the specific social purpose of production, then, for its measure of success.[170] Marx applies this to capitalism, concluding: 'Capitalist production finds its measure only in capital'.[171] Capitalism encompasses a number of measures, each based on value: value, expressed as price; surplus value, expressed as profit; rate of surplus value; rate of profit; rate of capital accumulation; rate of interest and more. Since capital is its own measure and capital grows only quantitatively, it is the rate of capital accumulation that is the definitive measure of wealth for capitalism.[172]

Marx endorses Aristotle's analysis of the significance of the two commercial circuits C-M-C and M-C-M' with respect to the measure of wealth, but he goes beyond Aristotle on a decisive point. In the *Urtext* Marx observes:

> Aristotle regards the form of circulation C-M-C ... as natural and reasonable, and brands the form M-C-M, the chrematistic one, as unnatural and inappropriate. What is here being attacked is only exchange value which becomes the content and end-in-itself of circulation, i.e. the setting up

169 The conclusion I arrived at in the General Introduction to *Reflections on Commercial Life* was: 'the most fundamental question under discussion in this anthology [is]: What is the measure, the limit, the end of wealth?' (Murray 1997b, p. 13). Amartya Sen and Martha Nussbaum take up the question of the proper measure of wealth (Sen and Nussbaum 1993 and Nussbaum 2000); they criticise the restriction of current discourse about wealth to matters of quantity and distribution. In the tradition of Aristotle's practical philosophy, their capabilities approach assesses wealth qualitatively, measuring it by what good human functioning requires. Their account, however, lacks Marx's attention to the significance of the specific social form and purpose of wealth.

170 Marx does just that when he distinguishes between productive and unproductive labour based on the specific purpose of production in capitalism, surplus value: 'Looked at from the simple standpoint of the labour process, labour seemed productive if it realized itself in a product, or rather a commodity. From the standpoint of capitalist production we may add the qualification that labour is productive if it directly valorizes capital, or creates surplus-value' (Marx 1976b, pp. 1038–9).

171 Marx 1968b, p. 520.

172 See Arthur 2002a, p. 147.

> of exchange value as something independent, and value as such becoming the aim of exchange ... Use value is the aim of selling for the sake of buying; and value itself, of buying for the sake of selling.[173]

Each circuit has its measure, but the two are poles apart:

> The simple circulation of commodities – selling in order to buy – is a means to a final goal which lies outside circulation, namely the appropriation of use values, the satisfaction of needs. As against this, the circulation of money as capital is an end in itself, for the valorization of value takes place only within this constantly renewed movement. The movement of capital is therefore limitless [*masslos*].[174]

Where these consequences of the two forms of the circulation of money and commodities are concerned, Marx agrees with Aristotle. At the beginning of Chapter Five of *Capital*, Marx marvels at the difference between the two circuits: 'How can this purely formal distinction change the nature of these two processes as if by magic'?[175] He even mentions the commonplace observation that would reduce the two circuits to a simple exchange that is selling for actor A and buying for actor B: 'A and B would declare that the whole series [M-C-M'] was superfluous and nothing but hocus pocus'.[176]

Now we come to where Marx departs from Aristotle. Aristotle conceived of the two circuits as separable, as if one could have generalised commodity production, thus C-M-C, without M-C-M'. Marx argues that the two are inseparable: the chrematistical or moneymaking circuit necessarily exists 'alongside' the C-M-C circuit, in which money functions merely as means of circulation. Marx argues that simple commodity circulation can be sustained only by constantly introducing new commodities, which requires that wealth be produced in the commodity form. Producers, in turn, need commodities to make new commodities, and commodities are acquired by buying them. Consequently,

---

173 Marx 1987b, p. 488.

174 Marx 1976a, p. 253. Since '*Mass*' is German for 'measure', '*masslos*' might be translated as 'measureless' rather than 'limitless'. See also the footnote on Aristotle in Marx 1976a, pp. 253–4, n. 5.

175 Marx 1976a, p. 258. On the role of formal causality in Marxian theory, see Murray 1997a, included in the present volume as Chapter 2.

176 Marx 1976a, p. 259. The claim that the different circuits are 'hocus pocus' is another way of reducing value to use value. For an account of how Marx responds to that commonplace view, see Campbell 2013.

the production of commodities commences with money. Given that starting point, producers will want more money at the end of the circuit than they put up at the start. So, simple commodity production presupposes the production of wealth on a capitalist basis: C-M-C presupposes M-C-M′. The circuit of capital, then, is necessarily found 'alongside' the circuit of simple commodity production, C-M-C. The generalization of the commodity-form of wealth and the production of wealth on a capitalist basis are inseparable. So, while Marx accepts Aristotle's conclusions regarding the implications of the two circuits for the measure of wealth, he rejects the notion that one can generalise the use of money as a means of circulation while avoiding the use of money as a means to make money.[177]

Marx's argument cuts not only against Aristotle but also against liberals, such as F.A. Hayek, who endorse simple commodity exchange (the market) as just, precisely because it does not impose any collective purpose on individuals. If Marx's argument holds, simple commodity circulation is just the benign face of a deeper, more encompassing actuality, the capitalist mode of production, which imposes the boundless end of capital accumulation on all who live under its dominion. The idea of a society without a collective compulsory good is a liberal mirage summoned by 'the illusion of the economic'.

Chris Arthur calls attention to the uniqueness of capital as the measure of wealth: 'the form-determination of capital as inherently self-expanding makes capitalism utterly different from any other mode of production'.[178] Martha Campbell traces the boundlessness of capital to the peculiar abstractness of value and links it to domination:

> In contrast to the varied and material goods that actually satisfy needs, value – the capitalist illusion of wealth – is insubstantial ('phantom-like' or 'ghostly', as Marx calls it (1976a, p. 128)). Because value exists apart from all particular goods, their relation to it is accidental. For this reason, capitalism is indifferent to all particularity, of goods, activities and individuals. Finally, because value is qualitatively uniform, it is purely quantitative and therefore infinite. Because human beings are harnessed

177 Thus, Marx argues in Chapter Four of *Capital* Volume I (as earlier in Section Six 'Transition to Capital' of the *Urtext*) that there is a dialectical transition from the forms of money associated with simple commodity circulation, the subject of Chapter Three, and money as capital. For a reconstruction of Marx's argument for the transition from money to capital, see Campbell 2013.

178 Arthur 2002a, p. 148.

to the creation of something endless that is indifferent to their needs, they are not the subjects of their economic life.[179]

Indifferent to human needs and the specific goods produced to meet them, value is not a peculiar, abstract form of wealth so much as it is 'the illusion of wealth'. Since it abstracts from every useful quality, value lacks that which Marx identifies as necessary for any useful thing: 'the usefulness of a thing makes it a use-value … It is conditioned by the physical properties of the commodity, and has no existence apart from the latter'.[180] In arguing to the conclusion that abstract labour is the substance of value, Marx flatly states that, *as a value*, a commodity is not a useful thing: 'As use-values, commodities differ above all in quality, while as exchange-values [values] they can only differ in quantity, and therefore do not contain an atom of use-value'.[181] Capitalism presents us with the irony that value, its measure of wealth, is not a form of wealth; on the contrary, bereft of all useful properties, value is the antithesis of wealth. When he uses phrases such as 'a void at the heart' or pictures the inverted, downward spiral into nothingness at the core of capital's accumulation process as a 'hellish dialectic', Chris Arthur conjures up what is terrifying in value's absolute separation from use.[182]

6 Toward a New Measure of Wealth

If capital is the mismeasure of wealth, what is its proper measure? What can an approach to Marx and Marxian theory that puts the spotlight on social form and purpose contribute to the project of fundamental social change? At the beginning of this introduction, we saw that Marx's historical materialism tells

179 Campbell 2004, p. 86.
180 Marx 1976a, p. 126.
181 Marx 1976a, p. 128.
182 See the chapter 'The Spectre of Capital', in Arthur 2002a, pp. 153–74. See also Riccardo Bellofiore's essay 'A Ghost Turning into a Vampire: The Concept of Capital and Living Labour' (Bellofiore 2009). Echoing Hegel's account of how the Enlightenment party of 'pure insight' devolves into 'absolute freedom' and then the Terror, Marx warns: 'Appropriation through labour and exchange of equivalents appears as the law of appropriation in this sphere [simple commodity circulation], so that exchange simply gives back the same value in other material. In short, here all is "lovely" ["*sheene*"], but, just like that, it will end in terror [*Schrecken*], and that as a consequence of the law of equivalence. We come, namely, to … *Capital*' (Marx 1954a, pp. 90–1; my translation).

us that 'Production … always has a double character': a mode of production is a 'way of life'. A 'way of life' always involves specific social forms and purposes, purposes which, following Aristotle, function as measures for a way of life. The failure to recognise this double character of production, to recognise that a mode of production involves a way of life, results in the truncated view that I call 'the illusion of the economic'. The idea of 'the economic' is the idea of production that is no particular mode of production, is production in general, and, by the same token, involves no particular social forms and no particular way of life. We have seen that the peculiar social forms and purpose of a capitalist society make it appear to be the economy in general, such that 'the illusion of the economic' comes naturally to participants in capitalist societies. 'The illusion of the economic' closes off the questions that drive Marx's inquiry in *Capital*: What are the specific social forms and purposes of wealth and the production of wealth and what are their consequences? The result is the now familiar narrowing of the horizons of scientific and public discourse to questions about how much 'wealth' there is and, perhaps, how it is distributed.[183]

With 'the illusion of the economic' comes the liberal illusion that a commercial society imposes no compulsory collective good on its participants – for many liberals, that is precisely what makes a commercial society just. In showing that, where wealth generally takes the commodity form, wealth is produced on a capitalist basis, Marx shows that a commercial society is actually a capitalist one. Consequently, a commercial society has a compulsory collective good, namely, the measureless accumulation of capital. We all know what happens to commercial societies when capital's accumulation process breaks down. When we see through the liberal illusion and recognise that a society without any collective purpose is a mirage, not the shining city on the hill, then we cannot avoid the question of what is the most humanly appropriate purpose around which to organise society.

What I call 'use-value Romanticism' and technological naïveté are likewise bound up with 'the illusion of the economic'. 'Use-value Romanticism' incorporates the illusion of liberalism into thinking about a post-capitalist society. If the problem with capitalism is its never-to-be-satisfied hunger for profits, which it extracts through exploiting the class of wage labourers, then – for one conception – surplus value must be ended, either by distributing the surplus back to the workers who produced it, or by redistributing the means of pro-

183 The point of my anthology, *Reflections on Commercial Life* (Murray 1997b), is to make available some outstanding contributions opposed to that narrowing of discourse.

duction such that no surplus-value is produced in the first place. A deeper conception recognises – as Left Ricardians and Proudhonists did not – that value is a specific social form inextricable from surplus value; it calls for doing away with value. But what will take the place of value and surplus value (and the other social forms that go with them), if we somehow rid ourselves of them? The answer, whether given explicitly or implicitly, seems to be use value itself. Production will no longer be production of value for the sake of accumulating surplus value; rather, it will be production for the sake of use value. This is what I call 'use-value Romanticism'; it is caught in the liberal illusion that we can have a society without any definite collective end. Production for the sake of use value is too indefinite to be an organising end; it sidesteps the implications of Marx's point about the double character of production. A mode of production is a way of life, but producing use values lacks the specific social forms and the social and moral substance of a way of life. Production for use value is meant to be an alternative to capitalism, but it is devised from illusions that capitalism generates. It is as if the disappointment with capitalism were that, because it is bound up in profit making, it fails to be the economy in general, which truly would be all about the provision of use values.

Technological naïveté comes with the 'commerce and industry picture' that is one more manifestation of 'the illusion of the economic'. Technological naïveté is the notion that technology develops free of specific social forms and purposes and is simply directed at the ever-more efficient production and delivery of use values. Marx's notions of the formal, and more particularly the real, subsumption of labour under capital undercut technological naïveté and the ordinary notion of 'industry' by making the point that specific social purposes – in capitalist societies, the production of surplus-value for the accumulation of capital – infuse and direct the course of technological development. An important and troubling consequence of this recognition for those working toward a society beyond the capitalist type is that the technology inherited by any new social formation will have been shaped by the imperative to increase surplus value. Recognising this, unfortunately, yields no obvious answers as to what to do with the existing production techniques.

These are some of the negative lessons about anti-capitalism taught by an inquiry into social form and purpose in Marxian theory. If production for the sake of use value is a false substitute for production aimed at accumulating capital – a shadow of capital's scary substantiality – what can take the place of capital? Answering that question requires a worldwide engagement – free of illusions – with the question: What way of life is most appropriate for human beings as co-inhabitants of Earth with its diversity of creatures? The search for humanly appropriate specific social forms and purposes of production presents itself as the pressing focus for the ongoing interpretation of human life in nature and history.

PART 1

The Essays

CHAPTER 1

Value, Money and Capital in Hegel and Marx*

Some years ago I was surprised to receive a package in the mail from a former student.[1] It took me a moment to recognise what was inside, a green ceramic ΔM. I had a good laugh. From our study of *Capital*, the student had gotten the idea loud and clear how preoccupied Marx is with ΔM, or what he calls 'surplus value'. In thinking over Hegel's treatment of property, contracts of exchange and civil society in the *Philosophy of Right* and earlier writings, I am struck by a simple fact: Hegel just does not seem to be interested in ΔM.[2] Hegel is aware that 'gain' or 'profit' motivate what he calls the 'reflective estate' of trade and industry. And he recognises that civil society is naturally expansive, with firms developing products and technologies in order to accumulate wealth. But the topic of surplus value simply does not move Hegel on grounds either of science (where does ΔM come from?) or social justice (what justification can be offered for ΔM?).

Why did the topic not strike a chord for Hegel?[3] Aristotle had posed the problem of its source plainly enough in Book One of his *Politics*, a passage to which Marx responds in *Capital*. And in his treatment of contracts of exchange, Hegel strongly affirms the principle of commutative justice, namely, that items

---

* Originally published as 'Value, Money and Capital in Hegel and Marx', in *Karl Marx and Contemporary Philosophy*, edited by Andrew Chitty and Martin McIvor (Basingstoke, Hampshire: Palgrave Macmillan, 2009), pp. 174–87, reprinted with the kind permission of Palgrave Macmillan.

1 An early version of this paper was presented to the Marx and Philosophy Society Annual Conference on 10 September 2005. Joe McCarney, one of the originators of the society, kindly sent me helpful, thought-provoking remarks on the presentation. I regret that his untimely death put an end to our exchange.

2 Those earlier writings include the Jena *System of Ethical Life* of 1802/3 and the Jena *First Philosophy of Spirit* of 1803/4 (both in Hegel 1979), along with the Jena *Lectures on the Philosophy of Spirit* of 1805/6 (Hegel 1983), and the recently unearthed Heidelberg lectures on *Natural Right and Political Science* (Hegel 1995), the earliest version of the *Philosophy of Right*. Jerry Muller observes, 'For Hegel, the market was the central and most distinctive feature of the modern world' (Muller 2002, p. 139). Hegel and Marx are alike in that they both thought and wrote about topics related to modern commerce throughout their adult lives.

3 Hegel writes about the 'surplus' in the Jena *System* (Hegel 1979, p. 118 ff.), but he is referring to commodities, not to surplus value.

of equal value be exchanged.[4] Yet that basic principle of commercial justice appears incompatible with capital's circuit, M-C-M+ΔM; which is exactly how Aristotle judged it to be.[5] Let me propose, tentatively, two possible reasons why ΔM didn't stir Hegel.

1. After a period of wrestling with the phenomena of modern commercial life as a young man, Hegel reconciled himself to it; ΔM comes with the territory, including ΔM in the form of interest paid to lenders.
2. The key to understanding the source of ΔM is to draw the distinction between labour and labour power and to comprehend the class distinction between capitalists and wage workers. Like John Locke, Hegel gave wage labour the moral stamp of approval; Marx quotes him on that point.[6] But Hegel neither drew the distinction between labour and labour power nor did he think of capitalists and wage workers as two classes. Rather, Hegel clumps them together under the rubric of the 'estate of trade and industry' [*Stand des Gewerbs*].[7] That categorization is doubly antiquated because Hegel is still thinking in terms of estates [*Stände*] rather than classes [*Klassen*] and because he does not distinguish between capitalists and wage labourers as classes.[8]

Hegel's disinterest in ΔM is one manifestation of a fact about his social theory that has been dawning on me for some time: Hegel does not have an adequate, clearly articulated concept of capital.[9] Readers of T.M. Knox's translation of

4 In rejecting the objectivity of value, Richard Winfield rejects Hegel's view here. Instead, for Winfield, commutative justice, if we can use the term, reduces to the requirement that exchanges be voluntary. See Winfield 1988, pp. 109ff.

5 Marx 1976a, p. 267. In particular, Aristotle railed against usury, whose circuit is compressed to M-M+ΔM.

6 Marx 1976a, pp. 271–2, n. 3.

7 Hegel 1991a, § 204. Winfield 1988 criticises Hegel for including the category of 'estates' in his philosophy of right.

8 Hegel divides the estates 'in accordance with *the concept*' into three: 'the *substantial* or immediate estate; the reflecting or *formal* estate; and lastly, the *universal* estate'. These correspond to agriculture, commerce and industry, and the state, respectively (Hegel 1991a, § 202). Hegel subdivides the 'reflecting or *formal* estate', the estate of trade and industry, into (1) the estate of craftsmanship, (2) the estate of manufacturing and (3) the estate of commerce. He draws no distinction between merchant capital and financial capital.

9 Winfield argues that Hegel is right to conceive of the commodity, not capital, as the centrepiece of modern commerce and industry (civil society). He writes, '[Hegel] works out the total structure of commodity relations without subsuming them under a system of capitals whose

Hegel's Philosophy of Right will object that the third subsection under the heading 'The System of Needs' is entitled 'Capital [and class-divisions]' and that, in § 199, Hegel refers us back to an earlier discussion of 'capital' in connection with the family.[10] But Hegel's term here is not '*Kapital*' but rather '*Vermögen*'. (Also, the term that Knox refers to with 'class-divisions' is not '*Klassen*' but rather '*Stände*'.) H.B. Nisbet's translation improves on Knox by translating '*Vermögen*' as 'resources' and '*Stände*' as 'estates'.[11] Paragraph § 199 recalls Adam Smith, as Hegel points to the way that the universal necessarily mediates the particular (Smith's 'invisible hand'). The self-interested efforts of the butcher, the brewer, the baker and others simultaneously allow them and countless strangers to meet their needs while they all maintain and augment (*vermehrt*) the 'universal and permanent resources' (*allgemeine, bleibende Vermögen*).[12] This is as close as Hegel comes to adequate concepts of capital and surplus value, including the idea of the aggregated social capital and its accumulation process. But resources are not necessarily capital, not even resources that accumulate. Admittedly, Hegel does situate resources within civil society, which means that he conceives of them as existing in the commodity form. But capital is more than resources in the commodity form that pile up like the 'heap of commodities' to which Marx refers in the opening sentence of *Capital*. Capital, in Marx's concise phrase, is 'self-valorizing value'; it is a peculiar social form of wealth that is inherently, and boundlessly, dynamic.[13]

---

profit derives from wage-labour commodity production. Although Hegel does make brief mention of the relationship of capital and labour, he treats it as a subordinate element within the market economy. In contrast to Marx, he does not view it as a privileged determining structure that envelops and orders all commodity relations within its process of capital accumulation' (Winfield 1988, p. 99).

10 Hegel 1952, §§ 199, p. 170.

11 Hegel 1991a, § 199.

12 In the same vein Locke and Smith wrote of the 'common stock of mankind'.

13 Moishe Postone writes, 'Marx's category of capital refers to an alienated, dualistic structure of labour-mediated relations in terms of which the peculiar fabric of modern society, its abstract form of domination, its historical dynamic, and its characteristic forms of production and work can be understood systematically. For Marx, capital, as the unfolded commodity form, is the central, totalising category of modern life' (Postone 1993, p. 352). It may seem ironic for me to charge that Hegel lacks a concept of capital, since, with Postone, Chris Arthur and others, I have argued that Marx sees Hegel as the philosopher of capital (Murray 1988a). But the 'of' in this case means that Hegel was unwittingly expressing in his logic of the concept – and more particularly in his logic of the idea – the logic of capital's subsumption of nature and humanity. Having capital on the brain did not require of Hegel that he undertake an exposition of capital and its consequences.

1 Capital and Marx's Critique of Bourgeois Philosophy of Right

In *Marx's Theory of Scientific Knowledge*, I argued that Hegel's *Philosophy of Right* is a crucial book for students of Hegel and Marx.[14] The *Philosophy of Right* is where Hegel's way of doing philosophy should really pay off. Of his four published books, the *Phenomenology* introduces the system; the *Science of Logic* confines itself to the shadowy realm of pure abstractions; and the *Encyclopaedia of the Philosophical Sciences* treats logic and the 'real sciences' of nature and spirit in a satisfactorily encyclopaedic fashion.[15] The *Philosophy of Right*, then, is Hegel's only full-dress version of a philosophical real science (*Realwissenschaft*). Here is where he had better deliver. And it was to Hegel's *Philosophy of Right* that the young Marx turned in 1843 after his abbreviated career as editor of the *Rheinische Zeitung*.

In the period between his dissertation and the *Grundrisse*, Marx was perhaps never more intellectually engrossed than in his uncompleted critique of Hegel's *Philosophy of Right*, which he considered the best book bourgeois social theory had to offer. Characteristically, Marx saw here an opportunity to criticise simultaneously the leading theory of the modern world along with that world itself: 'The critique of the German philosophy of right and of the state, which received its most consistent, its richest, and its final comprehension through Hegel, is ... the critical analysis of the modern state and of the actuality connected with it'.[16] Marx's work on the *Philosophy of Right* set his future course. (1) He locked into Feuerbach's critique that Hegel imposed logic onto reality. (2) It convinced Marx that the key to comprehending modern life lay in the anatomy of civil society. (3) It educated him more deeply in certain of Hegel's ways of thinking, prompting him to attend to the content and dialectic of social forms. (4) The series of 'brochures' that Marx announced in the 'Preface' to his *Paris Manuscripts* had their roots in his encounter with Hegel's *Philosophy of Right*, and the six 'book' scheme that he projected in the *Grundrisse* descends from those youthful plans. *Capital* is the first, and last, installment of Marx's mature critique of Hegel's *Philosophy of Right* and bourgeois philosophy of right generally. The concept of capital is central to that mature critique.

14 Murray 1988a, pp. 27–43.

15 Unlike the 'shadows' examined by the science of logic, the objects of the 'real sciences' of nature and spirit are actual. The task of the real sciences is to work out dialectically the basic concepts enabling scientific understanding of the relevant region of reality.

16 Marx 1970, pp. 136–7.

Closely linked to his focus on ΔM is Marx's choice to organise his presentation of capitalist society in terms of two spheres, the sphere of commodity circulation and the sphere of capital's circulation. Lacking an explicit, articulated concept of capital, Hegel does not draw this distinction. In Marx's theory, *value* is the dominant concept in the first sphere, *surplus value* in the second. Already Marx's *Grundrisse* is structured in terms of two books, the book on money and the book on capital. Upon finishing the *Grundrisse*, Marx wrote the 'Original Text' (*Urtext*) and then rewrote it for publication as the *Contribution to the Critique of Political Economy*. Both texts concerned commodities and money, the sphere of simple circulation.[17] One reason why Marx took this approach was because he expected his theory of capital to create a furore.[18] Though he first presented his account of the sphere of circulation separately (in the *Critique*), one of *Capital's* chief claims is that the sphere of simple commodity circulation is an abstraction from the sphere of capital's circulation; there is a conceptual distinction between the two, not a real one. As Chris Arthur has urged, *Capital* does not posit the existence of some precursor to capitalism called simple commodity production.[19] Rather, *Capital* shows that generalised commodity circulation, value and money are inseparable from capital, surplus value and wage labour. There are not actually two spheres; there are two ways of conceiving the marketplace.

Marx has several reasons for adopting the two-sphere mode of presentation. One concerns his phenomenologically based, systematic dialectical presentation; another concerns ideology critique. In the 'Original Manuscript' (*Urtext*) and again in *Capital*, Marx makes the dialectical argument that the sphere of simple commodity circulation cannot stand alone; rather, it presupposes production on a capitalist basis. Marx's approach in *Capital* to the bourgeois theory of right is to show that it is an ideology and to reveal how the peculiar social forms of capitalist society present themselves in ways that naturally foster this ideology. Here is where the two-sphere construction figures in: because commodity circulation is an easily recognizable and understandable moment of the circulation of capital where liberty, equality, property and Bentham appear to reign, it is easily mistaken for an independent sphere and even for the full reality of capitalist society.[20] Marx discloses the bourgeois theory of right to

17 The 'Original Text' contains several pages of a draft of Chapter Three, on capital. This part was dropped in the *Contribution to the Critique*.

18 See Marx's letter of 28 March 1859 to Lassalle.

19 Arthur 2002a, Chapter Two, especially p. 19.

20 In the final paragraph of the part of *Capital* Volume 1 dealing with the transformation

be, in the main, the ideology of the sphere of simple commodity circulation wrenched free from the circulation of capital, of which it is, in truth, only an aspect.

The two spheres are coupled by ΔM. In *Capital* Volume I, Marx devotes Part Two, 'The Transformation of Money into Capital', first to setting up the puzzle posed by the circuit of capital, M-C-M+ΔM – how can ΔM arise without offending commutative justice? – and then to supplying the distinction between labour and labour power required to solve it: 'The form of circulation within which money is transformed into capital contradicts all the previously developed laws bearing on the nature of commodities, value, money and even circulation itself'.[21] When he completes the solution late in Chapter Seven, 'The Labour Process and the Valorization Process', Marx insists on the point that capital's valorisation process can leave the sphere of commodity circulation's rule of justice intact: 'Every condition of the problem is satisfied, while the laws governing the exchange of commodities have not been violated in any way. Equivalent has been exchanged for equivalent'.[22] Hegel, by contrast, makes no distinction of spheres and pays the puzzle no heed. Hegel's attention never turns to ΔM.

Marx pulls up the two main planks of the bourgeois conception of right, both of which are incorporated into Hegel's *Philosophy of Right*. One concerns the principle of appropriation, the other the principle of exchange. The bourgeois principle of appropriation was famously enunciated by Locke in Chapter Five of his *Second Treatise of Government*: my labour entitles me to property. Hegel restates it in the *Philosophy of Right*: 'To give form to something is the mode of taking possession most in keeping with the idea, inasmuch as it combines the subjective and the objective'.[23] The bourgeois principle of exchange is that of commutative justice: equal values are to be exchanged. Hegel enunciates this principle in connection with contracts of exchange:

of money into capital, Marx writes, 'this sphere of simple circulation or the exchange of commodities … provide[s] the "free-trader *vulgaris*" with his views, his concepts and the standard by which he judges the society of capital and wage-labour' (Marx 1976a, p. 280).

21 Marx 1976a, p. 258.

22 Marx 1976a, p. 301; see also p. 731.

23 Hegel 1991a, §56R. Bernard Cullen observes that Hegel's first reference to economic activity was due to his reading of Locke and 'the Lockean concept of property as the embodiment of the personality of the labour was to reappear – practically unmodified – in vitally important sections of the *Philosophy of Right*, almost thirty years later (see Hegel 1991a, §51)' (Cullen 1979, p. 16).

> Since each party, in a real contract, retains *the same* property with which he enters the contract and which he simultaneously relinquishes, that property which remains *identical* as having being *in itself* within the contract is distinct from the external things [*Sachen*] which change owners in the course of the transaction. The former is the *value*, in respect of which the objects of the contract [*Vertragsgegenstände*] are equal to each other, whatever qualitative external differences there may be between the things exchanged; it is their *universal* aspect.[24]

Marx accepts that definition, saying, 'The law of exchange requires equality only between the exchange-values of the commodities given in exchange for one another'.[25]

Marx argues that the bourgeois principle that property is acquired through one's own labour necessarily reverses itself. Those who labour, the wage labourers, acquire no property in their product, while all property goes to those who do not labour, namely, the capitalists. Property, which appeared, necessarily, as 'grounded in a man's own labour', now 'turns out be the right, on the part of the capitalist, to appropriate the unpaid labour of others or its product, and the impossibility, on the part of the worker, of appropriating his own product'.[26]

As for the bourgeois principle of exchange, Marx shows that surplus value, which derives from the surplus labour that the capitalist class can extract from the working class, need not entail any violation of the standards of commutative justice. In revealing that the sphere of commodity circulation depends upon the circulation of capital, however, Marx exposes the irony that the whole framework and rationale of commutative justice, inasmuch as it appeals to the existence of value, rests on the exploitation of the class of wage workers. For without surplus value, there is no value.

Moving on to the reproduction of capital and its accumulation, Marx demonstrates that, as the capitalist's original investment – at first assumed to be the result of his own labour – is replaced by accumulated surplus value, the exchange between capitalist and wage labourer devolves into 'the legal fiction of a contract'.[27] Marx summarises the shocking outcome of his investigation of the concept of capital for bourgeois theory of right: 'Therefore, however much the capitalist mode of appropriation may seem to fly in the face of the original laws of commodity production, it nevertheless arises, not from a violation of

24 Hegel 1991a, § 77.

25 Marx 1976a, p. 731.

26 Marx 1976a, p. 730.

27 Marx 1976a, p. 719.

these laws but, on the contrary, from their application'.[28] These points that Marx makes against bourgeois philosophy of right all turn on the concept of capital.

In the treatment of the process of 'so-called primitive accumulation' in the concluding part of *Capital* Volume I, Marx closes the circle of his mature critique of bourgeois philosophy of right by removing the assumption that the capitalist's original investment funds were the consequence of his own labour. To the contrary, Marx's exposé of the secret of the 'so-called primitive accumulation' of capital reveals the process to have been one of bloody usurpation.

2 Value, Money and the Market

It is a profound misreading of *Capital* to think that the critical element of the book enters with the shift from the sphere of commodity circulation to the sphere of capital's circulation. That is the Ricardian reading of Marx. Marx's theory of value exclusively concerns the social form of labour peculiar to capitalist societies, a topic that is not on Ricardo's radar. The point of *Capital* is not to redistribute surplus value, as with the Ricardian Socialists; it is to abolish value. The Ricardian interpretation misses Marx's critique of bourgeois theory of right: surplus value is not the result of violating commodity exchange's law of equality; on the contrary, it is the presupposition and necessary consequence of generalised commodity exchange. Surplus value is the condition for the existence of the law of value. But Marx's conceptions of value and of simple commodity circulation are already deeply critical at the level of commodity circulation. Obstructions to human freedom and community already populate the sphere of simple commodity circulation.

Hegel's ideas about commodity exchange, value and money anticipate many of Marx's points: both see modern commercial life as marked by abstraction (of needs, labour and social relations); cynical levelling; egoism and excess; poverty and dangerous inequalities of wealth; and the domination of individuals by blind, unstable abstract forces. Certain of Hegel's (early) formulations surpass Marx's language in vehemence. Here is Hegel's description of the system of needs from the Jena *First Philosophy of Spirit*:

> Need and labour, elevated into this universality, then form on their own account a monstrous system of community and mutual interdependence

28 Marx 1976a, p. 730.

> in a great people; a life of the dead body, that moves itself within itself, one which ebbs and flows in its motion blindly, like the elements, and which requires continual strict dominance and taming like a wild beast.[29]

By comparison, this correlative passage from *Capital* is rather tepid:

> The owners of commodities therefore find out that the same division of labour which turns them into independent private producers also makes the social process of production and the relations of the individual producers to each other within that process independent of the producers themselves; they also find out that the independence of the individuals from each other has as its counterpart and supplement a system of all-round material dependence.[30]

Though Hegel's and Marx's ideas regarding commodity circulation overlap a good deal, substantial differences remain. First, as we have seen, Hegel does not articulate a concept of capital; consequently, he draws no distinction between the sphere of commodity circulation and the sphere of capital's circulation. Neither, then, does Hegel see capital's circulation as the presupposition of commodity circulation. As a result, he does not recognise the challenges to the bourgeois philosophy of right or the fresh obstacles to human freedom and community that Marx's exposition of capital discloses. Second, as critical as Hegel is about modern commerce (civil society), he reconciles himself to it. That is true from his first Jena writings through to the *Philosophy of Right*, written almost 20 years later: 'Thus in this system what rules appears as the unconscious and blind entirety of needs and the modes of their satisfaction. But the universal must be able to master this unconscious and blind fate and become a government'.[31] In the *Philosophy of Right*, Hegel counts on several different mediating institutions, above all, the state, to buffer the ill effects of the clash of the particular and universal in what Smith called 'the great scramble' of the marketplace.

In thinking about Hegel as a philosopher of reconciliation, it may be helpful to distinguish where Hegel believes that he has found reconciliation *in* actuality and where he reconciles himself *to* social realities that resist recon-

29 Hegel 1979, p. 249. Compare the toned-down version in Hegel 1991a, §186. See also Hegel 1979, pp. 153–4.
30 Marx 1976a, p. 203.
31 Hegel 1979, pp. 167–8.

ciliation. Hegel's approach to civil society incorporates reconciliation in both senses. Like Smith, Hegel sees a certain reconciliation of self-seeking and the good of the community as inherent to the system of trading the products of the division of labour: 'In this dependence and reciprocity of work and the satisfaction of needs, *subjective selfishness* turns into a *contribution towards the satisfaction of the needs* of *everyone else*'.[32] He finds further conciliatory aspects to civil society in the expansion and refinement of wealth, capabilities and permanent resources available to members of civil society. Memberships in *estates* [*Stände*] and *corporations* are also important in reconciling self-interest and the common good. Hegel cautions that the estates 'are of special importance, because private persons, despite their selfishness, find it necessary to have recourse to others. This is accordingly the root which links selfishness with the universal, i.e. with the state, which must take care to ensure that this connection is a firm and solid one'.[33] Last, but definitely not least, Hegel counts on the intervention of the state, which, as he was aware, can take place in multiple ways.

All the same, civil society's discontents are not uprooted: 'civil society affords a spectacle of extravagance and misery as well as of the physical and ethical corruption common to both'; poverty, in particular, 'agitates and torments' civil society without end.[34] There remains much about civil society that Hegel believes we must reconcile ourselves *to* if we intend to defend the modern world's great advance, namely, 'the principle of the self-sufficient and inherently infinite personality of the individual [*des Einzelnen*], the principle of subjective freedom'.[35] Though Hegel reconciles himself to civil society, like Marx, his conception of value and the peculiar social form of labour that produces value is profoundly critical. Let us turn then to Hegel's ideas about value and money.

Hegel does not write a great deal about value, and it is hard to draw conclusions even about basic aspects of his theory of the kind of value that money measures: does he have a labour theory of value, or a utility theory, or neither?[36] In particular, the question of how value is determined quantitatively is left hanging.[37] Still, we can identify a number of features of value as Hegel con-

---

32 Hegel 1991a, §199.

33 Hegel 1991a, §201.

34 Hegel 1991a, §185.

35 Hegel 1991a, §185R.

36 For a sophisticated account of Hegel's theory of value that explores a range of his uses of the concept of value, see Deranty 2005.

37 While perhaps frustrating for his readers, it may be to Hegel's credit that his theory of

ceives of it. Unlike classical political economists, Hegel sees value as bound up with the particular way that the production and distribution of wealth is organised in civil society, whose emergence 'belongs to the modern world'.[38] Value is thoroughly modern, a feature of the bourgeois world. Before Marx, Hegel has a 'truly social' concept of value.[39] Hegel's approach to value is cut from different cloth than that of political economy: it is historical and dialectical.[40] Value presupposes private property.[41] Value presupposes an advanced division of labour. Value presupposes commodity exchange, a social practice of abstraction that validates all labours in abstraction from their concrete purposes and methods. Value presupposes a public, authoritative system of recognition of commodity exchangers as equals. Value presupposes that a multiplicity of needs, use values and labours are comparable, indeed comparable quantitatively, and commodity exchange treats useful things as sums of money, while the labour power used in producing them counts as an input with a price.[42] Value is something public, universal; it is substantial even though utterly abstract (Marx writes of value's 'ghostly objectivity'). Value is the subject matter of contracts; it can be owned in contradistinction to owning particular use values. Those who lend at interest own only the value lent, not the specific thing loaned.[43] Value is changeable; it is 'a perpetual wave, surging up and down'.[44] More specifically, Hegel recognises that value is responsive to demand and to technological change. The former suggests that Hegel recognises that value and price are inseparable, the latter indicates that Hegel has at least a rudimentary idea of the 'value treadmill', whereby the increasing productive power of labour does nothing to increase the rate at which value is produced.[45]

Something remarkable is taking shape here. As Chris Arthur successfully argues in his provocatively titled essay 'Hegel's Theory of the Value Form', Hegel,

---

value remains indeterminate, since there are serious problems with both subjective utility theories of value and with the classical labour theory of value.

38 Hegel, 1991a, § 182A.

39 See Murray 2000a, included in the present volume as Chapter 4.

40 Winfield 1988 rightly makes much of this point.

41 Hegel 1991a, § 63A.

42 Hegel 1979, p. 118; Hegel 1991a, § 80.

43 Hegel 1995, p. 89. The relevant text from Hegel 1995 is: 'Lending on interest [*Anleihen*] (*mutuum*) is the same as renting, except that lenders remain owners solely of the value but have divested themselves of the specific thing'.

44 Hegel 1979, p. 167.

45 On the 'value treadmill', see Marx 1976a, p. 137. As Marx observes, this effect is one of the important consequences of the fact that the substance of value is *abstract* labour.

like Marx, is a value-form theorist.[46] Value-form theory represents a fundamental break with classical political economy in that it recognises the inner connectedness of the commodity, value and money. Money is the necessary form of appearance of value, whose 'ghostly objectivity' is a consequence of the social sort of labour that produces commodities. Money is no mere technical device, a convenience to facilitate barter; money plays a role in the constitution of commodities and value. Hegel distinguishes barter from purchase and sale, which is the 'exchange of a commodity for money [*Geld*], i.e., a thing that is not specific but universal, or a commodity that only has value, with no other specific determination as to use'.[47] This suggests that Hegel grasps a key feature of the value form, namely, the necessary polarity of the expression of value: the commodity functions as a particular use value (in what Marx calls the 'relative value form'), while money functions as value incarnate (in what Marx calls the 'equivalent value form'). Hegel conceives of the relation between money and value such that we cannot speak of value in a barter system, 'since money abstracts from the [specific] commodity to pure value, a primitive people does not yet have money, and makes do with inconvenient barter'.[48]

Here is a passage on commodity exchange in which Hegel captures fundamentals of value-form theory: 'The universality of labour or the indifference of all labour is posited as a middle term with which all labour is compared and into which each single piece of labour can be directly converted; this middle term, posited as something real, is *money*'.[49] Commodity-producing labour is socially validated as labour in the abstract, establishing abstract labour as the inner measure of the value of commodities that is necessarily expressed in money, value's outer measure. Hegel, of course, also recognises money's function as a means of circulation. With his well-articulated account of how credit emerges naturally from commodity exchange, creating the necessity for money as means of payment in addition to money as means of circulation, Hegel again anticipates Marx.

46 Arthur 2002a; see Hegel 1991a, § 63A, pp. 203, 204.

47 Hegel 1995, pp. 87–8.

48 Hegel 1995, p. 88.

49 Hegel 1979, p. 154.

3 Conclusion

Hegel thought deeply about commodities, value and money as a young man and kept thinking about them throughout the rest of his life. How close he was to arriving at an adequate conception of capital is suggested by a passage from his early Jena *System*. Here Hegel conceives of the capacity of value to maintain itself in commodity exchange in terms of the logic of the concept (which belongs to Hegel's subjective logic):

> This is exchange ... Property enters reality through the plurality of persons involved in exchange and mutually recognizing one another. Value enters in the reality of things and applies to each of them as surplus [i.e. as a commodity, rather than a product to be used by the producer]; the concept enters as self-moving, annihilating itself in its opposite, taking on the opposite character in place of the one it possessed before.[50]

Hegel here has the exchange of two commodities (presumably mediated by money) in mind; ΔM does not come into the picture. By contrast, in *Capital* Volume I Marx makes quite a similar observation but with respect to the circuit of capital, M-C-M+ΔM. He writes:

> Both the money and the commodity function only as different modes of existence of value itself, the money as its general mode of existence, the commodity as its particular or, so to speak, disguised mode. It is constantly changing from one into the other, without becoming lost in this movement; it thus becomes transformed into an automatic subject.[51]

Marx argues that this self-movement of value in and out of the money and commodity forms makes sense only if it leads to offspring in the form of ΔM.[52] What is the point of something as abstract and homogeneous as value preserving itself in the course of its circulation unless that process results in a quantitative increase – ΔM?

Marx makes a powerful argument here based on the very considerations that Hegel identifies as operative in commodity exchange. Marx combines his insight (which Hegel shares) that money is the sole adequate form in which

---

50 Hegel 1979, p. 121.

51 Marx 1976a, p. 255; compare Marx 1987b, p. 501.

52 Marx 1976a, pp. 250–1, 255–6.

value can express its identity or its change over time with the idea of value becoming a 'dominant subject' within commodity circulation to argue that money is necessarily the starting point and end point of the circuits that value dominates:

> As the dominant subject [*übergreifendes Subjekt*] of this process, in which it alternately assumes and loses the form of money and the form of commodities, but preserves and expands itself through all these changes, value requires above all an independent form by means of which its identity with itself may be asserted. Only in the shape of money does it possess this form. Money therefore forms the starting-point and the conclusion of every valorization process.[53]

When, in Hegel's words, 'value enters in the reality of things [commodities]' and value becomes 'self-moving', M-C-M+ΔM is the only circuit of its movement that makes sense.[54] Money must beget money.[55]

How important is Hegel's failure to articulate the concept of capital to his standing as a theorist of modern life? Marx's discoveries regarding the implications of capital for the bourgeois philosophy of right suggest that it is very important. Hegel's treatment of modern commercial life (civil society) in the *Philosophy of Right* and its several forerunners remains a dense, brilliant and honest account of modern commercial life. But Hegel's disinterest in ΔM and his failure to articulate the concept of capital cast doubt on Allen Wood's unfettered praise: Hegel's 'penetrating analysis of the human predicament in modern society is perhaps unsurpassed among social observers of the past two centuries'.[56] No doubt, the *Philosophy of Right* is full of remarkable insights into modern life, but can a book that articulates no clear concept of capital be the most penetrating analysis of modern society to date? Is the concept of capital so trifling?

---

53 Marx 1976a, p. 255.

54 This means that simple commodity circulation presupposes the circulation of capital, one of the most important points Marx makes in *Capital*. This is why, as against Winfield, Marx sees the commodity as subordinate to capital and views capital 'as a privileged determining structure that envelops all and orders all commodity relations' (Winfield 1988, p. 99).

55 Marx 1976a, p. 256.

56 Wood 1991, p. xxvii.

CHAPTER 2

Redoubled Empiricism: The Place of Social Form and Formal Causality in Marxian Theory*[1]

The extraordinary importance of Karl Marx for philosophy and social theory today depends heavily on the role social form plays in his thought.[2] His understanding of social form is distinctive but deeply indebted to Aristotle and Hegel. This fact is what, unfortunately, makes Marx's thinking so inscrutable to many.[3] For Marx, like Aristotle and Hegel, is diametrically opposed to the mind-set that

---

* Originally published as 'Redoubled Empiricism: The Place of Social Form and Formal Causality in Marxian Theory', in *New Investigations of Marx's Method*, edited by Fred Moseley and Martha Campbell (Atlantic Highlands, N.J.: Humanities Press, 1997), pp. 38–65, reprinted with the kind permission of Humanity Books.

1 The phrase 'redoubled empiricism' (which replaces 'empiricism in second intension', the one I used in my *Marx's Theory of Scientific Knowledge*) requires some preliminary comments. First, to 'redouble' empiricism simply means to double, not quadruple it; the phrase carries the connotation of a renewal and intensification of the efforts of empiricism. The redoubling I have in mind pertains to the concepts employed in empirical studies. Ordinary empiricism takes these for granted and to that extent handles them in an unselfconscious, non-empirical and consequently dogmatic manner. Why it falls into this trap will be examined in the chapter. Redoubled empiricism steers away from this dogmatism by consciously and empirically reflecting on the fixation of concepts in their relations to one another. How this is done will not be the subject of this chapter.

It is a fair question as to whether or not such non-dogmatic empiricism should be called empiricism at all. Donald Davidson, who criticises the 'very idea of a conceptual scheme' as the third dogma of empiricism – W.V.O. Quine having criticised two others – wonders whether it makes sense to extend the term 'empiricism' to what remains once the dogmas have been eliminated (Davidson 1984, p. 189). I choose to keep the term and risk confusions for this reason: the criticisms of ordinary empiricism on the part of redoubled empiricism are internal to the original empiricist project, which was to avoid unexamined and empirically unsupported assumptions in order to combat dogmatism. Redoubled empiricism is truer to the empiricist project than 'empiricism' as it has generally been understood.

2 Among the growing number of interpreters of Marxian theory who are particularly attentive to the role of social form let me mention these: Georg Lukács, Karl Korsch, I.I. Rubin, Roman Rosdolsky, Furio Cerutti, David Harvey, Derek Sayer, Simon Clarke, George McCarthy, Moishe Postone and the contributors to *New Investigations of Marx's Method* and its predecessor, *Marx's Method in 'Capital': A Reexamination*.

3 This is a point Scott Meikle makes in no uncertain terms. See Meikle 1985.

spans modern rationalism, British empiricism and Kantianism, to the 'purist splits'[4] that remain the backbone of our modern philosophical and scientific culture, the splits between the conceptual and the empirical and the subjective and the objective. Because of this opposition, Marx rejects the purist philosophical underpinnings that govern classical and neoclassical economics and incapacitate them from taking the proper measure of social form.

Characteristically, 'purist splits' divide their adherents into opposing philosophical camps. Following Hegel's account of the different 'attitudes toward objectivity',[5] I will separate them into modern rationalism, which I will call 'purist objectivism' (or 'objectivism') and 'purist subjectivism' (or 'subjectivism'), which includes British empiricism and Kant's critical philosophy. Though our focus is on empiricism and, more generally, subjectivism, we will examine both branches of purism to see how each closes off the conceptual space needed to make intelligible Marx's redoubled empiricism, that is, his empirical approach to social form and his attention to formal causality. In Marx's critique of the 'purist splits' and the modern philosophical alternatives that derive from them, we find the deepest roots of his profound methodological and scientific differences with classical and neoclassical economics. To come to terms with the depth of Marx's critique of classical and neoclassical economics requires that we investigate his fundamental differences with the mind-set of the modern philosophers.

In this chapter, then, I try to get to the bottom of the distinctiveness and superiority of Marxian theory over against classical and neoclassical economics. It lies in the fact that Marx takes a radically different – and philosophically and scientifically more satisfactory – approach to social form. Investigating Marx's understanding of social form opens the door to: (1) his philosophical rejection of the 'purist splits', (2) his revival of Aristotelian social forms and formal causality (which means that social forms make a difference in the world), and (3) his redoubled empiricism, wherein the social forms of needs, production, distribution – and not just the behaviour of objects already subsumed under forms – along with the powers and interconnections of these forms, are themselves subjects for experience-based inquiry.

The six key and interrelated concepts for this chapter, then, are: 'purist split', objectivism, subjectivism, social form, formal causality, and redoubled empiricism. My argument comes to this: both objectivism and subjectivism are rooted in 'purist splits' between the empirical and the conceptual and between the

4 I borrow this term from Collins 1972, pp. 14ff.

5 See Hegel 1975, pp. 47–112.

objective and the subjective that block redoubled empiricism and any philosophically or scientifically adequate account of social form. Modern rationalism, by prizing the purely conceptual over against the empirical, chokes off any possibility of redoubled empiricism. It can allow for objective social forms but not for an empirical inquiry into them. Subjectivism undercuts the notion of objective social form, for, on its terms, concepts are purely subjective and what is purely subjective has no objective correlate, such as a social form. With the same stroke, subjectivism renders nonsensical both formal causality (nonexistent forms can have no effects) and redoubled empiricism (if concepts are purely subjective, there is no point in submitting them to empirical scrutiny). I claim that Marx, following Aristotle and Hegel, rejects objectivism and subjectivism and their shared purist assumptions about concepts and facts, subjectivity and objectivity, and that he thereby discloses the space for social forms, formal causality and redoubled empiricism. Marx's position is not only philosophically more attractive, putting Marx in the company of the most astute 'post-dogmatic' empiricists – it also pays off scientifically.[6]

Classical and neoclassical economics are scientifically deficient, in the Marxian view, precisely because they harbour the purist assumptions of modern philosophy and, consequently, fail to advance from ordinary to redoubled empiricism: 'With all later bourgeois economists, as with Adam Smith, lack of theoretical understanding needed to distinguish the different forms of economic relations remains the rule in their coarse grabbing at and interest in the empirically available material'.[7] Conversely, in appealing to specific social forms (e.g., value, wage labour, capital) and their power (formal causality), Marx is able to identify, explain, and predict social phenomena that theories like classical and neoclassical economics fail even to recognise, and he provides superior accounts of aspects of phenomena recognised by all parties (e.g. the intensification of the labour process or movements in the rate of profit).[8] The net result of Marx's integration of social form into his theory is that, as Martha Campbell starkly and rightly observes, 'there are no counterparts to Marx's economic concepts in either Classical or utility theory'.[9] It is a fact much to the credit of Marxian theory.

6 Compare Bernstein 1971, p. 72.

7 Marx 1971a, p. 92.

8 The significance of speaking here of 'aspects of' phenomena will come clearer later in the chapter.

9 Campbell 1993b, p. 34. This is so precisely because Marx conceives of production as a social relation having a determinate form.

Beyond this superior first-order explanatory power, Marx's account of social forms enables him to identify where the basic shortcomings of classical and neoclassical economics lie and to offer a historical materialist explanation of their source. These two abilities, joined to the first-order explanatory superiority of Marxian theory, add up to a powerful case for the cogency of Marx's redoubled empiricism.

1 A Brief Account of 'Purist Splits' in Modern Philosophy

Subjectivism is based on two 'purist splits' and their correlation: (1) separating the subjective from the objective; (2) splitting the conceptual from the empirical; and (3) correlating the conceptual with the subjective and the empirical with the objective.[10] Since the relevant purist assumptions play themselves out throughout the modern period (Bacon and Descartes through German critical philosophy), it is best to present an account of the subjectivism of modern empiricism and critical (Kantian) philosophy in the broader context of modern philosophy as a whole. Let us begin, then, with a brief account of the purist objectivism of modern rationalism.

1.1 *Purist Objectivism: Modern Rationalism*

An earmark of modern rationalism (Descartes, Leibniz, Spinoza, Malebranche) is its 'purist split' between intellect or understanding, on the one hand, and sensation and imagination on the other. In the train of that separation comes the famous doctrine of innate ideas, for innate ideas are precisely those ideas which are formed by the intellect or understanding alone. Innate ideas are radically independent of sensation and imagination; they are the autonomous ideas of the pure subject.[11] They are, accordingly, purely subjective but only in the sense of being purely non-empirical;[12] this does not imply that they are not objective in the sense that they do not correspond to anything in the real world. On the contrary, consider Descartes' insistence that the objective properties of material beings (their 'primary qualities') are knowable only by the concepts of

10 As we will see, this is true of Kantian philosophy only in a qualified way.

11 This dual assertion about innate ideas does not hold for Leibniz, since he classifies all ideas, including those of sensation and imagination, as innate.

12 Thus Descartes, in his famous study of the bit-turned-blob of wax in the second of his *Meditations*, reaches the conclusion: 'We must therefore agree that I cannot even conceive what this bit of wax is by means of the imagination, and that there is nothing but my understanding alone which does conceive it' (Descartes 1960, p. 88).

pure intellect. Modern rationalism, then, is purist objectivism; purist because it cleaves the conceptual and the empirical from one another and objectivist because it holds that pure concepts provide objective knowledge, that is, knowledge of things as they are in themselves.[13]

While modern rationalism and subjectivism agree in their purism that the conceptual is non-empirical, they draw diametrically opposed consequences as to the objective validity of concepts: modern rationalism holds that it is precisely these purely subjective (non-empirical), innate concepts that comprehend the nature of things in themselves and thus are objective; whereas, for subjectivism, because concepts are non-empirical and purely subjective, they do not admit of objective validity. The present grip over our imaginations held by subjectivist thinking, for which subjectivity simply excludes objectivity, makes it tricky even to formulate the position of purist objectivism or the Hegelian position, which is objectivist but anti-purist. For both of the latter, though they differ importantly, there is a sense in which it is true that 'the more subjective, the more objective'.[14] That way of thinking makes no sense to a subjectivist. In modern rationalism, the sensuous or empirical is identified with the non-objective, with things as they seem to us, with anthropomorphism; whereas in subjectivism the purely empirical, the purely 'given', is the purely objective.

1.2 *The First Form of Subjectivism: Modern Empiricism*

Modern empiricism blasted away at the rationalists' doctrine of innate ideas and their related assertion that there is an intellectual faculty, namely intellect or understanding, that is categorically distinct from sensation and imagination and yields truth about the world – and, from a post-subjectivist standpoint such as Hegel's or Marx's, rightly so.[15] The irony, however, was that, leaving aside cer-

---

13 Hegel praises this objectivism of rationalist metaphysics: 'This metaphysical system took the laws and forms of thought to be the fundamental laws and forms of things. It assumed that to think a thing was the means of finding its very self and nature: and to that extent it occupied higher ground than the Critical Philosophy which succeeded it' (Hegel 1975, p. 48).

14 Hegel makes this criticism of rationalism: its 'purist split' between the conceptual and the empirical closes off the space for 'redoubled empiricism' – which calls for empirical scrutiny of concepts – and thereby leaves its concepts dogmatic and empirically inadequate (Hegel 1975, p. 60).

15 Caution must be taken with categories like 'modern rationalist' and 'modern empiricist'. These are philosophical 'ideal types', and the modern philosophers do not fit neatly under one or the other type (see Loeb 1981 and Collins 1972). John Locke, for example, comes

tain developments stemming from Locke's revolutionary and implicitly post-subjectivist doctrine of signs, the modern empiricists failed to extricate themselves from the quagmires of purism. How so? Because they too insisted on the 'purist split' between the conceptual and the empirical, merely adopting a stance opposite to that of the rationalists.

The modern empiricist view of concepts is nominalist: concepts are purely subjective; they have no objective correlates.[16] This amounts to an attack on Aristotelian forms insofar as forms are taken to be the objective correlates of certain concepts. As Francis Bacon puts the nominalist conclusion: 'forms are fictions of the human mind': forms are simply projections, like gods in Feuerbach's philosophy.[17] In the *Holy Family*, Marx calls attention to this feature of modern empiricism as found in Hobbes: 'Hobbes, as Bacon's continuator, argues thus: if all human knowledge is furnished by the senses, then our concepts, notions, and ideas are but the phantoms of the real world, more or less divested of its sensual form'.[18]

Similarly to Bacon and Hobbes, Locke splits the several workings of the mind (the purely conceptual and subjective) off from simple ideas (the purely empirical and objective). But, as Hegel was quick to point out, and as we will have further occasion to see, purists are prone to flip-flops and double-talk. Locke's is a highly influential – but hardly unequivocal – joining of nominalism with the subjectivist critique of Aristotelian 'real essences' or forms. Locke seems to be talking out of both sides of his mouth in his theory of 'nominal essences' in the third book of the *Essay Concerning Human Understanding*. Sounding like a razor-sharp nominalist, Locke writes that 'general and universal belong not to the real existence of things; but are the inventions and creatures of the understanding, made by it for its own use'.[19] Only two sections later, however, we

---

quickly to mind as an empiricist; indeed he famously attacked the rationalist doctrine of innate ideas, yet Berkeley heartily criticised his Cartesian materialism. From Marx's point of view this is an important observation, for two reasons: he identified Locke as the chief philosophical underlabourer for classical political economy, and Marx conceived of the classical labour theory of value along the lines of the purist objectivism of Descartes' theory of matter. (See Murray 1988a, p. 149, and Postone 1993, p. 142.) Classical political economy, as practiced by Locke, claims to follow an empiricist epistemology but defends an objectivistic theory of value as 'intrinsic worth', much as the empiricist Locke defends a largely Cartesian and objectivistic theory of matter.

16 In *The Holy Family* Marx observes: 'Nominalism is a main component of English materialism and is in general the first expression of materialism' (Marx and Engels 1975a, p. 127).

17 Bacon 1994, p. 49.

18 Marx and Engels 1975a, p. 128.

19 Locke 1975, p. 414.

find Locke hedging this stark nominalism, supplementing the subjectivist contention that nominal essences are '*the workmanship of the understanding*' with the proviso that they '*have their foundation in the similitude of things*'.[20] Here we see Locke's subjectivism being buffeted about. He cannot help but want it both ways: concepts (nominal essences), with their generality and universality, are *purely* the work of the subjective understanding, Baconian 'fictions of the human mind' – but they are 'also' determined by the objective similarities of things.

Redoubled empiricism, i.e., the empirical scrutiny and fixing of concepts in relation to other concepts, makes no sense if we stand by the subjectivist tenet that concepts are purely the work of the understanding. If that were so, experience could not play any role in the determination of concepts. Locke's anti-subjectivist – and contradictory – proviso, however, opens the space for redoubling empiricism, by allowing objective properties ('*the similitude of things*') to enter into the constitution of concepts.

We find the 'purist splits' of empiricism ready to hand once again in David Hume's seminal critique of causality. Hume accepts the data of sense perception as perfectly objective, but he is unable to find the impression of necessary connection anywhere in that objective world of sense. When he eventually does locate the impression of necessary connection, he identifies it as a purely subjective feeling implicated in a habit or custom of mind, which we unwittingly project onto the objective world.[21] Hume's identification of the purely subjective with the strictly non-objective makes this a shocking refutation of objective claims about causal connections. But this shock value relies on an inadequate phenomenology in which 'purely subjective' impressions keep turning up. Whenever we come across talk of the 'purely subjective' – and we will hear it prominently in neoclassical economics' notion of utility – we should look to see where a 'distinction of reason',[22] notably, the one between the subjective and objective, has been hypostatised into a 'real' separation. So, for all its bold and well-meaning forays against modern rationalism, modern empiricism missed the deeper issue of purism and yoked itself to the vain abstractions of the subjectivist mind-set.

20 These phrases come from Locke's title to Book III, section 13 (Locke 1975, p. 30).

21 For a powerful challenge to Hume's subjectivist employment of this rhetoric of projection, see Stroud 1993.

22 Hume sets forth the important notion of a 'distinction of reason' in two pages at the beginning of his *Treatise of Human Nature* (Hume 1989, pp. 24–5). 'Distinctions of reason' occur when we can distinguish but not separate, as, to use Hume's example, between the whiteness and the roundness of a marble globe.

1.3 *The Second Form of Subjectivism: Critical (Kantian) Philosophy*

In one sense, little needs to be said about critical philosophy and subjectivism, as it was Kant who crystallised the doctrine in his 'Copernican Revolution'; however, we want to see how this second type of subjectivism distinguishes itself from the first (modern empiricism). Following up on Hume's assertion that sense perception taken strictly can provide no warrant for universality or necessity, Kant reasoned – implicitly accepting Hume's presupposed identification of sense perception with objectivity (of one sort, at least)[23] – that, since in fact we have experience of universality, it must come from the subject, the knower, and from the knower alone. In the *Critique of Pure Reason* Kant identifies space and time as non-empirical,[24] purely subjective forms of sensibility and the twelve categories of the understanding as non-empirical, purely subjective functions necessary for the synthesis that is experience. Where Kant's critical philosophy differs from empiricism is: (1) in the assertion that what is given, the purely empirical, cannot be determined in total abstraction from the concepts of the understanding and the forms of sensibility: intuitions without concepts are blind.[25] (2) This insight leads Kant to the claim that the phenomenal world is co-constituted by what is given in intuition and by the purely subjective forms of intuition in conjunction with the categories of the understanding as they are schematised by the (transcendental) imagination. Hence, these purely subjective forms and categories have a sort of objectivity. That counts as a half-step away from modern empiricism's stance that subjective forms and concepts are not objective at all, and a half-step back in the direction of modern rationalism's doctrine that pure thought discovers the object-

---

23 Of Hegel's three meanings of objectivity this is the first: 'First it means what has external existence, in distinction from which the subjective is what is only supposed, dreamed, etc. Secondly, it has the meaning, attached to it by Kant, of the universal and necessary, as distinguished from the particular, subjective and occasional element which belongs to our sensations. Thirdly … it means the thought-apprehended essence of the existing thing, in contradistinction from what is merely *our* thought' (Hegel 1975, p. 68).

24 By 'non-empirical' I mean that they are not arrived at empirically, not that they have no place in experience; on the contrary, Kant insists that neither the forms of intuition nor the categories of the understanding directly yield any knowledge apart from experience.

25 This comes very close to a rejection of the 'purist split' between the conceptual and the empirical. For it is not obvious what is the difference between saying, on the one hand, that you can split the conceptual and the empirical but once you do you have nothing to say about either and, on the other hand, saying that the conceptual and the empirical are inseparable.

ive nature of the world. But it is only a half-step, because the objectivity that Kant allows to purely subjective forms and categories restricts comprehension of the universal and necessary to sensible things. 'Critical' objectivity is compromised by the sceptical qualification that it pertains only to things as they appear to us (phenomena), not things as they are in themselves (noumena).

Despite its differences with modern empiricism, what makes Kant's critical philosophy a type of subjectivism? It is, first, the now familiar claim to have identified purely non-empirical, purely subjective forms.[26] Second, it is the fact that, despite Kant's half-measures of granting phenomenal objectivity to purely subjective forms and categories, in the end, Kant denies that they apprehend in thought the essence of phenomenal things, the truth of them.[27] These half-measures inevitably (and rightly) raise the suspicions of both traditional empiricists and 'post-dogmatic' empiricists that Kant's critical philosophy is really no more licit than either the modern rationalism or empiricism it was meant to supersede.[28] Kant is at once too dogmatic – in putting the forms of sensibility and the concepts of the understanding beyond the pale of any empirical criticism (out of bounds for redoubled empiricism) – and too sceptical, for insisting on the impassable gulf between phenomena and things in themselves. This conjuncture of opposite excesses is characteristic of 'purist splits'.

26 Marx reacted strongly against this dualism of form and matter as early as the letter he wrote as a nineteen year old to his father. There he criticised his own 'Kantian-Fichtean' sketch of a science of jurisprudence: 'The mistake lay in my belief that matter and form can and must develop separately from each other, and so I obtained not a real form, but something like a desk with drawers into which I then poured sand' (Marx 1975d, p. 15). Getting at 'real forms' is what redoubling empiricism is all about. For an excellent study of the topic of form in Kant see Pippin 1982.

27 Hegel comments: 'But after all, objectivity of thought, in Kant's sense, is again to a certain extent subjective. Thoughts, according to Kant, although universal and necessary categories, are *only our* thoughts – separated by an impassable gulf from the thing, as it exists apart from our knowledge' (Hegel 1975, p. 67).

28 For the more traditional empiricists, see Reichenbach 1951. For the 'post-dogmatic' empiricist view, see Waismann's critique of Kant (Waismann 1968, pp. 48 ff.).

2 Critiques of Subjectivism

2.1 *The Aristotelian Conceptions of Form and Social Form*

Form is that in reality which answers to a concept that says *what* a thing is. Form involves necessity, universality (kind) and quality. For example, in Marx's theory, value is the social form of the product of labour in capitalism; this social form is an actual feature of the world that answers to Marx's concept of value. Value is qualitative in that it is socially necessary abstract labour that constitutes it; it involves universality as it is the social form that all products tend to take in capitalism; and it involves necessity in a number of ways, one being the necessary connection between value and money.[29]

Subjectivism supposes that a thing can exist even without any determination of what it is. Kant's 'thing-in-itself' is the epitome of this supposition. The Aristotelian tradition – and I locate Hegel and Marx in this tradition – rejects this blank ontology. Making just such an Aristotelian criticism, Elizabeth Anscombe writes:

> Such views are based on the unconscious assumption – which we have seen in Locke – that one can identify a *thing* without identifying it as a such-and-such – or that if one cannot do this, this is because *we* are incapable of conceiving substance except as having some qualities. The thing, then, that is taken to be postulated becomes a thoroughly mysterious entity which *in itself* has no characteristics: a 'somewhat we know not what' which is postulated as *underlying* the characteristics that it is said to 'have' and which alone enable us to conceive it.[30]

The subjectivist separation of what a thing is 'in itself' (the objective) from what it is as determined 'for us' (the subjective) is a vain abstraction.[31] What is truly absolute – where the buck always stops – is the inextricability of 'in itself' and 'for us'.

Hegel insists on this absolute:

> The tendency of all man's endeavors is to understand the world, to appropriate and subdue it to himself: and to this end the positive reality of the world must be as it were crushed and pounded, in other words, idealized.

29 On this see Murray 1993b, included in the present volume as Chapter 8.

30 Anscombe 1961, pp. 10–11.

31 It is the separation of the two that is objectionable; a 'distinction of reason' can be made.

> At the same time we must note that it is not the mere act of *our* personal self-consciousness which introduces an absolute unity into the variety of sense. Rather, this identity is itself the absolute.[32]

Reasoning again along Aristotelian lines, Hegel concludes that the 'what it is' of a thing cannot to be severed from the 'that it is', as subjectivism would have it. And a thing's form is what answers to the 'what it is' question. Hegel writes:

> But neither we nor the objects would have anything to gain by the mere fact that they possess being. The main point is not *that* they are, but *what* they are ... Laying aside therefore as unimportant this distinction between subjective and objective, we are chiefly interested in knowing what a thing is: i.e., its content, which is no more objective than it is subjective.[33]

This plain, but not innocent, conclusion – that in knowing we want to know what things are – is echoed in Donald Davidson's stunning finale to his unravelling of the subjectivist mind-set: 'In giving up the dualism of scheme and world, we do not give up the world, but re-establish unmediated touch with the familiar objects whose antics make our sentences and opinions true or false'.[34] 'Unmediated' only in that the 'purist split' between 'in itself' and 'for us' proves to be idle; only in that their nexus proves to be absolute.

Aristotle recognised that the 'what is it' question bears on society as well as nature: for this Marx praises him as 'the great investigator who was the first to analyze the value-form, like so many other forms of thought, society and nature'.[35] Aristotle's *Politics*, among others of his writings, is a seminal inquiry into social and political forms. Aristotle's text deals with the content of social forms, as well as with their consequences and relationships with other such forms – which means that it is an ancient yet instructive case of redoubled empiricism. Marx's pivotal observation that 'All production is appropriation of nature on the part of an individual within and through a specific form of society', is profoundly Aristotelian.[36] Furthermore, as a careful, experi-

32 Hegel 1975, p. 69.
33 Hegel 1975, p. 71, my emphasis in italics.
34 Davidson 1984, p. 198.
35 Marx 1976a, p. 151.
36 Marx 1973, p. 87.

ence-based study of the social forms constitutive of capitalist societies, *Capital* is an Aristotelian work.[37]

There is an important terminological point to be made in connection with this brief exposition of the Aristotelian conceptions of form and social form. It is a caution about the use of the terms 'determine' and 'modify'. It is easy to slide over the conceptual distinction between the two. 'Determine' pertains to what makes a thing what it is; something indeterminate (for example 'need', 'wealth', 'labour') lacks form – and therefore, on Aristotelian principles, actuality. 'Modify' operates at a different metaphysical and conceptual level; here we are dealing with something actual, something that is determinate, has form, and is undergoing some alteration. In this case the issue is not: *What is it?* but, assuming we already know that, *How does it behave?*[38] Ordinary empiricism targets this latter sort of question; redoubled empiricism takes on both.

2.2 *Pragmatism and 'Post-Dogmatic' Empiricism*

Pragmatists and 'post-dogmatic' empiricists such as William James, Friedrich Waismann, W.V.O. Quine, and Donald Davidson make common cause with Aristotelians against subjectivism around these fundamental points: (1) they recognise that the subjectivist position turns on the purist claims that the objective can be filleted from the subjective, the empirical from the conceptual, and (2) they find these claims untenable (or, in some cases, unintelligible).[39] A clear statement of this second point is found in William James's lecture 'Pragmatism and Humanism'. 'Humanism', to which James gives the pragmatist endorsement, turns out to be precisely the rejection of the subjectivist split between the subjective and the objective. James defines 'humanism' as 'the doctrine that to an unascertainable extent our truths are man-made products'.[40] The crucial phrase for present purposes is 'to an unascertainable extent', for it rules out the subjectivist separation of subjective from objective, conceptual from empirical. For the subjectivist image of human contributions as extractable weeds in the garden of knowledge, James exchanges that of a river and its

37 This claim is examined in detail in the second of two excellent studies of Marx's relationships to Aristotle, McCarthy 1990 and McCarthy 1994.

38 Compare this conceptual distinction to the Lakatosian one between propositions in the core and those in the periphery, as discussed in Smith 1997.

39 This means that pragmatism and 'post-dogmatic' empiricism involve more than a criticism of empiricism or even subjectivism; they address the underlying 'purist splits' that cut across modern philosophy.

40 James 1981, pp. 116–17.

banks: 'Does the river make its banks, or do the banks make the river? ... Just as impossible may it be to separate the real from the human factors in the growth of our cognitive experience'.[41] James's critique of subjectivism is a phenomenological one.

Contemporary 'post-dogmatic' empiricists are thinking along much the same lines. In his renowned article 'Two Dogmas of Empiricism', W.V.O. Quine concludes:

> My present suggestion is that it is nonsense, and the root of much nonsense, to speak of a linguistic component and a factual component in the truth of any statement. Taken collectively, science has its double dependence upon language and experience; but this duality is not significantly traceable into the statements of science taken one by one ... The unit of empirical significance is the whole of science.[42]

Quine's rejection of separable 'components' disqualifies subjectivism at the starting blocks, and his final statement succinctly expresses the outlook of redoubled empiricism.

Donald Davidson (sounding much like Hegel – or Marx) provides a yet more thorough excavation of the subjectivist terrain:

> There is the idea that *any* language distorts reality, which implies that it is only wordlessly if at all that the mind comes to grips with things as they really are. This is to conceive language as an inert (though necessarily distorting) medium independent of the human agencies that employ it; a view of language that surely cannot be maintained. Yet if the mind can grapple without distortion with the real, the mind itself must be without categories and concepts. This featureless self is familiar from theories in quite different parts of the philosophical landscape. There are, for example, theories that make freedom consist in decisions taken apart from all desires, habits, and dispositions of the agent; and theories of knowledge that suggest that the mind can observe the totality of its own perceptions and ideas. In each case, the mind is divorced from the traits that constitute it; an inescapable conclusion from

41 James 1981, pp. 122, 120. This illustrates Hume's point regarding 'distinctions of reason'.

42 Quine 1953, pp. 64–5. Compare Friedrich Waismann's comment: 'People are inclined to think that there is a world of facts as opposed to a world of words which describe these facts. I am not too happy about that' (Waismann 1968, p. 54).

> certain lines of reasoning, as I said, but one that should always persuade us to reject the premisses.[43]

These pragmatists and 'post-dogmatic' empiricists do not disagree with subjectivism that there is a human or subjective ingredient in cognition as well as an empirical or objective one; they just think that all attempts to separate one ingredient from another are in vain: as Hume recognised with his 'distinctions of reason', what can be distinguished cannot always be separated.

Marx concurs on both points. He loudly applauds the tradition of German Idealism, which itself famously builds upon insights of modern empiricism (and rationalism for that matter), precisely for recognising the constitutive role of human activity in knowing, at the same moment he criticises its purist conception of that activity. That is the unmistakable message of the 'Theses on Feuerbach', whose first thesis begins:

> The chief defect of all hitherto existing materialism (that of Feuerbach included) is that things [*Gegenstand*], reality, sensuousness are conceived only in the form of the *object or of contemplation*, but not as *sensuous human activity, practice*, not subjectively. Hence, in contradistinction to materialism, the *active* side was set forth abstractly by idealism – which, of course, does not know real, sensuous activity as such.[44]

This critique of subjectivism and its purist premises puts Marx at the philosophical cutting edge, among the 'post-dogmatic' empiricists.

3 Assessing the Marxian Theory of Redoubled Empiricism, Social Form and Formal Causality

The strength of the Marxian approach to social form rests first in its definite[45] and sound underlying philosophy: Marx was a self-conscious and highly sophisticated 'post-dogmatic' empiricist long before logical positivism ever reared its head. Now I want to consider further strengths of Marxian theory. (1) Once

---

43 Davidson 1984, pp. 185–6.

44 Marx 1976c, p. 3.

45 As opposed, say, to Simmel's wild swings between subjective and objective accounts of social form, as depicted by David Frisby in his Introduction to Simmel's *Philosophy of Money* (Frisby 1978). Given the neo-Kantian horizon of Simmel's thought, such swings might be expected.

our eyes are opened to how central social form and scientific explanation in terms of formal cause are to Marxian theory, we begin to appreciate the tremendous range of phenomena that the Marxian theory of capitalism explains and successfully predicts: phenomena which, as a consequence of Martha Campbell's point noted earlier, classical and neoclassical economics fail to acknowledge and are methodologically – not to mention politically – debarred even from recognising. (2) Marxian theory discloses exactly what is wrong with its competitors (classical and neoclassical economics) and where they have gone wrong. This explanatory power must count heavily in favour of Marxian theory when it comes to any comparison of the merits of competing research programs. Marxian theory provides a historical materialist explanation of why classical and neoclassical economics go wrong – something always appropriate and to be welcomed in dealing with inadequate theories. The case for this particular advantage of Marxian theory is too involved to be made in this chapter.[46]

3.1 *Marxian Theory's Explanatory Power*

I do not attempt here a thorough, much less a thoroughly comparative, assessment of the explanatory strength of the Marxian theory of capitalism. My affirmation of Martha Campbell's statement about the lack of counterparts to Marx's concepts in classical or utility theory suggests that comparative assessment is, in one sense, not an easy matter; yet once the Marxian theory of social form has been appropriated, it is easy enough to see what perfect non-starters are those two competitors to Marxian theory. And for this simple reason: if there always is a determinate social form of production, distribution, needs, etc., it will always have its effects (formal causality); to fail to theorise social form, then, is to fail to grasp the movements of the actual society under scrutiny (not to mention the causes of those movements).[47] Here, I will limit myself to some observations on how the considerations of this chapter bear on the evaluation of Marxian theory's explanatory power. These observations will take the form of a few comments on two papers by Fred Moseley, in which he contributes to the comparative assessment of Marxian theory by defending its explanatory power against separate criticisms made by Daniel Hausman and Mark Blaug.[48]

---

46 The thrust of the argument is that the peculiarly abstract social forms of capitalism promote the abstract understandings of labour and thought that characterise classical political economy and modern philosophy, respectively.

47 For Aristotle change of (social) form is a type of movement, the sort Marx thematises with his concept of formal subsumption.

48 Moseley 1993a and Moseley 1995.

The tendency in Moseley's two defences is to make the comparisons as if the theories operated on the same playing field. That misses the significance of Campbell's observation: there is a sense in which Marxian theory is not talking about the same sorts of things as classical or utility theory. As it happens, this is good news for Marxian theory, which talks about determinate realities, while the other two rattle on about hypostatised abstractions (notably 'labour' and 'utility'). When, for example, Moseley concludes: 'Neoclassical theory provides much less empirical content than Marx's theory', he supposes that the domain conditions for the two theories are well established and identical.[49] For Moseley, the difference is that in that supposed domain Marx explains more. While I agree with Moseley's affirmation of the explanatory superiority of Marxian theory, the considerations of this chapter suggest that the presuppositions framing the judgment need re-examination.

The domains of the competing theories are radically different; Marxian theory deals with actual social life in its definite forms while classical and neoclassical theory, by neglecting social forms, do not come to grips with actual social life; at best they deal with aspects of phenomena. Marxian theory contrasts with them not as apples to oranges but as apples to the colour red. In Marxian social theory specific social forms determine (they do not merely modify) the phenomena to be identified, explained and predicted. The subjectivist underpinnings of neoclassical theory bar it from thematising the phenomena in this way. A much stronger case for Marxian theory's empirical superiority (with 'empiricism' now understood in a more comprehensive sense) results from considerations of this kind.

Moseley's presentation of the case for the empirical superiority of Marxian theory underplays the crucial dimension of social form and formal causality.[50] Consider this text Moseley cites in making his case that, contra Hausman, Marx has a good explanation for why the rate of profit does not drop to zero:

> The law of capitalist accumulation, mystified by the economists into a supposed law of nature, in fact expresses the situation that the very nature of accumulation excludes every diminution in the degree of exploitation of labor, and every rise in the price of labor, which could seriously imperil the continual reproduction, on an ever larger scale, of the capital-relation.[51]

---

49 Moseley 1993a, p. 12.

50 I say 'underplays' because Moseley also invokes points that turn on social form, for example, Marx's account of the necessary connection between value and money.

51 Marx 1976a, pp. 771–2.

I take this appeal to 'the very nature' of (capital) accumulation, to involve explanation by formal causality: the most fundamental law of capitalist accumulation is that it is capital that is accumulated, that is, wealth in a determinate social form (hence the law of capitalist accumulation is no 'law of nature'), and that the specific kind of social relation between capitalists and wage labourers is reproduced in the process of accumulation. Setting aside periods of crisis or collapse, the Marxian theory of capital accumulation predicts that the 'capital relation', that determinate form of social relation between capitalists and wage labourers, will persist and be extended. Surely this is a terrifically successful prediction – but, due to the ascendancy of subjectivism with its blind eye to social form, it is also a prediction that is seldom noticed.

In surveying the empirical superiority of Marxian over neoclassical theory, Moseley draws attention to inherent technological change and inherent conflict between capitalists and workers over the length of the working day. These two are expressions of capital's drive to increase relative surplus value and absolute surplus value.[52] Attention to the role of social form and formal causality should not be set aside or ignored here. Its relevance manifests itself in two ways. First, that technological change, an aspect of the phenomenon of capitalist production recognisable to all, is inherent to capitalism depends, in Marx's account (I do not supply the account here), upon the causal role of the value form of social production. That there are the described conflicts between capitalists and wage labourers, an aspect of capitalist work relations recognizable to all, is likewise explained in terms of formal causality: the conflict proceeds from the determinate social form of the relationship. Second, it is not just that Marx successfully predicts 'technological change', where neoclassical theory does not; Marx identifies and predicts the social form of the change in technology. For the new technology is not just new 'instruments of production' (a

52 According to Marx the work day is divided into two parts, necessary labour time and surplus labour time. The necessary labour time is that part of the work day spent in producing an amount of value equivalent to the value of the worker's labour power; this is the source of the worker's wages. The surplus labour time is the remainder of the work day, and it is the source of surplus value (distributed as profits, interest and rent). The concepts of absolute and relative surplus value pertain to the two ways surplus value can be increased: shortening the part of the work day devoted to necessary labour (usually through increased productivity in the production of those commodities that enter into the value of labour power) – relative surplus value – or by increasing the part of the work day devoted to surplus labour, while leaving the other part unchanged – absolute surplus value. Marx further distinguished between increasing absolute surplus value by lengthening the work day and by intensifying it.

general, indeterminate concept). Rather the 'instruments of production' always have a determinate social form; Marx identifies that social form, capital, and accurately predicts that the new 'instruments of production' will be determined by it.

Similarly, the struggle to increase absolute surplus value is a struggle governed by the specific capitalist forms: the point of the capitalist drive to lengthen and/or intensify the work day is not adequately characterised by saying that it is about increasing 'surplus product'. It *is* about increasing 'surplus product', but a surplus product must have a determinate social form, and in capitalism that form is value. Marx does not simply predict that capitalists will constantly war with wage labourers to pump out more surplus; he shows that the surplus will have the form of surplus value. What reinforces these points (concerning inherent technological change and conflict in the workplace) is that Marx explicitly conceptualises capital's inherent drive to increase relative and absolute surplus value as, respectively, the real and the formal subsumptions of technology and labour under the social form of capital.[53] When we set aside the determinate social form of 'technology' or 'labour', we fail to come to grips with the pertinent 'what is it' questions and overlook the whole domain of formal causality, i.e. the power of social forms. Therein lies the terrible, empirical failure of classical and neoclassical economics. Marxian theory's success in addressing these questions is its triumph.[54]

3.2 *Where Classical and Neoclassical Theories Go Wrong*

Marxian theory discloses how debilitating the purist underpinnings of classical and neoclassical economics are. First, in a general way, these disciplines preclude any honest, clear-headed, and experiential approach to social form. This is a serious defect if Marx is right both that 'All production is appropriation of nature on the part of an individual within and through a specific form of society' and that social forms affect what happens in the world (formal causality).[55]

---

53 Formal subsumption of a labour process under capital means that the distinctive capitalist/wage labourer relationship obtains and that the process aims at the production of surplus value. Real subsumption means that the labour process undergoes a technical transformation in order better to pump out surplus value. See Marx 1976b, pp. 1,019 ff.

54 It should not be thought that Marxian theory has a monopoly on the market where careful observation and articulation of social forms or explanation through formal causality are concerned. Brilliant contributions come from many corners. See Murray (ed.) 1997b.

55 Marx 1973, p. 87. Notice the contrast between Adam Smith's talk of the 'wealth' of nations, which remains silent on the question of the form of that wealth, and the sentence with

Second, 'purist splits' (mis)shape the constitution of the foundational concepts of labour and utility themselves. Purism, especially in its classical empiricist form, undergirds and encourages a methodological attitude of neglect in relation to matters of form: within the orbit of classical empiricism, 'what is it' questions get faint and slurred responses. That is where this second, more specific, disabling feature of one-sided empiricism comes into play. For as Hegel observed, scientific empiricism is only kidding itself if it thinks that it gets along without concepts and forms, or if it thinks that concepts and forms play no constitutive role in science.[56] Science never has done without 'metaphysics', that is, without drawing on the necessary and universal character of its concepts, on 'the content of its concepts' – nor can it. (Of course it is possible to try to hide this reality from oneself, to engage in self-deception, as scientific empiricism does). So we can expect purist prejudices to emerge wherever classical and neoclassical economists attempt to clarify their concepts, most notably their respective conceptual foundation stones, 'labour' and 'utility'. And this is exactly what happens.

3.2.1 Classical Economics

Classical political economy is known for its labour theory of value: labour is the source of all value. What remains unclear in this simple statement is what either labour or value *is*. But inquiries into the form of labour and value are exactly what the assumptions of subjectivism prevent its adherents from carrying out. Nevertheless, questions concerning the nature of labour and value come up. And, in their own mixed-up ways, thinkers in the hold of the classical mind-set do attempt to answer these questions. We will see what a muddle they sink into and what role subjectivism and purism play in their blurring the distinction between wealth (and wealth-producing labour) and value (and value-producing labour) and their adopting an abstract (idealistic) conception of labour.

---

which Marx begins *Capital*: 'The wealth of societies in which the capitalist mode of production prevails appears as an "immense collection of commodities"; the individual commodity appears as its elementary form' (Marx 1976a, p. 125). For more on the significance of this opening, see Mattick Jr 1997.

56 'The fundamental illusion in scientific empiricism is always this, that it uses the metaphysical categories of matter, force, those of one, many, universality, also infinity, etc. Furthermore, [it] extends *implications* along the thread of such categories, whereby [it] presupposes and applies syllogistic forms, and in all this [it] does not know that it itself carries on and contains metaphysics and uses those categories and their connections in a fully uncritical and unconscious manner' (Hegel 1975, p. 62).

For several reasons, I would like to proceed in a somewhat indirect manner and take up a passage from Locke's *Second Treatise*. Locke's philosophy (at least the official version) is well-nigh definitive of the subjectivistic field within which classical political economy operates, and we are interested in the connections between the purism of modern philosophy and the purism of classical economics.[57] On this score, Locke is particularly appropriate because both Locke and classical political economy hitch purist objectivism in their ontologies of matter and value to the purist subjectivism of empiricist epistemology. Locke's labour theory of property may be seen as one of Marx's primary targets in the first volume of *Capital*.[58] In his thinking on economics Locke is commonly, and not without reason, seen in company with Petty, Berkeley, and Hume as a forerunner of the classical labour theory. Fair enough, but Locke was a great mind, and the great minds often feel something fishy is fishy, even when they cannot tell what it is exactly that stinks. With the hindsight provided by the Marxian theory of value, I believe that we can see that Locke was not an adherent of the strict, classical labour theory of value, not because he was born too soon or because he lacked the penetration of a Ricardo or Mill, but because he was thinking more deeply: because he sensed the confusions afflicting the classical labour theory even though he himself remained subject to them. There is greater virtue in his resistance to the classical labour theory than in the classical theory itself.

Locke's text reads:

> An Acre of Land that bears here Twenty Bushels of Wheat, and another in America, which, with the same Husbandry, would do the like, are, without doubt, of the same natural, intrinsick Value. But yet the benefit Mankind receives from the one, in a Year, is worth 5 £ and from the other possibly not worth a Penny, if all the Profit an Indian received from it were to be valued, and sold here; at least, I may truly say, not 1/1000. 'Tis Labour then which puts the greatest part of Value upon Land, without which it would scarcely be worth any thing: 'tis to that we owe the greatest part of all its useful Products.[59]

---

57 Compare Marx's observation: 'On the whole … the early English economists sided with Bacon and Hobbes as their philosophers, while, at a later period, Locke became "the philosopher" *par excellence* of political economy in England, France and Italy' (Marx 1976a, p. 513).

58 See Marx 1976a, especially pp. 733–4.

59 Locke 1960, p. 316.

The muddles Locke finds himself in here are characteristic of classical political economy; they turn on confusions over the concepts of wealth and value. Wealth is a general, universally applicable but indeterminate, concept; whereas value is the concept of the determinate social form of wealth in capitalism. (Thus, while uncultivated land is intrinsically a source of wealth, it is given *value* only within certain – commercial – social forms). Neither Locke nor the classical political economists properly register this distinction or the correlative one between wealth-producing labour and value-producing labour, these two distinctions being the fountainheads of Marx's critique of classical political economy.

Following this lead we can detect the following fundamental problems with classical economics, already visible in Locke's words: (1) the failure to fix the distinction between value and wealth (Locke wanders from value and price to usefulness and worth); (2) the correlative failure to distinguish between wealth-producing labour and value-producing labour (the text falsely suggests that all wealth-producing labour is value-producing); (3) the (at that time unavoidable) failure to recognise that value and wealth, value-producing labour and wealth-producing labour, are of two different logical types (in each pair the former is a determinate, the latter a general, abstraction); (4) the consequent tendency to reify 'wealth', i.e., to treat it as if it really were something actual, when in fact it is not – not when abstracted from any and every determinate social form (such as value);[60] (5) the tendency simply to identify wealth and value, wealth-producing labour and value-producing labour; (6) the misconception that value is intrinsic to objects in the same way as are those properties that make them useful to us; (7) the consequent failure to recognise the internal relation between value and money,[61] namely, that value must appear as something other than itself, as a use-value – there being no such connection between wealth and money – and that there can be no manifest, invariable

60 On this tendency to reify general abstractions see Derek Sayer's excellent book *The Violence of Abstraction* (Sayer 1987).

61 With this in mind there is something to be said for Locke's own non-classical theory of value, which is geared to the market considerations of supply and demand. Locke rightly sees that the market conditions play a constitutive role in the determination of value; so the (indeterminate) classical notion of 'labour' as the source of value will not work. Thus Marx observes that the Ricardians could make no convincing reply to Samuel Bailey's attack on Ricardo's 'absolute' theory of value 'because they are unable to find in Ricardo's own works any elucidation of the inner connection between value and the form of value, or exchange-value' (Marx 1976a, p. 177, n. 38).

measure of value;[62] and (8) the faulty presumption – it comes with slurring the difference between wealth and value – that wealth may be tallied up, as can value's necessary form of appearance, money.

Though he makes no clear distinction between wealth and value, I think it is Locke's sense of the difference that is one thing that keeps him from affirming the strict labour theory of value. Petty's famous line about labour being the father of material wealth and the earth its mother may be nagging at Locke.[63] There is no place for Petty's observation within the purist horizon of the classical theory of value, according to which it is labour pure and simple that is the source of value. But, then, so much the worse for the classical theory of value, and for the Ricardian socialists who adopt it, for, as Marx bitingly observed in the *Critique of the Gotha Programme*: 'labour is *not the source* of all wealth. *Nature* is just as much the source of use-values (and it is surely of such that material wealth still consists!) as is labour'.[64] Though Locke does not toe the Ricardian line, his own thinking about wealth is nonetheless stuck within a subjectivist conceptualization of labour, according to which the 'value-added' by (pure) labour may be distilled and its proportion mathematically ascertained,[65] and an objectivist conception of value as an intrinsic property of goods. Still, in his stumbling way, Locke does refuse to cave in unreservedly to the purist conceptions of labour and value, to the 'unalloyed abstractions' (to borrow a phrase from Hegel), definitive of the strict classical approach.

To sum up: (1) the ordinary empiricist horizon of classical economics blinds it to the reality of social form; no wonder then that it fails to make the all-important distinctions between value and wealth, value-producing labour and wealth-producing labour, or any of the crucial points that depend upon these distinctions; (2) operating in the grip of purist assumptions, classical political economy comes up with a suitably purist conception of labour that attributes

62 Compare Martha Campbell's treatment of the invariable measure of value in Ricardo in Campbell 1997.

63 Cited in Marx 1976a, p. 134. Cross-referencing that comment of Petty's with Locke's proportions may reveal something about the gender politics in play here.

64 Marx 1966a, p. 3.

65 The purism that persists in Locke's view may be accented by contrasting his talk of numerically identifying the proportion of (pure) labour's contribution to wealth with James's anti-purist defense of 'humanism', according to which the portion of the subjective ingredient in knowing is 'unascertainable'. Locke's view of wealth may usefully be likened to Kant's theory of knowledge: knowledge always involves both intuition (Nature) and the work of the transcendental ego (labour), and the critique of pure reason ascertains exactly what that contribution of the knowing subject is.

'supernatural creative power' to (pure) labour: it is the source of all wealth; (3) like Locke, who is an empiricist in epistemology but a purist objectivist (Cartesian) when it comes to matter, classical political economy is empiricist in epistemology but purist objectivist in its theory of value as 'intrinsic' to goods; (4) though Locke can sensibly be read as a forerunner of classical political economy, it turns out that several of his differences with the classical theory harbour intimations of Marx's critique of the classical theories of labour, value and wealth.

3.2.2 Neoclassical Economics

The ordinary empiricist and (more broadly) the subjectivist horizons of neoclassical economics lead it into the same two sorts of problems found in classical political economy: failures stemming from inattention to social form and a subjectivist conceptualisation of its foundational category (utility). Where classical political economy failed to fix the distinction between wealth and value, neoclassical economics fails to distinguish between use value and utility. And where the classical conception of labour is of pure labour, the 'supernatural creative' source of all wealth, neoclassical economics prides itself on its 'purely subjective' conception of utility.

A full treatment of the Marxian claim that neoclassical economics rests on a failure to distinguish between use value and utility, the former a general abstraction, the latter a determinate one, cannot be given here.[66] Marx refers to utility as an 'apparently metaphysical abstraction': 'metaphysical' (here in the bad sense) because it purports to stand for some single, qualitatively homogeneous and measured actuality and 'apparently' because this bad abstraction does point to the reality of the practices of generalised commodity exchange.[67] As opposed to utility, the general concept of use value makes no assumptions about the commensurability of all use values. Utility is a concept with ties to societies having a specific social form, namely those in which commodity exchange has been generalised.[68] Hobbled by the ordinary empiricist prejudices against social form, neoclassical economics fails to recognise the difference between use value and utility and the connections between utility and the social form of generalised commodity exchange.

---

66 I treat this topic at length in my unpublished paper 'The Difference between Use-value and Utility and the Difference it Makes: Grounds for a Marxian Critique of Neoclassical Theories of Value and Price' (Murray 1993a).

67 Marx and Engels 1976b, p. 409.

68 Marx further argues that it is only with the dominance of capital as a social form that this generalisation takes place.

In the circles of neoclassical economics, Marx's contention that use value is a property of useful objects counts as a piece of old-fashioned, metaphysical (= bad) objectivism, a real 'howler'. And yet Marxists can observe with amusement as neoclassical authors play out the inexorable and irredeemable perplexities of their subjectivist fancies. When neoclassical authors bother to try to pin down what it is they pretend to be talking about, utility, they necessarily end up ceaselessly equivocating. I say 'necessarily' because they are hung up by their subjectivist prejudices. C.E. Ferguson writes: 'if one sought a single criterion to distinguish modern microeconomic theory from its classical antecedents, he would probably decide it is to be found in the introduction of *subjective value theory*'.[69] Similarly, Antonietta Campus, writing in the *New Palgrave* dictionary of economics, pithily characterises utility as: use value 'reinterpreted in subjective terms'.[70] What manner of 'reinterpretation' is this? What is this '*subjective value theory*'? It is the concept of use value nailed to the cross of subjectivism's vain dualisms. Watch what happens when you try to make sense of this supposed 'reinterpretation'.

Ferguson states: 'Economists define "utility" as that quality which makes a commodity desired'.[71] That quality of what? Of the commodity? But a quality of a commodity is *its* quality, not one of a subject, and therefore is something objective in an intelligible sense of that word. Yet we also find Ferguson heedlessly identifying utility with satisfaction and saying 'any good or service deliberately consumed by a household provides utility'.[72] One sees how consuming a good can provide satisfaction to members of a household, but if the satisfaction is what utility is, how is that a quality of the commodity? Flip-flop; flip-flop.

Of the early marginal utility theorists Gossen, Jevons and Walras, Ferguson writes that they regarded utility 'as a measurable quality of any commodity', implying that utility is a property of a commodity, not of a subject.[73] Consider, then, just how well Ferguson's statement fits in with his or Campus's pronouncements about '*subjective value theory*' being the pivotal innovation of neoclassical microeconomics! C. Welch carries these shenanigans even further in his contribution to the *New Palgrave* when he writes that the early marginalists held the 'notion of pleasure as a quality inherent in a good', a pro-

69 Ferguson 1972, pp. 20–1.
70 Campus 1987, p. 320.
71 Ferguson 1972, p. 20.
72 Ferguson 1972, pp. 18, 21.
73 Ferguson 1972, p. 21.

position that suggests that the pioneers of neoclassical theory went altogether through the looking glass into a topsy-turvy world where pleasure is a property of things![74]

In his contribution to the *New Palgrave*, R.D. Collison Black displays the (bad) abstractive proclivities of the subjectivist mind-set in action: 'Utility in the sense of desiredness is a purely subjective concept, clearly distinct from usefulness or fitness for a purpose'.[75] Black possesses the wit to call attention to confusions among utility theorists over this distinction. But evidently the distinction is not so well fixed in Black's own mind as to keep him from writing in the sentence before the one quoted that 'desiredness' is 'the capacity of a good or service to satisfy a want, of whatever kind' (that being a sensible definition of use value, more or less identical to Marx's definition on the first page of *Capital*!). Are such capacities of goods to serve the purpose of our satisfaction 'purely subjective'? So Black is no more consistent than the utility theorists he chides. Nor is he in any position to be, since he is equally hung up by the subjectivist assumption that 'purely subjective' is a phrase that picks out something actual.[76] Give up that prejudice and the neoclassical idea of a 'subjective value theory' loses its point.[77] Out with that goes the misconception that neoclassical economics has a leg to stand on.

74 Welch 1987, p. 772.

75 Black 1987, p. 776.

76 Marx explicitly attacks this subjectivist assumption when he writes at the beginning of the first chapter of *Capital*: 'The usefulness of a thing makes it a use-value. But this usefulness does not dangle in mid-air. It is conditioned by the physical properties of the commodity, and has no existence apart from the latter' (Marx 1976a, p. 126). Utility theories want to make usefulness 'dangle in mid-air'; they want to abstract from the notion of usefulness all properties of the object – precisely by relying on the bad abstraction of the 'purely subjective'. Marx means to confute the very idea of a usefulness that is 'purely subjective'. And he polishes off the first chapter of *Capital* by yoking the 'purist objectivism' of classical value theory (value is an intrinsic property of objects) with the 'purist subjectivism' of utility theory (use value is independent of an object's properties): 'So far no chemist has ever discovered exchange-value either in a pearl or a diamond. The economists who have discovered this chemical substance, and who lay special claim to critical acumen, nevertheless find that the use-value of material objects belongs to them independently of their material properties, while their value, on the other hand, forms a part of them as objects' (Marx 1976a, p. 177). The point of the present chapter has been to uncover the deepest conceptual sources of these erroneous beliefs.

77 This Marxian critique pulls utility theories up by the root: the neoclassical innovation of 'marginal' utilities is useless, as is the later neoclassical abandonment of intersubjective utilities.

4 Conclusion

In this chapter we have explored the deep philosophical differences that set Marx off from the mainstream of modern philosophy and from those scientific research traditions, such as classical and neoclassical economics, which rely on the purist assumptions of their modern philosophical underlabourers, especially the empiricists. We found that Marx's rejection of the modern 'purist splits' between the conceptual and the empirical and between the subjective and objective opens the space for redoubled empiricism and for a conscious, realistic and experiential approach to social forms and their powers (formal causality). This enabled us to situate his thought in the company of Aristotle and Hegel, looking backward, and pragmatists and 'post-dogmatic' empiricists, looking forward. The latter part of the chapter investigated the significance of these abstruse philosophical matters for assessing the cogency of Marxian theory as a scientific research program in comparison to classical and neoclassical economics. By highlighting its attention to social form and formal causality, we found reasons to judge Marxian theory vastly superior to those two scientific competitors in its explanatory power, and we saw how the Marxian critique of purism uncovers where they go wrong to begin with. All of these considerations point up the philosophical and scientific vitality of Marxian theory.[78]

78 I would like to thank for their patient, diverse, and very helpful comments: Chris Arthur, Martha Campbell, Peter Fuss, Paul Mattick Jr, Fred Moseley, Geert Reuten, Jeanne Schuler and Tony Smith.

CHAPTER 3

Things Fall Apart: Historical and Systematic Dialectics and the Critique of Political Economy*

> In its mystified form, the dialectic became the fashion in Germany, because it seemed to transfigure and glorify what exists. In its rational form, it is a scandal and an abomination to the bourgeoisie and its doctrinaire spokesmen, because it includes in its positive understanding of what exists a simultaneous recognition of its negation, its necessary destruction; because it regards every historically developed form as being in a fluid state, in motion, and therefore grasps its transient aspect as well; and because it does not let itself be impressed by anything, being in its very essence critical and revolutionary.[1]

1 Social Form and 'The Illusion of the Economic'

Things Fall Apart, the title of Chinua Achebe's classic novel, expresses the nightmare side of the question that weighed on Marx's mind throughout his life: how does human life, which is irreducibly social in character, reproduce itself?[2] Humans are mortal, needy beings who reproduce sexually and meet (changeable) needs by engaging in definite, socially-structured transformations of the partly natural and partly already historically worked-up settings in which they find themselves. This production of wealth in the form of useful goods is a com-

---

* Originally published as 'Things Fall Apart: Historical and Systematic Dialectics and the Critique of Political Economy', in *New Dialectics and Political Economy*, edited by Rob Albritton and John Simoulidis (Basingstoke, Hampshire: Palgrave Macmillan, 2002), pp. 150–72, reprinted with the kind permission of Palgrave Macmillan.

1 Marx 1976a, p. 103.

2 'The human being is … not merely a gregarious animal, but an animal which can individuate itself only in the midst of society. Production by an isolated individual outside society … is as much of an absurdity as is the development of language without individuals living together and talking to each other. There is no point in dwelling on this any longer' (Marx 1973, p. 84).

mon factor in the reproduction of human life. Though it is a general, and rather banal, truth that to reproduce themselves humans must produce the things that answer their needs, there is no production in general.[3] Or, as Marx concisely expressed the seminal idea of historical materialism, 'All production is appropriation of nature on the part of an individual within and through a specific form of society'.[4]

Here lies Marx's fundamental contribution to the critique of political economy (or economics, as we now call it). It is also the taproot of both historical and systematic dialectics. 'Political economy is not technology ... production ... is always a certain social body, a social subject, which is active in a greater or sparser totality of branches of production'.[5] Production always has a definite social form and purpose.[6] What I call 'the illusion of the economic' is oblivious to this basic phenomenological truth. 'The illusion of the economic' is the notion that there is production in general, that there is a generic 'economy', as opposed to this or that historically specific mode of production. This illusion forms the basis of economics. Because it purports to offer a scientific account of production in utter abstraction from the specific social forms and purposes of actual modes of production, forms such as the commodity, money, capital, surplus value and wage labour, economics must be judged a pseudoscience. Consequently, Marx's critique of political economy or economics is not to be understood as a criticism of this or that 'economic' doctrine – though Marx is full of those sorts of criticisms too – but as a rejection of the horizon of inquiry that defines the discipline. As Paul Mattick Jr, puts it, 'Marx's critique – his "sci-

3 Marx 1973, p. 86.
4 Marx 1973, p. 87.
5 Marx 1973, p. 86.
6 On this point that specific *social forms* are bound up with definite *social purposes*, see Campbell 1993b, pp. 145–6. The idea that any social organization of production is purposive and that the purposes will vary with the form of that social organization of production sounds obvious enough. However, the rise of markets and capitalism has given rise to the illusion, seized upon by liberals, that free market societies lack any organising social purpose or have a social purpose only in the equivocal sense of being organised to address the individually determined schedules of needs of their members. I say that this is an illusion because, as Marx has shown, the truth of a market society is that it is a capitalist society. (This is because making a profit is the only reasonable explanation for why goods and services are produced as commodities.) The endless accumulation of capital is the compulsory social purpose of market societies. The real task for defenders of market societies, then, is not met by arguing, as F.A. Hayek does, that a market society is a just society precisely because it has no compulsory collective purpose. They have the more difficult task of showing that the endless accumulation of capital is the best achievable social purpose.

entific revolution" – therefore involved not merely a reworking of economic categories but the construction of another set of concepts, explicitly social and historical ones'.[7] In excluding historically specific social forms and purposes from its foundations, economics makes a mockery of any attempt to understand actual modes of production. The problem, then, comes to this: economics is missing an object of inquiry. For there is no 'production in general'; there is no 'economy'. There are only historically determinate modes of production and distribution, none of which can be understood on the basis of the few banal truths that in fact do cut across the many different historically specific modes of production.[8] Marx, then, was not a radical economist, but a radical critic of economics. Strictly speaking, terms such as 'Marxist economics' or 'Marxist political economy' are oxymorons.

'The illusion of the economic' usually takes the form of mistaking the capitalist mode of production for 'production in general'. So it is typical for texts in economics to bait and switch. They pretend to analyse 'the economy' and then quickly smuggle in the characteristic social forms and purposes of bourgeois society and the capitalist mode of production.[9] For example, an introductory microeconomics text once used at Creighton University obliviously reproduces the Trinity Formula on page seven. Appreciating the power of 'the illusion of the economic', Marx felt obliged to lead with his trump when he got to the final part of his three-volume book *Capital*:

> We have seen how the capitalist process of production is a historically specific form of the social production process in general. This last is both a production process of the material conditions of existence for human life, and a process, proceeding in specific economic and historical relations of production, that produces and reproduces these relations of production themselves, and with them the bearers of this process, their material conditions of existence, and their mutual relationships, i.e. the specific economic form of their society.[10]

Economics fails to grasp this basic truth because it is stuck in 'the illusion of the economic'.[11] In *The Poverty of Philosophy*, Marx expressed the dreary outlook of

7 Mattick Jr 1993, p. 124.

8 See Murray 1988a, Chapter 10.

9 See Marx's criticism of J.S. Mill in Marx 1973, p. 87.

10 Marx 1981, p. 957.

11 Why is the 'illusion of the economic' so common? Marx addresses this problem in his characteristic, historical materialist way. That is, he explains how specific features of

this way of thinking, 'Thus there has been history, but there is no longer any'.[12] Economics would bring history to a standstill, but history is not so obliging.

2 Systematic and Historical Dialectics and Their Relation

'The relation between a systematic and historical dialectic is obscure', writes Chris Arthur.[13] But not just their relation! Many questions arise regarding each term of the relationship and what place, if any, each has in Marx's thought. In this chapter I will try to identify and answer some of the most important of these questions. Let me briefly state in advance the chief conclusions that I reach.

1. Specific social form and purpose are the heartbeat of both systematic and historical dialectics. Consequently, we can expect no contribution to either systematic or historical dialectics from economics – except when it forgets itself.[14] To understand why things fall apart, we need to scrutinise the social forms and purposes involved in the various ways that the appropriation of nature to meet human needs have been socially organised and oriented socially.
2. 'Historical dialectics' is a phrase that points to aspects of necessity in historical change. I take it that the phrase refers to the sort of thing Marx was getting at in his remark that human beings make history but under circumstances not of their own choosing. As such, historical dialectics is a blunt concept, but I believe that it can be articulated further according to types of historical necessity. I distinguish five: (i) the historical dialectic involved in transformations from one mode of production to another; (ii) the historical dialectic involved in the actualization of a mode's social forms, entrenching

the society under consideration give rise to it. One of the peculiarities of the capitalist production process is that it presents itself in ways that encourage people to mistake it for production in general. The specific social forms of capitalist society seem to be written across it in invisible ink. For a detailed account of how capitalist social forms promote 'the illusion of the economic', see Murray 2002a, included in the present volume as Chapter 14.

12 Marx 1963b, p. 121.

13 Arthur 1993, p. 86.

14 Marx had already criticised economics in his 1844 manuscripts for failing to attend to the specific social forms and purposes of the capitalist mode of production (Marx 1975c, pp. 270–1), and he harps on about it for the rest of his life.

their dominance; (iii) the historical dialectic involved in the emergence of new forms, new necessities, as a dominant social form (mode of production) matures; (iv) the historical dialectic involved in the contradictory tendencies within a mode of production that destabilise it and push it apart; and (v) the historical dialectic involved in the struggles of participants in a particular mode of production, those within that mode of production and those against it.

3. Historical dialectics and systematic dialectics are not the same; neither is one reducible to the other. Mixing up the two has been the source of many problems.
4. Against those who contend that *Capital* is a work in Hegelian systematic dialectics, I argue that *Capital* is a work of Marxian systematic dialectics. Marxian systematic dialectics, I argue, distinguishes itself from the Hegelian (at least as Marx conceived of it) by recognising the limits of a dialectical presentation, specifically by recognising the natural and historical presuppositions of a systematic dialectical presentation, therewith rejecting the strictly Hegelian ideal of purely 'presuppositionless' science.
5. Against those, like John Rosenthal and Paul Mattick Jr, who reject systematic dialectics, I argue that Marx does offer a systematic dialectical account in *Capital*.
6. Since Marx distinguishes between the method of inquiry and the method of presentation, we may wonder whether or not there is a 'dialectics of inquiry' in addition to a (systematic) 'dialectics of presentation'. I argue that there is not, though one can prepare the mind for inquiries that result in a systematic dialectical presentation.
7. The stages in a systematic dialectical presentation are stages of a *conceptual* development that move from the abstract to the concrete; they are not actual stages, and their order should not be confused with the order of historical stages, even when the two orders sometimes overlap.
8. Theories of historical tendencies, historical stages or different 'regimes' of capital accumulation (for example, 'Fordism' or 'flexible accumulation') involve contingencies from which systematic dialectics abstracts; such theories depend upon systematic dialectics while supplementing it.
9. Talk of historical dialectics is pointless apart from a guiding conception of the human species as perfectible – Rousseau and Kant pioneered such thinking in the eighteenth century – and definite ideas regarding what human perfection involves. The question of the moral telos of humanity that sparks charges of 'Eurocentrism' cannot be sidestepped by Marxian theory.

3 Historical Dialectics

Since 'dialectics' spells necessity, does not the very phrase 'historical dialectics' turn human freedom into a paper tiger? Does not such terminology imply that historical materialism offers a deterministic 'science of history' (a phrase crossed out in the manuscript of *The German Ideology*)? Such a reaction represents a basic misunderstanding of what Marx is driving at with his conception of historical materialism. For Marx, necessity is an ingredient in history, but its presence does not exclude the exercise of human freedom. As Marx puts the point in his third thesis on Feuerbach, 'The coincidence of the changing of circumstances and of human activity can be conceived and rationally understood only as revolutionizing practice'.[15] Human beings 'make history', but they do so under circumstances that are not of their own making. The idea of a 'historical dialectic' begins with the thought that, in the human changing of human circumstances, the already given mode of production always plays a role:

> It is superfluous to add that men are not free to choose their productive forces – which are the basis of all their history – for every productive force is an acquired force, the product of former activity. The productive forces are therefore the result of practical human energy; but this energy is itself conditioned by the circumstances in which men find themselves, by the productive forces already acquired, by the social form which exists before they do, which they do not create, which is the product of the preceding generation.[16]

The already existing social form of production conditions human actions; here we see the link between Marx's fundamental insight into the significance of the specific social form and purpose of the reproduction of human life with his conception of historical dialectics:

> Because of this simple fact that every succeeding generation finds itself in possession of the productive forces acquired by the previous generation, which serve as the raw material for new production, a coherence arises in human history, a history of humanity which takes shape is all the more

15 Marx 1976c, p. 7.
16 Marx 1963a, p. 181.

> a history of humanity as the productive forces of man and therefore his social relations have been more developed.[17]

This grounding of historical dialectic in the ongoing entrenchment, transformation and even revolutionary overthrow of these social forms of the provisioning process invites us to discriminate between different types of historical dialectic with different degrees of necessity.

For heuristic purposes, I propose to differentiate five sorts of necessity that can be grouped under the concept of 'historical dialectics'.

(i) The transition from one mode of production to another is conditioned by the former mode of production and its problems in reproducing itself – the reasons why it falls apart – but here we find the greatest opportunity for freedom and creativity. Taking advantage of such opportunities requires a revolutionary leap, not only in circumstances but also in consciousness. Looking forward to the demise of the capitalist mode of production and the birth of communism, Marx and Engels write:

> Both for the production on a mass scale of this communist consciousness and for the success of the cause itself, the alteration of men on a mass scale is necessary, an alteration which can only take place in a practical movement, a revolution; the revolution is necessary, therefore, not only because the ruling class cannot be overthrown in any other way, but also because the class overthrowing it can only in a revolution succeed in ridding itself of all the muck of ages and become fitted to found society anew.[18]

(ii) The actualisation of the social forms bound up with a mode of production that is entrenching itself as dominant, spreading itself, deepening its hold, involves necessities that tend to be very strong, though the power of these social forms and the ways they work will depend on the particular mode of production in question and on pre-existing conditions. As the rhetoric of the *Communist Manifesto* proclaims, capitalist social forms are uniquely dynamic and expansive by nature.

(iii) Beyond the entrenchment and expansion of the social forms constituting a particular mode of production, there can be a growth of new forms, new necessities, as a mode matures. Here, too, the necessities may be quite strong,

17 Ibid.

18 Marx and Engels 1976b, p. 53.

but they will again depend upon the particular dynamism of the mode of production in question and pre-existing conditions.

(iv) As a historian, Marx was impressed with how things fall apart; as a dialectician he was keen to discover the extent to which the demise of a mode of production was a consequence of its pulling itself apart:

> Just as, on one side the pre-bourgeois phases appear as merely historical, i.e. suspended presuppositions, so do the contemporary conditions of production likewise appear as engaged in suspending themselves and hence in positing the historic presuppositions for a new state of society.[19]

The strength of these self-destabilising tendencies varies with the mode of production in question and, of course, their power grows as a mode of production's inner antagonisms grow.[20]

(v) Marx's assessment of the actual modes of production up through the capitalist one is that they have provided only either a narrow satisfaction, as in the case of the pre-capitalist modes, or no satisfaction, as in the case of the capitalist mode.[21] Dissatisfaction caused by a society's members chafing against the social forms and purposes of a certain mode of production leads to forms of opposition that mark a fifth sort of necessity involved in Marxian 'historical dialectics'. Some such conflicts involve inevitable features of the mode of production in question and take place more or less within its social forms. For example, in the capitalist mode of production, conflicts over the wage (which contains a historical and 'moral' ingredient), and over the length and intensity of the workday are unavoidable; they belong to how these capitalist forms function. Beyond these unavoidable conflicts, there is vast scope for opposition to the workings of capitalist social forms. For example, the insecurity of employment can be challenged in various ways – by, say, demanding state-enforced unemployment insurance. Commodification can be challenged by demands for the public provision of education, health care or other goods, or by restricting the commodification of natural or of culturally significant sites. These challenges can range from the mildly reformist to the revolutionary, at which point we circle back to item (i).

In the *Great Transformation*, Karl Polanyi was so shocked by the woes of unencumbered market society that he hypothesised its emergence as a 'double

19 Marx 1973, pp. 460–1.

20 I shall return to items (ii), (iii) and (iv) in the context of the diachronic aspect of systematic dialectics.

21 See Marx 1973, p. 162.

movement', the simultaneous creation of a 'disembedded' market society along with a host of reactions attempting to restrict its ill effects, such as overwork and child labour.[22] Within the Marxian tradition, Felton Shortall, working from the Uno-Sekine conception of the 'dialectic of capital', writes of the 'counter-dialectic' of the working class to the impositions of capital.[23] Shortall's term 'counterdialectic' seems problematic, however, given that he conceives of the 'dialectic of capital' as a systematic dialectic. 'Counterdialectic' suggests that the opposition of wage labourers to capital involves the sort of systematic necessities found in the 'dialectic of capital'. This appears to misclassify the sort of necessity involved in the opposition of wage labourers to capital's rule; the contingency, freedom and creativity involved in labour's 'counterdialectic' place it outside the scope of systematic dialectics, though not outside 'historical dialectics'.

A contrary problem with the Uno-Sekine approach adopted by Shortall requires a cautionary note regarding the distinction between items (iv) and (v). Given Marx's insistence on conceiving of 'revolutionizing practice' as 'the coincidence of the changing of circumstances and of human activity', we should not split item (v) from (iv), even if we can distinguish between them. Now the problem with the opposition between the 'dialectic of capital' and the 'counter-dialectic' of the working class is the opposite of the one just considered. Instead of too much necessity, now there is too little. Splitting the circumstances from the reaction against them underplays the disintegrative forces internal to capital and deflects attention from the ways these 'changing circumstances' shape forms of opposition to capital's dominance.[24] The less the 'dialectic of capital' discloses disintegrative tendencies, the more the 'counterdialectic' of the working class seems to be unhinged from 'changing circumstances'.[25]

---

22 Polanyi 1957.

23 Shortall 1994. On Shortall's relationship to the Uno-Sekine conception of the 'dialectic of capital', see Lebowitz 1998. See also the exchange between Shortall and Lebowitz in *Historical Materialism* (Lebowitz 2000 and Shortall 2000).

24 Compare Lebowitz's complaint (in Lebowitz 1998) against Shortall that he tends to flip-flop between too much necessity – internally begotten crises will bring the revolution – and too little – the heroic self-organised opposition of the proletariat will bring the revolution.

25 This disjuncture turns up in Chris Arthur's statement that 'The systematic approach need not lead to closure; for, critically presented, the logic of the capitalist system can be shown to be caught in a contradiction of positing as fully subsumed under its forms necessary conditions of its existence that exceed its grasp. I hope to show elsewhere that this is true of (a) its internal other, the proletariat; (b) its external other, nature' (Arthur 1997, p. 37,

4 Systematic Dialectics

The focus of systematic dialectics is one mode of production, considered (with qualifications, to be stated later) synchronically. The point of a systematic dialectical presentation of a mode of production is to identify and present in the most compelling way the essential moments of that mode of production, that is, those moments that are necessary for its reproduction.[26] *Capital* is, I argue, a systematic dialectical presentation of the capitalist mode of production. Marx worried that his systematic dialectical presentation in *Capital* would be mistaken for the sort of '*a priori* construction' for which he criticised 'German ideology'.[27] He was so concerned that, in December 1861, he wrote to Engels that the continuation of his *A Contribution to the Critique of Political Economy* (1859) 'will nonetheless be much more popular and the method will be much more hidden than in part 1'.[28] 'Hidden' implies present.

For Marx, a systematic dialectical presentation cannot be arrived at by 'applying' a pre-established 'dialectical logic' to some domain of inquiry. The only way to achieve a proper systematic dialectical presentation is through a rigorous, experience-based inquiry into the subject matter at hand. Such an inquiry 'has to appropriate the material in detail, to analyse its different forms of development and to track down their inner connection'.[29] I call such an inquiry 'phenomenological', for it goes beyond the ordinary empirical collection of facts organised under 'ready-made' concepts. It probes the concepts themselves, testing for 'inner connections'.[30] Only on this basis can the forms of the subject matter at hand be represented in a systematic dialectic of concepts.

---

n. 75). True, the proletariat and nature are posited by capital as 'others', and they are not fully subsumable, but this way of avoiding closure of the 'dialectic of capital' leaves us with abstract negations, whose oppositional force is, so far, left unrelated to disintegrative forces that build with the growth of capitalism. For a contrasting approach, see Postone 1993, where he develops the notion of 'shearing pressures' developing within capitalism.

26 Geert Reuten accurately defines the Hegelian (and Marxian) notion of a 'moment' as follows: 'A moment is an element considered in itself that can be conceptually isolated and analyzed as such but that can have no isolated existence'. See Reuten 1993, p. 92.

27 'If the life of the subject-matter is now reflected back in the ideas, then it may appear as if we have before us an *a priori* construction' (Marx 1976a, p. 102).

28 Marx, Karl, 'Letter to Engels (December 9, 1861)' as cited in Murray 1988a, p. 109.

29 Marx 1976a, p. 102.

30 For a more extensive treatment of this conception of Marx's conception of inquiry as phenomenological, see Murray 2000a, included in the present volume as Chapter 4.

The 'systematic' in 'systematic dialectic' refers to a presentation being orderly, coherent and complete. (With that last qualifier in mind, it is evident that there is at least one sense in which *Capital* fails to come up to the standard for systematic dialectics, since Marx did not finish *Capital*, which was intended as only the first of a six-book project.) The orderliness requirement echoes René Descartes' writings on method – as does the *Grundrisse* section on method – by calling for the introduction of concepts synthetically; that is, in order of their conceptual concreteness: simpler categories come before more complex ones. What 'systematic dialectics' adds to Descartes' account, and which greatly increases the systematicity of such a presentation, is that in such a presentation the structure of presupposition runs in both directions.[31] Not only do the complex categories presuppose the simple ones, which is the familiar point about synthesis; the simple categories also presuppose the complex ones, which is the phenomenological point. This two-way directionality of dialectical systematicity expresses the phenomenologically ascertained inseparability of multiple aspects of the object under examination. The dialectical movement from simpler to more complex categories reveals the latter to be presupposed by, and implicit in, the former. For example, the more complex category of commodity capital, which figures in the circuits of capital, treated in Part One of Volume II of *Capital*, is implicit in the simpler category of the commodity, with which *Capital* begins. It is one of the most significant developments of Marx's systematic dialectical presentation that the generalisation of simple commodity exchange is shown to presuppose the capitalist mode of production: commodities are produced as commodity capital.

So far, Marx's conception of systematic dialectics follows Hegel's. What, then, do we make of Marx's lifelong criticism of Hegel's dialectic as 'mystifying'? In the Postface to the second edition of *Capital*, Marx memorably contrasts his dialectic with Hegel's, while affirming that Hegel had the basics right:

> My dialectical method is, in its foundations, not only different from the Hegelian, but exactly opposite to it. For Hegel, the process of thinking, which he even transforms into an independent subject, under the name of 'the Idea', is the creator of the real world, and the real world is only the external appearance of the idea. With me the reverse is true: the ideal is nothing but the material world reflected in the mind of man, and translated into forms of thought ... The mystification which the dialectic suffers in Hegel's hands by no means prevents him from being the first

31 On this structure of mutual presupposition in *Capital*, see Bubner 1988 and Arthur 1997.

> to present its general forms of motion in a comprehensive and conscious manner. With him it is standing on its head. It must be inverted, in order to discover the rational kernel within the mystical shell.[32]

Faced with those metaphors, let me propose an interpretation of how Marx sees his dialectic differing from Hegel's. Hegelian dialectic, at least as Marx conceives of it, recognises no dependence of its object upon anything outside thought, no historical or material presuppositions limiting thought. It prides itself on its 'presuppositionlessness'. Marx's dialectic differs from Hegel's precisely in insisting on weaving material presuppositions, namely, historical presuppositions and those picked out by the 'general phenomenology' of the human condition, into the systematic dialectical presentation.[33] For example, in his opening account of the capitalist production process, in Chapter Seven of *Capital* Volume I, Marx begins with an account of the general features of human labour processes, and, in solving the mystery of the source of surplus value, Marx makes it clear that the existence of 'free' wage labourers is a factual, historical presupposition that is a condition for the systematic dialectical presentation of capital.[34]

We can summarise the chief features of Marxian systematic dialectics, then, as follows: (i) a systematic dialectical presentation will have identifiable premises or presuppositions given by nature and history; (ii) it will represent the moments of the object under study in their inseparability as uncovered by phenomenological inquiry into that object, and in so doing it will disclose the essence of what is under study; (iii) in introducing those moments, the

---

32 Marx 1976a, pp. 102–3.

33 This requirement of Marxian systematic dialectics appears to be incompatible with the more strictly Hegelian requirements as identified and embraced by Geert Reuten: 'All axioms are eschewed. Rather, anything that is required to be assumed, or anything that is posited immediately (such as the starting point), must be grounded. But it should not be grounded merely abstractly (i.e., giving arguments in advance), because this always leads to regress. That which is posited must be ultimately grounded in the argument itself, in concretizing it' (Reuten 1993, p. 92). I do not think that the sort of presuppositions Marx has in mind can be justified in the way called for here.

34 Against 'the Germans, who are devoid of premises' (p. 41), Marx and Engels write in *The German Ideology*, 'The premises from which we begin are not arbitrary ones, not dogmas, but real premises from which abstraction can only be made in the imagination. They are the real individuals, their activity and the material conditions of their life, but those which they find already existing and those produced by their activity. These premises can thus be verified in a purely empirical way' (Marx and Engels 1976b, p. 31).

presentation will proceed from the conceptually simpler to the conceptually more complex; and (iv) though the conceptual development proceeds from the conceptually simpler to the conceptually more complex, the former will be presented, at least implicitly, as presupposing the latter: there is a structure of mutual presupposition among the simpler and more complex categories.

5 The Myth of Systematic Dialectics?

Recent works by Paul Mattick Jr and John Rosenthal deny that *Capital* is a work of systematic dialectics.[35] Rosenthal regards dialectics as altogether a myth, while Mattick argues that 'Marx's dialectic' is strictly historical: there is no systematic dialectical presentation in *Capital*. For a defence of systematic dialectics against Rosenthal, I refer the reader to the critical review of his book *The Myth of Dialectics* by Tony Smith.[36] Here I shall make just a few points in reply to Mattick. Mattick maintains that Marx's dialectic 'is identified not with a logic of theory construction, but with the idea of the essentially historical character of social formations'.[37] This reduces any appearance of a systematic dialectic of presentation to historical dialectic. For Mattick, *Capital* is a systematic critique of the ideology of classical political economy, not a systematic dialectical presentation of the capitalist mode of production. I do not believe that these two purposes are mutually exclusive.

Mattick seems to think that, if *Capital* is making a systematic dialectical presentation, it must be applying a 'dialectical logic' like Hegel's to its subject. The trouble with this is that, for Mattick, there is really nothing to apply since 'even in the best cases, it must be said, the *necessity* … of the transition between categories in the Hegelian dialectic – and hence of its being a logic – has not been convincingly made. Hegel, at any rate, simply asserts it'.[38] A 'logic' that lacks necessity is no logic at all.

On this score, I think that Marx and Mattick are on the same wavelength, as Marx was always wary of efforts to 'apply' any abstract 'dialectical logic' to any subject matter. In his *Critique of Hegel's 'Philosophy of Right'*, Marx rebuked Hegel for attempting to impose an abstract, prefabricated 'dialectical' logic on his subject matter rather than let the necessities flow from a thoroughgoing

35 See Mattick Jr 1993 and Rosenthal 1998.
36 See Smith 1999 and the exchange that follows in *Historical Materialism*.
37 Mattick Jr 1993, p. 117.
38 Mattick Jr 1993, p. 125.

empirical investigation of his subject matter. For Marx, only the phenomenologically ascertained necessities of the matter under investigation can warrant a systematic dialectical presentation, not some abstract 'dialectical logic'. Interestingly, when Mattick looks at Marx's argument (in Section Three of Chapter One of *Capital*) for why value must appear as money, he concludes: 'The insufficiency of the simple form is not logical but practical and material: It would not suffice as a mode of representation of value'.[39] What is this 'practical' necessity but the engine of Marxian systematic dialectics in *Capital*, which is rooted not in some 'dialectical logical' necessity but in the capitalist mode of production's requirements for reproducing itself?

While Mattick's position captures the critical side of Marx's relation to Hegel's dialectic, it strikes me as unconvincing with regard to Marx's repeated affirmations to the effect that Hegel was 'the first to present its [the dialectic's] general forms of motion in a comprehensive and conscious manner'.[40] Moreover, there is so much in *Capital* that fits with the claim that it provides a systematic dialectical presentation of its subject matter, in particular the structure of mutual presupposition of categories, to which Marx often calls attention. Finally, I interpret the epigram to the present chapter to mean that the deepest outcome of the systematic dialectical presentation of the capitalist mode of production is the recognition of its transience.

6 A 'Dialectics of Inquiry'?

Marx made a point in the introduction to the *Grundrisse* and again in the Postface to the second edition of *Capital* of distinguishing between the method of inquiry and the method of presentation, writing of the latter:

> Of course the method of presentation must differ in form from that of inquiry. The latter has to appropriate the material in detail, to analyse its different forms of development and to track down their inner connection. Only after this work has been done can the real movement be appropriately presented.[41]

We may wonder, then, if we should think in terms of two kinds of dialectics, a dialectics of investigation and a dialectics of presentation. The title and con-

39 Mattick Jr 1993, p. 129.

40 Marx 1976a, p. 103.

41 Marx 1976a, p. 102.

tents of Bertell Ollman's book *Dialectical Investigations* recommend that approach to us.[42]

I believe that it is preferable to conceive of the phase of investigation as phenomenological, where 'phenomenological' is understood, as Marx suggests, to include both the work of analysis and the work of phenomenology construed more narrowly as the ascertainment of which aspects of the object of study are inseparable and essential. Phenomenological inquiry is what makes systematic dialectical presentation possible. As has already been indicated, we can identify definite features of the structure of a dialectical presentation; but, on the contrary, the method of investigation cannot be fixed in advance. I am reluctant to put much weight on the idea that Marx has a method of investigation.[43] Marx seems to agree with Aristotle and Hegel that the method of inquiry must take its lead from the object being investigated.[44] To say much in advance is to beg the important questions.

In *The German Ideology* Marx and Engels criticised German idealism's *a priori* handling of history:

> The difficulties begin only when one sets about the examination and arrangement of the material – whether of a past epoch or of the present – and its actual presentation. The removal of these difficulties is governed by premises which certainly cannot be stated here, but which only the study of the actual life-process and the activity of the individuals of each epoch will make evident.[45]

Marx returned to this thought in an 1858 letter to Engels regarding Ferdinand Lassalle:

> I see from this one note that the fellow plans in his second great work to present political economy Hegel-like. To his detriment, he will come to learn that it is a wholly other thing to bring a science for the first time to the point of being able to present it dialectically, through critique, than to apply an abstract, finished system of logic to hunches of just such a system.[46]

42 Ollman 1993.
43 See Murray 1988a, Chapter Eight, 'Why Did Marx Write so Little on Method?'
44 Hegel writes, 'it can only be the nature of the content itself which spontaneously develops itself in a scientific manner of knowing' (Hegel 1969).
45 Marx and Engels 1976b, p. 37.
46 Marx, K., 'Letter to Engels (February 1858)', as cited in Murray 1988a, p. 110.

Though it makes sense to be wary of positing a 'dialectics of investigation' alongside Marx's conception of systematic dialectical presentation, one can prepare the mind for phenomenological inquiry. In that spirit, Hegel called the study of logic 'the absolute education and breeding of consciousness'.[47] In addition to the study of logic, study of the history of philosophy and of the sciences helps to prepare the mind of the investigator. But these preparations function like physical training for quickness, speed, flexibility and strength; none guarantees that you can hit a curve ball or head a soccer ball into the corner of the net. There is no substitute for the encounter of scientific investigators with the actual movements of their object of inquiry.

7 Mix-Ups of Historical and Systematic Dialectics

The conflation of systematic and historical dialectics has caused Marxian theory problems for a long time. Here I shall briefly identify four such conflations. The first is the most infamous, Engels's influential conflation of the systematic and the historical into 'logical-historical method' – the exact phrase comes from R.L. Meek – according to which, the method of presentation tracks the historical order stripped of accidentals.[48] At the root of this confusion lies a serious mistake that has badly misled even readers of *Capital* who avoid the 'logical-historical' conflation. The mistake is to conceive of the various stages in the systematic presentation in *Capital* as describing several actualities rather than different levels of abstraction from actuality. Eugen Böhm-Bawerk's complaint of a 'contradiction' between Volume I's theory of value and Volume III's theory of prices of production and the misbegotten 'transformation problem' (transforming values into prices of production) are among the most egregious consequences of that misconception.[49]

The second type slurs the difference between a 'stage' or 'regime' theory of capitalism and a systematic dialectical theory of the capitalist mode of production. Such theories, while desirable, may obscure the distinction between contingent and necessary features of capitalism. Consequently, as Geert Reuten nicely puts it, 'When the regime goes into crisis, so does the theory'.[50]

---

47 Murray 1988a, p. 113.

48 For a critique of Engels and Meek, see Arthur 1997.

49 On the 'transformation problem' see Mattick Jr 1981, Moseley 1993 and Carchedi 1993.

50 Reuten made this remark at the 'New Dialectics and Political Economy' conference held at York University in the spring of 2001; it is quoted with his permission.

A third variety overlooks the difference between a tendency and a trend. Systematic dialectical theory can identify tendencies (and often countertendencies), but it is usually a matter of historical contingency when, or sometimes if, a tendency will result in an observable, historical trend. A systematic dialectical account of wage labour can identify a tendency to 'deskill' labour in order to cheapen it (the Babbage Principle); and this might lead one to posit a secular, historical trend towards 'deskilling', making Marxian theory unfairly vulnerable to refutation by disproving the existence of such a trend.[51]

A fourth mix-up has been pointed out by Tony Smith. The error here is to confuse primacy in systematic dialectical presentation with explanatory primacy in historical explanation. Against this misstep, Smith offers the proposition, 'There is an unbridgeable gulf between systematic dialectics and historical theorizing such that explanatory primacy in the former does not imply explanatory primacy in the latter'.[52] Applying this in the context of the debate over Robert Brenner's 'The Economics of Global Turbulence', Smith argues that the primacy of the class relationship between capital and wage labour in Marx's systematic dialectical theory in *Capital* in no way assures that class conflict, and not inter-capitalist competition, is the primary cause of the global downturn after the 'Golden Age' that followed the Second World War.

8 Historical Dialectics in Systematic Dialectics?

Systematic dialectics ordinarily is contrasted with historical dialectics, as the synchronic to the diachronic. I question whether that way of thinking does not let something important fall between the cracks – namely, the historical dialectics implicated in systematic dialectics. According to the usual conception, systematic dialectics provides a snapshot of a historically determinate mode of production (say, the capitalist mode of production), while historical dialectics takes up transitions from one mode of production to another (say, the feudal to the capitalist). *Capital*'s treatment of 'The So-called Primitive Accumulation' would thus be an excursion into historical dialectics supplementing a systematic dialectical presentation. Marx seems to encourage the synchronic conception of systematic dialectics:

---

51 For more on the tendency/trend distinction, especially with reference to the 'tendency of the rate of profit to fall', see Reuten 1997.

52 Smith 1999b, p. 166.

> In the succession of the economic categories, as in any other historical, social science, it must not be forgotten that their subject – here, modern bourgeois society – is always what is given, in the head as well as in reality, and that these categories therefore express the forms of being, the characteristics of existence, and often only individual sides of this specific society, this subject, and that therefore this society by no means begins only at the point where one can speak of it as such; this holds for science as well. This is to be kept in mind because it will shortly be decisive for the order and sequence of the categories.[53]

This pointed passage nicely debunks the old idea of the order of a systematic development tracking that of historical development, but there is something fishy about it. Was 'modern bourgeois society' really 'given' in 1857? 'Yes', because essential forms of 'modern bourgeois society' were present at that time and flexing their muscles, but 'no', in that, in 1857, the world, even England, was far from answering to the description of capitalist societies that *Capital* offers. To take a simple but important example, *Capital* is written as if the ordinary form of labour was wage labour, but that was far from being the case in 1857.[54] Then, in *Capital* Volume I we read of rampant 'Freedom, Equality, Property and Bentham' in the wonderfully ironic paragraph wrapping up the 'wisdom' of simple commodity circulation[55] – yet battles for basic freedoms, equalities and rights to property have raged ever since.

A passage in the *Grundrisse* provides a more accurate picture:

> While in the completed bourgeois system every economic relation presupposes every other in its bourgeois economic form, and everything posited is thus also a presupposition, this is the case with every organic system. This organic system itself, as a totality, has its presuppositions, and its development to its totality consists precisely in subordinating all elements of society to itself, or in creating out of it the organs which it still lacks. This is historically how it becomes a totality. The process of becoming this totality forms a moment of its process, of its development.[56]

---

53 Marx 1973, p. 106.

54 'In capitalist production the tendency for all products to be commodities and all labour to be wage-labour, becomes absolute' (Marx 1976b, p. 1,041).

55 Marx 1976a, p. 280.

56 Marx 1973, p. 278.

In other words, the systematic dialectic of *Capital* tells us not only what the capitalist mode of production is but points where it is going.[57] One cannot bleach the historical aspect out of systematic dialectics.

Historical dialectic, then, is implicated in the systematic dialectic of the social forms, the value forms (the generalised commodity, money, capital, wage labour and so on), presented in *Capital*. In the section on historical dialectics, I discriminated three sorts of necessity ((ii), (iii) and (iv)) that pertain here. Several related aspects of the historical dynamism posited by the capitalist mode of production may be mentioned here.

In the unfinished manuscript *Results of the Immediate Production Process*, Marx identified different forms of the subsumption of labour under capital, notably formal and real subsumption. Formal subsumption of labour under capital simply involves subjecting it to capital's purpose, the production of surplus value, while real subsumption of labour involves changing the technique or organization of the labour process in order to increase surplus value. Marx writes that it is only with real subsumption that we can speak of a 'specifically capitalist form of production'.[58] The historical dynamism of the capitalist mode of production is to keep expanding both formal and real subsumption. With the ongoing expansion of real subsumption, the mismatch between the capitalist measure of wealth (value, and more particularly, surplus value) and the mass of use values produced, grows.

It is only with the global reach of capital that the value forms actually become what the systematic dialectic of *Capital* posits their nature to be:

> Abstract wealth, value, money, hence abstract labour, develop in the measure that concrete labour becomes a totality of different modes of labour embracing the world market. Capitalist production rests on the *value* or the transformation of the labour embodied in the product into social labour. But this is only [possible] on the basis of foreign trade and of the world market. This is at once the precondition and the result of capitalist production.[59]

57 And some form of globalization is on the agenda: 'The tendency to create the world market is directly given in the concept of capital itself. Every limit appears as a barrier to be overcome' (Marx 1973, p. 408).

58 Marx 1976b, p. 1024.

59 Marx 1971a, p. 253. I am indebted to a paper by Tony Smith for calling this quote to my attention.

We should entertain the further possibility that, with the maturation of a mode of production, systematic dialectics may have to be responsive to the emergence of new necessities, and new social forms. Perhaps the credit card, the ATM (Automatic Transaction Machine) card and the debit card represent necessary new monetary instruments. If today's mass advertising can add use value to 'finished' products, perhaps adjustments in the account of circulation costs in Volume II of *Capital* are called for. Perhaps maintaining a moderate rate of inflation has become a necessary tendency, as Geert Reuten argues.[60]

9 Marx on Purpose in History: A Eurocentric View?

Marx's historical materialism, though a breakthrough in the scientific study of history, does not provide a template for a 'science of history'. Marx warns us not to 'metamorphose my historical sketch of the genesis of capitalism in Western Europe into an historical-philosophical theory of the general path every people is fated to tread'.[61] Marx's distaste for *a priori* theorising about history comes through strongly when he ridicules the very idea of a 'general historico-philosophical theory' providing a 'master key', 'the supreme virtue of which consists in being super-historical'.[62]

Still, things fall apart, and we want to know why. I believe that Marx responds to this question in various ways and on various levels. At the level of philosophical anthropology, Marx adopted Rousseau's conception of humanity from the *Second Discourse*: the essence of humanity is perfectibility. Our hearts are restless as long as the capacities for intelligent self-direction with which humans are endowed remain bottled up or perverted. The phenomenology of the human involved at this level of abstraction establishes a horizon within which more determinate explanations of historical change are situated. Marx has some quite general observations regarding the dynamics of historical development. Retooling a point Kant makes in his essay 'The Speculative (or Conjectural) Beginnings of Mankind', the following passage from *The German Ideology* envisions a spiralling dialectic of human needs and the measures taken to satisfy needs: 'The satisfaction of the first need, the action of satisfying and the instrument of satisfaction which has been acquired, leads to new needs; and

60 Reuten 2003.

61 Marx 1968a, p. 5.

62 Marx 1968a, p. 445.

this creation of new needs is the first historical act'.[63] In the *Grundrisse*, Marx returns to this thought, but puts something of a Malthusian-Darwinian spin on it:

> If the community as such is to continue in the old way, the reproduction of its members under the objective conditions already assumed as given, is necessary. Production itself, the advance of population (which also falls under the head of production), in time necessarily eliminates these conditions, destroying instead of reproducing them, etc., and as this occurs the community decays and dies, together with the property relations on which it was based.[64]

10 Things Fall Apart

Moving to a less general level, Marx recognises a bond between private property and individualism, and furthermore sees this pair as being corrosive of traditional societies. In particular, in *The German Ideology*, Marx and Engels see the gradual emergence of private property within the ancient communal mode of production as setting off a dynamic of dissolution: 'the whole structure of society based on this communal ownership, and with it the power of the people, decays in the same measure as, in particular, immovable private property evolves'.[65] Private property, of course, plays a crucial role in Marx's sketch of the historical dynamics of the decline of feudalism and the emergence of capitalism. The historical dynamism Marx attributes to private property and individualism appears too in his explanation of why the so-called 'Asiatic mode of production' is so resistant to change:

> The Asiatic form necessarily survives longest and most stubbornly. This is due to the fundamental principle on which it is based, that is, that the individual does not become independent of the community; that the circle of production is self-sustaining, unity of agriculture and craft manufacture, etc.[66]

---

63 Marx and Engels 1976, p. 42.
64 Marx 1973, pp. 82–3.
65 As cited in Marx and Engels 1978, p. 151.
66 Marx 1964, p. 83.

Obviously, this sort of immediate, unreflective and compulsory coincidence of the individual and the community is not Marx's cup of tea. The absence of private property and the stifling of the individual that Marx claimed to find in China, and more particularly in India, combine to arrest history. Unsurprisingly, Marx associates this shutdown with a short-circuiting of the dialectic of new needs we considered above: 'Absence of wants and predilection for hereditary modes of dress, are obstacles which civilised commerce has to encounter in all new markets.'[67] Here, again, we see Marx's philosophical anthropology making itself felt. In the purported stagnancy of the Asiatic mode of production, Marx does not detect counter-evidence to his Rousseau-inspired assertion of the human conatus of perfectibility; rather, he judges the Asiatic mode of production to be the sort of fetter on humanity that he and Engels described in *The German Ideology*:

> This fixation of social activity, this consolidation of what we ourselves produce into an objective power above us, growing out of our control, thwarting our expectations, bringing to naught our calculations, is one of the chief factors in historical development up till now.[68]

Where 'up till now' includes capitalism, of course.

If there is some rough teleological dialectic in the West leading from the emergence of private property and individualism toward bourgeois society and the capitalist mode of production, with the establishment of capitalism as the dominant mode of production on the face of the earth, the teleology and dynamics of history become much more definite and pushy. Capitalism knows where it is going – everywhere – and what it is going to do once it gets there – remake whatever's there into its own hectic form of life.[69] As Marx and Engels put it in the *Communist Manifesto*, the bourgeoisie 'draws all, even the most barbarian, nations into civilization. The cheap prices of its commodities are the heavy artillery with which it batters down all Chinese walls, with which it forces the barbarians' intensely obstinate hatred of foreigners to capitulate. It compels all nations, on pain of extinction, to adopt the bourgeois mode of

67 Marx 1968a, p. 18.

68 As cited in Marx and Engels 1978, p. 160.

69 'Wherever it takes root capitalist production destroys all forms of commodity production which are based either on self-employment of the producers, or merely on the sale of excess product as commodities. Capitalist production first makes the production of commodities general and then, by degrees, transforms all commodity production into capitalist commodity production' (*Capital* II, as quoted in Marx 1968a, p. 37).

production ... to become bourgeois themselves. In one word, it creates a world after its own image'.[70]

In its own perverse way, then, capitalism discloses several shortcomings of prior human history, while moving in contradictory ways towards overcoming them. As Marx sizes up capitalism's historic mission:

> The bourgeois period of history has to create the material basis of the new world – on the one hand the universal intercourse founded upon the mutual dependency of mankind, and the means of that intercourse; on the other hand the development of the productive powers of man and the transformation of material production into a scientific domination of natural agencies.[71]

Capitalism illuminates and addresses: (i) the narrowness and despotism of earlier social formations; (ii) their material poverty and the stifling of what David Hume fondly called the 'refinement' of human needs; (iii) their ignorance and superstition; and (iv) their subjection of humans to blind nature.

Why are pre-capitalist social formations destined to fall apart? Because they are too narrow, too parochial, too confining for humans. Marx harps on about the narrowness and fixity of all pre-capitalist social formations:

> In all these forms the basis of evolution is the reproduction of relations between individual and community *assumed as given* – they may be more or less primitive, more or less the result of history, but fixed into tradition – and a *definite, predetermined objective* existence, both as regards the relation to the condition of labour and the relations between one man and his co-workers, fellow-tribesmen, etc. Such evolution is therefore from the outset *limited*, but once the limits are transcended, decay and disintegration ensue.[72]

Marx adds, 'But free and full development of individual or society is inconceivable here, for such evolution stands in contradiction to the original relationship'.[73] (It turns out that capitalism also rests on too narrow a foundation for human flourishing, and that this poses problems for its capacity to keep reproducing itself.)

---

70 Marx and Engels, *Communist Manifesto*, as quoted in Marx 1968a, p. 2.

71 Marx 1968a, p. 13.

72 Marx 1964b, p. 83.

73 Marx 1964b, p. 84.

As Marx looks back over human history in the face of the emergence of a capitalist world market, the options have been (i) narrow satisfaction, in pre-capitalist societies or (ii) lack of satisfaction in capitalist society – which turns out to be based on its own very peculiar kind of narrowness. Capitalism's miserly pursuit of wealth as an end in itself suffers by comparison:

> The ancient conception, in which man always appears (in however narrowly national, religious, or political a definition) as the aim of production, seems very much more exalted than the modern world, in which production is the aim of man and wealth the aim of production.[74]

Marx continues his thought:

> Hence in one way the childlike world of the ancients appears to be superior; and this is so, in so far as we seek for closed shape, form and established limitation. The ancients provide a narrow satisfaction, whereas the modern world leaves us unsatisfied, or, where it appears to be satisfied with itself, is *vulgar* and *mean*.[75]

Where, then, does this leave Marx? It appears to leave him standing with Kant and Hegel:

> England, it is true, in causing a social revolution in Hindostan, was actuated only by the vilest interests, and was stupid in her manner of enforcing them. But that is not the question. The question is, can mankind fulfil its destiny without a fundamental revolution in the social state of Asia? If not, whatever may have been the crimes of England she was the unconscious tool of history in bringing about the revolution.[76]

Writing in 1968, with these and like passages in mind, Shlomo Avineri passed the following judgement: 'Marx's sole criteria for judging the social revolution imposed on Asia are those of European, bourgeois society itself'.[77] This remark, and the label 'Europocentric', with which Avineri then tags Marx, are intended to be pejorative.

---

74 Marx 1964b, p. 84.
75 Marx 1964b, p. 85.
76 Marx 1968a, p. 89.
77 Marx 1968a, p. 26.

I am not prepared to defend Marx's harsh judgment of mid-nineteenth-century Indian village life; but I would like to at least question Avineri's assertion, which he makes no effort to support, that Marx's criteria are European in a pejorative sense. I believe that the criteria to which Marx appeals in making his harsh judgments of both the British and the Indians may be found in the following passage:

> when the narrow bourgeois form has been peeled away, what is wealth, if not the universality of needs, capacities, enjoyments, productive powers, etc., of individuals, produced in universal exchange? What, if not the full development of human control over the forces of nature – those of his own nature as well as those of so-called 'nature'? What, if not the absolute elaboration of his creative dispositions, without any preconditions other than antecedent historical evolution – i.e. the evolution of all human powers as such, unmeasured by any *previously established* yardstick – an end in itself?[78]

To assess Marx's ideas about purpose in history, it would help to know what, if anything, is pejoratively European about this, and why.

---

78 Marx 1964b, p. 85.

CHAPTER 4

Marx's 'Truly Social' Labour Theory of Value: Part I, Abstract Labour in Marxian Value Theory*

> To make abstractions hold good in actuality means to destroy actuality.[1]

∴

Marx's theory of value addresses a multitude of ways in which labour performed within the force-field of capitalist social relations can be abstract. The root of this multiplicity is the profound abstractness of capital's urge endlessly to accumulate surplus value, as measured in money. The various ways that Marx conceives labour to be abstract due to the power of capital continue to perplex interpreters and so stand in need of identification and disentangling, tasks I undertake in this two-part article. Marx wasn't joking when he wrote of the commodity: 'it is a very strange thing, abounding in metaphysical subtleties and theological niceties'.[2]

The key to understanding Marx's thought on these topics is to grasp the role that social form plays. In thinking about wealth we commonly pose one or two questions: how much wealth is there? or, How is wealth distributed? In this snippet of dialogue between two schoolgirls in his novel *Hard Times*, Charles Dickens forcefully brings home the simple reason why the first question does not suffice:

> 'And he said, Now, this schoolroom is a Nation. And in this nation, there are fifty millions of money. Isn't this a prosperous nation, and a'n't you in a thriving state?' 'What did you say?' asked Louisa. 'Miss Louisa, I said I didn't know. I thought I couldn't know whether it was a prosperous nation

---

* 'Marx's "Truly Social" Labour Theory of Value: Part I, Abstract Labour in Marxian Value Theory', *Historical Materialism*, Number 6 (Summer 2000), pp. 27–65. Geert Reuten's reply, 'The Interconnection of Systematic Dialectics and Historical Materialism', appears in *Historical Materialism*, Number 7 (Winter 2000), pp. 137–65.

1 Hegel 1955, p. 425.

2 Marx 1976a, p. 163.

> or not, and whether I was in a thriving state or not, unless I knew who had got the money, and whether any of it was mine. But that had nothing to do with it. It was not in the figures at all', said Sissy, wiping her eyes.[3]

What the How much? and How distributed? questions neglect to raise is a fundamental, if elusive, question: what is the social form and purpose of wealth? Asking this third question presupposes a conception of human wealth as an intrinsically social phenomenon: wealth always has a specific social form and purpose. And what these are matters.

This presupposition is the quintessence of Marx's much misunderstood historical materialism.[4] Marx insists on it in principle, as, for example, when he writes in the *Grundrisse*, 'All production is appropriation of nature on the part of an individual within and through a specific form of society'.[5] And he insists on it in practice when he comes to study specific historical phenomena. Thus, *Capital* is largely a study of the nature, inner connections, and powers of value forms (commodity, money, capital, wages, etc.), that is, the specific social forms constitutive for the capitalist mode of production. This means that *Capital* is not a work in economics – 'Marxist economics' is a misnomer – rather, *Capital* is what Marx said it was: a critique of economics. The heart of that critique comes to this: economics pretends to do what cannot be done, to provide a scientific account of the production and distribution of wealth in utter abstraction from historically specific social forms. Of course, in order to explain things, economists turn around and sneak these forms back in, usually under cover of slurring the difference between specific categories like capital or wage labour and general ones like productive resources or labour.[6]

---

3 Martha Nussbaum and Amartya Sen quote this passage at the beginning of the introduction to their co-edited book, *The Quality of Life* (Nussbaum and Sen 1993). They go on to say why, in judging the quality of life, we want to know more than just how much wealth there is and how it is distributed.

4 For a critique of the standard, 'technological', misunderstanding that conceives of the 'forces of production' as asocial, see *The Violence of Abstraction*, Derek Sayer's book-length rejoinder to G.A. Cohen's *Marx's Theory of History*, and see Martha Campbell's remarks on pp. 144–6 of Campbell 1993b.

5 Marx 1973, p. 87.

6 The consequences of Marx's conception of social form for the social sciences extend beyond economics. In his eye-opening study *Marx, Marginalism and Modern Sociology*, Simon Clarke shows how the conceptual shortcomings of economics, specifically, neoclassical economics, crossed over to modern sociology in the work of Max Weber, Charles Parsons, and other leading sociologists. See Clarke 1982.

The failure to grasp the nature of Marx's theory of value matches the failure to recognise Marx as a critic of economics rather than a radical economist. Instead of seeing Marx's theory as a radical departure from the classical, or Ricardian, labour theory of value, commentators often see it as an improved, more consistent and radical version that lays bare, through the theory of surplus value, the exploitative class structure of capitalism. But Marx's theory of value is not so much a theory of wealth and labour as it is a theory of the peculiar social form of wealth and labour in capitalism. Indeed, *Marx's theory of value is nothing but his theory of the distinctive social form of wealth and labour in capitalism*. Where the classical labour theory of value is a completely asocial theory of value, Marx's is a thoroughly social one.

Ironically, we find commonly attributed to Marx precisely the asocial conception of value that he overthrew. James Bernard Murphy puts this upside down claim as plainly as possible: 'Value, for Marx, is not determined by our relations to persons but by our relations to natural objects.'[7] Jürgen Habermas asserts that, for Marx, labour is instrumental action, which Habermas characterises as a 'monological' (asocial) relation of humans to nature.[8] This likewise saddles Marx with precisely the asocial conception of labour and value that he overturned.

Many passages from Marx might be added to the following two to demonstrate that he actually possessed a 'truly social' conception of labour and value:

> Since the exchange-value of commodities is indeed nothing but a mutual relation between various kinds of labour of individuals regarded as equal and universal labour, i.e., nothing but a material expression of a specific social form of labour, it is a tautology to say that labour is the only source of exchange-value and accordingly of wealth in so far as this consists of exchange-value.[9]

> Hence he [Wagner] would have found that the 'value' of a commodity only expresses in a historically developed form, what exists in all other historical forms of society as well, even if *in another form, namely, the social character of labour*.[10]

7 Murphy 1993, p. 223. Richard Winfield's critique of Marx's theory of value as asocial is premised on the same inverted reading. See Winfield 1988. For a critique of Winfield, see Tony Smith's essay 'Hegel and Marx on Civil Society' in Smith 1993.

8 See Habermas 1971. Seyla Benhabib adopts this interpretation in Benhabib 1986.

9 Marx 1970a, p. 35.

10 Marx 1975e, pp. 206–7.

Notice, what is true of all historical societies is not that labour produces value but that labour always has some definite social form. Value, for Marx, is the consequence not of asocial 'labour' but of a specific social form of labour. This places Marx's theory of value far from thc discourse of economics.

Capital is wealth possessed of an imperious social form with an icy purpose. Tendencies to abstraction are endemic to capital. Indeed, Marx characterises the novelty of the capitalist epoch as the surpassing of regimes of personal dependence by the domination of all by abstractions of their own making. Marx conceives of the uncanny power of the capital form in terms of the different ways it subsumes and transforms wealth, its production, and its distribution. Wealth and its production and distribution always have some specific social form; with his concepts of the formal, real, ideal and hybrid types of subsumption under capital, Marx distinguishes different ways in which the social forms bound up with capital exercise their power.[11] These four categories of subsumption organise Marx's thinking about the various ways in which capital's propensities toward abstraction work themselves out.

Beyond these categories for sorting ways capital makes labour abstract, I will draw on Marx's notion of a 'shadow form' derivative from the capital form. I will identify two: utility and instrumental rationality. In calling these 'shadows' I mean that they are produced by the actual, capitalist forms of social life, but they can appear to be independent actualities, like Peter Pan's shadow. Thus, utility and instrumental action have only a 'shadowy' existence, and the common conceptions of them are best thought of as 'pseudo-concepts';[12] nonetheless, these 'shadows' and 'pseudo-concepts' have their own reality and effects. Any gardener knows that shade matters. Labour may become abstract by coming under these 'shadows' of capital. Like shadows, 'pseudo-concepts' such as utility and instrumental action can be cast more widely than the actual forms they mimic: thus, they get applied to human activities that are not subsumed under the forms bound up with capital, such as unpaid domestic activities. Such overshadowing can ease the transition to ideal or formal subsumption under value categories.

The present chapter, the first of two devoted to the topic, will focus on the meanings of 'abstract labour' to which Marx appeals in explicating his theory of value in the first chapter of *Capital*. This thorny topic concerns the type of

11 On these four types of subsumption see Marx 1976b, pp. 1019 ff.

12 Alasdair MacIntyre calls utility a 'pseudo-concept' in MacIntyre 1984. Tony Smith argues on the basis of texts from Max Weber that the concept of instrumental reason is derivative from the concept of value. See the Conclusion to Smith 1990, pp. 197–8. See also the section 'Labour and Instrumental Action', in Postone 1993, pp. 179–83.

labour that produces value. The second chapter, immediately following, spans the remaining forms of subsumption, including the 'shadow forms'. Because of its inherent interest, as well as its usefulness as a foil, I will also consider in the following chapter whether or not unpaid domestic labour can be considered abstract in any ways pertinent to Marxian value theory.

1 Only 'Practically Abstract' Labour Produces Value

In opposition to Samuel Bailey's polemics against Ricardian 'intrinsic value', Marx argued that, though exchange value is the necessary expression of value, it is not identical with value (as Bailey held). In thinking through what value could be, Marx concluded that, if it is not exchange-value, value can only be labour, or, more precisely, congealed 'abstract labour' – since concrete labours are incommensurable. Just what does Marx mean here by 'abstract labour' and what do different answers to that question tell us as to whether Marx's theory of value is social or asocial?

It has widely been assumed that 'abstract labour' is simply identical with value-producing labour. This assumption, which I previously shared, sets up what I will discuss below as 'Rubin's Dilemma'. I will argue that, while the concept of value-producing labour depends upon that of abstract labour, it is not the same concept. In fact, it is not the same sort of concept. Whereas labour of any concrete and historically specific social type can be viewed as labour in the abstract, only a historically specific sort of labour is abstract in practice, that is, receives its social validation precisely insofar as it counts as abstract labour. This concept of 'practically abstract' labour as a definite historical type of labour, namely, the labour that produces commodities and is socially validated once those commodities are exchanged for the universal equivalent (money), builds conceptually on the generally applicable notion of abstract labour. For we can tell whether labour is abstract in practice only if we first know what it means to be abstract. To judge whether a particular figure is a triangle, I need to know what a plane is. The fact that the concept of abstract labour is generally applicable does not imply that labour of every social sort produces value. Not all plane figures are triangles. Though labour can produce value only insofar as it is abstract, not every sort of labour produces value insofar as it is conceived of abstractly. Only 'practically abstract' labour produces value.

Correctly understanding Marx's theory of value depends upon making this distinction between the concept of abstract labour and that of 'practically abstract' labour. If one simply equates the concept of value-producing labour with the (general) concept of abstract labour, an asocial, naturalistic concept of value is inescapable. That is one horn of 'Rubin's Dilemma'. The second is this: if we identify abstract labour with value-producing labour and insist, rightly, that value-producing labour is of a historically specific social sort, then we must say that abstract labour is historically specific. The trouble here is that we get tripped up by the many passages in which Marx speaks of the general applicability of the concept of abstract labour. In other words, if we equate abstract labour with a historically specific sort, what can we make of Marx's talk of a generally applicable concept of abstract ('physiological') labour? But, when we recognise that: (i) Marx introduces the general, analytical category of abstract labour as a necessary step in expounding the concept of 'practically abstract' labour; and (ii) 'practically abstract' labour, not 'abstract labour', is value-producing, we escape 'Rubin's Dilemma' and remove misgivings about whether Marx's theory of value is 'truly social'.

The concept of abstract labour is 'analytical' because it identifies an aspect of any sort of actual labour rather than identifying a sort of actual labour, as the concept of 'practically abstract' labour does. There is no actual labour that is abstract as opposed to some other actual labour that is concrete. All actual labour is concrete and can be viewed as abstract. Thus, Ernest Mandel misunderstood the nature of these concepts. He argued that service labour cannot be value-producing because all such labour must be concrete, but service labour is not. In fact, however, all actual labour, service labour included, is concrete.[13] Gerlach, a would-be critic of Marx discussed by Rubin, thought he could refute Marx through experiments showing that 'human labour is always accompanied and conditioned by consciousness' so 'we must refuse to reduce it to the movement of muscles and nerves.'[14] But this only proves Marx's point: the concept of abstract ('physiological') labour abstracts from actual human labour, which is always consciously purposive (concrete). Actual labours, then, cannot be sorted into the concrete and the abstract (not in the sense of these terms presently under discussion). 'Practically abstract' labour, by contrast, is a sorting concept, it sorts actual labours into those that are 'practically abstract' and those that are not. Abstract labour and 'practically abstract' labour are not just different concepts, they are different kinds of concepts. Abstract labour is like extension; 'practically abstract' labour is like wax.

13 See my critique of Mandel in the Appendix to Murray 1998, pp. 57–61, included in the present volume as Chapter 12.

14 As quoted in Rubin 1972, pp. 132–3.

Drawing this distinction between abstract labour and 'practically abstract' labour clarifies Marx's relation to classical political economy. First, and most importantly, it reveals the profound difference between a generally applicable, asocial labour theory of value and a theory of value-producing labour as the historically specific social form of labour in capitalism, a 'value theory of labour' as Diane Elson terms it. There is a world of difference between the two. Second, it properly locates Marx's acknowledged debt to classical theorists like Smith and Ricardo. Marx credits the classical theorists with coming up with the concept of abstract labour, which his own very different conception of 'practically abstract' labour presupposes. Third, it gives us pause in speaking of Marx's distinction between the two sorts of labour involved in commodity-producing labour. Marx declared this to be the conceptual point on which the proper understanding of political economy turns; he regarded it as his own discovery and one of the best points in his book. If we understand the point to be simply the distinguishing of abstract from concrete labour, we reduce Marx's theory of value to a more lucid version of Ricardian value theory.[15] That makes

15 This appears to be the view that Paul Sweezy adopts. He writes, 'Abstract labour, in short, is, as Marx's own usage clearly attests, equivalent to "labour in general"; it is what is common to all productive human activity' (Sweezy 1942, p. 30). He follows up with an observation on Marx's relation to the classicals: 'In this, as in many other cases, Marx started from a basic idea of the classical school, gave it precise and explicit expression, developed it, and utilized it in the analysis of social relations in his own original and penetrating fashion' (p. 31). The trouble here is that Sweezy is pinned down by the assumption that there's just one idea in play, and that is the generally applicable concept of abstract labour. Consequently, Sweezy can conceive of Marx's advance over the classicals only in terms of cleaning up this one thought and putting it to work in a radical critique of capitalist social relations. Thus, as Marxists have so often done, Sweezy makes a left Ricardian of Marx. It might not seem so, for Sweezy goes on to quote Lukács to the effect that abstract labour is an abstraction 'which belongs to the essence of capitalism' (p. 31). And Sweezy calls attention to the sort of labour mobility characteristic of capitalism as if he is moving toward an idea of abstract labour as something specific to capitalism. Nevertheless, the trouble is that he is assuming that there is just one idea here, and he has already made it plain that it is generally applicable. So he is restricted to making this point in summation of his account of abstract labour: 'we may say that the reduction of all labour to abstract labour enables us to see clearly, behind the special forms which labour may assume at any given time, an aggregate social labour force which is capable of transference from one use to another in accordance with social need, and on the magnitude and development of which society's wealth-producing capacity in the last resort depends. The adoption of this point of view, moreover, is conditioned by the very nature of capitalist production which promotes a degree of labour mobility never before approached in earlier forms of society' (p. 32). Here we have expressed a thoroughly Ricardian (and Enlightenment) observation,

it hard to see where Marx thought his great innovation lay. Inasmuch as Marx grants that the classicals pioneered the concept of abstract labour, we have to wonder what he thought all the hubbub was about.

But the double-character of commodity-producing labour is not adequately expressed by talk of abstract versus concrete: commodity-producing labour is concrete and 'practically abstract'. The concept of 'practically abstract' labour piggybacks on the concept of abstract labour arrived at by the classical economists; so Marx was right to think of himself as standing on their shoulders. But Marx's idea that value comes not from labour but from a historically specific social form of labour, 'practically abstract' labour, is more than foreign to classical political economy; it thrusts the embarrassingly asocial presuppositions of economics into the light of day.[16]

In his 1993 essay 'The Difficult Labour of a Social Theory of Value', Geert Reuten argues that the theory of value presented in *Capital* is beset with ambiguity due to Marx's failure to recognise fully how fundamental was his own incipient break with the classical (Ricardian) labour theory of value. Reuten's essay is especially noteworthy for two reasons: first, Reuten is very sympathetic toward Marx's project in *Capital*, and he is a 'value-form' theorist himself (that is, he takes the theory of value to be a theory of the historically specific form of wealth in capitalist societies). Second, Reuten recognises both that Marx does invoke a generally applicable concept of abstract labour and that such a concept cannot serve as the basis for a 'truly social' theory of value. In this, Reuten challenges the assumptions behind what I am calling 'Rubin's Dilemma'. Reuten argues that Marx's theory is open to the interpretation that it is an 'abstract labour-embodied' theory of value and that such a theory does not differ fundamentally from Ricardian theory. It still conceives of value as

---

which speaks of 'wealth' and 'aggregate social labour' but is deaf to questions as to the specific social form of wealth and of labour. To this is joined the interesting point in the sociology of knowledge – one Marx makes – that the peculiar social practices of capitalism give rise to the generally applicable concept of abstract labour. Though Sweezy admirably goes on to discuss the fetishism of commodities and even quotes Marx as saying that this fetish character originates in 'the peculiar social character of the labour which produces commodities' (Marx, as quoted by Sweezy, p. 35), he has put himself in no position to make sense of this. Because his thinking is penned in by 'Rubin's Dilemma', Sweezy cannot but represent Marx's theory of value as fundamentally Ricardian and therefore not 'truly social'. Sweezy cannot put the puzzle together because, without knowing it, he is missing a piece: he lacks the concept of 'practically abstract' labour.

16 For an account of how radically Marx's theory differs from both classical and neoclassical economics see Campbell 1993b.

asocial. This is so, Reuten argues, because, in contrast to the determinate notion of 'value-producing labour' required by a true 'value-form' theory of value, 'abstract labour' is a general concept.[17]

Reuten's discrimination between a 'concrete labour-embodied' theory and an 'abstract labour-embodied' theory, seems to take into account Marx's advance over Ricardo (at least if we believe that Marx's innovation was to distinguish between concrete and abstract labour), while concluding that Marx did not unambiguously surpass Ricardo's asocial theory of value. If convincing, Reuten's interpretation would put the claim that Marx holds a 'truly social' theory of value under a question mark. So it forces readers like me who reject any assertion that Marx at best held confusedly and ambivalently a 'truly social' labour theory of value, to think further about abstract labour and value in *Capital*.

I will argue that Reuten is right to observe that Marx employs a notion of abstract labour that is general, and thus lacks the determinacy of value-producing labour, but wrong to think that Marx ever meant to identify this general notion of abstract labour with his concept of value-producing labour. Though the general notion of abstract labour is applicable to all human labour, it is only in a society where, as a rule, wealth takes the commodity form that the notion of abstract labour has practical significance. Only in such a society is labour validated as equally human in the same stroke as society treats the particular concrete character and purpose of the labour with utter indifference.[18] Is it any wonder that Americans have locked in on the phrase 'Whatever!'? Only such a society applies the category of abstract labour to itself in and through its own everyday practices. (This is not to say that members of such a society think of themselves as doing this; they do not.) For Marx, value-producing labour is 'practically abstract' labour, which is labour of a peculiar social sort.

Reuten associates the ambivalence he detects in Marx's theory of value with alleged confusions in Marx's mode of presentation: Is *Capital* really a work in

17 On the distinction between general and determinate abstractions see Murray 1988a, Chapter 10.

18 In the course of explaining why Aristotle was unable to solve the riddle posed by the expression of value, Marx observes: 'The secret of the expression of value, namely the equality and equivalence of all kinds of labour because and in so far as they are human labour in general, could not be deciphered until the concept of human equality had already acquired the permanence of a fixed popular opinion. This however is possible only in a society where the commodity-form is the universal form of the product of labour, hence the dominant social relation is the relation between men as possessors of commodities' (Marx 1976a, p. 152).

systematic dialectics or not? Reuten sees it falling well short of his expectations, which are Hegelian. I think Reuten is right to link the interpretation of Marx's theory of value to the question of how Marx has organised his presentation in *Capital*. But I think Reuten is wrong: first, to presume a strictly Hegelian standard, when, in *Capital*, Marx renews his early criticism of the Hegelian expectation of 'presuppositionlessness' in scientific presentation, and, second, to reach such a negative judgment regarding *Capital*'s claim to be a work of scientific dialectics.

The questions involved in understanding and assessing Marx's method do not pull away cleanly from the doctrines of *Capital*; how we answer them will guide us in how we read *Capital*. Consequently, I will offer a short guide to Marx's method before returning to Marx's theory of value, 'Rubin's Dilemma', and Reuten's challenge.

2 Phenomenology, Essentialism and Systematic Dialectical Presentation: A Package Deal

To explain what I mean by phenomenology, that is, the experience-based inquiry into what things are,[19] I begin with two heroes of analytic philosophy, George Berkeley and David Hume. Specifically, I take up Hume's notion of a 'distinction of reason', which he expressly derives from Berkeley's theory of abstraction. Hume's notion of a distinction of reason calls attention to the fact that, in experience, we find situations where we can conceptually distinguish aspects of something perceived, but these aspects cannot be separated in experience or even in imagination. Hume gives the example of a white marble globe: we can distinguish its whiteness from its spherical shape, but we cannot imagine having the one stand apart from the other. To give another example, Hume's theories of belief and of the (exclusive) division of our perceptions into impressions and ideas rely on the different 'manners' exhibited by our perceptions. These 'manners' are not separable from the perceptions they are the manners of (the vivacity or dullness of a perception does not stand apart from it); consequently, the notion of the manner of a perception involves a distinction of reason.

19 Phenomenological investigation is the 'redoubled' part of what I called Marx's 'redoubled empiricism' in my chapter 'Redoubled Empiricism: Social Form and Formal Causality in Marxian Theory', included in the present volume as Chapter 2.

In allowing for distinctions of reason, Hume presupposes an experience-based mode of inquiry capable of making judgments about how (that is, the manner in which) things are concrete. By something's being concrete I mean that it necessarily involves more than one conceptual determination or distinction of reason, as, for example, a sound involves tone and intensity or a commodity involves use-value and exchange-value. The properties that make something concrete in this sense are inseparable from it and can be identified as its essential properties. These are the properties that we ask for with the question: 'What is it?'[20] The experience-based inquiry that is presupposed by the claim that we can differentiate between a distinction of reason and the idea of a separable object is what I mean by the term 'phenomenology'. So phenomenology is the experience-based inquiry into the essence (or nature or form) of things. If essentialism is the belief that there are essences (or natures or forms), phenomenology is based on that belief; phenomenology is essentialist.[21]

If 'phenomenology' is the name for the experience-based inquiry into the essence or nature of things; 'systematic dialectical presentation' (or 'systematic dialectics') is the name for the most appropriate way to present the findings of phenomenology. So dialectical presentation is rooted in experience; it is not a matter of spinning webs *a priori*. Briefly, what the term 'dialectical' points to is that a presentation of this sort will show in a systematic way that those distinguishable aspects of the object under study that phenomenology has revealed to be essential to it (that is, actually inseparable from it) are essential and inseparable. Thus, for example, in *Capital*, Marx shows that value and price are inseparable and also that generalised simple commodity circulation is inseparable from the circulation of capital. Such a presentation serves as a much needed corrective to 'non-dialectical' ones, by which I mean presentations which rely on poor phenomenology, and which operate as if aspects of the object under study that actually are essential to it are not. Thus, *Capital* corrects the poor phenomenology underlying economics, which imagines that value and price are actually separable; that simple commodity circulation does not presuppose

20 Hegel stresses the primacy of this question, writing, 'But neither we nor the objects would have anything to gain by the mere fact that they possess being. The main point is not that they are, but what they are ... Laying aside therefore as unimportant this distinction between subjective and objective, we are chiefly interested in knowing what a thing is: i.e., its content, which is no more objective than it is subjective' (Hegel 1975, pp. 70–1).

21 On Marx as an essentialist, see Meikle 1985.

the circulation of capital; and, more generally, that human needs, labour and wealth are separable from their social forms and the representations of those forms.

The term 'systematic' refers to a presentation's being orderly, coherent and complete. (With that last qualifier in mind, it is evident that there is at least one sense in which *Capital* fails to come up to the standard for systematic dialectics.) The orderliness requirement echoes Descartes' writings on method – as does the *Grundrisse* section on method – by calling for the introduction of concepts synthetically, that is, in order of their conceptual concreteness: simpler categories come before more complex ones. The (broadly) Hegelian notion of 'systematic dialectics' adds to the systematicity of Descartes' mode of presentation by having the structure of presupposition run in both directions.[22] Not only do the complex categories presuppose the simple ones, which is the analytical point; the simple categories presuppose the complex ones, which is the phenomenological point. This two-way directionality of dialectical systematicity expresses the phenomenologically ascertained inseparability of multiple aspects of the object under examination.

This feature introduces a circularity into a systematic dialectical presentation that seems disturbing. And, it is at this point that Marx parts company with the Hegelian notion of systematic dialectics. Marx does not leave the circle of Hegelian systematic dialectics unbroken; famously, he objects to the 'presuppositionlessness' of Hegelian systematic dialectics and insists that science has premises, which he and Engels sketched in *The German Ideology*. These premises, which are given by nature and are not themselves subject to incorporation as 'results' of some more cosmic systematic dialectic, reappear in *Capital* and testify to Marx's explicit and frequently reaffirmed divergence from strictly Hegelian systematic dialectics (at least as he, questionably, understood Hegel).

In *Capital*, Marx offers both a general phenomenology of the human predicament and a specific phenomenology of the plight of humanity under capitalism. In this he does precisely what he roasts Jeremy Bentham for not doing:

> To know what is useful for a dog, one must investigate the nature of dogs. This nature is not itself deducible from the principle of utility. Applying this to man, he that would judge all human acts, movements, relations,

22 On this structure of mutual presupposition in *Capital*, see Bubner 1988 and Arthur 1997. In his treatment of Descartes' theory of the order of scientific presentation, James Collins argues that Descartes himself recognised a certain mutual reinforcement of concepts and claims that are introduced in an orderly fashion. See Collins 1972, pp. 68–71.

> etc. according to the principle of utility would first have to deal with human nature in general, and then with human nature as historically modified in each epoch. Bentham does not trouble himself with this.[23]

The brunt of Marx's spare general phenomenology comes in his tellingly brief remarks on use value in Chapter One (where he says little, out of respect for the diversity and historicity of human needs) and his lengthier general observations in Chapter Seven on the labour process. Supplementing those two accounts with observations that crop up elsewhere in *Capital*, we get the following general phenomenology of the human predicament: human beings are needy, self-conscious, symbolising, social, sexually reproducing animals who are in (and of) non-human nature, which they purposively transform according to their perceived wants. This general phenomenology comprises the truth of historical materialism. (i) It establishes a point of reference for judging all accounts of human life and activities: when these accounts depart from the full phenomenological complexity represented here, they err (as economics does on a grand scale). (ii) In exposing the self-conscious, symbolising, sexualised sociality of human beings, it shows why no general, ahistorical account of human phenomena will be adequate to them. Rather, the study of human life and activities will always require investigating specific social forms of human life (and its reproduction) and the ways participants in different societies represent their common life to themselves.

To see why we can take the preceding observations as a gloss on the section of the *Grundrisse* introduction devoted to the method of inquiry and the method of presentation,[24] we need a bridge from Hume's eighteenth-century terminology to the nineteenth-century terminology of Hegel and Marx. The term 'moment' provides this bridge. Geert Reuten accurately defines the Hegelian (and Marxian) notion of a 'moment' as follows: 'A moment is an element considered in itself that can be conceptually isolated and analyzed as such but that can have no isolated existence.'[25] So a Hegelian 'moment' is a Humean 'distinction of reason'. The difference between Hume and Hegel (and Marx) is that, though he engages in it, Hume allows no place in his official philosophy for phenomenology, whereas Hegel and Marx explicitly embrace it. Thus, I take it that, when Marx states '[t]he concrete is concrete because it is the concentration of many determinations, hence unity of the diverse',[26] he is making a phenomen-

23 Marx 1976a, pp. 758–9.

24 Marx 1973, pp. 100 ff.

25 Reuten 1993, p. 92.

26 Marx 1973, p. 101.

ological claim according to which these many 'determinations' are recognised as 'moments' or 'distinctions of reason', not as a bundle of separable elements. Commenting on this passage, Geert Reuten observes: 'Contingent phenomena cannot be explained as codetermining the internal unity of many determinants',[27] appropriately making the link between the determination of 'moments' and essentialism. For, to grasp the unity of these diverse determinations is to grasp the essence or nature of this concrete object of study. Marx's 'method of inquiry' includes phenomenology.

But phenomenology presupposes analysis; properly conceived, analysis is a moment of phenomenology. Better yet, analysis and phenomenology are coeval. Thus, in that same text Marx recognises that making appropriate distinctions of reason, which is the 'analytical' work indispensable for knowing, belongs to the 'method of inquiry'. Objects of knowledge may be presumed to be implicitly concrete, but it is the task of investigators to make that implicit complexity explicit through careful analysis, that is, by making good distinctions of reason. So Marx acknowledges his debt to thinkers in the tradition of political economy for having done so much of this analytical work. The problem with that tradition, however, was of the kind that so troubled Berkeley, namely, the tendency to hypostatise distinctions of reason, to think as though moments stand on their own. One way that Marx expresses this general complaint about the tradition of political economy is to chastise it for failing to attend to exchange value, money and capital as historically specific social forms. Instead, economics falsely proceeds as if wealth and its production were something actual in abstraction from specific social forms. By contrast, the object of *Capital* is a society of a certain type (a type still in the making as Marx wrote; still in the making as we read), one whose social form of production (in an inclusive sense) is capital. The task of *Capital* as a work of systematic dialectics is, in an orderly, coherent manner, to articulate that social form in its perplexingly abstract concreteness.

The present account of Marxian systematic dialectics holds that 'Marx's dialectic' is not solely a historical dialectic.[28] *Capital* is a work of systematic dialectics, but Marx does not believe that there is any *a priori* 'dialectical logic' for him to follow – an idea for which he pounced on Lassalle. Neither is *Capital* a work in strictly Hegelian systematic dialectics. On the contrary, I have argued that Marxian systematic dialectics is simply the most appropriate mode

27 Reuten 1993, p. 92.

28 For a contrasting view see Mattick Jr 1993. On the difference between historical and systematic dialectics, see Smith 1990.

of presentation for the results of phenomenology, that is, an experience-based investigation of some specific object of knowledge (capitalist society in the case of *Capital*), and that, in identifying the naturally given presuppositions of capitalist society, Marx rejects the presuppositionlessness of Hegelian systematic dialectics.

We can summarise the chief features of Marxian systematic dialectics, then, as follows. (i) A systematic dialectical presentation will have identifiable premises or presuppositions given by nature.[29] (ii) It will represent the moments of the object under study in their inseparability as uncovered by the analytical and phenomenological inquiry into that object. In so doing it discloses the essence (or nature or form) of what is under study. (iii) In introducing those moments, the presentation will proceed from the conceptually simpler to the conceptually more complex. (iv) Though the conceptual development proceeds from the conceptually simpler to the conceptually more complex, the former are presented, at least implicitly, as presupposing the latter.

In Marx, phenomenology, essentialism, and systematic dialectics come as a package deal.

In order to illustrate the significance of this way of understanding Marx's method and to establish a key Marxian doctrine that will set us on the right course as we interpret Marx's theory of abstract labour and value, I will consider how a generalised circulation of commodities, a market society, is related to the circulation of capital.

Marx's whole presentation of the commodity and generalised simple commodity circulation presupposes capital and its characteristic form of circulation. It is perhaps the foremost accomplishment of Marx's theory of generalised commodity circulation to have demonstrated – with superb dialectical reasoning – that a sphere of such exchanges cannot stand alone; generalised commodity circulation is unintelligible when abstracted from the circulation of capital.[30] In other words, properly conceived, the notion of generalised com-

29 This requirement of Marxian systematic dialectics appears to be incompatible with the more strictly Hegelian requirements as identified and embraced by Geert Reuten: 'All axioms are eschewed. Rather, anything that is required to be assumed, or anything that is posited immediately (such as the starting point), must be grounded. But it should not be grounded merely abstractly (i.e., giving arguments in advance), because this always leads to regress. That which is posited must be ultimately grounded in the argument itself, in concretizing it' (Reuten 1993, p. 92). I do not think that the sort of presuppositions Marx has in mind can be justified internally in the way called for here.

30 'Circulation considered in itself is the mediation of presupposed extremes. But it does not posit these extremes. As a whole of mediation, as total process itself, it must therefore

modity circulation marks a distinction of reason from the circulation of capital; it does not designate a form of life that could exist on its own. There is no sphere of generalised commodity production independent of capital.[31] Consequently, when Marx begins with the commodity and commodity-producing labour in Chapter One, the actual objects of inquiry are commodity capital and surplus-value-producing labour. It is just that, to respect the synthetic order of a systematic dialectical presentation, conceptually simpler categories must be introduced first.

Marx's elegant argument demonstrating why the circulation of capital is presupposed by the generalization of the commodity form of wealth goes as follows. If we assume that wealth generally takes the commodity form, then wealth will be produced and sold as commodities. But the wealth required to produce commodities (means and materials of production along with labour power) will, on our assumption, likewise be in the commodity form – it will have to be purchased before being put to use. This means that, in the course of the production of all goods and services, there will be a stretch that begins with money (spent to purchase the elements of production, since they are in the commodity form) and ends with money (returned upon the sale of the newly produced commodity). On these assumptions, for commodities to be produced, some party who has money – and, since this party is acting as a commodity exchanger, we assume a self-interested agent – must spend it to initiate a process that will terminate in the return of money. What would motivate a self-seeking possessor of money to initiate such a circuit? The prospect of getting more money at the end of the cycle. When wealth is generally in the commodity form, only capitalists will, as a rule, undertake to produce it.[32] It is the circulation of capital, then, that makes intelligible the generalised circulation of commodities.

---

be mediated. *Its immediate being is therefore pure guise*. It is the *phenomenon of a process going on behind its back*' (Karl Marx, *Urtext*, as cited in Murray 1988a, pp. 172–3).

31 Chris Arthur make a persuasive argument for this in Arthur 1997. For a contrasting view, see Winfield 1988.

32 Martha Campbell sees Marx as demonstrating this point with his answer to the question: 'What social purpose is served by generalizing the commodity form of wealth?' 'It can only be the accumulation of surplus value'. See Campbell 1993a.

3 Johnny Paycheck Meets USX: 'Practically Abstract' Labour[33]

Marx credits himself with having made a great discovery by distinguishing between concrete labour and abstract labour and then observing that it is abstract labour alone that creates value. What makes this a historic discovery and what does Marx mean here by 'abstract labour'?

Following the logic of Marx's thinking in the first chapter of *Capital* and drawing on remarks about abstract labour that he makes in the introduction to the *Grundrisse*, I propose that we read Marx as distinguishing between a generally applicable, analytical concept of abstract labour as 'physiological' labour and a concept of historically specific, 'practically abstract' labour. Marx's theory of value, then, claims that 'practically abstract' labour, and only 'practically abstract' labour, is value-creating labour. By making a distinction of reason, we may consider labour of any social type in the abstract. But by 'practically abstract' labour, a term of my own devising for which there is ample warrant in Marx's thoughts and words, I mean labour that a society treats as abstract – in the sense identified by the analytical concept of abstract labour – in practice.[34] 'Practically abstract' labour is socially validated in a way that shows society's actual indifference toward labour's specific character, that is, toward labour's specific ways of transforming nature and toward the specific use-value characteristics of its end product.[35] This, then, is a historically determinate social sort of labour, which shows that Marx's theory of value is not 'asocial' but rather a

---

33 USX is the corporation formerly known as U.S. Steel.

34 In a passage from the *Grundrisse* to which we will return, Marx observes that, in capitalism, 'this abstraction of labour as such is not merely the mental product of a concrete totality of labours' (Marx 1973, p. 104) and 'for the first time, the point of departure of modern economics, namely the abstraction of the category "labour", "labour as such", labour pure and simple, becomes true in practice. The simplest abstraction, then ... achieves practical truth as an abstraction only as a category of the most modern society' (Marx 1973, p. 105). In commenting on these passages in his *Dialectics and Labour*, Chris Arthur picks up on this idea of labour whose products are socially validated in the market as labour that is abstract in practice. Though his interpretation comes closer to Rubin's than to the present one, several of his formulations add credibility to the concept and terminology of 'practically abstract' labour. For example, Arthur writes: 'In commodity exchange these individual labours are not mere fractions at the start; they become fractions of the total labour of society only insofar as their universal character achieves practical truth in the value relations of the products entering into commodity exchange' (Arthur 1986, p. 99). See also pp. 100, 103.

35 As previously noted, all actual labour is concrete in the sense marked by Marx's contrast between concrete and abstract labour in Chapter One of *Capital*.

theory of social form. Hence Marx's theory of value must be understood as a contribution not to economics, which purports to bracket historically determinate social forms, but to the critique of economics.

What sort of social practice would validate labour in a way that fits this description of 'practically abstract' labour? What sort of society would actually be thoroughly indifferent to the specificity of use values and therewith to the specificity of the labour needed to produce desired use values? The 'Whatever!' world of generalised commodity circulation is such a society: the only one.

Think about generalised commodity circulation, the social arrangement that makes labour 'practically abstract'. To treat all wealth as commodities is to make the judgment that no particular use values – and, since commodities are, as a rule, products of labour, no particular types of concrete labour – have any privileged social standing: society is stoically indifferent toward the specific use-value aspects of human needs and labour. The market, where 'all that is holy is profaned', gives meaning to the term 'practically abstract' labour by subjecting the products of labour to its grinding indifference. Now the further question arises, what would make a society so indifferent to the specificities of human needs and to the sorts of labour required to satisfy those needs?[36] And how would participants in such a society represent the point of it to themselves? Consider two answers, the liberal answer and Marx's.

The classical liberal answer (which is also the answer of economics) is that society's indifference proves that there is no collective good being pursued in the marketplace; rather, the participants in the market act freely to satisfy their individually determined, self-seeking needs. Moreover, this indifference on society's part is admirable, because only by society's self-restraint in positing no collective good is individual liberty attainable.[37]

Marx answers: there are no social systems of production lacking a collective goal: social action always has its purposes.[38] The 'free market' is no exception to this rule: it only appears to be. But what odd collective good is it that requires complete indifference on the part of society to the specific nature of human needs and to the labour required to satisfy them? The collective goal of accumulating surplus value, which necessarily takes the form of endless moneymaking, fits the bill perfectly; uniquely, I believe. Indeed, we have seen

36 Here I follow Martha Campbell's line of thought in Campbell 1993a.

37 According to Friedrich A. Hayek, this is perhaps the greatest discovery mankind has ever made.

38 Compare Martha Campbell's observation that for Marx, 'property relations are relations for the collective use of both the elements and results of production. This collective use assumes different forms, each with its own goal' (Campbell 1993b, p. 146).

how Marx argues that capital accumulation is precisely the collective goal that makes sense of generalised commodity exchange (the 'free market').

Market practices belong to the social arrangements that render labour abstract; they function as a sort of 'labour-processing' plant. The 'free market' is not an independent phenomenon; it is a moment of capital's circulation. Consequently, any thought that the market alone makes labour 'practically abstract' misconceives the status of generalised commodity circulation in relation to the production process as a whole.[39] What it comes to is this: workers whose labour is 'practically abstract', i.e., workers who produce value, work for a wage for capitalists, who produce in order to make a profit. Johnny Paycheck, meet USX; it's a marriage made in heaven.

Clearly, 'practically abstract' labour is a historically determinate social form of labour. Non-capitalist modes of production are not based upon the market's actual indifference toward the specific characteristics of needs, labour, and wealth.[40] That is not because in those forms of production labour is concrete, as opposed to being abstract – as we have seen, this distinction between concrete and abstract labour does not sort actual types of labour – but because they have collective goals that do not require labour to be treated as abstract. So, if Marx means that only 'practically abstract' labour produces value, then he means that only a specific social form of labour produces value. In that case his theory of value is 'truly social'.

This is what he does mean, I conclude, but the matter is complicated and potentially confusing. For Marx has in play three different concepts, in fact, three different sorts of concepts, and they are liable to be run together in the mind of the reader. The three are: (i) the concept of abstract labour, (ii) the concept of 'practically abstract' labour, and (iii) the general concept of labour. The first and last are different, but both are generally applicable, while the second identifies a historically specific social sort of labour. Value is the product not of labour, not even of abstract labour (though labour produces value only insofar as it counts as abstract), but of 'practically abstract' labour, and only of 'practically abstract' labour.

39 Alfred Sohn-Rethel commits this error in his *Intellectual and Manual Labour*. For a critique of Sohn-Rethel along these lines see Postone 1993, pp. 177–9. Isaak Rubin anticipates and criticises the error of thinking that value is produced by exchange alone. See Rubin 1972, pp. 147–58.

40 István Hont and Michael Ignatieff's essay in their co-edited book *Virtue and Wealth* tells the bloody tale of how European societies moved from taking privately produced grain and distributing it publicly to treating grain with all the indifference due a true commodity. See Hont and Ignatieff 1983.

The concept of abstract labour differs from the concept of 'practically abstract' labour precisely in being generally applicable. Marx maintains that, though this general notion of abstract labour comes into full view only when society becomes actually indifferent to the specificities of labour and labourers (which explains why Aristotle could not solve the riddle of the value form), it is nonetheless applicable across all forms of social labour.[41] Its general applicability, however, does not imply that all social forms of labour involve actual social practices that validate particular labours *as* abstract labour. Only in societies with such practices do we find 'practically abstract' labour. It turns out that only in capitalism are particular labours validated by a practice that treats them as labour in the abstract. So 'practically abstract' labour is specific to capitalism.

Now, how does the concept of abstract labour differ from the general concept of labour that Marx sets forth in the seventh chapter of *Capital*, 'The Labour-process and the Valorization Process'? Marx spells out the general concept of labour as follows:

> The labour process, as we have just presented it in its simple and abstract elements, is purposeful activity aimed at the production of use-values. It is an appropriation of what exists in nature for the requirements of man. It is the universal condition for the metabolic interaction between man and nature, the everlasting nature-imposed condition of human existence, and it is therefore independent of every form of that existence, or rather it is common to all forms of society in which human beings live.[42]

41 On Aristotle see Marx 1976a, pp. 151–2. See also below.

42 Marx 1976a, p. 290. Marx's restatement of his point at the end, 'or rather ...' is meant to ward off the sort of misunderstanding widespread today due to the unfortunate legend of Marx's asocial, 'monological' theory of labour and production. At the close of the first paragraph of the section on the labour-process, Marx observes: 'The fact that the production of use-values, or goods, is carried on under the control of a capitalist and on his behalf does not alter the general character of that production. We shall therefore, in the first place [Marx's term is *zunächst*, which is meant to alert his reader to the fact that in discussing the labour-process in abstraction from all specific social forms he is making a distinction of reason], have to consider the labour-process independently of any specific social form' (p. 283). Then comes a sentence that begins: 'Labour is, first of all [*zunächst*], a process between man and nature ...' which is echoed immediately following the summary already cited: 'We did not, therefore, have to present the worker in his relationship with other workers; it was enough to present man and his labour on one side, nature and its materials on the other' (p. 290). The misinterpretation of such passages has bolstered the legend of

Though general, this concept is not nearly as abstract as the concept of abstract labour, which is identified in Chapter One. The concept of abstract labour in Chapter One abstracts altogether from society, from specific purposes of production and from nature to get down to 'pure labour'. By contrast to the thinness of that notion, the concept of labour in Chapter Seven is thick, though general. It explicitly incorporates, though in a general way, society and nature; as stated earlier, it presents Marx's general phenomenology of human labour, whereas Chapter One's concept of abstract labour abstracts entirely from the (actually inseparable) social and natural conditions of labour to get to 'pure labour' (labour 'in itself').[43]

The general concept of labour is a different sort of concept than either the concept of abstract labour or the concept of 'practically abstract' labour. The general concept of labour identifies and gathers, in a general way, the essential features of any actual act of human labour. This concept pulls together the results of a general phenomenological inquiry into human labour. As such, this

---

Marx the 'monological', asocial theorist of labour. What Marx is saying throughout is that some general observations regarding the distinctively human labour process can be made independently of, that is, in abstraction from, all specific social forms of the labour process. (Compare Marx 1973, p. 85, on 'production in general'). But, in making these observations, Marx is drawing a distinction of reason, attending to certain features that pertain, as he says, 'to all forms of society'. I call this a distinction of reason because, while Marx believes that some general observations regarding actual labour processes can be made in abstraction from their specific social form, he definitely does not believe either that there are any actual labour processes that lack a specific social form or that one can properly understand an actual labour process independently of its specific social form. As he puts it in the introduction to the *Grundrisse*, though we can make general observations regarding production, 'there is no production in general ... it is always a certain social body, a social subject' (Marx 1973, p. 86). The legend of Marx's asocial conception of labour would have us believe he thought otherwise. But the proof is in the pudding. Once Marx has presented, by drawing certain distinctions of reason, what he has to say in a general way about human labour, he proceeds, in the second part of Chapter Seven, to examine the specific social form of the labour process in capitalism. For Marx's account of the valorization process is his account of the specific social form of the labour process under capital. The idea of offering an account of any actual labour process in abstraction from its specific social form and then trying to pawn that off as a properly scientific account – as economics does – never enters Marx's mind.

43 This means that Sweezy was wrong in saying: 'Abstract labour, in short, is, as Marx's own usage clearly attests, equivalent to "labour in general"; it is what is common to all productive human activity' (Sweezy 1942, p. 30). The general concept of labour encompasses all that is common to productive activity; the concept of abstract labour is narrower than that.

concept obviously does not pick out any particular sort of labour. The general concept of labour might be compared to the general concept of, say, physical object or body.

The concept of abstract labour, by contrast, attends not to the manifold of essential features of human labour but narrows its focus to one aspect, the expenditure of human energies. In abstracting altogether from the sociality, conscious purposiveness, and natural conditions characteristic of all human labour, the concept of abstract labour makes a distinction of reason: the pure expenditure of human energies is nothing actual. Consequently, the concept of abstract labour is not a concept that separates actual labours into sorts. It is not as though some labours are abstract (in this sense) while others are not. In this sense, there simply is no abstract labour. If the general concept of labour is like the concept of physical object or body, the concept of abstract labour is like the concept of extension. We who inhabit capitalist societies live in perverse imitation of the residents of St. Augustine's two cities: no matter what our passport, we all live in the social Flatland ruled by capital's valorisation process.

The concept of 'practically abstract' labour does refer to actual labour of a specific type; it sorts actual labours into those that are 'practically abstract' and those that are not. It can be compared to the concept of wax: wax is one sort of physical object.

In distinguishing between the concepts of labour in Chapters One and Seven in the course of a commentary[44] on some sticky passages on abstract labour in the Introduction to the *Grundrisse*,[45] I asserted that 'the' concept of abstract labour in Chapter One is a determinate abstraction, unlike the general concept of labour of Chapter Seven. Now I think I was wrong and that my mistake lay in a failure to distinguish between the concept of abstract labour, which I now claim is general, and the concept of 'practically abstract' labour, which is historically determinate. Where previously I did not see a distinction to be made between these two, and I simply identified the concept of abstract labour with that of value-producing labour (which surely is historically specific), now I distinguish the general concept of abstract labour from the determinate concept of 'practically abstract' labour and identify only the latter with value-producing labour. The present interpretation, which sorts three concepts: (i) the (general) concept of abstract labour, (ii) the determinate concept of 'practically abstract' labour, and (iii) the general concept of labour, sticks to the main idea, that value-producing labour is of a historically specific type, while making better

44 In Murray 1988a, pp. 127–8.

45 Marx 1973, pp. 102–5.

sense of certain passages in the *Grundrisse* and *Capital*. To confirm this, let us look at a passage or two from each work.

The concluding paragraph of Section Two of Chapter One of *Capital*, the section entitled 'The Dual Character of the Labour Embodied in Commodities', reads as follows:

> On the one hand, all labour is an expenditure of human labour-power, in the physiological sense, and it is in this quality of being equal, or abstract, human labour that it forms the value of commodities. On the other hand, all labour is an expenditure of human labour-power in a particular form and with a definite aim, and it is in this quality of being concrete useful labour that it produces use-values.[46]

I take Marx to say here that there is a generally applicable concept of abstract labour (labour 'in the physiological sense') and that labour produces value only insofar as it is abstract in this sense. But if this concept of abstract labour is general, if it is applicable to all human labour, will that not imply that all human labour is value-producing? No. Marx does not say, 'abstract labour' produces value. Rather, he says that labour is value-producing only insofar as it is abstract. If labour is to be value producing, it will be so only insofar as it is taken in abstraction from its 'particular form' and 'definite aim'. In fact, Marx shows that there is a category mistake involved in the very proposition that all abstract labour produces value, for 'abstract labour' (in the sense relevant here) is not a sort of labour. The concept of abstract labour relevant here is not a sorting one; it is an analytical one pertinent to all human labour.

Neither should we forget what the subject of inquiry in Section Two of Chapter One is. The subject is not human labour in general, no more than the topic of Section One is wealth in general; it is the specific social sort of labour that produces commodities. Only that sort of labour, 'practically abstract' labour, is value-producing. Nonetheless, to make the point that commodity-producing labour produces value only insofar as it is abstract, Marx needs to develop the generally applicable concept of abstract labour.

The passage in *Capital* that most compellingly supports the present interpretation comes toward the beginning of the famous conclusion to the first chapter of *Capital*, 'The Fetishism of the Commodity and its Secret'. Lucio Colletti, in his important essay 'Bernstein and the Marxism of the Second International', rightly observed, 'Marx's theory of value is identical to his theory of

46 Marx 1976a, p. 137.

fetishism', to which he correctly added, 'it is precisely by virtue of this element … that Marx's theory differs in principle from the whole of classical political economy'.[47]

By the 'fetishism of the commodity', Marx points to the fact that, in capitalism, use values, the products of labour, come to be transubstantiated as values, objects possessed of peculiar social powers. Marx asks: '*What gives rise to the fetishism of the commodity?*' Following Colletti, we see that this amounts to the question, what gives rise to value? Marx rules out several possible responses. He says that the fetish character of the commodity comes neither from the use value of the products nor from 'the nature of the determinants of value'. Among those rejected determinants Marx cites three. The second is the duration of the labour process, a consideration which, Marx observes, must concern any society. The third is the fact that labour always has some social form: 'as soon as men start to work for each other in any way, their labour also assumes a social form'.[48] The first determinant that Marx rules out takes us right back to the closing paragraph of Section Two: 'however varied the useful kinds of labour, or productive activities, it is a physiological fact, that they are functions of the human organism, and that each such function, whatever may be its nature or form, is essentially the expenditure of human brain, nerves, muscles, and sense organs'.[49] In other words, Marx flatly asserts that value, or the fetish character of the commodity, is not a consequence of 'abstract labour', that is, labour does not produce value simply because it can be viewed as an expenditure of human capacities. The reason he rules out the three 'determinants of value' is precisely because they are general: human labour always has a specific social form; the duration of the labour-process always matters, though in different ways under different social forms; and human labour can always be regarded abstractly, as 'physiological' labour.

This passage demonstrates: (i) Marx does have a general concept of abstract labour (which he distinguishes from his general concept of labour) and (ii) Marx holds that, although labour is value-producing only insofar as it is abstract in this 'physiological' sense, the fact that all human labour may be thought of in this abstract manner does not imply that all human labour is value-producing labour. If Marx thought that value was 'abstract labour embodied' in the general sense of abstract labour (as Reuten claims), he would have already found the

47 Colletti 1972, p. 72. Despite these ringing declarations, Colletti ultimately failed to figure out just how radically Marx broke with political economy. For a critique of Colletti along these lines, see Moishe Postone 1993, pp. 146–8.

48 Marx 1976a, p. 164.

49 Ibid.

answer to his question as to the origin of the fetishism of commodities. Marx's account of the fetishism of commodities will not square with the notion that he held an asocial 'abstract labour-embodied' theory of value.

What, then, is the source of value, the fetish character of wealth in the commodity form? Marx answers:

> Clearly, it arises from this form itself. The equality of the kinds of human labour takes on a physical form in the equal objectivity of the products of labour as values; the measure of the expenditure of human labour-power by its duration takes on the form of the magnitude of the value of the products of labour; and finally the relationships between the producers, within which the social characteristics of their labours are manifested, take on the form of a social relation between the products of labour.[50]

There it is. Value is a consequence of the peculiar social form of wealth and labour in societies where wealth generally takes the form of commodities. The human labour whose equality with other forms of human labour is validated by the social practice of equating the products of those labours to one another in the market, through money, is abstract not in a general way; it is 'practically abstract' labour.

So as not to leave the slightest doubt as to whether or not this is a 'truly social' theory of value, Marx goes on to say, 'the commodity-form and the value-relation of the products of labour within which it appears, have absolutely no connection with the physical nature of the commodity and the material relations arising out of this. It is nothing but the definite social relation between men themselves which assumes, here, for them, the fantastic form of a relation between things'.[51]

One of the passages on abstract labour from the *Grundrisse* that I commented on in *Marx's Theory of Scientific Knowledge* was this: 'The simplest abstraction, therefore, which modern economics sets at the peak, and which expresses an ancient relation, valid for all forms of society, appears in this abstraction practically true, however, only as [a] category of the most modern society'.[52] I claimed that this 'simplest abstraction … valid for all forms of society …' was what I there called the 'abstract category of labour' and here call the 'general concept of labour', that is, the conception of labour that Marx expounds

50 Marx 1976a, p. 164.
51 Marx 1976a, p. 165.
52 Marx 1973, p. 105.

in Chapter Seven. The category of abstract labour that was 'in this abstraction practically true' only for modern society I called the concept of abstract labour. And, I further claimed that this was a determinate category and that abstract labour was value-producing labour. This now appears to me to be wrong.

We can make better sense of that passage by drawing the distinctions I now make among: (i) the general concept of labour, (ii) the concept of abstract labour, and (iii) the concept of 'practically abstract' labour. With these three different concepts in mind, we can see that this passage is not about the general concept of labour at all. That is not the 'simplest abstraction'; the concept of abstract labour is the simplest. It is the concept that modern economics 'sets at the peak', for only labour that counts as abstract in this sense is value-producing – and modern economics is all about value. This concept of abstract labour is general, since it is 'valid for all forms of society', but it is 'practically true' only in modern (market) societies. I take that to require the concept of 'practically abstract' labour as I have presented it. Though Marx has an analytical, generally applicable concept of abstract labour, it should be clear that he holds that only a historically specific social sort of labour, 'practically abstract' labour, produces value.

4 Escaping 'Rubin's Dilemma'

In his seminal book, *Essays on Marx's Theory of Value*, Isaac Rubin opens the chapter devoted to abstract labour with an observation that still has bite today: 'When we see the decisive importance which Marx gave to the theory of abstract labour, we must wonder why this theory has received so little attention in Marxist literature'.[53] But Rubin is disappointed by what he finds among those who do pay abstract labour some attention. Typical is Kautsky's approach, which Rubin describes as follows: 'Abstract labour is the expenditure of human energy as such, independently of the given forms. Defined in this way, the concept of abstract labour is a *physiological* concept, devoid of all social and historical elements.'[54] For Rubin, this way of thinking of abstract labour ends in an asocial, Ricardian theory of value that shows utter disregard for the 'truly social' theory of value that Marx sets forth in *Capital*.

53 Rubin 1972, p. 131. For example, Jon Elster is silent on the topic of abstract labour in his *Making Sense of Marx*, Elster 1985.

54 Rubin 1972, p. 132.

Rubin forcefully states the apparent dilemma that interpreters of Marx face:

> One of two things is possible: if abstract labour is an expenditure of human energy in physiological form, then value also has a reified-material character. Or value is a social phenomenon connected with a determined social form of production. It is not possible to reconcile a physiological concept of abstract labour with the historical character of the value it creates.[55]

To choose the first possibility, as so many Marxists and non-Marxists alike have done, is, as Rubin says, 'to arrive at the crudest interpretation of the theory of value, one which sharply contradicts Marx's theory'.[56] Rubin is thereby constrained to argue that there is no real dilemma here: abstract labour cannot be 'physiological labour'; in order to produce value, it must be a historically specific sort of labour.

I will not attempt to do what Rubin rightly calls impossible, namely, to 'reconcile a physiological concept of abstract labour with the historical character of the value it creates'. Instead, I will suggest why the dilemma Rubin poses is both more troublesome than he allows and altogether avoidable. The apparent dilemma is stickier than Rubin thinks because his solution forces us to say either that Marx did not have a generally applicable concept of 'physiological' labour or that he had one, but it ought not to be called a concept of abstract labour. Neither of those options is supportable, so Rubin's solution is not satisfactory.

There is a way out of 'Rubin's Dilemma', however. It is to reject the presupposition that gives rise to it. The presupposition is this: Marx has a single concept of 'abstract labour' in play in treating the dual character of commodity-producing labour, so 'abstract labour' must be flatly identified with 'value-producing labour'. I claim that Marx has two different concepts in play – indeed two different kinds of concepts – namely, the generally applicable concept of abstract ('physiological') labour and the historically specific concept of 'practically abstract' labour. While it is true that labour produces value only insofar as it is abstract in the 'physiological' sense, it is a simple fallacy to turn this around and claim that labour of whichever social sort produces value because the concept of abstract labour is generally applicable. Only 'practically abstract' labour may be identified with value-producing labour. So, while Rubin is right

55 Rubin 1972, p. 135.

56 Ibid.

to insist that the generality of the concept of abstract labour, understood to be 'physiological labour', is incompatible with the historically specific character of the value it is supposed to produce, he is wrong to think that such a claim is forced upon one who says Marx's concept of abstract labour is a generally applicable one. If we get our concepts and terminology straight, 'Rubin's dilemma' does not arise.

Does this put me in the unwelcome position of defending those whom Rubin criticises? I do agree with them that Marx's concept of abstract labour is generally applicable. However, because they share Rubin's mistaken assumption that Marx has one concept in play here, they are then forced into the egregious error of flatly identifying abstract labour (in this generally applicable sense) with value-producing labour. For that, Rubin rightly lambasts them.

My position is substantially in agreement with Rubin: what he calls 'abstract labour' is what I call 'practically abstract' labour. But this terminological difference is still significant. First, Rubin's terminology gets in the way of a convincing answer to those who say that Marx conceives of abstract labour as a generally applicable concept, so that if abstract labour simply is value-producing labour, value cannot be a socially specific form of wealth. It is not persuasive either to deny that Marx has a generally applicable concept of 'physiological' labour or to deny that it deserves to be called a concept of abstract labour. Second, it distorts Rubin's interpretation of what Marx is doing. Thus, Rubin writes of the 'physiological' concept of labour as 'the simplified conception of abstract labour' and as a 'preliminary definition'.[57] These phrases, especially the former, suggest that Rubin thinks that there is one concept in play, abstract labour, so that the concept of 'physiological' labour must be a simplification of the concept Marx is after. The concept of 'physiological' labour is simpler than the one Rubin calls 'abstract labour', but it is not a simplified version of that concept. It is a different concept, indeed a different sort of concept.

Failure to see this gets Rubin into a tangle. He says: 'Whoever wants to maintain Marx's well-known statement that abstract labour creates value and is expressed in value, must renounce the physiological concept of abstract labour'.[58] But what, exactly, are we to renounce? That there is a legitimate, generally applicable 'physiological' concept of labour? That such a concept deserves to be called a concept of abstract labour? That such a concept should be identified with the concept of value-producing labour? I agree with Rubin

57 Rubin 1972, p. 135.
58 Rubin 1972, p. 136.

that the concept of 'physiological' labour should not be identified with the concept of value-producing labour. But Rubin himself accepts the legitimacy and general applicability of the concept of 'physiological' labour. His constrictive terminology, however, does not allow him to call it a concept of abstract labour; he has reserved the term 'abstract labour' for value-producing labour. That unwarranted move causes confusion.

Rubin writes: 'But this does not mean that we deny the obvious fact that in every social form of economy the working activity of people is carried out through the expenditure of physiological energy'.[59] What is this but to admit that there is a legitimate, generally applicable concept of 'physiological' labour? But he follows this admission with some special pleading: 'Physiological labour is the presupposition of abstract labour in the sense that one cannot speak of abstract labour if there is no expenditure of physiological energy on the part of people. But this expenditure of physiological energy remains precisely a presupposition, and not the object of our analysis'.[60] This fails to make the point that the *concept* of abstract labour is presupposed by the *concept* of value-producing labour (what Rubin calls simply 'abstract labour' and what I term 'practically abstract' labour): we need to know what it means for labour to be abstract before we can tell whether or not a certain social type of labour is abstract in practice. So the 'physiological' concept of labour is a necessary object of analysis, even though it is not the ultimate object of analysis. Rubin has to pooh-pooh its significance because his concepts and terminology do not provide him the room to give it its due. Rubin's solution to the dilemma he poses is not without problems. But, by distinguishing between Marx's generally applicable concept of abstract ('physiological') labour and his concept of 'practically abstract' labour, we escape 'Rubin's Dilemma'.

5 On Reuten: Might Marx Have Held an 'Abstract Labour-Embodied Theory of Value'?

By now I hope to have presented a compelling case for the claim that Marx offers a 'truly social' labour theory of value. However, in his 1993 essay 'The Difficult Labour of a Social Theory of Value', Geert Reuten contends that ambiguities exist in Chapter One of *Capital* that allow for an interpretation that Marx held an 'abstract labour-embodied theory of value'. That would mean

59 Ibid.
60 Ibid.

Marx did not escape the orbit of Ricardian theory. In this closing section I attempt to answer the points that Reuten makes in support of his contention.

Reuten distinguishes three basic types of value theory swirling around in Marx and Marxism: (i) concrete labour-embodied theories, (ii) abstract labour-embodied theories and (iii) value-form theories. Though Reuten detects traces of the concrete labour-embodied theory in Marx, interpreting his theory in this manner would not begin to do justice to Marx's innovations in value theory. By contrast, the abstract labour-embodied theory takes into account Marx's insistence that only abstract labour is value-producing. Since Reuten recognises that Marx employs a generally applicable concept of abstract labour, he argues that a theory of value founded upon abstract labour in this general sense would fail to break with classical theory. Reuten emphasises that, if value were simply embodied abstract labour, it would have no inherent connection with the market. Such a theory would fail to provide a 'truly social' theory of value, which only the value-form theory of value can offer.

I agree with Reuten that an abstract labour-embodied theory is an asocial one that represents no fundamental break with classical political economy. But the evidence shows that Marx never held that theory, which is at such cross purposes to his objectives in *Capital*. Where Reuten's reasoning goes wrong, I believe, is in its failure to recognise that there are two concepts in play in Chapter One, the general concept of abstract labour and the concept of 'practically abstract' labour.[61] And Marx's account of value-producing labour is completed only with the latter: 'practically abstract' labour, not 'abstract labour', produces value. And, as we have seen, 'practically abstract' labour is inherently connected with the market.

Reuten makes three main points in support of his claim that Marx failed to achieve unambiguously a 'truly social' theory of value: (i) Marx repeatedly spoke of labour being 'embodied' in commodities; (ii) Marx repeatedly invoked the 'metaphor of substance'; and (iii) Marx is unclear about his method: he does not make clear whether his abstractions are analytical or dialectical. For Reuten, these first two points combine to show that Marx failed to break unequivocally with the naturalism of classical value theory. I find these first

61 Reuten does entertain a notion of 'practically abstract' labour; indeed he devotes to it a section of his essay, 'The Abstract-Labour Theory of Value: Abstraction in Practice'. However, he seems to take the notion of 'practically abstract' labour as a way of interpreting the concept of abstract labour as a determinate one, whereas I am arguing for two separate concepts, one general (abstract labour) and one determinate ('practically abstract' labour).

two points *prima facie* unpersuasive for this simple reason: I do not see how to avoid reading *Capital*, and the first chapter in particular, as an all-out assault on precisely the proposition that Reuten suggests Marx slips into defending, namely, that value is some asocial property of wealth.[62] As Marx sardonically comments in wrapping up the first chapter, 'so far no chemist has ever discovered exchange-value either in a pearl or a diamond'.[63] I cannot reconcile the clarity and confidence with which Marx ridiculed the very proposition that Reuten contends he might have been propounding with the idea he was ever propounding it.[64]

Still, why does Marx talk about 'embodiment' and 'substance'? I believe that Marx expects us to be shocked by the ludicrousness of the very proposition that abstract labour is 'embodied' in commodities: how can abstract labour be embodied? Is not the bodily the antithesis of the abstract? Marx says as much when he writes:

> If I state that coats or boots stand in a relation to linen because the latter is the universal incarnation of abstract human labour, the absurdity of the statement is self-evident. Nevertheless, when the producers of coats and boots bring these commodities into a relation with linen, or with gold or silver (and this makes no difference here), as the universal equivalent, the relation between their own private labour and the collective labour of society appears to them in exactly this absurd form.[65]

---

62 In commenting on Cornelius Castoriadis's essay 'From Marx to Aristotle', Moishe Postone observes that Castoriadis 'imputes an implausible degree of inconsistency to Marx. He implies that, in one and the same chapter of *Capital*, Marx holds the very quasi-natural, nonhistorical position he analyses critically in his discussion of the fetish' (Postone 1993, p. 171, n. 110). Though Reuten offers the 'abstract labour-embodied' reading only as a possible interpretation, he finds Marx's text ambiguous. Reuten, too, imputes 'an implausible degree of inconsistency' to Marx.

63 Marx 1976a, p. 177.

64 Though I disagree with Reuten that Marx was 'enmeshed in the physical substance-embodiment metaphor' (Reuten 1993, p. 110) – on the contrary, I think that Marx, with brilliant irony, exposed the fetishism involved in taking value to be a physical substance that 'transcends sensuousness' – Reuten is surely right to link the (profound misunderstanding of the) metaphor to the failure of many Marxists to recognise the theory of value as the theory of capitalist social forms. Even if Reuten's suspicions about Marx are unfounded, he sheds light on how Marx came to be so widely misunderstood, including by Marxists.

65 Marx 1976a, p. 169.

When Marx begins to speak of the fetish character of the commodity, he says that when something becomes a commodity 'it changes into a thing that transcends sensuousness';[66] commodities are, then, 'sensuous things that are at the same time suprasensible, social'.[67] But the suprasensible cannot be sensible, bodily; Marx does not believe in incarnation. Marx calls this 'embodiment' of 'congealed quantities of homogeneous human labour' a 'phantom-like objectivity'.[68] Did Marx believe in ghosts?[69] To treat commodities as if they 'embodied' abstract labour is to reify a distinction of reason; it is to treat an analytical abstraction as if it picked out some actual, natural or natural-like property of a product. Here we face one of those 'metaphysical subtleties'[70] to which Marx alerts us. In a capitalist society we act as though abstract labour were 'embodied' in products; the bizarreness of this social practice – even when seen through – does not stop it.

Marx's treatment of the fetishism of commodities in Section Four amounts to a commentary on the results of Section Three's investigation of the value-form, the necessary, polar form of expression of value in exchange-value. There Marx points up three 'peculiarities' of the value form: (i) value is expressed as use-value, (ii) abstract labour is expressed as concrete labour, and (iii) private labour is expressed as directly social labour. It is the second that is most pertinent here:

> The body of the commodity, which serves as the equivalent, always figures as the embodiment of abstract human labour, and is always the product of

66 Marx 1976a, p. 163.

67 Marx 1976a, p. 165.

68 Marx 1976a, p. 128.

69 In a qualified way one may answer 'yes' to this question. Recalling Marx's observation that to understand value 'we must take flight into the misty realm of religion. There the products of the human brain appear as autonomous figures endowed with a life of their own' (Marx 1976a, p. 165), consider this passage from Marx's notes to his dissertation: 'The ontological proof means nothing but: that which I actually present to myself, is an actual presentation for me that has its effect on me, and in this sense all gods, pagan as well as Christian, possess a real existence ... Kant's example [of the one hundred talers] could have made the ontological proof more forceful. Actual talers have the same existence as imagined gods [have]' (as quoted in Murray 1988a, p. 49). The 'ghostly objectivity' of value is real in the sense that it is posited by the actual practices of a capitalist society, and this positing of value has real effects. But this way of looking at the objectivity of value does not show that Marx mistook it for something natural; rather it confirms that he held a 'truly social' labour theory of value.

70 Marx 1976a, p. 163.

> some specific useful and concrete labour. This concrete labour therefore becomes the expression of abstract human labour. If the coat is merely abstract human labour's realization, the tailoring actually realized in it is merely abstract … Tailoring is now seen as the tangible form of realization of abstract human labour.[71]

This is very peculiar precisely because of the absurdity of thinking that tailoring just is abstract labour incarnate. Talk of 'embodiment' and 'substance' cannot be avoided in writing a critique of capitalist society, but let's not lose the irony.[72]

Rather than capitulating to naturalism, Marx's talk of abstract labour being 'embodied' bears directly on his theory of value as social form, as can be seen from his account of what gives rise to the fetishism of the commodity. The 'metaphysical' notion of abstract labour 'embodied' in products comes up precisely because Marx is dealing with a particular social form of production (capitalism) that validates actual labour only through the interaction of the products of labour. It is that peculiar social form of labour that forces upon us the weird notion of 'abstract labour embodied'.

We read earlier about what Marx thinks of the idea that value is a bodily property of products (commodities):

> the commodity-form, and the value-relation of the products of labour within which it appears, have absolutely no connection with the physical nature of the commodity and the material relations arising out of this. It is nothing but a definite social relation between men themselves which assumes here, for them, the fantastic form of a relation between things.[73]

I know of no place in *Capital* where Marx wavers from this view. When he speaks of 'substance', he qualifies it as 'social substance',[74] an expression that is inexplicable on the assumption that he is enmeshed in a naturalistic understanding of value. The fact that Marx speaks of 'substance' and 'embodiment' and 'congealed labour' only means he is doing what is necessary to present

---

71 Marx 1976a, p. 150.

72 Reuten illuminatingly observes (Reuten 1993, p. 97) that when Marx introduces the concept of value, he makes an unmistakable reference to the transubstantiation of the bread and wine at the Consecration of the Mass. This observation fits in well with my contention that Marx's talk of value 'substance' is laced with irony, but it is at sixes and sevens with Reuten's contention that Marx thought value was some sort of natural substance.

73 Marx 1976a, p. 291.

74 Marx 1976a, p. 128.

a critique of a society that acts as if such ideas made good sense. At the same time – this is a critique, after all – Marx's use of 'substance' is taunting. What a topsy-turvy sort of society it must be that is organised such that its social relations appear to be natural properties of things! Time for Ghostbusters!

I believe that there are further connotations in Marx's use of the term 'substance' with relation to value. As I argued in *Marx's Theory of Scientific Knowledge*,[75] Marx's account of the 'value substance' as the 'residue' that remains once all the concrete, natural properties of commodities have been abstracted away,[76] intentionally mimics Descartes' famous derivation of material substance (*res extensa*) from his analysis of the bit-turned-blob of wax at the end of the second Meditation.[77] Like Berkeley, Marx took a dim view of this sort of abstract, 'metaphysical' materialism, for it hypostatises 'distinctions of reason', extension, flexibility, moveability, and number, into 'abstract ideas'. Where abstract material substance makes a fetish of our abstractive capacities in thinking about natural objects (acting as though there actually were pure thought and objects of pure thought), value makes a fetish of the market's practical abstraction from the specific useful properties of commodities and of the concrete labour that produces them and treats 'congealed abstract (or pure) labour' as if it were something actual, instead of what it is, a socially enacted distinction of reason. Since we know that Marx was no fan of Cartesian materialism, we can see that he is deliberately undermining the naturalistic conception of value by invoking this Cartesian connotation of the word 'substance'.

In Hegelian language deriving from Aristotle, a society may be called a substance insofar as it possesses sufficient autonomy to reproduce itself. Marx was familiar with this usage and appealed to it in the course of writing his doctoral dissertation. He saw the Hellenistic philosophies (Stoicism, Scepticism, Epicureanism) to be outcomes of the breakdown of the substantial Greek societies that gave rise (in their decline) to Plato and Aristotle. Since Marx thought that the capital form was its own barrier, he saw limits to capitalist society's capacity to reproduce itself; nevertheless, especially in the unpublished *Results of the Immediate Production Process* and in Volume II of *Capital*, Marx made a point of demonstrating how capitalism is capable of reproducing itself materially and formally. So value deserves the name 'social substance' because

75 Murray 1988a, pp. 149–50, and Chapter 18.

76 Marx 1976a, p. 128.

77 See also Postone 1993, pp. 142, 175.

self-expanding value is the social form of capitalist production, and that social form is capable of reproducing itself – it is substantial. Obviously, this connotation of 'substance' indicates that Marx's theory of value pertains to the form of the society that posits it, not to a natural property of products of human labour.

Regarding Reuten's claim that Marx is confused as to whether or not his abstractions are analytical or dialectical, and, more generally, as to whether *Capital* is a work of systematic dialectics, I will address just two issues. First is the question of the status of the abstractions involved in Marx's value theory in Chapter One; the other concerns whether or not the commodity is the proper starting point for a systematic, dialectical account of capitalist society.

Worries over the apparent confusion as to the status of the abstractions involved in Marx's value theory are, I contend, rooted in a failure to see that Marx has three concepts going: the general concept of labour, the concept of abstract labour, and the concept of 'practically abstract' labour. The first two concepts are general, which means that they are analytical abstractions (and we have seen that the Marxian conception of systematic dialectics calls for the incorporation of such abstractions); while the determinate concept of 'practically abstract' labour, which is equivalent to the concept of value-producing labour, is a dialectical one. That this is so becomes clear in the course of the double movement of thought in the first chapter. Once Marx has arrived at the concept of value by starting from exchange value, he turns around in Section Three and shows that exchange value is the necessary form of appearance of value, which counts as a prime piece of dialectical reasoning.[78]

Reuten asks, 'is this, the commodity, the most abstract all-embracing concept for the capitalist mode of production'.[79] He answers: 'I doubt it'. He adds that 'Marx certainly develops from it the form of capitalist production (from Chapter 4 onwards)', but he claims that 'from a systematic dialectical point of view, this is not convincing'. I believe that the commodity, understood (as it is presented in the opening sentence of *Capital*) as the form that wealth generally takes, is just the right starting point for Marx's systematic dialectical presentation of capitalist society. Chiefly, this is because of Marx's demonstration that generalised commodity circulation and the circulation of capital presuppose

---

78 On this double movement, from exchange value to value and then from value to exchange value, see Murray 1993b, included in the present volume as Chapter 8. It is a telling fact about Reuten's essay that he does not talk about Section Three.

79 Reuten 1993, p. 96.

one another, which explains why Marx can make a dialectical argument that develops the concept of capital from that of generalised commodity circulation.[80]

80 An earlier version of this paper was presented at the seventh conference of the International Symposium on Marxian Theory, held in Tepozlan, Mexico, in June of 1997. I would like to thank the other participants, Chris Arthur, Riccardo Bellofiore, Martha Campbell, Paul Mattick Jr, Fred Moseley, Geert Reuten and Tony Smith for their comments. A version of the section on phenomenology and systematic dialectics was presented at the Radical Philosophy Conference held at San Francisco State University in November, 1998. I want to thank Jeanne Schuler and Peter Fuss for helpful comments. I would also like to thank the editors of *Historical Materialism* for their encouragement and well-considered suggestions.

CHAPTER 5

Marx's 'Truly Social' Labour Theory of Value: Part II, How is Labour That is under the Sway of Capital *Actually* Abstract?*

> To make abstractions hold good in actuality means to destroy actuality.[1]

1 Recapping Part 1

In the first part of this two-part article, I argued that, unlike the asocial classical (Ricardian) labour theory of value, Marx's labour theory of value is a 'truly social' one. In fact, it is a purely social one. Marx's theory of value is nothing but his theory of the social forms characteristic of the capitalist mode of production. Thus, we may speak of those forms as value forms, the (generalised) commodity, money (in its several forms), capital, wage labour, surplus value and its forms of appearance (profit, interest and rent) and more. The labour that produces value, then, is labour of a peculiar social sort. This thought is entirely foreign to the classical labour theory of value and, likewise, to Marxist accounts of value theory that mistake it for a radical version of Ricardian value theory. The gulf between the classical and the Marxian labour theories of value is wide.

Marx made much of the fact that his advance over the classical labour theory of value involved distinguishing between 'concrete' and 'abstract' labour. But, in interpreting the theory of value that Marx sets forth in *Capital*, we have to press beyond this signpost. For, as Geert Reuten observes, if we take the notion of abstract labour to be generally applicable, to leave matters here is to interpret Marx's as an 'abstract labour-embodied' theory of value that is as asocial as the classical one.[2]

---

* 'Marx's "Truly Social" Labour Theory of Value: Part II, How is Labour that Is Under the Sway of Capital *Actually* Abstract?,' *Historical Materialism*, Number 7 (Winter 2000), pp. 99–136.

1 Hegel 1955, p. 425.

2 Reuten 1993.

To make my case that *Capital* cannot plausibly be interpreted as setting forth an asocial 'abstract labour-embodied' theory, I showed in Part I how Marx distinguishes *three* relevant concepts. In fact, they are three different kinds of concepts. An accurate comprehension of Marx's 'truly social' theory of value requires getting these concepts into focus. The first is the general concept of labour, which expresses Marx's general phenomenology of human labour.[3] This phenomenology includes the fact that an actual labour process always has some specific social form and purpose, that the labour process involves materials and means of production as well as living labour and that the labour process always involves some specific sort of labour whose outcome is intended to meet some specific human want.[4] This concept is generally applicable, which means that, while it applies to capitalism, it also applies to every other mode of production.

The second is the (general) concept of abstract labour, or the concept of physiological labour. It is a reductive conception of human labour that conceives of it in utter abstraction from its material presuppositions, from its social

3 Marx presents this in Section I, 'The Labour Process', of Chapter Seven, 'The Labour Process and the Valorisation Process', of *Capital* Volume I.

4 Marx recognises that labour is always of some specific social kind when he calls attention to the fact that the general concept of labour, being general, abstracts from every particular social sort: 'The fact that the production of use-values, or goods, is carried on under the control of a capitalist and on his behalf does not alter the general character of that production. We shall therefore, in the first place, have to consider the labour process independently of any specific social formation' (Marx 1976a, p. 283). Following that abstraction from specific social form, Marx identifies the general features of the labour process: 'The simple elements of the labour process are (1) purposeful activity, that is work itself, (2) the object on which that work is performed, and (3) the instruments of that work' (Marx 1976a, p. 284). While Marx's general concept of labour encompasses these several complexities, it abstracts, precisely because it is general, from the specifics pertinent to them, whether that is the specific tools or materials the labour requires, its specific social form and purpose, or the labour's specific type and goal. That has led to the mistaken notion that Marx's general concept of labour abstracts from these complexities altogether.

Marx insisted on the intentional character of human labour in a noted passage distinguishing human labour from the work of bees. 'But what distinguishes the worst architect from the best of bees is that the architect builds the cell in his mind before he constructs it in wax. At the end of every labour process, a result emerges which had already been conceived by the worker at the beginning, hence already existed ideally. Man not only effects a change of form in the materials of nature; he also realises his own purpose in those materials. And this is a purpose he is conscious of, it determines the mode of his activity with the rigidity of a law, and he must subordinate his will to it' (Marx 1976a, p. 284).

form and purpose, from the social status of the labourer,[5] as well as from its definite technical form and purpose (e.g., sewing in order to make an item of clothing), leaving only the physiological exertion of human energies. Marx expresses this category so: 'however varied the useful kinds of labour, or productive activities, it is a physiological fact, that they are functions of the human organism, and that each such function, whatever may be its nature or form, is essentially the expenditure of human brain, nerves, muscles, and sense organs'.[6] This concept, though different from the first, is also generally applicable: an analyst can consider human labour in any society in this abstract way.[7] Consequently, if this is all there is to Marx's conception of value-producing labour, then Reuten is right. *Capital* could be interpreted as setting out an asocial, 'abstract labour-embodied' theory of value.

The third Marxian concept that I identify is 'practically abstract' labour. Neither 'labour in general' nor 'abstract (physiological) labour' is a kind of labour. Fruit is not a kind of fruit and length is not a kind of body. 'Practically abstract' labour does pick out a kind of labour. Labour of this type is treated in practice as if it were abstract in ways that overlap the second sense; that is, labour's material requirements and particular useful purpose (e.g., planting seeds in order to grow corn) and the social status of the labourer are matters of indifference – all that counts is that human labour is being done.[8] 'Practically abstract' labour does not bracket the social purpose of labour, which, in

5 This explains why, though the scope of the concept of abstract (physiological) labour is general, the concept came to the fore in modern times with the spread of egalitarianism. See Marx 1976a, pp. 151–2.

6 Marx 1976a, p. 164.

7 Thus, Marx writes: 'all labour is an expenditure of human labour-power, in the physiological sense, and it is in this quality of being equal, or abstract, human labour that it forms the value of commodities' (Marx 1976a, p. 137). This text shows not only that Marx considers this concept of abstract ('physiological') labour to be generally applicable but also what role it plays in working up the quite different concept of 'practically abstract', or value-producing, labour. For it explains what it means to treat labour as abstract, namely, to be indifferent to the specific purpose of the labour, treating it instead as a mere 'expenditure of human labour-power'. As argued in Part I of the present article, it is fallacious to reason as follows: since labour is value-producing only insofar as it is abstract, and since all labour can be analysed as abstract, physiological labour, all labour is value producing. Not only is such reasoning flawed, it attributes to Marx the incredible inconsistency of maintaining that *all* labour is value-producing in the very chapter where he takes pains to argue that value is a fetishistic result of a specific social form of labour.

8 'The value of a commodity represents human labour pure and simple, the expenditure of human labour in general' (Marx 1976a, p. 135).

this case, is the production of value, and, more to the point, surplus value.[9] That is quite different from the general applicability of the concept of abstract ('physiological') labour just discussed. As opposed to the first two concepts, 'practically abstract' labour is not generally applicable. Indeed, actual indifference to the particular useful purpose of labour and the social status of the labourer is rather peculiar.

What society treats labour with these sorts of indifference? Marx's answer to this question begins with the opening sentence of *Capital*, which reveals that this book, unlike the books of classical political economy, is not about 'wealth' but about wealth having a definite social form, the (generalised) commodity form. In restricting his inquiry to societies in which wealth generally takes the commodity-form, Marx restricts himself to labour of a definite social type, commodity-producing labour. Because commodity-producing labour is socially validated in an after-the-fact way, that is, by the sale of the commodities in the marketplace, it is actually treated in ways that overlap the physiological sense.[10] Commodity-producing labour is treated with indifference to its material requisites, its concrete purpose, and the social status of the labourer; all that matters is how much human labour goes into the commodity. Insofar as they are values, commodities differ only in quantity. Commodity-producing labour is, then, 'practically abstract', the type of labour that produces value, and Marx's theory of value is 'truly social'.

As *Capital* unfolds, we discover that the generalisation of the production of wealth in the commodity form presupposes the more complex value categories of capital and wage labour.[11] Goods and services are produced as commodities so that capitalists can pump out surplus value and accumulate capital.[12] As a rule, then, commodity-producing labour is wage labour and produces not only value but also surplus value. Since surplus value necessarily appears as money,

9 This is why value-producing labour is not simply abstract labour, but socially necessary abstract labour. And the social necessity is not generic – there is no society in general – but pertains to the specific aim of producing surplus value.

10 'It is only by being exchanged that the products of labour acquire a socially uniform objectivity as values' (Marx 1976a, p. 166).

11 'Had we gone further, and inquired under what circumstances all, or even the majority of products take the form of commodities, we should have found that this only happens on the basis of one particular mode of production, the capitalist one' (Marx 1976a, p. 273). See also Marx 1981, p. 1,019.

12 On why generalised commodity circulation presupposes the capitalist mode of production, see Murray 2000a, included in the present volume as Chapter 4, and Campbell 1993a.

moneymaking is the goal of the commodity-producing society. So we have an explanation for the mysterious social indifference to the concrete purposes of human labour and the status of labourers: they are beside the point. What matters is profit.

If the category of abstract labour is general, then labour in any society can be bracketed from its natural determinants and concrete purposes through a mental abstraction, but that in no way makes the labour actually abstract. Where wealth takes the commodity form, however, labour is abstract in practice inasmuch as it is socially validated only in roundabout fashion, namely, through the sale of its products. And 'practically abstract' labour may become actually abstract in various other ways that I will now identify. This real abstractness under the rule of capital manifests the power of the social forms that are the focus of Marx's theory of value.[13] The levelling power of the value forms can extend to human activities that are not formally capitalist. The following exploration, then, is meant to correct for what I.I. Rubin spotted as the basic error of Marx's critics – an error that stems from thinking of Marx as a radical economist, a 'Left Ricardian', or one more proponent of an asocial value theory – namely, 'their complete failure to grasp the qualitative sociological side of Marx's theory of value'.[14]

2 When Labour Becomes Actually Abstract: Three Rubrics

To sort the ways labour under capital can be actually abstract, I will invoke three rubrics. Each pertains to the 'qualitative sociological side of Marx's theory of value'. Because Marx's value-theory is widely thought not to be 'truly social', these rubrics are not as familiar as they deserve to be. Each needs some introduction.

First, I make use of Marxian categories for characterising how the powers of capital are exerted: formal, real, ideal, and hybrid subsumption under capital (or other value forms).[15] Formal subsumption means simply bringing some-

13 On the place of social forms and their powers in Marx's account of capitalism, see Murray 1997a, included in the present volume as Chapter 2.

14 Rubin 1972, p. 73. Jeanne Schuler and I call attention to this serious shortcoming of 'Left Ricardian' redistributionist thinking and develop a critique along these lines of Nancy Fraser's essay 'From Redistribution to Recognition? Dilemmas of Justice in a "Post-Socialist" Age' (Fraser 1997). See Murray and Schuler 2000.

15 I add 'or other value-forms' because, though capital is the encompassing social form – hence the title of Marx's book – it is instructive to articulate capital's power by discriminating effects of different value-forms.

thing under the scope of a value form. For example, if I bake a cake for dessert at home, it is not formally subsumed under the commodity form, whereas, if I sell my cakes around the neighbourhood, they are formally subsumed under the commodity form.

If I record music for a profitmaking recording firm, my music is formally subsumed not only under the commodity form but also under the capital form: it is commodity capital (that is, a commodity whose sale rounds out the profit-making circuit of capital). If I begin to refashion my music to reap greater profits (as suggested by the term 'corporate rock'), it undergoes real subsumption under capital. Real subsumption transforms needs, production processes, or products on the use-value level to better satisfy the requirements of some value form. The notion of 'McDonaldisation' roughly expresses real subsumption.[16] Thus, the newspaper *USA Today*, in which journalism adjusts to the demands of moneymaking (hence is really subsumed under capital), becomes 'McPaper'.[17] Capital's globalisation spells 'McWorld'.

Ideal subsumption takes us from actual subsumption to the land of 'as if'. Here, no real or even formal subsumption takes place; in ideal subsumption, something that is not actually subsumed under a value form is treated as if it were. In ideal subsumption, value forms reshape our imagination; they redefine and channel how we think, feel, and desire. Ideal subsumption is apt to incite formal and real subsumption.

Hybrid subsumption is like ideal subsumption in that it involves no formal or real subsumption, but it is like the latter two in that it involves actual, rather than ideal, transformations. Hybrid subsumption occurs when value forms reshape something that remains formally outside their orbit. Hybrid subsumption, like ideal subsumption, can be the wedge for formal and real subsumption.[18]

---

16 Ritzer 2000 conceives of 'McDonaldisation' along Weberian lines as an irrational process of rationalisation rather than in terms of the Marxian concept of real subsumption under capital. Ritzer is well aware of the profitmaking aspect of McDonald's, yet he characterises 'McDonaldisation' in terms of four traits that do not refer directly to value forms, namely, efficiency, calculability, predictability, and control. These four are drawn from the discourse of 'instrumental rationality', which is best understood as a shadow of the value forms.

17 When asked about the chances of *USA Today* winning awards for its journalism, former editor James Quinn remarked, 'They don't give awards for the best investigative paragraph' (as quoted in Postman 1985, p. 112).

18 In fact, Marx thinks of hybrid subsumption as, for the most part, a transitional form. See Marx 1976b, p. 1,023.

Second, the shadow forms of capital, such as utility and instrumental reason, can make labour (and more) actually abstract. These shadow forms are ideological silhouettes of the actual value forms.[19] There is irony in the very idea of value having shadow forms since Marx emphasises that values, as 'congealed quantities of homogeneous human labour',[20] are 'ghostly' (*gespenstige*) realities to begin with. By the same token, however, the phrase 'shadow form' is appropriate for depicting bourgeois ideologies. Just as fetish-producing practices of abstraction characterise capitalist social relations, the practice of reifying conceptual distinctions (mistaking shadows for actualities) pervades bourgeois ideologies.[21]

In contrast to the different types of subsumption, Marx does not explicitly develop the rubric of value's shadow forms. Still, the terminology of 'shadow form' offers a suggestive heading under which to arrange Marx's analyses of bourgeois ideologies. And there is a strong textual basis for the claim that Marx regarded utility as an ideological shadow cast by capitalist social forms.[22] Plausible cases can be made for a range of further shadow forms, including instrumental reason, social equality and the secular.

One reason for wanting to gather these several forms under the heading of shadow forms is this. They have a common origin not only in the value forms themselves but also in an appearance that the value forms naturally produce, namely, 'the illusion of the economic', or what Marx terms 'the religion of everyday life'. This true 'illusion of the epoch' is expressed in the idea advanced by Karl Polanyi that capitalism is the 'disembedded economy'.[23] Disembedded from what? From any authoritative social conceptions of what is sacred or good?[24] The 'disembedded economy' is, as it were, the economy 'as such',[25] 'in general', unadulterated by intrusive social customs or mores. But there is no

---

19 Capitalism's shadow forms, then, open a door on Marx's theory of bourgeois ideologies. *Capital* (including *Theories of Surplus-Value*) is the closest that Marx comes to a treatise on bourgeois ideology. As such, it leaves plenty of room for elucidation.

20 Marx 1976a, p. 136.

21 In the Humean language used in Murray 2000a, an abstraction is reified when a 'distinction of reason' (a conceptual distinction) is mistaken for an actual separation.

22 In *The Poverty of Philosophy* Marx refers to the 'equalitarian relation' as an 'embellished shadow' of commercial relations (Marx 1963b, p. 79).

23 See Polanyi 1968.

24 For F.A. Hayek, the free market is 'perhaps the greatest discovery mankind ever made' precisely because it (purportedly) refuses to organise society around any compulsory collective good.

25 Marx 1968b, pp. 528–9.

generic economy. As Marx writes, 'All production is appropriation of nature on the part of an individual within and through a specific form of society'.[26] The (bad) abstraction from determinate social form and purpose involved in this notion of an 'economy' where 'labour' produces 'wealth' to meet 'needs' results in the impoverished conceptual resources of economics and the shadow forms.

Capitalism propagates this pervasive 'illusion of the economic' precisely because its actual social forms are so bizarre. Consider the argument of the first chapter of *Capital*. The social form of the commodity is value, whose necessary mode of expression is money. Since the social form of the product of labour under capitalism appears as a thing alongside it, is it surprising when it is not recognised as such? 'The illusion of the economic' is the fantastical thought that the economy in general can actually exist and, what is more, that capitalism is it.[27] The shadow forms swirl out of this mist.

Third, labour is always situated in space and time. Due to the power of capital, space and time come to exist – and to be experienced – as abstract. This presents a further way in which value-producing labour becomes abstract.[28] Studying the different senses and ways in which time and place become abstract under the power of capital would be a many-sided and thorny task, far exceeding what can be undertaken here. Even the scope of these issues can only be suggested here. It would involve demographics: how many wage earners move? How often? How far? How do they feel about it? How do they settle in (or not settle in) to the places where they live and work? How might urbanisation and suburbanisation express the power of capital? Modern and postmodern architecture, city planning? Rates, patterns, and consequences of immigration? What role do value forms play in negotiating the boundaries between public and private places?

At the speculative end, it would involve looking into Newtonian concepts of absolute space and time and the overturning of those ideas by Einstein's theor-

26 Marx 1973, p. 87.

27 '[B]ourgeois or capitalist production ... is consequently for him [Ricardo] not a specific definite mode of production, but simply *the* mode of production' (Marx 1968b, p. 504n). See also Marx 1968b, pp. 527–8 and Marx 1978a, p. 172. It is as if capitalism were '*the* Fruit' existing alongside apples, oranges, and cherries (the various 'embedded economies').

28 Two illuminating historical studies on the theme of modern capitalism, work and time are Le Goff 1980 and Thompson 1967. For a more speculative and provocative look into the power of the value forms to transform time into 'abstract time', which is 'uniform, continuous, homogeneous, "empty" time ... independent of events' (Postone 1993, p. 202), see Chapter 5, 'Abstract Time', of Postone 1993.

ies of relativity. Philosophical theories, like McTaggart's theory of the unreality of time, would also have to be considered. How might capital change our experience of temporality? Looking into connections between advanced capitalism and postmodern sensibilities, Frederic Jameson speculates that capital is bringing about profound anthropological change. He writes of 'the disappearance of a sense of history, the way in which our entire contemporary social system has little by little begun to lose its capacity to retain its own past, has begun to live in a perpetual present and in a perpetual change that obliterates traditions of the kind which all earlier social formations have had in one way or another to preserve'.[29] Is capital compressing our temporal horizon into 'this grinding present tense'?[30]

Having opened the Pandora's Box of the third rubric, I want now to draw on a film and a memoir meant to fix a couple of the main ideas. I will then close the lid and end with a cautionary note.

Charlie Chaplin's film *Modern Times* cleverly depicts the actual abstractness of time in modern industry. The film opens with a close-up of a huge clock – time clocks figure prominently – and much is made of the mechanical way that work begins and ends with the blowing of the factory whistle. Pausing for a smoke in the lavatory is the moral equivalent of pilfering the cash register. Breaking for lunch is an intrusion on work time that the fanciful Billows automatic feeding machine means to stop.

In Maxine Hong Kingston's memoir *The Woman Warrior*, she recounts this exchange between her mother, an émigré from China, and herself:

> I have worked too much. Human beings don't work like this in China. Time goes slower there. Here we have to hurry, feed the hungry children before we're too old to work. I feel like a mother cat hunting for its kittens. She has to find them fast because in a few hours she will forget how to count or that she had any kittens at all. I can't sleep in this country because it doesn't shut down for the night. Factories, canneries, restaurants – always somewhere working through the night. It never gets done all at once here. Time was different in China. One year lasted as long as my total time here; one evening so long, you could visit your women friends, drink tea, and play cards at each house, and it would still be twilight. It even got boring, nothing to do but fan ourselves. Here midnight comes and the floor's not swept, the ironing's not ready, the money's not made. I would

29 Jameson 1983, p. 125.

30 The phrase is Jeanne Schuler's. See Schuler 1988–9, p. 65.

> still be young if we lived in China. 'Time is the same from place to place', I said unfeelingly. 'There is only the eternal present, and biology'.[31]

Later in that conversation, after it has been learned that the family's land back in China has been taken over, the daughter proclaims, '"Does it make sense to you that if we're no longer attached to one piece of land, we belong to the planet? Wherever we happen to be standing, why that spot belongs to us as much as any other spot"'.[32]

One caution – the abstract, value dimension in capitalist society never disengages from the concrete, use-value dimension: capitalism's double character can never be eliminated. Increasing abstraction with respect to time and place, then, will not tell the whole story, even when we bracket popular resistance to those processes.[33] Consequently, when contemporary geographers insist that location is not a matter of indifference, that specific places, notably 'world cities' such as Los Angeles, Tokyo, New York, Paris, Mexico City, Bombay, and Hong Kong matter in the process of 'globalisation', they need not contradict the Marxian disclosure of capital's power to make time and place abstract.[34]

3 Formal Subsumption

In societies where labour is 'practically abstract', wealth circulates not only as commodities but also as capital.[35] This means that commodity-producing labour, which is 'practically abstract', is, as a rule, labour that is formally subsumed under capital. Capitalist society tends to formally subsume ever more labour under capital and to really subsume labour that is formally subsumed.[36] In the final section of this chapter, we will explore the internal limitation on the spread of formal subsumption. As a rule, then, 'practically abstract' labour is

31 Kingston 1976, pp. 105–6.

32 Kingston 1976, p. 107.

33 On the theme of resistance to practices that homogenise time and place, see David Harvey's *Social Justice and the City* (Harvey 1973). The rise of historical malls like St. Louis's Union Station in the 1980s marked a corporate- and government-backed form of reaction to the homogenising of urban space and the obliteration of urban history. See Schuler 1988–9.

34 See, for example, the work of Saskia Sassen (Sassen 1998) or Manuel Castells (Castells 1989).

35 Marx 1976a, pp. 26–8.

36 See Marx 1976b, p. 1,036.

both formally subsumed under capital and really subsumed as well. Nonetheless, we may distinguish ways labour is actually abstract insofar as it is formally subsumed from those due to its being really subsumed under capital. Formal subsumption is our first topic.[37]

Though we know that commodity-producing labour is usually formally subsumed under capital, we can stick to the (simpler) conceptual level of commodity exchange and still identify ways in which it is actually abstract. We begin with these ways in which 'practically abstract' labour is actually abstract, which will involve some rehearsing of points made in introducing the concept of 'practically abstract' labour in Part I.

3.1 *Formal Subsumption under the Commodity and Commodity-Producing Labour*

'Practically abstract' labour is commodity-producing labour, and goods and services prove themselves as commodities only by being sold. Concrete labour involved in commodities that are not sold proves itself to be not 'socially necessary'. It fails to produce value. Thus, though the general idea of abstract (physiological) labour has nothing to do with the market or demand, market considerations definitely enter into the concept of 'practically abstract' labour.[38] Commodity-producing labour, by its nature, is attuned to the needs of others, but those needs exist here in a peculiar, abstract social form. Commodity-producing labour is actually abstract in answering to needs socially determined as 'demand'. Commodity-producing labour addresses human needs only through the cash nexus, which means (i) those whose needs are served exist in the anonymous role of the buyer, and (ii) the needs of the buyer count only when backed by money.[39]

---

37 The fact that there are various ways in which labour that is formally subsumed under capital is actually abstract shows that the problematic of actually abstract labour cannot be limited solely to 'technical' considerations. You need not work in Adam Smith's pin factory or on Ford's assembly line for your work to be abstract.

38 In Marxian value theory, value is not an independent variable that determines price, as in Ricardian value theory. This difference signals the 'truly social' character of Marx's theory of value. Marx recognises price as the necessary expression of the value of a commodity, that is, of the peculiar social form of the labour that produced the commodity. But labour does not exist independently of its social form, a reality to which Ricardian theory is oblivious.

39 The third element of wage labour that Marx discriminated in his early notes on James Mill (1843) concerned the abstract social form taken by the human needs that 'practically abstract' labour answers: 'the worker's role is determined by social needs which, however,

Since commodity-producing labour is socially validated by means of its products, there will be no point in rewarding commodity producers with more than the market price for their products. So, for a given labour period, the sale of products of less productive labour will result in less money, and vice versa for products of more productive labour. The mechanism of capitalist competition (which implicitly figures into the original account of value in the first chapter of *Capital*) spurs a race to raise the productivity of labour that turns out to be a rat race for the capitalist class taken as a whole. For, in the Flatland of the value dimension, it is not the actual (absolute) level of productivity that matters: value is altogether relative and a function of abstract labour. As higher levels of productivity get generalised across a branch of production, the amount of value produced per hour slides back to what it had been at the previous norm. This treadmill effect occurs because labour produces value only insofar as it is abstract labour. Abstract labour screens out the productivity of labour because productivity is a use-value consideration.[40] So commodity-producing labour is actually abstract in being rewarded in this roundabout way: it is treated as if it were labour in the abstract.

The disconnection between productivity and value brings home a fateful way in which 'practically abstract' labour is actually abstract.[41] For, to disconnect human labour from productivity is to break with labour's original

are alien to him and a compulsion to which he submits out of egoistic need and necessity, and which have for him only the significance of a means of satisfying his dire need, just as for them he exists only as a slave of their needs' (Marx 1975a, p. 220). Under the terms of this social arrangement, Marx observes further on in those notes, 'our *mutual* value is for us the *value* of our mutual objects. Hence for us man himself is mutually of no value' (Marx 1975a, p. 227). In the 1844 manuscript on the power of money, Marx is more graphic: 'Money is the *pimp* between man's need and the object, between his life and his means of life' (Marx 1975c, p. 323 [translation slightly revised]).

40 'Since productive power is an attribute of the concrete useful forms of labour, of course it can no longer have any bearing on that labour, so soon as we make abstraction from those concrete useful forms' (Marx 1976a, p. 264).

41 Moishe Postone singles this out as the locus of the primary contradiction in capitalism according to Marx: 'the difference between the two [wealth and value] is crucial to Marx's argument regarding the fundamental contradiction of capitalism. Increased productivity does not ... yield greater amounts of value per unit of time. For this reason, all means of increasing productivity, such as applied science and technology, do *not* increase the amount of value yielded per unit of time, but they *do* increase greatly the amount of material wealth produced' (Postone 1993, p. 197). This creates what Postone calls 'shearing pressures' within capitalism that keep it historically dynamic.

purpose, the provision of use values.[42] Likewise, the value-forms disconnect labour-saving technologies from their purpose of saving labour. Since the whole basis of capitalist society is the pumping out of surplus value, that is, the surplus labour-time of wage labourers, saving the labour of that class as a whole would asphyxiate capital, while choking off the income of workers. *The Man in the White Suit*, a British comedy starring the young Alec Guinness, drives home these perplexities inherent in the capitalist mode of production. When a labour-saving wonder fabric is discovered, both capitalists and workers recognise it as a threat to their profit- and wage-streams, respectively, so each tries to do the 'rational' thing: squelch it!

The difference between skilled and unskilled commodity-producing labour likewise comes to be socially recognised through commodity exchange. That means the difference gets recognised in quantitative terms, which is a highly abstract way to honour the merits of skilled labour. It breeds cynicism among workers: 'Plaques and praise, OK, but where is my raise?' Granting Marx's assumption that human labour is self-reflectively social in nature, this mode of recognition counts as a way in which 'practically abstract' skilled labour is actually abstract.

As commodity-producing, the goal of 'practically abstract' labour is to deliver goods and services to be sold, redeemed as money. Insofar as workers foresee this, there is something alarmingly abstract about their products and labour. Georg Simmel brilliantly portrays how money levels all things: 'money ... hollows out the core of things, their peculiarities, their specific values and their uniqueness and incomparability in a way which is beyond repair. They all float with the same specific gravity in the constantly moving stream of money. They all rest on the same level and are distinguished only by their amounts'.[43] Money's monotone muffles the sensibilities of participants in the money economy, resulting in the flattened affect that Simmel calls the blasé attitude.[44]

42 This break is contradictory because value-producing labour must also be concrete, use-value-producing labour – the double character of labour. Without use value there is no value: 'nothing can be a value without being an object of utility. If the thing is useless, so is the labour contained in it; the labour does not count as labour, and therefore creates no value' (Marx 1976a, p. 131).

43 Simmel 1971, p. 330. In his notes on James Mill of 1843 Marx likewise stresses the levelling effect of money: '*money* ... is completely indifferent both to the nature of the material, i.e., to the specific nature of the private property, and to the personality of the property owner' (Marx 1975a, p. 221).

44 Anxiety over this greying of affect, cloaked by hysteria over the Red Menace, gripped the original version of the film *Invasion of the Body Snatchers*.

The 'Protestant work ethic', which comes down to the blank maxim 'work hard', gives everyday expression to how the abstract purpose of commodity-producing labour leaches into the consciousness of the worker.[45]

3.2 *Formal Subsumption under Capital and Wage-Labour*

Now let us sort out those ways in which 'practically abstract' labour is actually abstract, using concepts from the level of capital rather than merely generalised commodity circulation.

Once we digest Marx's demonstration that generalised commodity circulation presupposes the circulation of capital, we discover a new way that 'practically abstract' labour is actually abstract. Not only does 'practically abstract' labour produce wealth destined to be redeemed for money, but the point of the production process is to make money. With this ironic description of the workings of a jukebox, John Steinbeck's *The Grapes of Wrath* brings home money's power over the production process:

> Bing Crosby's voice stops. The turntable drops down and the record swings into its place on the pile. The purple light goes off. The nickel, which has caused all this mechanism to work, has caused Crosby to sing and an orchestra to play – this nickel drops from between the contact points into a box where profits go. This nickel, unlike most money, has actually done a job of work, has been physically responsible for a reaction.[46]

This pecuniary motivation can only redouble the worker's sense of abstractness stemming from the fact that his or her products take the commodity form. The insinuation into the workers' consciousness of the profoundly empty truth (proclaimed by the new corporate name of U.S. Steel, USX) that endless moneymaking is the aim of their efforts, magnifies the actual abstractness of the work they perform. For, whatever sense workers can make of their labour, their private meaning is always overshadowed by the indispensable purpose it serves: to make money.[47] Therein lies the unique use value of wage labour.

Labour that is formally subsumed under capital is wage labour, since it is only wage labour that makes the production of surplus value possible. (Other

45 For all that, it remains true that 'practically abstract' labour must always be concrete and concretely purposeful (Marx 1976a, p. 137).

46 Steinbeck 1986, p. 158.

47 As James Roderick, then Chairman of U.S. Steel, put it: 'The duty of management is to make money, not steel'. So USX came by its new name honestly!

forms of surplus wealth do not require wage-labour). Wage labour is actually abstract in several ways other than its peculiar usefulness in producing surplus-value. Marx maintains that wage labourers must be free in two senses, and each holds implications for the actual abstractness of wage labour.

First, wage labourers must be free to dispose of their labour power as they choose. Their labour power is their property, which they can alienate (sell), never wholly, but only in portions that preserve their integrity as persons. In Chapter Six of *Capital* Volume I, 'The Sale and Purchase of Labour Power', Marx makes much of the fact that, as the sale and purchase of labour power takes place in the sphere of simple commodity exchange, wage labourer and capitalist meet as equals. One is in the role of seller, one is in the role of buyer. (Herein lies the basis of social equality as a 'shadow form').[48] Marx renews the criticism of 'human rights' that he began in 'On the Jewish Question' (1843) when he sarcastically calls simple commodity circulation 'a very Eden of the innate rights of man'. He continues: 'It is the exclusive realm of Freedom, Equality, Property and Bentham'.[49] 'Bentham' is Marx's shorthand for the following feature of the exchange between the seller and the buyer of labour power: 'Each looks only to his own advantage. The only force bringing them together, and putting them into relation with each other, is the selfishness, the gain and the private interest of each. Each pays heed to himself only, and no one worries about the others'.[50] The fact that the wage labourer, like the capitalist, acts out of narrow self-interest (at least insofar as the value forms determine the situation), turning a blind eye toward the promotion of the common good, discloses a morally disturbing way in which 'practically abstract' labour is actually abstract.[51]

48 The value forms engender the ideology of social equality – my money is as good as yours, so I must be a good as you – at the same time that they set up a class division between capitalists and wage labourers that functions beneath the radar of officially recognised distinctions. See Marx 1976b, p. 1,027.

49 Marx 1976a, p. 280.

50 Ibid. Though great moral philosophers count proper self-love among the most important virtues, it took creatures of the capitalist imagination like Ayn Rand and the 'egoist' Max Stirner (whom Marx and Engels lambast in *The German Ideology*) to propound the morally preposterous proposition that selfishness is a virtue.

51 Hegel understood this unmediated selfishness to be doubly problematic: (i) it promotes insecurity regarding one's own welfare and (ii) it is dishonourable precisely because it does not present the producer as making a socially recognised contribution to the common good. In his day, Hegel looked to 'corporations' (associations more like state-regulated guilds or professional groups than modern corporations) to provide workers with the missing security and social recognition. Of the member of a corporation Hegel writes: 'it is also recognised that he belongs to a whole which is itself a member of society in

Unless we accept the capitalist theodicy implicit in Adam Smith's image of an 'invisible hand' guiding the marketplace, which Marx ironically invokes in the continuation of the passage just quoted,[52] we must conclude that wage labour involves an abstraction – in human terms, a costly one – from the natural aim of social action, the common good.[53]

Second, wage labourers must be free of means of supporting themselves other than through the sale of their labour power. So, wage labourers are separated from the means and materials of production, in the sense that those conditions of production are privately owned by other parties (industrial capitalists and landowners).[54] The factors of production, inseparable within the labour process, are separated through the institution of private property.[55] This sets up a situation in which wage labourers, in selling their labour-power to capitalists, put themselves under the command of those capitalists or their surrogates (corporate managers).[56] For it is a feature of the contractual arrange-

---

general, and that he has an interest in, and endeavors to promote, the less selfish end of this whole. Thus, he has *his honour in his estate*' (Hegel 1991a, p. 271, § 253). By contrast, 'If the individual is not a member of a legally recognised corporation ... he is without the *honour of belonging to an estate*, his isolation reduces him to the selfish aspect of his trade, and his livelihood and satisfaction lack *stability*' (ibid).

52 'And precisely for that reason, either in accordance with the pre-established harmony of things, or under the auspices of an omniscient providence, they all work together to their mutual advantage, for the common weal, and in the common interest' (Marx 1976a, p. 280).

53 Even if we accept Smith's claim, moral difficulties remain. Hegel sympathised with Smith's vision of modern capitalism, but he did not accept the sublime thought of the 'invisible hand' as a moral refuge for the self-centred: 'it is necessary to provide ethical man with a universal activity in addition to his private end ... We saw earlier that, in providing for himself, the individual in civil society is also acting for others. But this unconscious necessity is not enough; only in the corporation does it become a knowing and thinking [part of] ethical life' (Hegel 1991a, p. 273, § 255).

54 The first determination of wage labour that Marx mentioned in his notes on James Mill was 'the estrangement and fortuitous connection between labour and the subject who labours' (Marx 1975a, p. 220).

55 On this topic see Campbell 1993b.

56 In his *Critique of the Gotha Programme*, Marx attacks the 'socialist' party plank that labour is the source of all wealth, calling it a 'bourgeois phrase' and observing, 'Labour is not the source of all wealth. Nature is just as much the source of use values ... as labour, which itself is only the manifestation of a force of nature' (Marx 1966a, p. 3). Endless confusion of wealth and value with one another is unavoidable for economics precisely because value is a peculiar social form of wealth and economics fails to incorporate social form all the way down. Economics is a truly asocial theory. Marx further discloses the gulf separating his 'truly social' labour theory of value from the classical labour theory of value:

ment between wage labourer and capitalist that the capitalist is in charge of the production process.[57] It is true that supervisory functions of the capitalist can be spun off to paid managers and corporate directors, a point emphasised by theorists of the 'managerial revolution'. Nonetheless, it remains the capitalist's prerogative to set the goals of production and to organise the process to meet those goals.

Of course, a capitalist already knows that the indubitable goal of production is to make money (to accumulate surplus value).[58] So this kind of abstractness recalls the prior point that wage labour is actually abstract because it submits to the abstract purpose of creating surplus value. The difference is this: there, the point was that labour is actually abstract because of its determining goal; here, the point is that labour is actually abstract because the labourers who produce commodities are denied the exercise of their capacity to set the (social) goals of their own labours or to determine how those goals will be achieved; they are hirelings. Setting the purpose of production is an aspect of work that is denied wage labourers and monopolised by capitalists.[59]

The labour contract not only puts the capitalist in charge; the fruits of production belong to the capitalist. They are (legally) removed from the hands of their wage-earning producers. This might dampen the effects mentioned above based on foreseeing the redemption of commodities for money: after all, those commodities, though produced by wage labourers, are not theirs – and we tend to care more about what is ours. The trouble is, when the fruits of one's labour are not one's to keep, what is? A wage.[60] Marx observes: 'Since

---

'The bourgeois have very good grounds for falsely ascribing *supernatural creative power* to labour; since precisely from the fact that labour depends on nature it follows that the man who possesses no other property than his labour power must, in all conditions of society and culture, be the slave of other men who have made themselves the owners of the material conditions of labour. He can work only with their permission, hence live only with their permission' (ibid.). So free wage labour is not so free.

57 Marx notes that factory workers in England were commonly known as 'hands' (Marx 1976d, p. 48).

58 For this reason, Marx speaks of the capitalist as the mere 'personification' of capital and regards capitalism a system of *impersonal* domination of all – though differently – by capital. If workers are 'hands', capitalists are 'pockets'.

59 Capitalists or their surrogates may see fit to involve workers in decision-making – after all, they are in charge!

60 The abstractness of the wage form has moral advantages that Marx recognises. In contrast to slaves, who subsist on use values selected by their masters, wage labourers have the choice and responsibility characteristic of all persons placed in the social role of the buyer. See Marx 1976b, p. 1,033.

the sole purpose of work in the eyes of the wage-labourer is his wage, money, a specific quantity of exchange-value from which every particular mark of use-value has been expunged, he is wholly indifferent towards the content of his labour and hence his own particular form of activity'.[61] When all it produces for you is cash, the sense of one's work being abstract comes through loud and clear: Johnny Paycheck works a 'job'.

Different wage forms (hourly wages, piece rates and salaries) and different pay periods (daily, weekly, biweekly or monthly) convey different messages regarding abstractness.[62] A detailed look at wage forms and pay periods goes beyond the scope of this chapter, but a few broad strokes can be made here. Hourly wages drive home the message that 'time is money'. They make the use-value aspect of one's work less palpable than in the case of salaried workers, for whom concrete activities are placed in the foreground. When the lunch whistle blows in *Modern Times*, the assembly-line workers stop in mid-motion. Laws that require overtime pay to workers paid by the hour, but not to salaried employees, reinforce this difference.[63] Hourly wages send the message that you work to get paid, whereas salaries suggest that the purpose of your work is more than pecuniary. The hourly wage encourages workers to feel more like 'time's carcass' than do salaried employees.[64] Piece rates fall in-between as they reward faster work – 'time is money' – while demanding successful accomplishment of concrete tasks, which accents the use-value dimension. The more this wage form is perceived by workers to be a capitalist ruse to intensify their work, however, the more it functions as a cynical variant of the hourly wage form.

As for pay periods, two observations may be made: (i) the shorter the pay period, the more emphatic the link between time and money, so that the shorter periods accent the abstractness of work for wages and (ii) monthly pay schedules weaken slightly the link between work time and money because of the infrequency of payment and because the month is not as uniform as the day or week.

---

61 Ibid. The fourth determination of wage labour that Marx noted in his notes on James Mill was 'that to the worker the maintenance of his individual existence appears to be the *purpose* of his activity and what he actually does is regarded by him only as a means' (in Marx 1975a, p. 120).

62 The different wage forms and pay periods link naturally with the problematic of abstract time.

63 Juliet Schor observes that many salaried workers work long hours of 'overtime'. See Schor 1992.

64 'Time is everything, man is nothing: he is at the most time's carcass' (Marx 1963b, p. 54).

A final type of actual abstractness that concerns the formal subsumption of labour under capital is the detachment or indifference resulting from the mobility of wage labour.[65] Marx writes in the *Grundrisse*:

> Indifference towards any specific kind of labour corresponds to a form of society in which individuals can with ease transfer from one labour to another, and where the specific kind is a matter of chance for them, hence of indifference. Not only the category, labour, but labour in reality has here become the means of creating wealth in general, and has ceased to be organically linked with particular individuals in any specific form.[66]

Remember the old question from the early days of television: What did Ozzie Nelson do for a living? The fact that viewers of the American sitcom *Ozzie and Harriet* did not know, tells us it does not matter. This indifference on the part of workers grows with the indifference of capitalist investment as announced by the corporate logo USX.[67] Commodity-producing labour is actually abstract, in the sense that those who perform it must be ready to abandon their jobs and relocate, retrain, etc., according to the demands of the market (that is, according to the demands of capital accumulation).[68] Talk to career counsellors for an earful on the need for today's wage-labourers to be 'flexible'.[69]

Formal subsumption is not an all-or-nothing proposition. It comes qualified with various restrictions that do not arise from the relevant value form. Alcoholic beverages are commodities, but the law prohibits their sale to minors. 'Blue laws' further hem in their status as a commodity by limiting their sale on the Sabbath. Houses may be commodities, but racist real estate practices do

65 The mobility of wage labour ties in naturally with the problematic of abstract space.

66 Marx 1973, p. 104.

67 Marx writes 'We can see this *versatility*, this perfect indifference towards the particular content of work and the free transition from one branch of industry to the next, most obviously in North America, where the development of wage labour has been relatively untrammeled by the vestiges of the guild system etc.' (Marx 1976b, p. 1,034).

68 *The Grapes of Wrath*, John Steinbeck's saga of the Depression-era Joad family's loss of their homestead in Oklahoma and subsequent journey to California in search of 'jobs with high wages', shows forces of capital ('the Monster') that impel workers to migrate, and it portrays the visceral reaction, especially among the elders, to being uprooted. Grandpa Joad does not survive the first day's travel, and Grandma expires as the Joads ride into the 'Promised Land' of California.

69 I recently heard that whereas in 1920 90 percent of adult Americans settled within 50 miles of their parents, today 90 percent settle more than 50 miles away from their parents.

not play by the rule that one person's money is as good as another's.[70] Marx identifies the medieval guild system as one where capital and wage labour are found, yet not in their unrestricted forms.[71] In particular, the relationship between master and journeyman or apprentice does not display the indifference to use value that characterises the relationship between capitalist and wage labourer – a guild called USX would be a joke:

> The *medieval guild system* ... is a limited and as yet inadequate form of the relationship between capital and wage-labour. It involves relations between buyers and sellers. Wages are paid and masters, journeymen and apprentices encounter each other as free persons ... The master does indeed own the conditions of production – tools, materials, etc. (although the tools may be owned by the journeyman too) – and he owns the product. To that extent he is a capitalist. But it is not as capitalist that he is *master*. He is an artisan in the first instance and is supposed to be a master of his craft ... His capital is bound to a definite kind of *use-value* and hence does not confront his own workers directly as *capital*.[72]

Marx notes a range of further restrictions on the role of the master/capitalist that do not belong to the capital form. He follows up: 'The purely formal conversion of production based on handicraft into capitalist production, i.e. a change in which for the time being the technological process remains the same, is achieved by the *disappearance of all these barriers*'.[73] So, even formal subsumption under capital and wage labour comes not in a rush but spans a historical course of increasing indifference toward specific use values and pre-existing social realities. Battles against barriers to participation in commercial activities based on race, ethnicity, religion, sex, marital status, sexual preference and more still rage.[74]

---

70 This example reveals an important progressive element in the abstractness of the commodity form and the social roles of buyer and seller. Social movements for civil rights go, for the most part, with the grain of the value forms, not against it. It is worth noticing that, without legal compulsion, high profile corporations have granted to same-sex 'domestic partners' benefits previously reserved for heterosexual married couples.

71 This discussion reminds us, first, that, while the words for the value forms may be applied to pre-modern societies, they do not point to the same realities and, second, that the social forms bound up with capital and the bourgeoisie are historically dynamic as forms.

72 Marx 1976b, pp. 1,029–30.

73 Marx 1976b, p. 1,031.

74 In *The Great Transformation*, Karl Polanyi points out that the rise of the free market

4 Real Subsumption

When considering actually abstract labour, our first thoughts likely turn to the detailed division of labour and the assembly line. Charlie Chaplin's manic, bolt-twisting, machine-fed, camera-monitored worker in *Modern Times* leaps to mind as do Smith's pin factory and F.W. Taylor's stopwatch. We know that workers voted with their feet on Henry Ford's introduction of the assembly line; the turnover rate over a year approached 100 percent until Ford spiked the wages. Even the great apologist for the detailed division of labour, Adam Smith, feared that, as its consequence, 'all the nobler parts of the human character may be, in great measure, obliterated and extinguished in the great body of the people'.[75] Friedrich Schiller expressed alarm at the division of labour in these dramatic words:

> Everlastingly chained to a single little fragment of the Whole, man himself develops into nothing but a fragment; everlastingly in his ear the monotonous sound of the wheel that he turns, he never develops the harmony of his being, and instead of putting the stamp of humanity upon his own nature, he becomes nothing more than the imprint of his occupation or of his specialised knowledge.[76]

The factory sequence in *Modern Times* brilliantly puts these words into the idiom of film.

Marx, too, was appalled by the dehumanising aspects of the detailed division of labour in modern industry. But he approaches the phenomenon quite differently. Marx treats this division of labour not simply as a technical matter but as a matter of social form, too. That explains why Marx's account of manufacture and modern industry comes under the heading of relative surplus value, which is his preferred rubric in *Capital* for handling the real subsumption of labour under capital. Treating the division of labour in this way certainly allows him

brought about a simultaneous struggle to rein in or compensate for its unwelcome consequences, especially those affecting people and land. In many areas, such as education, health care, pensions, public lands, scientific research and sex, formal subsumption under value forms remains hotly contested. Claus Offe makes much of the process of 'decommodification' that he observes taking place in the capitalist welfare state. See Offe 1984.

75 Smith 1979, pp. 783–4.

76 Schiller 1967, p. 35.

to protest its splintering effects, but it presses the point that the technical form of labour answers to its specific social purpose – under capitalism, moneymaking.

By attending to social form, Marx warns us not to jump on any one technical form of production as the truly capitalist one. Circumstances might arise such that shifts toward less fragmented labour would better serve the goal of capital accumulation.[77] 'De-depersonalised' labour can be 'good business'. The literature on 'post-Fordism' and 'flexible accumulation' addresses situations where wage labour becomes less abstract in its technical aspect. Such (re)humanising developments that occur within the context of real subsumption do not eliminate labour's actual abstractness, as those who overlook the power of social forms tend to assume.[78] Even formal subsumption under capital is sufficient to make labour actually abstract in various important ways.

5 Ideal Subsumption

Ideal subsumption refers to the practice of treating something not subsumed under the capital form (or some other value form) as if it were. When a young friend announces he brought home a $25 lizard from his camping trip, he engages in the most common form of ideal subsumption – treating something that is not a commodity as if it were one. Phrases like 'human capital' or 'social capital' invoke ideal subsumption with calls to 'invest' in our youth or our voluntary associations.[79] So-called 'negative externalities', such as air or water pollution, can be ideally subsumed and assigned price tags as discommodities. Such a move may cross over into actuality when governments implement policies such as fines, differential taxes, or 'pollution credits'.

Ideal subsumption routinely takes place within the circuit of capital, within firms themselves. In the 'ideal pre-commensuration' that projects an enterprise's profitability, all the factors of production, which, once purchased, func-

77 Consequently, Harry Braverman's narrative of a secular trend toward the deskilling of labour fails to appreciate the range of possibilities that Marx's conception of real subsumption encompasses. See Braverman 1974.

78 For a critique of the notion that 'flexible production' is putting an end to alienated labour, see Smith 1994 and Smith 2000.

79 For an application of the notion of 'social capital' to religious congregations, see Coleman 1996. Merchants impressed with the idea of 'social capital' may bring the non-commercial networks designated by that phrase, e.g., bowling leagues, yacht clubs, or Bible groups, within the circuits of capital by purchasing membership lists for advertising purposes.

tion as use values to produce new use values, must be treated as values or as value-adding.[80] Additionally, though between units of a capitalist corporation, goods and services usually are not actually exchanged as commodities, they may be reckoned as commodities. While a corporate lawyer working in a law firm sells legal services to paying customers, a staff lawyer at a capitalist corporation does not. Nonetheless, the corporation may, for whatever reason, choose to have the in-house lawyer compute 'billable hours' and 'charge' other departments of the firm. This practice of 'internal outsourcing' takes the operation of ideal pre-commensuration beyond the accountant's office and rubs workers' noses in the pecuniary aim of their work.

On the edge of the capitalist world are 'self-employed' persons who produce for the market. The term 'self-employed' belongs to the vocabulary of ideal subsumption, which superimposes the capitalist-wage labourer (employer-employee) relation onto a single person!

Of course, outside the capitalist world we find ideal subsumption as well. Thus Geert Reuten observes 'increasingly … household and leisure-time activities are at least being calculated in terms of value'.[81] By a parity of reasoning with formal subsumption, ideal subsumption makes labour (and other activities) more abstract. If working for wages as a child-care provider, a cab driver or a short-order cook introduces elements of abstraction, will they not cross over into domestic life if I ideally subsume my unpaid caring, carting and cooking under the wage form?[82]

6 Hybrid Subsumption

Hybrid subsumption is a catchall category for the power of capitalist social forms to cross over and transform needs, objects or practices that are neither formally nor ideally subsumed under those forms. Forms of production (e.g., family farms or other traditional types of production, co-operatives, not-for-profit corporations and state-socialist firms) that are not formally capitalist, but which compete with capitalist producers, experience the power of the capitalist forms. Competition pressures non-capitalist producers to assimilate new

80 On 'ideal pre-commensuration' see Reuten and Williams 1989, pp. 66–8.

81 Reuten 1993, p. 106.

82 As noted, liberating aspects come with the abstractness of wage labour. Liberal feminists including J.S. Mill and Simone de Beauvoir counted on the entry of women into the waged labour-force to be the backbone of women's liberation. Ideal subsumption of unpaid domestic labour taps into this emancipatory dimension of wage labour.

technologies and organisational forms, product innovations, pricing and marketing strategies, 'corporate cultures', etc. When that occurs, we have hybrid subsumption under value forms. Given the abstractness of capitalism's goal, hybrid subsumption planes these non-formally subsumed sectors and probably leads to formal and real subsumption. 'In one word, it [the bourgeoisie] creates a world after its own image'.[83] Historically, moneylenders and merchant capitalists who deal with non-capitalist producers have functioned as conduits for hybrid subsumption and as spearheads for formal and real subsumption.[84] Since capital emerges in a world not previously governed by value forms and since state-socialist societies exist in a world dominated by capital, hybrid subsumption has enormous historical significance.

7 Subsumption under Capital's Shadow Forms

Capitalism's shadow forms owe their currency to the capital form, and, I think, would not indefinitely endure after the eradication of the capital form; nonetheless, they have distinctive powers that deserve attention in examining the ways in which labour that comes under the sway of capital can be actually abstract.[85] The two I will consider are utility and instrumental reason.[86] Social equality, the secular, and 'wealth', 'work' (as in the Protestant ethic's 'work hard'), and 'production' may also be numbered among capital's shadow forms.[87]

---

83 Marx and Engels 1976a, p. 488.

84 See Marx 1976b, p. 1023.

85 This suggests that the right answer to Bernard Williams's plaintive question regarding utility theory: 'When will we hear the last of it?' may be: after we have heard the last of capitalism.

86 Other terms for 'instrumental reason' include 'technical reason', 'formal reason', and 'subjective reason'. I make no distinctions among them.

87 As noted, the shadow form of social equality stems from the egalitarian forms characteristic of simple commodity circulation: the commodity, money, buyer, and seller. On the secular, consider this passage from *The German Ideology* section on utility theory: 'The theoretical proclamation of the consciousness corresponding to this bourgeois practice, of the consciousness of mutual exploitation as the universal mutual relation of all individuals, was also a bold and open step forward. It was a kind of *enlightenment* which interpreted the political, patriarchal, religious and sentimental embellishment of exploitation under feudalism in a secular way ...' (Marx and Engels 1976b, p. 410). Marx and Engels were more succinct in the *Communist Manifesto*, when they summed up the consequences of the dominance of the bourgeoisie: 'All that is holy is profaned' (Marx and Engels 1976a,

(i) Utility. From early on (1845 at the latest), Marx considered utility a sham concept best explained as an afterimage of commodity circulation.[88] Thus, Marx and Engels write of utility: 'this apparently metaphysical abstraction arises from the fact that in modern bourgeois society all relations are subordinated in practice to the one abstract monetary-commercial relation'.[89] Indeed,

---

p. 487). In *Capital*, Marx linked 'practically abstract' labour with the closest Christian equivalent to secularism: 'for a society based upon the production of commodities, in which the producers in general enter into social relations with one another by treating their products as commodities and values, whereby they reduce their individual private labour to the standard of homogeneous human labour – for such a society, Christianity with its *cultus* of abstract man, more especially in its bourgeois developments, Protestantism, Deism, &c., is the most fitting form of religion' (Marx 1976a, p. 172). Writing with more hindsight, Max Weber sees the fitting subjective complement to capital's dominance as 'the ability to free oneself from the common tradition, a sort of liberal enlightenment' and indifference if not hostility toward religion (Weber 1958, p. 70). Capitalism breeds secularism. Vulgar economic ideas, what Marx calls capitalism's 'religion of everyday life', are wholly secular, 'fiction without fantasy' (Marx 1971a, p. 453).

Because of the bizarre character of its social forms, the value forms, capitalism presents itself as the economy in general, where 'wealth' (of no determinate social form) is created by 'labour' (of no determinate social form) in a production process that is equally generic. What is more, 'wealth', 'work', and 'production' each shadow capital's telos of endless accumulation by becoming fetishistic ends in themselves: 'material wealth as an end in itself' (Marx 1976b, p. 1,037), 'work hard!' (The Protestant Work Ethic) and 'production for the sake of production' (ibid). Quantitative bigness and the preoccupation with calculability that Max Weber calls 'the romanticism of numbers' (Weber 1958, p. 71) might be added to the list of shadow forms of value. Picture McDonald's tallying the billions of hamburgers they have sold.

88 This connection resurfaces in *Capital* when, in making his closing, ironic observations on the sphere of simple commodity circulation, Marx writes: 'The sphere of circulation or commodity exchange ... is the exclusive realm of Freedom, Equality, Property and Bentham' (Marx 1976a, p. 280). That Marx rejects the neoclassical notion of utility as 'purely subjective' is evident from his barbed observation 'The usefulness of a thing makes it a use value. But this usefulness does not dangle in mid-air. It is conditioned by the physical properties of the commodity, and has no existence apart from the latter' (Marx 1976a, p. 126).

89 Marx and Engels 1976a, p. 409. They precede this statement with the observation 'The extent to which this theory of mutual exploitation, which Bentham expounded ad nauseam, could already at the beginning of the present century be regarded as a phase of the previous one is shown by Hegel in his *Phänomenologie*. See there the chapter "The Struggle of Enlightenment with Superstition", where the theory of usefulness is depicted as the final result of enlightenment' (Marx and Engels 1976a, p. 409). Marx and Engels's contention that utility is a shadow form of generalised commodity circulation counts as a

it is not much of a leap from 'everything has its price' to 'everything has its utility'.[90] Recall what Simmel writes of money's power to level and hollow things out. Utility theory assumes that money has already emptied things out, that there are no definite, morally significant natures or any abiding collective good that set the horizon for making moral judgments.[91] In *Love's Knowledge*, Martha Nussbaum jars us with utility theory's proposal:

> It is a startling and powerful vision. Just try to think it seriously: this body of this wonderful beloved person is *exactly* the same in quality as that person's mind and inner life. Both, in turn, the same in quality as the value of Athenian democracy; of Pythagorean geometry; of Eudoxan astronomy. What would it be like to look at a body and to see in it exactly the same shade and tone of goodness and beauty as in a mathematical proof – *exactly* the same, differing only in amount and in location, so that the choice between making love with that person and contemplating that proof presented itself as a choice between having n measures of water and n + 100.[92]

historical-materialist critique of Hegel's reading of the Enlightenment: capital and 'practically abstract' labour are more fundamental than utility and Enlightened 'pure insight' to understanding the Enlightenment.

90 Actually, in capitalism, not everything has a price, nor can it. Unlike fractions of their labour power, free wage labourers do not have a price. And without free wage labourers there is no capitalism. Since capitalist society is organised around the collective 'good' of capital accumulation, and this goal is achievable only on the basis of free labour, a capitalist society is in no position to treat the (abstract) integrity of persons as a utility that could be traded off for some greater utility. This makes it hard to imagine utilitarian ethics getting the upper hand over Kantian ethics in a capitalist society.

91 On Marx's phenomenology of the human condition, utility theory engages in false abstraction. There are no such free-floating utilities or preferences because an authoritative collective good already exists. It is one thing to challenge that good, as Marx does in the case of capital; it is another to pretend it does not exist.

92 Nussbaum 1990, p. 116. Marx's neo-Aristotelian stance, rejecting the comparability of diverse goods, is clear in the following passage from *The German Ideology*, where Marx argues that the bogus notion of utility is a disguise for commercial (capitalist) society: 'Hence the actual relations that are presupposed here are speech, love, definite manifestations of definite qualities of individuals. Now these relations are supposed not to have the meaning peculiar to them but to be the expression and manifestation of some third relation attributed to them, the relation of *utility or utilisation*. This *paraphrasing* [*Umschreibung*] ceases to be meaningless and arbitrary only when these relations have validity for the individual not on their own account, not as spontaneous activity, but rather as disguises, though by no mean disguises of the category of utilisation, but of an actual third

'Optimising utility' is even more bizarre than the actual aim it shadows (the accumulation of capital): at least the latter has an actual, though unfixed, measure – money.[93] Suffice it to say, then, that applying utility theory to human labour, domestic life (as in the work of Nobel Laureate economist Gary Becker), or anything else, injects the abstractness of capital's goal into those forms of labour and life.[94]

(ii) Instrumental reason. The Weberian fear of 'social engineering' and the complete domination of instrumental reason is capitalism getting unnerved by its own shadow. The Kafkaesque idea of the 'totally administered society' smacks of science fiction. It supposes either that no collective good organises the society or that the collective good is something formal and empty like self-preservation (Horkheimer), control (Luhmann) or self-maintenance (Parsons). But those gossamer phrases dodge these questions: preservation of what form of life? Control over what? Self-maintenance of what sort of society? No society is generic – the idea is a fiction of the capitalist imagination. In truth, human labour is always concretely purposive and animated by definite social forms and purposes. So the worry about 'the totally administered society' is a worry that we will wriggle ourselves out of our own predicament.[95] It'll never happen! Better to worry about our actual plight.

---

aim and relation which is called the relation of utility' (Marx and Engels 1976b, p. 409). Later in the text, Marx and Engels write of the absurdity of the sort of comparison that goes on under the mask of utility: 'even though this absurd comparison has a real basis in the absurdity of present-day relations' (Marx and Engels 1976b, p. 440).

93 Already in *The German Ideology* Marx and Engels insisted that money was the actual measure presupposed by the notion of utility: 'The material expression of this use is money, which represents the value of all things, people and social relations' (Marx and Engels 1976b, p. 410); 'money – the means of comparison that acquires independent existence in practice' (Marx and Engels 1976b, p. 440). 'Money is the common measure for all, even the most heterogeneous things' (ibid.). Money explains utility, not the other way around.

94 This is not to claim that utility theory has no capacity to criticise capitalist society but only to say that mimicry of the capitalist mentality offers a spurious basis for critique. As Marx repeatedly observed in his criticisms of Proudhonism and 'left Ricardianism', value theory itself can be employed to criticise the capitalist class's pumping surplus value out of the working class. But such an approach fails to recognise either that value itself is fetishistic or that value ultimately makes no sense apart from surplus value: value presupposes surplus value. Compare Elizabeth Anderson's reservations regarding the critical potential of contemporary theories of rational choice in Anderson 1993, p. xii.

95 That fact that this worry looms so large in Jürgen Habermas's work, as evidenced by his antagonism toward the social engineering approach of Niklas Luhmann and, conversely, by his passion for communicative action as a counterweight to instrumental action,

In his concise treatment of instrumental reason, Tony Smith reminds us that Weber himself granted that the soul of 'rationalisation' was capital accounting (Reuten and Williams's 'ideal pre-commensuration'). In Weber's words, 'Rational capitalist calculation is possible only on the basis of free labour'.[96] In short, value forms dominate (as Marx also thought[97]) through the unprecedented emergence of free wage labour, and this in turn generates the notion of instrumental rationality. The horizon of instrumental reason, like the horizon of utility theory, is set by the liberal ideology that capitalism spawns, namely, that here exists a society without an authoritative collective goal.[98] Liberalism, economics, utility theory and instrumental rationality all share the bourgeois mind-set that shadows capitalist forms.

Most thinkers today are disposed to follow Kant in separating moral, pragmatic, and technical exercises of human intelligence. A truly critical thinker, however, adopts the encompassing notion of practical wisdom (*phronesis*). According to Aristotle's doctrine, practical reasoning (the so-called 'technical' included) can never be divorced from the imposing collective goals that inform the deliberations of practical wisdom.[99] Marx shares Aristotle's position, for his phenomenology asserts that human life is socially purposive, which means that it always has a definite form and collective goal.[100]

---

manifests his failure to recognise instrumental action as a shadow form of 'practically abstract' labour. The Frankfurt School discourse around the notion of instrumental reason turns on a miscomprehension of Marx's critique of value-producing labour. See Postone 1993. The 'traditional Marxism' of the Frankfurt School (setting Marcuse aside) has more in common with the neo-Kantian concepts of Weber than the neo-Aristotelian ones of Marx.

96 As quoted in Smith 1990, p. 198.

97 'The capitalist epoch is therefore characterised by the fact that labour-power, in the eyes of the worker himself, takes on the form of a commodity which is his property; his labour consequently takes on the form of wage-labour. On the other hand, it is only from this moment that the commodity-form of the products of labour becomes universal' (Marx 1976a, p. 274).

98 In *Marx, Marginalism and Modern Sociology*, Simon Clarke argues that modern sociologists, notably Weber, missed the key scientific revolution of the nineteenth century, namely Marx's 'truly social' theory of value, when they uncritically adopted the asocial (utilitarian) conceptual horizons of neoclassical economics (Clarke 1982).

99 Hence Aristotle calls political science the head of the practical sciences.

100 In recognising that collective goods are constitutive for individual lives, Marx understands that morality is like the weather: it is changeable but you always have it. The legend of 'Marx the amoralist', like the legend of Marx the theorist of asocial labour, rests on misconceptions.

For the Aristotelian, capitalism is a curiosity because the blinding actuality of individual choices in the marketplace makes it seem as though a market society lacks a shared aim. Consequently, practical reasoning in such a society seems to be as untethered as instrumental reason supposes. In truth, however, the free market has a collective goal (the expansion of value) and harbours a high-minded moral principle, the dignity of the (abstractly conceived) person. Instrumental reason, then, is more abstract than the actual form it shadows, capital. At least capital posits an actual (if terribly abstract) collective goal, as well as free wage labour; by contrast, instrumental reason presupposes that nothing is sacred and that we do not have an authoritative collective good at all. Consequently, handling labour under the shadow form of instrumental reason as, for example, in the 'scientific management' approach developed by F.W. Taylor, exaggerates the abstractness that already comes with labour's subsumption under capital.

8 'Honey, I Shrunk the Family': Abstract Labour and Domestic Life

'Rent a Lifestyle'. Thus ran the headline in my local newspaper advertising a 'swinging singles' apartment complex. It is a far cry from the older view of home as a haven from 'the great scramble' of commercial dealings. 'Rent a lifestyle' raises questions about the relationship between the value forms and domestic life: to what extent can domestic life be transformed by the power of value?[101] How far may capital pursue us home? We will see that for capital to subsume the household wholly would be self-defeating, since it would eliminate wage labour. This discloses in a new way that Marx's theory is 'truly social'.

Concerns about capital taking over the household should be specified: is the household being swallowed wholly or piecemeal? Wholly means the formal subsumption of the entire household under capital; piecemeal means bringing domestic functions under value forms bit by bit. I will argue that the wholesale subsumption of the household would be self-defeating since the accumulation of capital presupposes free labour. A gnawing piecemeal subsumption of domestic life, however, seems inevitable – capital is always on the lookout for new terrain for investment. Under capitalism, the family may be shrunk, but not sold.

---

101 Compare the compact discussion in Reuten and Williams 1989, p. 90, to which the present one is indebted.

Capital makes its presence felt as more and more household goods and services are store-bought. In basic areas like housing construction, clothing, and the provision and preparation of food, this is simply assumed. House cleaning and childcare are increasingly the functions of paid workers. In other areas, this piecemeal subsumption of the household still grabs our attention. We notice when parents arrange for a 'Chuck E. Cheeze' pizza and amusement parlour to put on their child's birthday party or when someone is hired to walk the dog. There are limit cases here: having Thanksgiving dinner catered is one thing, renting a womb, as in the Baby M case, is another. You may pay for the services of a marriage counsellor, but what is the sense in hiring a surrogate to go to marriage counselling for you? Comedians enjoy testing these limit cases. Years ago the American television show *Saturday Night Live* ran a skit in which a rich young man hires a commercial service to break off his romantic relationships for him. In cases of this sort, we deal not with wholesale subsumption of the household under capital but with 'contracting out'. The householders are still, at least formally, in charge.

Beyond the piecemeal formal and real subsumption of household goods and activities under the commodity capital form, the household is, of course, subject to ideal and hybrid subsumption under value forms. For example, children may be thought of as 'human capital' and expenditures for their development (like private tuition) can be considered as investments.[102] Statistics that compare the average lifetime earnings of a college graduate vs. a high school graduate encourage such thinking. Or you might imagine parents mentally tallying their expenses in raising a child – including, at market wages, the cost of their caregiving, while discounting, at market wages, for work done by the child – to figure out how much their child cost them. The title of Arlie Hochschild's study of American domestic life in the 1980s, *The Second Shift*, ironically engages in ideal subsumption, but the topic of her book is hybrid subsumption. What she calls the 'speed-up in the family' – more ironical ideal subsumption – is a consequence of the dramatic increase in the participation of American women in the waged labour force.[103] *The Second Shift* is all

102 Why is this not an actual investment? Why is this ideal, not formal subsumption? The reason is tricky. To view such expenditures as true investments treats my child's labour power as a whole as a commodity. But to make anyone's labour power as a whole into a commodity violates the rules of 'free' wage labour. A worker's labour power can be alienated as a commodity only by the part. (See Marx 1976a, p. 271, and note 3 on pp. 271–2.)

103 'Women's move into the economy is the basic social revolution of our time', writes Hochschild 1989, p. 239, echoing ideas of Mill and de Beauvoir.

about the power that capital exercises over the household without formally subsuming it – hybrid subsumption.

The domestic sphere, too, is subject to subsumption under capital's shadow forms: utility (as with Becker's approach to marriage) and technical reason. *Cheaper by the Dozen* humorously chronicles the home life of two leading American efficiency experts, Frank and Lillian Gilbreth, where instrumental reason meets the American family, but the scientifically managed household is not necessarily a happy one.

Answering the contested question: 'Does unpaid household work create value?' provides a good transition to our final question: 'Can the household be wholly subsumed under capital?' Marx's negative answer to both questions reveals his theory of value to be 'truly social'.

From the standpoint of Ricardian value theory, the exploitation involved in pumping surplus value out of wage labourers is nothing compared to the exploitation of those (usually women) whose household labours go unpaid. For, if value is embodied 'labour' or even embodied 'abstract labour' – household chores can be viewed from the physiological perspective – then, surely, value is being created as this unpaid household work is being done. If Marx accepted the asocial Ricardian labour theory of value, why has he nothing to say about how unpaid household labour creates value or surplus value, or about the capitalist exploitation of that labour? Silence on those questions is what we should expect, however, when we recognise Marx's theory of value as 'truly social', not Ricardian. Unpaid household work is not commodity-producing labour; it is not treated in practice as abstract labour; it is not 'practically abstract' labour.[104] So, while it is involved in the production of wealth, unpaid household work does not produce value. Again, this does not mean that unpaid household labour is not exploited, but only that it is not exploited in the way capital exploits wage labour.

Asking why household labour goes unpaid circles us back to our question concerning the limits to capital's subsumption of the household. The ordinary point of paying wages is to reap profits. But profits can be reaped from household labour only on the assumption that it produces commodities big with surplus value. But what would those commodities be? Wage labourers?

What would induce capital to swallow the household whole? A full-fledged takeover would be predicated on the production of labour-power as a profit-

104 It is tempting to say that unpaid household labour involved in rearing children is commodity producing because it is producing the labour power of the next generation of workers. But, again, that is to treat a child's labour-power as a whole as a commodity, and that violates the rules of wage labour.

able commodity – factories for breeding workers, if you will.[105] But that would eliminate one of the conditions for the sale of labour power by wage labourers, namely, the formal freedom of the worker. Capitalists cannot produce free workers, since capitalists produce commodities, and, if the worker is free, then the worker cannot be sold as a commodity. The wholesale formal subsumption of the domestic sphere under capital, then, is incompatible with the presupposition of capitalism that labour is, as a rule, done by (free) wage labourers.

Suppose the labourer is not free. If labourers are not free, they do not own their own labour power (do not have a 'property in their own persons', as John Locke would put it). In that case, the labourer has nothing to sell, so there will be no wages, for wages are paid to free workers, whereas the price of slaves (workers who are commodities) is paid to the capitalist who 'produced' them. In a system of unfree labour, you cannot exploit workers in the capitalist manner: without wages, there is no gap between wages and the value produced by workers.[106] Where there is no gap, there is no surplus value. (However, surplus wealth and exploitation may exist.) Without surplus value, there is no capital.

Look at it another way. Without wages, workers have no money. So all monetary exchanges will be between capitalists. But with all monetary exchanges going between capitalists, where will surplus value come from? In a monet-

105 The science fiction film *The Matrix* exploited the fear of the human race being bred for servitude by their creations.

106 When I first read this passage from Reuten and Williams, I thought it odd: 'It is because labour is the only element that takes on the form of value whilst it is not produced within the capitalist sphere of production that it potentially creates value-added' (Reuten and Williams 1989, p. 69). On further reflection, it turns out to be a gloss on Marx's account of surplus value. Surplus value (keeping in mind that surplus value is a particular social form of surplus wealth) arises from the difference between the value of labour power paid out to workers in wages and the value of the commodities produced by wage labour (less the value of constant capital). And Marx insists that for there to be wages, workers must be free (Marx 1976a, pp. 270–1). Were workers produced within the sphere of capitalist production, they would be commodities, hence not free. Since work animals are unfree and can be produced as commodities within the sphere of capitalist production, it follows from Reuten and Williams's claim that they do not create value. (The same holds for machines.) Were animals (or machines) to eliminate wage labourers, capitalism would collapse. This brings home the point once again that Marx's theory of value is 'truly social'. Only 'practically abstract' labour, not labour in its physiological aspect, creates value, for work animals exert themselves in the physiological sense without creating value. Because human wage labourers are socially recognised as free in a specific, abstract way, they can create value. Value is all a matter of social form.

ary exchange you either get equal value or not. If you do, you get no surplus value. If you have unequal exchange, then one exchanger gets surplus value at the expense of the other. But that contradicts the assumption that all parties to these exchanges are capitalists (i.e., those who increase value through exchange). Capitalists cannot have all the money; wage labourers must have money. Turning the household into a commodity would undo capitalism.

Since value can be expressed only in money, the same must be true of surplus value. Consequently, the exploitation involved in pumping surplus value out of workers must have a monetary expression. But, where workers have no money, there can be no such expression. So there can be no surplus value, hence, no capital. A new twist on the Midas myth awaits capitalists who would like to make everything a commodity.[107] Capitalism cannot evade a dialectic of respect and disrespect for workers, recognising their freedom while forcing them to turn the wheel of endless capital accumulation. Kant got the point when he allowed that we may treat people as means but never as mere means. Here lies a source of lasting moral friction in capitalist societies.

This demonstration may strike the reader as a conjuring trick: wait a minute! How can surplus value vanish just because workers are switched from one social role to another, from 'free' wage labourers to slaves? Do not slaves create surpluses for their masters? But this objection only reveals the stubbornness of Ricardian prejudices. We sense a hoax precisely because we slide back into the notion that 'labour' creates value – and for that, slave labour should serve as well as any other. That sort of thinking completely misses the point of Marx's critique of economics: value is entirely a matter of the social form of labour. If we really got that point we would expect value and surplus value to disappear with the elimination of a fundamental capitalist social form like free wage labour. And that is what the demonstration shows. It says, once more, that Marx holds a 'truly social' labour theory of value.

---

107 'Why not put everything up for sale?' begins Anderson 1993. One answer is clear: to do so would bring down capitalism and generalised commodity circulation with it. It would undermine itself.

CHAPTER 6

The Grammar of Value: A Close Look at Marx's Critique of Samuel Bailey

> It is naturally still more convenient to understand by value nothing at all.[1]

There is a buzz about 'value-added'. It springs from the world of business and flows into all manner of discourse. It seems that everyone is eager to 'add value', but just what do we add when we add value? About this, there is silence. It is a remarkable fact about contemporary life that so little thought is given to such a fundamental social reality as value. Or, perhaps it is not so remarkable after all, in view of how bizarre, elusive and complex value is. Marx observes:

> The objectivity of commodities as values differs from Dame Quickly in that 'a man knows not where to have it'. Not an atom of matter enters into the objectivity of commodities as values; in this it is the direct opposite of the coarsely sensuous objectivity of commodities as physical objects. We may twist and turn a single commodity as we wish; it remains impossible to grasp it as a thing possessing value.[2]

This elusive suprasensible nature of value is responsible for the poverty of much of our philosophical and social scientific discourse about modern society.[3] When the strange objectivity of value is denied (as by Bailey) or simply not noticed, the critical question of the specific social form and purpose of wealth is missed. Value, which accounts for why commodities and money are fetishes, is the inescapable consequence of the specific social form of labour in capitalist

1 Marx 1976a, p. 677, n. 6.

2 Marx 1976a, p. 138.

3 The suprasensible nature of value makes it a sitting duck for empiricists and anti-metaphysicians like Bailey.

societies.[4] Value belongs to the peculiar social form taken by wealth in the commodity form. Deny that value belongs to commodities, as Bailey does, and all that remains is bare use value, wealth without any particular social form.[5] But wealth exists only as some definite social form of wealth. What that social form is matters greatly; this is the deep phenomenological truth disclosed by Marx's historical materialism. Instead of investigating the content and implications of specific social forms of wealth, such as the commodity, money and capital, for the most part, philosophers and social scientists settle for the conceptually poor, hence non-illuminating, category of wealth.

Samuel Bailey (1791–1870) is not well known, but he was a perceptive critic of the classical (Ricardian) theory of value, one of the few modern investigators of the value form and a forerunner of subjective utility theories of value. Marx, in his unfinished history of political economy, *Theories of Surplus-Value*, examines Bailey's work carefully.[6] Bailey figures heavily in the first chapter of Marx's *Capital*, especially section three, 'The value-form or exchange-value', but his influence can be felt throughout *Capital*'s three volumes.[7] Marx singles out Bailey as one of the very few economists 'who have concerned themselves with the analysis of the form of value', though he is quick to add, '[they] have been unable to arrive at any result, firstly because they confuse the form of value with value itself, and secondly because, under the coarse influence of the practical bourgeois, they give their attention from the outset, and exclusively,

4 'This fetishism of the world of commodities arises from the peculiar social character of the labour which produces them' (Marx 1976a, p. 165).

5 The notion of bare use value, wealth without any particular social form, belongs to what I call 'the illusion of the economic'. The polarity of the expression of value in money creates the illusion that commodities are simply use values: 'The internal opposition between use-value and value, hidden within the commodity, is therefore represented on the surface by an external opposition, i.e., by a relation between two commodities such that the one commodity, whose own value is supposed to be expressed, counts directly only as a use-value, whereas the other commodity, in which that value is to be expressed, counts directly only as exchange-value' (Marx 1976a, p. 153). In particular, when money functions as money as such, 'as the only adequate form of existence of exchange value in the face of all the other commodities', those other commodities play 'the role of use-values pure and simple' (Marx 1976a, p. 227).

6 See Marx 1971a, pp. 124–68.

7 It is only in recent decades, thanks to the rediscovery of I.I. Rubin's *Essays on Marx's Theory of Value* (English translation, Rubin 1972) and to Hans-Georg Backhaus' seminal essay, 'On the Dialectics of the Value-Form' ['*Zur Dialektik der Wertform*'] (Backhaus 1969; English translation, Backhaus 1980), that Marx's theory of the value-form and its place in his unique, non-Ricardian theory of value has begun to get its due. See Arthur 2002a, pp., 11–13.

to the quantitative aspect of the question'.[8] Marx's first criticism fits Bailey perfectly, for Bailey flatly identified value with the exchange-value relation (among other things). Marx's second criticism points up the need for the 'third thing' argument, which Marx presents in the first section of Chapter One of *Capital*, in order to account for the possibility of quantitative comparisons of commodities.[9] There is a great deal to be learned from Marx's scrutiny of Bailey about problems with Ricardian value theory and with purely subjective theories of value; at the same time, there is much to gain in our understanding of Marx's unique, and still widely misunderstood, theory of value.

Marx's engagement with Bailey makes palpable the importance of the concept of value as well as the challenges of formulating it accurately, what Geert Reuten calls 'the difficult labour of a theory of social value'.[10] A concept holds together multiple determinations. Getting the concept of value right requires grasping all its necessary determinations – and in the right way. Bailey is perceptive enough to recognise what many of those conceptual determinations are; in particular, he recognises that the theory of the value form, exchange value, belongs to the theory of value. But putting these ideas together into an adequate concept of value is beyond him. As Marx examines Bailey's vacillating deliberations on value, he discovers an array of bad ideas (value is purely subjective), contradictory ideas (all commodities, indifferently, are money), incomplete ideas (value is a power of a commodity) and missing ideas (the polarity of the value form and the necessity of money as the exclusive commodity in the equivalent value form). Working through the jumble of Bailey's ideas and his constant flip-flopping (a consequence of never getting the concept of value right) sharpens Marx's thinking about commodities, value, exchange value, the value form and money. Watching Marx in his workshop enlivens our understanding of *Capital*.

The present chapter will address the following seven questions:

1. Why bother with Marx's critique of Bailey?
2. Why speak of the grammar of value?
3. How is the term 'value' used in ordinary language?
4. What are Bailey's chief criticisms of classical political economy?
5. What conceptions of value did Bailey put forward?

---

8 Marx 1976a, p. 141, n. 17.

9 See Murray 2006, included in the present volume as Chapter 17.

10 Reuten 1993.

6. What are Marx's key criticisms of Bailey?
7. What might Marx have learned from Bailey?

1 Why Bother with Marx's Critique of Bailey?

There are many good reasons to study Marx's critique of Bailey, some of which have been mentioned.

(i) It leads us to think hard about value, that is, the peculiar kind of value that commodities have as commodities, the kind of value that money expresses and measures. Bailey's ruminations expose anyone schooled in classical political economy to unrecognised complexities of value. Bailey wisely cautions, 'A false simplification in matters of fact can be of no service, and can only tend to perplex the mind of the inquirer'.[11] Unfortunately, Bailey cannot handle all the complexities of value.

(ii) Since Marx's theory of value is (wrongly) taken to be a version of Ricardo's labour theory of value, only driven to radical consequences, Bailey's criticisms of Ricardo's theory of value anticipate common criticisms of Marx's theory of value. Marx judges a number of Bailey's points (which include 'transformation problems' arising from different organic compositions of capital, different turnover times and monopoly pricing) to be telling criticisms of Ricardo. Bailey's criticisms serve as provocations to some of the most important theoretical initiatives that Marx undertakes in the three volumes of *Capital*.

(iii) His engagement with Bailey illuminates Marx's purposes in the first chapter of *Capital*. Bailey is around every corner of the argument, especially in the difficult third section, on the value form. Marx's critique of Bailey as value-form theorist highlights the importance of the polarity of the value form, the distinction between the relative value form and the equivalent value form and the exclusivity of the money form. Bailey rightly insisted that value is inherently relational, but he failed to grasp the necessary polarity of the expression of value – not all relations are polar relations – and thus failed to grasp the exclusivity of the money form. The root of these failures lay in his not seeing that value and exchange value (value's necessary form of expression) spring from the peculiarly asocial social form of labour in capitalism.[12]

---

11 Bailey 1967, p. 232.

12 'Political economy has indeed analysed value and its magnitude, however incompletely, and has uncovered the content concealed within these forms. But it has never once asked the question why this content has assumed that particular form, that is to say, why labour

(iv) The controversies among contemporary value-form theorists regarding the respective roles of production and exchange in the determination of value get their start in Bailey's insistence – against the classical labour theory of value's claim that value is created solely in production – that value exists only at the moment of commodity exchange.[13] In Bailey's theory of the value form, which represents a fundamental criticism of Ricardo, labour is no ingredient; it is all about commodity exchange. Bailey makes the examination of the value form, that is, the exchange-value relation, a feature of any adequate theory of value. In so doing, he bequeaths Marx the tricky problem of how to incorporate the value form as an ingredient of a labour theory of value, a task that never crossed Ricardo's mind.[14] Marx's examination of Bailey helps us to comprehend Marx's view of how value develops through production and exchange.

(v) Because Bailey may be seen as a forerunner of the subjectivistic approach to value taken by neoclassical economics, we can gain important insights into how Marx might have responded to neoclassical value theory.

2 Why Speak of the Grammar of Value?

There are several reasons to speak of the grammar of value. Bailey's critique of the Ricardian conception of value as intrinsic to the commodity rejects the ordinary grammar of value. So, too, does his purely subjective notion of the usefulness of things. We talk about the value of this or that, say of oil or corn, but Bailey makes a grammatical critique of such expressions. He insists that it is nonsense to talk of 'the value of A'; good sense limits us to 'the value of A in B.' This is what makes Bailey a value-form theorist. Bailey illustrates this shift by appealing to the grammar of 'distance'. Because distance is an inherently relational concept, it is ungrammatical – conceptually if not formally – to ask, 'What is the distance of Chicago?' as opposed to 'What is the distance from Winnipeg to Montreal?' Likewise, because value is inherently relational, the

---

is expressed in value, and why the measurement of labour by its duration is expressed in the magnitude of the value of the product' (Marx 1976a, pp. 173–4.)

13 See 'Avoiding Bad Abstractions: A Defence of Co-constitutive Value-Form Theory', included in the present volume as Chapter 15.

14 In *A Contribution to the Critique of Political Economy*, Marx calls attention to this perplexity: 'Thus a new difficulty arises: on the one hand, commodities must enter the exchange process as materialised universal labour-time, on the other hand, the labour-time of individuals becomes materialised universal labour-time only as the result of the exchange process' (Marx 1970a, p. 45). See also Marx 1976a, pp. 179–80.

expression 'the value of A' is ungrammatical. Marx, too, engages the debate on a grammatical plane. He observes of Bailey's insistence that value is the exchange-value relation, 'Relation of a thing to another is a relation of the two things and cannot be said to belong to either'.[15]

Marx spots a basic problem here that Bailey overlooked. If value is identified with the exchange relation itself (e.g., a gallon of milk exchanges with a gallon of gas), that rules out use of the phrase 'the value of milk'. But it also excludes 'the value of milk in gas' since the unacceptable phrase, 'the value of milk', is embedded in it, leaving Bailey tongue-tied. Bizarrely, according to Bailey, there is nothing for value to be the value of. When speaking of value Bailey tries to evade the possessive 'of', but the spurned grammar of possessives keeps returning; he keeps sliding back into 'the value of A' or 'its (A's) value'. Bailey is fighting a losing battle; possessives pop back up. The actual grammar of Bailey's formulations strains against his doctrine that there is nothing for value to be the value of.

Talk of grammar in a broader sense, one that turns on the content of concepts, may bring Ludwig Wittgenstein's 'philosophical grammar' to mind. Though the present chapter is not especially Wittgensteinian, it does draw on his practice of exploring the limits of sense in ways that go beyond formal grammatical analysis. To use an example from Marx, the phrase 'a yellow logarithm' does not make sense, not because the expression is ill-formed in any formal sense but rather because a logarithm is not the kind of thing that could be yellow.

The rubric of grammar stretches back to Bailey's empiricist precursor Bishop George Berkeley. Berkeley interpreted nature as God's language and called natural scientists 'grammarians of nature'. By the same token, economists might be spoken of as 'grammarians of society'. Bailey follows Berkeley, Locke and others in his determination not to allow language to impose upon our understandings.[16] Bailey warns of 'the chameleon-like properties of language', and he finds discussions of value to be perplexed by language:

> A singular confusion has also prevailed with regard to the ideas of measuring and causing value, and in the language employed to express them. The perpetual shifting from one notion to the other, the use of common terms for both ideas, and the consequent ambiguity, vacillation and perplexity,

15 Marx 1971a, p. 139.

16 Bailey invokes Locke's famous description of his task in the *Essay Concerning Human Understanding* as being to act as an 'underlabourer for science', when he writes that the 'rubbish must be removed, the ground cleared' (Bailey 1967, p. xii).

> exhibit a remarkable picture of the difficulty of thinking with closeness, as well as of the defects of language as an instrument of reasoning.[17]

Grammatical, in the broad sense of fixing the limits of sense, is a description that suits Bailey's conception of his critical inquiry into political economy.[18]

Add to the foregoing considerations Bailey's concern with tense in thinking about value. Bailey argues that, because value is relational and the relation between commodities (including money, which according to Bailey is not intrinsically different from any other commodity) cannot be established prior to the actual exchange of commodities, value exists only in the moment of exchange. Talk about value prior to the commodity's being exchanged is as senseless as saying: 'Yesterday, I walk to the post office.' Since commodity exchanges are momentary, any comparison of the value of a commodity (to slip into the possessive) across time is excluded in principle. Thus, ordinary questions such as 'Has the value of coffee declined over the past decade?' are ruled by Bailey to be grammatical errors. Curiously, this makes pointless – for grammatical reasons – the quest for a measure of value that is invariable. There is no grammatical space for questions concerning variations in value across time.

There is nothing wrong in principle with Bailey's inquiry into the grammar of value or with the idea that that inquiry might disclose problems with the ordinary grammar of value. For Marx, the trustworthiness of common sense is far from absolute. He neither dismisses common sense nor counts on its reliability.[19] One crucial instance of Marx's critique of common language concerns the phrase 'the value of labour' (as opposed to 'the value of labour-power'). The surface grammar is unobjectionable; the phrase is perfectly well formed. But a closer look reveals the confusion in it: 'On the surface of bourgeois society the worker's wage appears as the price of labour, as a certain quantity of money that is paid for a certain quantity of labour. Thus people speak of the value of

17 Bailey 1967, pp. vi, vii. Bailey's list of defects of classic works in political economy reads like a litany of empiricist complaints: 'Words used without determinate ideas, terms introduced without proper explanations, definitions abandoned almost as soon as enunciated, principles assumed without first being examined …' (Bailey 1967, p. viii).

18 'From the defects here imputed to the science, it is evident that in any work, which professes to examine and remove them, the points discussed must be questioned as to the use of terms, the distinction of ideas, the logical dependence of arguments, rather than questions of fact or evidence' (Bailey 1967, p. x).

19 See the discussion in Murray 2006, included in the present volume as Chapter 17.

labour'.[20] Marx contends that the phrase 'the value of labour' is grammatically flawed for two reasons: (1) only commodities have value, and labour is not a commodity. For labour to be sold as a commodity, the wage labourer would have to own it. But wage labourers are unable to labour until they get access to means of production. And that occurs only as a result of the sale of their labour power to the capitalist.[21] Labour is not a commodity for anyone.[22] (2) 'Labour is the substance, and the immanent measure of value, but it has no value itself'.[23] As the (immanent) measure of value, labour cannot have a value. You cannot measure something by itself; that violates the grammar of measure.[24] Marx pointedly concludes, 'In the expression "value of labour", the concept of value is not only completely extinguished, but inverted, so that it becomes its contrary. It is an expression as imaginary as the value of the earth'.[25]

An even more relevant example of Marx's grammatical investigations of value is his treatment of the value form (or exchange value) in Section Three of the first chapter of *Capital*. Here Marx presents his alternative to Bailey's grammar of value. Marx insists on the polarity of the value form and the conceptual distinction between the commodities occupying the two poles in the expression of value, i.e. the relative form of value and the equivalent form of value. The equivalent form proves to be the money form, that is, money exclusively occupies the equivalent value form and is thus immediately social and directly exchangeable with every other commodity. These polar forms, which are so fundamental to the grammar of commercial life and are rooted in the historical specificity of value, are absent from Bailey's grammar of value and continue to be overlooked in discourse about value.

Reference to grammar suggests something basic, pervasive, logical and perhaps even metaphysical. Language users who lack any scientific command of the subject can understand grammar in a lived way. Students of grammar usually speak more or less correctly, but they have to learn how to identify parts of speech. Likewise, value is pervasive in capitalist societies, and most members know it in a lived sense without having any scientific grasp of its nature and workings.[26] We also talk about value. How?

---

20 Marx 1976a, p. 675.

21 Marx 1976a, p. 677.

22 Marx 1976a, pp. 675 and 677, n. 6.

23 Marx 1976a, p. 677.

24 Marx calls this an 'absurd tautology' (Marx 1976a, p. 675).

25 Marx 1976a, p. 677.

26 I pursue the idea of the grammar of commercial life in the 'General Introduction' to my anthology, *Reflections on Commercial Life* (Murray (ed.) 1997b).

3 How is the Term 'Value' Used in Ordinary Language?

Let us do some analysis of ordinary language and try to spell out the grammar of the word 'value' as used in everyday talk about the kind of value that money measures. I will interpolate comments regarding Bailey's views – which largely oppose ordinary language – as we go. In common usage we employ the word 'value' in phrases such as 'the value of commodity A' or in questions such as 'has the value of commodity A gone up or down?' or 'Do commodities A and B have the same value?'

The ordinary usages of the term 'value' include the following features:

1. Value is public.[27] To talk about 'value for me' disregards the grammar of 'value' just as talk about 'truth for me' violates the ordinary grammar of 'truth'. My allergy to dairy products does not mean cheese has no value. Whatever value is, it is for everyone.
2. As suggested by the phrase 'the value of commodity A', value belongs to the commodity; it is a property intrinsic to it.
3. As suggested by the phrase 'the value of commodity A', value is singular; at a given time, the commodity has a certain value – not countless values, as in Bailey's talk of gold-value, corn-value, cloth-value, etc.
4. Furthermore, 'the value of the commodity A', assumes that value is measurable. Having a definite value at a given time requires having one socially valid measure of value. Though Bailey settles on money (gold) as the measure of value for practical considerations, since he does not properly grasp the exclusivity of the money form, he is actually committed to the view that every commodity is a measure of value different from the rest.
5. When we inquire about the Gross Domestic Product and its changes, we assume that we can aggregate the values of commodities and that we can compare these aggregates over time. On Bailey's approach we cannot say whether the value of the aggregate production is growing or not: (a) we cannot talk about the value of the aggregate in the first place and (b) even if we could measure aggregate value, we could not compare it from one moment to another.
6. Questions such as 'Do commodities A and B have the same value?' or 'What is the value of your inventory?' imply that value exists prior to the moment of exchange. Likewise, to the ordinary understanding, price

27 Prices, the necessary form of expression of value according to Marx, are public.

setters fit the price to the value of the commodity; according to Bailey, there can be nothing to fit.[28] When people talk of 'adding value', they do not think that it is all added in the twinkling of an eye at the moment when the product is sold.

7. As indicated by the question 'Has the value of commodity A gone up or down?' the value of a commodity can be compared across time. This is true even if the question is qualified 'Has the value of A in B gone up or down?' If, as Bailey insists, it makes no sense to compare the value of a commodity across time, then this ordinary question makes no sense. We will also struggle to make sense of money as a means of payment or a store of value. To eliminate the comparison of value across time is to undo capital altogether: valorization offends Bailey's grammar of value.
8. The question 'Do commodities A and B have the same value?' and the discourse of fair exchange or commutative justice – an exchange between two commodities is unjust when they are not of equal value – presuppose (a) that the value of one commodity can be compared with the value of another and (b) that two commodities could have the same value. If value simply is the exchange relation, as Bailey holds, then there is no room for unjust exchanges: if commodities A and B exchange for one another, there is only one relation, hence only one value. Bailey's grammar of value precludes injustice; it allows no grammatical space for an exchange between commodities of unequal value.
9. The subjective element cannot be eliminated from value. If you take away all desire for a commodity, its value vanishes.
10. The value of one commodity can change without necessarily changing the value of every (or even any) other commodity. Since, for Bailey, value is not only relative but also *only* relative, a change in the value of one commodity forces a simultaneous and opposite change in the value of the commodity for which it is being exchanged.

Bailey's thinking about value contravenes most of these features of the ordinary grammar of 'value', whereas Marx's theory of value accommodates most of them.

28 Compare Marx 1976a, p. 159.

4 What are Bailey's Chief Criticisms of Classical Political Economy?

Bailey's chief criticism of classical political economy is that, because value is strictly relative, value is not absolute and intrinsic to commodities. For Bailey, even the usefulness of a commodity is not intrinsic to it; rather, it is purely subjective; it is the feeling of approval that the commodity evokes in one's mind. Since he conceives of value as the exchange relation itself, Bailey denies that value is present prior to commodity exchange. That alone excludes the classical labour theory of value, according to which commodities gain their value in the production process. Because 'value' is short for 'the value of commodity A in commodity B', classical political economy's talk of a single value and of a single measure of value (labour time) is grammatically incorrect. There are as many measures of value as there are commodities.[29] Because value requires a current comparison of commodities, classical political economy goes down a grammatical *cul de sac* when it talks about comparing the value of money or commodities over time. Because value is nothing but the actual exchange relation, value is discontinuous. Bailey argues that the search for an invariable measure of value was not only futile; it was based on a misunderstanding of the grammar of value. Since value cannot be compared over time, 'invariable measure of value' is a senseless expression. Moreover, an invariable measure is unnecessary, since a variable measure could serve the purpose.[30] On this point Marx thought Bailey had a penetrating insight.

Bailey also criticised classical political economy at a less fundamental level. Bailey picks up on Ricardo's observation that firms with different organic compositions of capital will be differently affected by a rise in wages. This, Marx observes, is a particular manifestation of the incompatibility of two assumptions: (i) individual commodities sell at their value while (ii) firms with differing organic compositions of capital tend toward an average rate of profit. Bailey (again following Ricardo) noted a parallel problem with respect to differing turnover times.[31] He further observed not only that monopoly prices conflict

29 What Marx terms the 'total or expanded form of value' in Section Three of Chapter One of *Capital* expresses this aspect of Bailey's theory of value, to which Marx calls attention in note 25 on p. 155, where he goes on to comment that Bailey 'was under the delusion that by pointing to the multiplicity of the relative expressions of the same commodity-value he had obliterated any possibility of a conceptual determination of value'.

30 This is one of the points that Marx is making with his exposition of the general form of value in Chapter One of *Capital* (Marx 1976a, pp. 157–62).

31 Ricardo makes both observations in Section v of Chapter One of his *Principles of Political Economy and Taxation* (Ricardo 1951, pp. 38–43).

with the account of prices offered by the labour theory of value but also that this problem affects even non-monopolistic firms in so far as their inputs are affected by monopoly pricing. Indeed, Bailey recognised that all three phenomena – differing organic compositions of capital, differing turnover times and monopoly pricing – create 'transformation problems'. That is, he recognised that commodities which are inputs to the circuits of capital would be purchased not at their values but at prices that would be somehow 'transformed'. Marx accepted all three of these fundamental criticisms of Ricardian value theory.

5 What Conceptions of Value Did Bailey Put Forward?

What is value according to Bailey? Bailey's confounding texts offer several conceptions of value, whose adequacy and whose consistency with one another we will consider in turn. Though he did not sort them as I do, Marx drew most if not all of the distinctions noted here. Spelling them out in advance should be helpful when we turn to Marx's criticisms of Bailey. I will state them briefly and then examine each of them in more detail.

(i) The value of an object is the esteem in which it is held, with esteem understood as the purely subjective feeling the object evokes. Bailey quickly sheds this general, non-relative conception of value for one that better suits political economy and the investigation of commodities.

(ii) Value is a special feeling of relative esteem evoked by the comparison of two exchangeable things and expressed only through commodity exchange.[32] This concept of value suits the purposes of political economy, Bailey thinks.

(iii) Value is purchasing power, 'hence the value of A may be termed the power which it possesses or confers of purchasing B, or commanding B in exchange'.[33] Like the special feeling of relative esteem, purchasing power is expressed only through commodity exchange.

(iv) Value is the exchange relation itself. As Bailey's official definition, it may be more accurate to say that the exchange relation expresses the value, which is the special feeling of relative esteem. That would revert to (ii). As a

32 Since, as we will see in (iv), Bailey is prone to collapse the necessary expression of (purely subjective) value, namely, actual commodity exchange, with value itself, we may wonder about feelings of relative esteem that are not acted upon. Is this latent value that is actualised at the time of exchange? Or are only the feelings of relative esteem that are acted upon, that is, expressed in actual commodity exchanges, relevant to value?

33 Bailey 1967, p. 3.

purely subjective feeling, value still would be 'nothing positive or intrinsic' to any commodity.

(v) Sometimes Bailey writes as though value is not the exchange relation but rather the use value received in exchange; for example, the value of a gallon of milk is two loaves of bread. It may be more accurate to say that the use value received in exchange expresses the value of the commodity exchanged for it, though that would leave us still looking for what the value is.

(i) Bailey begins his *Dissertation* with the assertion that value is esteem. He conceives of the feeling of esteem in a typically modern way, that is, as purely subjective.[34] Bailey closes off any prospect of value's being intrinsic to the commodity with his opening definition, 'Value, in its ultimate sense, appears to mean the esteem in which any object is held. It denotes, strictly speaking, an effect produced on the mind'.[35] Bailey recognises that this is a perplexing conclusion to arrive at. We begin by inquiring into the value of some object. The grammar of the question 'what is the value of this commodity?' directs us to the relevant property of the commodity. Bailey's answer flies in the face of that expectation. Aware that his theory of value flouts common usage, Bailey offers this explanation of where ordinary language goes wrong:

> but as we are accustomed in other cases to give a common name to a feeling and to the cause which has excited it, and to blend them together in our thoughts, so in this case we regard value as a quality of external objects. Colour and fragrance, for example, are words which designate both the cause and the effect, both the material quality which produces the feeling in the mind, and the feeling produced. The philosopher, however, is the only one who discerns the distinction, and colour and fragrance are never thought of by the generality of men, but as qualities of external objects.[36]

34 David Hume states, 'If we can depend upon any principle, which we learn from philosophy, this I think, may be considered as certain and undoubted, that there is nothing, in itself, valuable or despicable, desirable or hateful, beautiful or deformed; but that these attributes arise from the particular constitution and fabric of human sentiment and affection' ('The Sceptic', in Hume 1985, p. 162).

35 Bailey 1967, p. 1.

36 Bailey 1967, pp. 1–2. Hume also compares values with 'secondary qualities' ('The Sceptic', in Hume 1985, p. 166, n. 3).

Bailey is swept along by the main currents of modern philosophy. He leaves no doubt that he means to extend to values the modern doctrine that 'secondary qualities' (colours, sounds, fragrances, tastes and feels) are purely subjective. 'It is precisely in the same way, that value is regarded as a quality belonging to the objects around us. We lose sight of the feeling of the mind, and consider only the power which the object possesses of exciting it, as something external and independent'.[37] Like Berkeley and other empiricists, Bailey traces the problem to the way that words impose upon our understandings. Because we have the same word for cause and effect, we conflate the two and believe that what is proper to the mind, namely the feeling of esteem, belongs to the object of that esteem.

Barry Stroud, in an essay examining the subjectivism of Bailey's forerunner David Hume, questions the coherence of this sweeping assertion that value is a purely subjective feeling and that, in themselves, all objects are indifferent. Stroud wonders what sense we can make of the idea that we 'project' value onto objects. If value is my feeling of esteem, when I judge that an object is valuable, what am I doing? Am I claiming to find that feeling of esteem in the object? How odd! But if this is not what I am doing, what account does the subjectivist like Bailey give of the ordinary thought, that objects have value? Stroud believes that no coherent subjectivist account of such thoughts has been offered, and he doubts that any will turn up.

Stroud points up the 'special problem' that thoughts about objects being valuable raise for modern subjectivists such as Hume and Bailey. This 'special problem' plagues Bailey's *Dissertation*:

> But the special problem which arises for the problematic thoughts we are interested in is that the impressions which are said to produce them cannot in that sense be impressions of 'anything, that does or can belong' to external objects. They are not 'of' anything that can be so, or that we can perceive to be so, in the world.[38]

The subjectivist account of value creates a grammatical conundrum: beauty or virtue are not the beauty or virtue 'of' anything. Likewise, Bailey leaves nothing for value to be the value 'of'. Subjectivists like Bailey do not so much explain value as explain it away. Since there is nothing for value to be the value 'of', we have to wonder what we were trying to explain in the first place. The whole inquiry into value seems to have been misguided.

37 Bailey 1967, p. 1.

38 Stroud 1993, p. 265.

(ii) Bailey shifts from value as esteem (which is non-relative, as Bailey recognises) to relative esteem (and to commodity exchange), but how? Robert Rauner offers this suggestion, 'Describing it [value] as a "simple feeling of esteem" did not fully convey the meaning of the term value, so Bailey carried his remarks further'.[39] But what was missing? Rauner does not say. Bailey's own transition offers little by way of justification:

> It is not, however, a simple feeling of esteem, to which the name of value, as used by the political economist, can be given. When we consider objects in themselves, without reference to each other; the emotion of pleasure or satisfaction, with which we regard their utility or beauty, can scarcely take the appellation of value. [Yet Bailey had written as if it could.] It is only when objects are considered together as subjects of preference or exchange, that the specific feeling of value can arise. When they are so considered, our esteem for one object, or our wish to possess it, may be equal to, or greater, or less than our esteem for another: it may, for instance, be doubly as great, or, in other words, we would give one of the former for two of the latter.[40]

Bailey includes 'preference' here as if it were equivalent to 'exchange', but we have preferences with regard to people and things that are not 'subjects of exchange'. Clearly, the feelings of relative esteem that Bailey intends here are directed at commodities. But why does Bailey choose to limit his field of inquiry to commodities? Apparently, because he takes that to be the practice of political economists, and he means to address political economists.

Bailey's convictions as a value-form theorist come through in this second definition: 'It is impossible to designate, or express the value of a commodity, except by a quantity of some other commodity'.[41] Value may be subjective but somehow it is also inherently relational. Since the simple feeling of esteem is not relational, it cannot be value. But we may yet wonder if 'the specific feeling of value' is relational. Is a purely subjective feeling about a relation, relational?

Bailey's claim that value simply is 'that specific feeling of value' raises the swarm of questions that surround modern conceptions of the self as pure subject, a world of its own somehow outside the natural and social world. Are

---

39 Rauner 1960, p. 5.

40 Bailey 1967, p. 2. Here Bailey anticipates the approach to the measurement of utility taken by von Neumann and Morgenstern 1953.

41 Bailey 1967, p. 26.

such feelings irredeemably private in the sense that they are open only to first-person inspection? Can the same (type of) special feeling of relative esteem exist for different pairings of commodities? A feeling of that odd type would have to abstract from the qualities of the different paired commodities. Is it plausible to assert that participants in commodity exchange are possessed of a set of such articulated and separately identifiable special feelings? Lacking a set of such feelings, can we talk about any two commodities having the same value – even for the same person? Turning to issues regarding 'other minds', are Bailey's special feelings private in the sense that no two persons could have the same 'specific feeling of value'? If these special feelings of relative esteem are private, then whenever we speak of value we really mean 'value for me'. All claims about value would have to be indexed accordingly. If, however, the same special feeling could be experienced by different persons, how would we know that they have the same feeling except by the pattern of their commodity exchanges? Doesn't the whole appeal to specific feelings of value come to nothing once Bailey shifts from talking about feelings of relative esteem to talking about value as the actual exchange relation?

Though Bailey targets his theory of value to commercial societies (societies whose wealth predominantly takes the form of commodities), when he speaks of value as 'the specific feeling of relative esteem', he imagines away the fact that the objects of our relative esteem are commodities, not fancied use values in general.[42] As a participant in a commercial society, my relative esteem for goods is not based on their use value alone. I consider their prices in arranging my preferences.[43] Would I rather have a box of chocolates or a new Mercedes? No matter how much I loved chocolate, I would be a fool not to prefer the car to the chocolates. Indexed to prices, my feelings of 'relative esteem' are saturated by money. Value cannot be explained in terms of relative esteem for (pure) use values because there are no use-values-in-general to esteem; wealth always has a specific social form and purpose, and social form and purpose always figure into the determination of our preferences. In conceiving of value, Bailey abstracts from money and prices in the wrong way; he pretends they do not exist. To pretend that use values in general are the objects of our preferences is to engage in bad abstraction.

(iii) Bailey approves of Smith's definition of value as purchasing power (which Ricardo affirmed), 'the definition of Adam Smith, therefore, that the

---

42 This is a serious problem for any system of measuring preferences.

43 Herein lies a general problem with efforts to explain value in terms of demand: demand must be indexed to prices and to the monetary resources of the buyer. But then money and prices are assumed rather than explained.

value of an object "expresses the power of purchasing other goods, which the possession of that object conveys", is substantially correct'.[44] Bailey describes purchasing power this way, 'Hence the value of A may be termed the power which it possesses or confers of purchasing B, of commanding B in exchange'.[45] Bailey observes of this definition that, like the conception of value as 'relative esteem', it insists on the relativity of value:

> According to this definition, it is essential to value that there should be two objects brought into comparison. It cannot be predicated of one thing considered alone, and without reference to another thing. If the value of an object is its power of purchasing, there must be something to purchase.[46]

From the fact that value 'cannot be predicated of one thing considered alone, and without reference to another thing', Bailey erroneously draws the inference that value cannot be predicated of a commodity. In that case, what are we to make of Bailey's talk of purchasing power as something that a commodity 'possesses' or 'confers'? If value is inherently relational, Bailey reasons, then it cannot be anything intrinsic to the commodity – as if it could not be intrinsic to the commodity that it stand in relation to other commodities or that there be property owners.

This third conception of value seems to conflict with Bailey's preferred one, that is, with (iv) on the present list. First, in some passages, purchasing power seems to be a power of a commodity, hence, a property of A. Consider Bailey's language, quoted above, 'the value of an object is its power of purchasing'. The possessive 'its' in this statement attributes purchasing power to the commodity. Bailey has even more emphatic formulations of the purchasing power of a commodity as 'the power which it possesses'. Second, as the purchasing power inherent in the commodity, value exists in the present tense; the power to purchase is present prior to any actual purchase. On Bailey's preferred, fourth, concept of value, value is the actual exchange relation, so value can exist only at the moment of exchange. Third, as a power inherent in the commodity, purchasing power is objective, a power that ownership confers on the owner and that goes with the commodity when it is transferred from owner to owner. (If value were my feelings of relative esteem, would they be transferred with the

44 Bailey 1967, p. 4.
45 Bailey 1967, p. 3.
46 Bailey 1967, p. 4.

commodity?) Smith and Bailey speak of the power possessed by the commodity – this is the power that Marx regards as the commodity's fetish character – being 'conveyed' to or 'conferred' on the owner of the commodity, who then exercises the power to purchase.[47] Bailey spells out the same idea in this way, 'He possesses riches who is the owner of commodities which themselves possess value; and, further, he is rich in proportion to the value of the objects possesses'.[48] This recognition of the commodity's objective, transferable social power stands Bailey's insistence that value is purely subjective on its head. The odd social objectivity of value is hard to shake.

(iv) Bailey expresses his fourth, his preferred, conception of value as follows, 'Value denotes consequently nothing positive or intrinsic, but merely the relation in which two objects stand to each other as exchangeable commodities'.[49] Here Bailey trims his second and third definitions of value in a move characteristic of his empiricist mentality. According to his definition (ii) above, Bailey conceived of value as purely subjective relative esteem that was necessarily expressed in 'the relation in which two objects stand to each other as exchangeable commodities'. According to definition (iii), 'the relation in which two objects stand to each other as exchangeable commodities', necessarily expresses value, which is defined as the purchasing power of the commodity. In Bailey's fourth conception, what was identified as the expression of value, now simply is value: value *is* the exchange relation.

Collapsing value into its necessary expression rids Bailey of problems for his official view that lurk in his second and third definitions of value. The problem in the second definition is this: if value is purely subjective, how can it be necessary to value that it be expressed in commodity exchange? Put the other way around, if appearance – the exchange of commodities – is inseparable from the essence (relative esteem), then value is not purely subjective after all. In the case of the third concept of value, sticking with its complexity would require Bailey to conceive of value as inherent to a commodity yet necessarily relational at the same time. Bailey is too much of an either/or thinker to be comfortable with that seemingly discordant thought. To Bailey's bifurcating mentality, if value is relational then it cannot be inherent, and vice versa. Abbreviating the more complex logic of his second and third conceptions of value, which discriminate between value and its necessary form of expression,

47 Smith's formulation, 'possesses and conveys' is more accurate than Bailey's 'possesses or confers'. It is because the commodity possesses purchasing power to begin with that it conveys that power to its owner.

48 Bailey 1967, pp. 165–6.

49 Bailey 1967, p. 4.

Bailey settles into this fourth, flattened conception of value: value just is the exchange relation, for example: one gallon of gas exchanges for one gallon of milk. With this fourth conception, the air has gone out of the balloon; instead of an essence appearing, we now have just appearance, the bare facts of exchange. Bailey's fourth, and official, definition of value leaves us with nothing to do but tabulate exchanges. But the phenomenon of value repels this urge to flatten it.

The consequences of this fourth conception of value wreak havoc on our ordinary expectations. If value just is the exchange relation, then the expression 'the value of commodity A' becomes grammatically unacceptable: a commodity does not have a relation; the relation is not something that belongs to the commodity. Strangely, it turns out that there is nothing that value can be the value of. Any inference that, because commodity A was exchanged for commodity B, they have the same value is based on grammatically unacceptable premises: how are we to compare 'their values' when there is only one relation, one value? Since commodity exchange is a momentary event, we cannot talk about the present value of a commodity, since value has no existence prior to the moment of exchange – and then vanishes with that moment. On Bailey's fourth conception of value, to ask if the value of commodity A has gone up, down or stayed the same over some time period is grammatically unacceptable.[50] And obviously so, since value is defined as the contemporary comparison of (different) commodities through actual commodity exchange. This fourth conception of value suggests that statements of value should be indexed not only to specific commodities (and to specific persons, if we keep relative esteem in the picture); value must be indexed to time. According to Bailey, then, the true grammar of 'the value of commodity A' is 'the value of commodity A in commodity B, for person X, at time t1'. But even in that expression the nagging 'of' remains.

(v) Bailey writes of the exchange relation, 'The value of A is expressed by the quantity of B for which it will exchange, and the value of B is in the same way expressed by the quantity of A'.[51] According to this fifth conception value is (necessarily) expressed as something else; here the value of A is expressed by the use-value of B, a formulation that points toward Marx's 'third thing'

---

50 Of course 'the value of commodity A' is not grammatically acceptable in the first place.

51 Bailey 1967, p. 3. 'We cannot speak of value, as I have before shown, without meaning value in something ... the value of A must mean its value in B' (Bailey 1967, p. 101). The grammar of the possessive – 'the value of A' and 'its value' – dogs Bailey despite his insistence that value is not intrinsic to the commodity.

argument, while ignoring the polar character of the value form.[52] On this fifth definition, either we must say there is no quantity of B that would be equal in value to A – which would be quite peculiar – or there is. In the latter case, A, as the expression of that quantity of B's value, and that quantity of B, as the expression of A's value, must be expressing the same thing, the same value. A cannot be the value of B and B cannot be the value of A, because the value of A and B are the same but A and B are not the same thing. Rather, there must be, as Marx writes, 'a common element of identical magnitude [that] exists in two different things'.[53] A and B must be 'equal to a third thing, which in itself is neither the one nor the other'.[54]

Bailey's several conceptions of value create multiple difficulties in addressing the ordinary question 'Is A equal in value to B?' Definition (ii), according to which value is relative esteem that is actualised in commodity exchange, has trouble making sense of the exchange of equivalents. If I exchange A for B, it is because I esteem B more highly than A, but then B is more valuable than A. Yet my partner in exchange must esteem A more highly than B, making A more valuable than B. According to definition (iii), value is purchasing power, which is expressed in commodity exchange. If A exchanges for B, we measure the purchasing power of A in B and B in A, respectively, which leads us into the same problem that turns up with definition (v): how do we know if B and A are equal? How do we even make sense of the question? On definition (iv), Bailey's preferred one, if A is exchanged for B, A and B cannot have different values since value is the exchange relation itself and where there is only one relation there is only one value. There is no grammatical space even to pose the question: Is A equal in value to B? Unjust exchange (that is, an exchange of unequal values) is excluded in principle. On definition (v) the problem is that, if A and B are of equal value, then, as expressions of that equal value, B and A must somehow be equal, but how? Bailey's theory provides no clue as to the 'common element of identical magnitude' that exists in B and A.

With all this trouble coping with the ordinary question 'Is A equal in value to B?' Bailey explains the origin of the expression and calls for its grammatical reform:

> But it will be found, that, in speaking of the value of A being equal to the value of B, we are led to use the expression by the constant refer-

52 Marx 1976a, p. 127.
53 Ibid.
54 Ibid.

> ence which we unavoidably make to the relations of these commodities to other commodities, particularly to money, and the import of our language, in its whole extent, is, that A and B bear an equal relation to a third commodity.[55]

The true grammar of the question 'Is the value of A equal to the value of B?' is 'Do A and B bear an equal relation to a third commodity?' I will argue that Bailey's attempted grammatical reform fails by his own lights. To do so, I will need to probe this notion of A and B bearing 'an equal relation to a third commodity'. Bailey elaborates as follows:

> Indeed, it is generally by their relation to a third commodity, that we can at all ascertain the mutual relation of two commodities which we are desirous of comparing. If we wish to know whether A and B are equal in value, we shall in most cases be under the necessity of finding the value of each in C; and when we affirm that the value of A is equal to the value of B, we mean only that the ratio of A to C is equal to the ratio of B to C.[56]

How can the ratio of A to C possibly equal the ratio of B to C unless A and B are commensurable? But in terms of what would they be commensurable? Bailey offers no clue.

A subtle bait and switch is going on here. Bailey conflates the ratio of the units of A to the units of C (say, 300 gallons of milk to one ounce of gold) with the ratio of the number of units of A to the number of units of C (300 to one). By eliminating the dimensions of A and C (milk and gold), the latter expression reduces to a number (300), which could be compared to the number obtained by handling the ratio of B to C in the same manner. If the numbers were the same – though there is no reason to think that they would be – we would say that A and B have the same value. But dropping the dimensions to arrive at this number is a gratuitous move. What, then, can we make of the former ratio (300 gallons of milk to one ounce of gold), which does not eliminate the dimensions of the units of A and C? The ratio will be x units of A over y units of C (300 gallons of milk over one ounce of gold). Likewise for the ratio of B to C (say, 300 gallons of gas over one ounce of gold). On what basis could we possibly say that the ratio of x amount of A to y amount of C was equal even to the ratio of x amount of B to y amount of C? On what basis can the dimensions A and B be equated? Bailey

55 Bailey 1967, p. 8.
56 Ibid.

offers none. To make Bailey's grammatical reform work, we need to make the assumption that, as values, A, B and C are homogeneous, they have a common dimension, so that the dimensions of A over C and B over C will cancel out. Nothing in Bailey's official conception of value allows us to do this.[57]

So, Bailey's attempted grammatical reform of the ordinary question 'Is A equal to B in value?' fails because the expression 'A and B bear an equal relation to a third commodity' turns out to be just as senseless as the one it was designed to replace. Give Bailey credit for the wit to recognise that his theory of value made the ordinary question grammatically unacceptable. However, his alternative expression, 'A and B bear an equal relation to a third commodity', flops.

6 What are Marx's Key Criticisms of Bailey?

Though Bailey harped on about the relational character of value, he did not recognise the polarity in the relational expression of value, even though some of his formulations might suggest it. So Bailey also lacks the distinction between what Marx calls the relative value form and the equivalent value form.[58] Bailey, then, does not adequately understand what Marx calls 'the simple value form' and is in no position to comprehend the more developed expressions of value, notably, the money form. Bailey talks about money, but it is not really money he means, since, according to him, money is not intrinsically different from other commodities. He regards every commodity as a different kind and different measure of value, so that each is 'equally real and equally nominal'.[59] So everything is money and nothing is money. Everything has a price and nothing has a price. Since Bailey has no way to get past this plethora of *kinds* of value, he has no way to get to (one) value. Without an exclusive measure of value,

57 Here is a perfect case of what Marx warns us against, 'we must, first of all, consider the value-relation quite independently of its quantitative aspect. The usual mode of procedure is the precise opposite of this: nothing is seen in the value-relation but the proportion in which definite quantities of two sorts of commodity count as equal to each other. It is overlooked that the magnitudes of different things only become comparable in qualitative terms when they have been reduced to the same unit. Only as expressions of the same unit do they have a common denominator, and are therefore commensurable magnitudes' (Marx 1976a, pp. 140–1).

58 See Marx 1976a, pp. 139–52.

59 Bailey 1967, p. 39. 'Money-value has no greater claim to the general term "*value*", than any other kind of value' (Bailey 1967, p. 58).

there is no money, so use values do not have prices, which means they are not commodities.[60] What is more, there is no value: the explanandum disappears. Marx's 'third thing' argument presupposes money, the presence of which, as Martha Campbell argues, Marx assumes from the beginning of *Capital*.[61]

Bailey is flatly wrong about money; money is different from other commodities. Only money has immediate social validity; it is directly exchangeable for all other commodities. Bailey does not register this readily observed difference between money and other commodities. Rather, he denies it. The narrowness of his theory induces Bailey to block out a fact of life in capitalism apparent to everyone: 'Everyone knows, if nothing else, that commodities have a common value-form which contrasts in the most striking manner with the motley natural forms of their use-values. I refer to the money-form'.[62] The root of the money form lies in the polarity of the expression of value (the value form); its polarity, in turn, is an unavoidable consequence of the asocial sociality of the production of commodities.

Bailey is unaware of the social antagonism at the root of the polarity of the value form. Ultimately, this is because he fails to recognise the capitalist mode as a specific – antagonistic – social form of production: Bailey treats the capitalist mode of production as if it were production in general. This is what I call 'the illusion of the economic'.[63] By contrast, Marx exposes the roots of the antagonisms involved in the specific social forms (the commodity, exchange value, value, money, wage labour and capital) and the specific purpose of capitalism, which require a system of commodity exchanges in order to mediate labour and its products:

> Because the product is not produced as an immediate object of consumption for the producers, but only as a *bearer of value*, as a claim, so to speak, to a certain quantity of all materialised social labour, all products as *values* are compelled to assume a form of existence distinct from their exist-

60 On the importance of Marx's assumption in *Capital* that commodities have 'valid prices', see Murray 2006, included in the present volume as Chapter 17.

61 Campbell 1997. Commodities have prices, so they presuppose money; bartered goods, goods that are directly exchanged, are not commodities: 'The direct exchange of products has the form of the simple expression of value in one respect, but not as yet in another. That form was x commodity A = y commodity B. The form of the direct exchange of products is x use-value A = y use-value B. The articles A and B in this case are not as yet commodities' (Marx 1976a, p. 181).

62 Marx 1976a, p. 139.

63 See Murray 2002a, included in the present volume as Chapter 14.

> ence as use-values. And it is this development of the labour embodied in them as social labour, it is the development of their *value*, which determines the formation of money, the necessity for commodities to represent themselves in respect of one another as money – which means merely as independent forms of existence of exchange-value – and they can only do this by setting apart one commodity from the mass of commodities, and all of them measuring their values in the use-value of this excluded commodity, thereby transforming the labour embodied in this exclusive commodity into general, social labour.[64]

There is no value without the qualitative transformation of privately undertaken labour into socially valid labour, and that transformation cannot be completed in the sphere of production: to complete the circuit of value, commodities must be sold. 'This necessity to express individual labour as general labour is equivalent to the necessity of expressing a commodity as money'.[65] Marx takes heed of Bailey's warning not to oversimplify value: value involves a circuit that spans production and exchange.[66]

Because Bailey treats production as production in general, he sees no particular connection between production and exchange. He has no idea that exchange value and value are the consequence of a particular social sort of labour. By contrast, Marx writes, 'But the labour which constitutes the substance of value is not only uniform, simple, average labour; it is the labour of a private individual represented in a definite product'.[67] Because Bailey's theory of value dissociates production and exchange, value is in no way determined in production, leaving the determination of value in exchange apparently arbitrary.[68] Production sets no limits on value that might hinder the smooth flow of commodity exchange. Marx counters with the ominous observation:

> in the midst of the accidental and ever-fluctuating exchange relations between the products, the labour-time socially necessary to produce

64 Marx 1971a, pp. 144–5; Marx 1974, p. 142. See also Marx 1974, p. 133.

65 Marx 1971a, p. 133; Marx 1974, p. 133.

66 See 'Avoiding Bad Abstractions: A Defence of Co-constitutive Value Theory', included in the present volume as Chapter 15.

67 Marx 1971a, p. 135; Marx 1974, p. 133.

68 Contrast Marx's observation on the phenomena of prices, 'It becomes plain that it is not the exchange of commodities which regulates the magnitude of their values, but rather the reverse, the magnitude of the value of commodities which regulates the proportion in which they exchange' (Marx 1976a, p. 156).

> them asserts itself like a law of nature. In the same way, the law of gravity asserts itself when a person's house collapses on top of him. The determination of the magnitude of value by labour-time is therefore a secret hidden under the apparent movements in the relative values of commodities. Its discovery destroys the semblance of the merely accidental determination of the magnitude of the value of the products of labour, but by no means abolishes that determination's material form.[69]

In denying the objectivity of value, that value is intrinsic to the commodity (because its social form is intrinsic to it), Bailey attributes a weightlessness to value that falsifies it.

I conclude this section with a summary of Marx's chief criticisms of Bailey:

(i) Bailey criticises Ricardo as a fetishist for believing that value is a property of products of labour. In fact, value is intrinsic to commodities not because they are products of labour but because of the peculiar asocial sociality of commodity-producing labour. Ricardo's value theory is a species of fetishism because it treats a purely social property of the commodity as if it were asocial, natural. Bailey turns out to be a fetishist because he identifies value with a relation between use values, turning value into a relation between things when, in reality, value is the consequence of a peculiar way in which people relate to one another when they produce wealth in the social form of the commodity.[70] Value is 'purely social'.

(ii) Bailey does not recognise the polarity of the value form.

(iii) Not recognising the polarity of the value form, Bailey does not recognise the social antagonism expressed by that polarity, namely, that while money is immediately socially validated and directly exchangeable, commodities are not. As Marx reminds us, 'We see then that commodities are in love with money, but that "the course of true love never did run smooth"'.[71] The root of this antagonism is the social form of production, namely, privately undertaken production for unknown others in the market.

(iv) Not recognising the polarity of the value form, Bailey does not recognise the two value forms, the relative value form and the equivalent value form; consequently, Bailey cannot grasp money, which is the commodity exclusively

69 Marx 1976a, p. 168.

70 See Marx 1971a, p. 147; Marx 1974, p. 145.

71 Marx 1976a, p. 202.

in the equivalent form. When he says that every commodity is a measure of value that is 'equally real and equally nominal', Bailey effectively denies that there is money because he denies that there is any commodity that exclusively has the equivalent value form. In this, the narrowness of Bailey's theory induces him to deny a readily observed fact of life in capitalist societies, namely, that there is money (in Marx's sense of the exclusive commodity in the equivalent value form). Though Bailey talks of money, and even wrote a separate book on the subject, he does not prepare the conceptual space for it; consequently, commerce is reduced to barter.[72]

(v) With a theory that excludes money, Bailey is in no position to argue for the existence of value, which requires a unitary, public measure of value. In this respect, though he is wrong on both counts, since there is money and value, his thinking has the unintended consequence of showing that money and value stand or fall together. Actually, the commodity also stands or falls with money and value, since it belongs to the commodity that it is commensurable with other commodities, and that requires a common, public measure of value, i.e., money. Use values exchanged in barter are not commodities. Money does not make commodities commensurable; value does, but there is no value without money. So we can extend the previous observation and say that though Bailey is wrong to conclude that there are no commodities, no money and no value, he helps us see how the three belong together.

(vi) Bailey sees no inherent connection between production and exchange. Here he commits one of the most fundamental errors of classical (and neoclassical) economics, an error that makes a tenable theory of value unachievable. The root of the problem here, as in classical and neoclassical economics, is Bailey's failure to recognise that production always has a specific social form and purpose.

(vii) Bailey's theory of value, according to which value is determined solely in exchange, is the opposite extreme to Ricardo's one-sided theory that value is determined solely in production. Neither is tenable; flip-flopping between the two is inescapable when production and exchange are conceived of as independent of one another. Instead, a developmental conception of value that encompasses production and exchange, such as Marx came up with, is required.

(viii) By making the comparison of value across time unintelligible, Bailey makes money's functions as means of payment, store of value and capital inexplicable.

72 Bailey 1837.

(ix) Bailey's subjectivist conception of use value is untenable: there is no use value in general, no utility, no usefulness in abstraction from the particular physical features of useful objects. Against Bailey, Marx presses the point:

> it is through its own properties, its own qualities, that a thing is a use-value and therefore an element of wealth for men. Take away from grapes the qualities that make them grapes, and their use-value as grapes disappears for men and they cease to be an element of wealth for men.[73]

Marx does not overlook utility; he rejects it as a bad abstraction, a 'pseudo-concept', as Alasdair MacIntyre calls it.[74]

7 What Might Marx Have Learned from Bailey?

Bailey is a forerunner of Marx, in particular of Marx as a critic of Ricardo and the classical theory of value.[75] (i) As Marx states, Bailey is a value-form theorist. (a) Bailey grasps that value must be expressed and that the exchange-value relation is the only way that value can be expressed. As Bailey puts it, 'It is impossible to designate, or express the value of a commodity, except by a quantity of some other commodity'.[76] On that fundamental of value-form theory, Marx and Bailey are in agreement.

(b) Bailey, then, makes the investigation of the value form, that is, the exchange-value relation, an ingredient of any adequate theory of value. Marx sharpens his own theory of value by identifying the shortcomings of Bailey's, principally that Bailey does not recognise the exchange-value relation to be a polar relation that posits value in two different (in fact, antagonistic) forms, which Marx calls the relative value form and the equivalent value form. That failure results in another. Without the insight into the polarity of the value form and the distinction between the two forms of value, Bailey cannot reach an accurate conception of money as the necessarily exclusive commodity in the equivalent value form. Bailey's shortcomings bring home to Marx the need for an integrated theory of the commodity, exchange value, value, money and capital. His engagement with Bailey may help to explain three interrelated

73 Marx 1971a, p. 129. See also Marx 1976a, 126.

74 MacIntyre 1984, p. 64.

75 Marx wrote of Bailey, 'Still, despite the narrowness of his own outlook he was able to put his finger on some serious defects in the Ricardian theory' (Marx 1976a, p. 155, n. 25).

76 Bailey 1967, p. 26.

differences between Marx's first published account of the value form, in the *Critique*, and the account he gives in *Capital*.[77] Marx now begins his analysis of the value form with the 'simple, isolated, or accidental value-form', e.g. 20 yards of linen = one coat, of which he writes, 'the whole mystery of the form of value lies hidden in this simple form. Our real difficulty, then, is to analyze it'.[78] He stresses the polarity of the value form, and he devotes most of the subsection to the relative value form and the equivalent value form.[79]

(c) Marx may have learned from Bailey's (one sided) insistence that value does not exist prior to the exchange of commodities. Denying the existence of value prior to exchange provides Bailey a potent reason to insist that value is nothing intrinsic to commodities. If it were intrinsic, it would exist prior to the actual exchange of commodities. Value-form theorists of all stripes can learn from Bailey's insistence that exchange belongs to value, and some (notably Eldred and Hanlon) join with Bailey and assert that value is constituted solely in exchange.[80] Marx considers Bailey's exclusive focus on exchange to be one sided, but he accepts an aspect of Bailey's thinking, the thought that commodity exchange plays a co-constitutive role in the formation of value. Bailey's insight requires Marx to devise a developmental conception of value that qualifies the sense in which we may speak of value being present in products prior to their sale. Thus Marx describes the value present in products prior to their sale as 'latent'.[81] For Marx value is not actualised until a commodity is sold: 'Only the act of exchange can prove whether that labour is useful for others, and its product consequently capable of satisfying the needs of others'.[82] Value stands the Heisenberg Uncertainty Principle on its head: only by being measured in the act of exchange does value become fully determinate!

77 See Marx 1970a, pp. 45–9 and Marx 1976a, pp. 138–63. In the first edition of *Capital*, Marx gave two versions of the value-form analysis, both of which were superseded by the version in the second and later editions.

78 Marx 1976a, p. 139. Accordingly, Marx devotes 15 of the 25 pages of Section Three 'The value-form, or exchange-value' to the simple value form.

79 Neither the polarity of the value form nor the two antagonistic value forms were identified in the *Critique*.

80 Some commentators identify this one-sided, exchange-only type of value-form theory (e.g. Eldred and Hanlon 1981), which goes back to Bailey, with value-form theory *per se*. For a criticism of that view, see 'Avoiding Bad Abstractions: A Defence of Co-constitutive Value Theory', included in the present volume as Chapter 15.

81 Marx 1970a, p. 45.

82 Marx 1976a, p. 180.

(d) Bailey recognised the specific social character of value inasmuch as the expression of value can occur only in a commercial society, where wealth takes the commodity form.[83] What is more, Bailey is aware of this. Writing of Torrens's excellent observation 'that value is not essential to the idea of riches', Bailey wonders 'whether it [value] is not always implied, and whether the latter term would have been invented in a state of society in which there was no interchange of commodities'.[84] Even this limited insight into value-form theory constitutes a decisive blow against the classical labour theory of value: value cannot simply be embodied labour. As Bailey appreciated, when Smith and Ricardo agreed to purchasing power as a definition of value, they might have seen that such a definition could apply only where wealth was generally in the commodity form.[85]

Though Bailey grasps the historical specificity of value, he does not link the necessity to express value in the exchange-value relation with the specific social form of labour that produces such wealth. Marx does make the link:

> From the analysis of exchange-value it follows that the conditions of labour which create exchange-value are social categories of labour or categories of social labour, social not however in the general sense but in the particular sense, denoting a specific type of society.[86]

Bailey fails to recognise that the determination of the provisioning process by specific social forms cuts across production and distribution; this failure is characteristic of classical and neoclassical economics.

83 But Bailey, as we have seen, does not develop the key concepts properly.

84 Bailey 1967, p. 166n.

85 When pressed, Ricardo saw the logic of this, but dug in his heels and reaffirmed his (socially generic) labour theory of value: 'You say if there were no exchanges of commodities they could have no value, and I agree with you, if you mean exchangeable value, but if I am obliged to devote one month's labour to make a coat, and only one week's labour to make a hat, although I should never exchange either of them, the coat would be worth four times the value of the hat; and if a robber were to break into my house and take part of my property, I would rather that he took three hats than one coat. It is in the early stages of society, when few exchanges are made, that the value of commodities is most peculiarly estimated by the quantity of labour necessary to produce them, as stated by Adam Smith' (Ricardo's letter to Trower [who held a position similar to Bailey's], 4 July, 1821, IX, pp. 1–2, as cited in Rauner 1960, p. 51). Obviously, Ricardo here asserts the independence of value from exchange value, something that both Bailey and Marx emphatically reject.

86 Marx 1970a, pp. 31–2.

(ii) We saw that Bailey's proposal for the measurement of value, by which the values of two commodities are to be measured by comparing their respective exchange ratios to a third commodity, does not work. The comparison equivocates between the ratio of two numbers and the ratio of two quantities of different types of use value: it fudges where the dimension of the ratio is concerned. Thinking through the problems with Bailey's 'third commodity' account of the measurement of value may have helped Marx to refine his 'third thing' argument for value.[87]

(iii) Though Marx repudiates Bailey's modern conception of use value as purely subjective, Marx recognised that Bailey is right to insist on the subjective aspect of value. Demand is an ingredient of Marx's theory of value that gives this subjective aspect of value its due.[88]

(iv) Marx's highest praise for Bailey is for his recognition that a commodity need not be invariable in value to serve as the measure of value.[89] Marx adopts this view: the value of money, the measure of value, is variable, and unavoidably so. By showing that the relative values of all other commodities could perfectly well be expressed in a commodity of variable value, Bailey shed light on a common confusion in classical political economy. The (true) need for an invariable internal measure of value, which could not itself be a commodity, was confused with the (futile) search for an invariable external measure, a commodity whose value did not change:

> The problem of an 'invariable measure of value' was simply a spurious name for the quest for the concept, the nature, of value itself, the defin-

---

87 We find the basics of the 'third thing' argument – the replaceability of commodities due to their quantitative congruence is evidence of a 'common denominator' – albeit without the phrase 'third thing', already developed in the *Critique*: 'Considered as exchange-value, one use-value is worth just as much as another, provided the two are available in the appropriate proportion. The exchange-value of a palace can be expressed in a definite number of tins of boot polish ... Quite irrespective, therefore, of their natural form of existence, and without regard to the specific character of the needs they satisfy as use-values, commodities in definite quantities are congruent, they take one another's place in the exchange process, are regarded as equivalents, and despite their motley appearance have a common denominator' (Marx 1970a, p. 28). That common denominator is not money but rather what money expresses – value. Perhaps Marx came to call this 'common denominator' the 'third thing' due to Bailey's insistence that measuring the value of a commodity in another commodity required a third commodity.

88 On the role of demand in Marx's theory of value see Murray 2005a, pp. 58–61, included in the present volume as Chapter 9.

89 Marx 1970a, pp. 71–2n.

> ition of which could not be another value, and consequently could not be subject to variations as value. This was labour-time, social labour, as it presents itself specially in commodity production.[90]

(v) Another way in which Bailey is a forerunner of Marx concerns the plural 'transformation' problems. Bailey recognised not only that firms with different organic compositions of capital would have different rates of profit if commodities sold at their values but also that the same is true for firms with different turnover times (and for monopolistic and non-monopolistic firms).[91] Consequently, the classical labour theory of value, which is directed at individual commodities, is untenable. Marx's discussion of Bailey's insights into these problems with Ricardian value theory shows his awareness of the so-called 'transformation problem', namely, that the input prices to the circuits of capital must be 'transformed' to reflect prices of production, rather than the supposed individual values of *Capital* I.[92] Marx was unperturbed: 'This important deviation of cost-prices from values brought about by capitalist production does not alter the fact that cost-prices continue to be determined by values'.[93] Marx's theory of prices of production in the third volume of *Capital* belongs to his rethinking of Ricardian value theory in order to cope with differing organic compositions of capital and differing turnover times. It represents another fundamental way in which he distances himself from the classical labour theory of value. Marx's mature labour theory of value overthrew the theory that Bailey rightly criticised, which held that the prices of individual commodities were determined by their individual labour values. As Marx observes, the labour theory of value holds, but it holds only at the level of the total capital. There is no 'transformation problem' because there is nothing to transform; Marx did not offer, in *Capital* I, a theory of individual values, which he long knew to be untenable.

For a minor figure in the annals of political economy, Samuel Bailey had a major impact on political economy's most profound critic, Karl Marx.

---

90 Marx 1971a, pp. 134–5; Marx 1974, p. 132.

91 At a lower level of abstraction than *Capital* III, perhaps one that Marx envisioned when he projected writing a book on competition, he would need to come to grips with the transformation issues Bailey raises concerning monopoly price.

92 See Murray 2014, included in the present volume as Chapter 13.

93 Marx 1971a, p. 168; Marx 1974, p. 167. Note that what Marx calls 'cost-prices' here is what he calls 'prices of production' in *Capital* III.

CHAPTER 7

Unavoidable Crises: Reflections on Backhaus and the Development of Marx's Value-Form Theory in the *Grundrisse**

> But within bourgeois society, based as it is upon *exchange value*, relationships of exchange and production are generated which are just so many mines to blow it to pieces.[1]

∴

One hundred fifty years after Marx stopped work on the *Grundrisse*, we find turmoil in financial markets linked to sub-prime mortgage lending practices and a remarkable real estate bubble. What motivated Marx to write the *Grundrisse* was the first world crisis of capitalism, beginning in 1857. Then, as now, proposals for banking reform arose in answer to the financial crisis. Marx begins the *Grundrisse* with an extended criticism of the proposals advanced by the Proudhonist Alfred Darimon. Darimon soon leads Marx to one of the most revealing topics of his analysis of the capitalist mode of production, the value form, or exchange value. In not grasping the value form, Darimon failed to recognise why capitalism requires money and is crisis prone. While financial reforms may help to forestall or better manage crises, they cannot root them out. In thinking that the troubles of the capitalist mode of production could be overcome by making changes to circulation, Darimon exemplified misconceptions regarding the relationships among production, distribution, exchange and consumption that Marx addressed in the general introduction to the *Grundrisse*.

For Marx, crises provide dramatic, recurrent evidence for the most fundamental claim of his critique of political economy, namely, that the capitalist mode of production is historically specific and transitory. Marx's stomach

---

* Originally published as 'Unavoidable Crises: Reflections on Backhaus and the Development of Marx's Value-Form Theory in the *Grundrisse*,' in *Marx's Laboratory. Critical Interpretations of the 'Grundrisse'*, edited by Riccardo Bellofiore, Peter Thomas, and Guido Starosta (Leiden/Boston: Brill, 2013).

1 Marx 1986, p. 96.

turned at the economists' pronouncement: 'Thus there has been history, but there is no longer any'.[2] As Marx came to see, recognition of the historically specific character of the capitalist mode of production begins with the value form of the wealth it produces:

> The *value-form of the product of labour* is the most abstract but also most general *form* of the *bourgeois* mode of production, which hereby is characterised as a *specific* type of *social* mode of production and thereby likewise as *historical*. Therefore, if one misperceives it for the eternal natural form of social production, one, then, naturally also overlooks what is specific in the value-*form*, thus the *commodity*-form, and, further developed, the money-*form*, the capital-*form*, etc.[3]

Notice the weight that Marx places on social form here. Marx has been widely misunderstood because the questions that preoccupy him, questions regarding the specific social form and purpose of labour and wealth, lie outside the discursive horizon shared by the mainstream of modern philosophy and the social sciences, notably economics. There, Marx's questions do not register; they gain no traction. No wonder Marx's account of the specific social form of wealth in capitalist societies, the value form, has been overlooked, ignored, shunned, garbled and parroted, due not simply to its conceptual complexity or any shortcomings of Marx's multiple efforts to explicate it, but primarily because it aims at answering questions that few ever ask.

Over the past four decades, however, this interpretive situation has been changing. Certain currents in recent Marxian theory and Marx scholarship have been labelled 'the new dialectics' or 'value-form theory'.[4] A seminal text emphasising the mutuality of dialectics and value-form theory is Hans-Georg Backhaus's 1969 essay 'On the Dialectics of the Value-Form' ('*Zur Dialektik der Wertform*'). Backhaus trenchantly diagnosed many deep misconceptions held by the bulk of Marx's interpreters, without sparing Marx from criticism. In Backhaus's judgement, despite multiple attempts to work out his radically new ideas, Marx's dialectic of the value form flopped. Backhaus points out that Marx published four versions of the dialectic of the value form: in the first chapter of the 1859 *Critique*, in the first chapter of the first edition of *Capital* Volume I, in an appendix to the first chapter of the first edition, and in the first chapter of the second and later editions. Whether the first draft of *Capital* Volume I, which

---

2 Marx 1963b, p. 121.

3 Marx 1966b, p. 275. All translations from 'Ware und Geld' are my own.

4 See Arthur 2002a.

is almost entirely lost, stated the dialectic of the value form in terms much different from the two versions that appeared in the first published edition, we do not know. In all likelihood, prior to the four published versions, there was a draft in the *Original Version* (*Urtext*) of the *Critique*; unfortunately, that part of the manuscript is also lost. Surely an *Urtext* version, which may or may not have differed significantly from the *Critique* itself, would have been based on relevant sections of the *Grundrisse*.[5]

The present chapter will consider to what extent Marx's exploration of the value form in the *Grundrisse* counts as an early version of the dialectic of the value form and lays the basis for its presentations in the *Critique* and *Capital*. First, in order to understand what we are looking for in the *Grundrisse*, I will point out the scope and main ideas involved in Marx's value-form theory, using the *Critique* and *Capital* Volume I as primary points of reference. Second, I will turn to Backhaus with several purposes in mind. (a) I begin by highlighting a number of his seminal contributions. (b) I argue that Backhaus is wrong to attribute the gross failures to understand Marx to Marx's own mistakes and omissions, even if Marx did make them. Misconceptions this deep must be attributed to the blind spots created by 'the bourgeois horizon', the discursive horizon that dominates modern philosophy and social science. It excludes realism about form, including social form; hence it lacks the conceptual space for forms and the 'content of forms', which is largely the focus of Marx's inquiry. (c) I argue that Backhaus is wrong to charge Marx with failing to present a coherent theory of value and with offering no dialectic of the value form. My criticism extends to those who have followed in Backhaus's footsteps on these counts, among them, the Konstanz/Sydney group (Eldred and Hanlon), Michael Heinrich and Geert Reuten. By contrast, I will defend Marx's argument in *Capital* regarding 'the analysis of the commodity' and, more particularly, the dialectic of the value form as presented in Section Three of Chapter One. In the third part of the paper I will survey the extent to which Marx's dialectic of the value form is developed in the *Grundrisse*.

1 The Scope and Main Features of Marx's Value-Form Theory

The key insight of historical materialism provides the conceptual context needed for understanding Marx's theory of the value form. Marx, in his early collaboration with Friedrich Engels, developed historical materialism not sim-

5 See Heinrich 2004, p. 2.

ply to insist on the significance of wealth and its production, but to call attention to the overlooked phenomenological point that wealth and its production always have historically specific social forms and purposes. Marx and Engels write in *The German Ideology*: 'This mode of production must not be considered simply as being the reproduction of the physical existence of the individuals. Rather it is a definite form of activity of these individuals, a definite form of expressing their life, a definite *mode of life* on their part'.[6] Here Marx and Engels oppose traditional attitudes that, precisely because they abstract from the definite social forms that belong to the production of wealth, dismiss the latter as bearing solely on the mere 'reproduction of the physical existence of human beings', rather than determining their '*mode of life*'.[7] The traditional view finds in the provisioning for human life little food for thought. Marx's complaint against traditional ways of thinking is that they ignore the fact that wealth and its production always have historically specific social forms and that those forms are pervasive and of great consequence. The idea that specific social form reaches all the way down and therefore must be an element in the fundamental concepts of a social theory is the watershed idea of Marx's historical materialism. The value form, or exchange value, is a specific social form of the products of labour where the capitalist mode of production predominates. It is inseparable from value-producing labour, which is a specific social form of labour under capitalism.

With this background in mind, let us turn now to indicating the scope and main features of Marx's theory of the value form. Marx's theory of the value form is one aspect of his analysis of the commodity. The double character of the commodity as a use value that has an exchange value, that is, a valid price, leads Marx to argue that exchange value is the expression of a 'third thing' that is common to commodities, namely value. There is a double movement to Marx's theory of value: he reasons first from exchange value to value and then from value to exchange value. The dialectic of the value form, which argues that value necessarily appears as exchange value, belongs to Marx's joint examination of value's substance, the determination of its magnitude and its form of appearance. These three, value's substance, magnitude and its form of appearance, are inseparable in Marx's account. Failure to recognise that

6 Marx and Engels 1976b, p. 31.

7 'The production of life, both of one's own in labour and of fresh life in procreation, now appears as a twofold relation: on the one hand as a natural, on the other as a social relation – social in the sense that it denotes the co-operation of several individuals, no matter under what conditions, in what manner and to what end' (Marx and Engels 1976b, p. 43).

inseparability, in particular by splitting off the form of value from its substance and magnitude, leads to interpretive blind alleys.

The crux of Marx's value-form theory lies in the proposition that money is the necessary form of appearance of value.[8] That means that the price form *is* the value form, for only in money can the value of commodities be expressed. Furthermore, it means that commodities, value, exchange value, money and prices constitute, for Marx, a whole from which no moment can be extracted. He titles the first Part of *Capital* Volume I 'Commodities and Money' for good reason. As Marx repeatedly insists, what is exchanged in barter are use values, not commodities; commodities are use values that have (valid) prices.[9]

The necessity of money (as distinct from commodities) for the expression of value reveals a fundamental, if hard to discern, feature of the value form: it is necessarily *polar*. Furthermore, the polarity of the value form harbours an antagonism that makes capitalism irremediably prone to crises: 'It is by no means self-evident that the form of direct and universal exchangeability is an antagonistic form, as inseparable from its opposite, the form of non-direct exchangeability, as the positivity of one pole of a magnet is from the negativity of the other pole'.[10] Recognising the necessary polarity of the value form and the necessarily antagonistic character of that polarity are among Marx's major, if overlooked, discoveries.

Commodities and money are the two poles of the value form, which is another way of saying that the price form *is* the value-form. The value form, or exchange value, is the expression of the value of a commodity in the only thing that can express it, money. Marx, apparently drawing on Ricardo's phrase 'relative value', terms the pole in which the commodity whose value is being

8 See Murray 1993b, included in the present volume as Chapter 8. Marx had the idea of the necessity of money at least by the time of *The German Ideology* (1845), where he and Engels write, 'money is a necessary product of definite relations of production and intercourse and remains a "truth" so long as these relations exist' (Marx and Engels 1976b, p. 203). The necessity of money figures heavily into Marx's 1846 critique of Proudhon, *The Poverty of Philosophy*.

9 'Their [the products of labour] taking the form of commodities implies their differentiation into commodities [on the one hand] and the money commodity [on the other]' (Marx 1976a, p. 188, n. 1). (Compare also Marx 1976a, p. 179.) Compare this passage from the *Critique*, 'Direct barter, the spontaneous form of exchange, signifies the beginning of the transformation of use-values into commodities rather than the transformation of commodities into money. Exchange-value does not acquire an independent form, but is still directly tied to use-value' (Marx 1970a, p. 50).

10 Marx 1976a, p. 161, n. 26.

expressed finds itself, the relative value form.[11] At the other pole, money, in which the value of the other commodity is being expressed, occupies the equivalent value form. Marx writes of these two forms: 'The relative form of value and the equivalent form are two inseparable moments, which belong to and mutually condition each other; but, at the same time, they are mutually exclusive or opposed extremes, i.e. poles of the expression of value'.[12]

As a consequence, money has no price. We are, perhaps, better acquainted with the peculiarities of the equivalent form, but the relative form of value expresses in its own way three features of value that Marx uncovers in the exploration of the substance and magnitude of value in Sections One and Two of Chapter One. Two conclusions that Marx drew regarding the substance of value were (1) it is congealed abstract labour and (2) it is 'purely social'. The relative form of value expresses both of these features of the substance of value. The relative value form also expresses Marx's conclusion that the quantity of labour a commodity contains determines the magnitude of its value: 'A given quantity of any commodity contains a definite quantity of human labour. Therefore the form of value must not only express value in general, but also quantitatively determined value, i.e. the magnitude of value'.[13]

The relative value form accomplishes this by equating a definite quantity of the commodity with a definite quantity of money, where those quantities are determined by the quantities of labour each contain. (How else can the quantities of the two be fixed?) Marx then explores the consequences for the relative form of the fact that changes in productivity may decrease or increase the amount of labour contained in the commodity or money or both. He concludes, 'Thus real changes in the magnitude of value are neither unequivocally nor exhaustively reflected in their relative expression, or, in other words, in the magnitude of the relative value'.[14]

This provides Marx's answer to those who seek a fixed measure of value: there can be no such thing.

Direct exchangeability is what characterises the equivalent value form: its three peculiarities are (a) 'use-value becomes the form of appearance of its opposite, value';[15] (b) 'concrete labour becomes the form of manifestation of

11 Regarding Ricardo, see Marx 1963b, p. 43 and p. 47, note.

12 Marx 1976a, p. 140.

13 Marx 1976a, p. 144.

14 Marx 1976a, p. 146.

15 Marx 1976a, p. 148.

its opposite, abstract human labour';[16] and (c) 'private labour takes the form of its opposite, namely labour in its directly social form'.[17]

In the notorious Section Three of the first chapter of *Capital* Volume I, 'The Value-Form or Exchange-Value', Marx presents a dialectical argument for the necessity of money in order to express value by 'working backwards' from the price form to 'the simple, isolated, or accidental form of value'.[18] In presenting the dialectic of the value form in Section Three, Marx begins with the simple value form and works his way up to the money form (or price form). The dialectic proceeds by identifying the defects of each of the first three candidates to serve as the expression of value: the simple form, the total or expanded form, and the general form. Each new form, culminating in the fourth and final form, the money form, represents an advance over the previous one inasmuch as it more adequately expresses value. Finding a fully adequate expression of value is what drives the dialectic in Section Three: defects and advances are judged against this standard. Clearly, the examination of the substance and magnitude of value in Sections One and Two are necessary in order to establish the standard. Until we know what value is, we cannot ascertain what can adequately express it.[19]

Marx's presentation in Section Three is open to misinterpretation. First, in actuality, there is only one value form, the price form; the three inadequate

---

16 Marx 1976a, p. 150.

17 Marx 1976a, p. 151.

18 See Marx 1976a, p. 163. The version of Chapter One in the first edition contains much of what is familiar from the second and later editions of *Capital*; however, it has no sections, and its exposition of the value form ends not with the money form but with a curious form in which the value of a quantity of each commodity is expressed by a disjunction – which is its equivalent value form – of certain quantities of all the remaining commodities. This form is judged to be defective because it allows for no socially valid occupant of the general equivalent form (a point made in the second edition in regard to the defectiveness of the general form). The version of the dialectic of the value form offered as an appendix to the first edition does not have that odd fourth form; it has sections and concludes with the money form.

19 In his translation of Volume I of *Capital*, Ben Fowkes makes a mistake in labelling the sections and subsections under (a) 'The Simple, Isolated, or Accidental Form of Value'. He has sections (1) '*The two poles of the expression of value: the relative form of value and the equivalent form*' and (2) '*The relative form*' right, as well as the two subsections of (2): '(i) *The content of the relative form of value*' and '(ii) *The quantitative determinacy of the relative form of value*' correct. But then he makes what should be sections '(3) *The equivalent form*' and '(4) *The simple form of value considered as a whole*' into subsections (iii) and (iv) of (2). This mistake does not occur in the Moore and Aveling translation of *Capital*.

forms leading up to the money form or price form are conceptual devices, designed by Marx to instruct the reader by unpacking the price form in order to establish that it alone can express value.[20] The movements, then, from one form to the next, are dialectical ones that should not be treated as directly historical, even if they may have implications for the genesis of money and commodities.[21] Another way that Marx indicates that this is how he understands these forms is that he dedicates Chapter Two, 'The Exchange Process', to the actual genesis of money.[22]

This, then, is a further feature of how Marx investigates the value form; he offers an account of the genesis of money in the process of exchange.[23] This

20 One indication of this is that Marx insists on distinguishing the simple value form from the similar form for the direct exchange of products (barter), 'The direct exchange of products has the form of the simple expression of value in one respect, but not as yet in another. That form was x commodity A = y commodity B. The form of the direct exchange of products is x use-value A = y use-value B. The articles [*Dinge*] A and B in this case are not as yet commodities' (Marx 1976a, p. 181). Since articles A and B are not commodities precisely for the reason that there is no universal equivalent, no money, we must conclude that the simple value form is abstracted out of a social context in which there is money.

21 'The historical broadening and deepening of the phenomenon of exchange develops the opposition between use-value and value which is latent in the nature of the commodity. The need to give an external expression to this opposition for the purposes of commercial intercourse produces the drive towards an independent form of value, which finds neither rest nor peace until an independent form has been achieved by the differentiation of commodities into commodities and money' (Marx 1976a, p. 181).

22 See the first edition of Chapter One of *Capital* Volume I for a final, transitional paragraph to the second chapter. (This paragraph was omitted from later editions.) In it Marx stipulates that the treatment of the contradictory character of the commodity has up to that point been 'analytical' and that Chapter Two will take up the 'actual' relations of commodities to one another in the exchange process (Marx 1966b, p. 246). See also Marx 1976a, p. 280.

23 'It [money] is a crystallisation of the exchange-value of commodities and is formed in the exchange process' (Marx 1970a, p. 48). In the *Critique* we find many of the ideas of the first three chapters of *Capital* Volume I. These include the double movement from exchange value to value (substance and magnitude) back to exchange value as the necessary form of appearance and a version of the dialectic of the value form that delineates the simple form, the expanded or total form, the general form, and the money form, along with their defects and advances. While the terminology of the polarity of the value form and the two poles of the relative form and the equivalent form are not established in the *Critique*, the basic ideas and hints of the terminology are present. Key ideas associated with Section Four of *Capital* Volume I on the fetishism of the commodity are present, though the phrase

historical chapter is required by the account he offers of the money form, for only social action in the sphere of exchange can validate one commodity as the sole, socially valid 'universal equivalent'. 'Money necessarily crystallises out of the process of exchange, in which different products of labour are in fact equated with each other, and thus converted into commodities'.[24] In the chapter on the exchange process, Marx makes explicit the conundrum latent in the joint theory of the substance, magnitude and form of value presented in Chapter One – value and exchange are inseparable:

> [The exchange of two commodities] puts them in relation with each other as values and realises them as values. Hence commodities must be realised as values before they can be realised as use-values ... On the other hand, they must stand the test as use-values before they can be realised as values ... Only the act of exchange can prove whether that labour is useful for others, and its product consequently capable of satisfying the needs of others.[25]

Much of the controversy within and over 'value-form theory' involves playing one aspect of this conundrum off against the other.

The fetishism of commodities, which was listed as the fourth peculiarity of the equivalent value form in the appendix to the first edition of Chapter One, belongs to the analysis of the value form and appears in all four versions of the value-form analysis noted by Backhaus.[26] For Marx the value form of the product of labour, and the commodity and money fetishisms that are inseparable from it, are rooted in the peculiar social form of labour in capitalist societies, 'As the foregoing analysis has already demonstrated, this fetishism of the world of commodities arises from the peculiar social character of the labour which produces them'.[27] This recognition illustrates the point that Marx was making in the general introduction to the *Grundrisse*, namely, that production, distribution, exchange and consumption are inseparable.

'fetishism of the commodity' is not. Points that appear in Chapter Two, 'The Exchange-Process', in *Capital* Volume I are also present in the *Critique*. All of this material is found in the *Critique*, without any sections, in Chapter One, 'The Commodity'.

24 Marx 1976a, p. 181.

25 Marx 1976a, p. 179.

26 For example, 'it is a characteristic feature of labour which posits exchange-value that it causes the social relations of individuals to appear in the perverted [*verkehrte*] form of a social relation between things' (Marx 1970a, p. 34).

27 Marx 1976a, p. 165. Compare Marx 1970a, pp. 31–2.

Backhaus opens the door onto the tremendous scope of Marx's theory of the value form when he writes, 'The analysis of the logical structure of the value form is not to be separated from the analysis of its historical, social content'.[28] So the investigation of the vast 'qualitative sociological' consequences of the value form, which, as we see now, encompasses the commodity form and the money form, belong to the scope of Marx's inquiry into the value form.[29] By the same token, Marx's theory of the value form has momentous implications for historical dialectics and the philosophy of history.

2 Hans-Georg Backhaus's 'On the Dialectics of the Value-Form'

2.1 *Backhaus's Contributions*

Any reflection on Backhaus's essay 'On the Dialectics of the Value-Form' must begin with an appreciation of its contributions. Already on the first page we encounter four potent observations. (1) Marx's theory of value has been mistakenly identified with the classical, or Ricardian, labour theory of value. Marx's theory is actually cut from different cloth; it is all about the specific social form of labour. (2) Marx has been mistaken for a political economist, when, in fact, he is a profound critic of political economy. (3) What Rubin called the 'qualitative sociological' side of Marx's theory of value has been missed. (4) Marx's theory of the value form has been ignored, misunderstood or parroted. On the next page appears another agenda-setting finding. (5) The dialectical nature of Marx's presentation in *Capital* has been either ignored or grossly misunderstood. These are five of the most important broad theses taken up by the best Marx scholarship of the last four decades. To these Backhaus adds several more. (6) 'It is first to be recalled that the use-values are always posited in the price-form'.[30] (7) 'Innumerable authors ignore the claim of the labour theory of value to derive money as money and thus to inaugurate a specific theory of money'.[31] (8) 'Ricardo's false theory of money is the quantity theory, whose critique is intended by the analysis of the value-form'.[32] (9) 'The analysis of the

28 Backhaus 1980, p. 107.

29 'The basic error of the majority of Marx's critics consists of: 1) their complete failure to grasp the qualitative sociological side of Marx's theory of value' (I.I. Rubin 1972, pp. 73–4).

30 Backhaus 1980, p. 105. Compare to Martha Campbell's observation, 'Although Marx never regards exchange value as anything but money price, he does not specify that it is until he shows what money price involves' (Campbell 1997, p. 100).

31 Backhaus 1980, pp. 102–3.

32 Backhaus 1980, p. 108. Compare to Campbell 2005, especially pp. 144–5.

logical structure of the value form is not to be separated from the analysis of its historical, social content'.[33] All in all, Backhaus's contribution in this essay is remarkable.

2.2 *'A Certain Blindness' is the Problem*

Very early in the essay Backhaus starts to spread the blame for the disordered interpretive situation to Marx himself. 'The deficient appraisal [*Rezeption*] of the value-form analysis, however, is not to be attributed solely to *a certain blindness* to the problem on the part of interpreters. The inadequacy of its presentations can only be understood on the presupposition that Marx left behind no finished version of the labour theory of value'.[34]

So, Marx had the idea for a post-Ricardian theory of value that included a dialectical presentation of the value form, but he botched the job. Backhaus expresses further reservations about Marx's presentation, this time emphasising Marx's faulty or absent dialectics:

> In the Foreword to the first edition of *Capital* Marx speaks explicitly of the fact that 'dialectics' characterises his presentation of the labour theory of value. If the conventional interpretations without exception ignore these dialectics, then the question must be gone into whether the 'defectiveness of the presentation' concerns not only the value form analysis [Section Three] but also the first two sections in the first chapter of *Capital*.[35]

For Backhaus, then, there is a reflux from the problems with Marx's dialectic of the value form back to his account of the substance and magnitude of value.

I find Backhaus's attempt to spread the blame to Marx implausible, and I believe the attempt is implausible even if Backhaus is right that there are serious lapses in Marx's presentation.[36] In the next section of the paper I

33 Backhaus 1980, p. 107.

34 Backhaus 1980, pp. 99–100, my emphasis.

35 Backhaus 1980, p. 100.

36 Marx did worry about how he was presenting the analysis of the commodity and the dialectic of the value form. In a letter to Kugelmann (13 October 1866), Marx wondered if something was 'defective' [*Mangelhaft*] in the 'analysis of the commodity' in the *Critique* (Marx 1954a, pp. 131–2, my translation). Like Backhaus, Marx was troubled by the fact that so many 'good minds' [*'gute Köpfe'*] did not catch on. Here I think that Marx may have paid too little attention to how 'a certain blindness' can effect even good minds. In any case, Marx did make at least three or four attempts at improving his analysis of the commodity. To mention a few changes that may count as improvements: making

will defend Marx from Backhaus's charges. But, setting this defence aside, I do not find it credible that shortcomings in Marx's presentation can explain how interpreters can altogether miss the topic of the value form, or fail to notice the conceptual gulf separating Marx from Ricardo, or remain unaware of the bearing of Marx's theory of value on his theory of money, or overlook the dialectical nature of Marx's presentation in *Capital*. It is more plausible to attribute misinterpretations of this magnitude to 'a certain blindness' to the value form and to dialectics. The problem is one of discursive horizons.[37]

Underlying the major failures of interpretation that Backhaus identifies is an incapacity to detect the topic of the specific social form and purpose of wealth and labour. Backhaus notes that 'the "economistic one-sidedness" chastised by Marx consists in the fact that economics operates as a separate branch of the scientific division of labour on the plane of pre-constituted economic objects'.[38]

Fine, but Backhaus does not explain how these 'economic objects' are 'pre-constituted' or why they are objectionable. What is wrong about the way that 'economic objects' are 'pre-constituted' is that they exclude specific social form and purpose. Because human needs, labour and wealth always have specific social form and purpose, by omitting them from its fundamental concepts, economics engages in bad abstraction. As a consequence, the discourse of economics, which purports to be generally applicable, is impoverished – or worse, false. Marx grants that some general observations may be made about the provisioning process, but they do not constitute a science. The idea that there can be a generally applicable science of economics is a terrible misapprehension. In *Capital*, Marx's critique of political economy, he informs his readers from the opening sentence that his undertaking is not of the purportedly general sort. Rather, what he provides is a thorough investigation of social forms and purposes specific to the capitalist mode of production, beginning with the ana-

explicit the distinction between value (essence) and exchange value (appearance); the introduction of sections into the chapter on the commodity; the separation of the dialectic of the value form into its own section; the separation of the dialectic of the value form from the treatment of the exchange process; and the treatment of the fetishism of the commodity in a separate section. I do not think that we should take Marx's worries and his efforts at improving his presentation as evidence that there is something seriously wrong with it, as Backhaus does. It seems to me that his basic line of thought is sound and remains much the same going back to the *Grundrisse*, perhaps even to *The Poverty of Philosophy*.

37 With his phrase 'the bourgeois horizon' and similar ones, Marx frames the difficulties in these terms.

38 Backhaus 1980, p. 107.

lysis of the commodity form. Marx's discourse, then, is a radically different and vastly richer one, freed from the bad abstractions of economics.[39]

2.3 *A Defence of Marx's Dialectic of the Value Form*

I begin with a couple more of Backhaus's criticisms of Marx, on which I intend to focus my reply:

> To me it seems that the mode of presentation in *Capital* in no way makes clear the expository (*erkentnisleitende*) motive of Marx's value-form analysis, namely, the question 'why this content assumes that form'. The defective mediation of substance and form of value is already expressed in the fact that in the development of value a gap can be shown. The transition from the second to the third section of the first chapter is no longer sensible as a *necessary* transition.[40]

Put more bluntly, 'Marx's analysis of the commodity, then, presents itself as an unmediated "jump from ... the substance to the form of appearance"'.[41] In that case, Marx fails to meet the standard that Backhaus spells out for dialectics, 'The dialectical method cannot be restricted to leading the form of appearance back to the essence; it must show in addition why the essence assumes precisely this or that form of appearance'.[42]

I agree with this expectation; moreover, this is the standard that Marx set for himself and thought that he met. 'Our analysis has shown that the form of value, that is, the expression of the value of a commodity, arises from the nature of commodity-value'.[43] But did Marx succeed? I believe so.

Marx repeatedly states his intention to pursue a double movement, from exchange value to value (substance and magnitude) back to exchange value or the value form.[44] Put more abstractly, his strategy is to move from appear-

---

39 As Martha Campbell observes, 'there are no counterparts to Marx's economic concepts in either classical or utility theory' (Campbell 1993, p. 152).

40 Backhaus 1980, p. 101.

41 Ibid.

42 Backhaus 1980, p. 102.

43 Marx 1976a, p. 152. Even more explicit is the concluding sentence to the presentation of the dialectic of the value form in the first edition of the first chapter, 'What was of decisive importance, however, was to uncover the inner, necessary conjuncture [*inneren notwendigen Zusammenhang*] of value-*form*, value-*substance*, and value-*magnitude*' (Marx 1966b, p. 240).

44 After determining the substance of value, Marx interjects, 'The common factor in the

ance to essence to the necessity of the appearance based on the essence. This is the course that Marx follows. To show the necessity of these appearances (exchange values, in this case), we first have to get to the essence (value). The only justification for positing value, though, is that it appears. So the analysis of the commodity must start from the appearance of value, that is, the valid [*gültige*] prices of commodities. In a two-step argument, Marx reasons that the replaceability of commodities as exchange values demonstrates that their exchange values express something equal and so must be manifestations of a 'third thing' underlying their disparate natural characteristics that makes them commensurable.[45] This he calls value. The second step is to argue that congealed abstract labour must be that 'third thing'; it constitutes the substance of value, which is utterly abstract and wholly social. Marx proceeds to argue that the magnitude of value is determined by the amount of labour time contained in the commodity. These, then, are the three salient points for the dialectic of the value form that emerge from Marx's account of the substance and magnitude of value: (1) value is wholly abstract; (2) value is a purely 'social substance'; and (3) values are quantitatively definite as determined by the amount of labour time in the commodity. These three features of value provide standards against which candidates for the value form are to be judged. In Section Three Marx keeps calling our attention to this fact. This fits Backhaus's expectation of dialectics, to show why this essence, value, must take exactly that form of appearance, exchange-value (price).

---

exchange relation, or in the exchange-value of the commodity, is therefore its value. The progress of the investigation will lead us back to exchange-value as the necessary mode of expression, or form of appearance, of value. For the present [*zunächst*], however, we must consider the nature of value independently of its form of appearance [*Erscheinungsform*]' (Marx 1976a, p. 128). Problems arise in value-form theory when one mistakes treating the substance of value independently of the form value with taking the substance of value to be independent of the form of value. It is not, which is why Marx keeps reminding us that the substance, magnitude and form of value all go together. Once Marx completes the examination of the magnitude of value, he gives us another reminder that the dialectic of the value form is still to come, 'Now we know the substance of value. It is labour. We know the measure of its magnitude. It is labour-time. The form, which stamps value as exchange-value, remains to be analysed' (Marx 1976a, p. 131). Lastly, at the outset of Section Three, Marx flags the double movement of his analysis of the commodity, 'In fact we started from exchange-value, or the exchange relation of commodities, in order to track down the value that lay hidden within it. We must now return to this form of appearance of value' (Marx 1976a, p. 139).

45 See Murray 2005b and Murray 2006, included in the present volume as Chapters 16 and 17, respectively.

Backhaus skates over the first three paragraphs of Section Three, which precede the introduction of the simple form of value, giving us the impression that Marx has nothing to say about the transition from value's substance and magnitude to its form. In fact, Marx is not drawing a blank; he is making key arguments in those paragraphs, with more arguments to come when he identifies the defects and advances involved with the different value forms.

As Hegel realised, essence must appear; what other justification can there be for positing essence in the first place? Accordingly, Marx begins Section Three:

> Commodities come into the world in the form of use values or material goods [*Warenkörpern*], such as iron, linen, corn, etc. This is their plain homely, natural form. However, they are only commodities because they have a dual nature, because they are at the same time objects of utility and bearers of value. Therefore they only appear as commodities, or have the form of commodities, in so far as they possess a double form, i.e. natural form and value form.[46]

Commodities are use values and values. Value is the specific social form of the commodity, but how does value present itself? The natural form of a commodity gives expression to its nature as use value, but how can its specific social character, its value nature, be expressed? Immediately, we face a twofold conundrum posed by the results of the investigation into the substance of value: how can what is wholly abstract present itself to us in the material make-up of a commodity and how can what is wholly social appear in the natural form of the commodity? Yet value must appear. I cannot express the value of linen in linen. As Marx says, 20 yards of linen = 20 yards of linen is not an expression of value.[47] How then? The solution to the twofold conundrum leads us to exchange value, to the price form.

Marx offers the answer, here in the version from the first edition, 'But commodities are material things [*Sachen*], whatever they are they must be either materially [*sachlich*] or they must show in their own relationships with material things'.[48] Since commodities cannot show their value nature materially – value is supersensible, not material, as Marx reminds us with a coarse reference to Dame Quickly – they must show it in their relationships with other material things, with other commodities: 'Since a commodity cannot be related to

46 Marx 1976a, p. 138.

47 Marx 1976a, p. 140.

48 Marx 1966b, p. 227.

itself as equivalent, and therefore cannot make its own physical shape into the expression of its own value, it must be related to another commodity as equivalent, and therefore must make the physical shape of another commodity into its own value form'.[49] That is the fundamental point, and, as Aristotle observed, it can be illustrated just as well by the simple value form, for example, 20 yards of linen = 1 coat, as the money-form. Marx nicely pulls together this line of dialectical reasoning in the first-edition version of Chapter One:

> The commodity is by nature a twofold thing, use-value and value, the product of useful labour and congealed abstract labour. In order to present itself as what it is, it must therefore double its form. The commodity comes by the form of a use-value naturally. It is its natural form. Value-form it comes by only in commerce with other commodities. But its value-form must itself also be an objective form. The only objective forms of commodities are their useful shapes, their natural forms. Since the natural form of a commodity, linen for example, is precisely the opposite of its value-form, it must make another natural form, the natural form of another commodity into its value-form.[50]

The solution to the first part of the conundrum, how to represent the supra-sensible value of a commodity in a commodity, is just what is needed to solve the second part, how to represent something 'purely social' in the natural form of a commodity.[51] Marx reminds us of the second outcome of his investigation of the substance of value: 'However, let us remember that commodities possess an objective character as values only in so far as they are all expressions of an identical social substance, human labour, that their objective character as values is therefore purely social'.[52]

Marx follows this up, reasoning again from specific properties of the essence (value) to a specific form of its appearance (exchange value): 'From this it follows self-evidently that it [value] can only appear in the social relation between commodity and commodity'.[53] Value, which is 'purely social', cannot be expressed in the natural form of a single commodity, and, yet, in what

---

49 Marx 1976a, p. 148.

50 Marx 1966b, p. 229.

51 Marx later calls attention to this fact, 'in the expression of value of the linen the coat represents a supra-natural [*übernaturliche*] property; their value, which is something purely social' (Marx 1976, p. 149).

52 Marx 1976a, pp. 138–9.

53 Marx 1976, p. 139.

can value be expressed but the natural form of *another* commodity? Marx concludes: 'The simplest value-relation is evidently that of one commodity to another commodity of a different kind (it does not matter which one). Hence the relation between the values of two commodities supplies us with the simplest expression of the value of a single commodity'.[54]

As indicated earlier, Marx's presentation of the relative value form divides into two subsections. These two are designed to track the results of Marx's investigations of the substance of value and its magnitude, respectively. The first subsection rehearses the points we have just covered. As Marx puts it, the relative form of value expresses, 'everything our analysis of the value of commodities previously told us'.[55] In other words, Marx says he is doing just what Backhaus says a dialectical presentation should do. The relative form of value expresses the two conclusions that Marx drew regarding the substance of value: (1) it is congealed abstract labour and (2) it is 'purely social'.

The second subsection addresses the conclusions Marx reached regarding the magnitude of value. That the quantity of labour a commodity contains determines the magnitude of its value is also expressed in the relative value form: 'A given quantity of any commodity contains a definite quantity of human labour. Therefore the form of value must not only express value in general, but also quantitatively determined value, i.e. the magnitude of value'.[56]

Marx explicitly appeals to the results of the investigation of the magnitude of value (the essence) as a standard for the expression of value (appearance). This is accomplished by a definite quantity of the commodity in the relative value form equating itself with a definite quantity of another commodity, where those quantities are determined by the quantities of labour each contain.[57]

The value form gives expression to the contradictions of the commodity form, the overarching topic of the analysis of the commodity. The commodity is at once a material use value and a supersensible thing, value. Producing value, the concrete labour involved in making the commodity counts as abstract labour. Thirdly, as value producing, the privately undertaken labour employed in making the commodity counts as directly social labour. The value form expresses these three contradictions of the commodity in the three peculiarities of the equivalent value form. In the equivalent value form, value, which is supersensible, is expressed in a concrete use value; abstract labour is expressed

54 Ibid.

55 Marx 1976a, p. 143.

56 Marx 1976a, p. 144.

57 This point returns in Marx's insistence, in Chapter Three, that, to serve as the measure of value, money must itself be a valuable commodity.

in (the product of) concrete labour; and directly social labour is expressed in (the product of) privately undertaken labour.

Marx's dialectic of the value form in Section Three is completed by identifying the defects and the advances involved in the several candidates to be the value form, culminating in the conclusion that only the price form adequately expresses value. The defect of the simple value form is obvious enough: 'The expression of the value of commodity A in terms of any other commodity B merely distinguishes the value of A from its use-value, and therefore merely places A in an exchange-relation with any particular single different kind of commodity, instead of representing A's qualitative equality with all other commodities and its quantitative proportionality to them'.[58]

In other words, an adequate expression of value must present (1) the commodity's qualitative equality with all other commodities and (2) its quantitative proportionality to all other commodities.

The expanded or total form does that, but it has its own defects:

> Firstly, the relative expression of value of the commodity is incomplete, because the series of its representations never comes to an end ... Secondly, it is a motley mosaic of disparate and unconnected expressions of value. And lastly, if, as must be the case, the relative value of each commodity is expressed in this expanded form, it follows that the relative form of value of each commodity is an endless series of expressions of value which are all different from the relative form of value of every other commodity.[59]

So, the expanded form establishes no uniform relative value form.

These defects are corrected by the general [*Allgemeine*] value form. 'The commodities now present their values to us, (1) in a simple form, because in a single commodity; (2) in a unified form, because in the same commodity each time. Their form of value is simple and common to all, hence general'.[60]

Reminding us again that it is the nature of value that guides his judgements about how value must appear, Marx adds that 'By this form, commodities are, for the first time, really brought into relation with each other as values, or permitted to appear to each other as exchange values'.[61] One way in which this

58 Marx 1976a, p. 156.
59 Ibid.
60 Marx 1976a, p. 157.
61 Marx 1976a, p. 158.

is true hearkens back to the conclusion of the investigation of the substance of value that it is 'purely social':

> The general form of value, on the other hand, can only arise as the joint contribution of the whole world of commodities. A commodity only acquires a general expression of its value if, at the same time, all other commodities express their values in the same equivalent; and every newly emergent commodity must follow suit. It thus becomes evident that because the objectivity of commodities as values is the purely 'social existence' of these things, it can only be expressed through the whole range of their social relations; consequently the form of their value must possess social validity.[62]

One defect of the general form remains, and it concerns the social validity of the commodity in the equivalent value form:

> The universal equivalent form is a form of value in general. It can therefore be assumed by any commodity ... Only when this exclusion becomes finally restricted to a specific kind of commodity does the uniform relative form of value of the world of commodities attain objective fixedness and general social validity.[63]

For any commodity to attain this fixed, general social validity as the universal equivalent is not a matter of conceptual dialectics; it requires social action in the process of exchange. Consequently, the examination of the exchange process, Chapter Two of *Capital* Volume I, belongs to the complete investigation of the value form.

3 Value Form in the *Grundrisse*

The second sub-section under the treatment of the general value form in Section Three provides a natural transition into the final section of this paper, on the value form in the *Grundrisse*. What Marx's dialectic of the value form shows is that the contradictions inherent in the commodity form require money and register social antagonisms. Marx writes:

---

62 Marx 1976a, p. 159.

63 Marx 1976a, p. 162.

> It is by no means self-evident that the form of direct and universal exchangeability is an antagonistic form, as inseparable from its opposite, the form of non-direct exchangeability, as the positivity of one pole of a magnet is from the negativity of the other pole. This has allowed the illusion to arise that all commodities can simultaneously be imprinted with the stamp of direct exchangeability, in the same way that it might be imagined that all Catholics can be popes. It is, of course, highly desirable in the eyes of the petty bourgeois, who views the production of commodities as the absolute summit of human freedom and individual independence, that the inconveniences resulting from the impossibility of exchanging commodities directly, which are inherent in this form, should be removed. This philistine utopia is depicted in the socialism of Proudhon.[64]

The 'inconvenience' of world economic crisis spurred Marx to begin the *Grundrisse* with the critique of Proudhon's disciple Darimon.

It does not take Marx long to get at the underlying point of his critique of Darimon. Marx describes the crux of Darimon's reform proposals as follows:

> abolish this privilege of gold and silver, demote them to the level of all other commodities. Then you do not abolish the specific evil of gold and silver money, or of notes convertible into gold and silver. You do away with all evils. Or rather promote all commodities to the monopoly status now possessed by gold and silver. Let the Papacy remain, but make everyone Pope. Do away with money by turning every commodity into money and endowing it with the specific properties of money.[65]

Darimon's discursive horizons are the problem: the most important questions are not questions for him. Marx observes:

> The answer can often consist only in the critique of the question, can often be provided only by denying the question itself.
>
> The real question is: does not the bourgeois system of exchange itself make a specific instrument of exchange necessary. Does it not of necessity create a special equivalent of all values? ... Darimon naturally passes over this question with enthusiasm.[66]

64 Marx 1976a, p. 161, n. 26.
65 Marx 1986, pp. 64–5.
66 Marx 1986, p. 65.

Of course, this question is the one that Marx takes up in the dialectic of the value form in *Capital*, and, as we have seen, his answer is yes, commodity exchange requires money. Moreover, money expresses the contradictions of the commodity form antagonistically. Marx gives the same answer in the *Grundrisse*, where, in his 'chapter on money', he works out so many of the ideas that appear in the first three chapters of *Capital* Volume I.

Darimon proposes to eliminate money and the inconveniences associated with it by replacing money with labour-time certificates.[67] Marx had already criticised the earlier 'labour money' schemes of Bray and Gray in *The Poverty of Philosophy*. Marx renews his criticism in the *Grundrisse*, observing:

> The first basic illusion of the champions of labour-time tickets consists in this: that by abolishing the nominal distinction between real value and market value, between exchange value and price, by expressing value in labour time itself instead of in a particular objectification of labour time, SAY, gold and silver, they also remove the real distinction and contradiction between price and value. On that basis it is self-evident how the simple introduction of labour-time tickets would remove all crises, all defects of bourgeois production. The money price of commodities = their real value; demand = supply; production = consumption; money simultaneously abolished and retained; the labour time whose product the commodity is, which is materialised in the commodity, would need merely to be stated to produce its corresponding counterpart in a token of value, in money, in labour-time tickets. Each commodity would thus be directly transformed into money, and gold and silver for their part reduced to the rank of all other commodities.[68]

The 'labour money' proposal denies the polarity of the value form; effectively, it wants all commodities to be in the equivalent form, that is, to be directly exchangeable, directly social. In arguing that price does not equal value, Marx is arguing that commodities are not directly exchangeable. Due to unavoidable fluctuations in supply and demand, prices fluctuate around values, while at the same time values may change due to changes in productivity. Marx reasons

67 The use of the word 'ticket' in the *Collected Works* translation of the *Grundrisse* is questionable since Marx's point in comparing Robert Owen's 'labour money' to theatre tickets was precisely to say that they had nothing in common with the 'labour money' of Bray, Gray, Proudhon and Darimon. See Marx 1976a, pp. 188–9, n. 1.

68 Marx 1986, p. 76.

that because price does not equal value, because commodities are not directly exchangeable, labour time cannot express value; money must:

> *Because price does not equal value, the element determining value, labour time, cannot be the element in which prices are expressed. For labour time would have to express itself at once as the determining and the non-determining element, as the equivalent and the non-equivalent of itself.* Because labour time as a measure of value exists only ideally, it cannot serve as the material for the comparison of prices. (This also explains how and why the value relationship assumes a material and distinct existence in [the form of] money. This point to be developed further.) The distinction between price and value demands that values as prices be measured by a yardstick other than their own. Price as distinct from value is necessarily *money price*.[69]

As this passage shows, Marx's response to Darimon is to reject 'labour money', to affirm the necessity that value be expressed in money prices and to set himself the task of working through the dialectic of the value form in order to explain 'how and why the value relationship assumes a material and distinct existence in [the form of] money'.

In the pages that follow, a section called 'The Origin and Essence of Money', Marx explores the dialectics of the value form, anticipating many of the points that are better articulated and more deliberately developed in the *Critique* and the first two editions of *Capital*. Since the form of value must express value, we must first know what value is. Marx answers that the value of the commodity is something 'different from the commodity itself' because as use values, commodities 'are of course distinct, possess different properties, are measured in different units, are incommensurable'.[70] Yet 'value is a commodity's quantitatively determined exchangeability'.[71] The quantitative determination of value presupposes that 'As values, all commodities are qualitatively equal and only quantitatively different, hence they can be measured in terms of each other and are mutually replaceable (exchangeable, convertible into each other) in definite quantitative proportions'.[72]

69 Marx 1986, pp. 77–8. As a consequence, speculative bubbles and related crises are unavoidable. The problem is that prices may not reflect values, but there is no reliable way to tell since price is the only observable measure of value.

70 Marx 1986, p. 78.

71 Ibid.

72 Ibid.

In *Capital* Volume I Marx appeals to this 'mutual replaceability' to prove that there is some 'third thing' that commodities have in common, which he calls 'value'.[73] Since as use values commodities are incommensurable, the 'third thing' must be something abstract, something other than any natural property of a commodity. Marx identifies labour as this 'third thing' and the quantity of labour time as the determinant of the magnitude of value: 'Its value ... is equal to the quantity of labour time realised in it'.[74] If value is nothing natural, what sort of thing is it? The answer anticipates *Capital* Volume I: 'value is their social relationship'.[75] In short order we have here in the *Grundrisse* the basics of Marx's account of the substance and magnitude of value in place: the substance of value is something abstract, 'labour', which is wholly social (non-natural). The magnitude of value is determined by the amount of labour time.

A phrase that Marx employs again and again throughout this section is 'as value, the commodity ...' Here is a revealing case:

> As value, the commodity is at the same time an equivalent for all other commodities in a particular ratio. As value, the commodity is an equivalent: as an equivalent, all its natural properties are extinguished; it no longer bears any particular qualitative relationship to other commodities, but it is the general measure, the general representative, and the general means of exchange for all other commodities. As value it is *money*.[76]

This 'as value' rubric is Marx's way here in the *Grundrisse* of working out the dialectic of the value form. For the whole point of the value form is to express the nature of the commodity as value.[77] Only money accomplishes that. We see here the terminology of the 'equivalent value-form' in development; in the exchange-value relation, it is precisely the role of money to function 'as value', that is, to be the equivalent.

---

73 Marx 1976a, p. 127.

74 Marx adds the qualification, 'This proposition is based on the assumption that exchange value = market value; real value = price' (Marx 1986, p. 78), just after he has been hammering away at the point that the difference between value and price is not nominal, as it would have to be for the 'labour money' schemes to work.

75 Marx 1986, p. 78.

76 Marx 1986, p. 79.

77 Marx later calls attention to this: 'In short, all the properties that are enumerated as particular properties of money are properties of the ... product as value as distinct from the value as product' (Marx 1986, p. 79).

Of course, Marx does not mean that the commodity is money; rather, and here he affirms the basic point of value-form theory, 'its property as value not only can, but must, at the same time acquire an existence distinct from its natural existence'.[78] Why?

> Because, since commodities as values are only quantitatively different from each other, every commodity must be qualitatively distinct from its own value. Its value therefore must also have an existence qualitatively distinguishable from it, and in the actual exchange this separability must become an actual separation, because the natural distinctions between commodities must come into contradiction with their economic equivalence; the two can exist alongside one another only through the commodity acquiring a dual existence. A natural existence and alongside it a purely economic one.[79]

Marx follows up with an 'as value' litany of the contradictions inherent in the commodity form, each of which demonstrates the necessity of money:

> As value, every commodity is uniformly divisible; in its natural existence, it is not. As value it remains the same, no matter how many metamorphoses and forms of existence it goes through; in reality, commodities are exchanged only because they are different and correspond to different systems of needs. As value, it is general, as an actual commodity it is something particular. As value, it is always exchangeable; in actual exchange it is exchangeable only if it fulfils certain conditions. As value, the extent of its exchangeability is determined by itself ... in actual exchange, it is exchangeable only in quantities related to its natural properties and corresponding to the needs of the exchangers.[80]

Among other points found here is the idea that direct exchangeability defines the equivalent (money).

Though Marx does not work up the four value forms that he employs from the *Critique* onwards, in effect, he calls attention to the defect of the simple value form when he writes: 'in order to realise the commodity at a stroke as exchange value and to give it the general effect of exchange value, its exchange

78 Marx 1986, p. 79.

79 Ibid.

80 Ibid.

for a particular commodity is not sufficient. It must be exchanged for a third thing which is not itself a particular commodity but the symbol of the commodity as commodity, of the commodity's exchange value itself; which therefore represents, say, labour time as such, say a piece of paper.'[81]

He follows this with the familiar observations that this 'symbol' 'presupposes general recognition', 'is a product of exchange itself, not the execution of a preconceived idea'.[82] Here Marx makes two key points in value-form theory: money requires social validation that comes only through the exchange process, and the emergence of money through the exchange process is spontaneous. 'In fact, the commodity which serves as the mediator of exchange is only transformed into money, into a symbol, gradually. As soon as that has happened, a symbol of the mediating commodity can in turn replace the commodity itself'.[83] This claim that money as means of circulation can be replaced by a non-commodity symbol, such as a paper bill, recurs in Marx's treatment of the topic in Chapter Three of *Capital* Volume I.

Marx then brings the foregoing investigation into the value form back to bear on his critique of Darimon's reform proposals:

> The exchange value of a product thus produces money alongside the product. Just as it is impossible to abolish complications and contradictions arising from the existence of money alongside specific commodities by changing the form of money … it is likewise impossible to abolish money itself, so long as exchange value remains the social form of products. It is essential to understand this clearly, so as not to set oneself impossible tasks, and to know the limits within which monetary reform and changes in circulation can remodel the relations of production and the social relations based upon them.[84]

Marx briefly alludes to what we recognise as the fetishism of the commodity and of money: 'In proportion as the producers become dependent upon exchange, exchange appears to become independent of them; the rift between the product as product and the product as exchange value appears to widen. Money does not create this opposition and this contradiction; on the contrary, their development creates the apparently transcendental power of money'.[85]

81 Marx 1986, p. 82.
82 Ibid.
83 Ibid.
84 Marx 1986, p. 83.
85 Marx 1986, p. 84.

As the commodity form is generalised, producers become increasingly subject to the power of the mutual relations of their own products, that is, to the price system. In the same process, social power concentrates in valuable commodities and money.

By way of exploring the consequences of the value form, Marx poses a follow-up question: 'The next question which confronts us is this: does not the existence of money alongside commodities contain from the outset contradictions inherent in this very relationship?'[86] He has already prepped us for the answer, which is 'yes'. First, he observes, 'the contradiction between its [the commodity's] specific natural properties and its general social properties, contains from the outset the possibility that these two separate forms of existence of the commodity are not mutually convertible'.[87] Marx will later express this point in terms of the polarity of the value form (of which there has been no mention through these parts of the *Grundrisse*), which dictates that only the commodity in the equivalent value form (that is, money) is directly exchangeable. Commodities, which are in the relative value form, are not. The next three consequences concern topics that Marx takes up in *Capital* after the first two chapters.

Second, the necessity of money to express value splits exchange into 'two mutually independent acts: exchange of the commodity for money, exchange of the money for a commodity, buying and selling ... their immediate identity ceases to exist. They may correspond or not ... It is possible that consonance between them may now be fully attained only by passing through the most extreme dissonances'.[88]

Crises, then, are native to the generalization of the commodity form of wealth.

Third, the separation of buying and selling opens the door to a merchant estate. The separation between the motives of merchants and consumers can give rise to trade crises.[89] Moreover, the rise of a merchant estate, whose characteristic form of circulation is M-C-M (actually, M-C-M + ΔM – the first form of capital), indicates the reversal consequent to the emergence of the value form (money), 'Money is originally the representative of all values; in practice it is the other way round, and all real products and all labour become representatives of money'.[90] Marx's statement that 'it is inherent in money

86 Ibid.
87 Ibid.
88 Marx 1986, p. 85.
89 Marx 1986, p. 86.
90 Marx 1986, p. 87.

… to turn itself from a means to an end' suggests that money presupposes capital.[91]

A fourth consequence of the value form is that 'money also comes into contradiction with itself and its determination because it is itself a particular commodity (even if only a symbol) and thus, in its exchange with other commodities, is again subject to particular conditions of exchange which contradict its universal unconditional exchangeability'.[92]

These difficulties, which might include recoinage issues, a dual monetary standard (silver and gold) and competing fiat currencies, bring home the problems involved in establishing the social validity required by the money form.

Marx's explorations in the *Grundrisse* of the 'qualitative sociological' and historical implications of the value form deserve separate treatment.[93] I will conclude by selecting just a few highlights from this rich material. Marx's observations concern people's attitude toward things, toward their own productive activities and toward other persons. Here Marx emphasises the venality that comes with the value form of the product of labour:

> The exchangeability of all products, activities, relationships for a third, *objective* entity, which in turn can be exchanged for everything without distinction – in other words, the development of exchange values (and of monetary relationships) is identical with general venality, with corruption. General prostitution appears as a necessary phase in the development of the social character of personal inclinations, capacities, abilities, activities. More politely expressed: the universal relationship of utility and usefulness.[94]

Regarding attitudes towards one's productive activities and toward other persons, Marx observes:

> The absolute mutual dependence of individuals, who are indifferent to one another, constitutes their social connection. The social connection is expressed in *exchange-value*, in which alone his own activity or his product becomes an activity or product for the individual himself. He

91 Marx 1986, p. 88.

92 Ibid.

93 A number of these insights turn up in Section Four of Chapter One, on the fetishism of the commodity.

94 Marx 1986, pp. 99–100.

> must produce a general product – *exchange value*, or exchange value isolated by itself, individualised: *money*. On the other hand, the power that each individual exercises over the activity of others or over social wealth exists in him as the owner of *exchange values*, of *money*. He carries his social power, as also his connection with society in his pocket.[95]

As indifferent to one another, participants in commerce are guided strictly by their private interest. But Marx is quick to disabuse us of the idea that this private interest is something natural, which commercial society has liberated from the encumbrances of traditional societies: 'The point is rather that private interest is itself already a socially determined interest and can be attained only within the conditions laid down by society and with the means provided by society, and therefore tied to the reproduction of these conditions and means. It is the interest of private persons; but its content, as well as the form and means of its realisation, are given by social conditions that are independent of them all'.[96]

The society in which the product of labour takes the value form as its social form is one where purely private interests clash with one another within an alienated system of 'absolute mutual dependence', a price regime in which people are 'ruled by *abstractions*'.[97] As such, the emergence of the value form as the specific social form of the product of labour marks a watershed in world history. Marx employs this observation to set out a three-stage account of world history, whose third stage lies in the future:

> Relationships of personal dependence (which originally arise quite spontaneously) are the first forms of society, in which human productivity develops only to a limited extent and at isolated points. Personal independence based upon dependence *mediated by things* is the second great form, and only in it is a system of general social exchange of matter, a system of universal relations, universal requirements and universal capacities, formed. Free individuality, based on the universal development of the individuals and the subordination of their communal, social productivity, which is their social possession [*Vermögen*], is the third stage. The second stage creates the conditions for the third. Patriarchal conditions and those of antiquity (likewise feudal ones) therefore decline with the

95 Marx 1986, p. 94.
96 Marx 1986, p. 95.
97 Marx 1986, p. 101.

> development of trade, luxury, *money*, *exchange value*, in the same measure in which modern society grows with them step by step.[98]

Marx underlines the point that the second stage creates the conditions for the third by observing: 'Universally developed individuals, whose social relationships are their own communal relations and therefore subjected to their own communal control, are not products of nature but of history. The degree and the universality of development of the capacities in which this kind of individuality becomes possible, presupposes precisely production on the basis of exchange value, which, along with the universality of the estrangement of individuals from themselves and from others, now also produces the universality and generality of all their relations and abilities'.[99]

In the recurrent crises precipitated by the value form, Marx saw catalysts for that third historical stage.

98 Marx 1986, p. 95.

99 Marx 1986, p. 99.

CHAPTER 8

The Necessity of Money: How Hegel Helped Marx Surpass Ricardo's Theory of Value*

Marx's theory of value has long been confused with Ricardo's labour theory, and, in the wake of Piero Sraffa's revival of Ricardian thought, we now discover a whole school of Marxist (or post-Marxist) economics operating on neo-Ricardian assumptions.[1] However, Marx's theory of value is cut from different cloth than Ricardo's, a point to which Marx called attention in the very first chapter of *Capital*. There he emphasised the centrality (and originality) of his distinction between concrete and abstract labour, further characterised the abstract labour that constitutes value as 'socially necessary', described value as a 'social substance' and a 'ghostly objectivity', and introduced a seminal yet seldom acknowledged innovation into political economy – the analysis of the value form. In this chapter I hope to make plainer the dialectical logic of the value form as Marx presents it. To accomplish this I trace the history of Marx's engagement with Hegel's philosophy – his logic in particular – showing how Marx acquired the conceptual resources that enabled him to overcome Ricardo's theories of value and capital. Unless the distinctive logic operating in Marx's theories of value and capital is appreciated, his unique achievements go unrecognised. Contrary to Joan Robinson's complaint that smatterings of 'Hegelian stuff and nonsense' litter *Capital*, I argue that it is precisely the lessons learned from Hegel that make *Capital* great.

Marx's critical engagement with Hegel's logic, particularly his logics of essence and the concept – both as pure theories and as Hegel put them into practice (notably in *The Philosophy of Right*) – was an early and decisive element in his intellectual development. Hegel characterised the study of logic as 'the absolute education and breeding of consciousness', and Marx's was a 'well-

---

* Originally published as 'The Necessity of Money: How Hegel Helped Marx Surpass Ricardo's Theory of Value', in *Marx's Method in 'Capital'*, edited by Fred Moseley (Atlantic Highlands, N.J.: Humanities Press, 1993), pp. 37–61, reprinted with the kind permission of Humanity Books.

1 I have treated topics of this chapter as well as related ones in my *Marx's Theory of Scientific Knowledge* (Murray 1988a) and 'Karl Marx as a Historical Materialist Historian of Political Economy' (Murray 1988b).

bred' consciousness.[2] Hegel pointed to the lack of this logical education as the chief shortcoming of scientific empiricism:

> The fundamental illusion in scientific empiricism is always this, that it uses the metaphysical categories of matter, force, those of one, many, universality, also infinity, etc. Furthermore, [it] extends *implications* along the thread of such categories, whereby [it] presupposes and applies syllogistic forms, and in all this [it] does not know that it itself carries on and contains metaphysics and uses those categories and their connections in a fully unconscious manner.[3]

Marx has this 'fundamental illusion' in mind when, in a footnote to his treatment of the value form in the first edition of *Capital*, he levels against the economists just that complaint:

> It is hardly surprising that the economists, wholly under the influence of empirical [*stofflicher*] interests, have overlooked the content of the form of the relative expression of value, when before Hegel, professional logicians even overlooked the content of the form of the paradigms of judgment and syllogism.[4]

By concentrating on certain episodes in Marx's development of a logically 'well-bred' consciousness in the first part of the chapter, I seek to identify what Marx learned from Hegel, as well as the criticisms he made of Hegel, in ways that will illuminate his mature critique of political economy, which is the focus of the second part.

I believe that Hegel's philosophy functioned as a heuristic guide as Marx worked out his critique of capitalism, a point best made by reference to the Paris manuscript critique of Hegel. Hegel surely aided Marx in understanding capitalism, but conceiving of him as the logician of capital may not have made Marx a more accurate interpreter of Hegel.[5] My purpose, however, is to explicate Marx's use of Hegel as he understood him, not to judge this interpretation.

---

2 Hegel 1969, p. 58, translation revised by P.M.

3 Hegel 1975, p. 62, translation revised by P.M.

4 Marx 1966b, p. 274; translation revised by P.M.

5 The fact that Marx read Hegel so much in the light of various Hegelians, including amateurs like Szeliga and Proudhon, also may have blurred his outlook on Hegel himself.

Since the Hegelian essence logic, whereby the essence necessarily appears as something other than itself, is the pivotal conceptual resource for Marx's theory of value – value necessarily appears as something other than itself, namely money (price) – it is the centre of attention in much of what follows.

1 Marx's Critique of Philosophy

1.1 *The Standard Essence-Appearance Model and Its Hegelian Critique*

The standard essence-appearance model mistakes essence for a real but strangely unobservable thing hidden behind the curtain of appearances, and it admits of no logical relationship between essence and appearance. (This is just the model operative in Ricardo's theory of value: value is something real and independent, 'embodied labour' secreted in commodities, and no thought is given to showing any logical connection between value and its appearance, price). In fact, these two features of the standard model amount to much the same thing. If the essence is reified, it stands alone, logically free of the appearances. The relationship between essence and appearances is conceived on the model of two types of thing: one, sensuously manifest yet dispensable (appearances); the other, real yet unobservable, except to pure reason (essence). In this model of essence and appearance, science must be a one-way street, externally (since there is no internal relation between independent entities) relating the appearances to their real basis in the world of essence. Just why this essence should have these appearances is never raised.

A prime example of this thinking is provided by Descartes' analysis of the bit-turned-blob of wax in his *Meditations*. After wondering how we know a bit of wax to be the same thing after all its sensuous appearances have been altered, Descartes concludes:

> The truth of the matter perhaps, as I now suspect, is that this wax was neither that sweetness of honey, nor that [pleasant] odor of flowers, nor that whiteness, nor that shape, nor that sound, but only a body which a little while ago appeared to my senses under these forms and which now makes itself felt under others.[6]

Descartes attributes the primary qualities (extension, flexibility, duration and movability) to the body of the wax. In making this famous distinction between

6 Descartes 1960, pp. 87–8.

primary and secondary qualities (colour, touch, taste, smell, sound), Descartes engages the standard model of essence and appearance that accounts for differing appearances by referring them to a common underlying essence.

In the Cartesian model, Hegel recognises a classic case of Enlightenment reification and forgetfulness. Hegel objects that Descartes recasts primary qualities into the logic of secondary qualities, that is, into the logic of immediacy (the logic of being). Hegel takes his clue from Descartes' own words:

> But what is here important to notice is that perception [or the action by which we perceive] is not a vision, a touch, nor an imagination, and has never been that, even though it formerly appeared so; but is solely an inspection by the mind.[7]

According to Descartes, perception is not a matter of (sensuous) imagination, but the activity of pure understanding. In one respect Descartes' observations do not differ from Hegel's, for Hegel recognises in Descartes' statements the admission that the distinction between essence and appearance – primary and secondary qualities – posits a distinction between two logics of thought: intuition and understanding. Descartes errs by reifying the concepts of the understanding (primary qualities), forcing them into the same mould as immediate intuitions or secondary qualities.[8] But primary qualities are – by Descartes' insistence – in principle non-observable, non-sensuous. Likewise, Descartes forgets that the concepts of the understanding arise only by abstracting from sensuous intuitions. In terms of Francis Bacon's witty metaphor, in thinking that he knows the wax solely by means of the understanding, Descartes the bee absentmindedly mistakes himself for a spider.[9]

In this light we see why Hegel writes that 'the essence must appear'. Essence must show itself in something that is not immediately itself, precisely because it has no immediate existence – it does not follow the logic of being. Essence must appear because it is a being of reflection, and it pertains to the logic of reflec-

---

7 Descartes 1960, p. 88.

8 Descartes writes: 'But when I distinguished the real wax from its superficial appearances, and when, just as though I had removed its garments, I consider it all naked' (Descartes 1960, pp. 89–90).

9 In aphorism XCV of *The New Organon*, Bacon writes: 'The men of experiment are like the ant, they only collect and use; the reasoners resemble spiders, who make cobwebs out of their own substance. But the bee takes a middle course: it gathers its material from the flowers of the garden and of the field, but transforms and digests it by a power of its own' (Bacon 1960, p. 93).

tion that something be given for reflection. That something is appearance. (How far, after all, would Descartes have gotten in knowing the wax without having sensed it?)[10] Under this dialectical conception of essence and appearance,[11] science is no longer a one-way street that externally relates appearances to essence; it works both from the appearances to the essence and from the essence to the appearances.[12] Appearances are no longer viewed as extraneous to the essence. Hegel's dialectical conception of essence thus overcomes the one-sidedness of the standard view, which overlooks the nature of reflection. Essence, for Hegel, includes the complete logical figure, the appearances (which are appearances only by being reflected) and that which is reflected in them. It would be a terrible mistake to conclude from Hegel's statement 'the essence must appear as something other than itself' that we should ignore the appearances precisely because they are not the essence. Rather, the appearances belong to the complete concept of the essence; appearance and essence are inseparable. This is precisely the logic that must be understood in order to grasp what sets Marx's theory of value off from the Ricardian.

1.2 *Marx's Criticisms of Hegel's Logic*

Though he draws heavily on Hegel's criticisms of conventional categories, Marx has a less optimistic understanding of the dialectic of essence than the one he attributes to Hegel. According to Marx, Hegel believes that the oppositions

---

10 Descartes states that imagination (taken here to include sensation) is non-essential to his thinking: 'I notice that this ability to imagine which I possess, in so far as it differs from their power of conceiving, is in no way necessary to my nature or essence, that is to say, to the essence of my mind' (Descartes 1960, p. 127).

11 I have no closing arguments for the notion of necessity operative here, but it is a fact of our use of language that non-causal claims of necessity are common, e.g., without property there can be no theft. A good deal of philosophical energy has been spent – notably by David Hume and Immanuel Kant – to account for these claims of necessity. The analytic-synthetic distinction put forward by Kant explains many such claims in terms of analyticity, that is, as tautologies. It took him most of a long, hard book to try to explain necessity of a non-tautological sort. It is fair to see in Hegel a forerunner of Quine in rejecting the analytic-synthetic distinction, and with it the nominalist effort to reduce all necessity to a matter of human conventions for the use of terms. Dialectical logic extends ordinary judgments about how concepts are connected, without either the 'dogma' of the analytic-synthetic distinction or any sweeping philosophical prohibitions against our ordinary attributes of necessity.

12 Marx pursues this double movement in his accounts of value and capital in *Capital*. See the treatment of value in the second part of this chapter.

inherent in essence can be reconciled through the mediation of a third party: For example, the state can reconcile the antagonisms provoked by civil society. For Marx, however, the very opposition of essence and appearance needs to be uprooted, not mediated; the logic of essence poses irreconcilable conflicts rather than a necessary differentiation that pushes on to higher unity. Third parties, such as heaven, the state, or money, signal submerged conflict, not achieved harmony. Marx's perceived differences with Hegel regarding the logics of essence and the concept are best examined in the context of two early works, namely his *Critique of Hegel's 'Philosophy of Right'* and the essay on Hegel's philosophy among the Paris manuscripts.

1.2.1 The Philosophy of Right

In Hegel's political philosophy, the incarnation of mediation in the state is the law-making power, where monarch and bureaucracy come into contact with the people, the atoms of civil society, to reconcile diverse and opposed interests. Marx assembles a host of empirical arguments against Hegel's theory of the law-making power as mediator, but we are after the logical implications of the discussion. Marx states them as follows:

> The rational relation, the *syllogism*, appears then to be complete. The *law-making power*, the middle term, is a *mixtum compositum* of both extremes: the sovereign principle and civil society, the empirical singularity and empirical universality, the subject and predicate. In general Hegel conceives of the *syllogism* as mediator, as a *mixtum compositum*. One can say that in his development of the rational syllogism the whole transcendence and mystical dualism of his system comes to the surface. The middle term is the wooden sword, the concealed opposition between universality and singularity.[13]

Here Marx traces the inadequacy of Hegel's conception of the law-making power back to a fundamental inadequacy in Hegel's logic of mediation, typified by the rational syllogism. The logic of the concept's promise of reconciliation proves an empty boast, a wooden sword.

For Marx, Hegel's is a logic of accommodation, for it passes beyond a given level without revolutionising it. The relation between civil society and the state is a case in point. Hegel's state transcends the inadequacy of civil society without transforming its logical atom, the abstract, egoistic individual. The

---

13 Marx 1970b, p. 85, translation revised by P.M.

contradictions of the political sphere result from not addressing the unreconciled contradictions of civil society.

1.2.2 The Paris Manuscript on Hegel

The Paris manuscript on Hegel pursues the argument that his philosophy provides a faulty reconciliation of particular and universal, of thought and nature: Hegel fails to escape the antinomies of the logic of essence as Marx construes it. Moreover, in this essay, Marx merges the logic of Hegel's philosophy with that of capitalist economic forms, thus anticipating the roles that his criticism of Hegel's logics of essence and the concept will play in *Capital*.

Marx explicitly associates Hegel with classical political economy:

> Hegel shares the standpoint of the modern national economists. He grasps labour as the essence, as the self-confirming essence of man; he sees only the positive side of labour, not its negative side. Labour is man's coming-to-be for himself within externalisation [*Entäusserung*] or as externalised man.[14]

This passage is deceptive because as yet Marx lacks a differentiated use of the term labour. As it reads, Marx seems to say that labour is by nature both positive and negative, that it always involves externalisation. To interpret labour in that way would make Marx's critique of Hegel unintelligible. By labour Marx means alienated labour, the specific social form of labour that exists under capitalism.

Marx's remark, then, is no more a naïve congratulation of Hegel for celebrating human self-creation in the *Phenomenology* than is Marx's theory of value an uncritical echoing of Ricardo's. The barb is that Hegel captures the essence of humanity under the conditions of alienated, abstract labour. The double character of capitalist society permeates both classical political economy and Hegel's philosophy; both achieve undeniable scientific insights, but always 'within the framework of externalisation [*Entäusserung*]'.

In *Capital* Marx develops the dialectic of the value form to demonstrate the necessity by which value has an external expression that is not identical with it. That expression is money. In Hegel's philosophy, logic is the external expression of abstract thinking, the money of spirit. The appearance of logic as a sphere of its own is for Marx a necessary consequence of the activity of abstract (alienated) thought:

14 Marx 1964a, p. 177.

> The positive thing that Hegel achieved here – in his speculative logic – is [to show] that the determinate concepts, the universal, fixed thought-forms in their independence over against nature and spirit are a necessary result of the universal alienation [*Entfremdung*] of the human essence, hence also of human thinking.[15]

Hegel's system of absolute idealism demonstrates for Marx the *necessary* connection between abstract, alienated thinking and a freestanding logic, just as Marx's later analysis of the value form demonstrates why, under the conditions of abstract, alienated labour (value-producing labour), we need money.

We can now see how Marx views the path of Hegel's system as a whole: The idea externalises itself as nature and spirit, only to return to itself as absolute in the end. The idea's story of externalisation [*Entäusserungsgeschichte*] parallels the dialectic by which money is transformed into capital: Money externalises itself in commodities (means of production and labour power) and returns to itself (with a surplus) in the valorisation process [*Verwertungsprocess*]. The logical idea externalises itself in nature and (human) spirit, but it recognises nature and (human) spirit only as representations of itself. 'Thus the whole of nature [and we could add 'spirit' here] only repeats for him [Hegel] the logical abstractions in a sensuous, external form'.[16]

When money is transformed into capital, it is externalised into natural objects, labour power and products of human labours on natural objects. In so doing, capital posits the earth and labour power (nature and human spirit) as values. At the end of its valorization process, capital returns to the fixated abstraction of its starting point – money. To the eyes of capital, the earth and human labour are valueless in themselves, just as in absolute idealism's scheme of things, '*Nature as nature ... is senseless*'.[17] By forgetting their sources, both the idea's course of externalisation, which treads the logical path of the negation of the negation on a grand scale, and capital's cycle of negations (buying, producing, selling) in the process of valorisation condemn themselves to a hellish running in spirals.

These last considerations set up an observation about *Capital* to which we will return, namely, that Marx frames the logic of capital in terms of his own construal of Hegel's logic of the concept, according to which it fails to break free of the antinomies of the logic of essence.

---

15 Marx 1964a, p. 189, translation revised by P.M.

16 Marx 1964a, p. 191, translation revised by P.M.

17 Marx 1964a, p. 190, translation revised by P.M.

1.3 *The Importance of Hegelian Logic to Marx's Early Work*

We now have the background to appreciate how decisive Marx's attention to Hegel's logic was for much of his early work. Already in his dissertation and associated notes, the logic plays an important role. Thus, Marx argues that Plato's transcendence, his creation of a world of ideas, the Absolute paralleling the sensible world, stems from his uncritical acceptance of the given. Moreover, this acquiescence leads Plato to create a mythology that uses given sense images as symbols and as myths for the Absolute. Thus, an unreconciled dualism necessarily expresses itself in a third party: Plato's myths. As for the central figure of his dissertation, Marx construes the Epicurean declination of the atom, its swerving from the regular path, as the necessary manifestation of the (defective) principle of the free, subjective individual that Marx identifies as the essence of Epicurus's philosophy.

'On the Jewish Question' is an extraordinary example of Marx's logic of essence set to work: Heaven is the necessary expression of the unreconciled divisions within Christian society; the modern state is the necessary expression of the unreconciled contradictions of civil and political life; and money is the necessary expression of the antinomies of the capitalist economy.

Marx's criticism of Feuerbach, and of the Young Hegelian approach to religion generally, is informed by his distinctive logic of essence. Feuerbach regarded religion as alienation precisely because it is the appearance of the human essence in something other than the human, namely, the divine. Marx, however, criticises Feuerbach for not seeing that alienation was the necessary result of the contradictory character of the human essence that is driven to religion:

> Feuerbach starts out from the fact of religious self-alienation, the doubling of the world into a religious one and a secular one. His labour consists therein, to dissolve the religious world into its secular foundation. But the fact that the secular foundation lifts itself up from itself and fixates itself as an independent realm in the clouds is only to be explained out of the self-rupture and self-contradicting of this secular foundation. This [foundation] must itself therefore be understood in its contradiction as well as be revolutionised in practice.[18]

It is the divisions among humans that necessarily give rise to religion: to eliminate the gods is not to eliminate those divisions. This insight, which encapsulates

18 Marx 1967c, p. 401, translation revised by P.M.

his logic of essence, sets Marx off from the program of the Young Hegelians. Attacking religion will not address the more fundamental problem of which religion is only the necessary expression. Analogously, Marx later rejects the Proudhonian analysis of the relationship between value and price and, consequently, rejects Proudhonian (and left-Ricardian) socialism.[19]

Let us take stock of Marx's thinking about the logic of essence:

1. An essence logic is in place in situations involving unreconciled dualisms, as, for example, between the private and the social aspects of labour in capitalism.
2. The dualism involved in an essence logic is not only unreconciled but irreconcilable until that dualism is overturned. Thus, Marx rejects Hegel's conception of the way the concept purports to reconcile the oppositions inherited from essence.
3. The essence must appear as something other than itself, as, for example, abstract labour (value) must appear as exchange value (money, price) and surplus value must appear as profit.
4. Because essence must appear as something other than itself, efforts to establish the identity of appearances with essence are necessarily one-sided. (This point comes into play in Marx's criticism of Proudhonian 'time-chit' proposals and generally with regard to value-price issues.) Appearances are indispensable to the essence; they belong to it. Thus, a scientific account moves not just from appearance to essence (as does Ricardo in his theory of value) but from essence to appearance (as Marx does in his account of the value form). Even this kind of talk can be misleading, for the essence is really the whole logical figure, the appearances and that which necessarily does not appear ('essence'). Thus, value-producing labour and price belong to a logical whole.
5. That the essence must appear as something other than itself tells us of its defects. So, for example, the analysis of the value form reveals something defective about value. Thus Marx consistently associates essence's 'logic of the third party' with religion and alienation.
6. As Tony Smith points out in his book *The Logic of Marx's 'Capital'*, 'an individual moment within an essence structure is thoroughly subordinate to the essence lording over it'[20] Essence logic is characterised by

19 H.G. Backhaus pursues this analogy in detail (Backhaus 1980, p. 108).
20 Smith 1990, p. 51.

relations of domination, domination by abstractions – a theme that lies at the heart of *Capital*.

2 Marx's Critique of Political Economy

I now want to show that Marx's attention to the logic of categories is just as vital to his critique of political economy as it was to his critique of philosophy. I begin with a few examples from his early work on political economy, then I show it in detail in some mature contributions to the critique of political economy.

2.1 *Marx's Early Work in Political Economy*

Toward the end of the unfinished Paris manuscript called 'Alienated Labour', Marx looks back over the course of his engagement with political economy:

> *Private property* is thus the product, result, and necessary consequence of *externalised labour*, of the exterior relationship of the worker to nature and to himself ... We have, of course, obtained the concept of *externalised labour* (*externalised life*) from political economy as the result of the *movement of private property*. But it is evident from the analysis of this concept that, although private property appears to be the ground and reason for externalised labour, it is rather a consequence of it, just as the gods are *originally* not the cause but the effect of the aberration of the human mind.[21]

In these passages we find rudiments of Marx's mature view that value-producing labour (essence) necessarily appears as something other than itself, namely, exchange value (appearance). Moreover, Marx here connects essence logic to religion, as he later does in his critique of Feuerbach.

Two paragraphs later, Marx links his construal of externalised labour to a preliminary but telling criticism of Proudhon:

> Political economy starts from labour as the veritable soul of production, and yet it attributes nothing to labour and everything to private property. Proudhon has drawn a conclusion from this contradiction that is favourable to labour and against private property. But we can see that

21 Marx 1964a, p. 117, translation revised by P.M.

> this apparent contradiction is the contradiction of *alienated labour* with itself and that political economy has only expressed the laws of alienated labour.[22]

What Marx here brings home is the futility of trying to eliminate private property without upending the dualism that pervades externalised labour, just as the Young Hegelians failed to rout the holy family by failing to revolutionise the earthly family. Externalised labour necessarily appears as private property. The essence logic operating in this early critique of Proudhon recurs in Marx's critique of Proudhonian time-chits in the *Grundrisse*.

Marx's comments on James Mill contain striking glimpses of his mature treatments of the value-price relation (more specifically, the price of production-market price relation) and of the value form.[23] The passage on the value-price (price of production-market price) relation offers a remarkable early example of Marx's essence logic at work in his reception of political economy:

> Mill makes the mistake – generally like Ricardo's school – of giving the *abstract law* without the variation and continuous suspension by which it comes into being. If it is an *independent* law, for example, that the costs of production ultimately – or rather with the periodic and accidental coincidence of supply and demand – determine price (value), it is equally an *independent* law that this relationship does not hold and that value [I take it that 'price' is what Marx actually has in mind here] and production costs have no necessary relationship ... This *actual* process, in which this law is only an abstract, accidental, and one-sided factor, becomes something unessential with the modern economists.[24]

Marx could hardly be more explicit in directing his own dialectical logic against the standard version operative in Ricardian value theory: The law whereby costs of production determine value does not exist independently; it comes into existence only by virtue of the actual oscillations of prices, the '*actual* process', which the Ricardians neglect as unessential.[25]

---

22 Ibid., translation revised by P.M.

23 Toward the end of the chapter I consider the relationship between the value-price issue as it comes up in *Capital*'s third chapter and the discussion of market value, price of production and market price in the third volume.

24 Marx 1967b, pp. 265–6.

25 When Marx writes that prices and production costs have 'no necessary relationship', it might appear that he directly contradicts my claim that there is a necessary connection

Here is the prefiguration of Marx's value-form analysis in *Capital*:

> Thus, on both sides, private property appears as representing private property of a different nature. It appears as the equivalent of another natural product, and both sides are interrelated in such a way that each represents the being of the other and both relate to each other as substitutes for themselves and the other. The being of private property has therefore as such become a substitute, and an equivalence. Instead of possessing a direct self-identity it is only a relation with something else ... Its existence as value is different from its immediate existence; it is exterior to its specific being, an externalised aspect of itself; it is only a relative existence of the same.[26]

Marx immediately comments: 'We must keep for another time a more precise definition of the nature of this value and also of the process by which it turns into a price'.[27] This is a date Marx kept in *Capital*, but only a few pages later Marx indicates that the end point of this early exploration of the value form lies in money: 'The complete domination of the alienated thing *over* man is fully manifested in *money*'.[28] The essence logic of value that culminates here in money is clearly identified by Marx as involving the domination of those persons who perform value-producing labour by abstract things: 'What was the domination of person over person is now the general domination of the *thing* over the *person*, of the product over the producer'.[29]

2.2 *Essence Logic at Work: Marx's Theory of Value*

Though the thought that Marx simply takes over Ricardo's labour theory of value still has currency, it is a profound misconception. The fact is, Marx overtakes Ricardo's labour theory. Appreciating Marx's distinctive logic of essence enables us to see how. In the following passage Marx draws our attention to his differences with the Ricardian labour theory of value:

---

between the law of value and the oscillations of price. However, I take him to mean that there is no necessity for an individual product with a certain production cost to have a certain price. On the contrary, non-identity of price and the monetary expression of production costs is the rule.

26 Marx 1967b, p. 274, translation revised by P.M.

27 Ibid., translation revised by P.M.

28 Marx 1967b, p. 276, translation revised by P.M.

29 Ibid., translation revised by P.M.

> It is one of the fundamental failings of classical political economy that it was never granted to it to discover from the analysis of the commodity, and especially of the commodity-value, the form of value, which precisely makes it exchange-value. Even in its best representatives, such as A. Smith and Ricardo, it handles the value-form as something entirely indifferent or external to the nature of the commodity itself.[30]

In addressing the value form, Marx's theory moves beyond classical theory's dependence on the traditional model of essence and appearance, which fails to show that essence (value) must appear (as money).

Another clue toward distinguishing Marx's dialectical theory from the Ricardian one comes at the beginning of the section of *Capital*'s first chapter entitled 'The Value-Form or Exchange-Value':

> Here, however, it is a matter of performing what was not once attempted by bourgeois economy, namely, to establish the genesis of this money-form, thus to follow the development of the value-expression contained in the value-relationship, from its simplest, least visible shape up to the blinding money-form. Therewith disappears likewise the riddle of money.[31]

Marx declares his intention dialectically to bring the category of money within the extended scope of the theory of value. Not only is exchange value the necessary form of value's appearance, money is the necessary end form of exchange value.

Marx presents his theory of value in two movements: First he moves from exchange value to value, that is, from appearances to the underlying essence that explains their behaviour; then, in the analysis of the value form, Marx shows why it is necessary that value appear as something other than itself, as exchange-value, a thing – money. Bridging the two movements – found in sections 1 and 3 of *Capital*'s first chapter, respectively – is the exposition in section 2 of the double character of the labour that produces commodities.

There is nothing particularly dialectical about the first movement. Marx starts out from the ordinary exchange relationship:

30 Marx 1976a, p. 174, translation revised by P.M.

31 Marx 1976a, p. 139, translation revised by P.M.

> Let us furthermore take two commodities, e.g., wheat and iron. Whatever their ratio of exchange, it is always presentable in an equation in which a given quantum of wheat is set equal to some quantum of iron, e.g., 1 quarter of wheat = *x* cwt. of iron. What does this equation purport? That a common element of the same magnitude exists in two different things, in 1 quarter of wheat and likewise in *x* cwt. of iron. Both are therefore equal to a third thing which is in and of itself neither the one nor the other. Each of the two, insofar as it is an exchange-value, must thus be reducible to this third thing.[32]

What is this 'third thing'? It is value, the 'mere congelation of undifferentiated human labour', a 'social substance':

> Now if one leaves the use-value of the commodities out of consideration, they retain only one property, that of being products of labour. However, the product of labour has already changed in our hands. If we abstract from its use-value, we abstract also from the material components and forms which make it a use-value. It is no longer a desk or a house or yarn or any other useful thing. All of its sensuous qualities are extinguished ...
>
> Now let us consider the residue of the products of labour. There is nothing of them remaining other than the same ghostly objectivity, a mere congelation of undifferentiated human labour, that is, the expenditure of human labour power without respect to the form of its expenditure ... As crystals of this their common social substance, they are values – commodity values.[33]

There is a striking, non-accidental resemblance between this passage and the one in which Descartes draws his conclusion about the bit-turned-blob of wax.[34] Descartes and Marx face similar conundrums: How can two objects totally dissimilar in their sensuous qualities – the bit and the blob of wax – be the same? How can two qualitatively dissimilar commodities be identical in terms of value? Descartes resolves his difficulty by appealing to the primary qualities of material substance: non-sensuous, non-imaginable qualities cognisable only by the pure understanding. Marx turns to the 'ghostly objectivity' of that 'social substance': [the] value of commensurate commodities. So

---

32 Marx 1976a, p. 127, translation revised by P.M.

33 Marx 1976a, p. 128, translation revised by P.M.

34 See the passage already cited (Descartes 1960, pp. 87–8).

for Descartes the residue of the wax, that which remains after we abstract from all the secondary qualities and that which makes the wax what it is, is something altogether abstract and intellectual – nothing at all sensuous or intuitive. Likewise for Marx: The way in which two commodities are identical, namely value, is something utterly abstract – the product of an actual social process of abstraction – and contains not a whit of concrete use value or useful labour.

This first movement captures the non-dialectical thinking about essence and appearance to which Ricardian value theory is confined. Not so for the second movement, which answers the question never raised in Ricardian theory: Why does value appear in the form of exchange value? Marx prepares his answer to this question by digging deeper into the nature of the labour whose 'congelation' is value. The crux of this preparation lies in recognising that value and value-producing labour are abstractions, 'beings of reflection', rather than anything immediate, natural, or sensuous.

Just as the commodity has a double character, use value and exchange value, the labour that produces commodities is double:

> Tailoring and weaving are constituent elements of the *use-values*, coat and linen, precisely through their *different* qualities; they are *substance* of coat-value and linen-value only insofar as one *abstracts* from their specific quality and both possess *equal quality*, the *quality of human labour*.[35]

Already in section 1, Marx had investigated the nature of this abstract, 'human labour'. The labour that congeals as value is abstract labour in the 'physiological' sense that it is the expenditure of human labour power without regard to any definite end. But, for an hour's labour to count as an hour's worth of value, it must meet several conditions:

1. It must be an hour of 'simple average labour'; hours of complex labour count for more. And what counts as simple average labour is historically variable, not naturally determined.
2. To be 'socially necessary', the hour of labour must produce the number of commodities equal to the number produced in an hour averaged across all producers of that commodity. An hour's labour that produces more commodities than the average counts as more value, and conversely.

35 Marx 1966b, p. 224, translation revised by P.M.

3. An hour of labour that is socially necessary in sense (2) is socially necessary in a further sense – one that builds demand into the very concept of value – only if the demand for that type of commodity matches the supply. If the supply of a commodity exceeds demand, an hour's labour on that commodity that is socially necessary in sense (2) produces less than an hour's value, and conversely. This third consideration, involving as it does a co-constitutive relationship between value and price,[36] is a deeply non-Ricardian element of Marx's value theory.[37] According to Ricardo's theory, prices are to be the variable completely dependent on labour inputs construed in a technical sense: there is no room in Ricardian theory for a dialectic of value and price.

What these three considerations mean is that Marx's theory of value cannot be construed as a labour theory in any ordinary or naturalistic sense. The labour that goes into the production of any particular commodity, the 'labour embodied', does not determine the value of that commodity[38] – for the three reasons just specified.[39] Value is not a concept appropriate for all human

36 Paul Mattick Jr writes: '"abstract labour" in Marx's sense is undefined except in relation to a system of prices' (Mattick Jr 1981, p. 777). In a similar vein, Guglielmo Carchedi writes: 'prices are not determined by values but rather are their concrete form of existence' (Carchedi 1986, p. 201).

37 As Carchedi writes: 'The basic difference between the Marxian and the neo-Ricardian notion of value is that for the latter value is embodied labour and is determined by the technical relations of production, independent of demand' (Carchedi 1988, p. 96).

38 That Marx's is not a 'labour embodied' theory is made plain in his polemics against Proudhon and the 'time-chitters'. This is discussed below.

39 Geert Reuten, who distinguishes essence-appearance models along the lines I do (i.e., between the 'ontological' and the 'conceptual dialectical'), worries that some 'abstract labour theorists' may still subscribe to a 'labour embodied' theory. This can happen if one thinks that value-producing labour is 'abstract labour' in the 'physiological sense', of which Marx writes: 'all labour is an expenditure of human labour-power, in the physiological sense' (Marx 1976a, p. 137, translation revised by P.M). If one thus characterises value-producing labour, setting aside the three considerations examined above, one could end up with an abstract labour embodied theory that sticks to the standard, or ontological, essence-appearance model and falls not far from the Ricardian tree. As Paul Mattick Jr observes, even the neo-Ricardian advocate Ian Steedman insists that it is 'abstract labour embodied' that neo-Ricardians sum in calculating labour values (Mattick Jr 1981, pp. 776–7). Thinking through the consequences of the three features of value-producing labour just considered forces upon us the dialectical model of essence-appearance and therewith the abandonment of labour-embodied thinking. See Reuten's Chapter Four in Moseley (ed.) 1993.

labour – as in naturalistic theory. It applies only when conditions (1) through (3) above are in force, that is, in competitive, market societies where all goods are produced as commodities. Value is Marx's term for the specific, puzzling and self-obscuring form that social labour takes under capitalism. He could hardly be more explicit than in this passage from *A Contribution to the Critique of Political Economy*:

> Since the exchange-value of commodities is indeed nothing but a mutual relation between various kinds of labour of individuals regarded as equal and universal labour, i.e., nothing but a material expression of a specific social form of labour, it is a tautology to say that labour is the only source of exchange-value and accordingly of wealth in so far as this consists of exchange-value.[40]

As an account of the specific social form of labour under capitalism, Marx's theory of value is definitely cut from different cloth than the classical labour theory culminating in Ricardo.

Marx describes his characterisation of the double character of commodity-producing labour as 'the linchpin [*Springpunkt*] to the understanding of political economy'.[41] His recognition that value and value-producing labour are abstractions that depend on the actual process of abstracting that transpires in capitalist production and distribution – not anything naturally, sensuously occurring – parallels Hegel's claim that Descartes' secondary and primary qualities are not logically similar: The former are immediate, the latter, reflective. Hegel teaches us that matter is not some substance underlying appearances that just happens not to be observable, rather it is no thing at all on the model of sensuous things. Matter is a being of reflection, an essence in the dialectical sense, that is, the kind of being that must appear as something other than itself. Marx's counterpoint to Ricardian value theory runs along just these lines: value-producing labour differs logically from concrete labour. The latter is immediate sensuous, particular; the former is reflective, abstract, universal. Because it is an abstraction, a being of reflection, value cannot appear immediately; it must appear as something other than itself.[42] Money proves to be the

---

40 Marx 1970a, p. 35, translation revised by P.M. A page later Marx writes, simply: 'the labour which posits exchange-value is a specific social form of labour' (Marx 1970a, p. 36, translation revised by P.M).

41 Marx 1976a, p. 132, translation revised by P.M.

42 Chris Arthur likewise connects Marx's theory of the value-form to his rejection of the

necessary form of value's appearance – and to be necessary for value's existence – yet money is not value. Indeed, there is no physically existing, fixed measure of value – and there cannot be one.[43]

Marx says of the turn from the first movement to the second in his exposition of value theory: 'The progress of the investigation will lead us back to exchange-value as the necessary mode of expression, or form of appearance, of value'.[44] Here we have an incontrovertible assertion of necessity on Marx's part. It is one of many.[45] The necessity involved here is neither the tautology of deduction nor causal necessity. Dialectical claims are of this non-tautological, non-causal sort.[46] What justification does Marx offer for this particular assertion of necessity? The answer lies in section 3, on the value form. There Marx reveals exactly how the exploration of the double character of commodity-producing labour prepares the way for the presentation of the value form:

> Not an atom of matter enters into the objectivity of commodities as values; in this it is the direct opposite of the coarsely sensuous objectivity of commodities as physical objects. We may twist and turn a single commodity as we wish; it remains impossible to grasp it as a thing possessing value. However, let us remember that commodities possess an objective character as values only in so far as they are all expressions of an identical social substance, human labour, that their objective character as values

---

standard essence-appearance model: 'If the necessity of a material form of appearance of value is not recognised then value theory becomes nothing but metaphysical essentialism' (Arthur 1979, p. 68).

43 As Geoffrey Pilling puts it: 'All those who think there can be some invariable measure of value in fact completely misunderstand the nature of capital' (Pilling 1980, p. 194). Pilling places Ricardians among those who do: 'It is no accident that there is no trace of the notion of fetishism in the work of what might be called the "Sraffa School", which has returned to Ricardo for some answers to the current crisis in economic theory. For it is precisely this school which has grappled with what we have tried to show is a quite mistaken problem – namely the search for some abstract standard of value – be it a "standard" or "composite" commodity' (Pilling 1980, pp. 195–6).

44 Marx 1976a, p. 128.

45 See, for example, the first footnote to Chapter Three of *Capital*. Later in that chapter Marx writes: 'The price-form entails the exchangeability of the commodity against money as well as the necessity of this exchange [*Veräusserung*]' (Marx 1976a, p. 198, translation revised by P.M). Claims of such necessity may be found in many passages from Marx already cited in this chapter.

46 Tony Smith is right to insist that 'Marx's theory, like Hegel's, includes claims of systematic necessity' (Smith 1990, p. 38).

> is therefore purely social. From this it follows self-evidently [*so versteht sich auch von selbst*] that it can only appear in the social relation between commodity and commodity.[47]

Once we recognise what value is, namely, an abstract, reflective, 'social' objectivity, it is evident that it can have no immediate appearance. The necessity here lies – as in Hegel's criticism of Descartes – in recognising the different *logics* of immediacy and reflection.

Marx begins the analysis of the value form with its simplest form: 'x commodity A values at y commodity B'. The seminal feature of this value expression is its polarity. Commodity A expresses its value in commodity B; A is active and B is passive. Commodity B is the mirror in which commodity A first recognises itself as a value. The value of A cannot appear in A itself; it can only be expressed relative to A in another commodity.[48]

> I cannot express, e.g., the value of linen in linen. 20 yards of linen = 20 yards of linen is no expression of value. The equation says much more reversed: 20 yards of linen are nothing other than 20 yards of linen, a specific quantum of the useful object, linen. The value of linen can then only be expressed relatively, i.e., in other commodities.[49]

Hence, Marx speaks of commodity A as in the relative value form. Commodity B, in which the value of A is mirrored, is in the equivalent form. Acknowledging that these two are necessarily polar is crucial in analysing the value form.

The value form is a social magnet: relative value form and equivalent form are extremes that belong to one another yet shut one another out. To say that the expression of value is necessarily polar means that the expression of value requires a reflective relationship. Marx's repeated use of 'mirror', or 'value-mirror', to characterise the commodity in the equivalent form highlights this feature. The polarity of the value form signals the essence logic. As the essence of exchange value, value must appear in something other than itself.

---

47 Marx 1976a, pp. 138–9, translation revised by P.M.

48 Samuel Bailey, with whose critique of Ricardian theory Marx was in certain respects impressed, observed this necessary polarity in the expression of value: 'It is impossible to determine or to express the value of a commodity except by a quantity of some other commodity' (Bailey as quoted in Backhaus 1980, p. 106). [Note to the present edition: No, Bailey recognised the necessity for value to be expressed, but he failed to see the necessary polarity of that expression. For Marx's critique of Bailey see Chapter 6 in the present volume.]

49 Marx 1976a, p. 140.

To appreciate fully Marx's account of the value form, we must be mindful that essence involves alienation. Essence appears only by giving itself over to something that is not itself – through alienation. Value recognises itself only in its reflection in another object. The labour that produces value is alienated labour. Fitting the pattern of alienation, the logic of value is inherently religious in Marx's critical sense. In discussing the relative value form, Marx refers explicitly to his critique of Feuerbach:

> Its existence [the existence of the linen, which is in the relative value form] as value appears in its equality with the coat as the sheep-nature of the Christian [does] in his equality with the Lamb of God.[50]

The Christian achieves fullness only mirrored in the Lamb of God, but the nature of the Christian thereby revealed is that of a sheep. For Marx, the religious alienation of the Christian is the necessary expression of the Christian's sheepish nature. Likewise, the fact that a commodity expresses its value only through another commodity manifests the alienation of the labour that produced it.

In this context we should emphasise the 'must' in Hegel's statement 'the essence must appear'. Essence is constrained to appear because it harbours within itself an unreconciled contradiction between immediacy and reflection. The practical point is this: change must be effected by recognising and resolving the contradiction immanent to the essence.

In the *Grundrisse*, Marx counter-poses the essence logic of value production to the quite different logic of communist production:

> On the foundation of exchange-value, labour is first posited as universal through exchange. On this foundation [communist society] labour would be posited as such before exchange, i.e., the exchange of products would not at all be the medium through which the participation of the individual in the general production would be mediated. Mediation must of course take place. In the first case, which starts out from the independent production of the individual – no matter how much these independent productions determine and modify each other *post festum* through their interrelations – mediation takes place through the exchange of commodities, exchange-value, money, all of which are expressions of one and the same relationship. In the second case, the presupposition is itself medi-

50 Marx 1976a, p. 143.

> ated, i.e., communal production, the communality as a foundation of production, is presupposed. The labour of the individual is from the very beginning posited as social labour. The product does not first have to be converted into a particular form in order to receive a universal character for the individual.[51]

In production governed by value, the particular is mediated by the universal, but only after it has been produced privately. The two determinations fall asunder and must be wrenched together by the price system. Mediation takes place in communist production as well, but the 'middle man' is avoided by the fact that the particular and universal determinations coincide. Particular use values produced communally are already universals inasmuch as they are decided upon by society as a whole. There is no further need to impose, at the level of exchange, a social determination on communally produced use values.[52]

2.3 *Value and Price in* Capital

It is sometimes assumed that in the first volume of *Capital* Marx simply identifies values with prices and that divergences between value and price turn up first with the third volume's discussion of prices of production. But in the first volume of *Capital*, as well as in related treatments in the *Grundrisse*, Marx insists on the necessary non-identity of value and price, a claim that he explicates in terms of his dialectical logic of essence.

Before delving into the theory of price presented in Volume I, its relationship to the discussion of market value, prices of production and market prices in Volume III should be aired. Böhm-Bawerk's famous critique that Marx's theories of value and price in the first volume were contradicted by the third displays several misconceptions. One is that the theories of value and price developed in the first volume are intended to apply to just any commodity. When Marx theorises about commodities and capital in the first volume, he assumes that an individual capital is an aliquot part of the aggregate capital and that an individual commodity is the product of such an average capital. When these qualifications are kept in mind, we realise that Marx did not forget to bring in market value and prices of production in Volume I; they do not belong there.

---

51 Marx 1973, pp. 171–2, translation revised by P.M.

52 See also Marx's first footnote to Chapter Three of *Capital*, in which he favourably contrasts Owen to Proudhon (Marx 1976a, pp. 188–9).

Notice that even though the category of price of production, which generally deviates from those of individual and market value, can have no place in Volume I, a discrepancy between value and price remains. Why? The non-identity of value and price in the chapter on money picks up the discrepancy not between values and production prices – under the assumptions of Volume I, this discrepancy cannot enter in – but between production prices and market prices in the third volume. Despite its name, production price is not a price at all, for prices are the money expression of value, whereas production price, like market value, is a value category. As such, production price must appear as something other than itself, namely market price. This is the necessity that is registered in the first volume's theory of price.

Marx's theory of price in the first volume insists that the difference between value and price is not nominal.[53] To call the distinction between value and price nominal is to obliterate, or leave unexplained, the differences between these two forms. Marx's theory of price explains the discrepancies by carefully examining the logic of the forms themselves.

We have seen the first, and decisive, phase of Marx's anti-nominalist theory of price in his theory of value, which shows the logical necessity for value to express itself in money. Since the value of a commodity is expressed through an alien, independent object (money), value and price are not, and cannot be, immediately identical. Their identity arises only in the gravitational pull that value exercises over the oscillations of price. The nominalist theory of price concentrates only on the identity of price and value; it disregards the fact that the reflective identity of price and value in the law of price operates only on the unavoidable presupposition of the immediate non-identity of price and value. Marx's theory, on the other hand, recognises both as equally essential.

In terms of Hegel's logic of essence, we can say that both the oscillation of price and the law of that oscillation are on the logical level of essence and that the proper comprehension of essence recognises the necessary unity of the two. Hegel writes in the section of his *Science of Logic* entitled 'The Law of Appearance':

> The law is therefore not on the other side of appearance, but rather immediately present in it; the realm of laws is the stable reflected image of the existing or appearing world. But even more so are both One Totality, and the existing world is itself the realm of laws, which, as the simply

53 As John Weeks writes: 'For Marx, the essence of the value-price relationship is their non-equivalence' (Weeks as quoted in Carchedi 1988, p. 99).

> identical, likewise is identical with itself in positedness or in the self-dissolving autonomy of existence.[54]

If we substitute 'law of price' for Hegel's 'law of appearance', 'the actual oscillations of price' for Hegel's 'existing or appearing world', and 'the constant negation of … itself [price] as the negation of the real value' for Hegel's 'the self-dissolving autonomy of existence', we have the basics of Marx's critical theory of price. Hegel's emphasis on the immanence of the law of appearance to the appearances themselves carries over into Marx's theory of price.

Like his critical theory of value and the value form, Marx's theory of price does not hypostatise value. As the law of price, value is not something beyond or outside of the actual movement of price, rather it is the tethering of price. Value does not exist as an actual, observable thing, but as the reflection of actual things. So Marx's theory of price reconfirms the non-metaphysical character of the theory of value that he puts forth in the first chapter of *Capital*, just as it underlines his debt to Hegel's logic.

Marx reminds us, in the third chapter of Volume I of *Capital*, not only that the distinction between price and value is a logical necessity but also that it indicates the social relations within a society characterised by these categories:

> The possibility of quantitative incongruence between price and value-magnitudes, or the deviation of the price from the value-magnitude, lies therefore in the price-form itself. It is no defect of this form, but rather, quite the opposite, that makes it the adequate form of a mode of production in which the rule can push itself through only as the blindly operating law of averages of irregularity.[55]

The divergence of price and value is not a surd, as in the nominalist theory; rather, it is identified as the necessary consequence of the commodity mode of production. By attending to the moment of non-identity of price and value, rather than abstractly fixating on their reflective identity in the law of price, Marx discloses the price form as a determinate and crisis-laden category of capitalist production.

To disregard prices, then, as 'mere appearances', or to set them aside on the grounds that, after all, they are something other than the essence, is the wrong consequence to draw from Marx's invocation of an essence-appearance

54 Hegel 1969, pp. 503–4, translation revised by P.M.

55 Marx 1976a, p. 196, translation revised by P.M.

model in order to conceive of the relation between value and price. The model of essence and appearance that Marx employs is dialectical. Appearances are necessary to the essence: there can be no value without price.

Since Proudhonism was such a powerful force within European socialism, Marx was particularly pleased with the polemical points his theory of price scored. Writing to Engels on 22 July 1859, Marx lists as the first outcome of *A Contribution to the Critique of Political Economy* 'that Proudhonism is eradicated'. Moreover, the body of the *Grundrisse* begins with an extensive critique of Alfred Darimon, a follower of Proudhon who wanted to supplant money with time-chits issued on the basis of how many hours an individual actually worked. If price were just a label for the labour embodied in a good, the proposal should work. But Marx links the problem with time-chits to a misunderstanding of the price form:

> The first fundamental illusion of the time-chitters consists therein, that by annulling the *nominal diversity* between real value and market value, between exchange-value and price – thus expressing the value in the labour-time itself instead of a specific objectification of labour-time, say, gold and silver – they also put aside the actual difference and contradiction between price and value.[56]

Along with Proudhon, Darimon takes the nominalist view of money, claiming that as the mediator of commodity exchange, money is a troublesome but removable contrivance rather than a logically necessary third party. Such theorists resent the interference of money at the same time as they champion commodity production and the egalitarianism found in the exchange of equal values. Marx takes that to mean that the utopian or 'bourgeois' socialists want to have their cake and eat it too, or as he puts it with respect to John Gray, 'The products are supposed to be produced as commodities, but are not to be exchanged as commodities'.[57] These 'unscientific socialists' simply fail to grasp the logical relations linking the categories of commodity, value and price.

2.4 *The Logic of Capital*

The logic of simple commodity circulation, which we have just examined, conforms to Hegel's logic of essence as well as to Marx's. I now argue that Marx

56 Marx 1973, p. 138, translation revised by P.M.

57 Marx 1970a, p. 85, translation revised by P.M.

deliberately presents capital in terms that evoke his early treatment of Hegel's logic of the concept and thereby reinforce his early criticism that Hegel's logic of the concept is a 'wooden sword', a defective reconciliation that leaves the opposed elements standing in their opposition to one another.[58]

When Marx speaks of value in the sphere of simple circulation, he speaks of (social) 'substance'. But Marx describes capital with the phrases 'automatic subject', 'here value becomes the subject of a process', 'the encompassing subject of such a process', and 'itself, self-moving substance'. In the concept of capital, substance reveals itself as subject, albeit an automatic one. Marx here recalls Hegel's criticism of Spinoza for conceiving of the Absolute as substance but not subject.

A comparison of the following two passages – the first, Hegel's description of the infinite as conceived on the logical level of the concept; the second, a description of capital from Marx's *Urtext* – brings out Marx's intention to identify the logic of capital with Hegel's logic of the concept:

> Only [*erst*] the veritable infinite, which posits itself as finite, reaches at the same time beyond itself as an other and remains therein, because it is its other, in unity with itself.[59]

> Its [money's] going into circulation must itself be a moment of its remaining-with-itself, and its remaining-with-itself must be a going into circulation.[60]

Marx underlines the identification of simple circulation with Hegelian essence logic and capital's circulation with the Hegelian logic of the concept (as he conceived of it) by appealing to the association of Judaism with the former and Christianity with the latter. At the same, time these associations bring home the point that, for Marx, the Hegelian concept is just as 'religious' as is essence. The association of capital with Christianity could not be more explicit than in this passage:

---

58 As Jeanne A. Schuler, Tony Smith and Geert Reuten have pointed out to me, there are very good reasons for doubting that Hegel's logic of the concept actually applies to capital. I am very suspicious about this myself, but here I restrict myself to what Marx saw himself doing with Hegel in *Capital*, not whether he was justified.

59 Hegel 1962, p. 183, translation revised by P.M.

60 Marx 1939b, p. 931, translation by P.M. [NOTE: at the time that I did this translation there was no English translation to revise.]

> It [value] differentiates itself as original value from itself as surplus-value, as God the Father from Himself as God the Son, and both are of the same age and constitute in fact only one person, for only through the surplus-value of 10 pounds sterling do the advance 100 pounds sterling become capital, and as soon as they have become this, as soon as the Son is created and through the Son, the Father, their difference disappears again, and both are one, 101 [*sic*] pounds sterling.[61]

Just before this passage Marx contrasted the logics of simple circulation and capital circulation with those of Judaism and Christianity, respectively:

> The capitalist knows that all commodities, no matter how ragged they always look, or how bad they always smell, are in faith and in truth money, innerly circumcised Jews, and moreover wonder-working means to make money out of money.[62]

The fact that, in *Capital*, Marx endeavours to associate the logic of capital with Hegel's concept and with Christianity demonstrates the continuing relevance of his early writings to his mature critique of political economy, in particular to his theory of capital.

Recall Marx wrote that Hegel's logic is the necessary result of his whole philosophy being governed by abstract thought: logic is the necessary form of appearance of abstract thinking – just as money is the necessary form of appearance of the abstract labour performed under the conditions of capitalism.[63] 'Logic is the money of spirit'. Following the consequences of these associations sheds light on the significance of the dialectical logic of the value form for Marx's theory of capital. As he criticised Hegel in the last of the Paris manuscripts, Marx simultaneously explored the logic of value, including, of course, the logic of capital. As we saw earlier, Marx associated the logical idea's externalisation in nature and spirit with the valorization process, whereby money is transformed into capital. Notice, now, that in both cases, the cycle begins – and ends – not with abstract thought or with value, but with their necessary forms of appearance, logic and money. What this tells us is that the dialectical logics of essence and of value are already integrated into Marx's conception of Hegel's philosophy of spirit and Marx's theory of capital. As value

61 Marx 1976a, p. 256, translation revised by P.M.

62 Ibid., translation revised by P.M.

63 See the discussion under 'The Paris Manuscript on Hegel' above.

striving to expand itself in an endless spiral, capital is not money, nor any production process, nor any commodity. What our exploration of Marx's theory of value has taught us is that, as a category of value, capital is itself necessarily non-apparent, non-observable, *and* that it must appear as something other than itself. What distinguishes capital from the logic of value at the level of simple commodity circulation is that, though it is identical to none of them, capital recognises itself in money, in production and in commodities. The formula M-C-M' (or more fully, M-C … P … C'-M') is the necessary form of capital's appearance.[64]

This embedding of the dialectical logic of the value form in Marx's introduction of the concept of capital implies that his theory of capital is at least as profoundly post-Ricardian as is his theory of value. Unaware of the significance of social form, the Ricardian theory of capital depicts capitalist production as 'the production of commodities by means of commodities', or C … P … C'. The givens in Marx's theory of capitalist production are not the physical quantities of the technical conditions of production and the real wages, as they are in Ricardian theory, but sums of money – value's necessary form of appearance – which are invested as capital.[65] Thus the logical lessons Marx learned from Hegel are central to his surpassing of Ricardo's theory of value, whether at the level of simple circulation or of capital.

64 This is a natural extension of the connections I pointed out regarding Marx's Parisian critique of Hegel, but it was Martha Campbell who helped me see this.

65 See Moseley's Chapter Seven in Moseley (ed.) 1993.

CHAPTER 9

Money as Displaced Social Form: Why Value Cannot be Independent of Price*

> Mediation must, of course, take place.[1]

∵

Money may be a mirror in which the value of a commodity is reflected, but Marx's theory of money is a window onto what is most distinctive about his theory of value and his critique of political economy. A widespread misconception holds that Marx adopted the classical (Ricardian) labour theory of value and then drew radical consequences from it in his theory of exploitation: surplus value is expropriated surplus labour. For Marx, value was strictly a 'social substance', a 'phantom-like objectivity', a congealed quantity of 'socially necessary' 'homogeneous human labour' of a particular social sort, namely, privately undertaken labour that produces goods and services for sale. Value necessarily appears as money. But, for the classical theory, labour of whatever social sort was the source of value, and money was an afterthought, a 'ceremonial form', as Ricardo called it; the answer to a merely technical problem. The radical Ricardian Thomas Hodgskin pushed this approach to the limit, expelling money from economic discourse:

> Money is, in fact, only the instrument for carrying on buying and selling and the consideration of it no more forms a part of the science of political economy than the consideration of ships or steam engines, or of any other instruments employed to facilitate the production and distribution of wealth.[2]

---

* Originally published as 'Money as Displaced Social Form: Why Value cannot be Independent of Price', in *Marx's Theory of Money: Modern Appraisals*, edited by Fred Moseley (Basingstoke, Hampshire: Palgrave Macmillan, 2005), pp. 50–64, reprinted with the kind permission of Palgrave Macmillan.

1 Marx 1973, p. 171.

2 As quoted in Marx 1970a, p. 51n.

This way of thinking about money – money is a clever invention to facilitate barter – stretches back to Aristotle, and it remains the commonplace view. According to Marx, this conception of money is deeply mistaken. Understanding why gives us a window onto what is wrong with the classical labour theory of value and leads us to the most profound error of economics, its failure to make the specific social form and purpose of needs, wealth and labour ingredients of its theory.[3]

According to Marx, value and money are inseparable yet not identical: without money there can be no value, yet money is not value. Marx's thesis of the inseparability of value and money overturns the classical theories of value and money and establishes new concepts governing the theory of price. These new concepts rule out the ordinary assumption of price theory: namely, that value is the independent variable that explains the behaviour of price, which is conceived to be the dependent variable.

Marx gets to this idea of the inseparability of value and money because he addresses the question, 'What is money?' Marx's perplexing answer to this question exceeds the discourse of economics: *money is the necessarily displaced social form of wealth and labour in those societies where the capitalist mode of production dominates*. This concept of money is not available to economics because economics understands itself as a general science; consequently it vacillates, either excluding altogether specific social forms of need, wealth and labour or including them under the false pretext that they are general. Marx's concept of money is not just substantively perplexing to economics; it is methodologically, even metaphysically, perplexing, because it challenges the nominalist empiricism underlying economics, a philosophy that has no truck with social forms or their power (formal causality). Marx's answer to the question, 'What is money?' tells us why money and value are inseparable yet not identical. It gives us that window onto the fundamental difference between Marx's theory of value and the classical one, and also onto what is fundamentally wrong with economics. If money is the necessary manifestation of the specific social form of labour and wealth in a capitalist society, then to conceive of labour and its products in a capitalist society as independent of money is to imagine that labour and wealth can exist without any specific social form. Herein lies the root of the problem with conventional value and price theories: their assumption that value and price are independent and dependent vari-

3 I use the term 'economics' to denote those inquiries into the provisioning process that do not make specific social forms ingredients of their theories.

ables, respectively, presumes that human needs, wealth and labour can exist without determinate social form, whereas they cannot.

Closely related to Marx's fundamental critique of economics for failing to make specific social forms of production and wealth ingredients of any inquiry into material production is his criticism of economics for failing to grasp the inseparability of production, consumption, distribution and exchange.[4] The reason why the latter are inseparable is that the specific social forms of each sphere have implications for each of the others. Take conventional price theory. By treating value and price as independent and dependent variables, respectively, conventional price theory violates Marx's doctrine of the inseparability of production and exchange. Conversely, Marx holds that money 'represents a social relation of production', and he traces the roots of the doubling of wealth in capitalist societies into commodities and money to the peculiar asocial sociality of labour under capitalism.[5]

Marx's theory of money is simultaneously a critique of ideology. Conceiving of money as necessarily displaced social form not only points to where classical political economy went wrong; in fact, it suggests why it went wrong. After all, money does not exactly have 'social form of labour' written all over it; neither does the value of commodities shout out 'social form'. On the contrary, Marx calls money a 'riddle' and the commodity a 'hieroglyphic'. Precisely because, in the capitalist mode of production, the peculiar social form of labour and its products necessarily gets displaced as the value property of commodities and as money (where they are unrecognizable as social forms), labour and wealth appear to be altogether without specific social form and purpose. 'Labour which manifests itself in exchange-value appears to be the labour of an isolated individual. It becomes social labour by assuming the form of its direct opposite, of abstract universal labour'.[6] Appearing not to be social at all, labour and wealth are not even candidates for the possession of definite social form and purpose. As a consequence, the capitalist mode of production naturally gives rise to the illusion that, being no particular social form of production, it is 'production in general' incarnate. This is what I call 'the illusion of the economic'.[7]

4 On this topic see particularly *The Poverty of Philosophy* (Marx 1963b, p. 78); the Introduction to the *Grundrisse*; and *Capital* Volume III, Chapter 51, 'Relations of Distribution and Relations of Production' (Marx 1981, pp. 1,017–24).

5 Marx 1970a, p. 35.

6 Marx 1970a, p. 34.

7 See Murray 2002a, included in the present volume as Chapter 14.

Marx's theory of money, of course, is a window onto not just the distinctiveness of his value theory and critique of economics, but also onto the distinctive, monetary, nature of the capitalist mode of production: 'all bourgeois relations appear gilded'.[8] Marx identifies two fundamental traits of the capitalist mode of production; both require money. (1) 'It produces its products as commodities. The fact that it produces commodities does not in itself distinguish it from other modes of production; but that the dominant and determining character of its product is that it is a commodity certainly does so'.[9] (2) 'The production of surplus-value [is] the direct object and decisive motive of production'.[10] Thinking of money as an instrument to facilitate the exchange of wealth badly misconstrues money's significance for the capitalist economy. Money cannot be merely an instrument in the capitalist mode of production, because money is necessary for the production of commodities and because the purpose of capitalist production, the endless accumulation of surplus value, can neither be defined nor pursued independently of money.[11] To posit money as an instrument is falsely to suppose that there could be a capitalist mode of production independent of money, to whose aid money could come.

1 Situating Marx's Theory of Money and His Critique of Economics

Marx's historical materialism involves a phenomenology of the human situation according to which concrete, useful labour (i.e., the transformation of given and previously worked-up materials in order to create new use values intended to meet human needs) is a universal and fundamental feature of the human situation.[12] Marx argues further that there is no production in general, and this is true in two respects, technically and socially.[13] (1) Production is always technically specific; it is always the production of this or that, cloth or clothes, in this or that way, weaving or sewing. We use 'widget' as a placeholder for any product, but there are no widget factories. (2) 'All production is appropriation of nature on the part of an individual within and through a spe-

8 Marx 1970a, p. 64.

9 Marx 1981, p. 1,019.

10 Marx 1981, p. 1,020.

11 Marx 1976a, p. 255.

12 By a phenomenology of the human situation I mean an experience-based inquiry into the inseparable features of human existence.

13 Marx 1973, p. 85. That there is no production in general does not mean that nothing can be said in general about production.

cific form of society'.[14] Human production always involves social relations and social purposes, but social forms and social purposes are always this or that. There is no sociality in general and there are no social purposes in general.

In this phenomenology of labour lies the basis of Marx's critique of economics. Its most telling point is that labour and wealth are inseparable from their specific social form and purpose. Economics is bogus because it separates wealth and labour from their specific social forms. Economics trades in bad abstractions. Economics is in the grip of 'the illusion of the economic', the idea that there is 'production in general', production with no particular social form or purpose.

2 The Polarity of the Commodity and Money Forms

Marx drew the disturbing conclusion that human relations in the sphere of commodity circulation match the Hegelian logic of essence. According to Hegel's essence logic, 'the essence must *appear*'.[15] According to Marx, value must appear as money. Ordinarily we assume that essence is independent of appearance. Hegel argues that the ordinary assumption is mistaken.[16] Being inseparable (essence *must* appear), essence and appearance do not face one another as independent to dependent variable. Likewise, Marx shows that value is not independent of price. Hegel judges the logic of essence critically, 'The sphere of Essence thus turns out to be a still imperfect combination of immediacy and mediation'.[17] That sums up Marx's judgment of the sphere of commodity circulation. This essence logic, expressed in the polarity of the value form (which shows itself in the polarity of the commodity and money forms), dominates Part One of *Capital* Volume I, 'Commodities and Money'.

Capital begins by exposing the root of the polarity, the double character of the commodity: it has use value and exchange value. The commodity's double character holds circulation's 'still imperfect combination of immediacy and mediation'.[18] Marx investigates the commodity form in a double movement

---

14 Marx 1973, p. 87.

15 Hegel 1975, § 131, p. 186.

16 'In reference also to other subjects besides God the category of Essence is often liable to an abstract use, by which, in the study of anything, its Essence is held to be something unaffected by, and subsisting in independence of, its definite phenomenal embodiment' (Hegel 1975, § 112, p. 164; see also § 114, p. 165).

17 Hegel 1975, § 114, p. 165.

18 See Marx 1970a, p. 48 and Marx 1976a, p. 180.

of thought, going first from exchange value to value, then reversing to go from value to exchange value.[19] The arc of the investigation leads from the commodity form to its polar form, the money form.[20] The analysis of the value form concludes that only in the money form does exchange value achieve a form adequate for the circulation of commodities. But Marx should not be understood as somehow arguing from barter to money.[21] Marx is careful to write the simple value form as 'x commodity A = y commodity B' and to contrast it with the equation for 'direct exchange' (barter), 'x use-value A = y use-value B'.[22] Use values exchanged in barter are not commodities. Why not? They do not have *an* exchange value, as commodities must. Martha Campbell points out, 'Although Marx never regards exchange value as anything but money price, he does not specify that it is until he shows what money price involves'.[23] In beginning *Capital* with the assumption that wealth takes the commodity form, Marx assumes a system of money and prices. Marx pulls a rabbit out of a cage, not – by some 'Hegelian' wizardry – out of a hat.[24]

Chapter Two, 'The Process of Exchange', confirms the conclusion reached conceptually in the first chapter: commodities and money are polar forms. The owners of commodities 'can only bring their commodities into relation as values, and therefore as commodities, by bringing them into an opposing relation with some one other commodity, which serves as the universal equivalent. We have already reached that result by our analysis of the commodity'.[25] Commodities, value and money prove mutually inextricable.

Chapter Three, 'Money or the Circulation of Commodities', examines different forms and functions of money: measure of value, standard of price, means of circulation and 'money as money' (hoards, means of payment, world money). All these forms match forms of Hegelian essence logic; the polarity of commodities and money persists throughout. This is true even of the final form, 'money as money', in which money seems to overcome polarity and orbit in godly freedom from the world of commodities.[26] Hegel calls this final shape

---

19 Marx points out that no one else thought to attempt this reverse movement (Marx 1976a, p. 139).

20 See Marx 1976a, p. 139.

21 See Campbell 1997. Her criticism of Levine and Ong applies to Murray 1988a.

22 Marx 1976a, p. 139; Marx 1976a, p. 181.

23 Campbell 1997, p. 100.

24 'Marx does not derive money from a nonmonetary context' (Campbell 1997, p. 100).

25 Marx 1976a, p. 180.

26 See Hegel 1975, § 112, p. 162.

of essence logic 'actuality'.[27] The truth that 'money as money' still belongs to the essence logic and bears a polar dependence on the world of commodities surfaces in the realisation that its bold claim simply to be value bursts on contact. 'If I want to hold on to it [money], then it evaporates in my hand into a mere ghost of wealth'.[28] Money as money is a mere *caput mortuum*, an empty thing-in-itself.[29]

To conclude this section we briefly consider implications of the polarity of the commodity and money forms:

1. Use values directly exchanged (barter) are not commodities. The commodity and money forms – and the necessity for them – develop in tandem with the growing scope and diversity of exchange.[30]
2. Value cannot appear except as something other than itself. This is not only because 'congealed homogeneous labour' is imperceptible but also because value cannot exist independently of money and commodity circulation. Value cannot be measured directly.
3. Money (price) is the necessary form of appearance of value.
4. As polar forms, the commodity form and the money form presuppose one another and exclude one another. (Here is the Hegelian essence logic in nuce: essence and appearance require one another but cannot be collapsed into one another.)
5. Money is the incarnation of value, but money is not value. In holding that money is value, rather than the expression of value, Samuel Bailey denied the polarity of the value form.[31]
6. Money is not value, but it is the only observable measure of value, so value can have no observable invariable measure.
7. Since neither money nor commodities are independent of one another, neither money nor commodities are mere things.[32] A coin remains a thing when it stops being money.
8. Value and price are not independent variables; so there can be no price theory of the conventional sort, which purports to explain the dependent variable, price, on the basis of the independent variable, value.

---

27 Chris Arthur links money with actuality (Arthur 2002a, p. 109). I thank him for a helpful exchange on this matter.

28 Marx 1939b, p. 920. See Arthur 2002a, p. 31.

29 Marx 1939b, p. 937; compare Hegel 1975, § 112, p. 162.

30 Marx 1976a, pp. 154, 181–3.

31 Compare Campbell 1997, p. 97.

32 'Money is not a thing, it is a social relation' (Marx 1963b, p. 81).

9. Since value cannot be measured directly, Marx's equation that price equals value multiplied by some constant cannot be established in a directly empirical manner. With no direct way of observing the value of commodities, the constant that relates value and price cannot be ascertained.[33]
10. Because of the peculiar social form of value-producing labour, value is inseparable from money. Nothing of the kind is found in Ricardian theory. Marx's truly social theory of value and money is incompatible with the asocial Ricardian theory of value and money.
11. Though value and the specific social form of labor that produces it are not possible without money, it is the transformation of the social form of labor into value-producing labor that accounts for the omnipresence of money.[34] Action is prior to its consequences.
12. Because commodities necessarily express their value in an external thing (money), things that have no value can have prices.[35]

3 Money, the Roundabout Mediator

Money is the consequence of a specific social form of labour. Money necessarily mediates private production and social need. Marx discusses the social form of labour that requires money first as commodity-producing labour and later as surplus value-producing labour. Because it does not grasp the topic of the specific social form and purpose of labour and wealth, economics fails to recognise the inseparability of the social sort of labour that produces commodities

---

33 This did not trouble Marx, as he believed that he had shown why value could only be congealed homogeneous human labour of a specific social sort: 'Since the exchange-value of commodities is indeed nothing but a mutual relation between various kinds of labour of individuals regarded as equal and universal labour, i.e., nothing but a material expression of a specific social form of labour, it is a tautology to say that labour is the only source of exchange-value and accordingly of wealth in so far as this consists of exchange-value' (Marx 1963b, p. 35). Marx's labour theory of value itself is not a tautology, but if it is true, exchange value, as the necessary expression of value, can represent only labour.

34 Marx 1976a, p. 152; compare Campbell 1997, p. 97.

35 Marx 1976a, p. 197. Marx, then, foresees and answers the common objection to his procedure at the beginning of Chapter One, where he seems to assume that all commodities (everything with a price on it) are products of labour and have value. This feature of the price form also opens the door to 'hybrid subsumption', that is, the incorporation, through the mediation of money, of non-capitalist forms of labour and wealth, e.g., slave labour and its products, into capitalism.

from money. By contrast, Marx's theory of commodities, exchange value, value, money and price is all about specific social forms, and all about the modes of mediation of labour and wealth in capitalist societies.

At the heart of that complex theory lies Marx's observation that commodity-producing labour is mediated in a roundabout fashion.[36] Commodity-producing labour has an asocial sort of sociality; it is social, because it produces for others but, as privately undertaken production, it is not directly social. Individuals produce commodities for their own purposes, but those particular purposes can be realised only if their products are socially validated as components of social wealth by being sold. Marx contrasts this asocial form of sociality, this roundabout type of mediation, with the directly universal, communist form of sociality:

> On the foundation of exchange-value, labour is first posited as universal through exchange. On this foundation [communist society] labour would be posited as such before exchange, i.e., the exchange of products would not at all be the medium through which the participation of the individual in the general production would be mediated. Mediation must, of course, take place. In the first case, which starts out from the independent production of the individual – no matter how much these independent productions determine and modify each other *post festum* through their interrelations – mediation takes place through the exchange of commodities, exchange-value, money, all of which are expressions of one and the same relationship. In the second case, the presupposition is itself mediated, i.e., communal production, the communality as a foundation of production, is presupposed. The labour of the individual is from the very beginning posited as social labour. The product does not first have to be converted into a particular form in order to receive a universal character for the individual.[37]

Value is inseparable from the system of money and prices because of the specific social form of the labour that produces commodities: 'On the foundation of exchange-value, labour is first posited as universal through exchange'. Value-producing labour must be universal, but, on the basis of 'the independent

36 In 'On the Jewish Question', Marx extended the Feuerbachian critique of religion as roundabout mediation to the modern state: 'Religion is precisely the recognition of man by detour through an intermediary. The state is the intermediary between man and his freedom' (Marx 1977, pp. 44–5).

37 Marx 1973, pp. 171–2.

production of the individual', this universality can be achieved only through exchange. The sale of commodities belongs to this particular social form of labour. Ricardian value theory and the Ricardian theory of money fail because they presume that value and money are separable. In assuming that labour produces value in production alone, Ricardian value theory treats labour as if it had no specific social form; it conceives of production not as the production of commodities or as capitalist production but as 'production in general'. But labour is not actual apart from a specific social form.[38] Ricardian value theory posits labour as existing without any determinate social form. This is its deepest mistake, a phenomenological error. Because Ricardian theory is lost in 'the illusion of the economic', it cannot understand money.

4 Demand, Value, Price

A common view holds that Marx thoughtlessly allots no role to demand.[39] After all, does not Marx have a labour value theory of price? And does not that mean that price is determined by labour? Is the price of a commodity not determined by the magnitude of the labour embodied in it? But the amount of labour that goes into a commodity is determined in production. What has that got to do with demand?

This popular conception mistakes Marx's theory of value for the classical or Ricardian one. Ricardian theory does neglect demand. However, a conceptual gulf separates Marx's theory of value from the Ricardian one. Where the Ricardian theory identifies unspecified 'labour' as the source (and true measure) of value, for Marx, value results from the specific social form of labour that produces wealth in the commodity form: 'The labour which posits exchange-value is a specific social form of labour'.[40] That specific social form of labour, the kind that produces commodities, is possible only if demand plays a role in the constitution of value.

Demand is not another word for desire; desire is common to all humans. Demand is a specific social form of desire found only in capitalist societies. Demand aggregates individually determined desires for goods and services. But

---

38 Hence Marx specifies that value is only 'latent' in the sphere of production; it becomes actual by passing the test of circulation (Marx 1970a, p. 45). What Marx calls 'individual values' are latent; they have not proven themselves as 'social values' (Marx 1981, p. 283).

39 I thank Fred Moseley and Duncan Foley for helpful exchanges on the topics of this section.

40 Marx 1970a, p. 36.

desires of this sort are not universal; neither is their aggregation.[41] Demand results from the atomization of society produced along with wealth in the commodity form.[42] Demand presupposes money and prices. Only when backed by money does desire count toward demand.[43] A vagrant's longing for housing creates zero demand. Take away money and demand vanishes. Demand cannot do even without the concept of money, for demand stretches desire across a monetary grid: to determine the demand for a commodity we need to know what individuals are willing to purchase at various prices. Take away prices and, again, demand vanishes. Finally, commodities are sold not only to consumers but also to capitalist producers. Their level of demand is inseparable from the rate of profit.

When Marx introduces value, he distinguishes between its substance and its magnitude. He identifies its substance as a 'phantom-like objectivity' and 'congealed quantities of homogeneous labour', labour of a specific social sort, commodity-producing labour.[44] Marx calls commodity-values 'crystals of this social substance'.[45] Labour produces value only if it is socially validated as abstract labour, and if it is 'socially necessary'. We learn that such validation occurs only in commodity circulation and that there is no way to tell whether labour is 'socially necessary' apart from the circulation of commodities. Because there can be no value without money and prices, and because the price system presupposes demand, value and demand are inseparable. Demand 'determines' value even before we get to the issue of the magnitude of value inasmuch as, without demand, there would be no substance of value to measure.

To understand how demand affects the magnitude of value and price, we need to know how it figures into the concept of 'socially necessary' labour. For, 'what exclusively determines the magnitude of the value of any article is therefore the amount of labour socially necessary'.[46] Marx's statement on 'socially necessary' labour, however, includes no mention of demand, 'Socially necessary labour-time is the labour-time required to produce any use-value under the conditions of production normal for a given society and with the

41 See Marx 1981, p. 295.
42 See Campbell 1997, p. 100.
43 Marx 1981, p. 282.
44 In assuming wealth in the commodity form, Marx assumes labour in the commodity-producing form.
45 Marx 1976a, p. 128.
46 Marx 1976a, p. 129.

average degree of skill and intensity of labour prevalent in that society'.[47] Nevertheless, demand constrains 'socially necessary' labour, a point that Marx signals cryptically at the end of the first section of Chapter One: 'If the thing is useless, so is the labour contained in it; the labour does not count as labour, and therefore creates no value'.[48] He addresses the matter more expansively at the beginning of Chapter Two. He observes that all commodities

> must stand the test as use-values before they can be realized as values. For the labour expended on them only counts in so far as it is expended in a form which is useful for others. However, only the act of exchange can prove whether that labour is useful for others, and its product consequently capable of satisfying the needs of others.[49]

Labour for whose product there is no demand is not 'socially necessary' and therefore produces no value.

Demand constrains value but not in the same way as do the production factors that determine whether or not labour is 'socially necessary'.[50] The average levels of technical development, skill and intensity give positive quantitative determinations of 'socially necessary' labour: they always matter. Demand affects the quantity of 'socially necessary' labour only when it does not balance supply. Insofar as demand matches supply, it stops influencing the magnitude of value and price.[51] (Even then, demand makes the determination of the magnitudes of value and price possible.) For expository purposes, Marx generally assumes that demand and supply balance. That puts demand on mute. Though he makes the heuristic assumption that demand and supply balance, Marx holds that, in reality, they do not.[52] Imbalance is to be expected in a system of roundabout mediation. Marx's theory of prices holds that, as supply and demand vacillate, prices will fluctuate around 'labour values'; the law of value, which states that price is determined by the quantity of 'socially necessary' labour, asserts itself only as the law of fluctuation of prices.[53] Marx argues that, due to competition, average prices over the long run will iron out the ups and downs of supply and demand, so that demand drops out as a factor in the

47 Ibid.

48 Marx 1976a, p. 131.

49 Marx 1976a, pp. 179–80. Compare Marx 1970a, pp. 45–6.

50 Marx calls attention to this difference: see Marx 1981, p. 283.

51 Marx 1981, pp. 290–1.

52 Marx 1981, p. 291.

53 Marx 1976a, p. 196.

quantitative determination of value and average price over the long run. These two considerations help explain why the place of demand in Marx's value theory is inconspicuous and not well understood.

Marx discusses demand at some length in Chapter Ten of *Capital* Volume III. He explains why as follows:

> To say that a commodity has use-value is simply to assert that it satisfies some kind of a social need. As long as we were dealing only with an individual commodity, we could take the need for this specific commodity as already given, without having to go in any further detail into the quantitative extent of the need which had to be satisfied. The quantity was already implied by its price. But this quantity is a factor of fundamental importance as soon as we have on the one hand the product of a whole branch of production and on the other the social need. It now becomes necessary to consider the volume of the social need, i.e. its quantity.[54]

In shifting levels of abstraction from the individual commodity as an aliquot part of the total social capital to the total social capital divided into branches of production and industrial capitals having differing organic compositions of capital, Marx introduces the concepts of market value and market price:

> Market value is to be viewed on the one hand as the average value of the commodities produced in a particular sphere, and on the other hand as the individual value of commodities produced under average conditions in the sphere in question, and forming the great mass of its commodities.[55]

The relation between market value and market price is, in the main, the now familiar one between value and price, 'if supply and demand regulate market price, or rather the departures of market price from market value, the market value in turn regulates the relation between supply and demand, or the centre around which fluctuations of demand and supply make the market price oscillate'.[56] Once again, demand drops out as a determinant of average prices over the long run.

54 Marx 1981, p. 286.

55 Marx 1981, p. 279.

56 Marx 1981, p. 282. See also Marx 1981, pp. 290–1.

Two complicating factors remain. (1) In extreme cases demand affects the magnitude of market value: 'Only in extraordinary situations do commodities produced under the worst conditions, or alternatively the most advantageous ones, govern the market value, which forms in turn the centre around which market prices fluctuate'.[57] (2) Demand appears to affect the average rate of profit and thereby prices of production. When a commodity 'is produced on a scale that exceeds the social need at the time, a part of the society's labour-time is wasted, and the mass of commodities in question then represents on the market a much smaller quantity of social labour than it actually contains'.[58] It seems to follow that the better that producers track demand, the less squandering of value occurs, resulting in fewer deductions from the total amount of surplus value and a higher average rate of profit and higher prices of production. Here we seem to have two ways in which demand can determine even the magnitude of market values and prices.

5 Money as Displaced Social Form and 'The Illusion of the Economic'

Marx's theory of money not only explains that economics falls into 'the illusion of the economic', it goes a long way toward explaining why. Marx says that the money form is 'blinding'.[59] What does it blind us to? Most of all, it blinds us to the polarity of the value form, which tells us that neither commodities nor money are mere things; they are things caught up in a peculiar network of social relations, social mediations, that they make possible. Marx stresses the point that, in capitalist society, social relations appear displaced onto the relations between things: 'it is a characteristic feature of labour which posits exchange-value that it causes the social relations of individuals to appear in the perverted form of a social relation between things'.[60] The point of Marx's theory of value and money is that we do relate to one another through our commodities and money. Nonetheless, it is *we* who associate in and through these things. Because value, which is something purely social, appears, first, to be a natural property of a commodity (the fetishism of the commodity) and, still more perversely, to be a thing, money (the money fetish) – social relations seem to be absent. The specific social form of labour and wealth in capitalism necessarily gets displaced onto money, a thing that does not look like a social

57 Marx 1981, p. 279. See also Marx 1981, pp. 280, 286.
58 Marx 1981, p. 289.
59 Marx 1976a, p. 139.
60 Marx 1970a, p. 34.

form at all![61] This sets the stage for 'the illusion of the economic' because it makes capitalist society, its labour and its wealth, appear to have no particular social form or purpose at all. 'It is however precisely this finished form of the world of commodities – the money form – which conceals the social character of private labour and the social relations between the individual workers, by making those relations appear as relations between material objects, instead of revealing them plainly'.[62] That not only generates 'the illusion of the economic', the belief that 'production in general' is actual, but it also naturally leads to the idea that capitalist production is 'production in general'.[63]

Marx brings out these ideas in his discussion of the money fetish in the closing paragraph of Chapter Two. I quote it in full for it synthesises so many of the ideas that we have been examining:

> We have already seen, from the simplest expression of value, x commodity A = y commodity B, that the thing in which the magnitude of the value of another thing is represented appears to have the equivalent form independently of this relation, as a social property inherent in its nature. We followed the process by which this false semblance became firmly established, a process which was completed when the universal equivalent form became identified with the natural form of a particular commodity, and thus crystallised into the money-form. What appears to happen is not that a particular commodity becomes money because all other commodities express their values in it, but, on the contrary, that all other commodities universally express their values in a particular commodity because it is money. The movement through which this process has been mediated vanishes in its own result, leaving no trace behind. Without any initiative on their part, the commodities find their own value-configuration ready to hand, in the form of a physical commodity existing outside but also alongside them. This physical object, gold or silver in its crude state,

61 Marx calls this situation '*verrückt*' (translated as 'absurd') (Marx 1976a, p. 169), which means 'displaced' and 'mad'. See Arthur 2002a, p. 173, n. 11.

62 Marx 1976a, pp. 168–9.

63 In *Capital* Volume III Marx points out that the division of surplus value into interest and profit of enterprise (which appears as the 'wages of superintendence') displaces the social form of the capitalist production process onto interest-bearing capital, 'The social form of capital devolves on interest, but expressed in a neutral and indifferent form; the economic function of capital devolves on profit of enterprise, but with the specifically capitalist character of this function removed' (Marx 1981, p. 506). Once again, specifically capitalist forms naturally create 'the illusion of the economic'.

> becomes, immediately on its emergence from the bowels of the earth, the direct incarnation of all human labour. Hence the magic of money. Men are henceforth related to each other in their social process of production in a purely atomistic way. Their own relations of production therefore assume a material shape which is independent of their control and their conscious individual action. This situation is manifested first by the fact that the products of men's labour universally take on the form of commodities. The riddle of the money fetish is therefore the riddle of the commodity fetish, now become visible and dazzling to our eyes.[64]

In money the social mediation of private labours vanishes into a thing, resulting in an atomistic condition of asocial sociality where capitalist social relations do not appear to be social relations. As Marx argued at the beginning of the *Grundrisse*, that helps explain the appeal of arguments that postulate a state of nature.

The mediating role of money makes capitalist social relations appear to be no social relations at all; likewise, the wealth produced on a capitalist basis appears to have no specific social form or purpose:

> Commodities first enter into the process of exchange ungilded and unsweetened, retaining their original home-grown shape. Exchange, however, produces a differentiation of the commodity into two elements, commodity and money, an external opposition which expresses the opposition between use-value and value which is inherent in it.[65]

So, in this polar form, the commodity appears as 'pure use-value', that is, use value stripped of any social form and purpose. Consequently, the commodity looks like 'natural wealth' or 'wealth in general', thus creating 'the illusion of the economic'. Commodity exchange works like a centrifuge, separating out the social aspect of the commodity as money, leaving the commodity to appear as purely private, mere use value.

Since the social form of wealth in the commodity form is displaced onto money, commodities themselves appear to be socially non-specific, to be wealth in general. Likewise, commodity-producing labour appears to be labour in general. The asocial, or indirect, sociality of commodity-producing labour appears as an absence of sociality rather than an unusual form of it. It is as

64 Marx 1976a, p. 187.

65 Marx 1976a, p. 199; see also p. 153.

if one failed to recognise indifference as one particular state of mind alongside love and hatred. Marx's theory of money, then, plays a pivotal role in his explanation of why capitalism exudes 'the illusion of the economic'. As the circulation process 'sweats out' money, 'the illusion of the economic' beads up.

CHAPTER 10

The Social and Material Transformation of Production by Capital: Formal and Real Subsumption in *Capital*, Volume I*

1 Why Wealth is a Poor Concept: On the Purpose of Production

What is the purpose of production in those societies where wealth is generally produced in the form of commodities, that is, in those societies where the capitalist mode of production predominates? Marx's answer to this simple, but commonly neglected, question enables him to begin the huge Chapter 15, 'Machinery and large-scale industry', by one-upping John Stuart Mill:

> John Stuart Mill says in his *Principles of Political Economy*: 'It is questionable if all the mechanical inventions yet made have lightened the day's toil of any human being'. *That is, however, by no means the aim of the application of machinery under capitalism*. Like every other instrument for increasing the productivity of labour, machinery is intended to cheapen commodities and, by shortening the part of the working day in which the worker works for himself, to lengthen the other part, the part he gives to the capitalist for nothing. *The machine is a means for producing surplus-value.*[1]

Mill's surprise only reveals his thoughtlessness regarding the specific purpose of capitalist production. Stocking up (unpaid surplus) labour, not saving labour, is the point of a system whose goal is the accumulation of capital. The cruel irony of capitalist development is that it is constantly driven to increase productivity for the purpose of appropriating more and more surplus labour.

---

* Originally published as 'The Social and Material Transformation of Production by Capital: Formal and Real Subsumption in *Capital*, Volume I', in *The Constitution of Capital: Essays on Volume I of Marx's 'Capital'*, edited by Riccardo Bellofiore and Nicola Taylor (Basingstoke, Hampshire: Palgrave Macmillan, 2004), pp. 243–73, reprinted with the kind permission of Palgrave Macmillan.

1 Marx 1976a, p. 492, my emphases.

Like economists generally, Mill is oblivious to the question that animates Marx's inquiry: 'What is the specific social form and purpose of wealth?'[2] Two questions about material wealth are well understood and widely asked. How much wealth is there? How is wealth distributed? While Marx is interested in these two, he focuses on the elusive, though more fundamental, question: What is the specific social form and purpose of wealth? Answering this third question, to which so many inquirers are oblivious, also provides the answer to the question: What is the specific measure of wealth? For capitalism, the purpose and measure is surplus value, the increment in value beyond the value invested by a capitalist. The capitalist's 'aim is to produce not only a use-value, but a commodity; not only use-value, but value; and not just value, but also surplus-value'.[3] By pressing this third question, Marx reveals that the everyday concept of wealth is impoverished.

In the *Grundrisse* Marx observes, 'all production is appropriation of nature on the part of an individual within and through a specific form of society'.[4] When we abstract from the specific social form and purpose of wealth (and from the specific social character of needs and labour), we lose our grip on actuality. That is what happens with wealth. Beginning with the first sentence of *Capital*, Marx announces that his topic is not wealth but rather a specific social form of wealth, wealth in the (generalised) commodity form. With that opening, Marx establishes the theme of the double character of wealth and production under capitalism – use value and value. The genius of *Capital* is that it maintains the theme of the double character of capitalism from start to finish; it never loses track of the powers of the peculiar social forms and purposes that animate the capitalist mode of production. By contrast, the concept of wealth is poor because it bleaches out social form.

The same difficulty arises when we come to capital. Oblivious to the topic of the specific social form and purpose of wealth, everyday thought and economics attempt to define capital on the basis of natural (socially nonspecific) characteristics. This leads to the common definition: capital is wealth capable of being used to produce more wealth.[5] It should be easy to see that this generally applicable definition of capital provides no bridge to understanding the

2 By 'economics' I mean any investigation into the production and distribution of wealth that does not incorporate specific social forms of needs, labour and wealth as ingredients of the theory. Classical and neoclassical economics both fit this description; 'institutional economics' does not. (On the latter point, see Campbell 2004.)

3 Marx 1976a, p. 293.

4 Marx 1973, p. 87.

5 See Marx 1973, pp. 85–6, for Marx's direct criticism of this conception of capital.

capitalist mode of production as historically specific. If the concept of capital is generally applicable, then what makes the capitalist mode of production distinctive has nothing to do with capital. So the everyday conception of capital, the one we find also in economics, is a nonstarter for understanding the capitalist mode of production.

The ordinary conception of capital is at once too broad and too narrow. It is too broad because it encompasses all human societies, but how is it too narrow? Marx's answer comes out most clearly in the *Results* and in Part One of Volume II of *Capital*. Marx observes that, under capitalism, wealth is produced not simply in the commodity form but in the form of commodity capital, that is, commodities whose sale realises surplus value. Since goods for individual consumption, including luxury items, are produced in the social form of commodity capital, not all commodity capital is suitable as a means for new production. According to the commonplace definition of capital, then, such goods and services must not be capital. Because of the role they play in the realisation of surplus value, however, they do function as capital. Here the commonplace definition is too narrow. Were economics and everyday discourse to include commodity capital as capital, their concept of capital would collapse into that of wealth, since there are no distinctive natural characteristics of wealth in the form of commodity capital. The effort to define capital in abstraction from specific social forms and purposes, then, breaks down in a twofold failure.

Recognising Marx's profound break with the discourse of economics opens the conceptual space needed to grasp what Marx means in talking of various forms of subsumption under capital. Talk of any sort of subsumption under capital is unintelligible on the basis of the commonplace conception of capital, which is silent on the question of the determinate social form and purpose of wealth. The whole point of Marx's discourse of different forms of subsumption is to reveal the diverse ways in which capital, as a specific social form of wealth, exercises its epoch-making power. Marx's discourse of subsumption drives home the point that *Capital* is fundamentally a study of the nature, inseparability, powers and consequences of the specific social forms belonging to the capitalist mode of production. The several subsumption concepts point to the diverse ways that capital, understood as a specific – and explosive – social form of wealth, revolutionises society, its goods and services and the ways they are produced.

2 Absolute Surplus Value and Relative Surplus Value

The middle third of the first volume of *Capital*, on which this chapter focuses, is devoted to two topics, absolute surplus value and relative surplus value. The present chapter relates these two, respectively, to the concepts of the formal subsumption and real subsumption of labour under capital. While mentioned in *Capital*, the terms 'formal subsumption' and 'real subsumption' are treated at greater length in Marx's manuscript of 1861–3 and in the intended, but unfinished, conclusion to Volume I, *Results of the Immediate Production Process* (*Results*).[6] In those manuscripts Marx also develops the concepts of ideal subsumption and hybrid subsumption, which we will examine. I argue that the changes to the production process that Marx identifies with increasing absolute surplus value involve simply formal subsumption, while those transformations required for relative surplus value involve real subsumption. Between them, formal subsumption and real subsumption under capital bring about a continual hubbub of social and material revolution, yet in the same stroke, they enforce social stasis because they strengthen and expand the hold of the law of value and capital's web of value forms. The middle third of *Capital* Volume I works out a surplus-value theory that provides a powerful theoretical explanation for the endless transformation of the globe by the bourgeoisie that Marx and Engels announced in the *Communist Manifesto*.

In 'The labour process and the valorization process', the first of the chapters that compose this middle third of Volume I, Marx shows how the capitalist is able to turn the trick of making money from money (valorisation). He begins by noting two fundamental characteristics of the capitalist form of production. First, simply by being the purchaser of labour power and of the means of production, the capitalist commands the production process. Second, the workers' entire product, including any surplus value realised by its sale, belongs to the capitalist.[7] The solution to the riddle of surplus value's source is this: the capitalist purchases labour power at its value but then commands its seller, the wage labourer, to keep producing value beyond the amount necessary to match the worker's wage. Remarkably, capital turns the trick of valorisation without putting a dent in simple commodity circulation's rules of fairness.[8] In this way

6 See Marx 1976a, p. 645; Marx 1976d, pp. 83–4; Marx 1982, pp. 2,130–59; and Marx 1976b, pp. 1019–38.

7 Marx 1976a, pp. 291–2.

8 'Every condition of the problem has been satisfied, while the laws governing the exchange of commodities have not been violated in any way. Equivalent has been exchanged for equivalent' (Marx 1976a, p. 301).

Marx discloses the irony of bourgeois justice: the whole sphere of commutative justice, that is, the exchange of equivalent values, which is the norm for simple commodity circulation, rests on the exploitation of those who sell their labour power by those who own the means of production. Bourgeois fairness is a counterfeit.

In explaining absolute surplus value and relative surplus value, Marx uses a divided line (ABC) to represent the working day. The first part of the line, AB, represents necessary labour, that is, the amount of labour required to produce enough value to match the value of the worker's labour power, the monetary expression of which is, by assumption, the wage. The second part of the line, BC, represents surplus labour, which creates surplus value for the capitalist. To increase surplus value the capitalist has three options.

1. Keep AB constant but increase BC by lengthening the working day; this is the strategy of absolute surplus value.
2. Keep AC constant but increase BC by decreasing AB. On the assumption that workers' wages cover the value of their labour power, only lowering the value of labour power can decrease AB.[9] That requires decreasing the value of the commodities that go into sustaining labour power.[10] The strategy of relative surplus value pumps out more surplus value by increasing the productivity of labour so as to cheapen labour power. For increasing the productivity of labour, the worker is 'rewarded' with a lower wage (in value terms). Wages that are lower in value terms need not be lower in use-value terms – indeed the assumption here is that, though the commodities consumed by workers contain less value, they will not be lower in use-value terms. With increased

9 As Marx well knows, this assumption need not be respected in reality.

10 Actually, there are other ways to lower the value of labour power. Capitalists can deskill workers for the purpose of lowering the value of their labour power. But this has its problems. First, deskilled labour does not produce as much value as skilled labour (Marx 1976a, pp. 304–5). Second, introducing more productive techniques may well require introducing new skilled labourers. Marx does not argue that deskilling is a necessary strategy in the production of relative surplus value. By contrast, he states unequivocally, 'Capital therefore has an immanent drive, and a constant tendency, towards increasing the productivity of labour' (Marx 1976a, pp. 436–7). Another possibility, a bloody one, is implicit in Marx's inclusion of a historical ingredient in the determination of the value of labour power (Marx 1976a, p. 75). Capital could try to turn back the hands of time and lower the minimal expectations of wage labourers. Or, more likely, in a world where workers of different sexes, ages, races, regions or nations have various minimal standards, capitalists can reduce the value of labour power by employing more workers with lower standards.

productivity, wages can simultaneously go down in value terms and up in use-value terms: capitalists and workers can split the relative surplus value.
3. Lengthen AC and shorten AB. Absolute and relative surplus value are 'flow' concepts; they discriminate, at any level of the development of productive power, whether an increase in surplus value is due to extending the working day (absolute surplus-value) or increasing the productivity of labour (relative surplus value).[11] Thus, highly productive firms can follow an absolute-value strategy by expanding the workday while holding productivity (and wages) constant. Marx thought it common for advances in productivity to lengthen the working day.[12]

The chief way to decrease the value of labour power that Marx studies in the middle third of Volume I is to increase the productivity of labour. Cooperation, division of labour, manufacture, machinery and large-scale industry are all ways of increasing productivity. But why, according to Marx, does increasing productivity reduce the value of commodities to begin with? Because abstract, not concrete, labour produces value. Productivity is a concrete, use-value consideration, so 'the productivity of labour does not affect the value'.[13] Consequently, as productivity increases across a given branch of production, more commodities are turned out, yet no more value is added per hour. It is only because of this 'value treadmill' that the values of the commodities that enter into determining the value of labour power decrease, opening the door to relative surplus value.[14]

Lowering the value of labour power, however, is not what motivates a firm to introduce a more productive labour process and thereby cheapen their goods. Capitalist firms that produce at higher than the average levels of productivity in their branch appropriate extra surplus value, because an hour worked in such firms counts as more than an hour of socially necessary abstract labour.[15]

---

11 See Marx 1982, pp. 2, 126.

12 Marx 1976a, p. 646.

13 Marx 1963c, p. 393.

14 Marx 1976a, pp. 436–7. Marx triumphantly observes, 'we have here the solution of the following riddle: Why does the capitalist, whose sole concern is to produce exchange-value, continually strive to bring down the exchange-value of commodities?' (Marx 1976a, p. 437).

15 In Chapter 12, 'The concept of relative surplus-value', Marx explains this by invoking a distinction between 'individual' and 'social' values. 'The individual value of these articles is now below their social value ... The real value of a commodity, however, is not its individual, but its social value; that is to say, its value is not measured by the labour-time

Notice that this mechanism gives even firms whose products do not enter into the determination of the value of labour power a good reason to keep looking for ways to increase productivity.[16] The 'value treadmill' and the logic of relative surplus value show that this drive to increase the productivity of labour is a powerful immanent tendency of the capitalist mode of production. Since Marx reaches this result solely by tracking the consequences of capital conceived of as a distinctive social form of wealth, we glimpse the power of his social-form approach.

Marx's use of a divided line to illustrate absolute surplus value in terms of extending the line and relative surplus value in terms of shortening its first division (necessary labour) is a neat pedagogical stroke. However, it has its risks. It could suggest that Marx's inquiry into surplus-value addresses solely quantitative considerations: What portion of the working day is devoted to 'necessary labour'? What portion to 'surplus labour'? What is the rate of surplus-value (surplus labour over necessary labour)? Concentrating on the lengths and proportions of the line segments can deflect attention from a prior question: What is the dimension of the line? Then it is easy for the bad habits of economics and everyday talk to slip in this answer: the divided line takes the measure of wealth and surplus wealth – instead of value and surplus value.

In this way, the divided line can play into the Ricardian socialist misreading of *Capital*, for which the all-consuming issue is the exploitative, class division of wealth. Because it is oblivious to the fundamental issue of the specific social form and purpose of wealth, Ricardian theory – including Ricardian socialism – fails to register the difference between wealth and value. If you overlook the fact that value is not wealth but a specific social form of wealth, then absolute surplus value looks applicable to any class society. Wherever one class lives off the labour of another, the labour of the servile class must be divided into necessary and surplus, and, holding the necessary constant, any lengthening of the working day will increase the surplus wealth appropriated by the dominant class.[17] The division between necessary and surplus labour forms the basis of any system of exploitation, but not just any social sort of labour produces value and surplus value.[18] Marx's divided line measures not 'wealth' but a definite social form of wealth, namely value, which is bound up with special social relations and purposes.

---

that the article costs the producer in each individual case, but by the labour-time socially required for its production' (Marx 1976a, p. 434).

16 Marx 1976a, pp. 434–5.

17 Marx 1976a, p. 344.

18 Marx 1976b, pp. 976–7.

Exploitation and class divisions are nothing new. Capitalism is unique in presenting itself as a universalistic and egalitarian society in which exchanges are governed by the law of commutative justice: equal value for equal value. In other words, capitalism presents itself precisely as the fair society that has rid itself of class and exploitation. One of *Capital*'s prime accomplishments is to place capitalist society among the ranks of exploitative, class societies. Ricardian socialism gets this right, but by collapsing value into wealth, surplus value into surplus wealth, it turns a blind eye to Marx's brilliant explorations of the effects of capital's web of distinctive social forms and purposes. Consequently, like many critics of *Capital*, Ricardian socialists squander what I.I. Rubin calls the 'qualitative sociological side of Marx's theory of value'.[19]

Connecting the concepts of absolute and relative surplus value with those of formal and real subsumption under capital helps us avoid the pitfall of a Ricardian socialist misreading of *Capital*. Why? Because the subsumption concepts force us to ask, subsumption under what? To that question the only plausible answer is specific social forms, notably, capital.

3 Marx's Four Subsumption Concepts: Formal, Real, Hybrid and Ideal

Marx discusses four different types of subsumption under capital: formal, real, hybrid and ideal.[20] Formal subsumption and real subsumption are central to the present chapter, but we will briefly consider hybrid and ideal subsumption. First, how are absolute and relative surplus value related to formal and real subsumption? Marx writes,

> The production of absolute surplus-value turns exclusively on the length of the working day, whereas the production of relative surplus-value completely revolutionizes the technical processes of labour and the groupings into which society is divided.
>
> It therefore requires a specifically capitalist mode of production, a mode of production which, along with its methods, means and conditions,

---

19 Rubin 1972, pp. 73–4.

20 To these four a fifth might be added. It might be called the subsumption of pre-capitalist commercial forms under capital. 'We see here how even economic categories appropriate to earlier modes of production acquire a new and specific historical character under the impact of capitalist production' (Marx 1976b, p. 950).

> arises and develops spontaneously on the basis of formal subsumption of labour under capital. This formal subsumption is then replaced by a real subsumption.[21]

While 'a merely formal subsumption of labour under capital suffices for the production of absolute surplus-value', the production of relative surplus value involves the real subsumption of labour under capital.[22] In other words, the middle third of *Capital* I is all about formal and real subsumption. More specifically, Part Three: 'The production of absolute surplus-value' treats of the formal subsumption of labour under capital, while Part Four: 'The production of relative surplus-value' deals with real subsumption of labour under capital. This second correlation implies that, since the three chapters devoted to cooperation, the division of labour and manufacture and machinery and large-scale industry (Chapters 13–15) all fall within Part Four, all three are forms of real subsumption.

Several of those authors who were among the first to write on formal and real subsumption reject this conclusion. Étienne Balibar and Derek Sayer identify 'simple' cooperation and manufacture with formal subsumption and large-scale industry with real subsumption.[23] Balibar claims, 'The "formal subsumption" which begins with the form of out-work on behalf of a merchant capitalist and ends with the industrial revolution includes the whole history of what Marx calls "manufacture"'.[24] Sayer writes along the same lines, 'Marx distinguishes what he calls manufacture and machine industry as successive historical stages … in the development of a specifically capitalist production process. These stages rest upon different historical forms of the labour/capital relation, which Marx refers to as formal and real subordination, subjection or subsumption of labour to capital respectively'.[25] Sayer does not recognise that Marx's phrase, 'specifically capitalist production' is equivalent to production that has undergone real subsumption. Consequently, if manufacture is a specific historical stage in the development of 'a specifically capitalist production process', then it must be a form of real subsumption. Sayer also fails to see that the terms 'formal subsumption' and 'real subsumption' refer first to concepts

21 Marx 1976a, p. 645.

22 Ibid. For similar statements see Marx 1976b, pp. 1,025 and 1,035, and Marx 1976d, p. 130.

23 Ernest Mandel, in his introduction to *Results*, concurs, 'Formal subsumption is characteristic of the period of manufacture; real subsumption is characteristic of the modern factory' (Mandel 1976, p. 944).

24 Balibar 1970, pp. 302–3.

25 Sayer 1987, pp. 30–1.

of subsumption and only secondarily – if at all – to historical stages of subsumption. Marx considers the possibility of a distinct historical stage of merely formal subsumption but finds no evidence of one. Neither does Marx think that there is any historical period of 'simple co-operation'.[26] Manufacture and large-scale industry are the only two historical periods of real subsumption that Marx acknowledges. Because they conceive of formal and real subsumption as historical stages rather than as concepts of subsumption, Sayer and Balibar lose sight of the fact that a production process must be formally subsumed under capital in order to be really subsumed.

With a thinker like Marx, the architectonic considerations alone make a strong case against Balibar and Sayer. But here are a couple of passages that directly undercut their view. Marx describes cooperation as 'the first change experienced by the actual labour process when subjected to capital'.[27] He goes on to remark that not only is cooperation the first form of real subsumption but that 'Co-operation remains the fundamental form of the capitalist mode of production, although in its simple shape it continues to appear as one particular form alongside the more developed ones'.[28] Though there is no period of 'simple' cooperation, cases of 'simple' cooperation occur. All forms of real subsumption are forms of cooperation; 'simple' cooperation is a type of cooperation, but so are manufacture and large-scale industry.

Where division of labour and manufacture are concerned, consider two passages. 'The division of labour in the workshop, as practised by manufacture, is an entirely specific creation of the capitalist mode of production'.[29] 'While simple co-operation leaves the mode of the individual's labour for the most part unchanged, manufacture thoroughly revolutionizes it, and seizes labour-power by its roots'.[30] These statements should remove any doubt: division of labour and manufacture are forms of real subsumption.

3.1 *Formal Subsumption*

Marx writes that the formal subsumption of labour under capital 'is the general form of every capitalist process of production'; real subsumption, then, always presupposes formal subsumption.[31] To begin to grasp capital's transformative power, we need to answer the following question: If formal subsumption

26 Marx 1976a, p. 454.
27 Marx 1976a, p. 453.
28 Marx 1976a, p. 454.
29 Marx 1976a, p. 480.
30 Marx 1976a, p. 481.
31 Marx 1976b, p. 1,019.

of labour under capital is the 'general form', what social and material transformations does it bring about? The social transformations involved in formal subsumption are epochal, but the material transformations are slight – until merely formal subsumption gives way to real subsumption. Formal subsumption assumes that labour takes the specific social form of 'free' wage labour and that wealth is generally in the commodity form. These conditions enable the capitalist both to monopolise the means of subsistence of wage labourers and to purchase all three factors of the production process: objects of production, means of production and labour power.[32] With formal subsumption:

> the process of production has become the process of capital itself. It is a process involving the *factors of the labour process* into which the capitalist's money has been converted and which proceeds under his direction with the sole purpose of using money to make more money.[33]

Marx dwells on the exact social character of the relation between capitalist and 'free' wage labourer:

> The pure money relationship between the man who appropriates the surplus labour and the man who yields it up: subordination in this case arises from the *specific content* of the sale – there is not a subordination underlying it in which the producer stands in a relation to the exploiter of his labour which is determined not just by money (the relationship of one commodity owner to another), but, let us say, by political restraints. What brings the seller into a relationship of dependency is solely the fact that the buyer is the owner of the conditions of labour. There is no fixed political and social relationship of supremacy and subordination.[34]

This means that capitalism announces the end of social classes as we knew them, where class membership was fixed by birth and received explicit political or social recognition. With the rise of capitalism, then, not only does class structure assume a new form, the very idea of class is radically transformed.

---

32 Marx 1976b, p. 1,026.

33 Marx 1976b, p. 1,020.

34 Marx 1976b, pp. 1025–6. On the other hand, not only do various forms of dependency based on religion, sex, race, ethnicity and 'birth' persist in actual capitalist societies, but they can serve various capitalist interests. Notably, they put downward pressure on wages and disrupt organised resistance to capital by workers.

In Chapter Six, 'The sale and purchase of labour-power', Marx had already emphasised the wage labourer's freedom to dispose of his labour power. In the marketplace, that 'Eden of the innate rights of man', the wage labourer and the capitalist meet as equals, one in the role of seller, the other buyer.[35] The perfect liberty and egalitarianism of that sphere are, of course, dealt a blow by the shift into the sphere of production, where the wage labourer is subordinate to the capitalist. But Marx's insistence that nothing other than the '*specific content* of the sale' enters into this unique type of subordination reveals how the characteristic social forms of simple commodity circulation condition the sphere of production.

Marx highlights the peculiar features of this social form of labour by contrasting the wage labourer with slaves, serfs and vassals; the independent peasant; and the medieval guild labourer. He points up several distinctive, and mostly liberating, aspects of wage labour:

1. Because of the voluntary and egalitarian aspects of the wage contract, wage labourers feel free.
2. The wage worker's livelihood and the livelihood of any dependents are the worker's own responsibility. Carrying the burden of this responsibility promotes a kind of self-reliance with the attendant ideologies and sensibilities. Positive social recognition and self-esteem also generally accompany these factors.[36]
3. The wage-worker is working for herself (as well as for her employer); her wages are hers to spend. While this increases self-esteem, it is also conducive to selfishness.[37]
4. Because wages are paid in money, it is up to the wage labourer to choose what to buy: 'It is the worker himself who converts the money into whatever

35 Marx 1976a, p. 280.

36 Simone de Beauvoir writes in *The Second Sex*: 'It is through gainful employment that woman has traversed most of the distance that separated her from the male; and nothing else can guarantee her liberty in practice ... with the money and the rights she takes possession of, she makes a trial of and senses her responsibility ... I heard a charwoman declare, while scrubbing the stone floor of a hotel lobby: "I never asked anybody for anything; I succeeded all by myself". She was as proud of her self-sufficiency as a Rockefeller' (de Beauvoir 1989, pp. 679–80).

37 Recall what Marx wrote of the participants in simple commodity circulation: 'each looks only to his own advantage. The only force bringing them together, and putting them into relation with each other, is the selfishness, the gain and the private interest of each. Each pays heed to himself only, and no one worries about the others' (Marx 1976a, p. 280).

use-values he desires; it is he who buys commodities as he wishes'.[38] Marx observes that this requires workers to develop self-control, while making it possible for them to break with a parochialism of needs.

5. In making his purchases, the worker re-enters the egalitarian sphere of commodity circulation, 'as the owner of money, as the buyer of goods, he stands in precisely the same relationship to the sellers of goods as any other buyer'.[39] We all call ourselves 'consumers'.
6. The variability of wages adds to the worker's perception that he is master of his fate, 'the size of his wage packet appears to vary in keeping with the results of his own work and its individual quality'.[40] The wage labourer's own talents can benefit him.
7. Marx points out a darker side of the wage: 'Since the sole purpose of work in the eyes of the wage-labourer is his wage, money, a specific quantity of exchange-value from which every particular mark of use-value has been expunged, he is wholly indifferent towards the content of his labour and hence his own particular form of activity'.[41] Even this indifference has its positive side: greater versatility on the part of workers.
8. As wealth increasingly takes on the commodity form, everyone needs money, so that '*money-making* appears as the ultimate purpose of activity of every kind'.[42] This leads to a slurring of the differences among the forms of revenue (wages, profits, interest and rent): everyone's a money-maker. This obscures crucial differences while promoting egalitarian ideologies and sensibilities among wage labourers.

Even though, as a consequence of the formal subsumption of labour under capital, 'the process of exploitation is stripped of every patriarchal, political or even religious cloak', Marx insists that 'a new relation of *supremacy and subordination*' takes the place of the outmoded ones.[43] A production process that has been formally subsumed under capital is one that is under the command of the capitalist and is so for no other reason than that the capitalist owns the factors of the production process. To what end does the capitalist command the production process? To the only end that capital knows – surplus value. The concrete production process and all the factors of produc-

38 Marx 1976b, p. 1,033.
39 Marx 1976b, p. 1,033.
40 Marx 1976b, p. 1,032.
41 Marx 1976b, p. 1,033.
42 Marx 1976b, p. 1,041.
43 Marx 1976b, p. 1,027.

tion are simply instruments for the valorisation of capital.[44] In this respect, capital holds particular use values and wage labourers in a calculated disregard. All the same, since the valorisation process requires concrete production processes, the capitalist does not have the luxury of ignoring the specifics of the products, the process of their production or the people who produce them.

The final social implication of formal subsumption to be mentioned is the mystification inherent in it. At the beginning of the fetishism section of Chapter One, Marx wrote of the commodity, 'it is a very strange thing, abounding in metaphysical subtleties and theological niceties'.[45] He went on to argue that 'the mystical character of the commodity' stems from the peculiarity of the commodity form as a specific social form of wealth. The peculiarly asocial social form of commodity-producing labour results in commodities being fetishes possessed – in addition to their sensible properties – of the occult power to provide their owners a share in the wealth of the commodity-producing 'community'. Commodities are use values that pack a social clout which, strangely, appears to be their inherent property. In the *Results*, Marx echoes the language of the fetishism section, writing, 'capital becomes a highly mysterious thing'.[46] The peculiar social forms and purposes involved in formal subsumption under capital result in capital becoming a more imposing fetish than the commodity:[47]

> Since – within the process of production – living labour has already been absorbed into capital, all the *social productive forces of labour* appear as the *productive forces* of capital, as intrinsic attributes of capital, just as in the case of money, the creative power of labour had seemed to possess the qualities of a thing. What was true of money is even truer of capital.[48]

Capital possesses the occult power not simply of command over some portion of social wealth but also of command over living labour, an uncanny consequence latent in the phrase 'subsumption of labour under capital'.[49]

---

44 Marx 1976b, p. 1,019.
45 Marx 1976a, p. 163.
46 Marx 1976b, p. 1,056.
47 For a reading of the three volumes of *Capital* as organised around the commodity fetish and the capital fetish, see Murray 2002a, included in the present volume as Chapter 14.
48 Marx 1976b, p. 1,052.
49 See Marx 1976a, p. 651.

As a consequence, all the socially developed productive powers appear to inhere in capital.

How, then, does formal subsumption transform the production process materially? Not much, says Marx. For all the social transformation involved, 'this change does not in itself imply a fundamental modification in the real nature of the labour process'.[50] What changes do occur are more of a quantitative than qualitative sort: the process becomes more continuous and orderly, less wasteful in the use of means of production. And, of course, there are those hallmarks of absolute surplus value, lengthening and intensifying the workday. Such slight changes characterise merely formal subsumption, that is, formal subsumption where real subsumption does not occur. This reminds us that we must be cautious with the terminology of 'formal subsumption', as it has two meanings.[51] 'It is the general form of every capitalist process of production; at the same time, however, it can be found as a particular form alongside the specifically capitalist mode of production [that is, production that has undergone real subsumption]'.[52] The first, and original, sense of 'formal subsumption' applies to all processes of production organised along capitalist lines; the second, merely formal subsumption, refers only to those where real subsumption has not taken place.

3.2 *Real Subsumption*

The social transformation of production involved in the formal subsumption of labour under capital lays the groundwork for the endless material (and social) transformation of production processes through their real subsumption under capital.[53] What is real subsumption of labour under capital, and what social

50 Marx 1976b, p. 1,021. See also Marx 1976b, p. 1,026.

51 A third sense of 'formal subsumption' would identify a historical period in which *merely* formal subsumption (the second sense) was the dominant mode of production. Marx finds no such period.

52 Marx 1976b, p. 1,019.

53 Marx 1976b, p. 1,035. Marx's concepts of formal and real subsumption challenge 'technological' versions of historical materialism such G.A. Cohen's. 'Technological' historical materialism misses the basic point of Marx's historical materialism when it falsely separates technology from specific social forms and purposes. Neither the conceptual point that specific social forms and purposes co-determine what the forces of production *are*, nor the specific historical point that merely formal subsumption precedes real subsumption fits 'technological' historical materialism. Cohen sees the latter problem and appeals to functional explanations to try to get around it. For a criticism of his attempt, see Sayer 1987.

and material transformations does it bring about? Real subsumption transforms, and keeps transforming, production processes materially (and socially) into forms that are more adequate to capital for the simple reason that they press out more surplus value.[54] This is why 'real subsumption' is matched with the phrases 'specifically capitalist mode of production' and 'capitalist production' (for short).[55] The term 'real subsumption' can apply (1) to the concept of materially transforming a formally subsumed production process for the purpose of increasing surplus value, (2) to a particular production process that has undergone real subsumption – McDonald's fast food 'restaurants' are so prominent a case that 'Mc' has become, so to speak, the prefix of real subsumption (hence *USA Today* is 'Mcpaper') – and (3) to a historical period characterised by real subsumption.[56]

Marx has a great deal to say about particular types of real subsumption. The three chapters devoted to cooperation, division of labour and manufacture and machinery and large-scale industry come to two hundred pages.[57] Marx defines cooperation as follows: 'When numerous workers work together side by side in accordance with a plan, whether in the same process, or in different but connected processes, this form of labour is called co-operation'.[58] While simple cooperation is a particular type of real subsumption, cooperation 'remains the fundamental form of the capitalist mode of production'.[59] The concept of cooperation, then, belongs to the systematic dialectical argument of *Capital*, while simple cooperation, manufacture and large-scale industry all pertain to historical dialectics.[60] Here, our focus will be on what we can say in general about real subsumption.

First, since real subsumption presupposes formal subsumption, everything that was said about the transformations it brings about applies to production processes that undergo real subsumption.[61]

Second, 'a definite and constantly growing minimum amount of capital is both the necessary precondition and the constant result of the specifically

54 Marx 1976b, p. 1,037.

55 See Marx 1976b, pp. 1,024 and 1,034–6.

56 Since Marx judges that there is no historical period of merely formal subsumption, the historical period of real subsumption largely coincides with modern capitalism.

57 Marx 1976a, pp. 439–639.

58 Marx 1976a, p. 443.

59 Marx 1976a, p. 454.

60 On systematic dialectics and historical dialectics see Smith 1990, Smith 2003 and Murray 2003, included in the present volume as Chapter 3.

61 Marx 1976b, p. 1,035.

capitalist mode of production'.[62] It is the enlargement of merely formally subsumed production processes that leads to the simplest, and the basic, form of real subsumption, cooperation.[63]

Third, in cooperation, the mere quantitative increase in the scale of production shifts into qualitative changes:

> A large number of workers working together, at the same time, in one place … in order to produce the same sort of commodity under the command of the same capitalist, constitutes the starting-point of capitalist production. This is true both historically and conceptually.[64]

By 'capitalist production' here Marx means the 'specifically capitalist mode of production': 'capitalist production' begins historically and conceptually with cooperation. All real subsumption involves cooperation.

What qualitative changes does cooperation bring about?

1. Only with an expanded scale of production do the different proficiencies of individual workers begin to level out enough so as to resemble the socially average character of labour for that branch of production. Only then does the law of valorization come 'fully into its own for the individual producer'.[65]
2. 'Even without an alteration in the method of work, the simultaneous employment of a large number of workers produces a revolution in the objective conditions of the labour process'.[66] Here Marx has economies of scale in mind.[67] The savings on means of production involved here cheapen commodities and thereby increase surplus value by lowering the value of labour power. Cooperation is a relative surplus-value strategy. At the same time, these savings on means of production (constant capital) raise the rate of profit by reducing constant capital.
3. Certain tasks can be undertaken only cooperatively; in such cases we have 'the creation of a new productive power, which is intrinsically a collective one'.[68]

---

62 Marx 1976b, p. 1,035.
63 Marx 1976b, p. 1,022.
64 Marx 1976a, p. 437.
65 Marx 1976a, p. 441.
66 Ibid.
67 Marx 1976a, p. 442.
68 Marx 1976a, p. 443.

4. Emending Aristotle's observation that the human is a political animal, Marx calls humans social animals, for whom 'mere social contact begets in most industries a rivalry and a stimulation of the "animal spirits", which heighten the efficiency of each individual worker'.[69]
5. Cooperation makes possible the accomplishment of huge tasks that must be completed quickly and at a particular moment, such as harvesting crops.
6. Other projects, building a large dam, for example, are so vast as to require the power of cooperative labour.
7. Cooperation can also allow for a spatial concentration of efforts that reduces incidental expenses.

Marx pulls all of these advantages together in a long paragraph culminating in the observation that whatever the source of cooperation's special productive power, it is 'under all circumstances, the social productive power of labour, or the productive power of social labour. This power arises from co-operation itself'.[70] This social productive power of cooperation costs the capitalist nothing. It is these new productive powers of social labour that make cooperation a strategy of relative surplus value. Real subsumption of labour under capital, then, is all about the development of the productive powers of social labour – on capital's terms and to serve capital's end. The mystification of social productive powers as inherent in capital increases with the progress of real subsumption.

Fourth, there is a (continual) transformation in the capitalist's command of the production process:

> We also saw that, at first, the subjection of labour to capital was only a formal result of the fact that the worker, instead of working for himself, works for, and consequently under, the capitalist. Through the co-operation of numerous wage-labourers, the command of capital develops into a requirement of carrying on the labour process itself, into a real condition of production.[71]

With real subsumption the workers' dependence on capitalists takes a material form; capitalists, not workers, take charge of the coherence and plan of operations in the workplace.

---

69 Marx 1976a, p. 443.
70 Marx 1976a, p. 447.
71 Marx 1976a, p. 448.

Leadership of the 'cooperative' production process falls to the capitalist because he is the capitalist – this much follows from formal subsumption. But the capitalist is not a generic leader: 'As a specific function of capital, the directing function acquires its own special characteristics'.[72] These special characteristics stem from the specific social form and purpose of the capitalist mode of production. The goal of the capitalist's 'industrial' leadership is 'the greatest possible production of surplus-value'.[73] A further important factor conditioning the capitalist's 'industrial' leadership is the antagonistic relationship between capital and wage labour. Here, Marx once again draws our attention to the double character of capitalist production:

> If capitalist direction is thus twofold in content, owing to the twofold nature of the process of production which has to be directed – on the one hand a social labour process for the creation of a product, and on the other hand capital's process of valorization – in form it is purely despotic.[74]

Due to the material changes to the production process, this despotism, which is capital's despotism personified, is exercised through the physical make-up of production processes.[75]

With his conception of the real subsumption of production under capital, Marx thinks of modern 'industry' in a profoundly new way. A common, everyday way to imagine modern capitalism is to picture it in terms of 'commerce and industry'.[76] Industry is thought of in generic terms as the process by which wealth with no particular social form or purpose gets produced. Commerce is treated simply as an efficient technique for distributing the 'wealth' that industry produces. Commerce and industry, then, are not internally related beyond the banal point that, without the wealth that industry produces, there would be nothing for commerce to distribute. Marx's claim that simple cooperation, manufacture and large-scale industry are all 'specifically capitalist' kinds

---

72 Marx 1976a, p. 449.

73 Ibid.

74 Marx 1976a, p. 450.

75 The opening factory scene of Charlie Chaplin's film *Modern Times* brings home the despotism of the assembly line, the time clock and electronic surveillance of workers. The fanciful 'Billows Feeding Machine', designed to prolong capital's despotism through the lunch break, turned out not to be 'practical'.

76 See Murray 1998, included in the present volume as Chapter 12. The present chapter reinforces that critique of the 'commerce and industry' picture by pointing out its incompatibility with subsumption concepts.

of production has no place in this picture. For the 'commerce and industry' picture, there is no 'specifically capitalist' kind of production: industry is industry. The fact that Marx adopts the ordinary terminology of simple cooperation, division of labour and manufacture and machinery and large-scale industry may lull his reader into believing that Marx too believes in the validity of that account. But once we appreciate the significance of formal subsumption and real subsumption and grasp what Marx means by 'the specifically capitalist mode of production', there can be no mistaking Marx's radical break with the 'commerce and industry' picture. Still, two deep conceptual mistakes interfere with our understanding of real subsumption.

One is the error of thinking that use-value and value categories are mutually irrelevant. In fact, use-value considerations enter into Marx's critique of political economy at many points, whether because the use-value considerations affect the value considerations, as in the case of the use value of the commodity labour power, or because the value considerations shape use-value ones.[77] Productivity is an interesting and pertinent case. Precisely because productivity is a use-value consideration and because the social kind of labour that produces value is abstract labour, changes in productivity across a branch of production do not affect the amount of value added per hour. As we saw, this is the 'value treadmill' effect. But that does not prove that changes in productivity have no effect on value considerations: the whole strategy of relative surplus value is to increase productivity in order to drive down the value of labour power. Increased productivity, a use-value consideration, allows capital to extract more surplus value from the same sum of new value added.

With real subsumption, production processes are transformed in use-value terms, materially, in order to satisfy capital's appetite for surplus value. I call the failure to recognise this phenomenon 'technological naiveté'. I pair that notion with 'use-value romanticism', the idea that socialism reduces to 'expropriating the expropriators', that is, eliminating surplus value by ending the monopoly of capitalists and land owners on the means of production. Once that is accomplished, the idea is that the means of production can be redirected to the production of use values ('wealth') instead of surplus value. This romantic conception fails to recognise that, if production for the sake of surplus value were overthrown, it would have to be replaced with some new and definite social form of production with a definite social purpose. That new purpose would have to be thicker than the mere production of use values. 'Use-value romanticism' misses the significance of real subsumption. With real subsump-

77 See Marx 1973, pp. 852–3. See also Arthur 2003 and Murray 1998, included in the present volume as Chapter 12.

tion, the distinctive social forms and purposes of the capitalist mode permeate and mould the material, technological make-up of the production process. A socialist society, then, would face the formidable challenge of undoing much of what real subsumption has brought about.[78]

Understanding real subsumption can also be blocked if we fail to see the inseparability of production and exchange. The false 'commerce and industry' picture of capitalism exemplifies that failure. One simple example of the inseparability of production and circulation is that the whole point of capitalist production, namely, the endless accumulation of surplus value, makes no sense without money and simple commodity circulation. Marx's criticism of economics on this point is original and profound.[79] It fits with his seminal contribution – to recognise the fundamental significance of the specific social forms and purposes of all actual production processes. Acknowledging the inseparability of production and exchange pressures us to drop the 'commerce and industry' picture and adopt the Marxian concepts of formal subsumption and real subsumption.

3.3 *Hybrid Subsumption*

Marx devotes one paragraph of *Capital* Volume 1 to what he calls the 'hybrid' [*Zwitter*] form of subsumption under capital.[80] Marx also discusses this form, though he does not use the term 'hybrid', in his manuscript of 1861–3 and in the *Results*.[81] In hybrid subsumption, capital appropriates surplus value without formal subsumption under capital occurring; indeed, Marx employs the concept of hybrid subsumption as one foil in his discussion of formal subsumption. Marx makes clear, both in the 1861–3 manuscript and in *Capital*, that capital's extraction of surplus value through hybrid subsumption, while it may well be more exploitative than under the conditions of formal subsumption, cannot be a form of direct, personal domination:

> It will be sufficient if we merely refer to certain hybrid forms, in which neither is surplus labour extorted *by direct compulsion from the produ-*

78 Chris Arthur makes this point, 'a considerable reworking of the use-value sphere would be necessary before a socialist mode of production could take root' (Arthur 2003, p. 149, n. 26).

79 See Marx 1973, pp. 94–100, and also Chapter 51, 'Relations of distribution and relations of production', in Marx 1981.

80 Marx 1976a, p. 645.

81 The heading used in the 1861–3 manuscript (Marx 1982, pp. 2, 152–9 and 2, 182) is 'transitional forms' (*Übergangsformen*). That term as well as the term 'accompanying form' (*Nebensformen*) come up in the *Results* (Marx 1976b, pp. 1,023, 1,044 and 1,048).

> *cer* nor has the producer been formally subsumed under capital. In these forms, capital has not yet acquired a direct control over the labour process.[82]

This condition, included in the definition of hybrid subsumption, directs us to two related points.

1. For Marx, it is one of the most decisive historic features of capitalism that it is not based on personal forms of domination. We saw that Marx makes a great deal of this in his discussion of the social effects of formal subsumption, in particular, of 'free' wage labour.
2. As Marx observes in the *Results*, with the spread of capitalism, the commodity and wage labour forms become 'absolute'; they predominate even where the commodity is not commodity capital and wage labour is not directly surplus-value-producing labour.[83]

With the spread of the commodity and wage labour forms, money tends to become the universal mediator in human exchanges. With the preeminence of money comes the erosion of personal domination: commercial exchanges presuppose formally free and equal persons, buyer and seller or borrower and lender. Money is the great leveller.[84] And in this passage from the 1861–3 manuscript, Marx insists that in hybrid subsumption the power of capital be mediated – as it always is – by money and the social roles of buyer and seller:

> We can speak of such transitional forms only where *formally* the *relationship of buyer or seller* (or, a modification, borrower or lender) between the actual producer and the exploiter predominates, where it is generally the case that the content of the transaction between the two parties is not conditioned by relationships of domination and submission [*Knechtschaft und Herrschaft*] but that they face one another as formally free.[85]

82 Marx 1976a, p. 645, my emphasis and amended translation.

83 Marx 1976b, p. 1,041.

84 Marx 1976a, p. 175.

85 Marx 1982, p. 2, 152. This requirement explains why, when Marx takes up examples of transitional subsumption, he does not mention the case of the apprentice-master relationship. Instead, he uses it to explain, by way of contrast, formal subsumption under capital. Because the relationship between apprentice and master does not reduce to a simple cash nexus, it fails to qualify as either formal or hybrid subsumption.

Marx recognises two types of hybrid subsumption, one he calls transitional [*Übergangsform*], the other, accompanying [*Nebensform*]. The transitional form refers to a kind of hybrid subsumption that is a bridge to modern capitalist social relations. Historically, two sub-types of transitional hybrid subsumption stand out: both involve ancient forms of capital, interest-bearing capital and merchant capital. In the former case, the usurer takes interest payments from producers who are not formally subsumed under capital; in the latter, the merchant capitalist profits by mediating between producers and consumers. As transitional hybrid subsumption moves labour processes toward formal subsumption under capital, it pulls them away from pre-capitalist forms of personal domination. Transitional hybrid subsumption's historic significance and scope of application is great even though the concept is marginal to *Capital*'s systematic dialectic. The accompanying type of hybrid subsumption refers to forms that keep appearing alongside established capitalist firms, as previously unsubsumed sectors of production come actually, though indirectly, under the power of capital. Hybrid subsumption endures, then, as a subordinate feature of life in a capitalist society.

3.4 *Ideal Subsumption*

The types of ideal subsumption under capital involve treating labour that is not actually subsumed under capital (whether formally or in a hybrid manner) as if it were. Ideal subsumption may be sorted as follows.

3.4.1 Ideal Subsumption of Pre-Capitalist Economic Formations under Capital

Because of their lack of attention to specific social form, which capitalism encourages by camouflaging itself, economists confuse the capitalist mode of production with production in general. Marx observes:

> The *determinate social character* of the means of production in capitalist production – expressing a particular *production relation* – has so grown together with, and in the mode of thought of bourgeois society is so inseparable from, the material existence of these means of production as means of production, that the same determinateness (categorial determinateness) is assumed even where the relation is in direct contradiction to it.[86]

86 Marx 1963c, p. 408.

Consequently, economists are prone to subsume pre-capitalist forms of production under the capital form. Marx catches J.S. Mill in a striking example of this, where Mill goes on about profit where there is no buying or selling.[87]

3.4.2 Ideal Subsumption of Non-Capitalist Processes of Production That Exist Side by Side with Capitalist Ones

> Within capitalist production there are always certain parts of the productive process that are carried out in a way typical of earlier modes of production, in which the relations of capital and wage-labour did not yet exist ... But in line with the dominant mode of production, even those kinds of labour which have not been subjugated by capitalism in reality are so in thought.[88]

The term 'self-employed' worker points to a type of ideal subsumption where a single person comes to regard herself as her own wage labourer and her own means of production as her capital.[89] This sort of ideal subsumption reveals the unseen power that specific social forms have over the imaginations of participants in capitalist societies.

3.4.3 Ideal Subsumption within Capitalist Firms

One curiosity of a capitalist production process is that, within it, goods and services no longer actually function even as commodities. However, goods and services functioning within a particular department within a capitalist firm may be ideally subsumed under the capital form and calculations made as if the department were its own capitalist firm, in order to locate the firm's profit centres. Because it is typical for industrial capitalists to rely on external financing, those who are self-financing may ideally subsume a portion of their own profits under the form of interest.[90]

---

87 Marx 1976a, p. 652.

88 Marx 1976b, p. 1,042.

89 Ibid.

90 Marx 1982, p. 2,180.

4 Results and Peculiarities of the Specifically Capitalist Drive to Increase Productivity

In the *Results* and in the 1861–3 manuscript, Marx identifies two chief consequences of relative surplus value (real subsumption) as (1) 'the development of the *social productive forces of labour*' and (2) 'to *raise the quantity of production* and *multiply* and *diversify the spheres of production* and their subspheres'.[91] Actually, Marx calls attention to this second development already in connection with formal subsumption's '*compulsion* to *perform surplus labour*', which increases production (not productivity) and both pushes the mass of products beyond the traditional needs of workers and creates the possibility of '*leisure time*' for human development outside the sphere of material production.[92]

At this point, one may want to respond to Marx, 'So you are saying that it is capitalism's nature constantly to increase the quantity of production, raise productivity and diversify products. Aren't these strong recommendations of capitalism?' There is an important truth expressed in this reaction, and Marx does find something deeply hopeful in these and other tendencies of capitalism. But the matter is not simple. The concept of 'the' drive to increase productivity – What could possibly be wrong with increasing productivity? – is problematic in just the same way as are the ordinary concept of wealth and the commonplace concept of capital. It shuns specific social form and purpose. There is something peculiar to the capitalist drive to increase productivity that makes it unexpectedly and elusively conflicted. We need to expose the troubling aspects of this drive to increase productivity and its tendency to camouflage itself as general and benign. Our purpose, once again, is to reveal that what may easily be taken as universal or natural, that is, not socially specific, in this case, 'the' drive for increased productivity, is specific. We want to see the capitalist colours of this drive to increase productivity.

4.1 *Production for the Sake of Production? Productivism and Wealthism*

Increasing productivity seems so unassailable a goal in a capitalist society precisely because, apparently devoid of any definite social purpose, capitalist production appears to be 'production for the sake of production'.[93] Because money is necessarily, if bizarrely, the way that the specific social form of the products

91 Marx 1976b, p. 1,037. See also Marx 1982, p. 2, 142–3.
92 Marx 1976b, p. 1,026.
93 Marx 1976b, p. 1,037.

of labour gets expressed in the capitalist mode of production, and because money appears alongside commodities, the capitalist production process and its products appear to lack specific social form. Production appears to be 'production in general', and wealth appears to be 'wealth in general'. Consequently, 'production' and 'wealth' appear as society's goals. Capitalism's specific social forms seem to be written in invisible ink.

I call 'production for the sake of production' *productivism*. By the same token, I call productivism's counterpart, 'wealth for the sake of wealth', or 'wealth as end in itself', *wealthism*.[94] As ways to represent the capitalist mode of production, both reveal and conceal truth. Marx notes that the ideologies of productivism and wealthism arise naturally as participants in a capitalist society represent their society to themselves.[95] Productivism and wealthism are what I call *shadow forms* of capital: they mimic the abstractness, quantitative focus and indifference of the value forms that cast them.

Productivism and wealthism in no way express universal truths. Quite the opposite, they are exclusively appearance forms of the peculiar purpose of capitalist production. Marx states:

> 'Production for the sake of production' – production as end in itself – enters in certainly already with the formal subsumption of labour under capital, as soon as it generally becomes the case that the immediate purpose of production is the production of the greatest possible amount of surplus-value.[96]

Marx conceives of 'production for the sake of production' as a necessary manifestation of the drive for surplus value, 'that the individual product contain as much surplus-value as possible, is achieved only through production for the sake of production'.[97]

By the phase 'production for the sake of production', Marx means production that is driven not by existing needs but rather by capital's imperative, 'Accumulate, accumulate'. As Marx puts it in the *Results*, 'instead of the scale of production being determined by existing needs, the quantity of products made is determined by the constantly increasing scale of production dictated by the mode of production itself'.[98] Capital's need to accumulate, not human needs,

94 Marx 1976b, p. 1,037.
95 Marx 1976a, p. 742.
96 Marx 1976b, p. 1,037.
97 Marx 1976b, p. 1,038.
98 Marx 1976b, pp. 1037–8.

is its mainspring. Marx's disaffection with productivism and wealthism echoes Aristotle and Aquinas: humans are not made for wealth; wealth is made for humans.

Marx nevertheless commends the transcendence of pre-existing limits on need; this is the positive side of capitalism, 'This is the one side, in distinction from earlier modes of production; if you like, the positive side'.[99] Here Marx sides with the moderns against the ancients. But the universality of needs under capitalism, while a progressive development, is, for Marx, an inadequate kind of universality. To be modern about human needs is not necessarily to be wealthist. Marx contrasts the modern, capitalist universality of needs, which is in thrall to the demands of surplus-value accumulation, with a new type of universality:

> When the limited bourgeois form is stripped away, what is wealth other than the universality of individual needs, capacities, pleasures, productive forces etc., created through universal exchange? The full development of human mastery over the forces of nature, those of so-called nature as well as of humanity's own nature? The absolute working-out of his creative potentialities, with no presupposition other than the previous historic development, which makes this totality of development, i.e. the development of all human powers as such the end in itself, not as measured on a predetermined yardstick? … In bourgeois economics – and in the epoch of production to which it corresponds – this complete working-out of the human content appears as a complete emptying-out, this universal objectification as total alienation, and the tearing-down of all limited, one-sided aims as sacrifice of the human end-in-itself to an entirely external end.[100]

The capitalist brand of universality inescapably subjects human beings to the imperious demands of their own creation, capital, and conceals barriers imposed by the demands of capital accumulation. Surplus value is its measure of success. Marx has a very different universal measure of wealth in mind, one that synthesises the Aristotelian emphasis on the development of human capabilities with the modern emphasis on universality and the openness of human nature.

---

99 Marx 1976b, p. 1,037.

100 Marx 1973, p. 488.

4.2 *The Drive's Selectivity*

In capitalism, production is not actually for the sake of production. The very idea of 'production for the sake of production' is false, the counterpart to the imaginary 'production in general'. So-called 'production for the sake of production' is actually undertaken for the sake of accumulating surplus value. Consequently, the capitalist drive to increase productivity is selective; it is directed where it conforms to the goal of increasing surplus value. If building Mcmansions for the comfortably housed is more lucrative than constructing homes for the homeless, 'production for the sake for production' will build Mcmansions.

4.3 *The Drive's Contradictory Character*

Because 'production for the sake of production' is actually production for the sake of surplus value, capital becomes a barrier to itself and proves contradictory.[101] Surprisingly, increased productivity can result in a reduction in the rate of profit, despite the strategy of relative surplus value.[102] Crises and overproduction manifest this contradictory nature: these phenomena bring home the stark reality that the capitalist mode of production imposes limits on itself. If production were simply for the sake of production, the very idea of overproduction would be a joke. In capitalism, of course, overproduction is no laughing matter. In crises, production declines because of its violation of its actual purpose (surplus value), not its violation of its purported purpose (production as an end in itself).

4.4 *The Drive's Exclusivity*

Because the purpose of the capitalist drive for increased productivity is singular, it gives the cold shoulder to other social objectives, for example, leisure time or time for domestic responsibilities; safe and attractive working conditions; preservation of natural beauty or historically significant sites. When accumulating surplus value is all that matters, workers get squeezed:

> On the other hand, the negative, or the contradictory character [of the drive]: production in contradiction to, and unconcerned for the producer. The actual producer as mere means of production, material wealth as

---

101 Marx 1976b, p. 1,037.

102 Marx relished his demonstration (in *Capital* Volume III) that a falling rate of profit can be a consequence not of diminishing productivity, as in Ricardo's theory, but of increasing productivity.

> end in itself. And the development of this material wealth, therefore, in contradiction to and at the cost of the human individual.[103]

Here Marx expresses just the idea we are after. What appears universal, 'the' drive to increase the productivity of labour, is (precisely in that abstractness) a manifestation of a specific mode of production, the mode of production organised around surplus value – not the illusory 'production in general'. By contrast, Marx points out how in the ancient world, 'where the worker counted as an end in himself', inventions were banned where they would break up the old social order. Protectionism and labour laws insuring job security echo those ancient practices.[104] As Marx coldly remarks, however, 'all of that is for the developed capitalist mode of production outdated and untrue, false perceptions'.[105]

4.5 *The Drive's Domineering Character*

There is something driven, something domineering, about the push to increase productivity within capitalism. Thus Marx writes, 'Productivity of labour in general [*überhaupt*] = maximum of product with minimum of labour, and therefore the greatest possible cheapening of commodities. This becomes the law, independent of the wills of individual capitalists'.[106] The heedless drive to increase productivity is imposed on participants in a capitalist society – capitalists included – by the impersonal demands of capital accumulation.

4.6 *The Drive's False Generality*

There are several features of the specific social forms of capitalism that ensure that the methods of increasing productivity of social labour brought about by real subsumption will be general, rather than parochial, but general in a particular way. Unlike other modes of production, capitalism necessarily posits a form of universalism. The social fetish of value itself is the consequence of the abstract way in which the universal equivalence of labour is recognised in capitalist society. Wage labour erodes patriarchal, political and religious forms of domination. Capitalist competition in the world market presses toward a cosmopolitan outlook: 'The intellectual creations of individual nations become common property. National one-sidedness and narrow-mindedness

103 Marx 1976b, p. 1,037.
104 Marx 1976b, p. 1,050.
105 Marx 1976b, p. 1,050.
106 Marx 1976b, p. 1,037.

become more and more impossible'.[107] We have already noted how the wage form and capitalism's push for product innovation burst the parochialism of needs.

Moishe Postone directs us to a tension between two sorts of generality that develop with capitalism, one that is radically indifferent to the particularities of use value and one that 'does not necessarily exist in opposition to particularity'.[108] The tension between these two sorts of generality may be the most hopeful product of real subsumption under capital. It creates what Postone calls 'shearing pressures' in capitalism that may yet, as Marx anticipated, open space for fundamental alternatives to capital.[109]

Appendix: On Relative Surplus Value and Inflation

In a recent essay, Geert Reuten proposes that a steady, low rate of inflation has become a systematic tendency of capitalism.[110] I would like to sketch an argument that may provide further support for his conclusion. Consider what the strategy of relative surplus value implies if there is no inflation. The strategy is to drive down the value of labour power, while continuing to pay wage labourers full value. But, where the value of money is constant, this requires lowering the nominal wage. Instead of being paid $100 per day, workers are now to be paid, say, $90. If we make the reasonable assumption that the price of labour power, the wage, is 'sticky', that is, workers balk at any lowering of their nominal wages, then the strategy of relative surplus value constantly runs into an obstacle.

The resistance of workers to a lowering of their wages in value terms is lessened by the ruse of a steady, low rate of inflation, which avoids 'sticker shock.' Inflation allows employers to cut wages in value terms while keeping the nominal wage steady or even rising. Thus, a zero percent raise will be presented as a 'wage freeze', not as the wage cut that it actually amounts to under even mildly inflationary conditions. As the inflation rate goes higher, however, the discrepancies involved in this deception become more noticeable and, let us assume, less effective. In fact, the ruse may turn counterproductive: if workers

107 Marx and Engels 1967, p. 84.

108 Postone 1993, p. 367.

109 For their valuable comments on earlier versions of this chapter I would like to thank Chris Arthur, Riccardo Bellofiore, Martha Campbell, Mino Carchedi, Paul Mattick Jr, Fred Moseley, Geert Reuten, Jeanne Schuler, Tony Smith and Nicky Taylor.

110 Reuten 2003.

come to anticipate ever higher rates of inflation, they will want to hedge against that prospect by demanding raises that shoot past the going rate of inflation. That is a recipe for a disruptive inflationary spiral.

CHAPTER 11

The Place of 'The Results of the Immediate Production Process' in *Capital**

1 Introduction

'The Results of the Immediate Production Process' ('Results'), the unfinished draft of a conclusion to *Capital* Volume I, which became available in German, Italian and French between 1969 and 1971 (in English in 1976), belongs to those recently available texts that continue to encourage a profound reinterpretation and re-evaluation of Marx's mature work.[1] Others include the *Grundrisse*, the *Urtext*, and the 1861–63 manuscript published in the MEGA. Reading these manuscripts, we encounter Marx in a different voice. He sounds less studied; more at home; more philosophical, dialectical and Hegelian; he is more prone to pursue incisive moral and sociological observations.[2] Above all, the topic of the specific social form and purpose of labour and wealth is explicit and emphatic.

* Originally published as 'The Place of "The Results of the Immediate Production Process" in *Capital*', in *Re-reading Marx: New Perspectives after the Critical Edition*, edited by Riccardo Bellofiore and Roberto Fineschi (Basingstoke, Hampshire: Palgrave Macmillan, 2009), pp. 163–77, reprinted with the kind permission of Palgrave Macmillan.

1 The 'Results of the Immediate Production Process' is the only 'chapter' of the 1863–4 draft (the 'third draft') of the first volume of *Capital* to come down to us, apart from some loose sheets from preceding chapters of that draft that were stuck in the manuscript of the 'Results'. The MEGA editors put the composition of the 'Results' in a time frame of 1863 to 1864 (MEGA editors 1988, p. 9*). The 'Results' was published simultaneously in German and Russian in *Arkhiv Marksa i Engelsa* Volume II (VII), pp. 4–266, in Moscow in 1939 (Editors of Marx 1969, p. i; Mandel 1976, p. 943). Maximilien Rubel published excepts in *Economie et Societes, Cahiers de L'Institut de Science Economique Appliquee, Serie Etudes de Marxologie*, no. 6, June 1967. In 1969 the 'Results' was published as a book in German (Marx 1969b) and in Italian (Marx 1969a). Complete translations into French (Marx 1971b) and English (Marx 1976b) followed. A new Italian translation is forthcoming in conjunction with the new Italian translation of *Capital* Volume I (Marx 2008).

2 In a letter of Marx to Lassalle of 12 November 1858, Marx writes that in the *Critique* (1859) he is not striving for an 'elegant presentation' but to write in 'my middling manner (*Durchschnittsmanier*)' (Marx and Engels 1954, p. 93; my translation). In a letter to Lassalle dated

Ever since the 'Results' entered the picture, the answer to the question of why Marx did not complete it and include it in *Capital* Volume I has remained a mystery. One purpose of the present chapter is to revisit this mystery in light of the MEGA. However, let me disappoint the reader straight away by saying that the MEGA editors have turned up nothing that addresses the question explicitly, leaving them and us to speculate. Commentators divide between those who argue that Marx had no theoretical reason for not including the 'Results' in *Capital* Volume I and those who maintain that Marx dropped the 'Results' either because changes to the plan of *Capital* Volume I made it superfluous or because material included in the 'Results' belonged elsewhere. I argue against the view that Marx had theoretical reasons to abandon the 'Results'. Most significantly, I reject the MEGA editors' claim that the treatment of the commodity as the product of capital does not belong in the 'Results' but only after the introduction of prices of production in *Capital* Volume III. That judgment rests on a paralysing mistake about Marx's dialectical method of presentation. While I hope to shed light on the 'Results', regrettably, neither my criticisms of existing literature nor my speculations dispel the mystery of what became of the 'Results'.

2 A Quick Overview of the 'Results'

The 'Results' runs just over 100 pages in the MEGA edition and nearly 120 pages in Rodney Livingstone's translation. Though still in rough form, the manuscript is organised in three parts, one devoted to each of these themes: (1) the commodity is the product of capital; (2) the aim of capitalist production is the production of surplus value; and (3) capitalist production reproduces specifically capitalist relations of production. Marx tells us that (1) is intended to come last, as it is unquestionably meant to be the transition to Volume II.[3]

Section (1) (26 pages) emphasises the circular nature of the argument in Volume I: 'As the elementary form of bourgeois wealth, the *commodity* was our point of departure, the prerequisite for the emergence of capital. On the

15 September 1860, Marx writes that the form of the sequel to the *Critique* will be somewhat more popular but 'in no way out of any inner drive from my side' (Marx and Engels 1954, p. 102; my translation).

3 Marx 1976b, p. 949. The 1933 German and Russian edition and the 1969 German edition take Marx's suggestion and place Section (1) last. The 1971 French translation and both English translations follow the order of the manuscript.

other hand, *commodities* appear now as the *product of capital*'.[4] Marx stresses the inseparability of (a) the generalised circulation of commodities, '(including money)'; (b) the generalization of wage labour; and (c) the capitalist mode of production. Marx provides an extended commentary on the difference between the commodity conceived of as independent, at the beginning of *Capital* Volume I, and the commodity conceived of as the product of capital.[5] To my knowledge there is nothing comparable to this portion of the 'Results' elsewhere in Marx's writings.

Section (2), easily the longest of the three (85 pages), rehearses a number of misconceptions about capital and reflects at length on the unity of the labour process and valorization process. That is followed by subsections on formal subsumption and real subsumption, productive and unproductive labour, net and gross product, the 'mystification of capital' and the transition from Sections II and III to Section I.[6]

Section (3), at six pages easily the shortest of the three, contains several pages on the relations between capital and wage labour relevant to the inversion of the bourgeois law of appropriation. It concludes with a one-paragraph subsection bearing the title of the manuscript. That short, final paragraph re-emphasises the point that capitalism reproduces its '*specific social* character' while reproducing itself materially.[7]

3 Getting the Right Question about the 'Results'

As Marx observed, asking the right question can be the key step in an inquiry. When it comes to the fate of the unfinished 'Results of the Immediate Production Process', we may wonder if Ernest Mandel's question 'But why was the originally planned Part Seven ['Results'] discarded?' jumps the gun.[8] Did

---

4 Ibid. The shift from 'the *commodity*' to 'commodities' here is important because, ordinarily, the product of capital is a mass of commodities where each counts as an aliquot part of the total product.

5 Ibid. See pp. 953–5 for three key differences.

6 Marx 1976b, p. 1058. An editorial note explains: 'Marx actually gave this section the heading "Transition from Sections I and II of This Chapter to Section II, Originally Treated as Section I", following his intention to re-arrange the order of sections as explained on p. 949. To avoid confusion we have retitled it to conform with the order in which the three sections are presented here' (Marx 1976b, pp. 1058–9, note).

7 Marx 1976b, p. 1,065.

8 Mandel 1976, p. 944.

Marx decide not to include the 'Results'? Of course, he did not include it, but the manuscript is unfinished; he could not have included it without completing it for publication. Marx gave up on simultaneously publishing all three volumes of *Capital* only reluctantly and late in the day. In allowing Volume I to be published independently, Marx was not deciding against the publication of Volumes II and III. In fact, there was little, if anything, that appeared consistently in his draft outlines of *Capital* that Marx decided not to include. As it is, Marx concluded the first edition of *Capital* Volume I by awkwardly appending a thumbnail sketch of the 'Results' that (1) highlighted the fact that the immediate result of the production process is the commodity, only now pregnant with surplus value; (2) called attention to the circling back of the investigation to its point of departure, the commodity; and (3) made the transition to Volume II by contrasting the simple circulation of commodities with the circulation of capital. In later editions this vestige of the 'Results' was excised.

Let us, then, adopt this general formulation of the question concerning the fate of the 'Results': Why did Marx not complete and publish the 'Results'? We should keep in mind that Marx did not stop work on Volume I of *Capital* in 1867, when it was first published. He reworked it for a second edition, which appeared in 1872. He also oversaw the French translation, which was published in instalments from 1872–5. Engels used Marx's notes and alterations for the French edition in publishing the third German edition in 1883, shortly after Marx's death. Without settling the issue, Marx's continued work on Volume I casts suspicion on the easy answer that Marx was simply too pressed for time to complete and include the 'Results' in *Capital* Volume I.

As mentioned, there are two basic answers to our question:

1. Marx decided, for one or another theoretical reason, to drop the 'Results'. In the literature we find two kinds of reasons why: (a) because Marx worked important points from the 'Results' into Volume I, so that it became superfluous; and (b) because important points from the 'Results' would have been out of place – by being introduced prematurely – in a conclusion to Volume I.
2. Marx never decided to drop the 'Results'; instead, one or another practical consideration kept him from completing and publishing the 'Results'. Perhaps Marx thought that including the 'Results' in the first volume would make the book too long; his publisher, Meissner, had given him a limit of 60 proof sheets [*Druckbogen*], and he expressed worry about length to Engels. Since the 'Results' was written as a bridge to Volume II, Marx's failure to complete Volume II might be thought to have made completing the bridge

to it seem less urgent.[9] Perhaps, but the unfinished state of Volume II did not affect Marx's rationale for constructing the 'Results' as a bridge from Volume I to Volume II.

4 Select Review of the Literature

Let us now consider some of the responses in the literature to the main question, namely, the editors' bibliographical notice to the 1969 German edition of the 'Results'; Ernest Mandel's introduction to the Livingstone translation; Allen Oakley's remarks; and, most importantly, the editors' introduction to the MEGA edition of the 'Results'.

4.1 *The Bibliographical Notice to 1969 German Edition*

The editors of the 1969 German edition write, 'Probably, during his final work up, Marx decided not to include the extensive sixth chapter in the first volume ... Therefore the content of the first volume of *Capital* concluded with the chapter (later, part) on the accumulation of capital.[10] Precisely in this chapter Marx adopted a series of theses whose draft is contained in the unpublished manuscript ['Results']'.[11] First, given its unfinished state, Marx could not have 'decided' to include the 'Results'. Second, if length – no doubt the manuscript is 'extensive' – is being offered as an explanation for why Marx did not publish the 'Results', the editors accept the second answer to the general question: practical considerations worked against including the 'Results'. But, third, the editors' further observation that Marx put a number of points from the 'Results' into *Capital* Volume I, suggests that, in so doing, he knowingly rendered the 'Results' superfluous. The editors, then, adopt type (a) of the first answer to our question about the fate of the 'Results': late additions to the text of Volume I made the 'Results' superfluous.

There are difficulties with the editors' suggestion, starting with their failure to identify the points from the 'Results' that are integrated into the treatment

9 Rodney Livingstone notes, 'presumably Marx would have finished the present chapter ['Results'] at this point when he had finally revised it [Volume II]' (Marx 1976b, p. 975).

10 The sixth and final 'chapter' of the first edition of *Capital* Volume I included sections on capitalist accumulation, the so-called 'original accumulation', and 'the modern colonial theory'. In later editions Volume I ends with two 'parts' on the topic of accumulation, Part Seven: The Process of Accumulation of Capital and Part Eight: So-Called Primitive Accumulation.

11 Marx 1976a, pp. 711, 716. Editors of Marx 1969, p. III.

of the accumulation of capital in *Capital*. Let me select some points treated in the 'Results' that appear in Part Seven of *Capital* Volume I: (1) that simple reproduction and accumulation involve not only material reproduction but also reproduction of the social forms specific to the capitalist mode of production; (2) the mysticism of capital; (3) that surplus value is the animating goal of capitalist production; (4) how prices, levels of productivity and productive force, the length of the working day and quantities and rates of surplus value interrelate; and (5) the inversion of the bourgeois law of appropriation.[12] Points (2) and (5) I will consider below in connection with the views of the MEGA editors.

Regarding point (1), some repetition of this sweeping observation in a capstone to Volume I would not be out of place. Regarding point (3), the idea that producing (and accumulating) surplus value is the specific aim of capitalist production is, of course, a major theme of Volume I, particularly once we get to Part Three. The 'Results' illuminates the significance of this specific aim of capitalist production by setting it in the context of Marx's basic complaint against political economy: it is oblivious to the topics of the specific social form and purpose of wealth and labour. And the 'Results' brings home the potential that this specific aim has for undoing the network of capitalist social relations.[13] In *Capital* Volume I, formal and real subsumption get nothing like the treatment that they get in the 'Results', where Marx treats them under the topic of surplus value as the defining aim of capitalist production.[14] Regarding point (4), as I will show, Marx's treatment of the commodity as the product of capital contains some of the most illuminating passages in the 'Results' and has implications for interpreting two of the most controversial turns in the dialectic of Volume I.

4.2 *Ernest Mandel*

In his introduction to the 'Results', Ernest Mandel writes, 'But why was the originally planned Part Seven discarded? … For the time being, it is impossible to give a definitive answer to that question'.[15] Thirty years later, even with the publication of the 'Results' in the MEGA, we still have no definitive answer. Mandel offers this two-sentence hypothesis in answer to the question of why

12 Marx's treatment of 'so-called primitive accumulation' is the *coup de grace* of his critique of the bourgeois theory of appropriation because it makes a mockery of Locke's idea of property being acquired originally through one's own labour.

13 See MEGA editors 1988, p. 16*.

14 The only explicit mention of formal and real subsumption in *Capital* Volume I occurs on p. 645.

15 Mandel 1976, p. 944.

Marx 'discarded' the 'Results': 'Possibly the reason lay in Marx's wish to present *Capital* as a "dialectically articulated artistic whole". He may have felt that, in such a totality, "Chapter Six" would be out of place, since it had a double didactic function: as a summary of Volume I and as a bridge between Volumes I and II'.[16]

I am not certain what to make of Mandel's suggestion. Is it that a 'summary' is out of place in a dialectical whole? We know from the Preface to *A Contribution to the Critique of Political Economy* (1859) that Marx decided against any anticipatory introduction.[17] I know of no comparable passage in which Marx renounces summaries, capstones or appendices; Mandel provides none. As its title announces, the 'Results' trades in retrospection more than anticipation, though, as a bridge to *Capital* Volume II, it has a moment of the latter. Moreover, we have other examples of retrospection in *Capital*. Section Four of the first chapter of *Capital*, 'The Fetishism of the Commodity and its Secret', reflects on the significance of the theory of value and the value form developed in the preceding three sections. The final section of *Capital* Volume III, 'The Revenues and their Sources', resembles the 'Results' in being a capstone, only this time to all three volumes of *Capital*.[18] In fact, each of the points of the 'Results' that define its three sections is concisely presented in Chapter 51, 'Relations of Distribution and Relations of Production'.[19]

Mandel is right that the 'Results' is a bridge. Marx makes this explicit as he calls attention to the circular nature of the presentation in *Capital*. What was the point of departure, namely the generalised commodity form of wealth, proves to be the necessary result of capitalist production. Only now the commodity is recognised as being capital in the commodity form, a fact whose significance is examined in the 'Results', which lays down the conceptual basis for the new set of determinations to be investigated in Volume II. Marx notes that the section on commodities as the product of capital should be placed last, 'because it forms the transition to Volume II', and he concludes the section: 'And in this respect their circulation, which is simultaneously the reproduction

16 Ibid.

17 Marx 1970a, p. 19.

18 Moreover, the fragmentary final Chapter 52 of Volume III, 'Classes', may have been conceived as a bridge to books on landed property and wage labour.

19 Marx 1981, pp. 1,019–23. The fact that Marx presents all three main points of the 'Results' there, could suggest that he intended for Chapter 51 of Volume III to serve in place of the 'Results'. I doubt that this is so: (1) Chapter 51 has a special purpose, as indicated by its title; (2) the dates of composition of the two capstones are close together; and (3) the treatment in the 'Results', at least of two of the points, is on a much larger scale.

process of capital, entails further determinations alien to the abstract description of the circulation of commodities. For this reason our next task is to turn to an examination of the *circulation process of capital*. This we shall do in the next volume'.[20] Why would a bridge from one volume to another go against the dialectical grain? Or is the problem the 'doubling of functions'? How so? The 'Results' discloses the dialectical structure of *Capital*; it does not sin against it.

4.3 *Allen Oakley*

'For some reason that is not clear, this vital concluding piece was left out of *Capital*, Book I, when it went to press', writes Allen Oakley.[21] After his description of the *'Results'* as 'vital' – unfortunately, he does not tell us what makes it so – Oakley adds, 'if the status of the 'Results' manuscript was as suggested above, the work (Volume I) was without its concluding chapter'.[22] Again, it is worth mentioning that the 'Results' was not in a publishable state: Marx could not just 'decide' to include it; he would have had to finish it first. Oakley says nothing about any decision on Marx's part to drop the 'Results'. On the contrary, in characterising the 'Results' as 'vital', Oakley adopts the second answer to the general question: Marx left the 'Results' out of Volume I, but not on any theoretical grounds. Beyond that, Oakley is silent.

4.4 *MEGA Editors*

The MEGA editors' introduction to the 'Results' comprises only six pages, but it is the most current and substantive contribution of those reviewed here. They begin their summary assessment of the importance of the 'Results' as follows, 'Therefore, the "Sixth Chapter" of the first book of *Capital* occupies an important place in the story of its coming to be and, more generally, in Marx's economic corpus'.[23] They highlight several points: (1) the 'Results' is where Marx first offers a thorough investigation of the commodity as the product of capital; (2) in doing so, Marx helps readers to recognise that his theory of value is not confined to the first section of Volume I but rather spans the three volumes of *Capital*; (3) the 'Results' presents the general characteristics of the capitalist mode of production, spells out the conditions of its origin and situates it historically; (4) the 'Results' points up the development within capitalist society of the material presuppositions for a post-capitalist future society; and

20 Mandel 1976, p. 949; p. 975.
21 Oakley 1983, p. 96.
22 Oakley 1983, p. 97.
23 MEGA editors 1988, p. 17*.

(5) from the 'Results' we can derive a better understanding of the Marxian method of research and presentation.

Despite their enthusiasm, the MEGA editors favour the first answer to the general question and offer three independent, though reinforcing, reasons as to why Marx decided to drop the 'Results'.[24] The first reason is type (b); the latter two are type (a): (1) Marx came to believe that to treat the commodity as the product of capital in the 'Results' was premature. The effort to distinguish the commodity as an individual from the commodity as an aliquot part of the mass of commodities produced by capital was misplaced, given that a full account of the commodity as the product of capital would have to wait until the introduction of prices of production in Volume III; (2) since Marx took up the 'mystification of capital' in the chapter on machinery, he made its treatment in the 'Results' superfluous; (3) because Marx addressed the issue of the inversion of the bourgeois law of appropriation in connection with the accumulation of capital, there was no need to treat it in the 'Results'. In these latter two points the MEGA editors agree with the editors of the 1969 German edition: Marx came to see the 'Results' as superfluous because he incorporated its ideas into the published Volume I. By contrast, the first point argues that Marx dropped the 'Results' because he came to see that it was premature, out of dialectical order. Let us consider each proposal in turn:

1. The MEGA editors are right, of course, that a full account of the commodity as the product of capital is not possible prior to the introduction of prices of production in Volume III. Is that a reason not to make the point in the 'Results' that the commodity as the product of capital counts as an aliquot part of the mass of commodities produced by capital? No. Marx warned against 'putting the science before the science'; he upbraided Ricardo for attempting the impossible – to answer every possible objection to his labour theory of value in his first chapter. But the reasoning of the MEGA editors lands us in the inverse kind of scientific futility. If we are not to offer a partial account, presumably because it falsifies, then, since we cannot give a complete account all at once, we condemn ourselves never to start – a Zeno's paradox of scientific presentation.[25] Against the MEGA editors, I argue: (a) the points that Marx makes in the 'Results' regarding the commodity as an aliquot part of the mass of commodities produced by capital are true

24 Curiously, the MEGA editors are silent on the question of why Marx would drop the sections on formal and real subsumption in the 'Results'.

25 In Murray 2005b, included in the present volume as Chapter 16, I criticise Chris Arthur for a similar assumption.

as far as they go; (b) they are worth making in a retrospective-prospective capstone to Volume I; and (c) they do not compromise Marx's development of more complex truths about the commodity as the product of capital later in *Capital*.

2. Regarding the topic of the 'mystification of capital', the MEGA editors argue that, since its causes were treated in the analysis of machinery, 'Their separate treatment proved itself theoretically superfluous'.[26] However, the chapter on machinery contains little that addresses the mystification of capital as explicitly as the 'Results'; indeed, the language of 'mystification' is absent.[27] Compare the benign title 'Machinery and Large-Scale Industry' to 'Mystification of Capital', the section heading in the 'Results'. While the machinery chapter is about the mystification of capital, its discursive level leaves room for gathering relevant points and reflecting on the mystification of capital. Thus, the 'Results' section begins with a three-point comparison of money fetishism with capital fetishism, showing why the latter is more deeply ingrained than the former.[28] Yes, Marx is examining the causes of the mystification of capital in *Capital* Volume I, but in the 'Results' he tells us that this is what he was doing.
3. Exposing the inversion of the bourgeois law of appropriation was pivotal to Marx's objectives in composing Volume I; I doubt that he would have published the book without accomplishing that. *Capital* is Marx's mature critique of bourgeois philosophy of right. Marx treats this topic emphatically in Chapter 23 ('Simple Reproduction') and Chapter 24 ('The Transformation of Surplus-Value into Capital'), as is unmistakable from the title of the latter's first section, 'Capitalist Production of a Progressively Increasing Scale. The Inversion Which Converts the Property Laws of Commodity Production into Laws of Capitalist Appropriation'. Surely, including this material took pressure off publishing the 'Results'.[29] I believe that this is an important ingredient of the answer to the general question of why Marx let Volume I to go to the printer without his finishing the 'Results'. This, however, is not to agree with the MEGA editors that, because Marx examined the inversion in Part Seven, he concluded that the 'Results' was superfluous: 'As a consequence,

26 MEGA editors of 1933a, p. 15*.

27 One of the most explicit passages is found on Marx 1976a, p. 548. Since the 'Results' devotes only eight pages to the mystification of capital, even if its treatment were superfluous, that would not be sufficient reason to shelve the 'Results'.

28 Marx 1976b, pp. 1,052–3.

29 Actually, there is little in the 'Results' on the inversion. We find a bit on p. 1,015 and then it is treated vigorously on pp. 1,062–4, in the third section.

the publication of the results of the immediate production process separately from *Capital* was once again made superfluous'.[30]

In a plan for Volume I drafted in January 1863, Marx foresees 'chapters' 5, 6 and 7 as follows: '5. Combination of absolute and relative surplus-value. Relation (proportion) between wage-labour and surplus-value. Formal and real subsumption of labour under capital. Productivity of capital. Productive and unproductive labour. 6. Reconversion of surplus-value into capital. Primitive accumulation. Wakefield's colonial theory. 7. Result of the production process'. To the latter he adds: '(Either under 6 or 7 the change in the form of the law of appropriation can be shown.)'.[31] What does this outline suggest? (a) If we assume that Marx intended to include formal and real subsumption and productive and unproductive labour in the 'Results', then, at least at this point, he was not opposed to returning to topics in the 'Results' that had been introduced in Volume I; (b) including the inversion was a priority in Marx's mind;[32] (c) contrary to the MEGA editors' proposal, at least at this point in time,

---

30 MEGA editors 1988, p. 16*.

31 Marx 1895; 1956, p. 414.

32 In two of the earliest plans for *Capital* – the first version of an index to the seven *Grundrisse* notebooks (Marx 1939a; 1941, pp. 855–9) and a plan drafted in February or March of 1859 after Marx had written *"Referate"* to the material in the *Grundrisse* that was not used in his *Contribution to the Critique of Political Economy* (Marx 1939a; 1941, pp. 969–74; see p. 950 for the dating) – Volume I culminates in the reversal of the bourgeois law of appropriation. There is no mention in either plan of the 'Results'; however, both include a final section to the first volume, 'Reversal [*Umschlag*] of the Law of Appropriation,' that follows a section on the 'primitive accumulation of capital'. Both plans call for sections on absolute surplus value and on relative surplus value (the second plan treats relative surplus value in three sections: cooperation, division of labour, and machinery), so that terminology goes back at least to 1858. But there is no section on absolute and relative surplus value and no mention of formal or real subsumption. Neither plan has a section on simple reproduction or the accumulation of capital. In the first plan there is a special section placed just before the 'transition from money to capital' entitled, 'The Law of Appropriation, as it Appears in Simple Circulation'. This section was written, using the exact number and title from the plan, in the *Urtext* (Marx 1939a; 1941, pp. 901–18). Marx eliminated the section when he rewrote the *Urtext* as the *Critique* (1859), and it did not reappear in *Capital*. Surely Marx's intention in 1858 was to use that section to set up the planned final section on the reversal. In the second plan the topic turns up in the title to the closing section of Volume I: 'Appearance of the Law of Appropriation in Simple Commodity Circulation: Reversal of this Law' (p. 974). In later plans – for example, the one from January 1863 – the reversal of the law of appropriation remains prominent; though now simple reproduction and accumulation are part of the plan, and Marx indicates that the reversal could be included

Marx did not think that choosing to include the inversion in what is here called Chapter Six (Parts Seven and Eight in *Capital* Volume I) meant dropping the 'Results'.

5 The Contribution of the 'Results'

The 'Results' teaches the crucial lessons of the newer, textually based, 'social form' interpretation of Marx's mature work. For the 'Results' is all about the specific social form and purpose of capitalist production, of the labour it presupposes and of the wealth it creates. True, *Capital* Volume I is about this too, but time and again the 'Results' tells us that this is what the book is about, making it easier to get the point. In part, the 'Results' teaches this crucial lesson because it is written in a voice more Marx's own. Primarily, though, it gets its message across because of the kind of writing it is. *Capital* Volume I is a work in systematic dialectics, comparable to Hegel's *Encyclopedia* and, more so, his *Philosophy of Right*. A less exact, but instructive, comparison is to Spinoza's *Ethics*. Like the body of *Capital* Volume I, these three works are dense, closely reasoned, 'scientific' texts that challenge readers first to follow the argument and then to situate it and appreciate its significance. Hegel and Spinoza aid their readers by complementing their spare, rigorous prose with prefaces, 'remarks', scholia and appendices (not to mention university lectures, in Hegel's case). A scholium is defined by *Webster's* as 'a remark or observation subjoined but not essential to a demonstration or a train of reasoning', while an appendix is 'supplementary material usually attached at the end of a piece of writing'. If such descriptions suit the kind of writing we find in the 'Results', as I believe they do, then we can understand why commentators might judge the manuscript to be 'superfluous': it does not advance the dialectical train of reasoning in *Capital*. But are such easier, 'supplemental' texts superfluous to the broader, rhetorical purposes of 'scientific' writers such as Spinoza, Hegel and Marx? I think not. Looking at our main question in this light suggests how,

---

either in the chapter on the accumulation of capital or in a new concluding chapter – the 'Results'. These facts reveal how important it was to Marx to expose the reversal of the bourgeois law of appropriation in *Capital* Volume I. Since Marx's harshest criticism – 'the exchange between capitalist and wage-labourer, the wage contract, devolves into "the legal fiction of a contract"' (p. 719) – requires the concepts of simple reproduction and the accumulation of capital, he may have decided to introduce accumulation and deviate from his plan to keep Volume I on the conceptual level of immediate production to give his critique of the bourgeois philosophy of right more power.

under pressures of space and time, Marx could let *Capital* Volume I go to the publisher without the 'Results', while not deciding that the text was out of place or 'superfluous'.

Each of the three sections of the 'Results' calls our attention to the topic of specific social form and purpose:

1. The section on the commodity as the product of capital focuses on the fact that the social form of the wealth produced by the capitalist mode of production is not simply that of a commodity but of one pregnant with surplus value. Much of the section is devoted to spelling out how the commodity as the product of capital differs, formally, from the commodity as it was conceived at the beginning of Volume I. This section emphasises the inseparability of the generalised commodity form of wealth, the wage labour form of labour and the capitalist mode of production.
2. The whole point of the second section is to insist on the peculiar social purpose of capitalist production; namely, the production and accumulation of surplus value. Marx exposes the failure of political economy to grasp that capital is not a thing but rather a specific social form of wealth with a specific aim. The categories of formal and real subsumption force the question – where the correlative terminology of absolute and relative surplus value does not – 'subsumption of what under what?' The only answer to the question 'under what?' is under a specific social form, notably, capital.[33] Likewise, the question *What is productive labour?* forces us to specify the

33 In fact, Marx discusses many more types of subsumption in the 'Results' than just (1) formal and (2) real. These include: (3) ideal; (4a and 4b) hybrid, of which he distinguishes two types, 'transitional' (to formal subsumption) and 'accompanying', in his more complete treatment of hybrid subsumption in the 1861–3 manuscript; (5) subsumption of pre-capitalist commercial forms, such as the commodity, money, even capital itself: 'We see here how even economic categories appropriate to earlier modes of production acquire a new and specific historical character under the impact of capitalist production' (Marx 1976b, p. 950); (6) what I will call non-formal subsumption, e.g., when, under conditions of capitalist agriculture, where seeds are generally in the commodity form, I use my own seeds to plant, they are subsumed under capital without taking on the 'value-form', that is, without ever having been sold; (7) non productive labourers are subsumed under the wage form; (8) some unproductive labour, notably, by government employees, which is paid for by taxes is subsumed under capital and even enters into the formation of prices (Marx 1976b, pp. 1,042–3). That Marx elaborated several subsumption concepts in the 'Results' should not lead us either to the conclusion that they apply only to the 'immediate production process' or that the fact that they pertain to the circulation of capital and to merchant and interest-bearing capital gave Marx a reason to discard the 'Results'.

social purpose of production. Under the capitalist mode of production, labour is productive only if it directly produces surplus value.
3. The whole point of this section is to distinguish between material reproduction and the reproduction of the social form of a particular mode of production.

Finally, Marx's stress in Section (1) on the circularity of Volume I brings out the systematic dialectical character of the presentation that Marx devised in *Capital*. In particular, Marx's stress on this circular – better, spiral – character of his presentation brings out the structure of mutual presupposition that characterises a systematic dialectical presentation.[34] The realization that Section (1) brings home is that the commodity with which *Capital* starts was actually one of the mass of commodities produced by the capitalist mode of production, an 'aliquot part' of that 'heap' of which Marx spoke in the book's opening sentence. Thus, capitalist production was presupposed from the beginning; all the same, capitalist production presupposes that wealth is in the commodity form: 'As the elementary form of bourgeois wealth, the *commodity* was our point of departure, the prerequisite for the emergence of capital. On the other hand, *commodities* appear now as the *product of capital*'.[35]

Let us return to the point that Marx makes repeatedly in Section (1): 'Only on the basis of capitalist production does the commodity actually become the *universal elementary form of wealth*'.[36] Since *Capital* begins with the assumption that the commodity is the 'universal elementary form of wealth', and Marx's arguments will not work without that assumption, we see that Marx presupposes capitalist production from the very beginning of *Capital*. The several consequences of this are profound:

1. *Capital* is about the capitalist mode of production from the start; as Chris Arthur has urged, the whole idea of generalised 'commodity production' as a stage on the way to capitalism is a myth.[37]

---

34 See Arthur 2002a.

35 Marx 1976b, p. 949. Already in the *Grundrisse* Marx commented on this structure of mutual presupposition between generalised commodity circulation and capital (Marx 1973, p. 227).

36 Marx 1976b, p. 951. Marx identifies this as the first of the three 'crucial points' in Section (1).

37 See Arthur 2002a. That, of course, is not to say that no commodities are produced prior to the capitalist mode of production, nor is it to deny that, historically, the emergence of capitalism presupposes a fairly developed level of commodity exchange.

2. Since the law of value can be established only on the basis of generalised commodity circulation, the law of value applies only to societies where the capitalist mode of production predominates.
3. That means: no surplus value, no value, which pulls the rug out from Proudhonism, Left Ricardianism and perhaps some forms of market socialism. It means that value, not simply surplus value, is the target of Marx's critique and his revolutionary intentions. Marx's goal is not to redistribute surplus value; it is to replace value with a new social form of wealth.
4. If a society where wealth generally takes the commodity form is necessarily one where the capitalist mode of production dominates, then the claim of liberal thinkers such as F.A. Hayek that it is the only possible free society, precisely because it has no compulsory collective aim, proves illusory. Because it must be capitalist, a market society must conform to capital's compulsion, the endless accumulation of capital.

Let us close with two examples that show how the 'Results' helps us understand two of Marx's most controversial moves in *Capital*. We will consider (1) Marx's argument in the first section of Chapter One that the 'third thing' common to all commodities must be (abstract) labour and (2) Marx's shift from C-M-C to M-C-M in Chapter Four.[38]

1. The only way to make Marx's argument for (abstract) labour as the substance of the 'third thing' work is to recognise that the commodity stands not for any individual commodity (which may or may not be the product of labour) but for an 'aliquot' part of the mass of commodities produced by capital.[39] But this is just the point that Marx drives home in Section (1) of the 'Results': as a product of capital, the commodity counts not as an individual but only as an aliquot part of the mass of commodities.[40] The commodity with which *Capital* begins proves to be such a commodity, a product of capital; however, it cannot be treated as such until the requisite categories have been developed. This is what mutual presupposition means in *Capital*: capital presupposes the commodity and the commodity presupposes capital; that means, we start from a commodity that is the product of capital. We just cannot say this at the outset of the presentation. That would be 'putting the science before the science'. The individual

38 Marx 1976a, pp. 127–8; p. 248.
39 See Murray 2005b, included in the present volume as Chapter 16.
40 Marx 1976b, p. 954.

commodity at the beginning of *Capital* must serve as a placeholder while we discover its true identity.

2. Marx's introduction of the circuit M-C-M appears unmotivated, to say the least.[41] Here is his transitional sentence: 'But alongside this form [C-M-C] we find another form, which is quite distinct from the first: M-C-M'.[42] The 'Results' teaches that it is not so unmotivated after all. It is an everyday observation in a market society to find M-C-M alongside C-M-C. But there is more to it: M-C-M must be there alongside C-M-C. Why? When wealth generally takes the commodity form, then all inputs into production, including labour power, are in the commodity form.[43] Consequently, the production of wealth on a capitalist basis must begin with money in order to purchase the needed labour power and means of production. In the 'Results' Marx goes out of his way to make the point that the consequence of the (simultaneous) generalisation of the commodity form and of wage labour is that all the inputs to production are found in the commodity form.[44] So production must begin with money. This explains why Section (1) of the 'Results' works as a transition to Volume II, which begins with the 'circuits of capital', of which the money circuit, M-C-M, is the first. Marx's transition from generalised commodity circulation to capital works, once we acknowledge that generalised commodity circulation presupposes capitalist production, i.e., that the (generalised) commodity form is both the presupposition and the consequence of capitalist production.[45]

---

41 Jacques Bidet claims that this transition lacks any argumentative basis: '*there is, in reality, no conceivable dialectical transition* ... Marx ... had to recognise that he could not proceed by *transition*, but only by *rupture*' (Bidet 2005, pp. 141–2). I contest this judgment.

42 Marx 1976a, p. 248.

43 Marx 1976b, p. 950.

44 Marx 1976b, pp. 950 ff. Marx also makes the contrasting point (Marx 1976b, p. 1,059).

45 I would like to thank the editors, Riccardo Bellofiore and Roberto Fineschi; the other members of the ISMT and other participants in the conference; and John Clegg. Tony Smith's generous comments were especially helpful.

CHAPTER 12

Beyond the 'Commerce and Industry' Picture of Capital*

Marx's goal in Volume II of *Capital* is to show that what circulates in a capitalist economy is capital and to flesh out the consequences. This is a taller order than it might seem, just because the pitfalls in getting to know capital are so many. A natural way of looking at the production and distribution of wealth in a capitalist society is to break it down into a generalised circulation of wealth, whose basic forms are money and commodities, buying and selling, and to imagine that this circulation accompanies a process of production that, without any determining social form, simply transforms material inputs to create new wealth. This outlook pictures a capitalist economy as a commercial and industrial one. Oddly, the picture excludes capital, for capital is not simply commodities, money or the use values needed for production (raw materials, labour and instruments of production). It does not belong to the nature of any of those to produce surplus value (profits, rents, interest), yet bearing surplus value is what defines capital.[1]

In this middle volume Marx deepens *Capital*'s initial analysis of the double character of the commodity (as a use value bearing an exchange value) to reveal and investigate the consequences of this fact: commodities in capitalism are use values that have the specific social form of capital. Capitalistically produced commodities do not have simply an exchange value; their sale realises surplus value. They are commodity capital, and this makes a world of difference. Similarly, money used to purchase the elements of capitalist production processes functions as money capital, and the easily neglected role of money capital in the circulation of industrial capital is closely examined. Finally, the purchased elements of capitalist production (means, materials and labour power) are recognised to exist in the form of productive capital. To call things what they are is a demand of science that Marx heeds.

---

* Originally published as 'Beyond the "Commerce and Industry" Picture of Capital', in *The Circulation of Capital: Essays on Volume Two of Marx's 'Capital,'* edited by Chris Arthur and Geert Reuten (London: Macmillan, 1998), pp. 33–66, reprinted with the kind permission of Palgrave Macmillan.

1 'Capital essentially produces capital, and it does this only as long as it produces surplus-value' (Marx 1981, p. 1,020).

A capitalist economy is necessarily a commercial one (that is, one where wealth generally takes the commodity form), but the much more revealing and complex truths that Volume II exposes are (1) that, in capitalism, all commercial transactions are, as a rule, caught up in the circuits of capital and (2) that a commercial economy is a capitalist one: there is no generalised commodity circulation apart from the circulation of capital. Regarding the first point Marx writes: 'The circuits of the individual capital, therefore, when considered as combined into the social capital, i.e. considered in their totality, do not encompass just the circulation of capital, but also commodity circulation in general'.[2] Where commodity circulation is generalised, as a rule, commodity exchanges involve capital either in the form of money capital or commodity capital (or both); nonetheless, Marx insists (a) that all commodity exchanges are governed by the rules of simple commodity circulation – equal values are freely exchanged – and (b) that the same exchange may belong to the circulation of capital for one bargainer but to simple commodity exchange for the other, as when a capitalist purchases labour power or when a capitalist sells consumption goods to either a capitalist or a wage labourer.

Regarding the second, more telltale point, Marx states, 'It is only on the basis of capitalist production that commodity production appears as the normal, prevailing character of production'.[3] The whole examination of generalised commodity circulation and the forms proper to it, then, must be seen as describing certain aspects of the actual phenomenon, namely, the circulation of capital, not an independent, free-standing phenomenon called 'generalised commodity circulation'. Herein lies the linchpin of Marx's deep critique of liberalism as the one-sided appreciation of capitalism's cheery and egalitarian commercial face.

The comforting but shortsighted 'commerce and industry' picture of capital's circulation is bound up with a blunder made by readers of *Capital*. It is to think that use value drops out of sight in *Capital* after the first page or two, once Marx has ascertained that a commodity both is a use value and has an exchange value. According to that view (held by Paul Sweezy and many others), once Marx dispatches the topic of use value with a handful of banal opening remarks,[4] he turns full attention to the social forms distinctive to capitalism, i.e., the value forms. And, there, use value purportedly becomes irrelevant.

2 Marx 1978a, p. 428.
3 Marx 1978a, p. 117.
4 See Marx 1976a, pp. 125–6.

Roman Rosdolsky debunked this error,[5] but it dies hard,[6] and the full scope of its debilitating effects needs to be made known. For, holding this view blocks efforts to learn what the distinctive social forms of capitalism (that is, the value forms) *are*; it inhibits attempts to recognise their powers; and it makes Marx's critique of capitalism either invisible or unintelligible.

In fact, use-value considerations never drop out of *Capital*, though, where they come into play, it is due to their involvement with specifically capitalist social forms, the value forms. This occurs in two ways: (1) when use-value factors enter into the make-up of a social form proper to capitalism – as they always do – and (2) when capitalist forms determine use values not just formally but materially, which is what 'real', in contrast to 'formal', subsumption under capital involves.

The fundamental case of the first type is the capital form itself. The use-value characteristics of what commodity exchangers bring to market, whether means or materials of production, labour power or consumption goods, are irrelevant in so far as market participants act simply as buyers and sellers. But they matter to the capital form: unless workers are separated from the means and materials of production, the indispensable use value for industrial capital, labour power, is missing from the marketplace. Here, in the determination of the capital form, class division enters simultaneously with specific use-value factors. Use-value factors enter into the determination of several other of the most important categories explored in Volume II: productive and unproductive labour, fixed and circulating capital (in contrast to the more fundamental pair, constant and variable capital), industrial capital's turnover time and the two departments of production (means of production and means of consumption) that structure Marx's account of the reproduction of the total social capital.

If capital presupposes a class division of specific use values such that the means and materials of production are in the hands of the capitalist class, its reproduction requires that the circulation of capital renew this class division of specific resources. With his reproduction schemes in Part Three, Marx demonstrates how capital accomplishes this by showing how the yearly product of Department II (means of consumption) is divided between the wage labourers and capitalists, while the entire product of Department I (means of production) circles back to the capitalist class. This nicely rounds out Volume II's exposition of the use-value factors constitutive of capital.

---

5 See Rosdolsky 1977.

6 Frederic Jameson advises: 'the reader needs to remember that "use-value" at once drops out of the picture on the opening page of *Capital*' (Jameson 1991, p. 231).

Marx's insistence on simultaneously addressing the material (use-value) and formal (value) dimensions of the circulation of capital stems from the fundamental, phenomenological assertion that underlies his 'historical materialism': 'All production is appropriation of nature on the part of an individual within and through a specific form of society'.[7] Marx is a materialist who believes in the reality and power of social forms.

(2) Real subsumption is all about the power of capitalist social forms materially to reshape wealth and its production. Attending to this phenomenon – which is inscrutable on the assumption that use-value considerations immediately drop out of the investigation of capital – highlights the pertinence of Volume II today for several reasons. The concept of the real subsumption of processes involved in industrial capital's turnover establishes the proper horizon for explaining the tendencies behind a variety of current trends, e.g. 'lean' and 'just-in-time' production, electronic financial transactions and new direct marketing schemes, that are attracting attention under headings such as 'post-Fordism' or 'flexible accumulation'.[8] And attending to phenomena of real subsumption reveals important historical dynamics to capitalist development that may put pressures on capitalism's capacity to reproduce itself over the long run.[9]

1 Picturing Capital's Circulation without Capital

Volume II of *Capital* tracks the turnover of industrial capital, first considering individual capitals and then, in Part Three, the total social capital. Marx emphasises how different (and how much more complex) a task this is than the examination of simple commodity circulation that he undertook in Chapter Three of Volume I:

> The way in which the various components of the total social capital, of which the individual capitals are only independently functioning components, alternately replace one another in the circulation process – both with respect to capital and to surplus value – is thus not the result of the

7 Marx 1973, p. 87.

8 See, for example, Harvey 1989.

9 Moishe Postone emphasises the historical dynamism of capitalism resulting from the real subsumption of use values under capital, and he theorises the build-up of 'shearing pressures' that could compromise the reproduction of capitalism (Postone 1993).

> simple intertwining of the metamorphoses that occurs in commodity circulation, and which the acts of capital circulation have in common with all other processes of commodity circulation, but rather requires a different mode of investigation.[10]

How use value figures into the analysis of the circulation of the total social capital is one crucial difference.

Part One paves the way by examining 'The Metamorphoses of Capital and Their Circuits'. Its purpose is properly to determine what capital is while dispelling misconceptions that capital is any one of these: commodities, money or means and materials of production united with living labour. Simply to identify capital with commodities or with money is wrongly to reduce an internally more complex value form (capital) to value forms proper to simple commodity circulation. To identify capital with means and materials of production united with living labour is to fail to recognise capital for what it is: not a thing, and not a historical constant, but a bizarre and astoundingly powerful (asocial) social form of wealth turned 'automatic subject':

> Capital, as self-valorizing value, does not just comprise class relations, a definite social character that depends on the existence of labour as wage-labour. It is a movement, a circulatory process through different stages, which itself in turn includes three different forms of the circulatory process. Hence it can only be grasped as a movement, and not as a static thing.[11]

The circulation of capital involves a flow not simply of materials but metamorphoses, a flow of forms. In the necessity of the metamorphoses of capital from money to the elements of production to commodities and back to money, further consequences of the value-form analysis from Chapter One of *Capital* are disclosed.

Marx's presentation of the three different forms that industrial capital necessarily inhabits and divests, money capital, productive capital and commodity capital, along with the three corresponding circuits, is intended (1) to demonstrate – in good Hegelian fashion – the dialectical unity of the three forms and circuits (which is to say it shows that each form and each circuit is an abstraction from the actual circulation of industrial capital) and (2) to expose

10 Marx 1978a, p. 194.

11 Marx 1978a, p. 185.

the peculiarities of (industrial) capital that naturally give rise to misinterpretations that one-sidedly fixate on one or the other of its necessary forms and circuits. Indeed, toward the end of his treatment of each of the three forms and corresponding circuits, Marx matches each with one or another school of political economy that fixates on that particular form and circuit: money capital with the Monetary System and mercantilism,[12] productive capital with classical political economy, and commodity capital with Quesnay's Physiocratic *Tableau économique*.[13]

The root of (industrial) capital's peculiarities, and in particular of the necessity for the three forms and three circuits, lies in the value form itself, that oddly asocial social form. Thus, in Volume I, Marx had already begun laying the groundwork for his criticism of the 'commerce and industry' picture of capital's circulation when he identified the failure of classical political economy to attend to the form (as opposed to the magnitude) of value as 'one of its chief failings'.[14] Marx examined the value form in the first chapter of *Capital*, concluding that value is the residue of the social form of labour in capitalism and that value's peculiar nature is to be (1) asocial in just the sense made famous by Adam Smith's metaphor of the 'invisible hand'; that is, the value-producing labour process is governed by the blind nexus of self-interested parties to 'the great scramble' of the market and (2) necessarily expressed as exchange value, as a thing, money.[15] The uncanny consequence of (1) and (2) is that the capitalist production process appears to lack a social form; it appears to be mere 'industry', to which 'commerce' is only a handy supplement. 'Commerce' can only supplement 'industry' because there is nothing about 'industry' to necessitate money and 'commerce'. By contrast, Marx argues that the capitalist production process does have a determinate social form, value, which, as it cannot appear itself – what does the residue of 'socially necessary abstract labour' look like? – must appear as money.

These oddities of the value form create a situation more baffling than that presented by a ventriloquist, for, while the ventriloquist appears not to be speaking, just as the capitalist production process appears not to have a social form, at least what is 'thrown' by a ventriloquist is recognizable as a voice. But who would identify what is 'thrown' by value, a bare thing, money, as a social form? Nevertheless, money talks.

12 See Marx 1978a, pp. 141–2.

13 See Marx 1978a, p. 179.

14 Marx 1976a, p. 174, n. 34.

15 See Murray 1993b, included in the present volume as Chapter 8.

In Volume II, Marx identifies how the value form shapes the circulation of (industrial) capital so as to make the 'commerce and industry' picture naturally appealing:

> As a specific and distinct form or mode of existence that corresponds to the particular functions of industrial capital, money-capital can perform only money functions, and commodity capital only commodity functions; the distinction between them is simply that between money and commodity. In the same way, industrial capital in its form as productive capital can consist only of the same elements as those of any other labour process that fashions products: on the one hand the objective conditions of labour (means of production), on the other productively (purposively) active labour-power. As industrial capital within the sphere of production can exist only in the combination corresponding to the production process in general, and thus also to the non-capitalist production process, so it can exist in the sphere of circulation only in the two forms of commodity and money that correspond to this.[16]

Owing to the value form, industrial capital necessarily takes the forms of money, which, insofar as it is money, behaves no differently than money generally does in commodity circulation; of commodities, which in so far as they are commodities behave no differently than commodities generally do in commodity circulation; and of means of production joined with active labour power, which is just what is generally the case in a production process – but with no sign of a distinctive social form governing that process. The capitalist production process thus appears to be 'disembedded' (in Karl Polanyi's terminology) from any specific social form or corporate conception of the good, though this appearance is only a *trompe l'oeil* caused by the actual social form of production (value) and its organisation around the peculiar and coercive collective 'good' of capital accumulation. Thus, due to the oddities of the value form, the circulation of industrial capital does offer footholds for the multiple errors of political economy and common sense that involve slurring the distinctions between money and money capital, commodities and commodity capital, the production process in general and the capitalist production process. Capital naturally casts the 'commerce and industry' shadowgraph.

---

16 Marx 1978a, p. 161.

Before considering how these natural misperceptions about capitalism rely on and reinforce the blunder about the role of use-value considerations in *Capital*, we now probe the 'industry' side of the 'commerce and industry' picture by elaborating on a match alluded to earlier: 'The circuit of productive capital is the form in which the classical economists have considered the circuit of industrial capital'.[17] This is to pursue the topic, just noted, of the slurring of the differences between the production process taken in abstraction from any determinate social form – the mere general abstraction that I have been marking with the term 'industry' – and the actual capitalist production process (which is governed by definite social forms, the value forms).[18]

In the middle of the chapter on the circuit of commodity capital, Marx returns to this identification of classical political economy with the circuit of productive capital and begins to fill in the picture for us:

> The general form of the movement P ... P' is the form of reproduction, and does not indicate, as does M ... M', that valorization is the purpose of the process. For this reason, classical economics found it all the more easy to ignore the specifically capitalist form of the production process [i.e. to treat capitalist production merely as 'industry'], and to present production as such as the purpose of the process – to produce as much and as cheaply as possible, and to exchange the product for as many other products as possible, partly for the repetition of production (M–C), partly for consumption (*m–c*). In this connection, since M and *m* appear here only as evanescent means of circulation, the peculiarities of both money and money-capital could be overlooked, the whole process then appearing simple and natural, i.e. possessing the naturalness of shallow rationalism [*flachen Rationalismus*].[19]

Fixating on the circuit P ... P', in which the role of money (even the commodity) as a determinate social form appears to be a matter of mere expediency, stiffened the classical political economists' disposition – one shared by the important critic of classical political economy, and forerunner of neoclassical economics, Samuel Bailey – to play down the significance of the commodity and money forms, thereby making their failure to grasp the nature of the value form more intractable. Oblivious to the necessity of money's role as

17 Marx 1978a, p. 166.

18 On general as opposed to determinate abstractions, see Murray 1988a, Chapter Ten.

19 Marx 1978a, p. 172.

the manifestation of the peculiar, asocial social form of capitalist production, value, they naturally enough pictured production as devoid of any particular social form, hence, as a 'simple and natural' process: 'industry' churning out 'wealth'.[20]

That picture of the capitalist production process as 'industry' pumping out 'wealth', suggested by the title of Adam Smith's masterpiece, *The Wealth of Nations*, deserves a few comments. First, the celebration of 'industry' and 'wealth' is an expression of what may be called 'wealth fetishism' or 'wealthism', inasmuch as it declares the endless spurting of decontextualised 'wealth', that is, use values purportedly lacking any definite social form traceable to the production process (such as the gift, commodity or commodity-capital form), to be the purpose of production. By contrast, in Book I of the *Politics*, Aristotle observed that true wealth is limited, making the point that nothing should count as wealth but what contributes to the attainment of some identifiable human good, which inescapably stands in relation to the good of the *polis*.[21] Second, the fiction of 'wealth' operative here is itself a by-product of the value form, which displaces the appearance of social form into a thing, money. Third, though 'wealthism' is a by-product of the value forms constitutive of the capitalist mode of production, the notion that what drives capitalism is the restless desire to accumulate 'wealth' is a falsehood perpetrated by the incapacity of common sense (and of various economic theories) to recognise the actual social forms ruling capitalism. For it is the uncanny impulsion to accumulate surplus value, not 'wealth', that keeps capital's heart throbbing.[22] Finally, 'wealthism' paints a conveniently false picture of the reality of capitalism; it

20 See Postone 1986 for a fascinating exploration of how the tendency to naturalise productive capital, while vilifying money capital and commodity capital, figured into Nazi anti-Semitism as part of a misguided and virulent form of anti-capitalism.

21 Compare these excerpts from Marx's *Grundrisse*: 'Do we never find in antiquity an inquiry into which form of landed property etc. is the most productive, creates the greatest wealth? Wealth does not appear as the aim of production ... The question is always which mode of property creates the best citizens. Wealth appears as an end in itself only among the few commercial peoples – monopolists of the carrying trade – who live in the pores of the ancient world, like the Jews in medieval society ... Thus the old view, in which the human being appears as the aim of production, regardless of his limited national, religious, political character, seems to be very lofty when contrasted to the modern world, where production appears as the aim of mankind and wealth as the aim of production' (Marx 1973, pp. 487–8). This passage should not be taken to imply that Marx envisions or urges a return to antiquity.

22 Consider the laconic remark of James Roderick, then Chairman of US Steel, 'The duty of management is to make money, not steel' (as quoted in Harvey 1989, p. 158).

gives capitalism a thin but tolerable story to tell about itself:[23] to speak with the French, it provides a 'metanarrative' of material progress that is only an 'alibi'.[24]

2 Use-Value Factors Constitutive for Value Forms

The 'commerce and industry' shadowgraph of the circulation of capital places generalised commodity circulation on one side (along with its characteristic value forms, the commodity and money, buying and selling) and a production process without any determinate social form on the other. This is a representation of capitalism that *leaves out capital*; and it is bound up with the blunder, analysed above, of denying the actual intermingling of use value and social form in capitalism. For, proper attention to the co-involvements of use value and value in capitalism compels us to outgrow the 'commerce and industry' picture. Conversely, that sketch omits those co-involvements.

Obliviousness to the use-value (and social class) factors constitutive of the capital form keeps the 'commerce and industry' picture in the dark about capital. In conceptualising simple commodity circulation, 'commerce', use value comes into play only in these three meagre ways: a commodity must be a use value of some sort (any old sort); it must be a use value for a stranger or someone being treated as a stranger;[25] and specific physical properties such as rarity, compactness and durability matter in the selection of the money commodity. On the 'industry' side of the picture, conceptualising the production process strictly in use-value terms allows no place for the determination – not the modification – of production by any specific social form.[26] So use value makes up

23 'Commerce' chimes in with a higher-minded story of human rights and the dignity of the person.

24 Jean-François Lyotard and Jean Baudrillard, respectively.

25 'A thing can be useful, and a product of human labour, without being a commodity. He who satisfies his own need with the product of his own labour admittedly creates use-values, but not commodities. In order to produce the latter, he must not only produce use-values, but use-values for others, social use-values' (Marx 1976a, p. 131). Engels elaborates on this passage, pointing out that these others are such as can be related to as buyers and sellers. This is the thought that I mean to convey when I use the word 'strangers'.

26 'Determine' pertains to what makes a thing what it is; something lacking form is indeterminate and therefore, on Aristotelian principles, lacks actuality. 'Modify' operates at a different metaphysical and conceptual level; here we are dealing with something actual, something that is determinate, has form, and is undergoing some alteration, which may

the 'industry' side of the picture and purports to stand alone independently of social form. (Recall that in *Capital* use value enters in at the point where it determines or is determined by the value forms.) However, as Marx observed in the *Grundrisse*, 'there is no production in general'; production always has a determining social form.[27] While it is useful to abstract general traits of production, 'industry' is a bad abstraction, a shadow pretending to be real. The irony is that the popularity of the representation of the circulation of capital as generalised commodity circulation paired with a production process lacking any particular social form is itself an ideological outcome of capital's takeover of production. Capital casts a shadow over itself.

Marx's achievement in Volume II is to take us out of the shadows, shedding the 'commerce and industry' picture in favour of the concept of the circulation of capital, and to educate us to the many instances of thick co-involvements of use-value and value factors as they affect the circulation of the total social capital. The following subsections will examine several of the most important such instances, beginning with capital itself.

2.1 *Capital*

Marx wastes little time in the first chapter of Volume II in getting to this key point: specific use value (and class) factors enter into the very constitution of capital and wage labour. As noted above, use value does enter into the constitution of the commodity, but only in highly abstract ways. And it is precisely the spell of that abstractness which deflects attention from the more specific use-value factors that make capital and wage labour possible. To the abstract patterns of thought to which generalised commodity exchange habituates us, capital just looks like money and the capitalist just looks like a buyer, while labour power is just one more commodity and its owner, the wage labourer, one more seller. So what's new about capitalism? Marx criticises the answer that says that what is new with capitalism is that labour power is paid in money, not 'in kind'. He writes:

> It is quite immaterial, as far as the money is concerned, what sort of commodities it is transformed into ... Thus once labour-power is found on the market as a commodity, its sale taking place in the form of a payment for labour, in the wage-form, then its sale and purchase is no more striking

or may not involve a change of form. In this case the issue is not: What is it? but, assuming we already know that, How does it act?

27 Marx 1973, p. 86.

> than the sale and purchase of any other commodity. What is characteristic is not that the commodity labour-power can be bought, but the fact that labour-power appears as a commodity.[28]

What must be presupposed for labour power to take the commodity form? That is the question, not what form the payment for that commodity takes.

That labour power appears as a commodity – and capital's existence hangs on the fact that it does – depends upon definite use-value and class factors:

> Before the sale, this labour-power exists in a state of separation from the means of production, from the objective conditions of its application. In this state of separation, it can be directly used neither for the production of use-values for its possessor, nor for the production of commodities which he could live from selling.[29]

The class aspect is that workers are separated from the means and materials of production, while capitalists own them. The use-value factor is so obvious it is easy to overlook: this class division pertains to those use values that make up the means and materials of production, those use values that we come to know in Part Three as the products of Department I. A class division based on some other use-value consideration (say, who gets luxury consumer goods and who does not) will not do. No separation of workers from the means and materials of production – no capital.[30]

Capital cannot afford the blasé marketplace mentality for which specifics about use values do not matter, for capital is all about the accumulation of surplus value, and surplus value, like value generally, originates in the production process. Because use-value considerations are intrinsic to the production process, they are intrinsic to capital as well:

> Whatever the social form of production, workers and means of production always remain its factors. But if they are in a state of mutual separa-

28 Marx 1978a, p. 114.

29 Ibid.

30 'The introductory act of circulation, the purchase and sale of labour-power, itself depends in turn on a distribution of the social elements of production which is the presupposition and premise of the distribution of social products, viz. the separation between labour-power as a commodity for the worker, and the means of production as the property of non-workers' (Marx 1978a, pp. 461–2). And the reproduction of the total social capital requires the reproduction of this separation of Department I goods from wage labourers.

> tion, they are only potentially factors of production. For any production to take place, they must be connected. The particular form and mode in which this connection is effected is what distinguishes the various economic epochs of the social structure.[31]

The capitalist way to make this connection involves generalised commodity exchange, the market, where workers appear as sellers of a commodity, labour power, and capitalists as its buyers. But because of the specific use-value factors in play here, namely that when the capitalist goes to market as capitalist it is to purchase the necessary elements of the production process, the money of the capitalist is transmuted into a new, more complex value form, money capital, and the commodities that compose the elements of the production process become, after purchase, productive capital.[32]

In his second chapter Marx recaps these points: 'the act M-C, insofar as it is M-L, is in no way simply the substitution of commodities in use form for commodities in money form, but includes other elements that are independent of the general circulation of commodities as such'.[33] Those 'other elements' are the use-value and class factors involved in the separation of workers from means of production. These factors are presupposed by the complex value form, capital. To fail to recognise this constitutive role for use-value factors thicker than those pertinent to the commodity and money forms, then, is to fail to grasp capital.

That failure, Marx observes, is endemic to the capital form, for generalised commodity circulation is the presupposition and constant by-product of the circulation of capital. And the erroneous belief that use-value factors quickly drop out of sight in *Capital* becomes an *idée fixe* through the power exercised over our imaginations by the abstract forms characteristic of generalised commodity circulation: the commodity and, especially, money. 'Money is the independent and palpable form of existence of value, the value of the product in its independent value-form, in which all trace of the commodities' use-value has been effaced'.[34] The unhinged money form is a 'frightful leveler', writes Simmel.[35] Money's glare whites out capital.

31 Marx 1978a, p. 120.
32 '[T]he money advanced functioned as money-capital because it was converted through circulation into commodities with a specific use-value' (Marx 1978a, p. 122).
33 Marx 1978a, p. 151.
34 Marx 1978a, p. 137.
35 See Simmel 1997.

2.2 *Productive and Unproductive Labour*

Marx defines productive labour as labour that figures into the 'immediate process of production' of capital or, what amounts to the same thing, as labour that produces surplus value. Unproductive labour is labour that is not productive labour. So the distinction between productive and unproductive labour is made within forms specific to capitalism; it has nothing to do with puritanical musings about what is 'truly useful' and what not.[36]

The distinction between productive and unproductive labour arises irresistibly because of the attention that circulation receives in Volume II. Several momentous consequences that commodity circulation has for the realisation, rate, distribution and accumulation of surplus value naturally give rise to the illusion that surplus value is produced in the sphere of circulation.[37] Marx emphatically opposes this error 'as it seems to provide it [political economy] with the proof that capital possesses a mystical source of self-valorization that is independent of its production process and hence of the exploitation of labour'.[38] Against this fetishising of capital, Marx insists: 'Circulation time and production time are mutually exclusive. During its circulation time, capital does not function as productive capital, and therefore produces neither commodities nor surplus-value'.[39] Marx recognises that circulation 'is just as necessary for commodity production as is production itself, and thus agents of circulation are just as necessary as agents of production'.[40] But the necessity of the labour involved in commodity circulation does not make it productive.

In the important Chapter Six, 'The Costs of Circulation', we find matters a bit more complicated than suggested thus far. Here Marx distinguishes between circulatory functions that are necessitated strictly by the peculiar formal properties of capital, that is, functions performed strictly to accomplish the metamorphosis of commodity capital into money or money capital into productive capital, and other functions. Those other functions include productive ones:

> Those circulation costs that proceed from the mere change in form of value, from circulation in its ideal sense, do not enter into the value of commodities. The portions of capital spent on them constitute mere deductions from the capital productively spent, as far as the capitalist is

36 For more on this topic, see the criticism of Ernest Mandel's views in the appendix to this chapter.
37 Marx lists several sources of the illusion; see Marx 1978a, p. 204.
38 Marx 1978a, p. 204.
39 Marx 1978a, p. 203.
40 Marx 1978a, p. 205.

> concerned. The circulation costs that we shall deal with now are different in nature. They can arise from production processes that are simply continued in the circulation sphere, and whose productive character is thus merely hidden by the circulation form.[41]

Transportation costs are of this latter, productive sort. Transportation adds value (and surplus value) because it affects the use value of commodities:

> the use-value of things is realised only in their consumption, and their consumption may make a change of location necessary, and thus also the additional production process of the transport industry. The productive capital invested in this industry thus adds value to the products transported.[42]

Storage costs are more complicated, but the appeal to the contrast between use value and social form is again decisive. Keeping a productive stock and a consumption-fund is common to all forms of social production. Expenditures on storage, then, are productive insofar as they are necessary, from the use-value point of view, for the free flow of industrial capital; they are unproductive when they result from interruptions of the formal changes from commodities to money.[43] The fact that, in capitalism, transportation and certain storage costs appear to belong to commodity circulation (though they actually belong to production) reinforces the illusion that the mere changes of form in commodity circulation can account for surplus value.[44]

The point remains that effort devoted strictly to the metamorphosis of commodity capital into money (*C'-M*) or money-capital into productive capital (*M-C*) is unproductive: 'The general law is that *all circulation costs that arise simply from a change in form of the commodity cannot add any value to it*'.[45] So, when Marx says that circulation excludes production, he means circulation in a restricted sense that pertains only to the formal changes capital must undergo; the broader, everyday understanding of circulation includes productive expenditures.

41 Marx 1978a, p. 214.
42 Marx 1978a, pp. 226–7.
43 See Marx 1978a, pp. 224–5.
44 Marx approvingly cites Ricardo's correction of J.B. Say on just this point. See Marx 1978a, p. 227, n. 9.
45 Marx 1978a, pp. 225–6.

No value, and *a fortiori*, no surplus value is created in the restricted sphere of circulation for a simple reason: in this sphere no use value is (preserved or) added to the commodity, and if no use value is (preserved or) added, no value is added. For, while a use value need not be a value, value depends on use value.[46] As a consequence, value-producing labour has a double character; it is 'socially necessary abstract labour' and it is 'useful labour'.[47] Just as throughout *Capital* Marx unpacks the significance of 'socially necessary abstract labour', he likewise continues to unfold the significance of the fact that value-producing labour is 'useful labour'. That is what is going on here. Use value figures into the determination of what counts as productive labour: for labour to be productive it must preserve or enhance use value. The labour required for circulation in the restricted sense does neither; that is why it is unproductive.[48]

2.3 *Fixed Capital and Circulating Capital*

The distinction between fixed and circulating capital falls within the category of productive capital and turns on how different elements of productive capital transfer value to products: fixed capital, having physically endured the production period, transfers only a portion of its value to the product in the course of the production period of a commodity and continues to function as a useful factor of production and transfer more of its value in one or more subsequent production periods; circulating capital, not having physically endured the production period, transfers all of its value to the product in each production period and is not able to function as a useful factor of production in a subsequent production period. Drawing this distinction correctly requires the

46 'A thing can be a use-value without being a value ... nothing can be a value without being an object of utility. If the thing is useless, so is the labour contained in it; the labour does not count as labour, and therefore creates no value' (Marx 1976a, p. 131). By 'an object of utility' we should understand simply a useful object. Marx considered utility theory to be an ideological by-product of capital's takeover.

47 'We use the abbreviated expression "useful labour" for labour whose utility [usefulness] is represented by the use-value of its product, or by the fact that its product is a use-value. In this connection we consider only its useful effect' (Marx 1976a, p. 132).

48 At this point we might ask: If the use-value considerations involved in determining whether or not labour is productive are this thin – the labour must preserve or add use value of some sort, any old sort – then why could the concept of productive labour not come within the purview of the 'commerce and industry' picture? The answer is that, in the concept of productive labour, the thin use-value notion of 'useful labour' is co-involved with a value category, namely, surplus value (or capital, if you like), which is more complex than any of the value categories of commerce (commodity, money, buyer and seller).

ability to grasp the actual co-involvement of value and use-value factors in capitalist production. The difficulty of the task is suggested by Marx's history of the efforts of political economists including Quesnay, Smith and Ricardo: they all fell into one pitfall or another and never did succeed in properly drawing the distinction.

Given the purposes of Volume II, the distinction between fixed and circulating capital holds plenty of interest in its own right, for differences between fixed and variable capital can have a tremendous impact on the turnover of industrial capital and thereby on the realisation, distribution, rate and accumulation of surplus value. What boosts the voltage of the whole discussion, however, is that political economy's failure to get the distinction right ties in with even more profound errors: its pervasive naturalisation of distinctively capitalist forms; its failure to grasp in a coherent theory the source of surplus value (which is equivalent to a failure to grasp capital); and, as a result, its abysmal readiness to attribute to capital the power to generate surplus value of itself. But just how are the errors in properly conceptualising the distinction between fixed and circulating capital tied in with these fundamental failures to know capital?

Within the tradition of political economy, Marx distinguishes several different mistakes stemming from the inability to grasp how use-value and value factors enter into the concepts of fixed and circulating capital. One mistake is to confuse circulating capital, which is a form of productive capital, with capital of circulation (commodity capital and money capital), a mistake that turns on not recognising the difference between the strictly formal metamorphosis that occurs when commodity capital is transformed into money or money capital into the elements of production (productive capital) and the material and formal metamorphosis that takes place in production when use values are altered and value is produced or transferred.[49] Thus a distinction that turns on

---

49 Marx makes these points in the following criticism of Adam Smith's views: 'What Adam Smith here calls circulating capital is what I intend to call capital of circulation, capital in the form pertaining to the circulation process, pertaining to the change of form mediated by exchange (material change and change of hands), i.e. commodity capital and money capital, in contrast to the form pertaining to the production process, that of productive capital. These are not particular ways in which the industrial capitalist divides his capital, but rather different forms that the same capital value, once advanced, successively assumes and discards throughout its *curriculum vitae*. Adam Smith lumps these together with the distinctions of form that arise within the circulation of the capital value, in its circuit through its successive forms, while the capital value exists in the form of *productive capital*' (Marx 1978a, p. 271). That last point is perhaps better expressed a few pages later:

the way that specific elements of the production process wear out and transfer their value to products gets jumbled up with one based on purely commercial considerations. As Marx observes, if circulating capital is mistaken for capital of circulation: 'It is impossible to see here why one particular kind of capital should be more fixed or more circulating than another'.[50] That is so because of the 'thinness' of the use-value considerations proper to commodity circulation – a commodity must be a use value, but any old use value will do – as opposed to the thicker use-value considerations proper to fixed capital. Here is one way the 'commerce and industry' picture intrudes on the proper understanding of this distinction.

If the first error erases the role of specific use-value factors in the distinction by collapsing the distinction between capital of circulation and productive capital (where the co-involvement of use-value and value factors is thicker), a second error rests on reducing the distinction to use-value features alone and thereby naturalising the distinction. Marx distinguishes two problems with this reduction of the distinction to use-value features:

> certain properties that characterise the means of labour materially are made into direct properties of fixed capital, e.g. physical immobility, such as that of a house. But it is always easy to show that other means of labour, which are also as such fixed capital, ships for example, have the opposite property, i.e. physical mobility.
>
> Alternatively, the formal economic characteristic that arises from the circulation of value is confused with a concrete [*dinglich*] property; as if things which are never capital at all in themselves, could already *in themselves* and by nature be capital in a definite form, fixed or circulating.[51]

The first problem is to think that particular use-value features, such as mobility and immobility, can settle the issue of whether something counts as fixed or circulating capital. But the distinction depends on function, not properties

'He [Smith] places the merely formal commodity metamorphosis which the product, the commodity capital, undergoes in the circulation sphere and which mediates the commodities' change of hands, on the same level with the bodily metamorphosis which the various elements of the productive capital undergo during the production process. Without further ado, he lumps together the transformation of commodity into money and money into commodity with the transformation of the elements of production into the product' (Marx 1978a, p. 275). See also Marx 1978a, pp. 247, 278, 280, 282, 290, 305.

50 Marx 1978a, p. 305.

51 Marx 1978a, p. 241.

alone: 'It is only the function of a product as a means of labour in the production process that makes it fixed capital'.[52] An ox used to pull the plough of a capitalist farmer is fixed capital, whereas an ox bred by a capitalist rancher to be sold for food is circulating capital. Thinking you could decide whether an ox is fixed or circulating capital just by inspecting its properties (e.g., durability) is like thinking that you could decide whether 'work' is a noun or a verb just by staring at the letters. The second problem is thinking that any use-value property could make something fixed or circulating capital independently of the social form of the production process in which it functions. To think in this way naturalises the distinction. But the determining factor in deciding whether or not something counts as fixed or circulating capital involves not simply use value functions but the way that value is transferred to products – and value is a determinate social form.[53] In the language of the present chapter, the trouble here amounts to mistaking a distinction within productive capital for an 'industrial' one. Once again, the 'commerce and industry' picture blocks understanding.

A third and especially devastating error is to mix up the distinction between fixed and circulating capital with an even more telling distinction within productive capital, that between constant and variable capital. Variable capital is the labour-power component of productive capital; it is called 'variable' since it is the one element within productive capital whose consumption *produces* (as opposed to *transfers*) value, and as such it is the sole source of surplus value. Constant capital is the rest of productive capital; while its value can be transferred, it does not produce any value or surplus value. Since the production of surplus value is the *raison d'être* of capital, the distinction between variable and constant capital is the key that unlocks the secrets of the capitalist mode of production. Because of the way that it gives value to products, variable capital (labour power) counts as circulating capital just as much as do

52 Marx 1978a, p. 240.

53 'This differing behavior of the elements of productive capital in the labour process, however, forms only the starting-point of the distinction between fixed and non-fixed capital, and not the distinction itself, as is already shown by the fact that it obtains equally for all modes of production, non-capitalist as well as capitalist. Corresponding to this different material role is *the way in which value is surrendered to the product*, to which further corresponds the way in which value is replaced by the sale of the product; and it is only this that constitutes the distinction in question. Thus capital is not fixed simply because it is fixed in the means of labour, but rather because a part of the value laid out on means of labour remains fixed in these, while another part circulates as a value component of the product' (Marx 1978a, p. 276).

those elements of constant capital that wholly transfer their value to products within a production period. This

> permits the similarity of form that variable capital and the fluid [circulating] component of constant capital have in the turnover to conceal the basic difference that they have in the valorization process and in the formation of surplus value, and in this way the whole secret of capitalist production is still further obscured.[54]

Once again we see Marx the social epistemologist at work, noticing how the peculiar social forms of capitalism throw its investigators off the track.

What really appals Marx is the compounding of the second and third errors, that is, the binding of the naturalisation of the distinction between fixed and circulating capital to the collapse of the constant vs. variable capital distinction. If the distinction between constant and variable capital is identified with the distinction between fixed and circulating capital, and if the latter distinction turns on use-value properties alone, then surplus value, hence capital, must spring from a strictly natural source and must have nothing to do with specific social forms. On the one hand, 'The capitalist production process is thus successfully transformed into a complete mystery, and the origin of the surplus-value present in the product completely withdrawn from view'.[55] On the other hand, in our ignorance we are led into the temptation of the 'Trinity Formula': led, that is, to attribute the power to produce surplus value to strictly natural factors (the means and materials of any labour process), thereby making a fetish of capital.

In wrapping up his remarks on this particularly sorry chapter in the history of political economy, Marx observes:

> What is also brought to fulfilment here is the fetishism peculiar to bourgeois economics, which transforms the social, economic character that things are stamped with in the process of social production into a natural character arising from the material nature of these things.[56]

That fetishism is a natural consequence of the persistent failures of the political economists to comprehend the actual and diverse co-involvements of use value

54 Marx 1978a, p. 278; see also pp. 296–7.
55 Marx 1978a, p. 303.
56 Ibid.

and value in the capitalist mode of production. In the commission of their errors they are aided and abetted by capital's shadowgraph, the 'commerce and industry' picture of the circulation of capital.

2.4 *The Turnover of Capital*

Time itself is the use-value factor of primary interest where the turnover of industrial capital is concerned, though the use-value features already encompassed in the distinction between fixed and circulating capital are important as well. Turnover time is the time it takes to complete a full circuit of industrial capital. That circuit includes the purchase, with money capital, of the elements of production; the completion of a production process (a production period); and the sale of the commodity produced. Turnover time is the sum of production time and circulation time proper. Production time can in turn be subdivided into working time and non-working production time (during which the work process is interrupted in order to accomplish some alteration, e.g. drying paint, necessary to produce the commodity), and circulation time proper can be subdivided into selling time and buying time.

The details of how different durations of these several periods affect capital's turnover become quite complicated, especially as the account must factor in the difference between fixed and circulating capital and the consequences of capital's necessary metamorphoses into and out of the money form during the course of its turnover, an aspect of the story that brings home some very practical consequences of the fact that value must be expressed in money, and which underlines the point that it is the capitalist production process that is under study, not the fiction 'industry'. For present purposes it is enough to recognise that the durations of the several components of turnover time have a profound effect on the realisation, distribution, rate and accumulation of surplus value – shorter is better – and that the durations of those periods depend upon a host of use-value factors including the availability and mix of labour power and materials, the state of scientific and technical development as it affects production time, the speed of communication and transportation, the effectiveness of marketing strategies and the sort of financial 'instruments' in use.

In Volume I of *Capital* the whole problematic of 'relative surplus value' uncovered a surplus-value-based scientific and technological dynamism to capitalist production. It is in the interest of the capitalist class as a whole to increase the productive power of labour in those industries whose products are consumed by wage labourers, in order to keep down or lower the cost of labour power and thereby, all things being equal, to maintain or increase the net amount of surplus value that capitalists realise. Furthermore, because of the competitive 'treadmill effect' involved with value-producing labour as 'socially necessary abstract labour' (if my workers are more productive than the average, each hour of their work counts for more than an hour's worth of value) it is in the interest of capitalists in whichever branch of production to increase productive power in order to increase their share of the total surplus value realised. The surplus-value-based drive for greater productive power disclosed in Volume I reveals an uncanny historical dynamic to the intermingling of use value and value in capitalism. The conclusions of Volume II regarding the velocity of capital's circulation – namely, that increased velocity can step up the realisation, rate and accumulation of surplus-value – redouble our reasons to recognise in capitalism's nexus of use-value and value a historical dynamism of unforeseen and unprecedented power. To Volume I's 'More'! Volume II answers, 'Faster'!

2.5 *Capital's Two Departments: The Reproduction Schemes*

The reproduction schemes of Part Three, showing how the total social capital can be reproduced, both materially and formally, are probably the best-known contribution of Volume II. Our limited objective in bringing them in here is to indicate how they round out Marx's Volume II presentation of the co-involvement of use value and value in capital. Up to the inquiry into the circulation of the total social capital, Marx could abstract from the issue of what sort of commodity any individual industrial capital was producing. Up to this point the 'commercial' assumption about the use value of commodities – that they have one – sufficed. When we come to the circulation of the total social capital, however, that thin condition is no longer good enough:

> As long as we were dealing with capital's value production and the value of its product individually, the natural form of the commodity product was a matter of complete indifference for the analysis, whether it was machines or corn or mirrors ... In so far as the reproduction of capital came into consideration, it was sufficient to assume that the opportunity arose within the circulation sphere for the part of the product that represented capital value to be transformed back into its elements of production, and therefore into its shape as productive capital, just as we could assume that worker and capitalist found on the market the commodities on which they spent their wages and surplus-value. But this purely formal manner of presentation is no longer sufficient once we consider the total social capital and the value of its product. The transformation of one portion of the product's value back into capital, the entry of another part into the individual consumption of the capitalist

> and working classes, forms a movement within the value of the product in which the total capital has resulted; and this movement is not only a replacement of values, but a replacement of materials, and is therefore conditioned not just by the mutual relations of the value components of the social product but equally by their use-values, their material shape.[57]

The question that our attention to the co-involvement of use value and value factors in Volume II can answer for us is this: In devising the reproduction schemes, why does Marx have two (and only two) departments, and why are they differentiated as they are, that is, between means/material of production (Department I) and means of consumption (Department II)? (After all, one can imagine any number of schemes for divvying the total yearly product up along use value lines into any number of departments). The answer takes us back to the purposes of Volume II and what we learned earlier of how thicker use-value (and class) factors enter into the capital form. The purpose of Volume II is to show how capital circulates and reproduces itself in and through its process of circulation. But capital is a nexus of material factors and social forms; its reproduction, then, requires that it must be reproduced materially and formally. We learned earlier that the capital form presupposes that those use values serving as the means and materials of production, the product of Department I, must be in the hands of the capitalist class to assure that labour power goes up for sale. The reproduction of the capital form, then, has a material (and social class) requirement, and it is this that requires Marx to make the distinction between the two departments as he does. To show that capital can reproduce itself formally, Marx has to show that Department I goods keep cycling back into the hands of the capitalist class, which is just what the reproduction schemes demonstrate.

3 Real Subsumption of Circulation under Capital[58]

Writing of formal and real subsumption under capital in the manuscript *Results of the Immediate Production Process*, Marx claimed that real subsumption presupposes formal subsumption.[59] Why should it? Both formal and real

57 Marx 1978a, p. 470. See also Marx 1978a, p. 508.

58 Circulation here includes the production process.

59 Marx 1976b, p. 1,019.

subsumption change use values. Formal subsumption alters them by changing their form – that which makes anything what it is – making them into something new, whether money capital, commodity capital, productive labour or circulating capital. Formal subsumption under capital, then, already involves the intermingling of use value and social form. Real subsumption involves material alterations of use values actuated by the demands of capital, say writing TV sitcoms around 'commercials', or interrupting televised sporting matches with 'TV time-outs'. Here lies our answer. Real subsumption presupposes formal subsumption because the whole reason for making the material changes is that they matter to capital: use value and value must already be involved with one another, that is, formal subsumption must already be in place. Notice that the 'commerce and industry' picture of the circulation of capital and the concomitant blunder of believing that use value drops out after the second page of *Capital* disable us from conceptualising either the formal or the real subsumption of circulatory functions under capital – which happen to be the chief topics of Volume II.

What we have been studying in the previous section can be fairly characterised, then, as an inquiry into the formal subsumption of circulatory (productive and distributive) functions under capital, which is where the brunt of the conceptual work takes place. Now we turn our attention from the formal to the real subsumption of circulation under capital.

The concept of the real subsumption of the circulation of socially produced wealth under capital discloses a multitude of surplus-value-based tendencies for the material transformation of circulatory functions that we can sensibly sort into three primary categories: (1) shortening turnover time; (2) reducing expenses associated with storage, whether incurred in the immediate production process or in commodity circulation proper; and (3) reducing the costs involved with money and accounting. These three, however, are not the only important ones. Two others worth mentioning are the tendency to develop technologies and labour-force management policies that help assure having the right technical mix of means/materials of production and labour power and the (perhaps surprising) tendency to break down production processes so that they can be expanded in small increments to alleviate both the problem of having to pool lots of money to expand and the problem of stagnating inventories.

The actual trends fanning out from these and other form-based tendencies are multiplying, as both the growing literature on 'flexible accumulation' and the daily business pages will attest. Volume II, then, adds new specificity to Marx's account of the consequences of real subsumption under capital for the shape, direction and velocity of technical innovation and change. My limited purpose here is to point to the concept of the real subsumption of the circulation of wealth under capital as a resource that can help us to know these changes for what they are.

4 Conclusion: What is Wrong with the 'Commerce and Industry' Picture and Why It Persists

Let us start with what is right about the 'commerce and industry' picture of the circulation of capital. 'Commerce' identifies a set of necessary aspects of the phenomenon of the circulation of capital: the circulation of capital encompasses, reproduces and generalises the sphere of simple commodity circulation, continually reinforcing the validity of its characteristic forms, the commodity, money, buyer and seller. Marx repeatedly states that insofar as capital operates within the horizon of commodity exchange (that is, in functioning as money capital and as commodity capital) it is governed by the laws of simple commodity circulation, the laws of 'commerce'. Moreover, certain functions that are necessary for the reproduction of capital are governed simply by those laws: the money that consumers (whether capitalists or wage labourers) spend 'unproductively' functions simply as money, not money capital. And – despite all the careless talk about human capital – the good that wage labourers bring to market, their labour power, functions for them strictly as a commodity, not as commodity capital. On the other side of the picture, 'industry' identifies use-value aspects of the capitalist immediate production process which belong to the phenomenon of the circulation of capital. Marx granted this truth already in his account of the labour process (as contrasted with the valorization process) in Chapter Seven of Volume I, but Volume II elaborates on that general presentation in many ways (as we saw, for example, in the discussion of productive labour above). For these reasons it is better to speak of the 'commerce and industry' representation of the circulation of capital as a shadowgraph, which does accurately represent certain aspects of an actual object, than as a mirage, which bears no such resemblance. Surely the elements of truth in the 'commerce and industry' picture partially explain its persistence.

Where the 'commerce and industry' picture goes wrong takes us back to Marx's fundamental observation: all production has a determining social form. The notion of 'industry' does not respect this truth. It does not recognise the force of Marx's dictum that the investigation of a mode of production must treat it as a nexus of material (use-value) factors and social forms – all the way down. Thus 'industry' is imagined to exist without any determining social form, and 'commerce' is consequently pictured as running alongside it rather than belonging to it. This fundamental misconception comes to the surface in many errors and shortcomings of the 'commerce and industry' picture.

The characteristic concepts of that picture – commodity, money, buyer, seller, industry – fail to answer correctly the ineluctable scientific question 'What is it?' What can you say for a picture of the circulation of capital that cannot tell what capital is? The representation leaves us equally tongue-tied when the time comes to speak of money capital, productive capital and commodity capital, of capitalist and wage labourer. Because this representation fails to grapple with the value form, it does not recognise money to be the necessary manifestation of the value (and surplus value) produced in the 'immediate production process of capital', and it thereby cannot grasp the necessity of the three distinct circuits of industrial capital and their consequences. In particular, obliviousness to the necessity of money in the capitalist mode of production yields a flurry of omissions and mistakes regarding the role of money capital. Among those mistakes is the promotion of 'wealthism': 'wealth' being what 'industry' pumps out, in contrast to Marx's judgment: 'Capitalist commodity production, for its part, whether we consider it socially or individually, similarly presupposes capital in the money form, or money-capital, both as the prime mover for each business when it first begins, and as a permanent driving force'.[60]

We have seen how the inability to think straight about the nexus of use value and social form (value) in capitalism, which is presupposed and reinforced by the 'commerce and industry' picture, resulted in the political economists' fumbling of key conceptual pairs: productive and unproductive labour, constant and variable capital, fixed and circulating capital. And the 'commerce and industry' picture's blindness to the co-involvement of use-value and social-form determinations in the turnover of industrial capital kept the whole phenomenon of real subsumption out of view, and with it, the social-form-based dynamism of capitalist production. Anyone confined to the 'commerce and industry' picture has to grasp at straws in order to explain the actual scientific and technological dynamism of capital.

The way of representing the circulation of capital that I have been calling here the 'commerce and industry' picture has the persistence and powers of propagation of a 'stink tree'. This is so for a variety of reasons, one of which I have already mentioned: it contains a number of important truths whose truth conditions are reproduced by the circulation of capital. Seeing what is false about it is difficult for a couple of reasons. It requires a readiness to

60 Marx 1978a, p. 431.

recognise the reality and power of social forms that is scarce in an intellectual milieu still largely defined by the war on forms waged by modern philosophy and science. The social forms characteristic of capitalism are bizarre and self-obscuring: these are points Marx makes much of, starting with his analysis of value and the value form in Chapter One of *Capital*. Money does not look like a social form; neither does the immediate production process appear to be organised by any definite social form or any definite social conception of the good; and the idea that there is a necessary relationship between money and the immediate production process in capitalism is not come by easily. Compared to the intellectual demands of the 'commerce and industry' picture, the degree of conceptual complexity demanded by the phenomenon of the circulation of capital is forbidding.

Finally, the uncomplicated world of 'commerce' is high-minded and progressive: 'The sphere of circulation or commodity exchange, within whose boundaries the sale and purchase of labour-power goes on, is in fact a very Eden of the innate rights of man. It is the exclusive realm of Freedom, Equality, Property and Bentham'.[61] What picture emanating from political economy could be more congenial to liberalism? And with 'industry' busily pouring out 'wealth', who wants to be the spoiler? Readers of *Capital* Volume II know the answer.[62]

Appendix: A Critique of Ernest Mandel on Productive and Unproductive Labour

Ernest Mandel addresses the topic of productive and unproductive labour in his introduction to David Fernbach's translation of *Capital* Volume II. The thrust of the position that Mandel develops there is that Marx's views on the distinction, particularly on how to classify service industries, fluctuated during the 1860s, until Marx settled on the position Mandel claims to find in Volume II: service industries (industries that produce no separable, free-standing product that could be taken to market) cannot involve productive labour. It will be argued that this is the wrong conclusion and, furthermore, that the reasoning Mandel offers in support of it is deeply flawed. This topic gains in importance as the fraction of for-profit business activities in the service sector increases.

61 Marx 1976a, p. 280.

62 For very helpful comments on an early version of this chapter, I want to thank Christopher J. Arthur, Martha Campbell, Mino Carchedi, Paul Mattick Jr, Fred Moseley, Geert Reuten and Tony Smith. I also want to thank Chris Arthur for a number of editorial suggestions that were right on the mark.

If Mandel is right that labour in the service sector is unproductive, then the expansion of that sector must represent a growing deduction from the total surplus value and put a worsening downward pressure on the rate of profit. If the service sector is productive, however, no such consequences follow. On the contrary, owing to short turnover times, service industries may even give profitability a boost.

Mandel offers this as the first of two definitions of productive labour between which Marx's thinking supposedly wobbled: 'all labour which is exchanged against capital and not against revenue'.[63] The second defines productive labour as 'Commodity-producing labour, combining concrete and abstract labour (i.e. combining creation of use-values and production of exchange-values)'.[64] This second definition cannot be right as it stands, since there can be commodity production apart from capitalism. More to the point here, Mandel believes that this second definition 'logically excludes "nonmaterial goods" from the sphere of value production'.[65] Why? Because of a basic thesis of *Capital*: 'there can be no production without (concrete) labour, no concrete labour without appropriation and transformation of material objects'.[66] Here we come to what will prove to be the nub of the problem with Mandel's view, namely, how he understands Marx's concept of concrete labour.

Mandel devotes special attention to the question of 'nonmaterial goods'. (Keep an eye on those scare quotes.) Attempting to build momentum for his interpretation that Marx was vacillating on how to distinguish between productive and unproductive labour, Mandel says that, in *Theories of Surplus-Value*:

> Marx tends to classify these [services] as commodities, in so far as they are produced by wage-earners for capitalist entrepreneurs. Although in Volume II he does not explicitly contradict this, he insists strongly and repeatedly on the correlation between use-values embodied in commodities through a labour process which acts upon and transforms nature, and the production of value and surplus-value.[67]

Mandel thinks that Marx comes to hold the view (arriving at it only with difficulty) that a commodity must be a use-value – which it must – but that a use value must be some independently existing object which is the result of

63 Mandel 1978, pp. 41–2.
64 Mandel 1978, p. 43.
65 Ibid.
66 Ibid.
67 Ibid.

'concrete labour' that 'acts upon and transforms nature'. Here is the wedge that will keep services from being considered commodities, hence service labour from being considered productive labour.

Mandel grants that Marx explicitly includes certain teachers as productive labourers,[68] but he draws this lesson:

> [that] only indicates that Marx had not yet completed his articulation of the contradictory determinants of 'productive labour' – on the one hand, exchange against capital rather than revenue, and on the other, participation in the process of commodity production (which involves the unity-and-contradiction of the labour process and the valorization process, use-value and exchange-value, concrete and abstract labour).[69]

But there are no 'contradictory determinants' to articulate. Rather, something is fishy about Mandel's whole suggestion of two different definitions of productive labour. On the one hand, surely Marx never thought that the mere production of a commodity (as opposed to commodity capital) qualified labour as productive; so the second definition is either flatly wrong or implicitly includes the first definition. On the other hand, the second definition is encompassed in the first, for, as Volume II stresses, the production and sale of commodities belongs to the circulation of capital, and capital exists only in its circulation.

Mandel finds evidence in the following text from Volume II of a general exclusion of 'personal service industries' from the realm of productive labour:

> If we have a function which, although in and for itself unproductive, is nevertheless a necessary moment of reproduction, then, when this is transformed, through the division of labour, from the secondary activity of many into the exclusive activity of a few, into their special business, this does not change the character of the function itself.[70]

The trouble is, this begs the question, which is: Are 'personal service industries' unproductive to begin with? For the same reason, Mandel's follow-up ('[i]f this is true of commercial travellers or book-keepers, it obviously applies all the more to teachers or cleaning services') is literally true, *if* the work of teachers and house-cleaners is non-productive.[71] But what Mandel means to

68 Marx 1976a, p. 644.
69 Mandel 1978, p. 43.
70 Marx 1978a, p. 209.
71 Mandel 1978, p. 43.

say, namely, that, if commercial travellers or bookkeepers are non-productive workers (as they are), then surely teachers and house-cleaners are, is simply a *non sequitur*. We need first to know why the former types are unproductive and then see if those considerations pertain to the latter types. Here we glimpse the false naturalisation of the concept of productive labour to which Mandel falls prey. Mandel begs the question because he has already resolved it in his own mind with the notion that the natural form of labour in 'personal service industries' (rather than its social form) gives grounds enough to exclude all such labour from being productive. Mandel acts as if there were a division based on natural characteristics between labours that are productive (or at least candidates for being productive) and those that are unproductive (or not candidates for being productive). This, I believe, is far from Marx's view. It amounts to a failure to think straight about how use value and value figure into the distinction.

The nub of the problem with Mandel's line of thought is that he treats the notion of 'concrete labour' as if it were a critical category, as if there were two types of actual labour, concrete and non-concrete; the former can produce commodities, the latter cannot.[72] (And labour in service industries is, by nature, of the 'non-concrete' sort.) That is not how the category of concrete labour works in Marx's thought. For Marx, all human labour is concrete in this general sense. There is no actual human labour to contrast with Marx's general category of concrete labour; there is no actual, 'non-concrete' labour, no labour that fails to involve the 'appropriation and transformation of material objects.' (What bad idealism to imagine there is!) So there is no natural class of actual labours which could be precluded from counting as productive by virtue of their failure to be concrete. No labour can be identified as non-concrete, and so no labour can be declared incapable of producing commodities on this basis.

Mandel's position trades on a peculiarity about the usage of the word 'commodity'. The term may mean a separable product, as Mandel takes it to be, or it may be, more generally, anything useful, including a 'useful effect', that has an exchange value – this second being the proper definition. Thus Marx writes, with the transportation industry in mind: 'There are however particular branches of industry in which the product of the production process is not a new objective product, a commodity'. Here Marx bows to the first usage of the term. But he goes on to say of the transport industry:

---

72 By the same token Mandel supposes a natural distinction between 'material goods' and 'immaterial goods'. There is a natural distinction to be made – it is the one between free-standing goods and 'useful effects' – but the way Mandel misconstrues the distinction is bad metaphysics and bad economics.

> The useful effect can only be consumed during the production process; it does not exist as a thing of use distinct from this process, a thing which functions as an article of commerce and circulates as a commodity only after its production. However the exchange-value of this useful effect is still determined, like that of any other commodity, by the value of the elements of production used up in it (labour-power and the means of production), plus the surplus-value created by the surplus labour of the workers occupied in the transport industry.[73]

This passage from Volume II simply contravenes Mandel's position: Marx says that the transportation industry (including the transportation of people) sells commodities and does so on a capitalist basis, meaning that transportation workers can be productive workers.[74]

Mandel's general rule is as follows: 'all forms of wage-labour which exteriorise themselves in and thus add value to a product (materials) are creative of surplus-value and hence productive for capitalism as a whole.'[75] I take this to mean that only free-standing products can be commodities and that only those workers who produce such products can be productive labourers. Hence service industry workers, who do not bring independently existing products to market, cannot be productive labourers. This is the wrong conclusion, drawn, as I have shown, for the wrong reasons. There is a difference between a free-standing product and a 'useful effect', but both are material. Likewise, we can distinguish between the labour that produces a free-standing commodity and the labour that performs a service for purchase, but both are concrete. The metaphysics underlying Mandel's normative notion of 'material goods' and concrete labour brings to mind the words of heavy-metal guitarist Ted Nugent, 'if I can't bite into it, it doesn't exist'. As for service industries, not only can they be productive of surplus value (adding to the aggregate surplus value) when organised capitalistically, but because for service industries that portion of the turnover time of industrial capital represented by *C'-M'* equals zero, it follows that, *ceteris paribus*, service industries would be favoured by capital.[76]

---

73 Marx 1978a, p. 135.

74 Mandel allows that transportation workers can be productive, but for a different reason. They can be productive when they complete the use value of some tangible product. The service of transportation itself cannot be a commodity by Mandel's lights.

75 Mandel 1978, p. 44. Here Mandel reverts to a position held by Adam Smith, who, unawares, did make the distinction between productive and unproductive labour on two incompatible bases.

76 It is true that in *Results of the Immediate Production Process*, Marx, while clearly granting

Mandel's fixation of the distinction between productive and unproductive labour on the natural difference between a useful effect that issues in a separable product and one that does not (as in the case of transportation) – his getting the relationship between use value and value categories wrong – not only leads him incorrectly to exclude true service industries from the category of productive labour; it also leads him to the opposite mistake, i.e. to count unproductive labour as productive because it issues in a tangible product:

> Similarly [to the production of films and television shows, the similarity being that they all result in independently existing products], wage-labour employed in making advertising films is productive, whereas the cajoling of potential clients to purchase or order such films is as unproductive as the labour of commercial representatives in general.[77]

But advertising is unproductive for the same reason as the cajoling is; namely, it is all about the formal change from *C'-M'*. The fact that in the course of their work advertisers produce tangible objects like films does not make their work productive.

---

that service labour could be productive, explicitly dismissed its economic significance: 'On the whole, types of work that are consumed as services and not in products separable from the worker and hence not capable of existing as commodities independently of him, but which are yet capable of being directly exploited in capitalist terms, are of microscopic significance when compared with the mass of capitalist production' (Marx 1976b, pp. 1,044–5). This empirical conclusion has no bearing on the conceptual issue at stake; moreover, there is no reason to think that, a hundred and thirty years later, we should arrive at the same factual judgment.

77 Mandel 1978, p. 45.

CHAPTER 13

The Secret of Capital's Self-Valorisation 'Laid Bare': How Hegel Helped Marx to Overturn Ricardo's Theory of Profit*

At the core of Marx's *Capital* lies his revelation of capital's secret, how capital makes money out of money, or, in Marx's more technical language, how value is valorised. In Marx's theory of surplus value, capital's secret is 'laid bare': money makes money by appropriating – without needing to violate commercial fair play – the unpaid labour of wage workers. Marx's theory of surplus value begins his complex theory of profit, which overturns both Ricardo's theory of profit and his individualistic theory of value. Profit includes incomes in the forms of profit of enterprise, interest and rent; the total annual profit is the sum of those incomes for the year.

Profit, and another basic capitalist social form, wages, keep capital's secret well hidden. Profit measures itself against the sum of money invested; the ratio of the two sums, of profit to investment, is the rate of profit. The rate of profit, then, appears to have nothing to do with what part of the investment goes to pay wages, much less with how much unpaid labour a capital appropriates. And this is not merely a matter of appearances. The action of competition among capitals all chasing higher rates of profit tends to bring about a general rate of profit, so the size of individual profits is determined by the size of the individual capital invested. Since capital *per se* appears as the variable determining profit, capital seems to valorize itself. A general rate of profit implies that the profit returned to an individual investment in fact bears no direct relationship to the fraction of the investment devoted to wages or to the unpaid labour appropriated through that investment. Turning to the wage, it presents itself as compensation for the labour done by a wage worker, as 'the price of labour'. That appearance puts a stop to the thought that profit arises from unpaid labour: there is none. The appearances and realities involved with profits and wages seem to torpedo Marx's claim that the source of profit is unpaid labour – and with it his theory of exploitation. But, as Marx was fond

---

* Originally published as 'The Secret of Capital's Self-Valorisation "Laid Bare": How Hegel Helped Marx to Overturn Ricardo's Theory of Profit', in *Marx's 'Capital' and Hegel's 'Logic'*, edited by Fred Moseley and Tony Smith (Leiden/Boston: Brill, 2014).

of saying in the face of an impasse, 'let us consider the matter more closely'. In order to overturn the extant theories of profit and wages, Marx has to introduce two key distinctions, between labour and labour power and between constant and variable capital, and to revolutionise (in a second way) the classical labour theory of value.

Marx had already put the labour theory of value on a new conceptual basis by identifying value as a historically specific social form. In *A Contribution to the Critique*, Marx writes, '[T]he labour which posits exchange-value is a specific social form of labour.'[1] With this conception of value as the consequence of the peculiar social character of commodity-producing labour, which necessarily appears as money, Marx reveals one of capitalism's secrets. Value is something strictly social, and money is the displaced social form of commodity-producing labour: 'Although it is thus correct to say that exchange-value is a relation between persons, it is however necessary to add that it is a relation hidden by a material veil.'[2] That 'material veil' is money and the price system. By revealing money to be the necessary expression of value, Marx demonstrates that 'money, though a physical object with distinct properties, represents ... nothing but a material expression of a specific social form of labour.'[3] To solve the conundrums that the general rate of profit poses for the classical labour theory of value, Marx first argues that *the labour theory of value is false at the level of individual commodities and capitals*. Marx responds not by abandoning a labour theory of value – that would be to give up on scientific understanding. Rather, he reconstitutes value theory, directing it at the level of the totality of commodities and prices, capitals and profits (and, by implication, their representative or aliquot parts).

Political economy's failure to reconcile the theory of value with the formation of a general rate of profit, like its tin ear for the social specificity of value and value-producing labour, is not accidental; inattention to matters of form show its confinement to the 'bourgeois horizon'. Marx's term 'bourgeois horizon' refers to the mind-set that was the target of his criticisms of the philosophy and economics of Proudhon's book *The Philosophy of Poverty*.[4] Of classical political economy Marx writes:

1 Marx 1970a, p. 36.

2 Marx 1970a, p. 34.

3 Marx 1970a, p. 35.

4 Marx writes to Annenkov: Proudhon 'does not rise above the bourgeois horizon' (Marx 1963a, p. 190).

> Yet even its best representatives remained more or less trapped in the world of illusion their criticism had dissolved, and nothing else is possible from the bourgeois standpoint; they all fell therefore more or less into inconsistencies, half-truths and unresolved contradictions.[5]

In the patterns of bourgeois thinking, Marx finds knots of unworkable bifurcations: mind versus world, form versus content, passive versus active, immediate versus mediated. These dualisms arise from the dogma that whatever can be distinguished in thought can exist separately. The bourgeois mind-set is always looking to factor out the purely subjective from the purely objective, pure form from pure content.

Hegel taught Marx to recognise and transcend the limitations of the 'bourgeois horizon', though Marx judged that Hegel ran afoul of his own criticisms of that mind-set.[6] At the age of 19, Marx wrote to his father about how, after gulping in Hegel, he understood the reason for the breakdown of his attempt to write a book on jurisprudence from the standpoint of Kant and Fichte. Marx explains, 'The mistake lay in my believing that the one (form) could and must be developed in separation from the other (matter), and consequently I obtained no actual form, but only a desk with drawers in which I then strew sand.'[7] By contrast, Marx discovered, in Hegel's concept, an alternative to the bifurcations of the bourgeois mind-set: 'The concept is indeed the mediating between form and content.'[8] Through Hegel, Marx developed the 'logical chops' to overturn the classical theories of value and profit. Of particular importance was Hegel's logic of essence: essence must appear as something other than itself.[9] In 'The Necessity of Money: How Hegel Helped Marx to Surpass Ricardo's Theory of Value', I argued that Hegel's logic of essence enabled Marx to break with Ricardo's theory of value and conclude that value must appear as money.[10] In the present chapter, I argue that Marx leans on Hegel's

---

5 Marx 1981, p. 969.

6 'Form and content are a pair of determinations that are frequently employed by the reflective understanding, and, moreover, mainly in such a way that the content is considered as what is essential and independent, while the form, on the contrary, is inessential and dependent. Against this, however, it must be remarked that in fact both of them are equally essential' (Hegel 1991b, §133, addition, p. 202). Marx's critique of the 'bourgeois horizon' echoes Hegel's criticism of the 'reflective understanding'.

7 Marx 1967, p. 43.

8 Ibid.

9 Hegel 1991b, §114, p. 165.

10 Murray 1993b, included in the present volume as Chapter 8.

logic of essence again: surplus value must appear as profit; profit is the transformed form of surplus value.[11]

In a letter to Engels of 16 January 1858, Marx writes, in the midst of work on the *Grundrisse*, 'I am getting some nice developments. For instance, I have thrown over the entire doctrine of profit as previously conceived. In the *method* of treatment the fact that by mere accident I have again glanced through Hegel's *Logic* has been of great service to me'. Marx follows up:

> If there should ever be time for such work again, I should greatly like to make accessible to the ordinary human intelligence, in two or three printer's sheets, what is rational in the method which Hegel discovered but at the same time enveloped in mysticism [*mystifiziert hat*].[12]

Let us look further into each of these provocative points.

Marx says that, with the aid of the rational aspect of the method that Hegel mystified, he has 'overthrown the entire doctrine of profit as previously conceived'. Marx's statement naturally raises several questions, which I will try to answer in order. 1. What did Marx mean by his statement that Hegel mystified his method? 2. What did Marx find to be rational in Hegel's method? 3. What were the shortcomings of the previous conceptions of profit? 4. What were the 'nice developments' that Marx made? 5. How did reacquainting himself with Hegel's *Science of Logic* help Marx to make these advances?

1 How, According to Marx, Did Hegel Mystify His Own Method?

What did Marx mean by Hegel's 'mystification of his method'? Let me indicate several aspects of Hegel's method, as Marx understood it, that he would have considered 'mystifying'.

1. Marx objected to Hegel for making logic into a discipline directed at freestanding logical entities. For Marx, this Platonist understanding of logical entities reifies what are properly conceived of as the logical aspects of worldly thinking. Marx adopts Feuerbach's assessment: 'Hegel sets out from the estrangement of substance ... from the absolute and fixed abstraction.'[13] Fixed thought-

---

11 'Marx shows in *Capital* ... the *necessity* ... for the category of value to be transformed into the category of price of production' (Murray 1988a, p. 263, n. 23).

12 Marx and Engels 1975b, p. 102. See also Marx 1976a, pp. 102–3.

13 Marx 1964a, p. 172.

abstractions, 'torn from *real* mind and from *real* nature', become the shadowy objects of inquiry in Hegel's logic.[14]

2. Marx traces the fixation of the abstractions investigated in Hegel's logic to his *Phenomenology of Spirit*, 'the true point of origin and the secret of the Hegelian philosophy.'[15] Marx identifies Hegel's standpoint in the *Phenomenology* as that of 'modern political economy': 'He grasps *labour* as the *essence* of man'; however, much as the labour that constitutes value is abstract labour, 'the only labour which Hegel knows and recognises is abstractly mental labour.'[16] Marx spells out the connection between Hegel's reduction of activity to 'sheer activity' and his positing of an independent realm of logical abstractions:

> The rich, living, sensuous, concrete activity of self-objectification is therefore reduced to its mere abstraction, *absolute negativity* – an abstraction which is again fixed as such and considered as an independent activity – as sheer activity. Because this so-called negativity is nothing but the *abstract, empty* form of that real living act, its content can in consequence be merely a formal content begotten by abstraction from all content. As a result there are general, abstract *forms of abstraction* pertaining to every content and on that account indifferent to, and, consequently, valid for, all content – thought-forms or logical categories torn from *real* mind and from *real* nature.[17]

To that accomplishment, Marx offers this left-handed compliment:

> Hegel's positive achievement here, in his speculative logic, is that the *definite concepts*, the universal *fixed thought-forms* in their independence *vis-à-vis* nature and mind are a necessary result of the general estrangement of the human essence and therefore also of human thought.[18]

Hegel's logic is the necessary outcome of his estrangement from the worldliness of human activity: 'His thoughts are therefore fixed mental shapes or ghosts dwelling outside nature and man. Hegel has locked up all these fixed mental forms together in his *Logic*.'[19] With Hegel, logic is the money of mind:

---

14 Marx 1964a, p. 189.
15 Marx 1964a, p. 173.
16 Marx 1964a, p. 177.
17 Marx 1964a, p. 189.
18 Marx 1964a, p. 189.
19 Marx 1964a, p. 190.

> *Logic* (mind's *coin of the realm*, the speculative or *thought-value* of man and nature – their essence grown totally indifferent to all real determinateness, and hence their unreal essence) is *alienated thinking*, and therefore thinking which abstracts from nature and from real man: *abstract* thinking.[20]

In these observations on abstraction and logic in the economy of Hegel's thought, we find a remarkable anticipation of Marx's mature theory of value as congealed abstract labour and of money as the necessary expression of value, indifferent to the particularities of commodities.[21]

3. Because Hegel reduces 'the rich, living, sensuous, concrete activity of self-objectification' to 'sheer activity', to abstract thought, the only sort of objectivity that he recognises is pure thinghood, a ghostly objectivity: 'it is equally clear that a *self-consciousness* ... can only establish *thinghood* (i.e. establish something which itself is only an abstract thing, a thing of abstraction and not a *real* thing).'[22] Marx goes on to describe such an object as 'only the *semblance* of an object, a piece of mystification.'[23] Likewise, Ricardo reduces wealth to congealed labour: 'The *independent, material form of wealth* disappears and wealth is shown to be simply the activity of men.'[24]

4. Marx objected to what he took to be Hegel's theological construal of logic. In describing Feuerbach's 'great achievement', Marx listed first '[t]he proof that philosophy is nothing else but religion rendered into thought.'[25] Hegel treats the abstract entities of his logic as ideas in the mind of God; they function as archetypes for the creation of nature and spirit.

5. Hegel, then, mystified logic by treating it as purely *a priori* – just as indifferent to the 'real determinateness' of nature and mind as value is indifferent to particular use values – as opposed to emerging by reflection on human reasoning about the world.

6. Following Feuerbach, Marx, in his early study of Hegel's *Philosophy of Right*, charged Hegel with imposing prefabricated logical forms onto his objects of study, such as the family, civil society and the state: 'He develops his thinking not out of the object, rather he develops the object in accordance with ready-

20 Marx 1964a, p. 174.
21 See Murray 1988a, p. 49.
22 Marx 1964a, p. 180.
23 Marx 1964a, p. 183.
24 Marx 1991, p. 345.
25 Marx 1964a, p. 172.

made thinking put together in the abstract sphere of logic.'[26] Marx insists that concepts must arise out of one's thinking over the objects of inquiry in the world – or reflection on that thinking engagement.

7. Marx objects to the 'presuppositionlessness' of Hegelian science.

8. Marx traces the mystification of the dialectic back to Hegel's logic, to his conception of the syllogism. Hegel's 'rational syllogism' reverts to the 'still imperfect combination of *immediacy* and *mediation*' characteristic of the sphere of essence:[27]

> In general Hegel conceives of the syllogism as mediator, as a *mixtum compositum*. One can say that in his development of the rational syllogism the whole transcendence and mystical dualism of his system comes to the surface. The middle term is the wooden sword, the concealed opposition between universality and singularity.[28]

Marx adds, 'Anything further than this belongs in the critique of Hegelian logic.'[29] If Marx were flatly opposed to logic, this task would be pointless.

2 What is Rational in Hegel's Method?

Though one might think that Marx was flatly opposed to logic in anything like Hegel's sense, evidence exists against that conclusion: not least, Marx's desire to write up what is rational in Hegel's method. Marx recognises the pertinence of logical categories and relations – not only those of ordinary formal logic. We do recognise common patterns in everyday and scientific reasonings whose content and movements can be attended to as such, though always as aspects of concrete reasoning about nature or spirit. In a passage from the first edition of *Capital*, Marx praises Hegel's attention to the content of some basic logical forms: 'before *Hegel*, professional logicians even overlooked the content of the form of the paradigms of judgment and syllogism.'[30] Attending to the content of forms belongs to the rational aspect of Hegel's method.

26 Marx 1970b, p. 14.

27 Hegel 1991b, § 114, p. 178.

28 Marx 1970b, p. 85. Hegel writes, 'the *rational* is nothing but the *syllogism*' (Hegel 1969, p. 665).

29 Marx 1970b, p. 89.

30 As quoted in Murray 1988a, p. 115.

In the chapter on wages in *Capital* Volume I, Marx writes, '[W]hat is true of all forms of appearance and their hidden background is also true of the form of appearance "value and price of labour", or "wages", as contrasted with the essential relation manifested in it, namely the value and price of labour-power.'[31] Here Marx finds a purpose for general observations regarding the categories of essence and appearance. The logical terminology of essence and appearance turns up in Marx's thinking about surplus value in relation to profit: 'Surplus-value and the rate of surplus-value are ... the invisible essence to be investigated, whereas the rate of profit and hence the form of surplus-value as profit are visible surface phenomena.'[32] To disclose profit as a necessary form of appearance, Marx first has to locate the source of all surplus value in surplus labour. Then Marx doubles back, reasoning from surplus value to profit, revealing profit to be the transformed form of surplus value.

As he does in his account of money as the necessary form of appearance of value, Marx finds rational aspects to Hegel's insight into the logic of essence. The conventional interpretation of the logic of essence sees only the one-way dependence of appearance on essence; it does not recognise essence's dependence upon appearance: essence *must* appear. Classical political economy recognises the scientific demand to go past everyday phenomena and explain them in terms of essential relations. But, confined to its conventional understanding of the logic of essence and appearance, classical political economy does not see the point of doubling back and developing the categories of appearance from those of essence.

3 The Shortcomings of Political Economy's Conceptions about Profit and the Rate of Profit

Classical political economy fails to develop a definitive conception of surplus value: it never gets to its '*absolute form*'.[33] Nonetheless, classical political economy makes progress. It topples the Trinity Formula, which imagines the three factors of production (land, means of production and living labour) to be the respective natural and independent sources of the three kinds of revenue (rent, interest/profit of enterprise and wages). It reduces rent and interest/profit of enterprise to surplus labour. Contrasting classical political economy with vulgar economics, Marx offers this complex assessment:

31 Marx 1976a, p. 682.
32 Marx 1981, p. 134.
33 Marx 1971a, p. 239.

> Classical political economy seeks to reduce the various fixed and mutually alien forms of wealth to their inner unity by means of analysis and to strip away the form in which they exist independently alongside one another. It seeks to grasp the inner connection in contrast to the multiplicity of outward forms. It therefore reduces rent to surplus profit, so that it ceases to be a specific, *separate* form and is divorced from its apparent source, the land. It likewise divests interest of its independent form and shows that it is a part of profit. In this way it reduces all types of revenue and all independent forms and title under cover of which the non-workers receive a portion of the value of commodities, to the single form of profit. Profit, however, is reduced to surplus-value since the value of the whole commodity is reduced to labour; the amount of paid labour embodied in the commodity constitutes wages, consequently the surplus over and above it constitutes unpaid labour, surplus labour called forth by capital and appropriated gratis under various titles.[34]

Here Marx allows that classical political economy has the three levels of concepts that he distinguishes in his own account: the particular appearance-forms of surplus value (profit of enterprise, interest and rent), profit and surplus value. For all that it accomplished, however, '[c]lassical political economy occasionally contradicts itself in this analysis. It often attempts directly, leaving out the intermediate links, to carry through the reduction and to prove that the various forms are derived from one and the same source.'[35] This is not accidental, says Marx:

> This however is a necessary consequence of its analytical method, with which criticism and understanding must begin. Classical economy is not interested in elaborating how the various forms come into being [*genetisch zu entwickeln*], but seeks to reduce them to their unity by means of analysis, because it starts from them as given premises. But analysis is the necessary prerequisite of genetical presentation, and of the understanding of the real, formative process in its different phases.[36]

34 Marx 1971a, p. 500.

35 Ibid. This lack of proper conceptual mediation is one of Marx's most common criticisms, 'As can be studied in the case of the Ricardian school, it is completely wrong-headed to seek directly to present the laws of the profit rate as laws of the rate of surplus-value, or vice versa' (Marx 1981, p. 136). See also Engels 1978, p. 93.

36 Ibid.

Classical political economy's failure to make sense of the development of categories shows its confinement to the 'bourgeois horizon'.

Ricardo was not the last word on profit and surplus-value from the Ricardian school. Commenting on a little-known 1821 pamphlet entitled *The Source and Remedy of the National Difficulties. A Letter to Lord John Russell,* Marx reflects on the limitations of Ricardo's theory of profit, identifies advances made by the author and brings out the limitations of the author's Ricardian standpoint:

> This scarcely known pamphlet ... contains an important advance on Ricardo. It bluntly describes surplus-value ... as '*surplus labour*', the labour which the worker performs gratis, the labour he performs over and above the quantity of labour by which the value of his labour-power is replaced ... Important as it was to reduce value to labour, it was equally important [to present] *surplus-value*, which manifests itself in *surplus product*, as *surplus labour*. This was in fact already stated by Adam Smith and constitutes one of the main elements in Ricardo's argumentation. But nowhere did he clearly express it and record it in an *absolute form*.[37]

This author's blunt description of surplus value as surplus labour counts as an advance over Ricardo. Marx identifies a second advance over Ricardo: 'He thus distinguishes the general form of surplus-labour or surplus-value from their particular forms, something which neither Ricardo nor Adam Smith [does], at least not consciously or consistently'.[38] The author self-consciously articulates the difference between surplus value and its several forms of appearance, whereas previous classical political economists were prone to mix up these different conceptual levels. Thus, this author makes some progress in addressing Marx's concern about a lack of proper mediation in thinking about surplus value, profit and surplus value's particular appearance-forms (profit of enterprise, interest and rent).

All the same, the pamphlet has its limitations:

> The pamphlet is no theoretical treatise ... It does not, consequently, make the claim that its conception of surplus-value as *surplus labour* carries with it a general criticism of the entire system of economic categories, nor can this be expected of it. The author stands rather on Ricardian

37 Marx 1971a, pp. 238–9.

38 Marx 1971a, p. 254.

> ground and is only consistent in stating one of the consequences inherent in the system itself.[39]

A 'general criticism of the entire system of economic categories' was the task that Marx undertook in *Capital*.[40]

Let us turn from Marx's general assessment to a number of specific shortcomings of classical political economy directly pertaining to surplus value and profit. These points specify the difficulties in 'the entire doctrine of profit as previously conceived'.

1. Where well thought-out concepts of surplus-value, profit and the specific forms of appearance of surplus value (profit of enterprise, interest and rent) and their conceptual relationships are needed, the discourse of political economy is loaded with confusions, inconsistencies and missing or mixed-up distinctions. 'At bottom, surplus-value – in so far as it is indeed the foundation of profit, but still distinct from profit commonly so-called – has never been developed'.[41] The 'General Observation' with which *Theories of Surplus-Value* begins is:

> All economists share the error of examining surplus-value not as such, in its pure form, but in the particular forms of profit and rent. What theoretical errors must necessarily arise for this will be shown more fully in Chapter III [*Capital* Volume III], in the analysis of the greatly changed form which surplus-value assumes as profit.[42]

2. Likewise, where well thought-out concepts of the rate of profit and the rate of surplus value and their conceptual relationship are needed, we again get conceptual confusion:

> Ricardo's disciples, just as Ricardo himself, fail to make a distinction between *surplus-value* and *profit* ... It does not occur to them that, even if one considers not capitals in different spheres of production but *each* capital separately, insofar as it does not consist exclusively of variable capital, i.e., of capital laid out in wages only, rate of profit and rate of

39 Ibid.

40 See Marx's letter to Lassalle of 22 February 1858 (Marx and Engels 1975b, p. 10).

41 Marx 1973, p. 385. On Ricardo see Marx 1968b, p. 168.

42 Marx 1963c, p. 40. See also Marx 1963c, pp. 82, 89.

> surplus-value are different things, that therefore profit must be a more developed, specifically modified form of surplus-value.[43]

3. Political economy lacked the idea that the concept of profit must be developed out of the concept of surplus value and shown to be a 'transformed form' of it. Hegelian ideas such as 'more developed forms' lie beyond the 'bourgeois horizon' of the classical political economists.

4. Political economy did not correctly draw the conceptual distinction between labour power and labour, which provides the necessary foothold for developing the concept of surplus value. Engels describes this failure:

> Labour is the measure of value ... Wages, the value of a definite quantity of living labour, are always smaller than the value of the product that is produced by this quantity of living labour, or in which this is expressed. The question [of 'the value of labour'] is insoluble in this form. Marx posed it correctly, and thereby answered it. It is not the labour that has a value ... It is not labour that is bought and sold as a commodity, but rather labour-power.[44]

5. Lacking the distinction between labour power and labour, political economy could not draw the distinction between constant and variable capital; instead, it tangled it up with the distinction between fixed and circulating capital.[45]

6. Lacking the distinction between constant and variable capital, political economy could not conceive properly of the rate of surplus value, the organic composition of capital, profit or the rate of profit.

7. Political economy, then, lacked the correct account of the qualitative source of profit and the quantitative determinants of profit and of the rate of profit. So, political economy could not answer the question: what determines the average rate of profit?

8. Classical political economy failed to reconcile the classical labour theory of value with the fact that capitals of a) differing organic compositions of capital and b) differing turnover-times tend to form a general rate of profit. Marx lays out the argument, concluding, 'The theory of value thus appears incompatible with the actual movement, incompatible with the actual phenomena of production, and it might seem that we must abandon all hope of

---

43 Marx 1971a, p. 85.

44 Engels 1978, p. 101.

45 See Marx 1968b, p. 170, and Engels 1978, p. 99.

understanding these phenomena'.[46] Ricardo recognised the problem in the first chapter of his *Principles*; in fact, Marx shows that Ricardo's examples actually prove that his theory of value cannot be reconciled with the general rate of profit.[47] However, as Marx sets forth in detail, Ricardo obfuscated this result by throwing the spotlight on secondary matters.[48] Other political economists, notably Malthus, recognised this basic contradiction without finding a way to overcome it. Instead, they a) rejected the labour theory of value (Malthus), b) argued that it applied to pre-capitalist societies but not to capitalism (Torrens) or c) tried unsuccessfully to reconcile the contradiction through one subterfuge or another (later Ricardians).[49] On this contradiction, Engels observes, classical political economy was shipwrecked: 'Around 1839, the Ricardian school foundered on surplus-value'.[50] At least by the writing of the *Grundrisse* in 1857–8, Marx knew that the labour theory of value in its individualistic conception is untenable: that was the truth at the other end of the stick that Marx got hold of in overturning the received conceptions of surplus value and profit. To throw 'over the entire doctrine of profit as previously conceived', Marx had to overthrow the classical labour theory of value and redirect it from individual commodities and capitals to the 'heap' of commodities and the total capital.

4 How Marx Addresses These Shortcomings of Classical Political Economy

Marx draws the necessary distinctions, develops the required concepts and discovers how to reconcile a reconceived labour theory of value with the formation of a general rate of profit among firms of differing organic compositions and/or turnover-times. Marx draws the distinctions between labour and labour power and between constant and variable capital, clarifying how the latter distinction differs from that between fixed and circulating capital. These distinctions open the conceptual space for an adequate concept of surplus value and of the rate of surplus value, which, in turn, are needed in order to develop the concepts of profit and the rate of profit as 'transformed forms' of surplus value and the rate of surplus value, respectively.

46 Marx 1981, p. 252.
47 Marx 1968b, pp. 190–1.
48 See Marx 1968b, p. 181.
49 Marx 1981, pp. 268–9. See also Marx 1968b, p. 191.
50 Engels 1978, p. 100.

To overthrow the existing doctrines of profit, Marx had to overthrow the individualistic classical labour theory of value; only then could he reconcile a labour theory of value with the general rate of profit. Marx replaces the failed labour theory of value, which explains individual prices as expressions of individual values, with a holistic labour theory of value that holds at the aggregate level, that is, for the total capital, and explains subordinate phenomena on that basis.[51] Individual prices do not match individual values; individual profits do not match individual surplus values. Still, the labour theory of value holds at the aggregate level and explains individual phenomena with transformed value categories: 'The sum of the profits for all the different spheres of production must accordingly be equal to the sum of surplus-values, and the sum of prices of production for the total social product must be equal to the sum of its values.'[52] Prices of production explain individual prices no longer in terms of individual values but rather on the basis of cost-price (the sum of constant and variable capital) plus profit, as determined by the average rate of profit, which depends on the aggregate surplus value (= aggregate profit), the ΔM of the total capital.[53] Individual profits are no longer explained by individual surplus values but by the transformed forms of surplus value and rate of surplus value, namely profit and rate of profit.

Marx expresses the crux of his objection to individualistic value theory, and also the chief points of his holistic labour theory of value, in a passage from his criticism of Ricardo (what Marx calls 'cost-price' here is what he calls 'price of production' in Volume III):

> Hence, if *profits* as a percentage of capital are to be equal over a period, say of a year, so that capitals of equal size yield equal profits in the same period of time, then the *prices* of the commodities must be different from their *values*. The sum total of these *cost-prices* of all the commodities taken together will *be equal to their value*. Similarly the total profit will

51 'Every section of the *aggregate capital* [*Gesamtkapital*] would in accordance with its magnitude participate in the aggregate surplus-value and draw a corresponding part [*aliquot Teil*] of it. And since every individual capital is to be regarded as shareholder in this aggregate capital, it would be correct to say *first* that its *rate of profit* is the same as that of all the others [because] capitals of the same size yield the same amount of profit … Competition more or less succeeds in this by means of its equalizations' (Marx 1968b, p. 29).

52 Marx 1981, p. 273.

53 'The production price of the commodity has also developed, as a transformed form of value' (Marx 1981, p. 263).

> be equal to the total surplus-value which all these capitals yield, for instance, during one year. If one did not take the definition of value as the basis, the *average profit*, and therefore also the cost-prices, would be purely imaginary and untenable. The equalisation of the surplus-values in different spheres of production does not affect the absolute size of this total surplus-value; but merely alters its *distribution* among the different spheres of production. The determination of this surplus-value itself, however, only arises out of the determination of value by labour-time. Without this the average profit is the average of nothing, pure fancy. And it could then equally well be 1,000 per cent or 10 per cent.[54]

Marx will not abandon a labour theory of value; without it, the general rate of profit, which is required to arrive at prices of production, is left unexplained. By the same token, we see why Marx objects to Ricardo's method, which treats value and the general rate of profit as being on the same conceptual level. The theory of value must account for the general rate of profit by accounting for the total surplus value (profit) before it can be used to explain the necessary transformation of values into prices of production.

4.1 *Implications of Marx's Overthrowing the Classical Doctrines of Profit and Value for the Organization of* Capital

Since overthrowing previous doctrines of profit required Marx to overthrow the individualistic classical theory of value and replace it with a holistic one, there are major implications for how Marx had to organise *Capital*. The classical labour theory of value fails not only as a theory of profit but also as a theory of prices. That conclusion might appear to consign the first volume of *Capital* to history's dustbin. Böhm-Bawerk claimed that Marx's theory of prices of production in Volume III contradicted his theory of value in Volume I, published in 1867. With what we know today, Böhm-Bawerk's claim looks quite different. But how shall we express this difference? Shall we say, simply, that Marx was well aware of a contradiction? After all, Marx had already recognised in the *Grundrisse* that Ricardian value theory is incompatible with a general rate of profit. Or shall we take what I argue is the more plausible route of denying any contradiction between the first and third volumes of *Capital*? But how can we do that? Suppose that, ten years after having overthrown Ricardo's individualist labour theory of value, Marx did not write hundreds of pages of *Capital* on the basis of it. Suppose that *Capital* is written, from the beginning, on the basis of

54 Marx 1968b, p. 190.

the new, aggregate theory of value. Then Marx's claims about value and surplus value pertain to the 'heap' of commodities and to the total capital or their aliquot parts, not to individual commodities or capitals.[55] Applied to each actual individual commodity or capital, virtually all the claims of the first two volumes of *Capital* are false; moreover, they were long known to be false by Marx.

If it can be avoided, why accept a reading of *Capital* Volumes I and II that has such a consequence? We can avoid it by reading *Capital* as written from start to finish from the standpoint of the holistic labour theory of value that Marx developed in overthrowing previous doctrines of profit. When Marx uses examples and writes of particular commodities and capitals in the first two volumes, he refers not to actual individual commodities or capitals but rather to representative commodities and capitals that are aliquot parts of the total 'heap' of commodities or capitals.[56] While it is generally false that individual commodities sell at prices determined by their individual values, it is true that an aliquot part of the heap of commodities would sell at a price determined by its value. Likewise, the profit realised by an individual capital will generally not be determined by the individual amount of surplus value created by the workers hired by that capital. But the profit to an aliquot part of the total capital would be determined by the surplus value created by the workers employed across all capitals. There is no contradiction between Volumes I and III because Marx never puts forward the individualistic theory of value that he had demonstrated to be false by 1858.

4.2 *Discordant Overlapping Discourses: Unmasking Capital's Pretence to be Self-Valorizing*

Marx organises the three volumes of *Capital* in order to expose the capital fetish, capital's pretence to match what Marx thought Hegel claimed for the concept. Marx organises this disclosure across the three volumes of *Capital*

55 See Murray 2005b, included in the present volume as Chapter 16. 'In capitalist production, each capital is assumed to be a unit, an aliquot part of the total capital' (Marx 1963c, p. 416; Marx 1991, p. 299). Fred Moseley comments that this passage 'clarifies the important point that the individual capitals which Marx often used as illustrations in Volume I of *Capital* … are not in fact individual capitals, but are instead ideal representatives of the total capital … and thus that the real subject of Volume I is this total capital' (Moseley 2009, p. 142).

56 In a letter to Engels (8 January 1868), Marx suggests the metaphor of the total social surplus value in solution, which neatly fits the idea of aliquot parts: 'I first deal with the general form of surplus-value, in which all these elements are still undifferentiated – in solution as it were' (Marx and Engels 1975b, p. 232).

by overlapping the apparent concept-logic of capital and the essence-logic of surplus value. He simultaneously develops the concept of capital, with its pretence to the self-contained development characteristic of Hegel's concept, self-valorisation, and lays out the essence-logic of surplus value, whereby surplus value necessarily appears as profit: 'profit is the form of appearance of surplus-value.'[57] The concept of surplus value incorporates the antagonistic and exploitative class relationship between capitalists and wage workers: it 'lays bare' capital's underpinnings. Marx calls attention to the disruption caused by the overlapping of the apparent concept-logic of capital and the essence-logic of surplus value:

> In surplus-value, the relationship between capital and labour is laid bare. In the relationship between capital and profit, i.e. between capital and surplus-value as it appears ... *capital appears as a relationship to itself*, a relationship in which it is distinguished as an original sum of value, from another new value that it posits. It appears to consciousness as if capital creates this new value in the course of its movement through the production and circulation processes.[58]

Identifying this disruptive overlap specifies how Marx both accounts for and exposes capital's pretence to be a concept-like 'self-valorizing' 'automatic subject'.

That capital appears to valorise itself arises naturally out of the way that surplus value necessarily appears, that is, as profit. Profit is measured against the value of capital's inputs into the production process (cost-price); consequently, due to the formation of a general rate of profit, the magnitude of profit is a function of the magnitude of capital invested. Since it is proportional to *its own* magnitude – and to nothing else apparent to everyday consciousness – capital's growth seems to be entirely its own doing. Marx's counter-discourse of surplus value exposes the truth about profit and capital's seemingly inherent power to valorize itself. The sole source of profit, hence of capital's valorization, is the unpaid labour of productive wage workers.

The phenomenon of wages, like that of profit, supports capital's fetishistic pretence to independence, to be 'self-valorizing value'. Marx reconceives wages

---

57 Marx 1981, p. 139.

58 Marx 1981, p. 139. 'Just as Marx rejects as illusory the presupposed independence from sensuous actuality that he finds in Hegel's philosophical logic, so, too, does Marx denude the concept of capital of its seeming independence from natural objects and living human labour' (Murray 1988a, p. 219).

as the transformed form of the value of labour power. Marx brings in the category of wages only after he has introduced surplus value, has distinguished between labour and labour power and between constant and variable capital, and has provided a thorough treatment of absolute and relative surplus value. The wage form includes features that are not present in the concept of the value of labour power. Marx introduces his examination of these features with this short paragraph: 'Let us first see how the value (and the price) of labour-power is represented in its converted [*verwandelte*] form as wages.'[59] The wage appears to be 'the price of labour', compensation for the labour done: 'On the surface of bourgeois society the worker's wage appears as the price of labour, as a certain quantity of money that is paid for a certain quantity of labour'.[60] Hence 'all labour appears as paid labour.'[61] Left unchallenged, this understanding of the wage as 'the price of labour' would thwart Marx's 'laying bare' of capital: his demonstration that unpaid labour accounts for profit.

The wage form blocks the distinction between labour and labour power; it leaves no way to account for surplus value and allows no conceptual space for the essential category of variable capital. Like profit and the rate of profit, the wage is an appearance-form that covers up the true source of profit:

> We may therefore understand the decisive importance of the transformation [*Verwandlung*] of the value and price of labour-power into the form of wages, or into the value and price of labour itself. All the notions of justice held by both the worker and the capitalist, all the mystifications of the capitalist mode of production, all capitalism's illusions about freedom, all the apologetic tricks of vulgar economics, have as their basis the form of appearance discussed above, which makes the actual relation invisible, and indeed presents to the eye the precise opposite of that relation.[62]

By first developing the essential categories of labour power and variable capital, and only later introducing the appearance-form of wages, presented as the transformed form of the value of labour power, Marx discloses the wage form to be the necessary form of appearance of relations of domination and exploitation. This is a blow to the Trinity Formula's assurance that all's well in the world of capitalist relations.

59 Marx 1976a, p. 697.
60 Marx 1976a, p. 675.
61 Marx 1976a, p. 680.
62 Marx 1976a, p. 680.

This pattern runs throughout *Capital*: Marx moves from observable phenomena interpreted in everyday ways, for example, wages and profits, to their essential determinants. He then works back and develops the appearance-forms as transformations of the essential forms. Of the revenue forms that Marx considers in the chapter on the Trinity Formula, the wage is the first he develops. Notice how he describes each of these revenue forms. In each case, the term 'transformation' [*Verwandlung*] signals that Marx is showing how an essential category, one of those that enable Marx to 'lay bare' capital's pretences, is (necessarily) transformed into a category of appearance that confirms capital's pretences. Of course, in the Hegelian conception, which Marx adopts, these transformed categories of appearance belong to the essence.

4.3 *On reading Chapters Four and Five of* Capital *Volume I*

What Marx called the 'Chapter on Capital' in the *Grundrisse*, begins in *Capital* Volume I with Chapter Four, 'The General Formula for Capital'. That formula is M-C-M + ΔM, and Marx calls ΔM, 'surplus-value'. As we learn in the first chapter of Volume III, 'Cost Price and Profit', this ΔM is numerically, but not conceptually, the same as what Marx calls 'profit'. ΔM is the profit to the total capital, M, which is identified in Chapter One of Volume III as total cost price. Cost price is the transformed form of the sum of constant capital and variable capital: 'If we call cost price k, the formula $C = c + v + s$ is transformed [*verwandelt sich*] into the formula $C = k + s$, or commodity value = cost price + surplus-value'.[63] In Chapter Four, then, Marx introduces the phenomenon that he intends to explain by developing the concept of surplus value and later showing that the category of profit is the 'transformed form of surplus-value'. It is the same phenomenon that Marx engages with at the beginning of Volume III.[64] The fact that Marx calls this ΔM 'surplus-value', not 'profit', and does not introduce the term 'profit' until the first chapter of Volume III, is important. It tells us much about how *Capital* is organised and to what ends.

Chapters Four and Five of Volume I are to be read in the light of the first two chapters of Volume III, where Marx introduces the concepts of cost price and profit and the rate of profit. The ΔM that Chapter Four introduces is not the ΔM of this or that individual capital but rather the net profit to all capitals. Or, it is the ΔM of an aliquot part of that total capital. Chapter Five of Volume I makes it clear that the ΔM of Chapter Four refers to the sum of the profits to all

63 Marx 1981, p. 118.

64 In the first draft of the chapter 'Cost Price and Profit', in the *Economic Manuscript of 1861–3*, Marx makes this explicit: 'We now return, therefore, to the point of departure from which we proceeded in considering the general form of capital' (Marx 1991, p. 80).

capitals – or to an aliquot part of the total capital.[65] Though the ΔM of this or that individual capital can be explained by the theory that surplus value arises out of circulation rather than production, by a 'mark-up' theory, the fact that there is a net surplus value to the total capital cannot be explained in this way.

In Chapter One of Volume III, ΔM appears as profit, a category that is conceptually paired with the category of cost price. This pairing distinguishes profit from the category of surplus value. Profit is defined as what remains after the cost price is deducted from the net proceeds from the sale of the commodities produced in the specified time-period: 'as an excess of the sale price of the commodity over its cost price'.[66] Marx argues that the category of cost price, by lumping constant and variable capital together, erases the essential distinction between the two.[67] It naturally produces the illusion that ΔM arises not in production but rather in circulation. 'Thus if commodity value is formed without any other element besides the capitalist's advance of value, there is no way of seeing how any more value is to come out of production than went into it, unless something is to come out of nothing'.[68] If ΔM cannot come out of production – as it cannot if the wage is 'the price of labour' – then it appears that it must somehow come out of circulation. Colonel Torrens thus insisted that profit must arise in circulation, while Ramsay rebuked him for implying that value could come out of thin air. Marx cites both Torrens and Ramsay in Chapter Five of Volume I and again in Chapter One of Volume III.[69] The way that Torrens accounts for ΔM (for the total capital), which flows naturally from the appearance-forms of cost price and profit, is shown in Chapter Five of *Capital* Volume I to fail: gains and losses cancel one another out. This leaves the questions of what gives rise to ΔM and what determines its magnitude unanswered. Not only are these questions unanswered, Marx charges that they are unanswerable without getting to the root of capital's appearance-forms (cost price, profit and rate of profit). He observes, 'But if we start from this rate of profit, we can never establish any specific relationship between the excess and the part of capital laid out on wages'.[70] So, Marx does not start *Capital* from the rate of profit.

---

65 In discussing in Volume III the notion that surplus value 'derives from the sale [of the commodity] itself', Marx observes, 'We have already dealt with this illusion in detail in Volume 1, Chapter 5' (Marx 1981, p. 128).

66 Marx 1981, p. 138.

67 Marx 1981, p. 253.

68 Marx 1981, p. 129.

69 Marx 1976a, p. 264, and Marx 1981, pp. 128–9, respectively.

70 Marx 1981, p. 138.

Marx starts from the phenomena that appear as profit and the rate of profit. These appearances, as Marx argues in Chapters One and Two of Volume III, naturally lead to 1) the conclusion that ΔM arises in circulation, not production, and 2) the attribution to capital of a mysterious power to throw off profits (to valorize itself). That pretence to self-valorization leads Marx in Chapter Two of Volume III to compare capital to Hegel's concept:

> We might say in the Hegelian fashion that the excess is reflected back into itself from the rate of profit, or else that the excess, which is characterised more specifically by the rate of profit, appears as an excess which the capital produces over and above its own value ... [c]*apital appears as a relationship to itself*, a relationship in which it is distinguished, as an original sum of value, from another new value that it posits. It appears to consciousness as if capital creates this new value in the course of its movement through the production and circulation processes.[71]

Toward the end of Chapter Four of Volume I, which takes up the same phenomena that will be examined in a very different light in the opening chapters of Volume III (namely as the necessary appearance of an essence, surplus value, as something other than itself), Marx describes capital as a concept-like 'automatic subject' that 'changes its own magnitude, throws off surplus-value from itself considered as original value, and thus valorizes itself independently ... [V]alue suddenly presents itself as a self-moving substance which passes through a process of its own'.[72] In Chapter Four of Volume I, Marx does not work through the reasons why profit seems to arise in circulation and capital seems to be an independent, self-moving substance, as he does in the opening chapters of Volume III. Marx does not introduce cost price, profit and rate of profit as categories of appearance until the beginning of Volume III, after he has developed the necessary essence-categories (labour power as opposed to living labour, constant capital and variable capital, surplus value and the rate of surplus value) and has explored the dynamics of surplus value at length. When Marx does introduce the categories of profit and the rate of profit, he introduces them as transformations of the essential categories of surplus value and rate of surplus value, which appear necessarily as something other than themselves, namely profit and the rate of profit.

---

71 Marx 1981, p. 139. 'But how this happens is now mystified, and appears to derive from hidden qualities that are inherent in capital itself' (Marx 1981, p. 139).

72 Marx 1976a, pp. 255–6.

We can compare what Marx does with surplus value and its form of appearance, profit, to what Marx does in Chapter One of *Capital* Volume I, with value and its form of appearance, money. Marx begins with a phenomenon that everyone is familiar with, namely, that a use value generally presents itself with a price. But he does not describe the phenomenon in that way; instead, he says that wealth in the form of a commodity has an exchange value.[73] At the beginning of Section Three, Marx again avoids using 'money' or 'price', saying that commodities 'possess a double form, i.e. natural form and value form'. So, when Marx introduces the money form as the culmination of the dialectic of the value form, he introduces it not as the familiar everyday phenomenon – commodities have prices – but rather as the necessary form of appearance of value, the transformed form of value, which has first been shown to be the essence of exchange value.

5 How Did Hegel Help Marx Surpass Ricardo's Theory of Profit?

Let us go to the crux of the matter before turning to some broader considerations. Marx writes of Adam Smith's thinking on surplus value and profit: 'Adam Smith … should certainly have seen from this [that he resolves surplus value into profit and rent, which are determined by quite different laws] that he ought not to treat [the] general abstract form as directly identical with any of its particular forms'.[74] As mentioned above, this failure to discriminate forms is one of the most fundamental criticisms Marx makes of the going theories of profit. Marx immediately attributes Smith's theoretical failure to a methodologically narrow empiricism:

> With all later bourgeois economists, as with Adam Smith, lack of theoretical understanding needed to distinguish the different forms of the economic relations remains the rule in their coarse grabbing at and interest in the empirically available material. Hence also their inability to form a correct conception of money, in which what is in question is only various changes in the form of exchange-value, while the magnitude of value remains unchanged.[75]

73 Martha Campbell observes, 'Although Marx never regards exchange value as anything but money price, he does not specify that it is until he shows what money price involves' (Campbell 1997, p. 100).

74 Marx 1963c, p. 92.

75 Ibid. Of Ricardo's method Marx says: 'But the faulty architectonics of the theoretical part

Here Marx associates the two chief failings of classical political economy: 1) it does not grasp the necessary formal difference between a commodity and the money for which it is exchanged; and 2) it does not grasp the necessary formal difference between profit and surplus value.[76]

Here lies the short answer to the question: how did Hegel help Marx surpass Ricardo's theory of profit? Hegel taught Marx to take matters of form in earnest, not to take given concepts for granted but to probe their content in a painstaking empirical and conceptually self-reflective way that I call 'redoubled empiricism'.[77] From Hegel, Marx learned to develop concepts, a thought foreign to the mind-set of the classical political economists; to show how one concept is the transformed form of another, as profit is the transformed form of surplus value; and to demonstrate the necessity of such transformations.[78] More particularly, Marx learned from Hegel's logic of essence not to treat essence and appearance as separable: essence must appear as something other than itself. Essence is not some imperceptible thing or force that stands alone, independent of its expression. Instead, the two are one complex reality.

5.1 *What Marx Learned from Hegel (An Incomplete List)*

1. *Immanent critique*: Marx learned from Hegel to advance science by way of an immanent critique of previous thinkers.[79] Marx's mature theory of profit is a case in point: he arrives at it by probing the failure, which had been seen by Malthus, Bailey and others, of the individualistic classical theory of value to account for the general rate of profit.

2. *Conceptual clarity*: Quite a few of the mistakes of the political economists involve lack of clarity about concepts; often their concepts are vague, confused

(the first six chapters [of Ricardo's *Principles*]) is not accidental, rather it is the result of Ricardo's method of investigation itself and of the definite task which he set himself in his work. It expresses the scientific deficiencies of this method of investigation itself' (Marx 1968b, p. 167).

76 'In elaborating [*die Entwicklung*] the concept of value, he [Ricardo] does not clearly distinguish between the various aspects, between the exchange value of the commodity, as it *manifests itself*, *appears* in the process of commodity exchange, and the existence of the commodity as value as distinct from its existence as an object, product, use-value' (Marx 1971a, p. 125). Marx also makes this kind of complaint regarding Ricardo's approach to surplus value and profit.

77 See Murray 1997a, included in the present volume as Chapter 2.

78 'This whole BLUNDER of Ricardo's … spring[s] from his failure to distinguish between *surplus-value* and *profit*; and in general his treatment of *definitions of form* is crude and uncomprehending, just as that of the other economists' (Marx 1989, p. 439).

79 Hegel 1969, p. 581.

or ambiguous. Hegel wrote, '[P]hilosophizing requires, above all, that each thought should be grasped in its full precision and that nothing should remain vague and indeterminate'.[80] Marx's mature theory of profit is again a case in point, since, before Marx, no clear conceptual distinctions were drawn between labour and labour power, constant and variable capital, surplus value and profit or the rate of surplus value and the rate of profit.

3. *Not taking concepts for granted*: Marx does not take categories for granted. Marx complains over and over about political economists taking concepts for granted rather than 'developing' them – the complaint reaches back to his first serious encounter with the political economists, in the *Paris Manuscripts*. One of Marx's basic criticisms of Ricardo is that he simply assumes the general rate of profit rather than probing it to determine its conceptual compatibility with his individualistic theory of value.[81] As we have seen, classical political economy made a bad showing where the category of wages was concerned:

> Classical political economy's unconsciousness of this result of its own analysis and its uncritical acceptance of the categories 'value of labor', 'natural price of labor', etc. as the ultimate and adequate expression for the value-relation under consideration, led it into inextricable confusions and contradictions, as will be seen later, while it offered a secure base of operations to the vulgar economists who, in their shallowness, make it a principle to worship appearances only.[82]

Because of his attention to forms, Marx's scientific agenda reaches far beyond the horizon of political economy. The idea that a system of categories needs to be criticised fits in perfectly with the aspirations of Marx's 'redoubled empiricism', but it is foreign to an empiricism unreflective about its categories.

4. *Essence must appear as something other than itself*: From Hegel's logic of essence Marx learned the basic conceptual figure: essence necessarily appears as something other than itself. Essence and appearance are recognised to be inseparable. Hegel supersedes the conventional understanding of the categories of the essence logic as 'products of the reflecting understanding, which both assumes the distinctions as *independent* and at the same time posits their relationality *as well* ... [I]t does not bring these thoughts together'.[83] Hegel's advance in grasping the logic of essence shows up in Marx's treatments of value

80 Hegel 1991b, § 80 addition, pp. 127–8.
81 See Marx 1968b, p. 174.
82 Marx 1976a, p. 679.
83 Hegel 1991b, § 114, p. 179.

and of surplus value: value necessarily appears as something other than itself, money; surplus value necessarily appears as something other than itself, profit.

5. *Systematic dialectic: to develop concepts and transform forms*: Marx learns from Hegel's logic to develop categories methodically, in a structure of mutual presupposition, not just to postulate them. Developing the necessary forms of appearance of essences is a crucial case of category development. Marx rebukes Ricardo for postulating a general rate of profit and then making a faulty effort to check to see if it is compatible with the law of value as Ricardo had (too narrowly, as it turns out) conceived of it.[84] Needless to say, 'How from the mere determination of the "*value*" of the commodities their surplus-value, the profit and even a *general rate of profit* are derived remains obscure with Ricardo'.[85] More generally, Marx complains that Ricardo's *Principles*, starting with the first chapter, is a conceptual hodgepodge.[86] Marx insists that the general rate of profit must be developed out of the theory of value, not simply postulated. The very idea of transformed forms is Hegelian in inspiration. When we move from the phenomena in their everyday interpretation to their essence, we move in order to comprehend them. In reversing directions and moving from essential categories to their necessary forms of appearance, we grasp appearance-forms, such as money and profit, as transformed forms of essential categories, value and surplus value, respectively. In proceeding in this way Marx develops categories and achieves a conceptually adequate representation of capitalist actuality – 'absolute form'.

84 Marx 1968b, p. 174. See also Moseley 1993a, p. 163.

85 Marx 1968b, pp. 190–1.

86 Marx 1968b, pp. 164, 168, 190.

CHAPTER 14

The Illusion of the Economic: The Trinity Formula and the 'Religion of Everyday Life'*

> Capital-profit (profit of enterprise plus interest), land-ground-rent, labour-wages, this trinity form holds in itself all the mysteries of the social production process.[1]

> The forms of revenue and the sources of revenue are the *most fetishistic* expression of the relations of capitalist production ... The distorted form in which the real inversion is expressed is naturally reproduced in the views of the agents of this mode of production. It is a kind of fiction without fantasy, a religion of the vulgar.[2]

Capital reaches its consummation in 'The Trinity Formula', the chapter that opens the seventh, and concluding, part of Volume III.[3] This unfinished chapter rounds out Marx's six-fold project in *Capital*: (1) to present and examine in the form of a systematic dialectic the social forms constitutive of the capitalist order, beginning with the (generalised) commodity; (2) to expose capitalist society, in its enlightened secularism, as idolatrous and fetishistic; (3) to reveal that the social egalitarianism of capitalist society harbours class dom-

---

* Originally published as 'The Illusion of the Economic: The Trinity Formula and the "religion of everyday life"', in *The Culmination of Capital: Essays on Volume III of Marx's 'Capital'*, edited by Martha Campbell and Geert Reuten (Basingstoke, Hampshire: Palgrave, 2002), pp. 246–72, reprinted with the kind permission of Palgrave Macmillan.

1 Marx 1981, p. 953.

2 Marx 1971a, p. 453.

3 In speaking of consummations in Volume III, we should not forget that what we know as the three volumes of *Capital* are far from fulfilling Marx's plan for a comprehensive critical investigation into capital. On some of the issues involved with the incompleteness of Marx's work, see Shortall 1994, Rosdolsky 1977, Rubel 1981, Oakley 1983, Lebowitz 1992 and Arthur 2002b and 2002c.

ination; (4) to examine and critically evaluate representations and theories of capitalism; (5) to show how capitalist social forms naturally exude ideological representations; and (6) to reveal capitalism to be a historically specific mode of production whose contradictory dynamics point toward its eventually giving way to a historically new mode of production. As such, the chapter sheds a great deal of light on Marx's purposes and accomplishments in *Capital* and on the structure of his exposition. The title 'The Trinity Formula' drives home Marx's master theme that capitalism is the secular epitome of Christianity's 'cult of man in the abstract'.[4]

According to Engels, the manuscript of the chapter on the Trinity Formula begins as follows:

> We have seen how the capitalist process of production is a historically specific form of the social production process in general. This last is both a production process of the material conditions of existence for human life, and a process, proceeding in specific economic and historical relations of production, that produces and reproduces these relations of production themselves, and with them the bearers of this process, their material conditions of existence, and their mutual relationships, i.e. the specific economic form of their society.[5]

This is an apt beginning to the conclusion of *Capital*, for those opening sentences express the most fundamental, if widely overlooked, point of the book: capitalism is not 'the economy in general'. That there is no economy in general follows from the complex statement that expresses perhaps Marx's most seminal insight: 'All production is appropriation of nature on the part of an individual within and through a specific form of society'.[6] The chapter's two opening sentences remind us of the double character of the capitalist mode

4 Marx 1976a, p. 172. The idea that secular capitalist society is the fulfilment of Christianity goes back to Marx's essay 'On the Jewish Question'. For Marx, 'criticism of religion is the premise of all criticism' (Marx 1975b, p. 175). Since Volume III, Part Seven, concludes with a brief, unfinished chapter on classes, we may wonder if the theme that capitalism is a class society (for all the egalitarianism radiated by the forms of simple commodity circulation) deserves pride of place. Perhaps it is best to see the 'master theme' as the congruity of these two seemingly incongruous ideas: capitalism is an egalitarian society and capitalism is a class society. See Marx and Engels 1975a, p. 78; Marx 1973, pp. 248–9; and Marx 1976a, pp. 164, 280.

5 Marx 1981, p. 957.

6 Marx 1973, p. 87.

of production. It is a particular instance of the human provisioning process and as such shares several features with all human modes of provisioning, features that Marx describes in treating of 'the labour process in general' back in the first part of Chapter Seven of Volume I. At the same time, the capitalist production process is a 'valorization process' with many socially distinctive features that Marx conceives of as the various value forms, e.g., the (generalised) commodity, exchange value, money, capital, wages, profit, interest and rent.

Marx's task in *Capital* is to stick with this original insight and to think through the capitalist production process (at a certain level of abstraction) in its actuality, that is, in its double character, its use-value and value dimensions. Among the chief results of this investigation is that the social forms determining the capitalist provisioning process (the value forms) have the power to reproduce and extend themselves, continually reweaving and widening the net of capitalist relations. In this, Marx returns to the point he made in a more preliminary way in *Results of the Immediate Production Process*, the manuscript apparently intended as the transition from the first to the second volume of *Capital*, 'This form of mediation is intrinsic to this [the capitalist] mode of production. It perpetuates the relation between capital as the buyer and the worker as the seller of labour'.[7] Similarly, the purpose of the reproduction schemes at the conclusion of Volume II is to respect the double character of capitalist production and show how, in its circulation process, capital can, simultaneously, reproduce and expand itself both materially and formally.[8] 'It is precisely here that the principal difficulty lies, in the analysis of reproduction and the relationship of its various components, both in their material character and in their value'.[9] It is not simply resources in: more resources out; it is capital in: more capital out.[10] The complex task of *Capital* is one that economists before, during, and after Marx's lifetime not only have not undertaken – it is a task they have failed even to recognise. The failure to grasp the theoretical need to sort general features of the provisioning process out from socially specific ones reaches gigantic proportions in the vulgar economists' 'Trinity Formula', but Marx is quick to remind us that, for all their insights into errors collected in the Trinity Formula, the classical political economists 'remained more or less

7 Marx 1976b, p. 1,063.

8 See Moseley 1998.

9 Marx 1981, p. 983.

10 See Marx 1971a, p. 514. To find out how prevalent this obliviousness to social form remains today, ask someone what capital is or look up the 'answer' in an introductory economics textbook.

trapped in the world of illusion their criticism had dissolved, and nothing else is possible from the bourgeois standpoint'.[11]

The first six parts of Volume III complete the systematic dialectic of capitalist social forms (at least at a certain level of abstraction) by working through the dialectical development of the necessary forms of appearance of surplus value. Surplus value, which Marx introduced in Chapter Four of Volume I, necessarily appears as something other than itself, namely profit, interest (and its counterpart, profit of enterprise) and rent. Volume III's lengthy exposition of the necessary forms of surplus value's appearance builds up to Part Seven as the capstone to all three volumes.

I will argue that this exposition of the necessary forms of appearance of surplus value closes the second, and much longer, of two circuits of thought that comprise *Capital*. Each circuit is organised around a fetish. The first explains how and why the product of the capitalist mode of production is a fetish. This circuit investigates the commodity and its twin fetish, money. 'Commodities and Money', Part One of Volume I, makes up the first circuit. Part Two, 'The Transformation of Money into Capital', provides the needed transition from the first to the second circuit, from the sphere of circulation to the sphere of production. The second circuit explains how and why the three factors of the labour process in general (raw materials, produced means of production and living labour) become fetishes inasmuch as each of the three appears to be an independent source of value and therewith of revenue (rent, interest and profit of enterprise and wages, respectively). This second circuit begins with the first chapter of Part Three of Volume I, 'The Labour Process and the Valorization Process', and culminates in the first chapter of Part Seven of Volume III, 'The Trinity Formula', which could well bear the subtitle, 'The Fetishism of the Factors of Production'.

Marx's probing of the variants of the Trinity Formula, a doctrine of vulgar political economy, discloses it to be a compendium of errors and ideological misrepresentations propagated by the capitalist mode of production. The most basic and pervasive of these is the history-stopping idea that capitalism is not a particular historical mode of production but rather the economy in general.[12] I will call this 'the illusion of the economic'; it is the basis of everyday, pseudo-scientific (as in the case of vulgar political economy) and even scientific misconceptions of the capitalist mode of production.

11 Marx 1981, p. 969.

12 Expressing the standpoint of classical political economy, Marx writes in *The Poverty of Philosophy*, 'Thus there has been history, but there is no longer any' (Marx 1963b, p. 121).

How can the vulgar representations of the capitalist mode of production, which Marx calls the 'religion of everyday life',[13] and even widely shared scientific ideas, such as those of classical political economy, be so riddled with half-truth and total miscomprehension? Marx addresses this problem in his characteristic, historical materialist way. That is, he explains which features of the society under consideration give rise to them. In this chapter, we will pay close attention to those aspects of capitalism that engender 'the illusion of the economic'.

A stubborn obstacle to reading *Capital*, and to reading 'The Trinity Formula' in particular, is the common, but mistaken, idea that Marx adopts the classical (Ricardian) labour theory of value and then drives it to radical conclusions in the theory of surplus value. The thought comes to this: Marx was a Left Ricardian. Removing this roadblock is exceedingly difficult. To state the difference between Marx and Ricardo bluntly, Marx's theory of value is his theory of the specific social form of labour under capitalism; Ricardo's labour theory of value is oblivious to the elusive problematic of social form. The gulf between the two theories is wide, and the consequences of not recognising it are grave. Unfortunately, the usual interpretation of 'The Trinity Formula' reinforces the misjudgement that Marx was a Left Ricardian.

On the Left Ricardian reading of *Capital*, the critique of the Trinity Formula packs quite a wallop. It is a résumé of what is taken to be the book's central achievement, the demonstration that capitalism is a system of class exploitation wherein control of land and the produced means of production by landowners and capitalists, respectively, enables them to expropriate surplus value from the class of wage labourers. The classical labour theory of value seems to serve this argument well. In fact, the leading Left Ricardian idea is that Marx's theory of exploitation is the logical outcome of classical value theory – its 'truth', as Hegel would say. The conventional reading of 'The Trinity Formula' has Marx teaming up with classical political economy – once Marx has corrected some of its basic errors – to smash the idols of vulgar economics. There is truth in this standard reading, but not nearly enough.

Ricardian value theory, when properly developed, seems to pull the rug out from under the vulgar economic ideas expressed in the Trinity Formula. If labour is the source of all value, then the class of wage labourers creates all value. This suggests two things: (1) since neither capitalists nor landowners add value, neither class deserves any revenue; and (2) the revenues they do get, rent and profit (interest and profit of enterprise), must be siphoned off from the

13 Marx 1981, p. 969.

class of wage labourers. Consequently, each of the Trinity Formula's three propositions governing the forms of revenue are false: (1) rents compensate the contribution of land (the proprietor of land), (2) interest compensates the contribution of capital (the capitalist) and (3) wages compensate the contribution of labour (the wage labourer). Ricardian value theory shows that in the first two cases, neither party adds value, so no compensation is justified. The problem in the case of wage labour is the reverse: since it adds more value than it receives, wages short-change workers. Such injustices call for redress. But of what sort?

Left Ricardians answer this question variously. But they have two things in common: (1) being inattentive to matters of form, they slur the difference between wealth and value and (2) they recommend some form of the redistribution of 'wealth'. Let me venture a rough typology of variants of Left Ricardianism. A reformist, social democratic sort of Left Ricardianism calls for the use of state power, usually the powers of selective and progressive taxation, to shift 'wealth' from landlords and capitalists to wage labourers. A more radical Left Ricardianism can take different forms. One involves the transfer of all surplus value into worker-run banks; another would involve the conversion of all firms into worker-owned cooperatives. Yet another recommends replacing money with 'time-chits', a move intended to smother surplus value. A revolutionary type of Left Ricardianism has more in common with a Marxian approach: it calls for a redistribution not of revenues but of land and the means of production.[14] This form of Left Ricardianism rightly despairs of creating a just society without overturning the property relations on which capitalism rests. Yet, even the revolutionary Ricardian project remains centred on remedying or eliminating exploitation, that is, the unjust appropriation of surplus value from workers by capitalists.

Ironically, the basic Left Ricardian conception of justice is the standard commercial one: equal value for equal value. Because Ricardian theory is oblivious to the problematic of the social form of wealth; because, consequently, Ricardian theory cannot help but run 'wealth' and 'value' together, it is the surplus, not the value, in surplus value that troubles the Left Ricardian. Value is not a problem; only its (mal)distribution is. But for Marx, value is a problem, a monster of a problem.[15]

14 Marx makes much of this difference in the penultimate chapter of *Capital*; see Marx 1981, p. 1,019.

15 This is not to suggest that Marx is not concerned about exploitation, the surplus in surplus value. On the contrary, the upshot of *Capital* is that, since generalised commodity circulation is inseparable from the circulation and accumulation of capital, the two are inseparable: no surplus value, no value.

Understanding Marx to be a radical Ricardian, while it coheres with some important aspects of Marx's criticism of the vulgar economists' Trinity Formula, obfuscates Marx's deepest ideas. This is to be expected, for those ideas reject Ricardian value theory on account of its bourgeois inattention to social form. Questions shunted away by Ricardian theory make up Marx's subject matter. Ricardian theory worries about whether 'wealth' is being distributed fairly. It does not trouble itself, however, about the social form of this wealth or the multiple implications of that social form. Economics of all varieties is terribly hard of hearing when it comes to the questions that preoccupy Marx. It simply cannot conceive of a question such as, What does it mean for a society that, generally, it produces wealth in the social form of the commodity? My objective in this chapter, then, is to offer an alternative exposition of 'The Trinity Formula', working from the assumption that Marx's own theory of value is a theory of capitalist social forms. Marx offers not a new improved version of the classical labour theory of value but a radical break with it. By examining the roots of 'the illusion of the economic', I hope to expose the sources of the plausibility of Ricardian ideas. Hopefully, this will make those ideas less believable.

1 Organising *Capital* around Two Fetishes: The Product and the Labour Process

Here is my hypothesis regarding the structure of *Capital*: it can be broken down into two 'from – to' movements of greatly different lengths. Each reveals a strand of the fetishism characteristic of the capitalist mode of production. The first movement shows how commodities, the products of the capitalist mode of production, are mysteriously possessed of social powers that appear to be natural properties. As value, the commodity has clout. Belonging to the same movement, money arises alongside the world of commodities. With its social power of immediate exchangeability seeming to spring right out of the earth, money is a fetish still more blinding than the commodity. The first movement starts from the double character of products in the characteristically capitalist form, proceeding from the use value and exchange value of the commodity to the necessity for one commodity's value to appear in the body of another commodity (exchange value as the necessary form of appearance of value), to the 'fetishism of the commodity' and to the money fetish.

The second movement tracks the fetishism caused by the social form of the labour process under capitalism. This movement extends from the double character of the capitalist labour process – labour process in general and valorization process – to the necessary forms of appearance of surplus value (profit of enterprise, interest and rent) and to the Trinity Formula, which expresses the fetishism of the three factors of the labour process under capitalism. My claim is that, just as Marx's exposition of the double character of the *product* of the capitalist production process, the commodity, sets up the treatment of the fetishisms of the commodity and money, Marx's exposition of the double character of the capitalist labour process itself (in the first chapter of *Capital* devoted to capital proper, Chapter Seven) intentionally sets up 'The Trinity Formula'.[16] The chapter on the Trinity Formula parallels Chapter One's section on the fetishism of the commodity in providing a retrospective and commentary on the results of the ponderous task of thinking through the double character of the labour process under capitalism. If the first movement penetrates the mystery whereby products, mere things, are possessed of social power, the clout of purchasing power, the second movement explains how the three personifications of the factors of the labour process taken in general (produced means of production, raw materials of production and labour; corresponding to the capitalist, the landowner and the wage labourer), draw revenues in the forms of interest, rent, and wages. For Marx it is to be expected that a fetish-ridden labour process will result in a fetishistic product.[17]

These parallel developments expose twin tendencies of capitalism: (1) to slur, in the minds of its participants, general features of both wealth and the production of wealth with historically determinate forms that both wealth and the production of wealth take – wealth with value; production with valorization and (2) to make a fetish of wealth and of the three factors involved in the production of wealth.[18] These two tendencies are actually two aspects of the same reality, capitalism's oddly asocial type of sociality.[19] Thus, in the first development, the commodity appears to be simply 'wealth' (or 'use value') devoid of social form because, strangely, its social form appears as a separate

16 Volume III was drafted in 1864–5, a couple of years before Volume I was published (1867).

17 In these respects, *Capital* echoes the Paris manuscript 'Estranged Labour'; see Marx 1964a, p. 279.

18 On the distinction between general and determinate abstractions, see Chapter Ten of Murray 1988a.

19 In Chapter 51 of Volume III, 'Relations of Distribution and Relations of Production', Marx identifies 'two characteristic traits' of the capitalist mode of production; they correspond to the parallel developments presently under discussion. The two are: (1) the dominant form of the product is the commodity, and (2) the production of surplus value is the decisive motive of production (Marx 1981, pp. 1,019–20). I take this observation as support for my thesis.

thing, money. So we slur the difference between wealth and commodities.[20] At the same time, wealth in the commodity form has an exchange value because it is a value, that is, a thing possessed of the power to exchange with all other commodities. Endowed as if by nature with this peculiar social power, wealth in the commodity form is a fetish.

In the case of the second development, again we find the slurring of general and determinate concepts: raw materials with landed property, means of production with capital, and labour with wage labour. By the same token, the division of the wealth created by the capitalist production process into the capitalist forms of revenue (rent, interest and profit of enterprise, and wages) is taken as the natural and inevitable outcome of there being three distinguishable factors of the production process. Herein, too, lies the fetishism of the factors of production. Each is taken to be an independent source of value, a conception Marx represents with the image of the three factors as three trees, each bearing its own sort of fruit. The consequences of the parallel developments, then, are (1) that both wealth and the production of wealth in capitalism appear to be devoid of specific social form, hence 'natural' – here is 'the illusion of the economic' – with the result that the specific social forms get slurred with general features of wealth and its production and (2) both the wealth produced and the three distinguishable factors in the production of wealth become fetishes.

Though this second movement of thought in *Capital*, devoted to the 'fetishism of the factors of the capitalist labour process', which is just what the Trinity Formula encapsulates, follows the first movement, dedicated to the commodity and money fetishes, the second encompasses the first, while the first presupposes the second.[21] For one result of the examination of the capitalist production process to which Marx gives special attention is that all its products take the commodity form, just as all its inputs enter as commodities.[22]

This 'two movements/two fetishes' reading adds a new facet to a more familiar idea, namely that *Capital* is composed of two 'books', one on commodities and money, and one on capital. Marx divided the *Grundrisse* into the 'chapter on money' and the 'chapter on capital', and *A Contribution to the Critique of Political Economy* was a version of that first 'chapter'. The first movement that I identify covers Part One of Volume I, 'Commodities and Money'. Part Two is

20 This is reinforced in everyday consciousness today through the practice of presenting the Gross Domestic Product as if it were a measure of the 'wealth' created over a year's time.

21 This is to be expected in a work of systematic dialectics; see Arthur 1997 and Bubner 1988.

22 Marx 1981, pp. 1,019–20.

transitional, covering the genesis of capital, wage labour and surplus value. And Part Three, which opens with Chapter Seven's account of the double character of the labour process under capitalism, begins the treatment of capital proper. This topic absorbs the rest of *Capital*.

What is distinctive in this reading is to see the Trinity Formula as the terminus for a movement of thought that was set up back in Chapter Seven of Volume I and to recognise the parallel with the movement that begins on *Capital*'s first page with the double character of wealth in the commodity form. The treatment of the general category use value in the first movement is matched by the treatment of the labour process in general in the second. Likewise, the treatment of the value dimension of the commodity in the first is matched by the treatment of the valorization process in the second.[23] A further parallel exists between the role played by the first chapter's section on the fetishism of commodities and the chapter on the Trinity Formula at the close of Volume III; each is basically a commentary on conceptual developments (the systematic dialectic) that have already taken place.

Marx calls attention to the 'two movement/two fetish' structure of *Capital* in summing up the results of his investigation of the Trinity Formula:

> We have already shown in connection with the most simple categories of the capitalist mode of production and commodity production in general, in connection with commodities and money, the mystifying character that transforms the social relations for which the material elements of wealth serve as bearers in the course of production into properties of these things themselves (commodities), still more explicitly transforming the relation of production itself into a thing (money) ... In the capitalist mode of production, however, where capital is the dominant category and forms the specific relation of production, this bewitched and distorted world develops much further ... Capital – profit (or better still capital – interest), land – ground rent, labour – wages, this economic trinity as the connection between the components of value and wealth in general and its sources, completes the mystification of the capitalist mode of production, the reification of social relations, and the immediate coalescence of the material relations of production with their historical and social specificity: the bewitched, distorted and upside-down world haunted by

23 In adopting this paired presentation of general categories (use value, process of production) with determinate categories (value, valorisation process) Marx abandoned an earlier plan, jotted down at the end of the method section of the *Grundrisse*. See Marx 1973, p. 108.

> Monsieur le Capital and Madame la Terre, who are at the same time social characters and mere things.[24]

Throughout *Capital* Marx sounds the theme of the necessary inversion of capitalism's abstract, enlightened secularism into a thoroughgoing fetishism that endows both the products and the process of production with uncanny powers. In this passage it reaches its crescendo.

2 The Trinity Formula: A Compendium of Errors and Illusions

For Marx, the Trinity Formula is a compendium of errors and illusions regarding the capitalist mode of production. It epitomises the misunderstandings endemic to everyday consciousness and language under capitalism and reconfirmed by those boosters of the 'religion of everyday life', the vulgar economists. The less apologetic, more scientific-minded, classical economists made real progress in dispelling some of the necromancy surrounding the Trinity Formula. But they, too, worked under the spell of the most deep-seated illusions operative in the Trinity Formula. To see both where the classical economists advanced and where they were bogged down, we need to pick apart the many errors and illusions involved in the several variants of the Trinity Formula. Let us consider them one at a time.

2.1 *The First Variant of the Trinity Formula*

The first versions of the formula (*capital – profit, land – rent, and labour – wages* and *capital – interest, land – rent, and labour – wages*) absurdly classify capital (a category specific to capitalist societies) with two factors of the labour process in general, land and labour, a mismatch that Marx derides: 'Their mutual relationship is like that of lawyer's fees, beetroot and music'.[25] This bumbling is not Marx's prime target, however; he is after the entrenched patterns of misperception and thoughtlessness underneath it.

2.2 *The Second Variant of the Trinity Formula*

When that initial match-up is altered (under pressure of trying to make some sense of capital – interest) by substituting 'produced means of production' for

---

24 Marx 1981, pp. 965–6, 968–9. Further textual support for this reading may be found in Marx 1981, pp. 963–4, 968–9, and 1,023–4, and in Marx 1971a, p. 510.

25 Marx 1981, p. 953.

'capital', the absurdity of the original combination is avoided, only for political economy to arrive at the 'uniform and symmetrical incongruity' that completes the circuit that begins with Chapter Seven of Volume 1, 'The Labour Process and the Valorization Process'. *Produced means of production – interest, land – rent, labour – wages*: this formula expresses the two mystifications that are Marx's two most fundamental targets, 'the illusion of the economic' and 'the fetishism of the factors of the capitalist labour process'.

2.2.1 Three Errors in the Phenomenology of the Production Process

The assumptions involved in this consistently incongruous formula include three key phenomenological errors that result from projecting certain perceived or real features of the capitalist production process onto the labour process in general. Foremost of these errors is to imagine that the labour process *in general* can stand alone, that it can actually exist independently of all determinate social form. This is 'the illusion of the economic'. It is akin to thinking that 'The Fruit' can exist alongside an apple or pear. The mistake here is to believe that there can be an actual labour process devoid of determinate social form and purpose. There can be no generic economy. That is why the idea of 'the economic' is an illusion. Furthermore, the assumption in the Trinity Formula is that the capitalist mode of production is 'production in general'. This illusion is shared by vulgar and classical economists alike. When Marx wrote of classical economists being prisoners of the 'bourgeois standpoint', he had 'the illusion of the economic' in mind as one of its defining features.[26]

One of the peculiarities of the capitalist production process is that it presents itself in ways that lead its observers to mistake it for that mirage, an actual production process in general. Marx's several explanations of how capitalist forms propagate this illusion reveal how seriously he takes the whole issue of the ways humans represent their forms of life to themselves. (One important lesson of *Capital* is to treat the ways that participants in a capitalist society represent their life to themselves as features that belong to a capitalist society and its capacities for reproducing itself.) Marx's explanations count as remarkable contributions to social epistemology and as models for further work.

26 We may wonder why evidence of non-capitalist modes of production does not dash this illusion. For one answer see Marx 1976a, p. 175, n. 35 and Marx 1981, p. 1,017. Marx's conception of 'ideal subsumption' or 'subsumption by analogy', supplies a second answer. 'Ideal subsumption' of non-capitalist social relations under capitalist forms makes the procrustean move of treating non-capitalist phenomenon as if they fit, say, the capitalist forms of revenue. See Marx 1981, p. 1,015.

In Volume I we learn that the specific social form of the product of the capitalist labour process (the commodity) necessarily gets expressed as a separate thing – money. It is not surprising that this bit of ventriloquism is not recognised for what it is. For the value objectivity of the commodity – its specific social character – is 'purely social' and 'supra-natural', it leaves no trace on the 'natural form' of the commodity. Instead, the commodity is thought to have no social form or purpose at all, an idea that conforms well to the conception of the market as a place where consumers with privately determined desires exercise their sovereign choices. Where does social form or purpose figure into that?[27]

In Volume II, Marx points out how a one-sided attention to the circuit of productive capital (as opposed to the circuits of money capital and commodity capital), which begins and ends with the use values requisite for the production process, misled the classical political economists into thinking that the capitalist production process was production in general:

> The general form of the movement P ... P' is the form of reproduction, and does not indicate, as does M ... M', that valorization is the purpose of the process. For this reason, classical economics found it all the more easy to ignore the specifically capitalist form of the production process, and to present production as such as the purpose of the process.[28]

In other words, isolating the circuit of productive capital from the flow of money capital and attending only to the former allowed the classical economists to shear the valorization process from the production process and present the latter as if it were production in general.

In Volume III Marx explains how the mitosis of the profit form into interest and profit of enterprise serves to make the capitalist production process look like production in general:

27 Left Ricardianism falls into this illusion in its own way when it imagines that, by ending production for the sake of surplus value, production 'for the sake of use value' would be left. I call this illusion 'Use-value Romanticism'. There is no use value in general. The specific purpose of the production of use values in capitalism is to produce and accumulate surplus value. Only another definite social purpose, with accompanying definite social forms, can replace it. Marxian theory's most profound challenge is to identify those new social forms and that new social purpose.

28 Marx 1978a, p. 172.

> Since the aspect of capital's specific social determination in the capitalist mode of production – capital ownership which possesses the capacity of command over the labour of others – becomes fixed, with interest appearing as the part of surplus-value that capital produces in this connection, so the other part of surplus-value, profit of enterprise, necessarily appears as if it does not derive from capital as capital, but rather from the production process independently of its specific social determination, which indeed has already obtained its particular mode of existence in the form of interest on capital. However, the production process, when separated from capital, is simply the labour-process in general. The industrial capitalist, as distinct from the owner of capital, appears therefore not as functioning capital but rather as a functionary independent of capital, as a simple bearer of the labour-process in general; as a worker, and a wage-worker at that.[29]

Just as the social form of the commodity appears as a separate thing, money, here the social form of the capitalist production process appears as a separate thing, again money, only this time it is money in the role of interest-bearing capital, the most fetishistic of all capitalist forms. The pattern is as follows: the social form of the product or the production process bizarrely and necessarily expresses itself as a separate thing, whether money *per se*, money capital or interest-bearing capital, leaving the impression that what remains lacks social form altogether. 'The illusion of the economic', then, is a by-product of the peculiarity of the value forms.

A second root error regarding the phenomenology of the production process is to imagine that each of the three necessary factors in any labour process (produced means of production, the earth's raw materials and living labour) can be productive on their own. While two of the three factors of the labour process (produced means of production and land) can exist independently, what Marx calls '"the" labour', is a mere abstraction. Within the labour process none of the three factors can act independently. Yet, in personifying the three necessary factors of the labour process, the Trinity Formula supposes otherwise:

> In the formula capital-interest, earth-ground-rent, labour-wages, capital, earth and labour appear respectively as sources of interest (instead of profit), ground-rent and wages as their products or fruits – one the basis,

29 Marx 1981, p. 505.

> the other the result, one the cause, the other the effect – and moreover in such a way that each individual source is related to its product as something extruded from it and produced by it.[30]

Marx expands on the image of fruit, saying of the three forms of revenue: 'They appear as fruits of a perennial tree for annual consumption, or rather fruits of three trees'.[31] This notion of three independent sources of revenue, the three perennial fruit trees, betrays a false phenomenology of the labour process, one that hypostatises distinguishable factors in the creation of new wealth into three independent sources owned by three different (classes of) persons.[32]

This bewitching idea of interest-bearing capital as an independent source of value captured my imagination as a boy of six, when my parents presented me with my first bank account. I remember being electrified by the thought that the bank intended to pay me three dollars a years for every one hundred dollars of my money that they were keeping safe for me. With a head swelling from my new-found bit of Trinitarian wisdom, I wondered why the government did not just advance every citizen a million dollars so that we could all live comfortably

---

30 Marx 1981, p. 955. Marx introduced this idea of revenue types as 'fruits' with separate sources back in his discussion of interest and profit of enterprise. See Marx 1981, pp. 497–8, 501, 516–17. See also Marx 1971a, p. 511. Though Marx speaks of one tree for capital in the discussion of the Trinity Formula, on p. 498 of *Capital* Volume III (Marx 1981) he speaks of two, one yielding interest and one profit of enterprise. Four trees, though, did not suit the rubric of the Trinity Formula.

31 Marx 1981, p. 960. I believe that Marx's use of the image of fruit and the fruit tree is not accidental here but rather a reference to his parody of Hegelian method in *The Holy Family*, according to which the speculative method attributes to the abstraction '"the" Fruit' the remarkable powers of producing actual apples and pears out of its own bosom (Marx and Engels 1975a, p. 60). When Marx takes up the third member of the 'trinity', labour, he writes '*"die" Arbeit*' (Marx 1972, p. 823) to mimic, I believe, '"the" Fruit'. This gets lost in Fernbach's translation of '"die" *Arbeit*' as 'labour' (Marx 1981, p. 954). We find this pattern elsewhere in Marx's work. See Marx 1966, p. 234, and Marx 1975e, p. 198.

32 Here David Hume's idea of a 'distinction of reason' is helpful. A distinction of reason identifies an *aspect* of something that is not actually separable from it. (Hegel would call this a 'moment'). In Hume's example we can make a distinction of reason between the whiteness and the spherical shape of a white marble globe, but the two cannot be separated (Hume 1978, p. 25). Determining what is actually separable and what is only conceptually distinguishable is the work of phenomenology. Marx's criticism of the Trinity Formula's picture of three separate sources of value, the three fruit trees, is based on his phenomenology of the production process, according to which materials, means and living labour are inseparable, though distinguishable, factors of production.

on the returns to the value our banked capital produced each year. As logical and appealing as my plan sounded, it smelled fishy.

The thought that land produces rent, which Marx terms 'the Physiocratic illusion', is a bit more difficult to dispel because of the imaginative association of rent with the fertility of the earth.[33] Writing on revenue forms in the third part of *Theories of Surplus-Value*, Marx observes:

> The *land* or *nature* as the source of *rent* ... is fetishistic enough. But as a result of a convenient confusion of use-value with exchange-value, the common imagination is still able to have recourse to the productive power of nature itself, which, by some kind of hocus-pocus, is personified in the landlord.[34]

It is easy enough to grow impatient watching for seeds to sprout; imagine waiting till rents shoot forth from the soil!

Marx's criticism of the Trinity Formula is different from, and more fundamental than, the criticism pioneered by classical political economy, that capital and land are not sources of value, hence not the sources of interest and rent. For Marx's point here is not that, taken separately, capital and land are not sources of revenue, while labour is. The point is not that 'labour' is the sole value-bearing tree. No, '"the" labour' is 'a mere spectre ... nothing but an abstraction and taken by itself cannot exist at all'.[35] Taken separately, none of the three factors are sources of use values, and without use value there is no value. To think otherwise is to adopt the bourgeois standpoint, which ascribes a '*super-natural creative power*' to labour, as Marx charged in his criticism of the Left Ricardianism of the Gotha Programme.[36]

A third phenomenological error is to imagine that the 'wealth (or use-value) added' by each of these three necessary components can be discriminated and quantified. One could avoid the previous error and grant that the three factors of the labour process in general do not act independently, yet still attempt to gauge their respective contributions to the 'use-value added'.[37] John Locke

33 Marx 1976a, p. 176.

34 Marx 1971a, p. 454.

35 Marx 1981, p. 954.

36 Marx 1966a, p. 3.

37 This is the approach taken in neoclassical economics, when it speaks of the 'marginal productivity' of the different factors of production. Geert Reuten and Michael Williams reject this neoclassical doctrine and point out that F.W. Taussig criticised J.B. Clark's neoclassical doctrine of the marginal productivity of capital (Reuten and Williams 1989, p. 72).

was fond of doing that for land and labour (produced means of production revealingly did not figure into his best-known examples), on different occasions allotting land one tenth, hundredth, or thousandth of the 'use-value added' (or 'improvement' as Locke liked to call it). In attempting to prove his point, however, Locke fell back on the different prices of the yield of uncultivated vs. cultivated land, thereby revealing how – and this is quite generally the case with utility theory – the entire thought experiment about the labour process was unwittingly conducted in the shadow of the price form and the valorisation process.[38] For Marx, no such apportionment of 'use-value added' is possible, because there is no homogenous measure for use value, no metric of wealth.[39] Utility is a sham concept, a shadow of price.[40] To think otherwise is to commit a basic phenomenological error.

2.2.2 The Fetishism of the Factors of Production

The second, 'symmetrically incongruous' formulation of the Trinity Formula best fits the description, the 'fetishism of the factors of the capitalist production process', because this variant presents the three factors of the labour process in general as mysteriously invested by nature with the social powers of yielding revenues in the forms of interest, rent and wages. 'Rent, profit and wages thus appear to grow out of the roles that the earth, the produced means of production and labour play in the simple labour process, considering this labour process simply as proceeding between man and nature and ignoring any historical specificity'.[41] In terms of the artistic structuring of *Capital* around the two fetishisms, here is where the other shoe drops.

2.3 *The Third Variant of the Trinity Formula*

Of course, the three factors of the labour process are far from having any such powers. What is really going on here is that the formula slurs over the distinction between the three factors of the labour process in general and the

38 See Chapter Five of Locke 1960.

39 For Marx, the idea of 'purely subjective' utility is a non-starter based on a false, one-sided phenomenology of desire. He writes in the opening pages of *Capital*, 'The usefulness of a thing makes it a use-value. But this usefulness does not dangle in midair. It is conditioned by the physical properties of the commodity, and has no existence apart from the latter' (Marx 1976a, p. 126). That there is no metric for those physical properties was the premise of Marx's argument that only abstract labour can explain what commodities have in common. This is Marx's answer to all forms of utility theory.

40 See Marx and Engels 1976b, p. 409.

41 Marx 1981, p. 964.

three chief protagonists of the capitalist production process: means of production with capitalist, land with landed property owner and labour with wage labourer. This personification of the three factors of the labour process in general, the 'economic three-in-one' as Marx calls it,[42] conflates the essential class structure of capitalism, whereby 'labour' is 'freed' of ownership of land and produced means of production, with the conditions necessary for any labour process. In superimposing the characteristically capitalist class configuration onto the three factors of the labour process, the third variant of the Trinity Formula conveniently bestows the inexorability of the latter on the former. So the Trinity Formula performs the ingenious ideological feat of simultaneously calling attention to what Marx, echoing Ricardo, calls 'the three great classes of modern society',[43] while doubly neutralising any suggestion of class conflict: once, by presenting the different revenues as fair compensations for 'value-added' from different, naturally occurring sources, and once again by collapsing the three classes into the three naturally occurring factors of the labour process.[44] Perhaps, then, it is no wonder that, when the manuscript to 'Classes', the short final chapter of the book, breaks off, Marx is preparing to explain why distinguishing classes on the basis of the different forms of revenue (as opposed to property relations) is a poor idea.[45]

2.4 *The Fourth Variant of the Trinity Formula*

If the inconsistency of the original formulas is avoided in the opposite manner to read: *capital – interest, landed property – rent*, and *wage-labour – wages*, the systematic incongruity is eliminated: now we have three *value* categories paired with three types of revenues in the value form. Something can be said for this formula. Capital does pump out interest, landed property does extract rent;

42 Marx 1981, p. 953.

43 Marx 1981, p. 1,025.

44 How many times have we heard the bromide 'capital and labour need each other', which rolls together two truths and two falsehoods? The two truths are: (1) any labour process requires both means of production and living labour, and (2) *capital* and *wage labour* need each other. The two falsehoods, familiar from the Trinity Formula, are (1) since means of production and living labour are inescapable conditions of the labour process, capital and wage labour are inescapable as well and (2) because we can conceptually distinguish between the means of production and living labour in the labour process, there must be two distinct economic roles and two types of property owners, the capitalist, who personifies – and owns – the means of production, and the wage labourer, who personifies labour and owns nothing with which to make a living but his or her own labour power.

45 Marx 1981, p. 1,026. For more on this topic see Mattick Jr 2002.

wage labour does pull down a wage – these fetishes work! – but the formula blocks all understanding of surplus value (capital's lifeblood), along with its necessary forms of appearance, profit of enterprise, interest and rent. Instead of recognising profit of enterprise, interest and rent as portions of surplus value that was produced originally by wage labourers, this fourth variant of the Trinity Formula announces that capital and landed property are independent sources of value that simply receive their due in the revenues of interest and rent, respectively, just as profit of enterprise is compensation (wages) for the capitalist's labour.[46]

At least this formula keeps consistently to the realm of value, but within that realm it gets everything twisted up. The falsehood of the Trinity Formula's conception of profits, interest and rent is what Marx had just written almost a thousand complicated pages to prove. I will not attempt here to rehearse that intricate account of the necessary, and necessarily deceptive, forms of appearance of surplus value. A prima facie case for the Trinity Formula's falsehood, however, reaches back to the beginning of Volume I. Since value is exclusively a matter of the social form of labour in capitalism, capital and landed property cannot be sources of value.[47] Labour is the source of all value, consequently, of all surplus value.

What makes this simple refutation hard to swallow, and what likewise can make the Trinity Formula's claim of triple sources of value seem more plausible, is the persistence with which wealth (use value) and value keep getting confused with one another. It seems flatly wrong to attribute the production of all wealth to labour. And it is! Not only is 'labour' (human labour taken in abstraction from the two other necessary factors in the labour process, produced means of production and raw materials) not the source of all wealth; it is not the source of any. Remember, Marx calls it 'a mere spectre.' '"The" labour' cannot produce anything. Marx states that land is a component in the production of use value: 'The earth, for example, is active as an agent of production in the production of a use-value, a material product, say wheat. But it has nothing to do with producing the *value of the wheat*'.[48] Marx immediately reminds us of the lesson from Chapter One on the polarity of the value form and the oddities of the equivalent form of value: 'In as much as value is expressed in wheat, the wheat is considered simply as a certain quantum of objectified social labour, this labour being quite indifferent to the particular material in which it

---

46 See Marx 1981, p. 965.

47 Marx 1970a, p. 35; 1976a, p. 176; 1976a, p. 176.

48 Marx 1981, p. 955.

is expressed or to the particular use-value of this material'.[49] Nothing that lacks use value has value; so 'labour' cannot create value on its own. Nevertheless, Marx insists that not one iota of use value enters into the constitution of value:

> the commodity-form, and the value-relation of the products of labour within which it appears, have absolutely no connection with the physical nature and the material [*dinglich*] relations arising out of this. It is nothing but the definite social relation between men themselves which assumes here, for them, the fantastic form of a relation between things.[50]

Remember, revenues are values.

It was with regard to this version, consistently formulated on the 'value' plane, that classical political economy made important advances in debunking the Trinity Formula, to which vulgar economists were so attached. The classical doctrine ruled out the notion of either capital or land being sources of value; implicitly at least, it was a theory of surplus value. And it explicitly theorised interest and rent as deductions from industrial gross profits (the surplus value pumped out by industrial capital). While it thereby struck a historic blow against the 'fetishism of the factors of the capitalist production process', classical political economy's own shortcomings were many and serious: it failed to recognise what value is (congealed socially necessary abstract labour) and why it necessarily appears as exchange value (hence it did not understand that – or why – money is an essential feature of capitalist production); it failed to reconcile its value theory with the needed theory of prices of production; it failed to provide a consistent theory of surplus value, for it failed to make the distinction between labour and labour power, an aporia that the Trinity Formula condenses into 'labour – wages'; it failed to discriminate clearly and consistently between surplus value and its forms of appearance (profit of enterprise, interest, rent); and, consequently, it failed to articulate a theory properly developing the conceptual relationships between surplus value and its necessary forms of appearance. On more basic levels, such as the level of 'the illusion of the economic', classical political economy entirely lost its advantage over vulgar economics.[51]

49 Ibid.
50 Marx 1976a, p. 165.
51 See Marx 1971a, pp. 500–1.

3 Conclusion: Beyond the Left Ricardian Interpretation of 'The Trinity Formula'

I have argued that Marx's chapter 'The Trinity Formula' is wrongly understood as a defence of Ricardian (classical) value theory against vulgar political economy. That ordinary interpretation blocks understanding of Marx's deeper purposes in *Capital*, and more particularly in its concluding part, Part Seven of Volume III. Marx wrote *Capital* as a critique of political economy, and, in the final part of his book, Marx draws together and highlights his fundamental criticisms of both vulgar and classical political economy. I want to close by considering the second to last chapter in Part Seven, 'Relations of Distribution and Relations of Production', for Marx's most fundamental criticism of vulgar and classical political economy alike is that they failed to recognise the capitalist order as a historically specific mode of production. In the more complicated cases of John Stuart Mill and the Left Ricardians, both of whom recognised the historical dimension of distribution, the mistake lay in not grasping the inseparability of production and distribution. This final consideration will provide the opportunity to reinforce what I have argued regarding 'the illusion of the economic', which forms the horizon of the secular 'religion of everyday life'. And it gives me the opportunity to gather several of Marx's chief criticisms of Ricardian theory. Since these criticisms apply to Left Ricardian theory, it will also be the occasion for a final effort to dislodge that stubborn obstacle to understanding *Capital*, namely, the mistaken idea that Marx was a Left Ricardian.

I will consider three deep criticisms that Marx makes of Ricardian theory: (1) it fails to understand value and the necessity for value to be expressed as something other than itself, namely as money; consequently, it does not understand money; (2) it fails to grasp either the distinction between labour power and living labour or the juridical and moral import of that distinction; consequently, its doctrine of surplus value is faulty and its political project doomed; and (3) it fails to recognise the point with which Marx intended to begin Part Seven, 'the capitalist process of production is a historically specific form of the social production process in general';[52] in other words, Ricardian theory is trapped in 'the illusion of the economic'. As we will see, Marx holds that this third criticism applies to John Stuart Mill and the Left Ricardians, even though they recognise the historical specificity of different modes of distribution.

52 Marx 1981, p. 957.

The first two criticisms of Ricardian theory go back to the early chapters of *Capital* – the first goes back to Chapter One and the second to Chapters Six and Seven.

1. Ricardian value theory failed to recognise that what constitutes value is not simply 'embodied labour' (or even 'embodied abstract labour'). If it were, then all human labour, under all historical circumstances, would produce value. That *value* is not a general feature of the human condition, as is labour, constitutes the crux of Marx's profound criticism of Ricardian theory. The point of Chapter One of *Capital* is to show that value is a fetish: value is the necessary consequence of the peculiarly asocial social form of labour under capitalism. Value is the outcome of commodity-producing labour, which we may call 'practically abstract' labour because it is socially validated only in a roundabout manner, namely, through the exchange of commodities. The point of the analysis of the value form in the third section of Chapter One is to demonstrate that the value of a commodity must appear as something other than itself, namely, as money. Ricardian theory, then, fails to understand that value is a consequence not of labour, but of the specific social form of labour under capitalism. Consequently, it is in no position to grasp the phenomenological point that value and money are inseparable – money is no mere technical aid to exchange; money is necessary to organise production based on value-producing labour.[53] Left Ricardian proposals such as eliminating money in favour of 'time-chits' (certificates of hours worked), which were intended to eliminate the exploitation involved in surplus value by insuring that the equalitarian rule that equal values be exchanged for equal values be followed, fail to recognise that hours of actual commodity-producing labour cannot be immediately socially validated. Writing in *The Poverty of Philosophy*, Marx complains that Proudhon fails to see that 'money is not a thing, it is a social relation', and he wonders, 'how can M. Proudhon go on talking about the constitution of a value, since a value is never constituted by itself? It is constituted, not by the time needed to produce it by itself, but in relation to the quota of each and every other product which can be created in the same time'.[54] The non-identity of value and money, value's necessary mode of expression, cannot be wished away.[55]

---

53 See Campbell 1997.

54 Marx 1963b, pp. 81, 83.

55 Marx 1973, p. 138.

2. The second two errors of Ricardian theory are both involved in the Left Ricardian proposal for 'the equalitarian application of the Ricardian theory'. The Left Ricardian idea that wage labourers are being short-changed is based on a failure to recognise the difference between the value of labour power and the value that labour power produces when it is consumed as living labour. Given the fact that the theory of surplus value lies at the heart of Left Ricardian thinking, this failure is doubly ironic. First, Left Ricardians never penetrated the secret of surplus value, and, second, they therefore failed to understand how surplus value can be expropriated without violating the commercial rule of thumb: exchange equal values for equal values. The point of Chapters Six and Seven of *Capital* Volume I is that the proper explanation of surplus value requires distinguishing between the commodity that wage labourers sell, their labour power, and the production of fresh value (including surplus value) when their labour power is consumed, as living labour, by capitalists who put them to work in a labour process that is likewise a valorisation process. While Marx ridicules the very idea of the value of living labour, comparing it to a yellow logarithm, labour power is a commodity whose value capitalists can pay in full even as they realise surplus value, simply by keeping workers at their task long enough. As Marx summarises his historic solution to the problem of the source of surplus value, 'Every condition of the problem is satisfied, while the laws governing the exchange of commodities have not been violated in any way. Equivalent has been exchanged for equivalent'.[56] So, if left-Ricardians *were* to understand the source of surplus value, the pipe dream of eliminating surplus value through an equalitarian application of the law of value would have to be discarded. A critique of the injustice of the capitalist mode of production cannot rely on the bourgeois canons of commutative justice.[57] Thus, in *The Poverty of Philosophy* Marx concludes his critical treatment of the Left Ricardian John Bray as follows: 'Mr. Bray does not see that this equalitarian relation, this *corrective ideal* that he would like to apply to the world, is itself nothing but the reflection of the actual world; and that therefore it is totally impossible to reconstitute society on the basis of what is merely an embellished shadow of it'.[58] If you want to change the world, it is best to understand it.
3. The deep mistake underlying the first error, the one involved in the 'time-chit' proposal, is the third Ricardian misconception and the last that will be

56 Marx 1976a, p. 301.

57 Marx 1981, pp. 460–1.

58 Marx 1963b, p. 79.

> considered here. As Marx writes of the Ricardian socialist John Gray, '*goods are supposed to be produced as commodities but not exchanged as commodities*'.[59] The mistake is the phenomenological error of tearing production and distribution asunder.[60] This error provides the subject matter of the penultimate chapter of *Capital*, 'Relations of Distribution and Relations of Production'. This chapter is set up by 'The Trinity Formula' inasmuch as the revenue forms are the forms of distribution. Marx first observes: 'In the customary view, these relations of distribution appear to be natural relations, relations arising from the nature of all social production, from the laws of human production pure and simple'.[61] Such a conception is, of course, nurtured by the Trinity Formula, according to which the (specifically capitalist) revenue forms sprout from the three factors of the labour process in general. But Marx believes that certain developments in classical political economy undermine this de-historicising conception of the forms of distribution. And, in John Stuart Mill, Marx finds 'a more developed and critical awareness' that 'concedes the historically developed character of these relations of distribution'. However, Marx goes on to observe that Mill 'holds all the more firmly to the supposedly constant character of the relations of production themselves, as arising from human nature and hence independent of all historical development'.[62] Mill's advance, the recognition of the historicity of the forms of distribution, is presupposed by the various redistributionist schemes of Left Ricardianism. So too, unfortunately, is Mill's great shortcoming. For the preoccupation of Left Ricardians with the surplus in surplus value signals their failure to recognise value as a historically specific relation of production.

The general truth of the matter, a truth that constitutes one of the primary phenomenological results involved in historical materialism, is this: relations of production and distribution are inseparable:

> The so-called relations of distribution, therefore, correspond to and arise from historically particular and specific social forms of the production process and of the relationships which men enter into among themselves in the process of reproducing their human life. The historical character of

59 Marx 1970a, p. 85.
60 Marx 1973, p. 87.
61 Marx 1981, p. 1,017.
62 Marx 1981, p. 1,018.

> these relations of distribution is the historical character of the relations of production, and they simply express one side of these.[63]

In *Capital*, Marx demonstrates the inseparability of production and distribution in the specifically capitalist mode of production by showing (a) that the purpose of capitalist production is valorisation, pumping out and accumulating surplus value, (b) that this is possible only when labour generally takes the specific social form of wage labour and (c) that profit (interest and profit of enterprise) and rent are the necessary forms of appearance of surplus value.

So Mill and the Left Ricardians strike a blow against 'the illusion of the economic', but an ineffectual one. Marx comments, 'The view that considers only the relations of distribution to be historical, and not the relations of production, is simply the perspective of a criticism of bourgeois economics that is incipient but still timid and restrained'. Where production is concerned, 'the illusion of the economic' lingers, as Marx goes on to say, due to 'a confusion and identification of the social production process with the simple labour process'.[64] Here Marx sends us back to the beginning of the second circuit of thought in *Capital*, Chapter Seven of Volume I, where he insisted that there is no labour process in general – the notion that there is one defines 'the illusion of the economic' – and that the capitalist labour process, while it shares features with labour processes throughout history, distinguishes itself from all others by being a valorisation process.

Marx concludes Chapter 51 by reminding the reader of the significance of this recognition of the falsehood of 'the illusion of the economic' and the truth of the historical materialist proposition that the production process always has a definite social form with definite historical implications: 'each particular historical form of this process further develops the material foundations and social forms. Once a certain level of maturity is attained, the particular historical form is shed and makes way for a higher form'.[65] The reasonable prospect that this is no less true of the capitalist mode of production animated Marx's hopeful critique of political economy and of the 'fiction without fantasy' spread by the 'religion of everyday life'.[66]

63 Marx 1981, p. 1,023. See also Marx 1963b, p. 79 and Marx 1973, pp. 87–100.

64 Marx 1981, p. 1,023.

65 Marx 1981, pp. 1,023–4.

66 I want to thank Geert Reuten and Martha Campbell, along with Chris Arthur, Riccardo Bellofiore, Paul Mattick Jr, Fred Moseley, Jeanne Schuler and Tony Smith for especially constructive criticisms of previous versions of this chapter.

PART 2

Critical Engagements

CHAPTER 15

Avoiding Bad Abstractions: A Defence of Co-constitutive Value-Form Theory

> We see then that commodities are in love with money, but that 'the course of true love never did run smooth'.[1]

Marxian value theory is a value-form theory. Since it was by asserting this that I came to be invited to participate in the present symposium, I will begin here.[2] Speaking in a general way, one could say that value-form theory encompasses any theory of the value form, where the value form is the expression of value, namely, exchange value. That Marx is a value-form theorist in this general sense is apparent from any number of facts, the most striking is that he devotes Section Three of the first chapter of *Capital* to 'The Value-Form, or Exchange-Value'. Marx discusses two theorists of the value form in this general sense, Aristotle and Samuel Bailey. Marx identifies Aristotle as 'the great investigator who was the first to analyse the value-form, like so many other forms of thought, society and nature'.[3] Aristotle recognised (1) that it takes the equating of two commodities to express value, though he did not notice the necessarily polar nature of the expression of value nor, consequently, did he analyse the peculiarities of either the relative or equivalent value forms; (2) 'that the money-form of the commodity is only the further developed figure [*die weiter entwickelte Gestalt*] of the simple form of value';[4] (3) that the equalities expressed in the form of

1 Marx 1976a, p. 202.

2 The assertion was made during a panel on value-form theory at the 2006 *Historical Materialism* conference in London that was sponsored by the journal *Critique of Political Economy*. The present chapter is a condensed version of my contribution to the symposium on value-form theory and the Temporal Single System Interpretation (TSSI), Murray 2011, which is published in the first issue of the online journal *Critique of Political Economy*. The other contributions to the symposium were Freeman 2011, Gonzalez and Posner 2011 and Kliman 2011.

3 Marx 1976a, p. 151.

4 Ibid., my revised translation.

value presuppose commensurability, so that there must be some quantifiable 'third thing' (as Marx calls it) common to all commodities, of which they represent various magnitudes; and (4) that this common thing cannot be either a physical property of a commodity or what we might term 'use-value in the abstract' (utility), since, as Marx puts the Aristotelian point, 'The usefulness of a thing ... does not dangle in mid-air. It is conditioned by the physical properties of the commodity, and has no existence apart from the latter'.[5] Utility is a mirage.

These are heavy debts that Marx owes Aristotle. But Aristotle's theory of the value form came to a halt when he could find nothing that worked as the 'third thing,' as value, in terms of which all commodities are commensurable. Marx explains Aristotle's failure to recognise that human labour in general is the substance of the 'third thing' in terms of his historical limitations: value could not be 'deciphered until the concept of human equality had already acquired the permanence of a fixed popular opinion'.[6] Not contending with the historical obstacles that Aristotle faced, Marx succeeds in solving the riddle of the value form.

Modern theorists of the value form are few, Marx observes; the most notable is Samuel Bailey.[7] In *Capital* Volume I Marx comments, 'The few economists, such as S. Bailey, who have concerned themselves with the analysis of the form of value have been unable to arrive at any result, firstly because they confuse the form of value with value itself, and secondly because, under the coarse influence of the practical bourgeois, they give their attention from the outset, and exclusively, to the quantitative aspect of the question'.[8] It is odd that the TSSI authors do not consider Bailey, for two reasons.[9] Firstly, Bailey held the extreme value-form theory that is their target. Secondly, Marx already criticises Bailey's value-form theory along lines followed by the TSSI authors. Marx writes, 'The most superficial form of exchange-value, that is the *quantitative relation* in which commodities exchange with one another, *constitutes*, according to Bailey, their value'.[10] Bailey is the originator of the

5 Marx 1976a, p. 126.

6 Marx 1976a, p. 152.

7 See also Chapter 6 in the present volume and Furner 2004 and Murray 2006, included in the present volume as Chapter 17.

8 Marx 1976a, p. 141, n. 17.

9 I will refer collectively to the proponents of the Temporal Single System Interpretation (TSSI) contributing to the value-form symposium, Alan Freeman, Maya Gonzalez, Andrew Kliman and Michael Posner, as 'the TSSI authors'.

10 Marx 1971a, p. 129.

idea that value is constituted exclusively in exchange, which collapses value and exchange value. A passionate critic of Ricardian value theory, Bailey was a determined opponent of the very idea that value is an intrinsic property of a commodity, present prior to its sale. Inasmuch as Bailey is the pioneer of the variant of value-form theory that troubles the TSSI authors, Marx has done much of their work for them.

I propose that we distinguish simply having some theory of the value form, as Aristotle did, from value-form theory in the more restrictive sense that is widely employed today. Value-form theory maintains that neither the value nor the magnitude of value of a commodity is constituted independently of its sale; put more generally, neither value nor the magnitude of value are constituted independently of money and the circulation of commodities. When I say that Marxian value theory is a value-form theory, this is the sense I intend. We sometimes find a narrower meaning in the literature, when the term 'value-form theory' is limited to the one-sided theory according to which value and the magnitude of value are constituted exclusively in exchange. Bailey, not Marx, is the originator of this extreme variant of value-form theory, which I will call the *exchange-only* view. Since Marx rejected the basic claims of this type of value-form theory, it ought not to be considered Marxian. By contrast, Marxian value-form theory holds that value and the magnitude of value are co-constituted in production and circulation. It takes what I will call a *co-constitutive* view. Value is a supersensible social property intrinsic to the commodity as a potential, arising out of production, whose magnitude is not fully determinate until that potential is actualised with the final act of social validation, the sale of the commodity. Marxian value theory reverses the logic of Heisenberg's Uncertainty Principle: only through the measurement of value in money, that is, only through the sale of the commodity, is value actualised and the magnitude of value finally determined. The term 'value-form theory' as I propose to use it, then, includes both the co-constitutive view and the exchange-only view.[11]

11 Value-form theory should not be identified with any of the following: (1) the claim that there are ambiguities, mistakes or contradictions in Marx's presentation of his theory of value (Arthur, Reuten, Heinrich and Eldred and Hanlon); (2) the claim that value is constituted exclusively in exchange; (3) reconstructing Marx, even though several value-form theorists engage in reconstruction.

1 From Straw Man to Paper Tiger

The TSSI authors endorse the idea that value is historically specific, which they find in all value-form theories, but they reject value-form theory in favour of what I will call a *production-only* conception of the constitution of value and the determination of the magnitude of value. They argue that both the magnitude of value and the price of commodities are determined prior to the sale of the commodity. Furthermore, they believe that this captures Marx's view; in other words, they argue that Marx was not a value-form theorist. There is a basic difficulty with the TSSI authors' engagement with value-form theory. Most, perhaps all – I am not certain about Eldred and Hanlon or Kay and Mott – of the value-form theorists with whom they engage hold a co-constitutive view.[12] The TSSI authors continually collapse the co-constitutive view into the exchange-only view; their arguments work only against the latter. They do this because they cannot take seriously the co-constitutive view, which regards value as intrinsic to the commodity but only latently present prior to the sale of the commodity. The TSSI authors are locked into an either-or logic: either the commodity has its value in full before it is sold or there is no sense in which it has value. If it does, it must have a determinate magnitude of value (and a determinate price); if it does not, the question of the magnitude of its value is moot.

Though they do not put the point so directly, the TSSI authors spurn the idea that the commodity's value is an intrinsic potential prior to its sale: potential is a metaphysical hoax. Likewise, the Marxian value-form proposition that value and price are both preconditions and results of commodity circulation is unthinkable to the TSSI authors. Value is either a precondition or it is a result; it cannot be both. For them, the co-constitutive value-form theory is a conceptual and metaphysical mishmash that would make of value an impossible changeling. In the minds of the TSSI authors, then, a hole gapes where I place Marxian value-form theory and any other co-constitutive value-form theory. Because their concepts allow no room for value-form theory to take any other form, the TSSI authors engage only the most one-sided conception of value-form theory, the exchange-only value-form theory. As a consequence of their either-or thinking, with its metaphysical aversion to real potentiality and indeterminacy and its conceptual aversion to value's existence as both precondition

12 In addition to Bailey, Sohn-Rethel adopts an exchange-only view (Sohn-Rethel 1978), but the TSSI authors do not discuss him. For a criticism of Sohn-Rethel's one-sided value-form theory, see Postone 1993, pp. 177–9.

and result, the TSSI authors cannot help but make a straw-man of value-form theory. They are bound to collapse value-form theory into its most extreme variant, which shares their belief that value does not exist potentially in commodities prior to their sale. Thereafter, the two part company; the extreme value-form theory reaches a conclusion opposite to that of TSSI: the value of a commodity and the magnitude of its value are constituted exclusively in the act of exchange. Consequently, to juxtapose the 'market-centred' (value-form theory) with the 'production-centred' (TSSI), as Andrew Kliman does, understates the contrast. The value-form view that he and other TSSI authors criticise is not just market-centred; it conceives of value and the magnitude of value as being determined exclusively in exchange, by the sale of the commodity whose value is at issue. Likewise, Kliman's TSSI view is not production-centred; it holds that value, the magnitude of value, and price are fully determined prior to the sale of the commodity. For TSSI, value is determined exclusively in production; it is a production-only theory. If the TSSI authors were correct, our choice would be a stark one: reject value-form theory in favour of their production-only view or accept the extreme, exchange-only variant of value-form theory.

Having made a straw man of value-form theory by collapsing it into its most extreme (and empty) version, the exchange-only variant, the TSSI authors turn it into a paper tiger. They inflate the exchange-only view by equivocating on the word 'determine'. We can distinguish two senses of 'determine'. In one sense price is determined in the sale of a commodity; how much money is exchanged for a commodity determines its price, say $10. This sense of 'determine' does not get us beyond tautology: price just is what a commodity sells for, so the sale of a commodity determines its price. But what determines why that price is $10 rather than $2 or $50? With this second sense of 'determine', we go beyond definition; we are looking for an explanation. But the exchange-only theory offers no explanation, hence its vacuity. As Gonzalez and Posner observe, 'In the hands of the value-form theorist, value is transformed from a predicate of real human activity into a mystical substance of unknown provenance'.[13] They add (correctly, with regard to the exchange-only version of value-form theory) that this 'reinstates the fetishism that Marx sought to overthrow in his critique of political economy'.[14] That was a dart Marx enjoyed throwing at Bailey, since, with his polemics against 'intrinsic value' – like other subjectivistic philosophers and economists, he even rejected the common sense notion that use value is intrinsic to goods – Bailey prided himself as the consummate anti-fetishist.

13 Gonzalez and Posner 2011, p. 207.
14 Gonzalez and Posner 2011, p. 214.

There is an equivocation involved in saying that, according to the exchange-only theory of value, value is determined in exchange. Thus, Kliman writes of value-form theory (by which he means, as we can read, the exchange-only version), 'total price is determined in and through exchange' since 'commodities only acquire their prices by being exchanged'.[15] The first statement equivocates; it suggests that exchange is somehow determining the price in the second, explanatory, sense of 'determine', when, really, this kind of value-form theory only states the tautology that the price of a commodity is how much money you get for it. The phrase 'determined in and through exchange' accentuates the equivocation by adding an idle 'through' to the 'in', as if mere exchange were somehow not only indicating that a commodity sold for $10 but also explaining why it sold for that and no other price. But the extreme value-form theory criticised by the TSSI authors has no such explanation to offer. The 'through' is a dead letter that lends the exchange-only theory the pretension to a scientific weight it lacks. Here is where the exchange-only value-form theory gets puffed up into a worthier foe than it is.

In the exchange-only value-form theory, we have what Alan Freeman terms an 'ontological collapse'. This extreme variant of value-form theory affords us no basis for distinguishing between value and price, so the talk of 'constituting' value and price 'through' the act of exchange only adds hype to the humdrum observation that commodities are sold at some price. At most the exchange-only version of value-form theory is a negative theory, as it was when Samuel Bailey introduced this strain of value-form theory; it is a rebuke to any intrinsic theory of value, including any labour theory of value. The 'theory' comes down to this: there is no value, only price, and there is no theory of price. A paper tiger.

Consequently, I agree with the criticisms that the TSSI authors make of the ideas to which they reduce value-form theory – i.e., the ideas which make up its extreme, exchange-only variant. The key ideas of Marxian value theory cannot be derived from this variant. The problem with the TSSI criticism of value-form theory is that – because of its either/or: the value of a commodity either exists whole and entire prior to its sale or it does not exist at all – it cannot countenance the co-constitutive kind of value-form theory originated by Marx. Yet that kind makes up the mainstream of value-form theory today.

---

15 Kliman 2011, p. 191.

2 Needed: Two Concepts of Abstract Labour

Gonzalez and Posner write, 'The crux of our argument against the value-form theory pivots on the theorization of abstract labor'.[16] It does, but the trouble is that they write as if there were just one concept of abstract labour at stake, when there are two – in fact there are two *kinds* of concepts of abstract labour in play in Marx's theory of value. With good reason, Gonzalez and Posner point to the difficulties that value-form theorists have in reconciling 'Marx's theorization of abstract labor as physiological human labor with Marx's view that abstract labor as the substance of value belongs to an historically specific "social formation in which the process of production has mastery over man, instead of the opposite"' (Marx 1976a, p. 174).[17] No doubt, we confront a difficult interpretive task. Trying to resolve the apparent difficulty just noted without distinguishing two concepts of abstract labour – two kinds of concept – results in what I call 'Rubin's dilemma'. If we allow only one concept of abstract labour, either we must deny that there is a generally applicable concept of abstract labour or we must deny that value-producing labour is labour of a specific social sort.

To escape 'Rubin's dilemma' we need to distinguish between (1) a generally applicable concept of abstract labour, which we can associate with human labour considered 'physiologically', and (2) what I term 'practically abstract' labour, which is labour that is socially validated in practice *as* abstract in the former sense. Once we have the concept of human labour in the abstract, the former concept is applicable to concrete labour of whatever social type. Abstract labour in this sense is not a kind of labour; it is a way of regarding any social or technical sort of concrete labour. So it is pointless to talk about someone doing abstract labour in this sense. It is a category mistake to contrast abstract labour (in this sense) to concrete labour, as if one person could perform concrete labour and another abstract labour. In this sense there simply is no abstract labour; there only is concrete labour. We do speak of concrete labour being more or less abstract; for example, the bolt-tightening work done by Charlie Chaplin's character in his film *Modern Times* counts as abstract. But a different sense of 'abstract labour' is in play here, one that distinguishes among types of concrete labour, not between concrete and abstract labour.

By contrast, 'practically abstract' labour is a specific social type of labour, namely labour that is socially validated in practice as abstract in the physiological sense. Value-producing labour is 'practically abstract' labour; so value-

16 Gonzalez and Posner 2011, p. 204.

17 Gonzalez and Posner 2011, p. 204.

producing labour is a specific social form of labour. On that point value-form theory and TSSI agree. But the social practice whereby labour is validated as abstract is commodity circulation. So value-form theory belongs to the concept of 'practically abstract' labour: value is inseparable from money and the circulation of commodities.

3 Commodity Fetishism without Money Fetishism?

Value-form theory and TSSI agree that value and value-producing labour are specific social forms of wealth and labour, but TSSI rejects the value-form theorist's claim that money and circulation are ingredient to this social specificity. More particularly, TSSI claims that the value of a commodity is fully determinate before it is sold. What alternative account, then, do TSSI theorists offer of the social specificity of value and value-producing labour? Gonzalez and Posner answer that what 'gives abstract labor an historically specific character and real existence in capitalism is the fact that this common equality of all human labor is transformed into an "objective characteristic" of the commodities themselves, "as … socio-natural properties of these things"'.[18] Obviously, they refer to what Marx calls the 'fetish character of the commodity'. But what shows us that the common, 'physiological' character of human labour has been 'transformed into an "objective characteristic" of the commodities themselves', and what is responsible for this peculiar transformation? How does congealed 'abstract labour' become an objective characteristic of commodities?

Gonzalez and Posner refer us to the 'value-relation of commodities', in which 'the various forms of concrete labor are not socially related as distinct and functionally reciprocal concrete labors which are productive of distinct useful objects, but only as *human labor as such*'.[19] They quote a passage from the appendix to the first edition version of the first chapter of *Capital* that brings out the inversion of concrete and abstract:

> Within the value-relation and the value expression included in it, the abstractly general counts not as a property of the concrete, sensibly real; but on the contrary the sensibly-concrete counts as the mere form of appearance or definite form of realisation of the abstractly general.[20]

---

18 Gonzalez and Posner 2011, p. 205. The citation from Marx is to Marx 1976a, pp. 164–5.

19 Gonzalez and Posner 2011, p. 205.

20 Gonzalez and Posner 2011, p. 206, n. 19, citing Marx 1978b, pp. 130–40.

Marx specifies that 'the value expression', that is, the sale of the commodity, is included in the 'value-relation'. So money and the circulation of commodities are ingredient to Marx's conceptions of value and value-producing labour. Commodity circulation, the buying and selling of commodities, is the social practice by which concrete labour is transformed into 'practically abstract' labour. Gonzalez and Posner have arrived at a value-form conclusion: the specific social forms, value and value-producing labour, are inseparable from money and circulation. Of course, it is not their intention to reach this conclusion.

Gonzalez and Posner veer away from a value-form conclusion when they insist that, despite the appearance created by the 'value-relation', the 'true subject' is not 'abstract human labor' (indeed, that is no subject at all); it is 'the definite, concrete forms of labor which alone possess the characteristic of being *human* labor, and are thus the true subject'.[21] This formulation omits what is all-important in Marx's theory of value, namely, the specific social form of that concrete labour. Since there is no concrete labour without a specific social form, socially unspecified concrete labour is also 'no subject at all'. It is merely a bad abstraction. By contrast, proponents of the co-constitutive version of value-form theory neither dissociate value-producing labour from concrete labour – since concrete labour is the only kind of labour there is, to do so would be to abandon a labour theory of value – nor do they separate concrete labour from its specific social form.

Later in their contribution Gonzalez and Posner drop the value-form theory conclusion to which they were led and adopt a position taken by Paul Sweezy. Sweezy tried to square the circle and reconcile a physiological conception of abstract labour with commodity fetishism and a socially specific conception of value.[22] They write, 'Again, the specificity of the capitalist mode of production is seen not in the existence of abstract human labor but in the transformation of this predicate of real human labor into the only form of labor's social existence'.[23] Here nothing is said about how this 'transformation of this predicate of real human labour into the only form of labor's social existence' takes place. The value-form theorist wonders: can this transformation occur without money and the circulation of commodities?

21 Gonzalez and Posner 2011, p. 206.

22 See the critique of Sweezy in Murray 2000a, pp. 33–4, n. 15. Murray 2000a is included in the present volume as Chapter 4.

23 Gonzalez and Posner 2011, p. 205, n. 18.

Like Sweezy, Gonzalez and Posner are penned in by 'Rubin's dilemma': they want one concept of abstract labour (the generally applicable one) to do the work of two. They write:

> we must say that the difference between abstract and concrete labor consists not in a difference between the lengths of time during which they are performed, nor in the supposed imperceptibility of abstract labor, but rather in the fact that when concrete labor is treated as *abstract* labor it is treated as 'human labor-power expended *without regard to the form of its expenditure*'.[24]

But who is treating concrete labour as abstract and how? Silence. What specific feature of capitalist production is responsible not only for making this abstraction but also for transforming abstract labour into a supersensible property of the commodity? They do not say. The value-form theory answer, which Gonzalez and Posner seemed to arrive at earlier in their paper, is that a capitalist society treats labour this way when wealth circulates as commodities, that is, when commodities are bought and sold. Thus, commodity-producing labour is 'practically abstract' labour, which is the peculiar social sort of labour that produces value.

Gonzalez and Posner go on:

> To make such an abstraction we take real, concrete human labor and *remove* all of its determinate qualities, leaving only the pure expenditure of undifferentiated human labor-power. This implies that abstract labor is one aspect of concrete labor, performed only when concrete labor is also performed: or, in other words, abstract labor is a part of the *real labor process*.[25]

We? Who is this we? And why couldn't this mysterious onlooker make the same abstraction regardless of the social form of the 'real labor process'? Gonzalez and Posner note, 'This abstraction from the specificity and determinate character of concrete human labor [Done how and by whom?] is precisely the

24 Gonzalez and Posner 2011, p. 208. Again, the very idea of abstract labour 'being performed' is wrongheaded. The idea being set up here, that we can measure value by counting up hours of concrete labour, would put Marx's all-important qualification, that value-producing labour must be 'socially necessary', out of play.

25 Gonzalez and Posner 2011, pp. 208–9.

"reductive abstraction" opposed by Geert Reuten' (Reuten 1993, p. 97). It is, but Reuten is right to oppose it. For the 'reductive abstraction' conception of value-producing labour forces us into the unacceptable conclusion that human labour produces value regardless of its social form.

Gonzalez and Posner resist that conclusion while trying to fend off value-form theory: 'But if abstract labor is seen both as a (socially) real substance and as existing prior to the market, then there is no need to refer to the market in order to treat it as "a real abstraction or abstraction in practice"'.[26] It is not a question of how abstract labour is seen. The question is whether or not (congealed) abstract labour is an actual social substance existing prior to the market. Gonzalez and Posner shed no light on why we should think it is. They reject Reuten's value-form claim that abstract labour attains actuality as a ghostly social substance only by means of the 'real' or 'practical' abstraction from use value (and useful labour) that occurs in the market. Nonetheless, Gonzalez and Posner argue that abstract labour achieves the status of a 'socially real substance' that exists prior to and, I take it, independently of the market. But they do not point to any socially specific feature of the capitalist production process that would explain why abstract labour is 'a (socially) real substance existing prior to the market', much less why that substance must be incarnated in money. In effect, they leave commodity fetishism unexplained, and they disconnect commodity fetishism from money fetishism. Marx does not; he specifies that 'the enigmatic character of the product of labor, as soon as it assumes the form of a commodity ... arises from this form itself'.[27] But the commodity form of the product is inextricable from money and circulation. Following in the footsteps of Sweezy, Gonzalez and Posner offer us a 'physicalist' (Freeman) conception of value against their own intentions. And a 'physicalist' conception of value is a fetishistic one; it treats a strictly social property or power as if it were naturally occurring.

Abstract labour is inseparable from concrete labour, say Gonzalez and Posner; I agree. But they reason fallaciously from this truth:

> It therefore follows, contra Reuten, that we are able to add together one hour of one form of concrete labor (tailoring, for example) and one hour of another form of concrete labor (such as weaving) to arrive at two hours of labor performed; when we do this, however, we abstract from the differences between the two concrete labors, and thereby reduce the two

26 Gonzalez and Posner 2011, p. 208, n. 21, quoting Reuten 1993, p. 97.

27 Marx 1976a, p. 164.

> *different* types of labor to their commonality as physiologically human labor *in general*, i.e. human labor in the abstract.[28]

The fact that all hours of abstract labour that are socially validated derive from concrete labour does not imply its converse, namely, that each hour of concrete labour counts as an hour of abstract labour. A necessary condition – that concrete labour be performed in order for there to be socially necessary abstract labour – is not a sufficient condition.

Counting hours of concrete labour to determine the magnitude of value is subject to the criticisms that Marx made against the various 'time chit' or 'labour-money' schemes of John Bray, John Gray and Proudhonians such as Alfred Darimon. And for the same reason. They all failed to appreciate the inseparability of value from the value form, the core thesis of value-form theory. Marx observes, 'John Gray was the first to set forth the theory that labor-time is the direct measure of money in a systematic way'.[29] On that conceptual basis he proposed that banks issue 'labour-money' certifying the hours of concrete labour performed. 'Every commodity is immediately money; this is Gray's thesis which he derives from his incomplete and hence incorrect analysis of commodities'.[30] Every hour of concrete labour is immediately valid as value-producing labour: that is the thrust of Gonzalez and Posner's thinking as well.

Marx's critique commences with the point that he makes not only against Gray, Bray and Proudhonists but also against the whole of 'bourgeois' political economy: they never investigated the money form, so they never recognised the necessary polarity of the value form, of commodities and money:

> Since labor-time is the intrinsic measure of value, why use another extraneous standard as well? Why is exchange-value transformed into price? Why is the value of all commodities computed in terms of an exclusive commodity, which thus becomes the adequate expression of exchange-value, i.e., money? This was the problem that Gray had to solve. But instead of solving it, he assumed that commodities could be directly compared with one another as products of social labor.[31]

---

28 Gonzalez and Posner 2011, p. 209. They refer to Reuten 2005, p. 87. Once again the enigmatic 'we' appears. Who is doing the counting?

29 Marx 1970a, p. 83.

30 Marx 1970a, p. 85.

31 Marx 1970a, p. 84.

Marx explains why commodities cannot be treated as if they were money and hence why the polarity of commodities and money cannot be eliminated: 'But they are only comparable as the things they are. Commodities are the direct products of isolated independent individual kinds of labour, and through their alienation in the course of individual exchange they must prove that they are general social labour'.[32] Gray failed to grasp the social implications of producing wealth in the commodity form because he failed to comprehend the inseparability of value and the value form. He lacked a value-form theory of value. We should not repeat Gray's mistake.

4 Capitalism as a Monetary System

Kliman criticises value-form theory for identifying money and the monetary character of capitalism as its distinguishing feature. He writes, 'This is particularly pronounced in the work of Arthur (Arthur 2006, pp. 8–9), who argues that "capitalism is essentially a monetary system" and that money is "the actuality of value". In short, "Money rules"'.[33] But capitalism *is* essentially a monetary system: money and circulation are essential to it. And, money is the 'actuality of value', inasmuch as value cannot be actualised without it: this is a central point of value-form theory. In Arthur's account it is capital, not money, that rules, but there is no capital without money and circulation. Conversely, only when capital rules can there be a monetary system. Arthur's value-form reasoning goes like this: capital is self-valorizing value, so there can be no capital without value, but, because only the sale of the product can validate value-producing labour as socially necessary, money and circulation are essential for capital. So, 'capitalism is essentially a monetary system'. Arthur is critical of how Marx develops the concepts of value, money and circulation, and he offers a reconstruction of that development, but he agrees with Marx that they are all necessary manifestations of the capitalist mode of production. For Arthur, surplus value and capital are the truth of value and money, a truth that presupposes wage labour as the dominant social form of labour. Arthur agrees with Marx that money and circulation are presupposed by capitalist production and presuppose capitalist production. The latter point is the conceptual basis for his rejection of the very idea of a system of non-capitalist commodity production.

32 Marx 1970a, pp. 84–5. See also Marx 1976a, pp. 188–9, n. 1.

33 Kliman 2011, p. 184.

Though money and circulation, on the one hand, and capitalist production, on the other, are mutually presupposing – Arthur argues that *Capital* generally follows a logic of mutual presupposition – one could say that the capitalist mode of production is the deeper phenomenon precisely because it has the capacity for reproducing itself, a power that the sphere of commodity circulation, taken alone, lacks. Arthur's conception of value, then, is not confined to circulation; if anything, like Marx's, Arthur's theory of value is production-centred. In both cases this truth may be lost sight of because of the nature of a systematic dialectical presentation. But the order of presentation must not be mistaken for an ontological order. The fact that the commodity, exchange value, value, money and circulation are presented before capital, surplus value, wage labour, etc. does not mean that they are independent of the latter, much less that they have ontological priority – if anything, the reverse is the case.

Kliman argues that neither money nor circulation is 'the distinctive feature of capitalism'. Rather, Kliman counters, 'What he [Marx] singled out as capitalism's distinctive feature was, of course, that labor-power appears as a commodity'.[34] On this score he is doubly wrong: (1) it is distinctive to capitalism that it is a monetary system and (2) it is wrongheaded even to want to choose between these two features, since both are unique to capitalism. True, 'capitalism's characteristic feature' is that wage-labourers are continually separated from the means of production and forced to sell their labour power, but circulation and the generalisation of the commodity form make that possible – and necessary. Writing in the concluding part of *Capital* Volume III, Marx identifies two 'characteristic traits' of capitalist production. That surplus value is the direct objective of production is the second; of the first Marx writes:

> It produces its products as commodities. The fact that it produces commodities does not in itself distinguish it from other modes of production; but that the dominant and determining character of its product is that it is a commodity certainly does so. This means, first of all, that the worker himself appears only as a seller of commodities, and hence as a free wage-laborer – i.e. labor generally appears as wage-labor.[35]

Here Marx calls special attention to a point that value-form theorists highlight: the generalisation of the commodity form of wealth is an earmark of capitalism. Kliman's contest misses the point: the generalisation of the commo-

34 Kliman 2011, p. 185.

35 Marx 1981, p. 1,019.

dity form (the monetary system) and the generalisation of wage labour are mutually presupposing.

5 TSSI's Mutually Reinforcing Bad Abstractions

Hegel's logic of essence, according to which the essence necessarily appears as something other than itself, possesses the conceptual complexity needed to understand Marx's theory of value and money.[36] Exchange value (money) is the necessary form of appearance of value (which is congealed, socially necessary abstract labour); consequently, value is not independent of exchange value (money). 'Money as a measure of value is the necessary form of appearance of the measure of value which is immanent in commodities, namely labor-time'.[37] This, I believe, is the central proposition of co-constitutive value-form theory. That value is not actual and that the magnitude of value is not determinate prior to the sale of a commodity are consequences of this proposition. Exchange value (money) is not value: money is measured in ounces of gold or in dollars; value is measured in hours (of congealed socially necessary abstract labour time). Essence necessarily appears as something other than itself – value as money.

Hegel's conception of essence opposes conventional thinking about essence, which Hegel would identify with *Verstand* thinking (thinking that treats as separable what is actually only distinguishable). According to conventional thinking about essence, essence stands alone; essence appears, yes, but appearance does not belong to what essence is. Appearance manifests essence (price expresses value), but appearance is in no way constitutive of essence; essence is exactly what it is quite apart from appearance. Hegel's insight about essence is twofold. Appearance is necessary for essence. What reason would there be for asserting the existence of an essence that did not appear? But, if appearance is necessary for essence, then essence is inseparable from appearance: appearance belongs to essence; essence is not independent of appearance. To assert the independence of essence from appearance is to engage in bad abstraction. Bad abstraction – treating what is only distinguishable as separable – is the basic problem with the TSSI authors, for in rejecting value-form theory they falsely assert the independence of value from the value form, money.

---

36 See Murray 1993b, included in the present volume as Chapter 8, and Chapter 11 in Murray 1988a.

37 Marx 1976a, p. 188.

Bad abstraction recurs in the interpretive practice of TSSI authors as they read Marx and other value-form theorists. The pivotal case concerns the interpretation of Marx's account of what determines the magnitude of value. Marx reaches this conclusion: 'What exclusively determines the magnitude of the value of any article is therefore the amount of labor socially necessary, or the labor-time socially necessary for its production'.[38] Torn out of context – here is the bad abstraction – this quote sounds like a ringing endorsement of the TSSI position. But what is the missing context? Marx switches topics from the substance of value to the magnitude of value – the decisive issue for the TSSI authors – with this caution:

> The common factor in the exchange relation, or in the exchange-value of the commodity, is therefore its value. The progress of the investigation will lead us back to exchange-value as the necessary mode of expression, or form of appearance, of value. For the present, however, we must consider the nature of value independently of its form of appearance.[39]

The TSSI authors either overlook this caution or misunderstand it by taking it to mean that the magnitude of value is actually determined independently of its necessary mode of appearance, money. Eldred and Hanlon wrongly draw the conclusion that Marx is asserting the independence of the magnitude of value from the expression of value in money.[40] But to *consider* value apart from the value form is not to assert that value *is* independent of the value form. For Marx, the *substance*, *magnitude* and *form of appearance* (the value form) are distinguishable but inseparable aspects of value.

Marx is making what David Hume called a 'distinction of reason', that is, he distinguishes between aspects of something that are actually inseparable.[41] Hume gives the example of a spherical white marble globe: I can distinguish, or consider apart, the whiteness and the spherical shape of the globe, even though this whiteness and spherical shape are actually inseparable. Making a distinction of reason is of course an act of abstraction; what saves it from being a bad abstraction is that it recognises the inseparability of the aspect in question from what it is an aspect of. Before discussing what determines the magnitude of value, Marx gives us notice that he is making a distinction of reason when he considers the magnitude of value in abstraction from value's

38 Marx 1976a, p. 129.

39 Marx 1976a, p. 128.

40 Eldred and Hanlon 1981, pp. 25–6; see also 35 ff.

41 Hume 1978, pp. 24–5.

necessary form of appearance (i.e., money). In considering the magnitude of value independently of money, value's necessary form of appearance, Marx is not asserting that value is actually independent of money. On the contrary, the point of his cautionary introduction is to remind the reader that value is not independent of money, the value form. When Marx writes that exchange value is 'the necessary mode of expression, or form of appearance, of value', he is invoking the full conceptual complexity of Hegel's logic of essence. If exchange value (money) is the necessary form of appearance of value, then there is no value without money: value is not independent of money. That is the basic contention of value-form theory, which is why Marx is a value-form theorist.

'Violent abstraction' is Derek Sayer's arresting term to describe the cleaving of a mode of production into 'forces of production' and 'relations of production' that is characteristic of the conventional understanding of Marx's historical materialism.[42] 'Violent' or bad abstraction is the root of the problem in the present debate between TSSI and value-form theory as well. For Marx, the cleaving of production from distribution is one of the violent abstractions that plague economics. This point is the focus of Chapter 51 of *Capital* Volume III, 'Relations of Distribution and Relations of Production'.[43] Marx observes, 'the relations of distribution are essentially identical with these relations of production, the reverse side of the same coin, so that the two things share the same historically transitory character'.[44] A couple of pages later, Marx spells out implications for the capitalist mode of production, 'The character (1) of the product as a commodity, and (2) of the commodity as the product of capital, already includes all the relations of circulation, i.e. a specific social process which products must pass through and in which they assume specific social characters'.[45] Marx makes it clear that products of capital must pass through commodity circulation in order to assume their specific social character, that is, their character as value. So, both the TSSI production-only theory and the exchange-only value-form theory are one-sided; both engage in bad abstraction. Both cleave production from distribution.

The three bad abstractions of TSSI theorists are complementary and mutually reinforcing: (1) they falsely separate value from its necessary form of appearance, exchange value (money), (2) they falsely separate Marx's exposi-

42 See Sayer 1987.

43 See also Marx 1973, pp. 88–100.

44 Marx 1981, p. 1,018.

45 Marx 1981, p. 1,020. I have replaced 'involves' as a translation of '*einschliessen*' with 'includes.'

tion of the magnitude of value from his exposition of the value form, and (3) they falsely separate production from distribution. TSSI's bad abstractions are reminders of how difficult it is to get free of *Verstand* thinking, or what Marx called 'the bourgeois horizon'.

CHAPTER 16

The New Giant's Staircase*

As the investigation of capital in Christopher Arthur's *The New Dialectic and Marx's 'Capital'* culminates, in Chapter Eight, 'The Spectre of Capital', Arthur introduces two chilling images. First, Arthur writes, 'there is a void at the heart of capitalism'.[1] The second image draws in Cynthia Willett's idea that Hegel's logic holds the possibility of a 'hellish dialectic', an inverted, downward spiral into falsity and nothingness, the shadow of the upward-pointed spiral of being's movement toward truth and fullness of being.[2] For Arthur, value is

> a form without content, which yet takes possession of our world in the only way it can, through draining it of reality, an ontological vampire that bloats his hollow frame at our expense.[3]

In money, value appears as one more thing alongside wealth in the particular; it is as if 'the Fruit' lay next to an apple and a pear:

> If we treat value as the spiritual essence of the capitalist economy, its range of incarnations all centre on a single origin, namely money, the transubstantiated Eucharist of value.[4]

Marx calls money 'a born leveller and cynic',[5] and Georg Simmel vividly elaborates on money's capacity to drain reality from things: money

* The present chapter, 'The New Giant's Staircase', was originally published, along with six other contributions and a reply by Arthur, as a contribution to 'Debating the Hegel-Marx Connection', a symposium on Arthur's *The New Dialectic and Marx's 'Capital'*, edited by Jim Kincaid, in *Historical Materialism*, 13, 2: 61–83.

1 Arthur 2002a, p. 153.

2 In imitation of Dante's warning to those who enter the inferno, Marx hangs a warning over the threshold between the sphere of simple commodity circulation and 'the hidden abode of production', where 'we shall see not only how capital produces, but how capital itself is produced' (Marx 1976a, p. 280).

3 Arthur 2002a, p. 167.

4 Ibid.

5 Marx 1976a, p. 179.

> hollows out the core of things, their peculiarities, their specific values and their uniqueness and incomparability in a way which is beyond repair. They all rest on the same level and are distinguished only by their amounts.[6]

If value is wealth whose particularity has been boiled off, gelatinous stuff that hardens into money, then capital is value juiced up from substance to money-mad subject: active, self-relating, enlarging.[7] Capital is a spectre whom our practices have summoned into being but who now lords over us. Relentless moneymaking – capital's only unqualified 'good' – plunges in a downward spiral.

Charles Dickens shared Arthur's idea that the most disturbing aspect of capitalism is satanic indifference toward the world of particulars. His novel *Hard Times* only secondarily concerns the inequities of capitalism, the plight of factory 'hands' and the ecological and aesthetic blight brought on by capitalism's 'Coketowns'. Primarily it exposes the nihilism of capitalism and its chief ideologies, political economy and utilitarianism. *Hard Times* examines the effects of the Gradgrind educational philosophy, which insists on the facts, allows nothing to the imagination, trusts only in self-interest and treats political economy and utilitarianism as gospel truth:

> It was a fundamental principle of the Gradgrind philosophy that everything was to be paid for. Nobody was ever on any account to give anybody anything, or render anybody help without purchase. Gratitude was to be abolished, and the virtues springing from it were not to be. Every inch of the existence of mankind, from birth to death, was to be a bargain across a counter. And if we didn't get to Heaven that way, it was not a politico-economical place, and we had no business there.[8]

In Book II of *Hard Times*, Dickens introduces Mr James Harthouse, a 'fine gentleman' whose boredom with everything else left him 'going in' for the 'hard Fact fellows' of the Gradgrind party. 'He was a thorough gentleman, made to the model of the time: weary of everything and putting no more faith in anything than Lucifer'.[9] Arriving in Coketown, he drifts into seducing Thomas Gradgrind's eldest daughter, Louisa, who is married to the town's leading capitalist,

6 Simmel 1997, p. 340.

7 Max Weber quotes Ferdinand Kürnberger's remark: 'They make tallow out of cattle and money out of men' (Weber 1977, p. 353).

8 Dickens 1990, p. 212.

9 Dickens 1990, pp. 91–2.

the blustery Mr Josiah Bounderby. With Harthouse enter Arthur's two images. Harthouse's name invokes the first; he is a mere housing for a heart: 'He was touched in the cavity where his heart should have been'.[10] The second appears as Mr Bounderby's bitter housekeeper, Mrs Sparsit, imagines Louisa's seduction by Harthouse as her twisting down 'the new Giant's staircase' into the abyss.[11] Louisa's education in the Gradgrind philosophy had already thrust her into a tailspin:

> Upon a nature long accustomed to self-suppression, thus torn and divided, the Harthouse philosophy came as a relief and justification. Everything being hollow and worthless, she had missed nothing and sacrificed nothing. What did it matter, she had said to her father, when he proposed her husband. What did it matter, she said still. With a scornful self-reliance, she asked herself, What did anything matter – and went on.[12]

What is demonic about Harthouse is the indifference that creates the funnel in the cavity where his heart belonged:

> And yet he had not, even now, any earnest wickedness of purpose in him. Publicly and privately, it were much better for the age in which he lived, that he and the legion of whom he was one were designedly bad, than indifferent and purposeless. It is the drifting icebergs setting with any current anywhere, that wreck the ships.[13]

Indifference, what Simmel called 'the blasé attitude', accompanies capital's draining our world of its reality. Capital is the new, spectral giant, and the descending new giant's staircase threatens our humanity. 'The void at the heart of bourgeois life results in the most accomplished irony: accumulation as an infinite increase in emptiness is mistaken for a plenitude of wealth'.[14]

Since value is parasitical on concrete wealth and labour, the ontology of capital is more complex than this downward spiral; indeed, the competitive dynamics of capital accumulation unleash an explosion of growth. Marx identi-

10 Dickens 1990, p. 172.

11 See Dickens 1990, p. 153, n. 5.

12 Dickens 1990, p. 125.

13 Dickens 1990, p. 135. At the bottom of the giant-ringed ninth circle of Dante's inferno is ice created by the flapping of Satan's wings. I take it that Marx had this in mind in describing commodities in so far as they are values as 'merely congealed quantities of homogeneous human labour' and 'crystals of this social substance' (Marx 1976a, p. 128).

14 Arthur 2002a, p. 172.

fies two chief consequences of capitalist accumulation as (i) 'the development of the social productive forces of labour'[15] and (ii) 'to raise the quantity of production and multiply and diversify the spheres of production and their sub-spheres'.[16] But this upward spiral of expanding wealth, new types of wealth and ever-higher levels of productivity is haunted by the vacuity of its aim and its unquenchable demand for surplus labour. These contrary spirals define our historical situation, its possibilities and its impoverishments.[17]

1 Capital as Social Form

What opens the space for Arthur's inquiry into the twisted ontology of capital is his manner of answering the question: What is capital? The textbook response that capital is wealth that can be used to produce new wealth is too generic. Arthur's answer is that capital is a peculiar social form, self-valorising value, with extraordinary powers and consequences.[18] Arthur describes social form as 'one of the central concepts of the book'.[19] I would call it the central concept not only of Arthur's book but also of *Capital* and historical materialism.[20] The idea that social form reaches all the way down into a mode of production and, therefore, must be an element in the fundamental concepts of a mode of production, is Marx's watershed idea.[21] Marx succinctly makes the point in the *Grundrisse*, 'all production is appropriation of nature on the part of an individual within and through a specific form of society'.[22] Marx's deepest criticism of political economy (or economics, as we call it today) is that it is oblivious to the inescapable reality of specific social forms and purposes. Economics goes on as if its topic were the economy in general; Marx's point

15 Marx 1976d, p. 1,037.

16 Marx 1976d, p. 1,037.

17 See Postone 1993 on the 'shearing pressures' these contrary spirals create.

18 'The form-determination of capital as inherently self-expanding makes capital utterly different from any other mode of production' (Arthur 2002a, p. 146).

19 Arthur 2002a, p. 15.

20 Since Arthur writes, '[T]he question of social form is central to the Marxian understanding of economic systems' (Arthur 2002a, p. 86), any difference between us may be one of emphasis.

21 The idea that social form reaches all the way down contradicts the typical, 'technological' conception of historical materialism, according to which the 'forces of production' are not social-form-determined but, on the contrary, are the ultimate determinant of the 'relations of production'.

22 Marx 1973, p. 87.

is that there is no such thing.[23] Production always has a specific social form and purpose, from which scientific inquiry dare not abstract.

Arthur puts the phrase 'new dialectic', one he coined, into the title of this book; more particularly, he writes, '[T]his book combines two mutually supportive new trends in Marxist theory, that of systematic dialectic and that of value-form theory'.[24] These are helpful terms for classifying work in Marxian theory and Arthur's in particular. Fundamental is the divide between those who see Marxian theory as centrally about specific social forms and those who do not. Value-form theory is a theory of the specific social forms of capitalism, the value forms, that insists – against Ricardian theory, for which value is determined solely in production – that any adequate Marxian theory of value must incorporate commodity exchange and money. And systematic dialectic, as it bears on Marxian theory, aims at the most satisfactory presentation of the specific social forms of the capitalist mode of production. One gets to systematic dialectic only after first recognising that the focus of the Marxian investigation is the totality of specific social forms that constitute the capitalist mode of production and then discovering that this totality defies a linear presentation. What a Marxian systematic-dialectical presentation presents is a system of categories describing specific social forms.[25] Value-form theory and systematic dialectic are 'mutually supportive'; both belong to the social-form approach.

2 Arthur's Contributions

Arthur's contributions turn on his recognition of the centrality for Marxian theory of the specific social forms of needs, labour, wealth and so forth. It is an understatement to say that Arthur reaches his goal of vindicating the fruitfulness of his general approach. The renewal of Marxian theory to which Arthur contributes has far-reaching consequences not only for Marxism but more broadly for social and political theory, the philosophy of social science and moral philosophy.[26] I will identify several of Arthur's main contributions before evaluating two of his initiatives at reconstruction.

(i) It has become commonplace not only among mainstream authors but also among Marxists or authors sympathetic to Marx either to ignore his the-

23 'It is only in virtue of differences in social form that Marx can insist that there is no such thing as "economics" in general' (Arthur 2002a, p. 86).

24 Arthur 2002a, p. 15.

25 'Essentially, then, the presentation is of a system of categories' (Arthur 2002a, p. 85).

26 Arthur begins to explore the consequences for moral philosophy in Chapter Ten, 'Whose Reason? and Whose Revolution?'.

ory of value or to dismiss it offhandedly. Such authors usually assume that Marx adopted the untenable Ricardian labour theory of value.[27] By showing that value is all about specific social forms, Arthur makes untenable the assumption on which Marx's value theory is discarded. Marx's value theory is a world apart from Ricardo's. Because value has been misunderstood, even within Marxism, so, too, has capital, self-valorising value. Capital is not simply wealth that capitalists own and use to make more wealth. Capital is a unique and powerful social form of wealth; it has such a mind of its own that it reduces capitalists to its 'personifications'. Overthrowing capital, then, is not simply a matter of redistributing 'wealth'; it requires discovering a new social form and purpose of wealth.[28]

(ii) Arthur makes a compelling case for reading *Capital* as a systematic-dialectical presentation. What is more, he shows that systematic-dialectical presentation is required by the nature of the object under investigation. The defining social forms of capitalism form a totality; they are inseparable, which explains why they cannot be properly presented in linear fashion.

(iii) Systematic dialectic and value-form theory are 'mutually supportive',[29] just as linear presentation and Ricardian theory reinforce one another. Arthur shows why we cannot separate issues of method and presentation from substantive issues, for example, Marx's theory of money.

(iv) What is new about the 'new dialectic' is that it rejects the forced, 'Diamat' conception of dialectics as a universally applicable formalism. 'New dialectic' adheres to the Aristotelian insistence that method follow the object under study. Though Arthur holds that there is no general dialectical logic, he has much to say in general about systematic-dialectical presentations. (a) The object of a systematic-dialectical presentation – from start to finish – is a totality.[30] (b) It is imperative in such a presentation to get the right starting point. It should be sufficiently simple to be grasped immediately by thought and yet sufficiently historically determinate to lead to the other categories that structure this specific society.[31]

---

27 Some authors who accept Marx's value theory identify it with Ricardo's, 'Marx constructed his argument using "classical" value theory, the standard theory of his day, which had developed from Adam Smith through David Ricardo – the "labour theory" of value' (Schweickart 2002, p. 25).

28 In Chapter Ten: 'A Clock without a Spring: Epitaph for the USSR', Arthur explains the collapse of the Soviet Union as a failure to discover such a new social form and purpose.

29 Arthur 2002a, p. 15.

30 On capital as an organic totality see Meaney 2002.

31 Arthur 2002a, p. 27.

The commodity serves Marx's purposes because he shows that only with the capitalist mode of production does wealth generally take the commodity form. (c) Systematic-dialectical presentation moves from the conceptually more abstract to the more concrete.[32] (d) Systematic dialectic has a definite method of advance; in Arthur's words:

> systematic dialectic is based on observing whether or not the characteristic provisionally identified, in this case value as a universal property of commodities, can be objectively grounded in the stage of development (here of exchange) under review.[33]

(e) In advancing the way it does, a systematic-dialectical presentation posits the later categories as presuppositions of the earlier categories, which are themselves presuppositions of the later: it articulates 'a logic of mutual presupposition'.[34] (f) Placeholders, or 'markers',[35] such as the qualification 'socially necessary', allow for the development of concepts.[36]

---

32 'From the start the object of investigation is the capitalist totality, and this is grasped first of all abstractly and then more and more concretely' (Arthur 2002a, p. 40).

33 Arthur 2002a, p. 30. See also p. 67.

34 Arthur 2002a, p. 64. Marx rejects as idealistic the Hegelian demand that a systematic-dialectical presentation be altogether presuppositionless. I am not sure where Arthur stands on this. He quotes Marx from the *Urtext*, 'the dialectical form of presentation is right only when it knows its own limits' (Arthur 2002a, p. 74). Then he cites a *Grundrisse* passage that combines the points about mutual presupposition and the limits to presuppositionlessness: 'In the completed bourgeois system every economic relation presupposes every other in its bourgeois economic form, and everything posited is thus also a presupposition ... This organic system itself, as a totality, has its presuppositions' (Arthur 2002a, p. 74). But, Arthur wants to dissociate those presuppositions from the systematic-dialectical presentation: 'This logic does not depend in any way upon the historical development that first threw up the elementary preconditions of the system [such as the existence of 'doubly free labour'] for these are articulated and grounded within the logical ordering itself' (Arthur 2002a, p. 75). And later, in criticising Marx's (supposed) presupposition that all commodities are labour products, Arthur allows that it could be justified through an appeal to broader historical materialist considerations. But he objects that such an appeal would violate Hegelian standards for systematic-dialectical presentation: 'for any attempt to follow the model of Hegel's dialectic an absolute beginning without imposed conditions is needed' (Arthur 2002a, p. 158).

35 Arthur 2002a, p. 58.

36 'Socially necessary labour time' is 'insufficiently determinate' at the outset (Arthur 2002a, p. 40).

(v) Since the object of a systematic-dialectical presentation is a totality, 'the order of Marx's presentation is not that of a sequence of models of more and more complex objects, but that of a progressive development of the forms of the same object, namely capitalism, from a highly abstract initial concept of it to more and more concrete levels of its comprehension'.[37]

By showing that *Capital* is about capital from the beginning, Arthur demolishes the myth that Part I is about 'simple commodity production', adding the revelation that Engels was the source of the one mention of 'simple commodity production' in *Capital*. Arthur pursues the issue further, arguing that, even if we imagine a pre-capitalist society of commodity producers, there would be no value because no mechanisms would exist to enforce the law of value.[38] He closes the book on 'simple commodity production' with a quote from Marx that confirms his reading of *Capital* as a systematic-dialectical presentation:

> the concept of value wholly belongs to the latest political economy, because that concept is the most abstract expression of capital itself and of the production based upon it.[39]

Consider what this means for the bourgeois conception of (commutative) justice as equal value for equal value. If there is no value without capital, there is no value without surplus value, so the exploitation of wage workers becomes the condition of bourgeois justice.

(vi) Lenin made famous the idea that not only Hegel's conception of systematic dialectic but also his logic is vital to the construction of *Capital*. Several of Arthur's most distinctive contributions concern how to think about the relation between *Capital* and Hegel's logic:

> It is a running theme of this book that interesting, and illuminating, connections may be drawn between Marx's *Capital* and aspects of Hegel's idealist philosophy, because capital itself is a very peculiar object, requiring conceptualization in forms analogous to those of Hegel's 'Idea'.[40]

It is not simply that capital is peculiar in being a totality; that is enough to require a systematic-dialectical approach. The abstract quality of the value

37 Arthur 2002a, p. 18. See also, Arthur 2002a, pp. 33–4.
38 Arthur 2002a, p. 19.
39 Arthur 2002a, p. 24. Marx 1986, pp. 159–60.
40 Arthur 2002a, p. 137.

forms, their self-movement, and their power to subsume concrete wealth and labour resemble Hegel's logical categories. 'The logic of the value-forms in their self-relating abstraction is an incarnation in social terms of the self-movement of thought in Hegel's logic'.[41] For Arthur, this is so much the worse for capital:

> The very fact that capital is homologous with the Idea is a reason for criticising it as an inverted reality in which self-moving abstractions have the upper hand over human beings.[42]

Still, the homology is not complete: capital only mimics the Idea; it cannot succeed in encompassing all its presuppositions. The recalcitrance of nature and wage workers to capital's designs may be managed but not eliminated:

> [N]o genuine unity in difference is achieved, and ... the material and ideal sides of the economy remain estranged from one another no matter how much mediating complexes attempt to secure 'room to move' for the contradictions.[43]

3 Evaluating Two Reconstructive Initiatives

Though 'new dialectic' is characterised by a return to sources, primarily Hegel and Marx, and, though Arthur describes *Capital* as 'a veritable treasure of dialectic',[44] he, like others pursuing a systematic-dialectical approach to capital, finds reasons to reconstruct Marxian value theory. First, Arthur fixes the meanings of value and capital as 'pure forms' before introducing labour. Second, drastically altering Claudio Napoleoni's idea, he proposes a twofold concept of exploitation that situates it primarily in production rather than exchange. I do not find either reconstruction necessary. Neither do I share the lingering suspicion that I think motivates them, namely, that *Capital* falls short of being a thoroughgoing rejection of Ricardian value theory's obliviousness to the value forms.[45] I will explain my reasons, beginning with the first initiative; it requires a complicated response.

41 Arthur 2002a, p. 106.
42 Arthur 2002a, p. 8.
43 Arthur 2002a, p. 108.
44 Arthur 2002a, p. 3.
45 See Arthur 2002a, p. 85 for a passage in which Arthur is quick to blend Marx into the Marxist tradition, much of which is Ricardian Marxist.

3.1 *Deferring the Introduction of Labour: Value and Capital as 'Pure Forms'*

Arthur sketches his first reconstruction:

> Now as to my own work presented here. One thing which I see as consequent on value-form theory is that, if it is predicated on analysis of exchange-forms in the first place, it should not be in too much of a hurry to address the content. It is notorious that Marx dives down from the phenomena of exchange-value to labour as the substance of value in the first three pages of *Capital* and people rightly complain they do not find any proof there. So I argue in several places here that we must first study the development of the value-form and only address the labour content when the dialectic of the forms itself requires us to do so.[46]

Several points can be sorted here. (i) Arthur thinks that he can, indeed he must, determine what the value form is independently of any content. (This is problematic for the usual Aristotelian reasons: as pure as they are, even Hegel's logical forms are forms of thought). Likewise, Arthur thinks that he can, and must, determine what the value form is in terms of the sphere of exchange independently of production. (This is problematic in light of Marx's insistence on the inseparability of production and exchange). (ii) The charge that Marx is 'in too much of a hurry' to get to the labour content is, as it stands, a gripe, not an argument. Its source, I think, is Arthur's suspicion that *Capital* is tainted by Ricardian value theory and a Ricardian Marxist preoccupation with exploitation, understood simply as unjust distribution.[47] (iii) In the background lies the charge, made explicitly elsewhere, that, in order to introduce labour in the opening pages of *Capital*, Marx must make either the false assumption that all commodities are products of labour or the gratuitous one that only such commodities matter. (iv) Arthur argues that, because of the provisional nature of

46 Arthur 2002a, p. 12. 'I refuse to find it necessary to come to labour until after the conceptualization of capital as a form-determination' (Arthur 2002a, p. 85). *Refuse* to find it necessary?

47 Consider these two passages. 'Marx moves so quickly to his "substance" of value that we lose sight of the fact that value is actual only in the fully developed concept (namely capital). Hence sometimes the impression is given in his discussion that a prior content, labour, reduces the value-form to its mere phenomenal expression' (Arthur 2002a, p. 105). 'He [Marx] has a critique of form (fetishism) as well as a critique of content (exploitation); but in his anxiety to relate value to production he had already jumped – far too hastily – to labour as its substance' (Arthur 2002a, p. 87).

the early stages in a systematic-dialectical presentation, Marx cannot prove, at the conceptual level of commodity circulation, even the necessity that there be value as distinct from exchange-value.

I evaluate this initiative in three steps. First, I consider why Arthur stresses commodity exchange and money.[48] Second, I spell out what Arthur believes is ill-conceived in Marx's presentation and follow up with a defence of Marx. Third, I consider Arthur's reconstruction itself.

'Material abstraction' is Arthur's term for describing what happens in commodity exchange and for thinking about the nihilistic twist that value gives capitalist society:[49]

> This 'material abstraction' ... produces an 'inverted reality' in which commodities simply instantiate their abstract essence as values; and concrete labours count only as lumps of abstract labour.[50]

The crucible of 'material abstraction' is commodity exchange, where concrete use value is transubstantiated into abstract value incarnate in money. Money makes value possible. Measuring value in money works in just the opposite way to the Heisenberg Principle; instead of measurement introducing uncertainty, the determination of merely 'latent' value is impossible without measurement.[51]

In his zeal to avoid Ricardian insensitivity to social form, Arthur, I believe, overshoots his goal and arrives at a position in between Marx's and the one-

---

48 Alfred Sohn-Rethel's way of thinking about commodity exchange as a social process of abstraction from use value analogous to intellectual abstraction surely is an influence.

49 I propose 'practical abstraction' as a preferable term to Arthur's 'material abstraction'. 'Practical' seems more descriptively accurate, since the abstraction takes place in the practice of commodity exchange. The phrase 'practical abstraction' would also affirm the legitimacy of the term 'practical' in Marx's materialism, on which Arthur casts doubt. He complains that Marx 'gives an "idealist" reading even of concrete labour, as a "form-giving fire" that freezes into fixity' (Arthur 2002a, p. 169). Calling this 'idealist', even if in scare quotes, is surprising. Marx is talking here about action. There is nothing 'idealist' in that unless we assume that Marx's materialism excludes action and form from the world. But Marx distanced himself from such materialism in his *Theses on Feuerbach*. Finally, 'practical abstraction' matches what I have argued – drawing on work by Arthur – is our best way to talk about the specific social form of labour that produces value, namely, as 'practically abstract' labour (Murray 2000a, included in the present volume as Chapter 4).

50 Arthur 2002a, p. 80.

51 'The actuality of value and its expression or measure develop together at the same time' (Arthur 2002a, p. 96).

sided type of 'value form' position associated with Michael Eldred and the Konstanz-Sydney group.[52] To explain, let me sketch four positions on value and money; the first altogether overlooks the topic of the value form; the last three represent different versions of value-form theory.

(i) The Ricardian position is that value is embodied labour; value is fully determined qualitatively and quantitatively in the sphere of production. Value is independent of money (indeed it is the independent variable that explains price, the dependent variable); money serves merely as a label for value and a convenient instrument for exchange. (ii) Eldred's type of value-form theory is the polar opposite of the Ricardian. It confines the qualitative and quantitative determination of value to the sphere of commodity exchange. Any mention of value prior to exchange is out, and any talk about value in terms other than monetary ones stops making sense. As Arthur says of it, 'the labour theory of value as a (causal) theory of price determination is dispensed with'.[53] (iii) Marx's theory insists on the inseparability of value, whose substance is congealed abstract labour of a particular social type, 'practically abstract' labour (labour that is socially validated – in commodity exchange – *as* abstract), from money, which is value's necessary form of appearance. (Consequently, though time is the 'inner' measure of abstract labour, value can be observed only in the movements of price). According to Marx's theory, the qualitative and quantitative determination of value overlaps production and exchange (in keeping with the inseparability of production and exchange), so that value is 'latent' in the sphere of production; it can be actualised only by being sold.[54] Value

52 Arthur 2002a, p. 14. Overreaction to Ricardian neglect of social form is detectable in this passage: 'the question of form is so crucial that the presentation starts with the form of exchange, bracketing entirely the question of the mode of production, if any, of the objects of exchange' (Arthur 2002a, p. 86). Why assume that proper attention to social form requires bracketing production? Is not production form-determined by value? Is there a Ricardian slip in Arthur's reasoning? And what happens to the inseparability of production and exchange? Something is fishy about the 'if any' too. Are we seriously to entertain the hypothesis that a society's 'heap' of commodities can be renewed with no mode of production, no labour? If we are, then why not entertain the same hypothesis when we get to capital, where, in order to bring labour into his presentation, Arthur has to reject that very hypothesis: 'The activity of production is an activity of labour' (Arthur 2002a, p. 105). Labour is just as necessary for renewing the 'heap' of commodities as it is for accumulating capital. When Marx brings labour into the presentation near the beginning, he is not lacking justification.

53 Arthur 2002a, p. 14.

54 Marx 1970a, p. 45. Marx expresses the overlapping as follows, 'on the one hand, commodities must enter the exchange process as materialised universal labour-time, on the other

and price, though bound in a causal nexus, are not related as independent to dependent variable, respectively. (iv) Arthur's position is close to Marx's in that, in the end, he attributes the quantitative determination of value – still necessarily actualised by money and exchange – to (socially necessary) abstract labour. Closer to the Eldred position is Arthur's insistence that the value form itself is determined exclusively in exchange, independently of labour and the sphere of production. For Arthur, value is a pure, contentless form, which necessarily subsumes labour, whereas, for Marx, we cannot abstract the value form from a peculiar social type of labour:

> I differ from Marx in that I believe it is possible, through the power of abstraction, to push back the beginning beyond 'the commodity form of the product' to the world of commodity exchange as such.[55]

For Marx, positing a 'world of commodity exchange as such' involves bad abstraction; the real world of generalised commodity exchange is inseparable from the capitalist mode of production.[56] The parallel to Hegel for Marx is not between contentless logical forms and contentless value forms but between forms of pure thought and forms of pure labour.

Arthur emphases the similarities between 'material abstraction' and abstract thinking:

> I lay great stress on the way exchange abstracts from the heterogeneity of commodities and treats them as instances of a universal, namely value. This parallels the way the abstractive power of thought operates; and it gives rise to a homologous structure to logical forms, namely the value-forms.[57]

Worry over abstractions in modern thought animated the philosopher George Berkeley. He cautioned philosophers, scientists (political economists included) and mathematicians against 'abstract ideas' and what he saw as their primary

hand, the labour-time of individuals becomes materialised universal labour-time only as the result of the exchange process' (Marx 1970a, p. 45).

55 Arthur 2002a, n. 24, p. 36.

56 'The production and circulation of commodities ... by no means require capitalist production for their existence, on the other hand it is only on the basis of capitalist production that the commodity first becomes the general form of the product' (Marx 1988a, pp. 312–13).

57 Arthur 2002a, p. 8.

ill consequences: scepticism, materialism and atheism (and, in the economic sphere, mercantilism and prejudice against paper money). Because we can separate in words what we cannot separate in reality, our language can trick us into treating as actual what are only 'abstract ideas'. Berkeley arrived at his immaterialism by arguing that material substance, understood as pure extension, is not actual because we have no perceptions of pure extension; perceptions involving extension always include at least tactile feelings or sensations of colour. Material substance and other 'abstract ideas' haunted the modern mind, warned Berkeley.[58]

If 'abstract ideas' weighed on Berkeley's mind, Arthur's is engulfed by 'material abstraction': it is our lives and world, not simply our minds and theories, that are under the spell of false abstractions:

> With the ever-extending commodification of all material things and persons, and the inscribing of all relations within the value-form, then mere abstraction is loosed upon the world. Pure forms ... are objectively present in a realm other than pure thought.[59]

The 'material abstraction' that occurs in commodity exchange is the forge from which emerges the metallic giant, capital – '[T]he spirit is made metal and stalks among us' – an abstraction not only incarnate but gyrating along its course of relentless self-expansion.[60] We inhabit an inverted world where 'individuals are now ruled by abstractions'.[61] It is a world chronically wasting away as we descend the new giant's staircase, for, as Hegel said, '[T]o make abstractions hold good in actuality means to destroy actuality'.[62]

---

58 On the parallel between Marx's argument in Chapter One for abstract labour as the 'substance' of value and Descartes' famous analysis, in the second of his *Meditations*, of material substance in the bit-turned-blob of wax, see Murray 1988a, p. 132, and Postone 1993, p. 142.

59 Arthur 2002a, p. 107.

60 Arthur 2002a, p. 167. Dickens depicts Bounderby as a giant with a metallic laugh.

61 Marx 1973, p. 164. Marx highlights the perversity of this situation: 'What chiefly distinguishes a commodity from its owner is the fact that every other commodity counts for it only as the form of appearance of its own value. A born leveler and cynic, it is always ready to exchange not only soul, but body, with each and every other commodity, be it more repulsive than Maritornes herself. The owner makes up for this lack in the commodity of a sense of the concrete, physical body of the other commodity, by his own five and more senses' (Marx 1976a, p. 179).

62 Hegel 1955, p. 425.

Now we turn to consider two of Arthur's objections to Marx. The foremost, and familiar, complaint goes back to Böhm-Bawerk. In order to arrive at labour as the one and only thing that all commodities have in common, Marx must make either the false assumption that all commodities are products of labour or the gratuitous one that only they deserve consideration. Marx barely starts his 'masterwork' and already he has flubbed it – so the story goes. Arthur appears to accept this, writing, 'this commodity form attaches to things that are not even products of labour ... even if these are excluded by fiat'.[63] But Marx neither assumes, falsely, that all commodities are products of labour nor assumes, gratuitously, that only such commodities deserve consideration. As for the former, not only is there something unlikely about Marx missing a point obvious to the casual observer, there is the glaring fact that in his 1859 *Critique*, Marx writes:

> the last, and apparently decisive objection [to any labour theory of value] ... is this: if exchange-value is nothing but the labour-time contained in a commodity, how does it come about that commodities which contain no labour possess exchange-value.[64]

Marx goes on to say that his answer to the objection lies in his theory of rent (which he developed – unbeknownst to Böhm-Bawerk – before the publication of the first volume). So Marx's plan is to incorporate non-products into his value theory.

A second striking fact shows that Marx does not exclude non-products. In Chapter Three: 'Money or the Circulation of Commodities', Marx calls attention to the fact that the price form applies to products and non-products alike:

> The price-form ... may also harbour a qualitative contradiction, with the result that price ceases altogether to express value, despite the fact that money is nothing but the value-form of commodities ... Hence a thing can, formally speaking, have a price without having a value.[65]

What Marx holds to be compatible, indeed unavoidable, Arthur takes as compelling evidence against Marx's position:

63 Arthur 2002a, p. 28. See also, Arthur 2002a, p. 36, n. 24, and p. 86.

64 Marx 1970a, p. 63.

65 Marx 1867, p. 197.

> the argument that there is indeed a content to the value-form in labour cannot be correct as far as the pure form of exchange is concerned because many non-products are coherently inscribed within the form.[66]

Marx's two-step argument counters the prima facie plausibility of Arthur's objection. First, wealth generally takes the form of a commodity, that is, has a price, only because of the specific social form of labour, so the price form is not a 'pure form' independent of production. Second, it belongs to the nature of the price form (due to the independence of money from a commodity) that non-products can have prices.

This response throws into question Arthur's assertions:

> Marx failed to grasp that this implies a method of exposition which engages the value-form first, and then provides reasons to narrow the focus of the enquiry to products, rather than one that starts from production, i.e. 'value', and then inexplicably allows the scope of the commodity form to include non-values.[67]

But Marx doesn't 'narrow the focus of the enquiry to products', and he doesn't start *Capital* with 'production'; he starts simultaneously with exchange and production, in keeping with his insistence on the inseparability of production and exchange.[68] Arthur tries to give Marx a Ricardian collar here by referring to 'production' and 'value' in a one-sided way that ignores the context in which Marx brings in labour and value, namely, the context of wealth in the commodity form. Arthur charges that Marx 'inexplicably' expands the scope of the commodity form to include non-commodities. But Marx never excludes the non-products, so there is no need to expand the scope. As for their inclusion being 'inexplicable', Marx's account of the price form provides an explanation. Arthur writes as if Marx stumbles into an embarrassing admission about non-

66 Arthur 2002a, p. 157. By talking about non-products being inscribed in the 'pure form of exchange', I take it that Arthur just means that non-products have prices.

67 Arthur 2002a, p. 157.

68 By starting with wealth in the commodity form, Marx begins with exchange. He begins with production inasmuch as he assumes that, though some commodities will not be products, production is required to keep the 'heap' of commodities streaming into the market. Moreover, production will be value-form-determined. Insofar as Marx starts with production, then, he does not start with production in general or production independent of exchange; by the same token, the labour that produces value is not some generic labour. Marx's beginning is not presuppositionless.

products when, in fact, he knows exactly where he is going and why. To summarise, neither the charge of leading with a falsehood nor that of theorising 'by fiat' will stick. What, then, is Marx doing?

At the beginning of *Capital*, Marx indicates that he will examine the commodity as the 'economic cell-form' of capitalist society, while, in his plan for *Capital*, Marx intends to consider capital in general first. Interpretive charity, along with these and other systematic considerations, suggests the following answer: where the 'heap' of commodities and capital in general are concerned, Marx's claims about commodities and capitals do not hold for each commodity or capital taken individually but to commodities and capitals as representative parts of the sum of commodities and capitals, respectively. The 'heap' of commodities will include both produced and non-produced commodities, while the total social capital will include industrial, merchant and interest-bearing capitals. The only way that a representative part of the 'heap' would not be a product of labour would be if no commodities were products of labour. Since we are assuming that wealth generally takes the commodity form, this amounts to saying that a society's wealth could be renewed with no labour. Likewise, the only way that a representative part of the total social capital would not involve labour would be if no capital employed labour. Since Marx assumes that labour is required to meet human needs, he assumes that a representative commodity will be a product of labour and that a representative capital will employ labour. Understood in this way, Marx's claims are neither false nor gratuitous.

This heuristic, 'representative-part' strategy serves Marx's systematic-dialectical purposes well. It allows Marx to establish truths about the 'heap' of commodities that do not hold for each commodity in it and truths about capital in general that do not hold for each capital. Consider what this strategy implies in two other cases. First, take the apparent contradiction between the Volume I theory that commodities sell at their values and the Volume III theory that they sell at their prices of production. The conventional notion is that the theory of prices of production that Marx introduces in Volume III in order to solve the problem of the different organic compositions of capital supersedes – in the sense of falsifying – what he claims about the value of commodities in Volume I. But if the Volume I theory applies not to all commodities taken individually but rather to a heuristic, representative commodity, then the claims of Volume I, though superseded by more complex truths, are not falsified. Second, the representative-part strategy forces us to reconsider the assumptions of the traditional 'transformation problem'. This supposed problem assumes that, in Volume III, Marx retracts the earlier assertion that all individual commodities sell at their values for the new claim that they do not;

rather they sell at their prices of production. I do not think that Marx ever asserts that individual commodities sell at their values, which he knows to be false. (Marx developed his theory of prices of production before Volume I was published.) Marx did not organise *Capital* by deliberately making false claims (e.g. that all commodities are products of labour, that only such commodities matter or that individual commodities sell at their values) that he knew his own theory would force him to retract. The representative-part strategy saves Marx from such embarrassments. Marx develops his concepts and theory as he goes along in *Capital* – so we rightly think of the earlier stages as being superseded by the latter – but not at the price of retracting what he established earlier.[69]

In a second objection to Marx, Arthur argues that the provisional nature of the early stages in a systematic-dialectical presentation keeps Marx from proving, at the conceptual level of commodity circulation, that value must exist as distinct from exchange value. I believe that Arthur wrongly makes proving something at an earlier stage depend on grounding it at later stage. Arthur seems to think that, because the reality of value can be grounded only once the concept of capital has been introduced (a point I accept), no proof of value can be offered at the level of commodity circulation.[70] But we can accept the early proofs and still grant, in the context of the full presentation, that they are provisional. They may be provisional in the manner discussed above: truths about heuristic representative parts are superseded by more differentiated truths (as prices of production supersede values). Or they may be provisional in the sense that the earlier truths incorporate terms that function as placeholders – as 'socially necessary' functions in the definition of value-producing labour –

69 In discussing Hegel's *Philosophy of Right*, Arthur concludes with an observation along the lines of what I am arguing here: 'This illustrates ... a general point about systematic dialectic: that nothing is lost, that every "refuted" position is yet preserved within a more comprehensive form of realisation of the concept in question, here that of "right"' (Arthur 2002a, p. 70). I present Marx's representative-part strategy as one way in which truth is preserved.

70 Arthur writes: 'The existence of value is a condition of market exchange being more than an aggregation of accidental transactions, but a systematically unified and ordered process, with some stability, permanence and continuity'. This looks like a proof of value, yet he discounts it, 'But at this stage of the presentation this is by no means secured' (Arthur 2002a, p. 94). However, Marx assumes market exchange that is 'a systematically unified and ordered process, with some stability, permanence and continuity'. So we do have a proof, though we have not yet shown that this market system presupposes the capitalist mode of production. We can know that value exists without full knowledge of why.

whose meanings are specified in the course of the presentation. Systematic dialectic builds truth on truth, not on a scaffold of 'maybes'.[71]

Arthur's criticisms of Marx largely supply his reasons for deferring the introduction of labour. We may note two disadvantages that Arthur's deferred introduction of labour has in comparison to Marx's presentation. The commodity raises questions of quality and quantity. We want to know not only how it is that diverse commodities exchange for one another but also why each has the specific exchange value it does. Because he insists that the value form is without content, Arthur's answer to the first question teeters on tautology: commodities are mutually exchangeable because they have the '*quality* of being exchangeable'.[72] As for the quantitative question, Arthur refuses any answer other than 'exchangeability is measured by exchangeability'[73] until much later. Second, when Arthur introduces the formula for capital, M-C-M', he can offer no explanation for the monetary increment in M'.

I may not fully understand Arthur's way of bringing labour back into the theory of value. When, after describing wage workers as uniquely recalcitrant toward capital's objectives, he writes, '[T]his is why, for a theory grounded on the social form of the economy, labour is to be correlated with value',[74] I do not see the argument. In any case, Arthur does not introduce labour as the content of the value form – according to Arthur it has none – but as a content subsumed under it (albeit necessarily so). I see why, on Arthur's way of developing the systematic dialectic, labour must be subsumed (formally and really) and thereby form-determined by value, but I do not see why that makes labour the sole source of value and labour time the magnitude of value. A simpler point eludes me. How could value have any magnitude at all if it is pure, contentless form? Arthur wants to keep the value form contentless and yet have labour determine the magnitude of value; I do not see how he can have it both ways.[75]

71 By contrast, Arthur writes, 'Thus every move in my argument was not one from an established truth to a valid implication but, contrariwise, a movement towards truth from a hopelessly provisional starting point' (Arthur 2002a, p. 107).

72 Arthur 2002a, p. 90.

73 Ibid.

74 Arthur 2002a, p. 54.

75 Arthur appears to recognise the problem when he writes: 'But in so far as value is – as yet – determined as pure form, there is nothing substantial (analogous to mass or extension) to measure' (Arthur 2002a, p. 100). This 'as yet' suggests that his plan is to conceive of value as pure form only provisionally, but I do not grasp the strategy for reconceiving value once he introduces labour. See also Arthur 2002a, pp. 105–6, where Arthur writes of the value form sinking into the matter and 'then' developing it 'as its own content' and of the value form seeking 'to stabilise itself through subsuming the matter and turning it into a bearer

3.2 *A New Concept of Exploitation*

In a second reconstructive initiative, Arthur advances a new concept of exploitation that eliminates the extremes of Claudio Napoleoni's proposal. Reacting to Ricardian Marxist disregard of social form, in particular of the formal and real subsumption of production and labour under capital, Napoleoni went so far in stressing capital's grip on production as to claim that labour is reduced to a mere instrument of production. He therefore attributed all 'productive power' to capital. With capital, not labour, as the source of all value and surplus value, the usual conception of exploitation as the expropriation of surplus value produced by workers must be abandoned. Napoleoni's new concept of exploitation concerns production alone; it amounts to renaming the phenomena of alienation, inversion and domination by capital.[76]

Arthur rejects Napoleoni's extreme assertions:

> Albeit that the production process is really subsumed by capital, the problem for capital is that it needs the agency of labour. It is not really a matter of reducing the worker to the status of a mere instrument of production, like a machine, or like an animal whose will has to be broken. It is a matter of bending the will to alien purposes ... They act for capital, indeed as capital, but still in some sense act.[77]

Arthur calls the labour of wage workers 'counterproductive' to emphasise their resistance to capital, which he describes as 'ontologically constitutive'[78] of capital. Still, he grants that they do produce value: 'I do not follow Napoleoni in abandoning entirely the labour theory of value, or the possibility of a measure of exploitation in surplus-value'.[79] Arthur does affirm Napoleoni's shift to production as the primary site of exploitation. So Arthur ends up with a twofold notion of exploitation:

> Exploitation in production is in effect not dissimilar to alienation in that it involves the subjection of workers to alien purposes; it goes on throughout

---

of self-valorization'. These depictions of the value form seem to posit it as already existing before sinking into or subsuming content.

76 'By a neat twist Napoleoni reintroduced the term 'exploitation' as the appropriate characterisation of the very alienating relationship that makes nonsense of the old definition!' (Arthur 2002a, p. 50).

77 Arthur 2002a, p. 52.

78 Arthur 2002a, p. 57.

79 Arthur 2002a, p. 52.

> the day. Exploitation in distribution arises from the discrepancy between the new wealth created and the return to those exploited in production.[80]

Arthur's first notion, like Napoleoni's original proposal, just renames alienation, while the second doubles back to the traditional conception. Arthur's twofold conception of exploitation has the awkward consequence that exploitation goes on all day in one sense and doesn't in another. Though the substance of Arthur's view is right, the renaming device seems unnecessary and confusing. Arthur might do better to stick with his point – against Ricardian Marxism – that Marx's theory of value is already a theory of alienation, inversion and domination and then let exploitation come in, as Marx does, with the concept of surplus value.[81]

4 Conclusion: 'The Void at the Heart of Bourgeois Society'

Above all, Arthur is the ontologist of value and capital, which is self-valorising value. Since value, money and capital are peculiar social forms involving peculiar social purposes, it is his attention to social form that makes Arthur's ontological project possible.[82] By contrast, the obliviousness of economics to social form is responsible for its barren concept of capital as wealth-producing wealth and closes off the ontological investigation. This is not surprising, since the capitalist mode of production presents itself as if it were 'production in general,' a point to which Marx returns throughout *Capital*. Because 'new dialectic' holds to the Aristotelian demand that method follow the nature of the object of investigation, ontology must take the lead: it is the self-reflexive and totalising character of capital that requires a systematic-dialectical approach.

80 Arthur 2002a, p. 56.

81 'I argued that the critical edge of his [Marx's] work does not merely lie in substantive demonstrations of just how exploitation is possible in a system founded on equal exchanges but penetrates to the very structures of the value-form, whose logic is a manifestation of the fact that capital is a structure of estrangement founded on the inversion of form and content, universal and particular etc. insofar as exchange-value dominates use-value' (Arthur 2002a, p. 106).

82 Though they got it better than anyone else, neither Hegel nor Marx, writes Arthur, 'understood just how "peculiar" a money economy is' (Arthur 2002a, p. 9). I believe that Arthur underestimates Marx; it is one more expression of his suspicion of residual Ricardianism in Marx.

Adam Smith described the marketplace as 'the great scramble'. It is an image well suited to reinforce the idea that the market is a clearinghouse for the satisfaction of individual preferences. As a value-form theorist, Arthur takes an intense interest in commodities, money and the market, since – here is the point Ricardian value theory misses – they belong to the spectral ontology of value and capital. Combining systematic dialectic with value-form theory, Arthur shows that money and the market are not mere commercial instruments for the 'efficient' distribution of 'wealth' produced by 'industry' ('production in general'); they are necessary to a form of production gripped by the 'false infinite' of endless moneymaking. The liberal idea that the market establishes a place free of any commanding social purpose is exposed as an illusion. On the contrary, what Arthur shows is that 'the great scramble' of the market has a purpose; it is capital's purpose, and it sucks us dry.[83]

83 I would like to thank Jeanne Schuler for her help.

CHAPTER 17

In Defence of the 'Third Thing Argument': A Reply to James Furner's 'Marx's Critique of Samuel Bailey'*

Examining Marx's theory of value through his critique of Samuel Bailey, James Furner intends to undermine Marx's 'third thing argument' – that exchange value expresses value – and to support Chris Arthur's proposal to reconstruct Marxian theory by introducing labour into the theory of value at the conceptual level of capital.[1] Furner concludes, 'It would therefore be surprising if Marxists were to continue to give much positive weight to the "third thing argument"'.[2] I believe that it is a serious mistake to dismiss the 'third thing argument'. Marx's theory of value cannot do without it, and if you are going to do without Marx's theory of value, you might as well do without his critical theory of the capitalist mode of production.

Furner separates his discussion of value theory into three parts, looking first at the simple commodity, then at money and capital. He claims that Marx's case in Chapter One of *Capital* against Bailey's identification of value with exchange value – and in favour of his own (labour) theory of value – is fallacious. According to Furner, Marx's polemic against Bailey's value theory, a forerunner of modern utility theories, becomes effective only when we advance to the theory of money (Marx's value theory explains the necessity of money where Bailey's does not) and, all the more so, when we move to the level of capital, where Bailey's insistence that comparisons of value across time are

* * Originally published as 'In Defence of the "Third Thing Argument": A Reply to James Furner's "Marx's Critique of Samuel Bailey"', in *Historical Materialism*, Volume 14, Issue 2 (2006), pp. 149–68. James Furner's, 'Marx's Critique of Samuel Bailey' appeared in *Historical Materialism*, 12, 2 (2004), pp. 89–110.

1 Marx's critique of Bailey is part of the manuscript of 1861–3; it was published in Part III of *Theories of Surplus-Value* (Marx 1971a, pp. 124–68).

2 Furner 2004, p. 108. It is not clear how much weight the argument is given presently. Allen Wood suggests (implausibly) that Marx himself did not take it very seriously, 'Despite its prominent place in *Capital*, Marx's "proof" of the law of value is not taken seriously as such by its author. I think it is best regarded as an expository device, part of Marx's avowed attempt to "popularize" his discussion of value in *Capital*' (Wood 1981, p. 228).

nonsensical makes any understanding of capital impossible. Furner writes, with Chris Arthur and others in mind:

> Many discussions of Marx's theory of value focus on a couple of pages in Section One of Chapter One of *Capital*. In these passages, Marx is quick to distinguish between exchange-value and value as a purely social aspect of commodities and to identify its source in (abstract) labour. A number of contemporary advocates of Marx's theory of value stress that neither issue can be resolved at this point.[3]

Furner is not arguing that Marx's value theory – in particular, the claims that value is a 'purely social' objectivity belonging to commodities that is distinguishable, though inseparable, from their exchange value; and that value's 'source' is (abstract) labour – is indefensible. On the contrary, Furner writes as an advocate of Marxian value theory. His point is that Marx's theory cannot be established at the conceptual level of the commodity (Chapter One) and by means of the 'third thing argument' but only as we move to the more complex phenomena of money and capital.

Furner is right to contrast my view with Chris Arthur's:

> With regard to the relation between value and 'abstract' labour, a difference emerges between Patrick Murray's turn to Section Four of Chapter One on commodity fetishism, in which Marx sets out from a system of production organised in private yet materially dependent units in order to

3 Furner 2004, pp. 89–90. The idea that Marx identifies '(abstract) labour' as the 'source' of value is problematic since Marx calls '(abstract) labour' the 'substance' of value. Source and substance are two different concepts. The moon is the source of tides but not their substance; the connection between moon and tides is empirical, not conceptual. Marx argues that socially necessary 'abstract' labour of the social sort that produces commodities belongs to what value is. In Chapter One Marx distinguishes three inseparable aspects of the complex phenomenon of value and treats each in turn: the substance of value, the measure of value and the form of value. Marx identifies 'abstract' labour as the substance of value, labour time as the immanent (not directly observable) measure of value and exchange value as the form of value. That Furner says 'source' where Marx has 'substance' is not accidental; it exposes a dilemma facing Arthur's proposal for reconstructing Marxian value theory. If we can know what value is without any reference to labour, then labour ('abstract' labour) does not belong to the concept of value. Consequently, when labour is brought in (once we get to the level of capital, in Arthur's proposal), it will have to be brought in as value's 'source' rather than its 'substance'. If we cannot know what value is at the level of simple commodity exchange, how will we develop Marx's concepts of money and capital?

> demonstrate why commodities acquire an 'objectivity as values' [*Wertgegenständlichkeit*], and Chris Arthur's account turned towards the category of capital.[4]

Furner's conclusion that Marx's 'third thing argument' fails, and that it must do so, supports Arthur's reconstructive initiative. Since I maintain that Marxian value theory does not require the reconstruction Arthur proposes – what is more, I do not see how the reconstruction can work – I need to show that, where these conclusions are concerned, Furner is mistaken.[5] That is what I propose to do here.

1 Do Commodities 'Have' Exchange Values?

Furner argues that Marx's 'third thing argument', which is presented in the first section of Chapter One of *Capital*, begs the question. Furner first cites the passage where Marx reasons from the fact that a given commodity has multiple exchange values to the conclusions that 'the valid exchange-values of a particular commodity express something equal, and secondly, exchange-value cannot be anything other than the mode of expression, the "form of appearance", of a content distinguishable from it'.[6] Furner comments:

> This passage begins by considering the fact of a given commodity's exchange with many other commodities. These exchange-values are said to be exchange-values the wheat 'has'. To say that the exchange-values belong to the wheat is taken to imply that there is something of which the wheat is further possessed by virtue of which it has exchange-values. To grant the wheat such an intrinsic property allows one to say that there is a constancy that x boot-polish or y silk or z gold each represent and which makes them 'of identical magnitude'. There is thus more to Marx's reference to equality than the fact that a diverse set of commodities exchange

4 Furner 2004, p. 90. If Furner's contrast is meant to imply that I adopt the traditional interpretation that Chapter One is about a pre-capitalist system of 'simple commodity production' – I am not sure that it is – it is mistaken. *Capital* is about the capitalist mode of production from the start.

5 I criticise Arthur's reconstructive initiative in 'The New Giant's Staircase', my contribution to *Historical Materialism*'s symposium on Arthur's book *The New Dialectic and Marx's 'Capital'*; see Murray 2005b, included in the present volume as Chapter 16.

6 Marx 1976a, p. 127, as cited in Furner 2004, p. 93.

> for the same amount of wheat. There is said to be some intrinsic aspect to a commodity that any number of other commodities may represent such that in representing it they are equal.[7]

Furner thinks that Marx begs the question by claiming that a given commodity 'has' an exchange value: 'To say that the exchange-values belong to the wheat is taken to imply that there is something of which the wheat is further possessed by virtue of which it has exchange-values'. Furner seems to be using the term 'imply' as equivalent to 'means'. In other words, Marx does not argue to the existence of a 'something of which the wheat is further possessed by virtue of which it has exchange-values'; he assumes it in assuming that exchange value is something that the wheat 'has'.[8] But Marx is not begging the question; he is arguing from something that commodities are observed to have, namely, 'valid' exchange values, to something further, something intrinsic to the commodity, value.[9]

---

7 Furner 2004, p. 93.

8 I am not confident that I understand Furner's line of thought here. Furner may be using 'imply' in the usual way, but then it seems that Marx does just what he proposes to do, namely, argue from exchange values to value. Perhaps Furner thinks that Marx begs the question just by saying that a commodity 'has' exchange values. That criticism does not work either. To see why will require a closer look at what Marx means by claiming that commodities 'have' exchange values.

9 Value is intrinsic to the commodity not as a use value – it is not one more natural or physical property – value is purely social and supersensible. It is an unavoidable consequence of the peculiar social form of the commodity. Bailey cannot conceive of a property that is wholly social yet intrinsic to the commodity. In denying that value is anything intrinsic to the commodity, Bailey is trying to dispense with the reality of the commodity's social form. Neoclassical economists, in conceiving of value as something purely subjective, likewise deny that value is in any way intrinsic to the commodity. In doing so, they, like Bailey, try to brush off the reality of the commodity's social form. Ironically, in doing so, both Bailey and neoclassical economists pride themselves on overcoming what they regard as a double fetishism regarding commodities. First, they expose the supposed fetishism of classical (Ricardian) value theory, which claims that value is intrinsic to the commodity. Second, swept up in the subjectivism of modern philosophy, Bailey and the neoclassical economists consider the attribution of use value to commodities a further, less apparent, case of fetishism: usefulness, according to them, is purely subjective. Common sense, which takes usefulness to be objective (though not purely so), is living in a fool's paradise according to Bailey and the neoclassical economists. Marx shows this speculative daring to be based on two phenomenological errors. It is a mistake to think that usefulness can be wholly separated from the specific properties of a commodity. As for value's being intrinsic to the commodity, Marx would agree that there is something metaphysical in the derogatory sense about value.

Furner inverts Marx's reasoning. It is not the question-begging assumption of some 'intrinsic property' to the commodity that 'allows one to say that there is a constancy that x boot-polish or y silk or z gold each represent and which makes them "of identical magnitude"'.[10] Marx's argument is that the fluctuations of actual exchange values – it is the fluctuations in the prices of commodities that Marx has in mind – display a pattern.[11] Only on that basis do commodities have 'valid [*gültige*]' exchange values, and only on the basis of commodities having 'valid' exchange values does Marx claim that they are 'mutually replaceable' 'as exchange-values'.[12] If the 'valid' exchange value of a gallon of milk is three dollars and the 'valid' exchange value of a gallon of gasoline is three dollars, I can replace the milk with gasoline by selling the milk and buying the gasoline.[13] Marx takes the mutual replaceability of commodities to be sufficient evidence of their identical magnitude.[14] But if these diverse commodities share some magnitude, what is its dimension? It cannot be milk, money or oil. Since commodities have no sensible (phys-

---

But Bailey and the neoclassical economists mistake the source of the problem; they blame it on a propensity to the metaphysical on the part of Ricardo and other classical value theorists. While Marx rejects as asocial the classical labour theory of value, he agrees with Ricardo that value is intrinsic to the commodity. In developing his purely social labour theory of value, Marx explains that this fetishism of the commodity, this intrinsic supersensible value that gives the commodity its clout, is an inescapable consequence of the peculiar social form of the labour that produces commodities. Value is intrinsic to the commodity because the commodity's specific social form is intrinsic to it. That is why the denial by Bailey and the neoclassical economists that value is intrinsic to the commodity amounts to a denial that the commodity's social form is intrinsic to it. Therein lies their second phenomenological error: they think that wealth can exist without any specific social form. They fall into what I call 'the illusion of the economic', that is, the illusion that the economy in general, the economy with no particular social form, can actually exist. Capital, not some metaphysical penchant on the part of economists, is the root of the bad metaphysics of value.

10 Furner 2004, p. 93.

11 See Campbell 1997 for the argument that Marx begins *Capital* with the assumption that there are commodities and money in the sort of society he is examining.

12 Furner says nothing about Marx's adjective 'valid'.

13 'Valid' exchange values require money. Only with money is there a unitary measure of value to provide a common scale with which to identify the fluctuations in exchange value.

14 'But although the commodity has a thousand different kinds of value, or a thousand different prices, as many kinds of value as there are commodities in existence, all these thousand expressions always express the same value. The best proof of this is that all these different expressions are equivalents which not only can replace one another in this expression, but do replace one another in exchange itself' (Marx 1971a, p. 147).

ical) feature in common, the dimension must be a 'supersensible' one. Marx's argument, then, goes from the observable replaceability of specific quantities of commodities (as determined by their 'valid' exchange values) to the identity of their magnitudes (taking replaceability as the test of identity of magnitude). Magnitude is always magnitude of; it always has a dimension, but the various commodities do not share a use-value dimension. Milk is not money; money is not oil. Consequently, argues Marx, there must be a supersensible 'third thing' intrinsic to commodities, whose dimension is common to them.[15]

What does Marx mean by talking about a commodity 'having' exchange values? Furner starts his commentary saying, 'This passage begins by considering the fact of a given commodity's exchange with many other commodities'.[16] This understates Marx's claim. Marx asserts not simply that commodities are exchanged but that they have 'valid' exchange values.[17] In assert-

15 Marx's argument is complicated by the fact that some commodities, land, for example, are not products of labour. This point has long been taken as an obvious objection to Marx's argument that the 'third thing' that commodities have in common is 'abstract labour', and it is an important consideration in Chris Arthur's call for a reconstruction of Marxian value theory. In 'The New Giant's Staircase' (Murray 2005b, included in the present volume as Chapter 16) I point out that this seeming objection was anticipated by Marx – he spells it out in his *A Contribution to the Critique of Political Economy*, 'the last, and apparently decisive objection [to any labour theory of value] ... is this: if exchange-value is nothing but the labour-time contained in a commodity, how does it come about that commodities which contain no labour possess exchange-value' (Marx 1970a, p. 63) – and I argue that Marx answers the objection not only with his theory of rent but also with his strategy that makes capital in general, and the commodity as a representative (or aliquot) part of the 'heap' of commodities, the subject of investigation. Following that argumentative strategy, Marx need not make the claim, which he knows to be false, that every commodity is a product of labour. I know of no other strategy by which a Marxian labour theory of value can be developed.

16 Actually, this is misleading because it suggests a barter situation. Since it is a capitalist society Marx is writing about, all exchanges are between commodities and money. Marx does not consider goods exchanged in barter to be commodities, 'The direct exchange of products [barter] has the form of the simple expression of value in one respect, but not as yet in another. That form was x commodity A = y commodity B. The form of the direct exchange of products is x use-value A = y use-value B. The articles A and B in this case are not as yet commodities' (Marx 1976a, p. 181).

17 Marx takes it as a fact about the sort of society he is investigating, capitalist society, that wealth takes the commodity form and that commodities have prices. (That, of course, means that he takes the existence of money to be a fact of life in capitalism.) He writes, 'the endless series [of exchanges between money and all other commodities] is a socially

ing that commodities have 'valid' exchange values, Marx asserts that there are patterns to the fluctuations of exchange values. Indeed, Marx insists that the only way that 'valid' exchange values (prices) can exist is amidst fluctuations:

> The possibility, therefore, of a quantitative incongruity between price and magnitude of value, i.e. the possibility that the price may diverge from the magnitude of value, is inherent in the price-form itself. This is not a defect, but, on the contrary, it makes this form the adequate one for a mode of production whose laws can only assert themselves as blindly operating averages between constant irregularities.[18]

Marx's assertion that commodities 'have' exchange values is an empirical claim, not a question-begging assumption. Marx's 'third thing argument' cannot be made on the basis that goods exchange with other goods. If there were no money and prices and if there were no regularity to price fluctuations – if the law of value did not force its way through – there would be no 'valid' exchange values. Then there would be no basis on which Marx could assert that commodities can replace one another, hence no basis for asserting that they are of identical magnitude. That would eliminate the observational basis for asserting a 'content' ['*Gehalt*'] intrinsic to commodities that is distinguishable from their properties as use values. Without observable constancy in the fluctuations of prices, Marx's 'third thing argument' for value cannot be made.

That Furner fails to recognise what Marx means by the 'valid' exchange values of a commodity – hence fails to understand the observational basis for and

given fact in the shape of the prices of the commodities' (Marx 1976a, p. 189). It belongs to Marx's concept of a commodity that it 'has' a price. Marx says of the products of labour that 'their taking the form of commodities implies their differentiation into commodities [on the one hand] and the money commodity [on the other]' (Marx 1976a, p. 188, n. 1). In limiting the scope of *Capital* to those societies where the commodity form is dominant, Marx begins with a fact about capitalism: commodities 'have' prices. In *A Contribution to the Critique of Political Economy* Marx makes no bones about this: 'The busiest streets of London are crowded with shops whose show cases display all the riches of the world, Indian shawls, American revolvers, Chinese porcelain, Parisian corsets, furs from Russia and spices from the tropics, but all of these worldly things bear odious, white paper labels with Arabic numerals and then laconic symbols £ s. d. This is how commodities are presented in circulation' (Marx 1970a, p. 87).

18 Marx 1976a, p. 196.

the logic of the 'third thing argument' – shows itself in a point he makes against Andrew Kliman's defence of Marx. Furner distinguishes between 'actual price and average price over a certain period' and goes on to say: 'One does not need to think of average price as something a commodity "has"'.[19] True, but this is because the concept of 'average price' is purely mathematical; it applies whether there is a pattern to the prices of a commodity or not. Furner does not grasp Marx's concept of a 'valid' exchange value (price): 'valid' price and 'average price' are not the same. Every commodity has an 'average price' simply as a matter of computation; to have a 'valid' price, the fluctuations in a commodity's actual prices must display patterns, which we take to reveal something about the commodity. These patterns, to which Marx refers with his concept of the 'valid' exchange value (price) of a commodity, provide the evidence for Marx's argument that value is intrinsic to commodities. Reasoning along these lines, Kliman observes, 'whenever exchanges are merely contingent, ephemeral events', a commodity cannot be said to 'have' an exchange value.[20] Kliman adds:

> Marx could not successfully have derived the equivalence of commodities to one another from the mere phenomena of exchange ... he instead derived it from a particular fact about capitalism – commodities 'have' exchange-value.[21]

So it is not surprising that Furner – overlooking Marx's concept of 'valid' exchange-value and the evidence to which he appeals – concludes that Marx's argument begs the question. Furner is right that it makes no sense to say that a commodity 'has' an average price, but it does make sense to say of a commodity whose prices present a pattern that it 'has' a 'valid' price.

Furner recaps his case for why Marx's 'third thing argument' begs the question, 'As the above discussion hoped to show, Marx actually begins his "third

19 Furner 2004, p. 96.

20 Kliman 2000, p. 101, n. 46.

21 Kliman 2000, p. 102, n. 46. What Kliman goes on to say, namely, that in capitalism 'we *think* and *say*' that a commodity has a price, is a step removed from Marx's point. In saying that commodities 'have' exchange values, Marx claims that prices exhibit patterns, not that people think that they do – though that is true too. Furner has a point, then, when he objects to Kliman's appealing to common sense to establish this premise as a 'fact' of everyday experience (Furner 2004, p. 95). The fact relevant for Marx's argument is a fact about prices, not what people think about them.

thing argument" by supposing exchange-values to be had by a commodity'.[22] I agree that Marx asserts that a commodity 'has' (replaceable) exchange values but disagree that he begs the question when he argues for value as distinct from exchange value. What Marx means is that commodities 'have' 'valid' exchange values, that is, fluctuations in their prices can be observed to show patterns. Furner does not recognise this; instead he interprets the meaning of 'has' in a way that leaves Marx begging the question. But there is nothing question begging in asserting that commodities 'have' 'valid' exchange values and arguing on that basis that they must have the supersensible, strictly social property of value.

Furner is no more convinced by Marx's follow-up argument, where he takes any two commodities that are exchanged for one another and represents their exchange as an equation. Marx argues that such an equation implies that there is a third thing, value, which is neither the one commodity nor the other, but exists in both. Furner focuses on a phrase that comes up on p. 152 of *Capital* (the 'third thing argument' comes up on p. 127), where Marx praises Aristotle for 'his discovery of a relation of equality in the value-expression of commodities'. Furner jumps on the phrase 'the value-expression of commodities', charging, 'With this phrase, exchange can no longer be seen as the logical starting-point of Marx's argument. Instead of value depending upon an equality, it is equality that is said to be found in the expression of value'.[23] Furner detects a circular argument that moves from value, to equality expressed in exchange-value, then back to value, but his case is forced. Marx makes his argument that exchange value presupposes value and is value's expression some twenty-five pages prior to his use of the phrase to which Furner objects! Actually, Marx's second argument builds on his first. If every commodity 'has' a 'valid' exchange value, every commodity is mutually replaceable with every other commodity having the same 'valid' exchange value. Mutually replaceable commodities, argues Marx, have the same magnitude. But two commodities having the same magnitude are equal to one another with respect to that magnitude. This allows Marx to represent their exchange as an equation, and that leads him to the 'third thing' (value) in answer to the question: What are these equal magnitudes, magnitudes of?

22 Furner 2004, p. 94.

23 Furner 2004, p. 95.

2 On Appealing to Common Sense

Furner reprimands Kliman for appealing to common sense:

> What lends this argument [Kliman's] a certain strangeness is that, at no point in Chapter One of *Capital*, could Marx be construed as providing a principled claim about extending validity to commonplace ideas. If anything, the way in which the idea of an intrinsic value is first introduced in contrast to what exchange-value 'appears to be [*scheint*]' suggests the inappropriateness of such an attempt.[24]

But Kliman does not assert that Marx considers common sense to be always reliable; neither is such a strong claim required to make his case. What is Furner's point? That Marx does not endorse common sense beliefs across the board? Who would doubt that? That no appeal to common sense beliefs is allowable unless all are? Why accept that? Furner's talk of the 'inappropriateness' of Kliman's appeal to certain common sense beliefs hardens later on: 'It is neither desirable nor possible to rescue Marx's "third thing argument" by appealing to commonplace patterns of thought'.[25] Is Furner suggesting that Marx excludes all appeals to common sense beliefs? But Marx regularly calls upon them, including in Chapter One. A striking example comes up in the context of Marx's praise for Aristotle's attention to the value form. Marx argues that Aristotle was unable to discover the truth about value 'because Greek society was founded on the labour of slaves, hence had as its natural basis the inequality of men and of their labour-powers'.[26] It was only the shift in common sense toward egalitarianism that made it possible to move forward:

> The secret of the expression of value, namely the equality and equivalence of all kinds of labour because and in so far as they are human labour in general, could not be deciphered until the concept of human equality had already acquired the permanence of a fixed popular opinion.[27]

Suspicion regarding some common sense beliefs is compatible with trusting others.

---

24 Furner 2004, p. 96.
25 Furner 2004, p. 97.
26 Marx 1976a, p. 152.
27 Marx 1976a, p. 152.

Furner argues against Kliman's claim that common sense and behaviour take 'commodities to have a worth independent of their actual exchange'.[28] (Or does Furner want to argue that common sense need not draw such a conclusion?) Furner maintains that one need not conceive of an unusually high or low price as lying above or below some price that the commodity 'has' and consequently being a 'rip-off' or a 'bargain.' Furner rightly connects the question of whether a commodity 'has' an exchange value with the question of justice in exchange. If there is no exchange value that a commodity 'has', there can be no question of its being sold above or below that exchange value: the discourse of justice and injustice in commercial transactions loses its grip. In place of a discourse of just and unjust exchanges based on commodities' 'having' exchange values, Furner recommends that we think of prices as either ordinary or unexpected, 'the only distinction that needs to be made is the distinction between actual price and average price over a certain period'.[29] Here Furner follows Bailey: since there is only exchange value (price), exchange value is not the expression of anything intrinsic to the commodity. Consequently, there can be no discrepancy between price and intrinsic value. Unjust exchange is thereby excluded in principle.[30] But common discourse pertaining to justice in commercial exchange cannot be collapsed into talk about ordinary and unusual prices.[31] Someone who says that a certain price is unjust does not mean that it is unusual.[32] Ordinary discourse is incompatible with Bailey's contention that value is established exclusively in the act of exchange.

---

28 Furner 2004, p. 96. One must be cautious in speaking of commodities having value prior to or independently of exchange. For Marx the potential value of a commodity is actualised only in exchange. To insist without qualification that value is independent of exchange is to slip into a Ricardian conception of value.

29 Furner 2004, p. 96.

30 Thus, Marx concludes from Bailey's theory of value, 'A commodity cannot be sold below its value any more than above it, for its value is what it is sold for' (Marx 1971a, p. 154).

31 St. Thomas Aquinas's statement 'it is contrary to justice to sell goods at a higher price than their worth, or to buy them for less than their value' (in Murray 1997b, p. 100) is representative of the common view.

32 'If 3 lbs. of coffee exchange for 1 lb. of tea today or would do so tomorrow, it does not at all mean that equivalents have been exchanged for each other. According to this, a commodity could always be exchanged only at its value, for its value would constitute any quantity of some other commodity for which it had been accidentally exchanged. This, however, is not what people generally *mean*, when they say that 3 lbs. of coffee have been exchanged for their equivalent in tea. They assume that after, as before, the exchange, a *commodity of the same value* is in the hands of either of the exchangers. The rate at which

In support of his claim that nothing in common sense or common practice requires us to hold that commodities 'have' prices, Furner cites this passage from Marx's critique of Bailey: '[T]he most ordinary merchant does not believe that he is getting the same value for his £1 when he receives 1 quarter of wheat for it in a period of famine and the same amount in a period of glut'.[33] But Marx's point here is the opposite of Furner's. It is not that the ordinary merchant sees that wheat does not 'have' an exchange value, so that all there is to say is that prices in conditions of famine or glut differ from the average price for wheat. Marx's point is that the merchant knows that the value of a measure of wheat – and, with the value, the price that the wheat 'has' – is not fixed: it will be greater in times of famine than in times of glut. The context of Marx's observation is his criticism of Bailey's identification of the value of one commodity with the amount of another commodity received in exchange for it (as opposed to the amount of *the value of* the other commodity); for example, the value of a day's labour power is a quarter of wheat. That makes the quantity of the latter commodity the (invariable) measure of the value of the first. Marx's point is that even an ordinary merchant knows that a quarter of wheat changes value in times of famine or glut; it is no fixed measure of value.[34] Correctly understood, this case of the ordinary merchant proves Furner wrong when he complains that it is 'neither desirable nor possible' to argue on the basis of 'appealing to commonplace patterns of thought'.[35] In this case of the ordinary merchant, that is exactly what Marx is doing. He refutes Bailey's assertion that the quantity of one commodity is an invariable measure of the value of a second commodity by appealing to fact that even the most ordinary merchant knows better.

3 *Must* the 'Third Thing Argument' Fail?

Furner pushes his criticism of Marx's 'third thing argument' further, arguing that defences of it 'necessarily fail' because, at the level of the argument in Chapter One of *Capital*, Marx cannot defeat Bailey's rival subjectivistic theory of value as 'relative esteem'.[36] Even if we grant Marx's contention that 'the

two commodities exchange does not determine their value, but their value determines the rate at which they exchange' (Marx 1971a, p. 132).

33 Marx 1971a, p. 150.

34 See Marx 1976a, p. 130.

35 Furner 2004, p. 97.

36 Furner 2004, p. 98. Furner passes over in silence the complications for Bailey's theory of

exchange of commodities in given proportions could not proceed if it were not underpinned by some sort of qualitative homogeneity', that will not prove that there is some supersensible property, value, that is intrinsic to commodities.[37] Furner's intention is not to defend Bailey's theory that the 'qualitative homogeneity' underlying commodity exchanges is nothing intrinsic to commodities but rather purely subjective relative esteem. Furner is simply proposing that, at this level of argument, Marx cannot defeat Bailey and establish his own (labour) theory of value. But, like generations of interpreters and critics of Marx going back to Böhm-Bawerk, Furner overlooks the fact that, both in *Capital* and in his critique of Bailey, Marx mocks the very idea of subjective value theory. Here is what Marx has to say (in the fifth paragraph of *Capital*) about the idea that usefulness is something purely subjective, that is, wholly separable from all particular features of the useful thing, 'The usefulness of a thing makes it a use-value. But this usefulness does not dangle in mid-air. It is conditioned by the physical properties of the commodity, and has no existence apart from the latter'.[38] The brevity of Marx's critique does not detract from its profundity and finality. The idea that usefulness is something 'qualitatively homogeneous' is simply a non-starter. Marx does answer subjective value theory in the first chapter of *Capital*; it is just that few seem to notice.[39]

---

value raised by introducing 'relative esteem'; for example, if value is 'relative esteem', then the exchange relation is not value – as in Bailey's official theory – but the expression of value.

37 Furner 2004, p. 99.

38 Marx 1976a, p. 126. Marx directs this point explicitly against Bailey's subjectivistic theory of use value, 'it is through its own properties, its own qualities, that a thing is a use-value and therefore an element of wealth for men. Take away from grapes the qualities that make them grapes, and their use-value as grapes disappears for men and they cease to be an element of wealth for men' (Marx 1971a, p. 129). See also Marx 1971a, p. 144. Marx closes Chapter One of *Capital* on this point, chiding those economists – he has just quoted Bailey – who 'find that the use-value of material objects belongs to them independently of their material properties' (Marx 1976a, p. 177).

39 In this criticism of subjective value theory, we glimpse Marx's rejection of the subjectivism of modern thinking, what Marx often called the 'bourgeois horizon' common to modern philosophy and political economy. Conversely, it may be taken as an indication of Marx's renewal of Aristotelian philosophy, which opposes the bifurcations of modern thinking. Perhaps that explains why it has been overlooked.

4 Is Bailey's Theory of Value Transhistorical?

Furner examines and sets aside one possible argument for the superiority of Marx's value theory over Bailey's, namely, the charge that Bailey uses 'a transhistorical category', relative esteem, 'to explain a historically specific phenomenon'.[40] After granting that there is a 'real slackness about the way in which Bailey jumps from using transhistorical to historical terms', Furner lets him off the hook because 'in practice, Bailey used the concept of esteem in connection with terms particular to commodity production such as market competition'.[41] Here, I think Furner underestimates Bailey. Bailey's conception of 'relative esteem' is not transhistorical even in theory.

In his *Critical Dissertation on Value* (1825), Bailey introduces 'relative esteem' as follows:

> It is only when objects are considered together as subjects of preference or exchange, that the specific feeling of value can arise. When they are so considered, our esteem for one object, or our wish to possess it, may be equal to, or greater, or less than our esteem for another; it may, for instance, be doubly as great, or, in other words, we would give one of the former for two of the latter.[42]

Bailey does slur 'preference' into 'exchange', proving Furner's point about his 'slackness'; still, it is fair to say that Bailey believes that 'the specific feeling of value' arises only where we have a social practice of commodity exchange. In putting the term 'exchange' into his explanation of 'relative esteem', he introduces the idea that value exists only where there is generalised commodity exchange. In fact, Bailey says as much. Writing of Torrens's 'excellent' observation 'that value is not essential to the idea of riches', Bailey wonders 'whether it [value] is not always implied, and whether the latter term would have been invented in a state of society in which there was no interchange of commodities'.[43] This conceptual link between 'relative esteem' and commodity exchange is further confirmed by Bailey's praise for Smith's definition of value as purchasing power, 'the definition of Adam Smith, therefore, that the value of an object "expresses the power of purchasing other goods, which the possession of that

40 Furner 2004, p. 100.
41 Furner 2004, p. 100.
42 Bailey 1967, p. 2.
43 Bailey 1967, p. 166, n.

object conveys", is substantially correct'.[44] Bailey's conception of value as 'relative esteem' incorporates the phenomenon of commodity exchange; contrary to Furner, it is not transhistorical, even in theory.[45]

We might say that, when Bailey insists that 'relative esteem' must be expressed in the exchange of commodities, he injects value-form theory into a conception of value meant to be purely subjectivistic. But how can value-form theory, which conceives of exchange value (price) as the necessary form of appearance of value, be an ingredient of a purely subjectivistic account of value? Commodity exchange is an objective and historically specific social practice. If commodity exchange belongs to the concept of value, as it appears to in Bailey's theory, the intent to frame a purely subjective theory of value is violated. Value-form theory is incompatible with any purely subjectivistic value theory. So Bailey's stab at a subjectivistic theory of value does not represent a viable alternative to Marx's value theory, as Furner claims. If Bailey's theory of value were transhistorical, Marx would be justified to criticise it as such, as Furner grants. But not being transhistorical does not make Bailey's theory of value a viable option; instead, the theory implodes.

5 Money

Furner is correct that Marx's theory of money is superior to Bailey's because he explains what money expresses and why it exists. This provides a good reason to judge Marx's theory of value to be superior to Bailey's. Equally, though, it can be said of Bailey's theory of value that it fails to explain why value exists. Though Bailey recognises value as specific to societies where there is commodity exchange, he has no account of why there is such a practice, hence why there is value, any more than he has an account of why there is money – and for the same reason. Bailey has no notion of the inseparability of forms of production and forms of distribution (exchange). Bailey is oblivious to the topic of the social form of production. Lacking that idea, Bailey cannot say why commodity exchange attains prominence in a society, which on his terms is the same question as why there is value. This counts against Furner's claim that the superiority of Marx's theory of value first appears when he gets to money. Marx can account for why there is value; Bailey cannot.[46]

44 Bailey 1967, p. 4.

45 Compare Marx 1971a, p. 163.

46 Consequently, Bailey's theory of value is, as Marx calls it, fetishistic: 'Bailey is a fetishist

Furner's critique of Bailey's thinking about money sidesteps several of its severe shortcomings. (i) Bailey does not understand what money is; that is, he lacks the proper concept of money.[47] Bailey does not recognise that money must be the exclusive commodity in what Marx calls the general equivalent form of value; money is the one and only commodity that is 'directly social', that is, directly and universally exchangeable.[48] This connects to Bailey's failure to recognise that commodities 'have' exchange values, since that is possible only where there is money (properly understood). (ii) Bailey cannot get money right because – though in identifying value with exchange value, he insists on the relational character of value – he does not see the *polarity* of exchange value.[49] He misses its polarity because he does not recognise the root of that polarity, the double character of commodity-producing labour. Consequently, as Marx points out in a passage that Furner quotes,[50] Bailey fails to see that money, and money alone, answers the need for a qualitative transformation of commodity-producing labour, from privately undertaken into socially valid labour. (iii) Bailey's theory of money as the measure of value will not work because his general theory of measuring the value of any two commodities in a third commodity does not work. (iv) Because Bailey excludes the possibility of comparing the value of any commodity (the money commodity included) across time, he cannot make sense of money's functioning as a measure of value

---

in that he conceives value, though not as a property of the individual object (considered in isolation), but as a relation of objects to one another, while it is only a representation in objects, an objective expression, of a relation between men, a social relation, the relationship of men to their reciprocal productive activity' (Marx 1971a, p. 147).

47 Furner observes: 'Marx claims that Bailey cannot say what money is an expression of and thus why it exists at all' (Furner 2004, p. 102). True, but Marx claims that Bailey does not even understand what money is.

48 Marx 1976a, p. 161. This involves an observational lapse on Bailey's part, for the exclusivity of money's character as directly and universally exchangeable is observable to the ordinary participant in a capitalist society: 'Everyone knows, if nothing else, that commodities have a common value-form which contrasts in the most striking manner with the motley natural forms of their use-values' (Marx 1976a, p. 139). It is a singular strength of Marx's theory of money that it accounts for this phenomenon.

49 Furner never mentions the polarity of the value form. Polarity comes up in Marx's treatment of the simple form of value (in section three of Chapter One), which constitutes a reply to Bailey (Campbell 1997, p. 94): 'The relative form of value and the equivalent form are two inseparable moments, which belong to and mutually condition each other; but, at the same time, they are mutually exclusive or opposed extremes, i.e. poles of the expression of value' (Marx 1976a, pp. 139–40).

50 Furner 2004, p. 101.

or a store of value (means of payment).[51] Let us consider the first and third points in more detail.

(i) One could say that Bailey's is not so much a theory of money as a denial that money exists.[52] Money, according to Marx, is the commodity that exclusively occupies the universal equivalent form of value and thereby directly incarnates value. According to Bailey, there is no such thing. Bailey regards each commodity as a new kind and a new measure of value:

> The value of any commodity denoting its relation in exchange, we may speak of it as ... corn-value, cloth-value, according to the commodity with which it is compared; and hence there are a thousand different kinds of value, as many kinds of value as there are commodities in existence, and all are equally real and equally nominal.[53]

With Bailey, everything is money and nothing is money.

(iii) Furner is right to trace Bailey's theory of money back to his idea that the values of two commodities, A and B, can be compared only by seeing how each relates to C, a third commodity. Bailey explains:

> If we wish to know whether A and B are equal in value, we shall in most cases be under the necessity of finding the value of each in C; and when we affirm that the value of A is equal to the value of B, we mean only that the ratio of A to C is equal to the ratio of B to C.[54]

But the ratio of A to C (say, ten gallons of milk to one ounce of gold) cannot equal the ratio of B to C (say, ten gallons of gas to one ounce of gold) unless A and B are commensurable. A subtle bait and switch is going on here. Bailey conflates the ratio of the units of A to the units of C with the ratio of the number of units of A to the number of units of C (ten to one). By eliminating the dimensions of

51 See Marx 1971a, p. 162.

52 Likewise, one can say that Bailey's is not so much a theory of value as the denial that value exists. (i) Bailey denies that value is any one thing; rather, there are as many kinds (and measures) of value as there are commodities. (ii) Against Ricardo, Bailey insists that value is not a property of commodities; in fact, it is not a property of anything: nothing has value.

53 Bailey 1967, p. 39. Furner does not mention this passage, though Marx quotes it in Marx 1976a, p. 155, n. 25. Bailey gets even more explicit in rejecting the exclusivity of money, and thereby rejecting money's existence, 'Money-value has no greater claim to the general term "*value*", than any other kind of value' (Bailey 1967, p. 58).

54 Bailey 1967, p. 8.

A and C (milk and gold), the latter expression reduces to a number, ten, which could be compared to the number obtained by handling the ratio of B to C in the same manner. If the numbers are the same, we say A and B have the same value. But there is no justification for dropping the dimensions to arrive at this number. That leaves us comparing a ratio of ten gallons of milk to one ounce of gold with a ratio of ten gallons of gas to one ounce of gold.[55] There is no way to equate these two ratios and determine that A and B have the same value except to make the assumption that, as values, A, B and C are homogeneous: they have a common dimension. Only then would the dimensions of A over C and B over C cancel out. But, to concede that A, B and C have a common dimension is to concede the point of Marx's 'third thing argument'. Nothing in Bailey's official conception of value allows us to do this.[56]

6 Capital

In his section on capital, Furner points up problems that Marx identifies in Bailey's theory of profit. One problem goes to capital's root: determining profit involves comparing the value of one's investment with the value of the return, but Bailey excludes comparison of values across time.[57] No doubt, this counts heavily against Bailey's theory of value. Furner raises a further problem with Bailey's theory of profit. Due to the multiplicity of kinds and measures of value in Bailey's theory, profit, understood as the capitalist's portion of the commodities sold, could go up while the value of profit could go up, stay the same, and go down – all at the same time – depending upon which measure of value one employs. Furner quotes Marx: 'It merely amounts to a repetition by Bailey of his proposition that value is the quantity of articles exchanged for an article'.[58]

---

55 Furner even quotes a passage from Marx where he effectively makes this argument: 'The value of A expressed in B must be something quite different from the value of A in C, as different as B and C are. It is not the same value, identical in both expressions, but there are two relations of A which have nothing in common with each other, and of which it would be nonsense to say that they are equivalent expressions' (Marx 1971a, p. 150, as quoted in Furner 2004, p. 99).

56 That Bailey has no way to compare the values of different commodities is one more count against his theory of value.

57 'Is it not a fact that, in the process of circulation or the process of reproduction of capital, the value of one period is constantly compared with that of another period, an operation upon which production itself is based?' (Marx 1971a, p. 154).

58 Furner 2004, p. 104.

Referring to this passage Furner mentions 'the confusion between use-value and value that arises within Bailey's discussion at the level of the commodity'.[59] Ironically, by identifying value with the use value of the commodity for which another commodity is exchanged, Bailey finds himself making that use value an invariable measure of value.[60] If, in the course of a year, wages go from one bushel of wheat to two, they have doubled according to Bailey's thinking. But, as Marx pointed out in his appeal to the common merchant, everyone knows that the value of a bushel of wheat does not remain constant. Value is not use value. By identifying value with use value, Bailey wants the impossible – to wipe away the inescapable fetish character of the commodity form of wealth without changing the social form of production. Contrary to Furner's thrust, this gives us a good reason to prefer Marx's theory of value to Bailey's even at the level of the commodity.

There is a problem with Furner's argumentative strategy that cuts across his sections on money and capital. He reasons that Marx's theory of value is superior to Bailey's since, in the case of money, it can explain what money expresses and why it exists, while, in the case of capital, Marx's theory of value allows, as Bailey's does not, for comparisons of value across time, without which the circuit of capital makes no sense. All true, but one wants to know with what justification Furner introduces Marx's theory of value in these sections. After all, he has argued that Marx's own case for his theory of value, which goes through the 'third thing argument', begs the question. So how do we get to Marx's theory of value at all?[61] Furner provides no alternative line of argument. Rather, value drops into his sections on money and capital like a *deus ex machina*.

I have tried to make the case that Furner is wrong to think that, in assuming commodities 'have' exchange values, Marx's 'third thing argument' begs the question. It is wrong to think that there is any level at which Bailey's subjective value theory can compete with Marx's labour theory of value. With regard to the latter point, I have argued both that Marx directly attacks the idea that value can be purely subjective – the very idea of purely subjective utility is

---

59 Furner 2004, pp. 104–5.

60 Actually, this is doubly ironic: first, because Bailey was so critical of Ricardo's search for an invariable measure of value, and, second, because Bailey's insistence that comparing value across time is senseless puts the whole issue of the variability or invariability of value out of bounds. On the latter point, see Marx 1971a, pp. 150–1.

61 Marx emphasises the necessity to develop the concept of value at the level of the commodity, not capital, toward the end of his critique of Bailey, Marx 1971a, pp. 164–5. See also p. 131.

bogus – and that, because Bailey's value theory incorporates the idea that value ('relative esteem') must be expressed in the exchange of money and commodities, it undermines its own claim to be purely subjective. One purpose I have in defending the way Marx develops his theory of value is to show that a reconstruction of Marx's value theory along the lines suggested by Chris Arthur is unnecessary. I hope that none of this will detract from the service Furner has done by calling attention to Marx's critique of Samuel Bailey and by forcing us to think through what it means for a commodity to 'have' an exchange value.

CHAPTER 18

Reply to Geert Reuten*

It was Geert Reuten's essay 'The Difficult Labour of a Theory of Social Value' (1993) that got me to rethink whether, for Marx, value-producing labour was simply 'abstract labour'.[1] Reuten pointed out that, as any social sort of labour can be regarded in the abstract ('physiologically'), an 'abstract labour-embodied' theory of value would fail to be a 'truly social' theory of value.[2] I concluded that 'abstract labour' is a general, not a determinate, category. It must be distinguished from the determinate category of 'practically abstract' labour, that is, labour that is actually socially validated as abstract.[3] Value-producing labour, as Marx conceives of it, is 'practically abstract' labour, so Marx's theory of value is 'truly social'. In fact, it is exclusively about the specific social form and purpose of labour in societies where the capitalist mode of production dominates. In my article 'Marx's "Truly Social" Labour Theory of Value: Part I',[4] I argued for these ideas and criticised Reuten for insisting that Marx could be interpreted as offering an asocial, 'abstract labour-embodied' theory of value. Now I have Geert Reuten to thank for a thoughtful and thought-provoking reply to that article.

In responding I will address three main issues: (i) historical materialism and systematic dialectics, (ii) Marx's theory of value and (iii) why Marx's theory of value has long been interpreted as an asocial, Ricardian theory of value, when it is not. Before turning to these topics, I want to say something about Reuten's repeated admonition that we should be prepared to reconstruct Marx. I agree, even if I tend to find less call for this than Reuten does, but a general admonition, such as this, is no help in determining where, specifically, Marx needs to be reconstructed. If I find that in *Capital* Marx presents us with a 'truly social' labour theory of value, this does not prove that I am treating him with kid gloves. Likewise, Reuten's general observation that it is extremely difficult to make a clean break with previous conceptions when one introduces

* Originally published as 'Reply to Geert Reuten', *Historical Materialism*, Volume 10, Issue 1 (2002), pp. 155–76. Geert Reuten's 'The Interconnection of Systematic Dialectics and Historical Materialism', appeared in *Historical Materialism*, Number 7 (Winter 2000), pp. 137–65.

1 Reuten 1993.

2 Reuten himself rejects an asocial, 'abstract labour-embodied' theory of value.

3 On general and determinate abstractions see Chapter Ten of Murray 1988a.

4 Murray 2000a, included in the present volume as Chapter 4.

a revolutionary new scientific conception does not give a warrant to any specific conclusions regarding where Marx's efforts to break with the old ideas may have failed. Generalities will not make Reuten's case. So let us examine the particular points he makes.

1 Historical Materialism and Systematic Dialectics

Reuten notes that I rarely refer to historical materialism. In one sense, that is true. Historical materialism in general does not have much to say. And what it has to say may sound banal, despite its exceptional importance. In my article I expressed the general, phenomenological truth of historical materialism as follows: 'human beings are needy, self-conscious, symbolising, social, sexually reproducing animals who are in (and of) non-human nature, which they purposively transform according to their perceived wants'.[5] The task of a historical materialist investigator is to explore the specific social ways that human beings reproduce themselves and purposively transform nature to meet their wants. I do not believe that there is a great deal to be said in general about how such an investigation is to be carried out.[6] Reuten seems to agree; apart from the directives (1) to sort general from determinate abstractions and (2) to set forth how a society reproduces itself, 'historical materialism provides no methodological indication of *how* to set up the study of a particular "historical material constellation"'.[7] Historical materialism tells us what to do but does not offer much advice on how.[8] Reuten observes that, by contrast, systematic dialectics provides much more direction as to 'the exposition of the object of inquiry',[9] at least where capitalism is concerned. I agree.

Reuten offers this general characterisation of systematic dialectics: 'Systematic dialectics aims to show the essential working of the object: the whole in essence. The whole in essence is the interconnection of all the moments *necessary* for the *reproduction* of the object'.[10] I accept this, given the reminder he

5 Murray 2000a, p. 39. Reuten comments that 'this "general phenomenology" is perplexingly thin' (p. 148). In my article I called it 'spare' (p. 30) but went on to observe that, rather than being 'perplexing', this thinness holds space open for historically diverse ways of living.

6 For a contrasting view see Ollman 1993.

7 Reuten 2000, p. 141.

8 Compare Chapter Eight, 'Why Did Marx Write so Little on Method?', in Murray 1988a.

9 Reuten 2000, p. 141.

10 Reuten 2000, p. 142.

provides in a footnote that 'moments' 'can have no isolated existence'.[11] At this point I begin to have some difficulties following Reuten. He hedges: 'for me, phenomenological research is a mainly *analytical* stage of inquiry prior to the research of the dialectical *Darstellung* [presentation]'.[12] In footnote 20 Reuten elaborates: 'I adopt the term "analysis" in a broad sense ... Thus the stage of phenomenological analysis involves more than "analysis" in the narrow sense of merely indicating *difference*, it also involves provisional outlines of the inseparability of phenomena'.[13] If that is so, what was the function of the qualifier 'mainly' in the previous citation? As I understand it, Reuten's broad conception of 'phenomenological analysis' matches what I called 'phenomenology'. I used the term 'analysis' in what Reuten here calls the narrow sense. I agree that the word 'analysis' can be used in the restricted sense, where it is contrasted with 'synthesis', or in a broad sense, where it means careful, methodical thinking, as in, 'What is your analysis of the situation?' I believe that the narrow sense is to be preferred here; Reuten appears to vacillate between the two senses.

Reuten writes, 'the phenomenological research is the prior stage that Marx refers to as *Forschungsweise*, "the way of inquiry"'.[14] There it sounds as if Reuten is going to identify phenomenological research with inquiry – I take it that inquiry and research mean the same thing (*Forschung*) – and systematic dialectics with presentation, which is the way I have it in my article.[15] But Reuten employs the perplexing phrase 'the research of the dialectical *Darstellung*', which suggests (1) that the stage of inquiry (research) does not consist only of phenomenological analysis and (2) that systematic dialectics belongs to research as well as to presentation. What does not add up for me is Reuten's statement that 'the distinction of necessary moments from contingencies ... goes at the heart of the systematic dialectics proper: it is the result of

11 Reuten 2000, p. 142, n. 16.

12 Reuten 2000, p. 143.

13 Reuten 2000, p. 143, n. 20.

14 Reuten 2000, p. 143.

15 This description seems to fit Marx's own statement in the Postface to the second edition of *Capital*, quoted by Reuten on p. 150: 'Of course the method of presentation must differ from that of inquiry. The latter has to appropriate the material in detail, to analyse its different forms of development and to track down their inner connection. Only after this work has been done can the real [*wirkliche*, i.e. actual] movement be appropriately presented. If this is done successfully, if the life of the subject matter is now reflected back in the ideas, then it may appear as if we have before us an a priori construction'. 'To analyse [the material's] different forms of development and to track down their inner connection' is the work of what I term 'phenomenology' and identify with inquiry.

the research of the dialectical *Darstellung*'.[16] Did not Reuten's broad conception of phenomenological analysis include working up 'provisional outlines of the inseparability of phenomena'? Does that not involve distinguishing 'necessary moments' from 'contingencies'? If so, I do not understand how Reuten's 'research' component of systematic dialectics differs from the work of 'phenomenological research' (what I call 'phenomenology'). Consequently, I do not see either what is missing from my account or what is to be gained by Reuten's. Is the point of talking about 'the research of the dialectical *Darstellung*' that a systematic dialectical presentation is revisable, the sort of thing that goes through drafts? Think, for example, of the treatments of the commodity in the *Urtext*, the *Critique*, the several editions of *Capital* Volume I. I take that point for granted. In any case, it appears that this is not what Reuten has in mind. For, when he speaks of '"essays" (try-outs) in dialectics',[17] he states that the research involved in systematic dialectics should be identified with Marx's work prior to the *Critique* (1859), or even prior to the *Grundrisse* (1857–8). I see neither where Reuten makes a clear distinction between the synthetic dimension of what he calls 'phenomenological analysis (or research)' and the supposed research dimension of systematic dialectical presentation nor where a clear distinction is to be drawn. If there is one, I have missed it.

Reuten criticises my identifying the simple/complex distinction with the abstract/concrete distinction. He is right that I identify the (conceptually) simple with the (conceptually) abstract and the (conceptually) complex with the (conceptually) concrete. However, I believe that I address, at least to some extent, the point that Reuten finds lacking. Of the requirement that a systematic dialectical presentation move from the abstract to the concrete, Reuten says,

> Here, the dialectical layering of concepts comes in ... If you want to present the whole you must start from the whole. That is, you must start from the abstract whole ... Concretisation, foundation and reproduction are the aspects of the one process that drives the systematic dialectic forward in stages.[18]

I believe that what I identify as the fourth requirement of a Marxian systematic dialectical presentation,[19] namely, that simpler categories presuppose the

16 Reuten 2000, p. 143.
17 Reuten 2000, p. 146.
18 Reuten 2000, pp. 143–4.
19 Murray 2000a, p. 41.

more complex ones, covers the main point Reuten is driving at here. In order for the simpler categories to presuppose the more complex ones, the whole must be present at the beginning and at every step in the systematic dialectical presentation. Reuten's idea that a systematic dialectical presentation goes forward in increasingly concrete stages is, I believe, a consequence of the combination of what I identify as the third and fourth requirements of a Marxian systematic dialectical presentation.[20] Reuten speaks of 'major stages' and of the movement from more abstract wholes to more concrete ones in a systematic dialectical presentation. Such descriptions fit the make-up of *Capital* well, but I am not sure that there is an additional requirement involved here, or, if there is, exactly how to characterise it.

Reuten's vacillation with regard to the term 'phenomenological analysis' turns up in his Section 2.4. There he contrasts the 'phenomenological analytical stage' with 'the synthetics of the dialectical *Darstellung*'.[21] This contrast suggests that Reuten here takes 'phenomenological analysis' in the narrow sense, whereas, in footnote 20, he claimed to understand the term in a broader way that included synthesis.[22] This suggestion is reinforced when Reuten says of phenomenological analysis that 'this stage of thorough analysis results in abstractions and ultimately ends up with an "abstract universal"'.[23] That sounds like analysis in the narrow sense, while what Reuten calls the second research stage, the 'research dimension of systematic dialectics', explores how the abstract determinations hold together to form a concrete whole. But was that not the business of working up 'provisional outlines of the inseparability of phenomena'[24] that Reuten included in the broader meaning of 'phenomenological analysis'? Again, I do not see the basis for a distinction between the broader meaning of 'phenomenological analysis' and what Reuten wants to call the research aspect of systematic dialectics.

Reuten states that I object to the 'two-way directionality of dialectical systematicity'.[25] I do not; on the contrary, I identify the mutually presupposing character of categories as the fourth requirement of a Marxian systematic dialectical presentation. I say, recognising the dominance of one-way (linear) thinking, that the circle of presuppositions in a systematic dialectical presenta-

20 Ibid.
21 Reuten 2000, p. 145.
22 Reuten 2000, p. 143.
23 Reuten 2000, p. 145.
24 Reuten 2000, p. 143, n. 20.
25 Murray 2000a, p. 147.

tion 'seems' disturbing,[26] not that it is. I agree, given an important qualification, with Reuten's claim that 'systematic dialectics does not presuppose, assume, the truth of the starting point: its truth has to be proven in the course of the presentation'.[27] I agree that the truth of the starting point of *Capital*, namely, the (generalised) commodity form, is proven in the course of the presentation, when it is shown that the generalisation of the commodity form presupposes the capitalist mode of production, even as the capitalist mode of production presupposes the generalisation of the commodity form of wealth. But, to understand my qualification, we need to look more closely at this starting point, which is a nexus of general and determinate categories (use value and exchange value), and at the presuppositions of a Marxian systematic dialectical presentation.

Reuten cites Jairus Banaji, who quotes Marx (from the *Urtext*) as follows, 'the dialectical form of presentation is only correct when it knows its own limits'.[28] Banaji and Reuten both take this to refer to *historical* presuppositions, and that is what Marx has in mind in the passage. Thus, the systematic dialectical presentation that Marx offers in *Capital* has specific historical presuppositions, notably the historical transformation of unfree labourers into 'free' labourers, who can sell their labour power piecemeal to capitalists. I agree with Reuten and Banaji that this is one sense in which Marx understands his systematic dialectical presentation in *Capital* to be limited by presuppositions that do not belong to its dialectical network of mutually presupposing categories. But it is not the only one.

Reuten distinguishes two senses of 'presupposition'. One is the sense of a requirement.[29] Reuten identifies this sense in the context of discussing the way that stages in a systematic dialectical presentation are mutually presupposing. So, in Reuten's example, the accumulation of capital presupposes the circulation of capital, and the circulation of capital presupposes the accumulation of capital; they require one another. The second sense of 'presupposition' refers to 'postulates, assumptions, axioms'.[30] Since postulates are also requirements, I believe that Reuten means to draw a distinction between a one-way, linear or analytical conception of presupposition and a two-way, dialectical conception of presupposition. In a demonstrative science, the linear conception forces one back to postulates or axioms that are stipulated. Reuten, like Hegel, sees this

26 Murray 2000a, p. 38.
27 Reuten 2000, p. 147.
28 Banaji 1979, p. 31.
29 Reuten 2000, p. 147.
30 Ibid.

as a shortcoming of a linear presentation.[31] If I am right to construe Reuten's distinction in this way, then it appears to leave out a third sort of presupposition, one that is neither part of a network of mutual presuppositions nor one baldly stipulated. These are observable facts. The historical presupposition of 'free' labour is a presupposition of this sort. The genesis of 'free' labour belongs to no systematic dialectical account that Marx offers, but 'free' labour is not merely stipulated; it is a historical fact that conditions the systematic dialectical presentation in *Capital*. But that presentation is conditioned not only by historical fact.[32]

I argue that Marx's systematic dialectical presentation in *Capital* is not 'presuppositionless' in a second sense: it presupposes the facts about the human situation that make up what I call the 'general phenomenology' of historical materialism. Reuten takes this thought in two contrary directions. One is to concede the point; the other is to try to confine its application to 'historical dialectics', or 'historiography', as opposed to a true systematic dialectical presentation. Thus, in note 40,[33] Reuten, crediting Tony Smith, observes that in the *Phenomenology of Spirit* Hegel accepts the same 'general phenomenology' of the human condition as Marx. So how does Marx 'part company' with Hegel, wonders Reuten. But, in that case, Hegel's systematic dialectics would not be 'presuppositionless', and Marx's objection to Hegel would simply be misplaced. In the same vein Reuten says, 'At some point, all of the "general" transhistorical requirements (Murray's general phenomenology) must be incorporated into the systematic dialectical presentation in their determinate *social form* (specific phenomenology)'.[34] Why? How can they be 'incorporated'? I take this to be my point, for this requirement reveals that a Marxian systematic dialectical presentation presupposes historical materialism's 'general phenomenology' of the human condition. Aspects of that 'general phenomenology' turn up at various points in *Capital*, in the discussions of use value, of the labour process in general, of the reproduction of labour power.[35] Like the

31 Reuten 2000, p. 150.

32 With this in mind, my formulation of the first requirement of a Marxian systematic dialectical presentation (Murray 2000a, p. 41) should include history as well as nature, to read: '(i) A systematic dialectical presentation will have identifiable premises or presuppositions given by nature and history'.

33 Reuten 2000, p. 148.

34 Reuten 2000, p. 151.

35 In the *Grundrisse* Marx set out a plan according to which he would begin his 'Economics' by pulling together all 'the general, abstract determinants which obtain in more or less all forms of society' (Marx 1973, p. 108). But he did not follow that plan in *Capital*.

historical ones, these presuppositions belong to the third type, a type omitted by Reuten. These general facts about the human situation are neither part of the network of mutual presuppositions (as are the determinate social forms) nor merely stipulated postulates. I believe that the requirement to incorporate the general facts about the human situation shows that, as one should expect, Marx's systematic dialectical presentation in *Capital* knows two types of limits; it has historical presuppositions and it has general, transhistorical presuppositions. Insofar as Reuten follows this line of thought, he grants that (Hegelian) systematic dialectics does recognise that it has factual presuppositions, in which case Marx had no business objecting to Hegel's presuppositionlessness.

Elsewhere, Reuten retracts this line of thought and insists on the presuppositionlessness of systematic dialectical presentation, 'the synthetic stage of systematic dialectics ... is, subject to failures, presuppositionless'.[36] Here, I take it, Reuten reaffirms what I called the 'strictly Hegelian requirements'[37] on systematic dialectical presentation that he stated in his 1993 essay:

> All axioms are eschewed. Rather, anything that is required to be assumed, or anything that is posited immediately (such as the starting point), must be grounded. But it should not be grounded merely abstractly (i.e., giving arguments in advance), because this always leads to regress. That which is posited must be ultimately grounded in the argument itself, in concretising it.[38]

What has happened to the historical presuppositions of the systematic dialectical presentation in *Capital*? What has happened to the requirement that the general facts of the human situation must be incorporated into the systematic dialectical presentation?

Reuten charges that I provide no reference for my statement that Marx 'objects to the "presuppositionlessness" of Hegelian dialectics', adding, 'I assume that there is none'.[39] However, he follows up the reference I make to *The German Ideology* and locates the following passage from my book, *Marx's Theory of Scientific Knowledge*:

---

36 Reuten 2000, p. 151.

37 Murray 2000a, p. 41, n. 29.

38 Reuten 1993, p. 92. Notice that this earlier formulation likewise allows for only two types of presupposition.

39 Reuten 2000, p. 149.

> Marx's criticisms of speculative method and the philosophical anthropology of absolute idealism establish a context for his attack on speculative historiography and for his own materialism. To see this connection, let us consider a celebrated passage from the *German Ideology* in which Marx expounds his historical materialism at the expense of speculative historiography, 'With the presuppositionless Germans we must begin with ascertaining the first presuppositions of all human existence, therefore also of all history, namely the presupposition that man must be in a position to live in order to "make history"'.[40]

Reuten comments, 'Murray himself indicates, this objection to "presuppositionlessness" is set out in the criticism of speculative historiography',[41] and he remarks that Hegel's theory of history is obviously no exercise in systematic dialectics and that no historiography can do without presuppositions. But that is not quite what I wrote; I refer to 'Marx's criticisms of speculative method' as providing a 'context' for criticisms of speculative historiography, not that Marx's criticism limited itself to speculative historiography. I take the phase 'the presuppositionless Germans' as striking a blow against 'speculative method' generally. Indeed the main thrust of the first part of my book, 'Marx's Critique of Philosophy', was to show that Marx saw himself as both a pupil and a serious critic of Hegel's philosophy generally.

The evidence that Marx saw himself as developing a deep criticism of Hegel, beginning early in his intellectual development; that he took this critique to be an important ingredient in his critique of political economy; and that he stood by it throughout his life, is overwhelming. In his unfinished *Critique of Hegel's 'Philosophy of Right'* and in the final 1844 manuscript, 'The Critique of Hegel's Philosophy as a Whole', Marx develops fundamental criticisms of Hegel. These he followed up with more polemical critiques of Hegelians in *The Holy Family, The German Ideology*, and *The Poverty of Philosophy*. In his critique of the *Philosophy of Right*, Marx diverges from Hegel not only on substantive political matters, but he specifically criticises Hegel's method for failing to mediate concept and object, and he rejects Hegel's logic of the 'rational syllogism' as phony mediation. Marx writes, respectively, 'He [Hegel] develops his thinking not out of the object, rather he develops the object in accordance with ready-made thinking put together in the abstract sphere of logic'[42] and 'One

40 Ibid.

41 Ibid.

42 Marx 1970a, p. 14.

can say that in his development of the rational syllogism the whole transcendence and mystical dualism of his system comes to the surface'.[43] In his final Paris manuscript Marx criticises Hegel's conception of human self-consciousness as abstract, idealistic: 'But that a self-consciousness through its externalization can posit only thinghood, i.e., only an abstract thing, a thing of abstraction, and no actual thing, is just as clear'.[44] In a remarkable anticipation of the direction his future work, Marx observes that in adopting this abstract conception 'Hegel shares the standpoint of the modern national economists'.[45] Criticising Mr Szeliga in *The Holy Family*, Marx reiterates the charge that Hegelian speculation fails to mediate concept and object properly and consequently turns conservative:

> In Mr. Szeliga we also see a brilliant illustration of how speculation on the one hand apparently freely creates its object a priori out of itself and, on the other hand, precisely because it wills to get rid, by sophistry, of the rational and natural dependence on the object, falls into the most irrational and unnatural bondage to the object, whose most accidental, most individual determinations it is obliged to construe as absolutely necessary and universal.[46]

In the foreword to the *Paris Manuscripts*, Marx writes of 'critique's necessary coming to terms with its birthplace – Hegelian dialectic and German philosophy altogether'.[47] In a letter to Leske of 1 August 1846, Marx writes of the importance of his criticism of Hegel and German philosophy generally for his 'Economy':

> It seemed to me very important to send in advance of the positive development, a polemical writing against German philosophy and German socialism up to now. This is necessary in order to prepare the public for the standpoint of my 'Economy', which positions itself opposite the preceding German science.[48]

43 Marx 1970a, p. 85.
44 Marx 1964a, p. 180.
45 Marx 1964a, p. 177.
46 Marx and Engels 1975a, p. 61. See also Marx 1963, pp. 106–7, for a critique of Hegel's 'absolute method.'
47 Marx 1964a, p. 64.
48 Marx 1954b, p. 13.

Marx, then, made fundamental criticisms not only of speculative historiography but also of Hegel's philosophy, his dialectic and his conception of (presuppositionless) science.

In the method section of the *Grundrisse*, Marx renews his criticism of Hegel's idealism:

> The concrete is concrete because it is the concentration of many determinations, hence unity of the diverse. It appears in the process of thinking, therefore, as a process of concentration, as a result ... In this way Hegel fell into the illusion of conceiving the real as the product of thought concentrating itself, probing its own depths, and unfolding itself out of itself, by itself.[49]

I take it that Marx's point here pertains to the question of 'presuppositionlessness'. Hegelian dialectic, at least as Marx conceives of it, recognises no dependence of its object upon anything outside thought, no historical or material presuppositions limiting thought. Marx's dialectic differs from Hegel's precisely in insisting on incorporating material presuppositions (namely, historical presuppositions and those picked out by the 'general phenomenology' of the human condition) into the systematic dialectical presentation.[50] In the Postface to the second edition of *Capital*, Marx reaffirms his respect for Hegel while contrasting his dialectic with Hegel's, recalling – with no hint of retraction – the critique of 'Hegel's dialectic' that he had developed thirty years previously:

> My dialectical method is, in its foundations, not only different from the Hegelian, but exactly opposite to it. For Hegel, the process of thinking, which he even transforms into an independent subject, under the name of 'the Idea', is the creator of the real world, and the real world is only the external appearance of the idea. With me the reverse is true: the ideal is nothing but the material world reflected in the mind of man, and translated into forms of thought.
>
> I criticised the mystificatory side of the Hegelian dialectic nearly thirty years ago, at a time when it was still the fashion. But just when I was working at the first volume of *Capital*, the ill-humoured, arrogant and

49 Marx 1973, p. 101.

50 Again, if Hegel's dialectic actually admits of such presuppositions, then Marx was wrong about Hegel.

> mediocre epigones who now talk large in educated German circles began to take pleasure in treating Hegel in the same way as the good Moses Mendelssohn treated Spinoza in Lessing's time, namely as a 'dead dog'. I therefore openly avowed myself the pupil of that mighty thinker, and even, here and there in the chapter on the theory of value, coquetted with the mode of expression peculiar to him. The mystification which the dialectic suffers in Hegel's hands by no means prevents him from being the first to present its general forms of motion in a comprehensive and conscious manner. With him it is standing on its head. It must be inverted, in order to discover the rational kernel within the mystical shell.[51]

I claim that Marx's insistence on incorporating his 'general phenomenology' of the human situation, along with relevant historical presuppositions, into his systematic dialectical presentation of the capitalist mode of production reveals precisely how he sees his dialectic differing from Hegel's. This insistence is what I call attention to as the first requirement of a Marxian systematic dialectical presentation.

I do not understand how Reuten can ignore all of this and act as though Marx had never uttered a disparaging word regarding Hegel's dialectic.

In concluding his section on historical dialectics and systematic dialectics, Reuten charges: 'he [Murray] redefines systematic dialectics as "Marxian systematic dialectics", which, apparently, is what Marx does. This largely immunises *Capital* against improvements'.[52] First, it should be clear from numerous passages cited above that, rightly or wrongly, Marx distinguishes his dialectics from Hegel's. Second, I spell out in general terms what I take to be the basic requirements of Marxian systematic dialectical presentation.[53] So, third, there is no 'immunization' of *Capital* against improvements – where needed!

---

51 Marx 1976a, pp. 102–3. Marx makes much the same point in a letter to Kugelmann of 6 March 1868, writing, 'my method of development [*Entwicklungsmethod*] is not the Hegelian since I am a materialist and Hegel an idealist. Hegel's dialectic is the basic form [*Grundform*] of all dialectic, but only after its mystical form is stripped off, and this is just what distinguishes my method' (Marx 1942, p. 234).

52 Reuten 2000, p. 152.

53 See the four-point summary in Murray 2000a, p. 41.

2 Marx's 'Truly Social' Labour Theory of Value

Reuten finds it 'astonishing'[54] that I offer my account of the difference between the general concept of abstract labour and the determinate concept of 'practically abstract' labour as an interpretation rather than a reconstruction of Marx. I believe, however, that my case is very strong. Though I will add to the specific texts that count in favour of my view, we need first to keep the big picture in mind. I will make four 'big picture' points, then address specific criticisms that Reuten makes.

(a) Marx tells us again and again, going back at least to the *Paris Manuscripts*, that he is a critic of political economy. The fundamental point of his criticism goes hand in hand with the seminal idea involved in historical materialism, namely: 'All production is appropriation of nature on the part of an individual within and through a specific form of society'.[55] Though there are some, rather banal, general truths about production, there is no production in general, and there is no science of production in general. That, however, is precisely what political economy (and 'economics' generally) purports to be. Just as there is no production in general, there is no labour in general; on the contrary, the crux of a historical materialist account of a particular social form of production is to identify the specific social form and purpose of labour within that type of production. In *Capital*, Marx does just that, identifying labour in capitalism first as value-producing labour and then, more definitely, as surplus-value-producing labour. If Reuten is right, when Marx came to think about labour and value in *Capital* – whoops! – he lost track of his most profound discovery, one he had emphatically spelled out at least ten years earlier (in the *Grundrisse*), but a discovery, I would argue, that went back over twenty years. *Capital* is brilliant precisely because it puts the fundamental insight of historical materialism to work.

(b) The subtitle of *Capital* announces that it is to be a 'critique of political economy', and the opening sentence of the book implicitly makes the fundamental critique: there is no science of production in general; there is no 'economics'. Marx tells his reader right off that the subject matter of his book will be those societies wherein goods and services are generally provided in the specific social form of commodities, adding that in such societies the capitalist mode of production dominates. There is an obvious consequence of this, so obvious as to be easily missed. The opening sentence of *Capital*, in effect, tells

54 Reuten 2000, p. 155.

55 Marx 1973, p. 87.

us that, just as the book is all about wealth in the commodity form, so too it is all about labour in the commodity-producing form. And commodity-producing labour is 'practically abstract' labour. In other words, Marx implicitly begins *Capital* with the determinate concept of commodity-producing labour. In order to recognise commodity-producing labour as 'practically abstract' labour, that is, labour whose social validation involves recognising it as abstract labour, Marx later introduces the general concept of abstract labour.

(c) Reuten's hypothesis cannot make good sense of Section Three ('The Value-form or Exchange-Value') and Section Four ('The Fetishism of the Commodity and its Secret') of the first chapter of *Capital*. The question Marx intends to answer in those two sections is one that Ricardian value theory fails even to ask, namely, why must value appear as exchange value, as money? Marx's answer to the question is that value-producing labour is a specific social kind of labour, commodity-producing labour, which we can term 'practically abstract' labour; it is a bizarrely asocial social type of labour for which social validation comes *post festum*, in the marketplace, not at the point of production.[56] The social character of value-producing labour necessarily appears as a thing, as a commodity's exchange value.

In his reply Reuten addresses Section Three, saying, 'the crucial value-form theoretic in Section Three can be skipped as a tedious historical account of the emergence of money'.[57] I do not understand how it can be. For a start, it is a conceptual, not a historical, analysis, and Marx describes his task as one 'never even attempted by bourgeois economics'. Are we to believe that Marx thought that bourgeois economists never discussed the history of money? Reuten claims that Section Three need not be inconsistent with interpreting Marx's theory of value as an asocial 'abstract labour-embodied' one, but I do not see what support he offers for that assertion. Reuten corrects my misstatement that he does not talk about Section Three in his 1993 essay.[58] He devotes one page to it. However, Reuten's main point there is based on this assumption:

56 Marx already had the basic idea in *The Poverty of Philosophy*, where he wrote of Proudhon, 'M. Proudhon has presupposed the existence of money. The first question he should have asked himself was, why, in exchanges as they are actually constituted, it has been necessary to individualise exchangeable value, so to speak, by the creation of a special agent of exchange. Money is not a thing, it is a social relation … this relation is a link, and, as such, closely connected with a whole chain of other economic relations … this relation corresponds to a definite mode of production neither more nor less than does individual exchange' (Marx 1963b, p. 81).

57 Reuten 2000, p. 157. Reuten does not think that it should be dismissed so easily.

58 Reuten 2000, p. 157, n. 66.

'Let us say, for the sake of argument – I do not agree with it – that value is a genus and that exchange value is its species'.[59] Since for Marx, as well as for Reuten, the relationship between value and exchange value is not that of genus and species but of essence and its necessary form of appearance, nothing can be built on this assumption. So I do not see where Reuten establishes any plausible interpretation of Sections Three and Four that shows them to be consistent with interpreting Marx's theory of value as an asocial 'abstract labour-embodied' theory.

(d) A final broad consideration that makes Reuten's hypothesis far-fetched is the fact that, from at least the time of *The Poverty of Philosophy* (1847), Marx was a vocal critic of various forms of Ricardian socialism, from Bray and Proudhon to the Gotha Programme. At the heart of Marx's criticisms was a rejection of Ricardo's asocial labour theory of value. Thus, Marx writes:

> how can M. Proudhon go on talking about the constitution of a value, since a value is never constituted by itself? It is constituted, not by the time needed to produce it by itself, but in relation to the quota of each and every other product which can be created in the same time.[60]

This insight that value is a social relation and is constituted through the process of commodity exchange[61] lays the basis for Marx's harsh criticism of the 'equitable-labour-exchange bazaars' established by followers of John Bray[62] and the 'time-chit' proposals of Alfred Darimon, a follower of Proudhon. The crux of his criticism is that the 'time-chitters' follow Ricardo in understanding value to be determined individually in production, prior to exchange, thereby swallowing the bourgeois, asocial conception of value. Once again, Reuten would have us believe that in painstakingly seeing the first chapter of *Capital* through various drafts and editions, Marx lost his grip of these ideas that he insisted on for over twenty years!

On page 154 of his reply, Reuten gives three quotes, each of which he takes to set out the general concept of abstract labour. I agree that this is the purpose of the first quote, but notice his transition to the second: 'Second, with the introduction of the concept of value, abstract labour is further specified'.[63] Does this not suggest, as I argue, that the general concept of abstract labour alone

59 Reuten 1993, p. 101.
60 Marx 1963b, p. 83.
61 Marx 1963b, pp. 64–5.
62 Marx 1963b, p. 79, note.
63 Reuten 2000, p. 154.

does not make up the concept of value? Now look at the last sentence of the second quotation: 'As crystals of this social substance, which is common to them all, they are values – commodity values' [*Warenwerte*].[64] Marx states that value is a 'social substance', an unintelligible remark on the assumption that value is asocial, and he reminds us of the horizon within which he develops his theory of value, namely, that it is a theory of wealth in a particular social form, the generalised commodity form.

Reuten says that I interpret 'Marx's *one* term of abstract labour, to have *two* separate meanings, one general and one determinate'.[65] I do not; rather, I say that Marx's concept of abstract labour is general and that his concept of value-producing labour is determinate. I call value-producing labour 'practically abstract' labour because the thrust of Marx's argument is that commodity-producing labour is value-producing precisely because it is 'practically abstract', that is, because it involves a social practice, the market, that validates individual labours *as* human labour in the abstract. Marx writes, 'It is only by being exchanged that the products of labour acquire a socially uniform objectivity as values, which is distinct from their sensuously varied objectivity as articles of utility'.[66]

In footnote 66[67] Reuten attempts to discount what I describe as the most compelling quotation in support of my position.[68] I do not think that he succeeds. In the quoted passage Marx says that the 'mystical character of the commodity', which just is its value character, does not spring from the fact that human labour, which can always be viewed in the abstract ('physiologically'), is involved in its production. Of this Reuten says, 'I find it not very convincing to derive a core argument from something that is *not* said'.[69] He confuses not saying something with saying that something is not the case. Marx does the latter, which provides strong evidence. Then, Reuten examines the part of the quotation in which Marx says that the value character of the commodity arises from the commodity form and asserts that you can find confirmation there of the asocial 'abstract labour-embodied' theory. I do not see

64 Marx 1976a, p. 128. Compare this passage from Section Three, 'let us remember that commodities possess an objective character as values only in so far as they are all expressions of an identical social substance, human labour, that their objective character as values is therefore purely social' (Marx 1976a, pp. 138–9).

65 Reuten 2000, p. 155.

66 Marx 1976a, p. 166.

67 Reuten 2000, pp. 155–6.

68 Marx 1976a, p. 164.

69 Reuten 2000, pp. 155–6, n. 64.

how. Marx says, 'Whence, then, arises the enigmatic character of the product of labour, as soon as it assumes the form of a commodity? Clearly it arises from this form itself'.[70] The specific social form of wealth is what gives rise to value.[71]

Does Marx have a generally applicable concept of abstract labour? Reuten and I agree that he does. Does Marx have a concept of commodity-producing labour? (Here is where the problem of obviousness creeps in.) Of course he does. Can that be the same as his concept of abstract labour? Only if Marx thinks that all labour produces commodities, which he does not. Does Marx hold that commodity-producing labour, a socially specific form of labour, produces value? He does. Does Marx hold that commodity-producing labour produces value because it fits the description of being 'practically abstract', or rather, does Marx think that commodity-producing labour produces value precisely because it socially validates individual labours *as* abstract? He does. Is Marx's theory of value 'truly social'? Yes.

3 Why Marx Has been Mistaken for a Radical Ricardian

Reuten believes that I 'must be able to explain'[72] why Marx has been widely interpreted as a proponent of an asocial (radicalised) Ricardian labour theory of value. I do not think so; I believe that my interpretation is convincing on its own merits. Fifty million fans may not have been wrong about Elvis, but most interpreters have badly misunderstood Marx. Nevertheless, Reuten's question is a good one, and I will sketch some answers. (a) The key one is that the asocial standpoint of Ricardian value theory – and of 'economics' generally – is the natural ideology of capitalism. Marx observes:

> something which is only valid for this particular form of production ... namely the fact that the specific social character of private labours carried on independently of each other consists in their equality as human labour, and, in the product, assumes the form of the existence of value, appears to those caught up in the relations of commodity production ... to be just as ultimately valid as the fact that the scientific dissection of

70 Marx 1976a, p. 164.

71 'The characteristic which objects of utility have of being values is as much men's social product as is their language' (Marx 1976a, p. 167).

72 Reuten 2000, p. 157.

> the air into its component parts left the atmosphere itself unaltered in its physical configuration.[73]

Just because someone hangs up a shingle that says 'socialist' or even 'Marxist' does not mean that he or she has escaped the gravitational force of this ideology.

(b) It is not only that capitalist social relations naturally reproduce the ideologies of vulgar and classical political economy; they engender the many faces of bourgeois philosophy generally (e.g., revivals of the Hellenistic philosophies stoicism, scepticism and epicureanism; classical empiricism; Kant; utility theories; and 'state of nature' and social contract theories). Marx identified the British empiricist John Locke as the bourgeois philosopher within whose scope bourgeois political economy moved.[74] Bourgeois philosophy blocks understanding of neo-Aristotelian thinkers like Marx (and Hegel, for that matter.) Forms and formal causality fell into disgrace with bourgeois philosophy, but Marx and Hegel are all about forms.[75]

(c) Reuten correctly points up the inseparability of Marx's 'method' from the substantive points he makes in the critique of political economy. But, if Marx's 'method' is that of systematic dialectics, should we be surprised either that his 'method' or that his critique of political economy has been so misinterpreted, when Hegel has been a 'dead dog' for one hundred and seventy years? Joan Robinson's ridicule of 'Hegelian stuff and nonsense' is typical. How many philosophers and social scientists of the twentieth century have turned to Hegel because his philosophy is more scientific? How many have shared Marx's view that 'the mystification which the dialectic suffers in Hegel's hands by no means prevents him from being the first to present its general forms of motion in a comprehensive and conscious manner'?[76]

(d) Reuten fairly observes that in the twentieth century, classical political economy gave way to neoclassical economics, so students of economics would not have been steeped in the Ricardian labour theory of value. But that misses the deeper point about Marx's critique of 'economics'. That classical political economy dropped off the scene in favour of neoclassical economics (based on the pseudo-concept of 'utility' and a revival of vulgar ideas including the 'Trinity Formula') does not change the fact that 'economics' is bourgeois ideology.

---

73 Marx 1976a, p. 167.

74 Marx 1976a, pp. 512–13, n. 27.

75 On this topic see Meikle 1985 and Murray 1997a, included in the present volume as Chapter 2.

76 Marx 1976a, pp. 102–3.

Reuten's remark sidesteps the force of Marx's fundamental critique: there is no production in general; neither is there any science of production in general, yet that is exactly what 'economics' purports to be. Anyone, which was just about everyone, who missed the force of this fundamental criticism was in no position to catch the profound difference between Ricardo's asocial labour theory of value and Marx's exclusively social value theory of labour. As Paul Mattick Jr observes, 'Marx's critique – his "scientific revolution" – therefore involved not merely a reworking of economic categories but the construction of another set of concepts, explicitly social and historical ones'.[77] Training in 'economics' blocks out this truth.

(e) Language compounds these difficulties, for Marx generally uses the same terms as the political economists. 'Value' and 'labour theory of value' are cases in point: it is easy to think, 'same phrase, same concept.' Marx may compound this problem by not always being as critical of Ricardian theorists as he might. Then again, he was also eager to praise them for the advances they had made. Diane Elson's nice turn of phrase, 'value theory of labour', is helpful as it rotates one in the direction of thinking that Marx offers a theory of a particular social sort of labour.[78]

(f) Ricardo's value theory involves much simpler and more familiar ideas. It suits the ordinary scientific mentality, which wants to explain a dependent variable (price) in terms of an independent one (value). Marx's theory of value, according to which price and value are not independent, leaves that mentality perplexed and without the satisfaction it was seeking.

(g) As Felton Shortall points out, the fact that, after Marx first introduces the concepts of exchange value, value and price through a theory of abstract social value, for much of *Capital* he brackets important implications of that theory. He assumes that prices are simply the monetary expression of value, and he abstracts from any kind of 'devalorisation'. Both give the appearance of a 'quasi-embodied labour' theory of value.[79]

(h) Inertial factors in the reception of Marx should not be discounted. As for Sweezy's role in that history, I do not 'assume' that Sweezy 'does no justice to Marx'.[80] In my footnote 15,[81] I show that Sweezy does about as much justice

77 Mattick Jr 1993, p. 124. Or, as Martha Campbell puts it, 'there are no counterparts to Marx's economic concepts in either classical or utility theory' (Campbell 1993, p. 34).

78 See Elson 1979.

79 Shortall 1994, p. 303.

80 Reuten 2000, p. 157.

81 Murray 2000a, pp. 33–4.

to Marx as one can while still operating with a Ricardian mind-set. But that is not nearly justice enough.

Reuten is right that, as significant as our disagreements may be, when set against mainstream views they are 'very moderate indeed'.[82] Hopefully, we can sort out what differences remain; more importantly, we can hope that the 'truly social' theory of value and the criticism of 'economics' (and in particular of its blindness to specific social forms) will receive the hearing that they deserve.

82 Reuten 2000, p. 162.

CHAPTER 19

The Trouble with Ricardian Marxism: Comments on 'The Four Drafts of *Capital*: Towards a New Interpretation of the Dialectical Thought of Marx' by Enrique Dussel*

'We are perhaps nearer to Marx than ever', writes Enrique Dussel, hopefully. I believe that he is right and that this is so for several reasons. (1) The real subsumption of the globe under capital and its brood of social forms is further under way today than ever before. The world Marx foresaw is coming ever more into being. We even have a handy street name for it: 'McWorld'. (2) Many defective Marxisms, notably Stalinism, have come and, for the most part, gone. (3) As Dussel emphasises, the publication of previously little or unknown drafts of *Capital* puts us in a more favourable position than ever before to make fresh and better interpretations of Marx's thought. The *Paris Manuscripts* of 1844 and the *Grundrisse* have already made quite an impact on our understanding of Marx, and Dussel expects the publication in German and in English of the *Manuscript of 1861–3*, the 'second draft' of *Capital*, along with the publication (in German) of the *Manuscript of 1863–5*, the 'third draft' of *Capital*, to open a new era in Marxian scholarship. To these three I would like to add a fourth reason, one that Dussel tellingly does not mention.

(4) The fourth reason is the development of a current of interpreting Marx and his theory of value that stems from the work of I.I. Rubin, Roman Rosdolsky, Paul Mattick Sr, Hans-Georg Backhaus, Hans-Jürgen Krahl, and others, and that flows against the dominant current of interpretation. According to the dom-

---

* Originally published as 'The Trouble with Ricardian Marxism: Comments on "The Four Drafts of *Capital*: Towards a New Interpretation of the Dialectical Thought of Marx", by Enrique Dussel', *Rethinking Marxism*, Volume 14, Number 3 (2002), pp. 114–22, reprinted with the kind permission of the journal *Rethinking Marxism*.

This is a reply to 'The Four Drafts of *Capital*: Towards a New Interpretation of the Dialectical Thought of Marx' by Enrique Dussel and to 'Introduction to Dussel' by Fred Moseley, *Rethinking Marxism*, Volume 13, Number 3 (2001), pp. 10–26 and 1–9, respectively. Fred Moseley's reply to the present reply, 'The "Heart and Soul" of Marx's Critique of Capitalism: Exploitation or Social Form – or Both', appears in *Rethinking Marxism*, Volume 14, Number 3, pp. 122–8.

inant interpretation, Marx adopted the classical (Ricardian) labour theory of value and drove it to radical conclusions with his theory that surplus value results from the exploitation of wage workers by capitalists. The kind of Marxism that results from this misinterpretation of Marx's critique of political economy we can call Ricardian Marxism. As we will see, certain of his ideas involve Dussel in Ricardian Marxism. Moishe Postone, in his remarkable book *Time, Labor, and Social Domination*, which germinated in his reading of the *Grundrisse* in the mid-seventies, terms this dominant interpretation, 'Traditional Marxism'. Postone offers a penetrating reinterpretation of Marx's critical theory that brings us much nearer to Marx and begins to expose the extraordinary ability of Marxian theory to get to grips with the world of the twenty-first century. So I am wary of Dussel's judgment that the new access to the *Grundrisse* only 'somewhat modified the traditional vision of Marx'.[1] The crux of Postone's reinterpretation is that Marx's theory of value is not a theory of 'labour', as both 'Traditional Marxism' and classical political economy would have it, but a theory of the specific social form of labour in capitalism. There lies the key distinction between Ricardian Marxism and Marxian theory; quite a gulf separates the two. Though this fourth development is, in part, a consequence of the third, notably with respect to the *Grundrisse*, I would argue that it is the more significant of the two.

(5) Dussel argues that the urgency of social change arising from the growing poverty and immiseration of the 'peripheral' or 'underdeveloped' world also draws us nearer to Marx. While there is good sense to this observation, I have some misgivings about it. Did the misery of a war-ravaged Russia in 1917 draw it nearer to Marx? Yes, but ... The plight of impoverished people may make Marx attractive to them, but why should we expect those who live in enforced hunger and ignorance to be the ones to push past the facile understandings of Marx? Simone Weil scolded Marx on this score, wondering where he ever got the idea that dehumanisation – 'absolute poverty' – was the training ground for a more humane society. Criticism may well start from the negativity of the victim, but there is no royal road to science. Marx's *Capital* may be the most outstanding contribution to social science we have, but it poses enormous intellectual challenges.

Let me turn now to several brief and diverse remarks and work toward a couple of sustained critical points. Perhaps I am oversensitive on the matter, but Dussel's talk of Marx's constructing his categories and working up a dialectical construction, worries me.[2] As it is widely used today, the term 'con-

---

1 Dussel 2001, p. 11.

2 Dussel 2001, p. 16.

struction' belongs to a sceptical, bifurcating discourse that splits subjectivity from objectivity, conceptual schemes from what we seek to know. By contrast, I believe that Marx sided with Hegel when the latter wrote:

> But neither we nor the objects would have anything to gain by the mere fact that they possess being. The main point is not that they are, but what they are ... Laying aside therefore as unimportant this distinction between subjective and objective, we are chiefly interested in knowing what a thing is: i.e., its content, which is no more objective than it is subjective.[3]

For Marx, as for Hegel, the truth of our concepts was the focus of concern. Perhaps Dussel shares my worries here, because by page 16 he places the word 'construction' in scare quotes.

To bolster his thesis (which will be examined below) that the dialectic of *Capital* begins not with the commodity and money but with the transformation of money into capital, Dussel makes two dubious factual claims. First, of the topics addressed in Part I of *Capital* – namely the commodity, value and money – Dussel writes: 'for ten years (from 1857 to 1867), Marx did not return to this subject'.[4] Does this not overlook Marx's strenuous engagement in *Theories of Surplus-Value* with Samuel Bailey's criticism of Ricardian value theory? Second, Dussel asserts: 'Marx began the four drafts with the "chapter on capital"'.[5] This seems to be both false and misleading. False because the *Grundrisse* counts as the first draft, yet it begins with the 'chapter on money', and misleading because Marx had already written the *Urtext* and published *A Contribution to the Critique of Political Economy* when the three later drafts were written.

Dussel writes of Volume III being elaborated 'from the more concrete perspective of "competition"'.[6] I would be interested in Dussel's further thoughts on the relationship of the different parts of Volume III to Marx's plan to write a separate treatise on competition. I may have this wrong, but the passage suggests that Dussel thinks that the concept of 'price of production' in Volume III brings in what Marx called 'competition'. I am inclined to disagree. I think that by 'competition' Marx had in mind a more conceptually concrete level than that of 'prices of production'. But I would like to have a more definite idea of

3 Hegel 1975, p. 71.
4 Dussel 2001, p. 15.
5 Dussel 2001, p. 18.
6 Dussel 2001, p. 16.

what Marx did have in mind by 'competition' on which to base a judgment. The remarks Dussel makes on page 18, however, suggest that he believes that competition reaches beyond Volume III.

Dussel observes that Marx spells out the concept of real subsumption in the *Manuscripts of 1861–3*,[7] a topic that he takes up again in the portion of the *Manuscripts of 1863–5* that we know as the 'Unpublished Chapter VI' or *The Results of the Immediate Production Process*. And Dussel later observes that formal and real subsumption come up in Chapter Five of the 'fourth draft' of *Capital*.[8] I would like to make a couple of brief observations in this regard. First, I wonder if Dussel's research has shed light on either why Marx chose not to publish the *Results* with Volume I or why, in *Capital*, Marx seemed to back off from the terminology of formal and real subsumption, letting the concepts of absolute and relative surplus value, respectively, do the work instead. Dussel remarks that the problem of formal and real subsumption remained 'insufficiently addressed in the "Fourth Draft" due to the elimination of the "Unpublished Chapter VI"',[9] but I wonder if he has more to say as to why this happened. Second, I would add that in these two manuscripts, Marx introduces not only the concepts of real and formal subsumption of labour under capital but also the important concepts of ideal and hybrid or transitional subsumption. Ideal subsumption involves conceiving of some phenomenon as if it were subsumed under capital when it actually is not. When we talk of a wage earner's labour power as his or her 'human capital' or when we talk of social networks (even bowling leagues and church organisations) as 'social capital', we engage in ideal subsumption. Hybrid subsumption occurs when non-capitalist phenomena are subjected to the power of capital as, for example, when non-capitalist forms of production (whether these be state socialist or patriarchal familial or other) throw their wares into the world market. For the 'peripheral world' these concepts of ideal and, especially, hybrid subsumption deserve considerable attention from Marxian theorists.

Dussel runs two different points together when he insists, first, that 'the person or the subjectivity of "living labour" ... by not being [a product] of labour, cannot have any exchange value' and, second, that 'living labour' cannot have exchange value.[10] Here Dussel's humanism gets the better of his good judgment. These are two different claims; moreover, while the second is true

7 Dussel 2001, p. 17.
8 Dussel 2001, p. 19.
9 Dussel 2001, p. 17.
10 Dussel 2001, p. 22.

and an important Marxian thesis, the first is false. Slaves can be bred and sold. That fact does not take away from Marx's point that capitalism is based on free wage labour.

Dussel writes provocatively of Marx's 'great Hegelian precision' and his being '"Hegelianized" more and more until 1880',[11] but I would like to know what exactly he understands by 'Hegelian precision' and also what he thinks remains of Marx's early criticisms of Hegel.

So much for the diverse remarks.

One of Dussel's main and most controversial theses is the following:

> *Capital*, its dialectical, logical, essential discourse begins with the 'transformation of money into capital.' On this will rest the fundamental aspect of our pretension to a total reinterpretation of the dialectical discourse of Marx ... The question of the commodity and money were necessary assumptions for the 'explanation' (that is, to know what money is: 'objectified' living labour), but *Capital* begins when, from circulation and as a contradiction, 'living labour' [*lebendige Arbeit*] is 'subsumed' in a labour-process that is the first emergence of capital by the negation of money as money (in the payment of the first wage).[12]

The little word 'begins' causes big problems in interpreting and evaluating the claim Dussel makes here. As Fred Moseley says, 'I am not sure exactly what Dussel means here by "starting point"'.[13]

While I agree with the criticism Moseley makes of one interpretation of Dussel's claim, I will defend Dussel in a qualified way by appealing to a different sense of 'starting point'. I will go on to make some critical comments that I think go beyond Moseley's critique. To begin, I note a revealing ambiguity that Moseley reproduces without comment when he writes that for Dussel the real conceptual starting point of *Capital* is 'living labour, or the confrontation between living labour and capital as objectified labour'.[14] Which one is it: 'living labour' or the confrontation between it and capital? The two are far from being the same: the first leaves capital out of the starting point; the second brings it in. Though Dussel is often keen on saying that 'living labour' is Marx's true starting point (I will say more on that later), in the passage just given, that

11 Dussel 2001, p. 17.

12 Dussel 2001, pp. 18–19.

13 Moseley 2001, p. 6.

14 Ibid.

is not what he writes. According to that passage, the beginning of *Capital* is not simply 'living labour' but rather the subsumption of 'living labour' under capital.

What does Dussel mean when he says that *Capital's* 'dialectical, logical, essential, discourse' begins not with the commodity, value and money but with the subsumption of 'living labour' under capital? I suggest that he means two things, one defensible and one not. First the defensible idea. In the introduction to the *Grundrisse* Marx writes:

> In the succession of the economic categories, as in any other historical, social science, it must not be forgotten that their subject – here, modern bourgeois society – is always what is given, in the head as well as in reality, and that these categories therefore express the forms of being, the characteristics of existence, and often only individual sides of this specific society, this subject, and that therefore this society by no means begins only at the point where one can speak of it *as such*; this holds *for science as well*. This is to be kept in mind because it will shortly be decisive for the order and sequence of the categories.[15]

So *Capital* starts from – and never quits – the reality of modern capitalist society, and Marx is perfectly clear that the subsumption of 'living labour' (in the specific social form of free wage labour, I would add) under capital is what makes modern capitalism possible. Insofar as Dussel means to call these facts to mind, his point is well taken.

But what can we make of the claim that *Capital's* 'dialectical, logical, essential, discourse begins with the "transformation of money into capital"'?[16] The following, I think: Dussel judges Marx's whole treatment of the commodity, money and generalised simple commodity circulation in Part I of Volume I of *Capital* to be 'inessential'; moreover, Part I does not belong to the dialectical development of categories in *Capital*. Dussel cordons off Part I as some purely analytical preliminary to the real, the dialectical, action of *Capital*. Moseley's criticism of this move is based on a point that Dussel concedes – namely, that the concepts developed in Part I are 'necessary assumptions' for the real starting point.[17] Moseley writes: 'it seems to me that this introduction is nonetheless logically necessary. One cannot simply pass over the analysis in part I

15 Marx 1973, p. 106.
16 Dussel 2001, p. 18.
17 Dussel 2001, p. 18.

and start with part 2'.[18] By insisting on the logical necessity to begin with Part 1, Moseley naturally concludes that Part 1 is the logical starting point of *Capital*. For Moseley, logically necessary assumptions are logically prior: Dussel simply fails to draw the proper conclusion from a point that he himself makes.

I agree, but I believe that Dussel's thesis is more problematic than Moseley indicates, for it reveals a mistaken conception of the nature of Marxian dialectics, one that leads to substantive errors and omissions. Dussel fails to recognise two distinctive, mutually implicating features of Marxian dialectical presentation: (1) it rejects the ordinary scientific conception of the essence as independent of appearance and (2) it forsakes a linear, Euclidean conception of the build-up of a scientific presentation. By contrast, Marx adopts a conception of essence that recognises appearance as essential; as Hegel says, the essence must appear as something other than itself. For example, Marx conceives of the sphere of simple commodity circulation as a necessary appearance form of the circulation of capital. Consequently, Marx conceives of the development of the dialectic of the categories as involving mutual presupposition; for example, the circulation of capital presupposes the generalisation of commodity exchange, and the generalisation of commodity exchange presupposes the generalisation of the circulation of capital. This structure of mutual presupposition throws the very idea of a starting point into a cocked hat. Where does a circle of mutually presupposing categories 'start'?

The trouble with Ricardian Marxism – notably, its inability to see the gulf separating Marxian value theory from the Ricardian labour theory of value; to recognise that, for Marx, human emancipation is to be achieved only by overthrowing value, not by eliminating surplus value through a fancied equitable redistribution of value – cannot be separated from Ricardian Marxism's failure to grasp the dialectical nature of Marx's concepts and mode of presentation in *Capital*. Failing to understand that Marx conceives of appearance as essential to the essence, Ricardian Marxism fails to grasp that price is the necessary form of appearance of value, so that price cannot be conceived of in the way that ordinary value theories (including Ricardian value theory) do. Price is not the dependent variable and value the independent variable. The point of Marxian value theory is that value and its necessary form of appearance, price, are not independent. Consequently, the upshot of Marxian value theory is that there can be no price theory in the ordinary sense – that is, no theory wherein price is the dependent variable explained by value, the

18 Moseley 2001, p. 7.

independent variable. The further implications of this line of thought – for example that there is no 'transformation problem' – are considerable.

To recognise that simple commodity circulation is a necessary aspect of a deeper, more complex reality – the circulation of capital – opens up two important insights. (1) There is no 'simple commodity production', so the very idea of 'market socialism' becomes problematic. (2) If the market is a necessary aspect of the reality of capitalist accumulation, then the liberal idea that the 'free market' is devoid of compulsory social goals is an illusion. Market societies live under the compulsion to keep capital accumulating; as Marx was quick to point out, capitalist crises (depressions) bring this truth home all too convincingly.

Dussel's ambiguity as to the real starting point of *Capital* – is it 'living labour' or is it the subsumption of 'living labour' under capital? – turns into outright vacillation in one section of his paper, '"Living labour" versus "objectified labour": the logic of *Capital*'. He writes: 'The dialectical logical movement of *Capital* begins in the radical contradiction of "living labour" and "objectified labour" as capital'.[19] For this to be true, capital must belong to the starting point of Marx's dialectic: without capital there is no contradiction. But next we read of 'living labour, as the absolute point of departure of the dialectical discourse, prior to the existence of capital'.[20] Here capital is excluded from the 'absolute point of departure of the dialectical discourse'. It should be noted that the two quotes Dussel provides in defence of his position support only the first claim, not the second. Nevertheless, a page later Dussel writes, '"Living labour" ... is the generative category for all of Marx's remaining categories'.[21] Writing in the same vein another page later, Dussel elaborates: 'The development of the concept of capital ... is accomplished, step by step, departing from "living labour" and subsequently unfolding all the moments of "objectified labour": value, surplus value, etc.'.[22] Marx's dialectic does not proceed this way, nor could it. None of the value categories that Marx develops in *Capital* can be unfolded from 'living labour'. It would seem that Dussel unintentionally concedes this later on when he effectively grants that 'living labour' is a general category. He writes that 'living labour' can be subsumed under capital or under existing socialism, which surely implies that the categories specific to capitalism cannot be unfolded from it.[23]

19 Dussel 2001, p. 20.
20 Dussel 2001, p. 21.
21 Ibid.
22 Dussel 2001, p. 22.
23 Dussel 2001, p. 23.

Dussel vacillates not only in his claims about the true beginning of *Capital* but also in his use of 'living labour'. Sometimes 'living labour' functions as what it is, a general category making no reference to capitalist relations; at other times it functions surreptitiously as a category specific to capitalist society. When Dussel writes, 'living labour is absolute poverty',[24] he must be thinking of wage labour. The root of Dussel's second vacillation is his readiness to treat 'living labour' as an actual kind of labour, when it really is just a general abstraction applicable to any human society. The dilemma for Dussel comes to this: if he takes 'living labour' to be a general category, there is no way to extract all – or any – of the value categories out of it. (You cannot squeeze juice out of 'the Fruit'.) If, on the other hand, he takes 'living labour' to mean the specific social sort of labour characteristic of capitalism – that is, free wage labour – then he must abandon the idea of 'living labour' independent of capital as the absolute starting point of Marx's dialectic.

The role that Dussel assigns to 'living labour' betrays the Ricardian Marxist cast of his thinking. How? Because 'living labour' is a generally applicable category, not a socially and historically determinate one like wage labour, and what is characteristic of Ricardian, including Ricardian Marxist, value theory is that it conceives of value simply as 'objectified' or 'embodied' labour. Marx conceives of value in a radically different way: value is a social fetish that is a necessary by-product not of 'labour' but of the peculiar social sort of labour characteristic of capitalist societies. Is there anything that goes beyond Ricardian value theory in Dussel's references to 'objectified labour' or his statement: 'The "law of value" indicates that exchange value can have no other source than "living labour"'?[25] I do not see it. Ricardian value theory and Marxian value theory are worlds apart: Marx's theory is entirely a matter of the specific social form of wealth and of labour in capitalism; Ricardian value theory is oblivious to the problematic of social form. Where Marxian theory looks to a revolution in the social form of wealth, a revolution against value, Ricardian Marxism overlooks the problematic of the social form of wealth. It attends only to the 'How much'? and 'How distributed'? questions. Ricardian Marxism misses Marx's critique of value as a peculiar social form of wealth and imagines the political task as bringing about a just redistribution of 'wealth'.

The hallmark of Ricardian Marxism is that it takes the theory of surplus value to be the heart and soul of Marx's critique of capitalism. So it is not surprising that, when Dussel comes to put his finger on the pulse of Marx's 'ethical

---

24 Dussel 2001, p. 21.

25 Dussel 2001, p. 22.

critique' of capitalism, it turns out to be the unjust appropriation of 'unpaid labour' by capitalists. Dussel writes: 'The "unpaid" component of labour that produces surplus-value as surplus labour is invisible to bourgeois "morality". But it is not invisible to Marx's critique (to the transcendental "ethic")'.[26] But this 'unjust appropriation' was visible to any number of Left Ricardians going back at least to the 1840s, when, in *The Poverty of Philosophy*, Marx harshly criticised Proudhon and others for the attempt to turn value, the bourgeois measure of wealth and standard of justice, against bourgeois society. Of the English Ricardian socialist John Francis Bray, Marx comments:

> Mr. Bray does not see that this egalitarian relation, this corrective ideal that he would like to apply to the world, is itself nothing but the reflection of the actual world, and that therefore it is totally impossible to reconstitute society on a basis which is nothing but an embellished shadow of it.[27]

The radical redistributionist program of Ricardian Marxism is a mirage of capital's own making. Marx reissued that barbed criticism late in his life when he railed against the 'bourgeois phrases' of the authors of the Ricardian socialist *Gotha Programme*, who proclaimed: 'Labour is the source of all wealth'. Marx replied:

> Labour is *not the source* of all wealth. *Nature* is just as much the source of use values ... The bourgeois have very good grounds for fancifully ascribing *supernatural creative power* to labour, since it follows precisely from the fact that labour depends on nature, that the man who possesses no other property than his labour power must, in all conditions of society and culture, be the slave of other men who have made themselves the owners of the material conditions of labour.[28]

For Marx, far from being invisible to bourgeois 'morality', Dussel's Ricardian Marxist condemnation of the extraction of surplus value falls within its orbit.

Ricardian thinking and the sort of humanism that Marx criticised in Feuerbach belong to the same (bourgeois) mind-set, so it is not surprising that we find an abstract humanism at the core of Dussel's conception of Marx's 'ethical' critique. Marx wrote:

---

26 Dussel 2001, p. 24.
27 Marx 1963b, p. 144.
28 Marx 1966a, p. 3.

> For a society of commodity producers, whose general social relation of production consists in the fact that they treat their products as commodities, hence as values ... Christianity with its religious cult of man in the abstract, more particularly in its bourgeois development, i.e. in Protestantism, Deism, etc., is the most fitting religion.[29]

An 'ethical critique' from the 'transcendentality of living labour' must be quite abstract in nature, precisely because 'living labour' is a general category applicable across human history.[30] I do not say that such a category is without critical power; neither do I believe that Marx dismissed it. But to concentrate on it alone is to fail to see the force of Marx's point, made in the 'Theses on Feuerbach', that the human essence is not to be taken in abstraction from the specific social relations in which humans find themselves. The fact that 'living labour' is not the 'absolute starting point' of *Capital* tells us that Marx took his own ideas to heart.

If, as Dussel hopes, the emancipatory potential of Marxian theory is to come to fruition in the twenty-first century, it will take a rethinking that moves beyond the mind-set of Ricardian Marxism and abstract humanism to which Dussel's own concepts retain a lingering attachment.

29 Marx 1976a, p. 172.

30 Dussel 2001, p. 23.

Bibliography

Albritton, Robert, and John Simoulidis (eds.) 2003, *New Dialectics and Political Economy*, Basingstoke: Palgrave Macmillan.

Alderman, Liz, and Landon Thomas Jr 2012, 'In Europe, Stagnation as a Way of Life', *New York Times*, February 10, p. B1.

Anderson, Elizabeth 1993, *Value in Ethics and Economics*, Cambridge: Harvard University Press.

Anscombe, G.E.M. 1961, 'Aristotle', in *Three Philosophers*, by G.E.M. Anscombe and Peter Geach, Ithaca: Cornell University Press.

Aristotle 1946, *The Politics of Aristotle*, translated by Ernest Barker, Oxford: Oxford University Press.

Arthur, Christopher J. 1979, 'Dialectic of the Value-Form', in *Value: The Representation of Labor in Capitalism*, edited by Diane Elson, Atlantic Highlands, NJ: Humanities Press.

——— 1986, *Dialectics of Labour: Marx and his Relation to Hegel*, Oxford: Basil Blackwell.

——— 1993, 'Hegel's *Logic* and Marx's *Capital*', in *Marx's Method in 'Capital': A Reexamination*, edited by Fred Moseley, Atlantic Highlands, NJ: Humanities Press.

——— 1997, 'Against the Logical-Historical Method: Dialectical Derivation versus Linear Logic', in *New Investigations of Marx's Method*, edited by Fred Moseley and Martha Campbell, Atlantic Highlands, NJ: Humanities Press.

——— 2002a, *The New Dialectic and Marx's 'Capital'*, Leiden/Boston: Brill.

———2002b, 'Capital in General and Marx's *Capital*', in *The Culmination of Capital: Essays on Volume III of Marx's Capital*, edited by Martha Campbell and Geert Reuten, Basingstoke: Palgrave Macmillan.

——— 2002c, 'Capital, Competition, and Many Capitals', in *The Culmination of Capital: Essays on Volume III of Marx's Capital*, edited by Martha Campbell and Geert Reuten, Basingstoke: Palgrave Macmillan.

——— 2003, 'The Problem of Use-Value for a Dialectic of Capital', in *New Dialectics and Political Economy*, Basingstoke: Palgrave Macmillan.

——— 2004, 'Money and the Form of Value', in *The Constitution of Capital: Essays on Volume I of Marx's 'Capital'*, edited by Riccardo Bellofiore and Nicola Taylor, Basingstoke: Palgrave Macmillan.

——— 2006, 'Money and Exchange', *Capital & Class* 30, 3: 7–35.

Arthur, Christopher J. and Geert Reuten (eds.) 1998, *The Circulation of Capital: Essays on Volume Two of Marx's 'Capital'*, Basingstoke: Macmillan.

Augustine 1995, *Against the Academicians* and *The Teacher*, translated by Peter King, Indianapolis: Hackett Publishing Company, Inc.

Avineri, S. (ed.) 1968, *Karl Marx on Colonialism and Modernization*, Garden City, NY: Doubleday.

Backhaus, Hans-Georg 1969, 'Zur Dialektik der Wertform', in *Beiträge zur marxistischen Erkenntnistheorie*, edited by Alfred Schmidt, Frankfurt: Suhrkamp Verlag.

——— 1980, 'On the Dialectics of the Value-Form', *Theses Eleven*, 1: 99–120.

Bacon, Francis 1960 [1620], 'The New Organon', in *The New Organon and Related Writings*, edited by Fulton H. Anderson, Indianapolis: Bobbs-Merrill.

——— 1994 [1620], *Novum Organum*, edited and translated by Peter Urbach and John Gibson, Chicago: Open Court.

Bailey, Samuel 1837, *Money and Its Vicissitudes in Value*, London: Effingham Wilson, Royal Exchange.

——— 1967 [1825], *A Critical Dissertation on the Nature, Measure, and Causes of Value*, New York: Augustus Kelley Publishers.

Balibar, Étienne 1970 [1968], 'The Basic Concepts of Historical Materialism', in *Reading 'Capital'*, translated by Ben Brewster, New York: Pantheon Books.

Banaji, Jairus 1979, 'From the Commodity to Capital: Hegel's Dialectic in Marx's *Capital*', in *Value: The Representation of Labour in Capitalism*, edited by Diane Elson, London: CSE Books.

Baudrillard, Jean 1975, *The Mirror of Production*, translated by Mark Poster, St. Louis, MO: Telos Press.

——— 1981, *For a Critique of the Political Economy of the Sign*, translated by Charles Levin, St. Louis, MO: Telos Press.

——— 1997, 'Consumer Society', in *Reflections on Commercial Life: An Anthology of Classic Texts from Plato to the Present*, edited by Patrick Murray, London: Routledge.

Becker, Gary 1976, *The Economic Approach to Human Behavior*, Chicago: University of Chicago Press.

Bellofiore, Riccardo 2009, 'A Ghost Turning into a Vampire, The Concept of Capital and Living Labour', in *Re-reading Marx: New Perspectives after the Critical Edition*, edited by Riccardo Bellofiore and Roberto Fineschi, Basingstoke: Palgrave Macmillan.

Beneria, Lourdes, and Catharine Stimpson (eds.) 1987, *Women, Households and the Economy*, New Brunswick, NJ: Rutgers University Press.

Benhabib, Seyla 1986, *Critique, Norm, and Utopia: A Study of the Foundations of Critical Theory*, New York: Columbia University Press.

Berkeley, George 1948, *The Works of George Berkeley, Bishop of Cloyne*, edited by A.A. Luce and T.E. Jessop, London: Nelson.

——— 1957 [1710], *A Treatise Concerning the Principles of Human Knowledge*, edited by Colin M. Turbayne, Indianapolis: The Bobbs-Merrill Company, Inc.

Bernstein, Richard 1971, *Praxis and Action*, Philadelphia: University of Pennsylvania Press.

Bidet, Jacques 2005, 'The Dialectician's Interpretation of *Capital*', *Historical Materialism*, 13, 2: 121–46.

Black, R.D. Collison 1987, 'Utility', in *The New Palgrave: A Dictionary of Economics* in four volumes, edited by John Eatwell, Murray Milgate et al., London: Macmillan.

Bonefeld, Werner, et al. (eds.) 1995, *Emancipating Marx, Open Marxism* 3, London: Pluto Press.

Braverman, Harry 1974, *Labor and Monopoly Capital: The Degradation of Work in the Twentieth Century*, New York: Monthly Review Press.

Bubner, Rüdiger 1988, 'Logic and Capital: On the Method of a "Critique of Political Economy"', in *Essays in Hermeneutics and Critical Theory*, translated by Eric Matthews, New York: Columbia University Press.

Burns, Tony, and Ian Fraser (eds.) 2000, *The Hegel-Marx Connection*, Basingstoke: Macmillan.

Campbell, Martha 1993a, 'The Commodity as Necessary Form of Product', in *Economics as Worldly Philosophy: Essays on Political and Historical Economics in Honor of Robert L. Heilbroner*, edited by Ron Blackwell, Jaspal Chatha and Edward J. Nell, New York: St. Martin's Press.

——— 1993b, 'Marx's Concept of Economic Relations and the Method of *Capital*', in *Marx's Method in 'Capital': A Reexamination*, edited by Fred Moseley, Atlantic Highlands, NJ: Humanities Press.

——— 1997, 'Marx's Theory of Money: A Defense', in *New Investigations of Marx's Method*, edited by Fred Moseley and Martha Campbell, Atlantic Highlands, NJ: Humanities Press.

——— 2002, 'The Credit System', in *The Culmination of Capital: Essays on Volume III of Marx's 'Capital'*, edited by Martha Campbell and Geert Reuten, Basingstoke: Palgrave Macmillan.

——— 2004, 'Value Objectivity and Habit', in *The Constitution of Capital: Essays on Volume I of Marx's 'Capital'*, edited by Riccardo Bellofiore and Nicola Taylor, Basingstoke: Palgrave Macmillan.

——— 2005, 'Marx's Explanation of Money's Functions: Overturning the Quantity Theory', in *Marx's Theory of Money: Modern Appraisals*, edited by Fred Moseley, Basingstoke: Palgrave Macmillan.

——— 2013, 'The Transformation of Money into Capital in Marx's *Capital*', in *Marx's Laboratory. Critical Interpretations of the 'Grundrisse'*, edited by Riccardo Bellofiore, Peter Thomas and Guido Starosta, Leiden/Boston: Brill.

Campbell, Martha, and Geert Reuten (eds.) 2002, *The Culmination of Capital: Essays on Volume III of Marx's 'Capital'*, Basingstoke: Palgrave Macmillan.

Campus, Antonietta 1987, 'Marginalist Economics', in *The New Palgrave: A Dictionary of Economics* in four volumes, edited by John Eatwell, Murray Milgate et al., London: Macmillan.

Carchedi, Guglielmo 1984, 'The Logic of Prices as Values', *Economy and Society* 13, 4: 431–55.
——— 1986, 'The Logic of Prices as Values', in *The Value Dimension*, edited by Diane Elson, London: Routledge & Kegan Paul.
——— 1988, 'Marxian Price Theory and Modern Capitalism', *International Journal of Political Economy* 18, 3: 6–112.
——— 1993, 'Marx's Logic of Inquiry and Price Formation', in *Marx's Method in 'Capital'*, edited by Fred Moseley, Atlantic Highlands, NJ: Humanities Press.
Cassidy, John 1997, 'The Return of Karl Marx', *The New Yorker*, October 20 and 27.
Castells, Manuel 1989, *The Informational City*, London: Blackwell.
Castoriadis, Cornelius 1978, 'From Marx to Aristotle, from Aristotle to Marx', *Social Research* 45, 4: 667–738.
Cerutti, Furio 1984, 'The "Living" and the "Dead" in Karl Marx's Theory', in *Rethinking Marx*, edited by Sakari Hänninen and Leena Paldán, Berlin: Argument-Verlag.
Clarke, Simon 1982, *Marx, Marginalism and Modern Sociology*, Basingstoke: Macmillan.
Cohen, Gerald A. 1978, *Karl Marx's Theory of History: A Defense*, Princeton: Princeton University Press.
Coleman, John 1996, 'Under the Cross and Flag', *America*, May 11, 16: 6–15.
Colletti, Lucio 1972, 'Bernstein and the Marxism of the Second International', in *From Rousseau to Lenin*, translated by John Merrington and Judith White, New York: Monthly Review Press.
Collins, James 1972, *Interpreting Modern Philosophy*, Princeton: Princeton University Press.
Cullen, Bernard 1979, *Hegel's Social and Political Thought: An Introduction*, New York: St. Martin's Press.
Davidson, Donald 1984 [1974], 'The Very Idea of a Conceptual Scheme', in *Inquiries into Truth and Interpretation*, New York: Oxford University Press.
de Beauvoir, Simone 1989 [1949], *The Second Sex*, edited and translated by H.M. Parshley, New York: Vintage Books.
Deranty, Jean-Philippe 2005, 'Hegel's Social Theory of Value', *The Philosophical Forum*, 36, 3: 307–31.
Descartes, René 1960 [1641], *The Meditations Concerning First Philosophy*, in *Discourse on Method and Meditations*, translated by Laurence J. Lafleur, Indianapolis: The Bobbs-Merrill Company, Inc.
——— 2000, *Philosophical Essays and Correspondence*, edited by Roger Ariew, Indianapolis: Hackett Publishing Company, Inc.
Dickens, Charles 1990 [1854], *Hard Times*, edited by George Ford and Sylvere Monod, New York: W.W. Norton & Company.
Dobb, Maurice 1968, *Political Economy and Capitalism: Some Essays in Economic Tradition*, Routledge and Kegan Paul: London.

Dussel, Enrique 2001, 'The Four Drafts of *Capital*: Toward a New Interpretation of the Dialectical Thought of Marx', *Rethinking Marxism*, 13, 1: 10–26.

Eatwell, John, Murray Milgate and Peter Newman (eds.) 1987, *The New Palgrave: A Dictionary of Economics* in four volumes, London: Macmillan.

Editors of Marx 1969, 'Bibliographical Notice' to Marx, in *Resultate des unmittelbaren Produktionsprozesses*, Archiv Sozialistischer Literatur 17, Frankfurt: Verlag Neue Kritik.

Eldred, Michael, and Marnie Hanlon 1981, 'Reconstructing Value-Form Analysis', *Capital & Class*, 13: 24–60.

Elson, Diane 1979, 'Marx's Value Theory of Labour', in *Value: The Representation of Labour in Capitalism*, edited by Diane Elson, London: CSE Books.

Elster, John 1985, *Making Sense of Marx*, Cambridge: Cambridge University Press.

Engels, Friedrich 1976 [1886], Preface to the English Edition, in Karl Marx, *Capital: Volume One*, translated by Ben Fowkes, Harmondsworth: Penguin Books.

——— 1978 [1884], 'Preface' to *Capital: Volume Two*, translated by David Fernbach, London: Penguin.

Ferguson, C.E. 1972, *Microeconomic Theory*, third edition, Homewood: Richard D. Irwin, Inc.

Fine, Ben, and Dimitris Milonakis 2009, *From Political Economy to Economics: Method, the social and the historical in the evolution of economic theory*, London and New York: Routledge.

Fraser, Nancy 1997 [1995], 'From Redistribution to Recognition? Dilemmas of Justice in a "Post-Socialist" Age', in *Justice Interruptus: Critical Reflections on the 'Postsocialist' Condition*, London: Routledge.

Freeman, Alan 2011, 'Money, Labour and Logic: A Critical Comparison', *Critique of Political Economy*, 1: 155–76.

Frisby, David 1978, 'Introduction', in *The Philosophy of Money*, translated by Tom Bottomore and David Frisby, London: Routledge and Kegan and Paul.

Furner, James 2004, 'Marx's Critique of Samuel Bailey', *Historical Materialism*, 12, 2:89–110.

Grossman, Henryk 1992 [1929], *Law of Accumulation and the Breakdown of the Capitalist System*, London: Pluto Press.

Gonzalez, Maya, and Michael Posner 2011, 'Capitalist Production and Social Form: The Paradox of the Value-Form Paradigm', *Critique of Political Economy*, 1: 197–216.

Habermas, Jürgen 1971, *Knowledge and the Human Interests*, translated by Jeremy J. Shapiro, Boston: Beacon Press.

Harvey, David 1973, *Social Justice and the City*, Baltimore: Johns Hopkins University Press.

——— 1982, *The Limits to Capital*, Oxford: Basil Blackwell.

——— 1989, *The Condition of Postmodernity*, Oxford: Basil Blackwell.

Hegel, G.W.F. 1952 [1821], *Hegel's Philosophy of Right*, translated by T.M. Knox, Oxford: Oxford University Press.

——— 1955, *Lectures on the History of Philosophy III*, translated by E.S. Haldane and Frances H. Simson, New York: The Humanities Press, Inc.

——— 1962, *Lectures on the Philosophy of Religion* [1821, 1824, 1827, 1831], Volume I, translated by E.B. Speirs and J. Burdon Sanderson, edited by E.B. Speirs, Atlantic Highlands, NJ: Humanities Press.

——— 1969 [1812, 1813, 1816], *Hegel's Science of Logic*, translated by A.V. Miller, Atlantic Highlands, NJ: Humanities Press.

——— 1975 [1817], *Hegel's Logic*, translated by William Wallace, Oxford: Clarendon Press.

——— 1977 [1806–7], *The Phenomenology of Spirit*, translated by A.V. Miller, Oxford: Clarendon Press.

——— 1979, *System of Ethical Life (1802/3) and First Philosophy of Spirit (Part III of the System of Speculative Philosophy 1803/4)*, edited and translated by H.S. Harris and T.M. Knox, Albany: State University of New York Press.

——— 1983, *Hegel and the Human Spirit: A Translation of the Jena Lectures on Philosophy of Spirit (1805–6)* with commentary by Leo Rauch, Detroit: Wayne State University Press.

——— 1991a [1821], *Elements of the Philosophy of Right*, edited by Allen W. Wood, translated by H.B. Nisbet, Cambridge: Cambridge University Press.

——— 1991b [1817], *The Encyclopedia Logic*, translated by T.F. Geraets, W.A. Suchting and H.S. Harris, Indianapolis: Hackett Publishing Company, Inc.

——— 1995, *Lectures on Natural Right and Political Science: The First Philosophy of Right* (Heidelberg 1817–18), translated by J. Michael Stewart and Peter C. Hodgson, Berkeley and Los Angeles: University of California Press.

Heinrich, Michael 2004, 'Ambivalences of Marx's Critique of Political Economy as Obstacles for the Analysis of Contemporary Capitalism', available at http://www.oekonomiekritik.de/310Ambivalences.rtf.

——— 'Reconstruction or Deconstruction? Methodological Controversies about Value and Capital, and New Insights from the Critical Edition', in *Re-reading Marx: New Perspectives after the Critical Edition*, edited by Riccardo Bellofiore and Roberto Fineschi, Basingstoke, Hampshire: Palgrave Macmillan.

Hochschild, Arlie 1989, *The Second Shift*, New York: Avon Books.

Hont, István, and Michael Ignatieff (eds.) 1983, *Wealth and Virtue: the Shaping of Political Economy in the Scottish Enlightenment*, Cambridge: Cambridge University Press.

Horkheimer, Max 1974 [1947], *Eclipse of Reason*, New York: Seabury Press.

Hume, David 1978 [1739, 1740], *A Treatise of Human Nature*, second edition, edited by L.A. Selby-Bigge, Oxford: Clarendon Press.

——— 1985, *Essays: Moral, Political, and Literary*, edited by Eugene F. Miller, Indianapolis: Liberty Classics.

——— 1989 [1739, 1740], *A Treatise of Human Nature*, edited by P.H. Nidditch, Oxford: Clarendon Press.

James, William 1981 [1907], *Pragmatism*, edited by Bruce Kuklick, Indianapolis: Hackett Publishing Company.

Jameson, Fredric 1983, 'Postmodernism and Consumer Society', in *The Anti-Aesthetic*, edited by Hal Foster, Port Townsend, Washington: Bay Press.

——— 1991, *Postmodernism, or, The Cultural Logic of Late Capitalism*, Durham: Duke University Press.

Jevons, William Stanley 1970 [1871], *The Theory of Political Economy*, edited by R.D. Collison Black, Harmondsworth: Penguin Books.

Kant, Immanuel 1965 [1787], *The Critique of Pure Reason*, translated by N. Kemp Smith, Atlantic Highlands, NJ: Humanities Press.

Kicillof, Alex, and Guido Starosta 2007, 'On Materiality and Social Form: A Political Critique of Rubin's Value-Form Theory', *Historical Materialism*, 15, 3: 9–43.

Kingston, Maxine Hong 1976, *The Woman Warrior: Memoirs of a Girlhood among Ghosts*, New York: Vintage.

Kliman, Andrew 2000, 'Marx's Concept of Intrinsic Value', *Historical Materialism*, 6: 89–113.

——— 2011, 'On Capital's Historical Specificity and Price Determination: Comments on the Value-form Paradigm', *Critique of Political Economy*, 1: 177–96.

Korsch, Karl 1970 [1923], *Marxism and Philosophy*, translated by Fred Halliday, New York: Monthly Review Press.

Lear, Jonathan 1988 *Aristotle: The Desire to Understand*, Cambridge: Cambridge University Press.

Lebowitz, Michael 1992, *Beyond Capital: Marx's Political Economy of the Working Class*, London: Macmillan.

——— 1998, 'Explaining the Closure of Marx', *Historical Materialism*, 3: 171–88.

——— 2000, 'Answering Shortall', *Historical Materialism*, 6: 125–32.

Le Goff, Jacques 1980, 'Merchant's Time and Church Time in the Middle Ages', in *Time, Work, and Culture in the Middle Ages*, translated by Arthur Goldhammer, Chicago: University of Chicago Press.

Likitkijsomboon, Pichit 1995, 'Marxian Theories of Value-Form', *Review of Radical Political Economics*, 27, 2: 73–105.

Locke, John 1960 [1690], *Two Treatises of Government*, edited by Peter Laslett, Cambridge: Cambridge University Press.

——— 1975 [1690], *An Essay Concerning Human Understanding*, edited by P.H. Nidditch, Oxford: Oxford University Press.

Loeb, Louis E. 1981, *From Descartes to Hume*, Ithaca: Cornell University Press.

Lukács, Georg 1971 [1922], *History and Class Consciousness*, translated by Rodney Livingstone, Cambridge: The MIT Press.

Lyotard, Jean-François 1984, *The Postmodern Condition: A Report on Knowledge*, translated by Geoff Bennington and Brian Masummi, Minneapolis: University of Minnesota Press.

MacIntyre, Alasdair 1984 [1981], *After Virtue*, second edition, Notre Dame: University of Notre Dame Press.

Mandel, Ernest 1976, 'Introduction to *Results of the Immediate Production Process*', in *Capital: Volume One*, translated by Ben Fowkes, New York: Vintage Books.

——— 1978, 'Introduction to *Capital, Volume II*', in *Capital: Volume Two*, translated by David Fernbach, Harmondsworth: Penguin Books.

Marx, Karl 1939a; 1941 [1857–8], *Grundrisse der Kritik*, Frankfurt: Europaische Verlagsanstalt.

——— 1939b; 1941 [1858], *Urtext*, in *Grundrisse der Kritik*, Frankfurt: Europaische Verlagsanstalt.

——— 1942, 'Marx to Kugelmann, 6 March 1868', in *Karl Marx, Friedrich Engels: Briefe über 'Das Kapital'*, Berlin: Dietz Verlag.

——— 1954a, *Briefe über 'Das Kapital'*, Berlin: Dietz Verlag.

——— 1954b, 'Marx an Leske, 1. August 1846', in *Karl Marx, Friedrich Engels: Briefe über 'Das Kapital'*, Berlin: Dietz Verlag.

——— 1963a, 'Letter to P.V. Annenkov (December, 28, 1846)' in *The Poverty of Philosophy*, New York: International Publishers.

——— 1963b [1847], *The Poverty of Philosophy*, New York: International Publishers.

——— 1963c [1862–3], *Theories of Surplus-Value, Part I*, edited by S.W. Ryazanskaya, translated by E. Burns, London: Lawrence & Wishart.

——— 1964a, *Economic and Philosophic Manuscripts of 1844*, edited by Dirk J. Struick, translated by Martin Milligan, New York: International Publishers.

——— 1964b [1857–8], *Pre-Capitalist Economic Foundations*, translated by Jack Cohen and E. Hobsbawm, New York: International Publishers.

——— 1966a [1875], *Critique of the Gotha Programme*, edited by C.P. Dutt, New York: International Publishers.

——— 1966b [1867], 'Ware und Geld' (*Das Kapital*, 1. Auflage 1867, 1. Buch Kapital 1), in *Karl Marx, Friedrich Engels: Studienausgabe in 4 Bänden, Band 2: Politische Oekonomie*, edited by Iring Fetscher, Frankfurt: Fischer Taschenbuch Verlag.

——— 1967a [1837], 'Letter to his Father: On a Turning-Point in Life', in *Writings of the Young Marx on Philosophy and Society*, edited by Lloyd Easton and Kurt Guddat, New York: Anchor Books.

——— 1967b [1844], 'From Excerpt-Notes of 1844', in *Writings of the Young Marx on Philosophy and Society*, edited by Lloyd Easton and Kurt Guddat, New York: Anchor Books.

——— 1967c [1845], 'Theses on Feuerbach', in *Writings of the Young Marx on Philosophy and Society*, edited by Lloyd Easton and Kurt Guddat, New York: Anchor Books.

——— 1967d, *The Communist Manifesto* [1848], translated by Samuel Moore, Harmondsworth: Penguin Books.

——— 1968a, 'Letter of 1877', in *Karl Marx on Colonialism and Modernization*, edited by Shlomo Avineri, Garden City: Doubleday.

——— 1968b [1862–3], *Theories of Surplus-Value, Part II*, edited by S.W. Ryazanskaya, translated by Renate Simpson, London: Lawrence & Wishart.

——— 1969a [1863–4], *Il Capitale: Libro I, capitol VI inedito*, edited by Bruno Maffi, Florence: La Nuova Italia.

——— 1969b [1863–4], *Resultate des unmittelbaren Produktionsprozesses*, Archiv Sozialistischer Literatur 17, Frankfurt: Verlag Neue Kritik.

——— 1970a [1859], *A Contribution to the Critique of Political Economy*, edited by Maurice Dobb, translated by S.W. Ryazanskaya, New York: International Publishers.

——— 1970b [1843], *Critique of Hegel's 'Philosophy of Right'*, edited by Joseph O'Malley, translated by Annette Jolin and Joseph O'Malley, Cambridge: Cambridge University Press.

——— 1971a [1862–3], *Theories of Surplus-Value, Part III*, edited by S.W. Ryazanskaya and Richard Dixon, translated by Jack Cohen and S.W. Ryazanskaya, London: Lawrence & Wishart.

——— 1971b [1863–4], *Un Chapitre inedit du Capital*, edited and translated by R. Dangeville, Paris: Union générale d'Éditions

——— 1972 [1894] *Das Kapital: Kritik der politischen Okonomie, Band III, Der Gesamtprozess der kapitalistischen Produktion*, edited by Friedrich Engels, *Marx Engels Werke*, Volume 25, Berlin: Dietz Verlag.

——— 1973 [1857–8], *Grundrisse*, translated by Martin Nicolaus, Harmondsworth: Penguin Books.

——— 1974 [1862–3], *Theorien über den Mehrwert: Dritter Teil*, in *Marx Engels Werke*, Volume 26.3, Berlin: Dietz Verlag.

——— 1975a [1844], 'Comments on James Mill, *Elements d'économie politique*', in *Karl Marx, Frederick Engels: Collected Works*, Volume 3: *Marx and Engels: 1843–4*, New York: International Publishers.

——— 1975b [1844], 'Contribution to the Critique of Hegel's Philosophy of Law: Introduction', translated by Martin Milligan and Barbara Ruhemann, in *Karl Marx, Frederick Engels: Collected Works*, Volume 3: *Marx and Engels: 1843–4*, New York: International Publishers.

——— 1975c, *Economic and Philosophic Manuscripts of 1844*, in *Karl Marx, Frederick Engels: Collected Works*, Volume 3: *Marx and Engels: 1843–4*, New York: International Publishers.

——— 1975d, 'Letters from Marx to His Father', in *Karl Marx, Frederick Engels: Collected Works*, Volume 1: *Karl Marx: 1835–43*, New York: International Publishers.

——— 1975e, 'Notes (1879–80) on Adolph Wagner', in *Karl Marx: Texts on Method*, edited and translated by Terrell Carver, New York: Harper and Row.

——— 1976a [1894], *Capital: Volume One*, translated by Ben Fowkes, Harmondsworth: Penguin Books.

——— 1976b [1863–4], 'Results of the Immediate Production Process', translated by Rodney Livingstone, in *Capital: Volume One*, translated by Ben Fowkes, Harmondsworth: Penguin Books.

——— 1976c [1845], 'Theses on Feuerbach', in *Karl Marx, Frederick Engels: Collected Works*, Volume 5: *Marx and Engels: 1845–7*, New York: International Publishers.

——— 1976d, *Zur Kritik der Politischen Ökonomie (Manuscript 1861–3)*, in *Karl Marx, Friedrich Engels, Gesamtausgabe* (MEGA), Zweite Abteilung, Band 3, Teil 1, Berlin: Dietz Verlag.

——— 1977 [1843], 'On the Jewish Question', in *Karl Marx: Selected Writings*, edited by David McLellan, Oxford: Oxford University Press.

——— 1978a [1885], *Capital: Volume Two*, translated by David Fernbach, Harmondsworth: Penguin Books.

——— 1978b [1867], 'The Value-Form', *Capital & Class*, 4, Spring.

——— 1981 [1894], *Capital: Volume Three*, translated by David Fernbach, Harmondsworth: Penguin Books.

——— 1982, *Zur Kritik der Politischen Ökonomie (Manuscript 1861–3)*, in *Karl Marx, Friedrich Engels, Gesamtausgabe* (MEGA), Zweite Abteilung, Band 3, Teil 6, Berlin: Dietz Verlag.

——— 1986 [1857–8], 'Economic Manuscripts of 1857–8', edited by Larisa Miskievich, translated by Ernst Wangermann, in *Karl Marx, Frederick Engels: Collected Works*, Volume 28, London: Lawrence and Wishart.

——— 1987a [1857–8], 'Economic Manuscripts of 1857–8', edited by Larisa Miskievich, translated by Victor Schnittke and Yuri Sdobnikov, in *Karl Marx, Frederick Engels: Collected Works*, Volume 29, London: Lawrence and Wishart.

——— 1987b [1858], 'Original Text' (*Urtext*), in 'Economic Manuscripts of 1957–8', edited by Larisa Miskievich, translated by Victor Schnittke and Yuri Sdobnikov, in *Karl Marx, Frederick Engels: Collected Works*, Volume 29, London: Lawrence and Wishart.

——— 1988a, *Economic Manuscript of 1861–3*, edited by Larisa Miskievich, translated by Ben Fowkes and Emile Burns, in *Karl Marx, Frederick Engels: Collected Works*, Volume 30, New York: International Publishers.

——— 1988b, 'Letter to Engels (December 9, 1861)', in *Marx's Theory of Scientific Knowledge*, Atlantic Highlands, NJ: Humanities Press.

——— 1988c [1863–4], *Resultate des unmittelbaren Produktionsprozesses*, in *Karl Marx and Friedrich Engels: Gesamtausgabe* (MEGA), Section II, Volume 4.1, Berlin: Dietz Verlag.

——— 1989, *Economic Manuscript of 1861–3 (Continuation)*, edited by Salo Ryazanskaya, translated by Emile Burns, Renate Simpson and Jack Cohen, in *Karl Marx, Frederick Engels: Collected Works*, Volume 31, New York: International Publishers.

——— 1991, *Economic Manuscript of 1861–3 (Continuation)*, edited by Salo Ryazanskaya and Larisa Miskievich, translated by Ben Fowkes, Emile Burns, Renate Simpson, and Jack Cohen, in *Karl Marx, Frederick Engels: Collected Works*, Volume 33, New York: International Publishers.

——— 1994 [1863–4], 'Results of the Direct Production Process', in *Karl Marx, Frederick Engels: Collected Works*, Volume 34, translated by Ben Fowkes, New York: International Publishers.

——— 2008 [1863–4], *Risultati del processo di produzione immediate*, in *Il Capitale: Libro I*, edited by R. Fineschi, translated by G. Sgro, Rome/Naples: La citta del Sole-Editori Riuniti.

Marx, Karl and Friedrich Engels 1954, *Karl Marx, Friedrich Engels: Briefe über 'Das Kapital'*, Berlin: Dietz Verlag.

Marx, Karl, and Friedrich Engels 1956–73, *Karl Marx, Friedrich Engels: Werke* (MEW), 39 Volumes, Berlin: Dietz Verlag.

——— 1975a [1845], *The Holy Family*, translated by Richard Dixon and Clemens Dutt, in *Karl Marx, Frederick Engels: Collected Works*, Volume 4: *Marx and Engels: 1845–7*, New York: International Publishers.

——— 1975b, *Karl Marx and Frederick Engels: Selected Correspondence: 1846–95*, translated by Dona Torr, Westport: Greenwood Press, Publishers.

——— 1975c, *Karl Marx, Frederick Engels: Collected Works*, Volume 3: *Marx and Engels: 1843–4*, New York: International Publishers.

——— 1976a, *The Communist Manifesto* [1848], in *Karl Marx, Frederick Engels: Collected Works*, Volume 6: *Marx and Engels: 1845–8*, New York: International Publishers.

——— 1976b [1845–6], *The German Ideology*, translated by Clemens Dutt, W. Lough et al., in *Karl Marx, Frederick Engels: Collected Works*, Volume 5: *Marx and Engels: 1845–7*, New York: International Publishers.

——— 1976c [1845], *The Holy Family*, in *Karl Marx, Frederick Engels: Collected Works*, Volume 4: *Marx and Engels: 1845–7*, New York: International Publishers.

——— 1978 [1972], *The Marx-Engels Reader*, second edition, edited by Robert C. Tucker, New York: W.W. Norton & Company.

Mattick Jr, Paul 1981, 'Some Aspects of the Value-Price Problem', *Économies et societies* (Cashiers de I'SMEA Series), 15, 6–7: 275–81.

——— 1986, *Social Knowledge: An Essay on the Nature and Limits of Social Science*, Armonk, NJ: M.E. Sharpe.

——— 1993, 'Marx's Dialectic', in *Marx's Method in 'Capital': A Reexamination*, edited by Fred Moseley, Atlantic Highlands, NJ: Humanities Press.

——— 1997, 'Theory as Critique: On the Argument in *Capital*', in *New Investigations of Marx's Method*, edited by Fred Moseley and Martha Campbell, Atlantic Highlands, NJ: Humanities Press.

Mauss, Marcel 1990, *The Gift*, translated by W.D. Halls, New York: W.W. Norton.

McCarthy, George 1990, *Marx and the Ancients: Classical Ethics, Social Justice, and Nineteenth-Century Political Economy*, Savage, MD: Rowman & Littlefield.

——— 1994, *Dialectics and Decadence: Echoes of Antiquity in Marx and Nietzsche*, Savage, MD: Rowman & Littlefield.

Meaney, Mark 2002, *Capital as Organic Unity: The Role of Hegel's 'Science of Logic' in Marx's 'Grundrisse'*, Dordrecht: Kluwer Academic Publishers.

MEGA editors 1988, 'Introduction' to Marx, *Resultate des unmittelbaren Produktionsprozesses*, in *Karl Marx and Friedrich Engels: Gesamtausgabe* (MEGA), Section II, Volume 4.1, Berlin: Dietz Verlag.

Meikle, Scott 1985, *Essentialism in the Thought of Karl Marx*, LaSalle, Ill: Open Court Publishing Co.

——— 2009, 'Marx, the European Tradition, and the Philosophic Radicals', in *Karl Marx and Contemporary Philosophy*, edited by Andrew Chitty and Martin McIvor, Basingstoke, Hampshire: Palgrave Macmillan.

Menger, Carl 1950, *Principles of Economics*, edited and translated by J. Dingwell and B.F. Hoselitz, Glencoe, Illinois: Free Press.

Milios, John, Dimitri Dimoulis and George Economakis 2002, *Karl Marx and the Classics: An Essay on Value, Crises and the Capitalist Mode of Production*, Aldershot, Hampshire: Ashgate.

Mill, John Stuart 1994 [1836], 'On the Definition of Political Economy and the Method of Investigation Proper to It', in *The Philosophy of Economics*, second edition, edited by Daniel M. Hausman, Cambridge: Cambridge University Press.

Miller, Arthur 1977 [1949], *Death of a Salesman*, edited by Gerald Weales, New York: Penguin Books.

Mohun, Simon (ed.) 1994, *Debates in Value Theory*, Basingstoke: Macmillan.

Morishima, Michio 1973, *Marx's Economics*, New York: Cambridge University Press.

Moseley, Fred 1993a, 'Marx's Logical Method and the "Transformation Problem"', in *Marx's Method in 'Capital': A Reexamination*, edited by Fred Moseley, Atlantic Highlands, NJ: Humanities Press.

——— (ed.) 1993b, *Marx's Method in 'Capital': A Reexamination*, Atlantic Highlands, NJ: Humanities Press.

——— 1993c, 'Explanatory Progress or Retrogression in Economics? A Marxian Response to Hausman', paper presented at Mt. Holyoke College, June 1993.

——— 1995, 'Marx's Economic Theory: True or False? A Marxian Response to Blaug's

Appraisal', in *Heterodox Economic Theories: True or False?* Aldershot, Brookfield: Edward Elgar Publishing.

——— 1998, 'Marx's Reproduction Schemes and Smith's Dogma', in *The Circulation of Capital: Essays on Volume Two of Marx's 'Capital'*, edited by Christopher J. Arthur and Geert Reuten, Basingstoke: Macmillan.

——— 2000, 'The New Solution to the Transformation Problem: A Sympathetic Critique', *Review of Radical Political Economics*, 32, 2: 282–316.

——— 2001, 'Introduction to "The Four Drafts of *Capital*: Toward a New Interpretation of the Dialectical Thought of Marx"', *Rethinking Marxism*, 13, 1: 1–9.

——— 2004, 'Money and Totality: Marx's Logic in Volume I of *Capital*', in *The Constitution of Capital: Essays on Volume I of Marx's 'Capital'*, edited by Riccardo Bellofiore and Nicola Taylor, Basingstoke: Palgrave Macmillan.

——— 2009, 'The Development of Marx's Theory of the Distribution of Surplus-Value in the Manuscripts of 1862–3', in *Re-reading Marx: New Perspectives after the Critical Edition*, edited by Riccardo Bellofiore and Roberto Fineschi, Basingstoke: Palgrave Macmillan.

Moseley, Fred, and Martha Campbell (eds.) 1997, *New Investigations of Marx's Method*, edited by Fred Moseley and Martha Campbell, Atlantic Highlands, NJ: Humanities Press.

Muller, Jerry 2002, *The Mind and the Market: Capitalism in Modern European Thought*, New York: Alfred A. Knopf.

Murphy, James Bernard 1993, *The Moral Economy of Labor: Aristotelian Themes in Economic Theory*, New Haven: Yale University Press.

Murray, Patrick 1983, 'Marx Minus Hegel: Further Discussion of [Derek] Sayer', *Philosophy of the Social Sciences*, 13, 4, 487–99.

——— 1988a, *Marx's Theory of Scientific Knowledge*, Atlantic Highlands, NJ: Humanities Press International, Inc.

——— 1988b, 'Karl Marx as a Historical Materialist Historian of Political Economy', *History of Political Economy*, 20, 1: 95–105.

——— 1993a, 'The Difference between Use-Value and Utility and the Difference it Makes: Grounds for a Marxian Critique of Neoclassical Theories of Value and Price', unpublished paper presented at Mt. Holyoke College, June 1993.

——— 1993b, 'The Necessity of Money: How Hegel Helped Marx Surpass Ricardo's Theory of Value', in *Marx's Method in 'Capital': A Reexamination*, edited by Fred Moseley, Atlantic Highlands, NJ: Humanities Press.

——— 1997a, 'Redoubled Empiricism: Social Form and Formal Causality in Marxian Theory', in *New Investigations of Marx's Method*, edited by Fred Moseley and Martha Campbell, Atlantic Highlands, NJ: Humanities Press.

——— (ed.) 1997b, *Reflections on Commercial Life: An Anthology of Classic Texts from Plato to the Present*, London: Routledge.

——— 1998, 'Beyond the "Commerce and Industry" Picture of Capital', in *The Circulation of Capital: Essays on Volume Two of Marx's 'Capital'*, Basingstoke: Macmillan.

——— 2000a, 'Marx's "Truly Social" Labour Theory of Value: Part I, Abstract Labour in Marxian Value Theory', *Historical Materialism*, 6: 27–65.

——— 2000b, 'Marx's "Truly Social" Labour Theory of Value: Part II, How is Labour that Is Under the Sway of Capital *Actually* Abstract?', *Historical Materialism*, 7: 99–136.

——— 2002a, 'The Illusion of the Economic: The Trinity Formula and the "religion of everyday life"', in *The Culmination of Capital: Essays on Volume III of Marx's 'Capital'*, edited by Martha Campbell and Geert Reuten, Basingstoke: Palgrave Macmillan.

——— 2002b, 'The Trouble with Ricardian Marxism: Comments on "The Four Drafts of *Capital*: Toward a New Interpretation of the Dialectical Thought of Marx"', *Rethinking Marxism*, 14, 3: 114–22.

——— 2002c, 'Reply to Geert Reuten', *Historical Materialism*, 10, 1: 155–76.

——— 2003, 'Things Fall Apart: Historical and Systematic Dialectics and the Critique of Political Economy', in *New Dialectics and Political Economy*, edited by Robert Albritton and John Simoulidis, Basingstoke: Palgrave Macmillan.

——— 2004, 'The Social and Material Transformation of Production by Capital: Formal and Real Subsumption in *Capital*, Volume I', in *The Constitution of Capital*, edited by Riccardo Bellofiore and Nicola Taylor, Basingstoke: Palgrave Macmillan.

——— 2005a, 'Money as Displaced Social Form: Why Value cannot be Independent of Price', in *Marx's Theory of Money: Modern Appraisals*, edited by Fred Moseley, Basingstoke: Palgrave Macmillan.

——— 2005b, 'The New Giant's Staircase', *Historical Materialism*, 13, 2: 61–83.

——— 2006, 'In Defence of the "Third Thing Argument": A Reply to James Furner's "Marx's Critique of Samuel Bailey"', *Historical Materialism*, 14, 2: 149–68.

——— 2009a, 'The Place of "The Results of the Immediate Production Process" in *Capital*', in *Re-reading Marx: New Perspectives after the Critical Edition*, edited by Riccardo Bellofiore and Roberto Fineschi, Basingstoke, Hampshire: Palgrave Macmillan.

——— 2009b, 'Value, Money and Capital in Hegel and Marx', in *Karl Marx and Contemporary Philosophy*, edited by Andrew Chitty and Martin McIvor, Basingstoke, Hampshire: Palgrave Macmillan.

——— 2011, 'Avoiding Bad Abstractions: A Defense of Co-constitutive Value-Form Theory', *Critique of Political Economy*, 1: 217–48.

——— 2013, 'Unavoidable Crises: Reflections on Backhaus and the Development of Marx's Value-Form Theory in the *Grundrisse*', in *Marx's Laboratory: Critical Interpretations of the 'Grundrisse'*, edited by Riccardo Bellofiore, Peter Thomas and Guido Starosta, Leiden/Boston: Brill.

——— 2014, 'The Secret of Capital "Laid Bare": How Hegel Helped Marx Overcome

Ricardo's Theory of Profit', in *Marx's* Capital *and Hegel's* Logic: A Reexamination, edited by Fred Moseley and Tony Smith, Leiden/Boston: Brill.

Murray, Patrick, and Jeanne Schuler 2000, 'Recognizing Capital: Some Barriers to Public Discourse about Capital', in *Race, Class, and Community Identity* (Volume 1 of *Radical Philosophy Today*), edited by Andrew Light and Mechthild Nagel, Amherst, MA: Humanity Books.

——— 2008 'Karl Marx and the Critique of Bourgeois Philosophy', *The Modern Schoolman*, 85: 163–80.

——— n.d., *False Moves: Basic Problems with Philosophy*, unpublished book manuscript.

Napoleoni, Claudio 1975 [1973], *Smith, Ricardo Marx*, Oxford: Blackwell.

Nussbaum, Martha 1990, *Love's Knowledge: Essays on Philosophy and Literature*, Oxford: Oxford University Press.

——— 2000, *Women and Human Development: The Capabilities Approach*, Cambridge: Cambridge University Press.

Nussbaum, Martha, and Amartya Sen (eds.) 1993, *The Quality of Life*, Oxford: Clarendon Press.

Oakley, Allen 1983, *The Making of Marx's Critical Theory: A Bibliographical Analysis*, London: Routledge and Kegan Paul.

Offe, Claus 1984, *Contradictions of the Welfare State*, edited and translated by John Keane, Cambridge, MA: MIT Press.

Ollman, Bertell 1971, *Alienation: Marx's Conception of Man in Capitalist Society*, Cambridge: Cambridge University Press.

——— 1993, *Dialectical Investigations*, New York: Routledge.

Pilling, Geoffrey 1980, *Marx's 'Capital': Philosophy and Political Economy*, London: Routledge & Kegan Paul.

Pippin, Robert 1982, *Kant's Theory of Form*, New Haven: Yale University Press.

Polanyi, Karl 1957 [1944], *The Great Transformation*, Boston: Beacon Press.

——— 1968, 'Aristotle Discovers the Economy', in *Primitive, Archaic, and Modern Economics: Essays of Karl Polanyi*, edited by George Dalton, Garden City: Doubleday.

Postone, Moishe 1986, 'Anti-Semitism and National Socialism', in *Germans and Jews since the Holocaust*, edited by Anson Rabinbach and Jack Zipes, New York: Holmes and Meier.

——— 1993, *Time, Labour, and Social Domination: A Reinterpretation of Marx's Critical Theory*, Cambridge: Cambridge University Press.

——— 1999, 'Contemporary Historical Transformations: Beyond Postindustrial and Neo-Marxist Theories', *Current Perspectives in Social Theory*, Volume 19.

Postman, Neil 1985, *Amusing Ourselves to Death*, New York: Penguin Books.

Quine, W.V.O. 1953 [1951], 'Two Dogmas of Empiricism', in *From a Logical Point of View*, New York: Harper Torchbooks.

Rauner, Robert 1960, *Samuel Bailey and the Classical Theory of Value*, London: The London School of Economics and Political Science.

Rawls, Johns 1970, *A Theory of Justice*, Cambridge: Harvard University Press.

Reichelt, Helmut 1995, 'Why did Marx Conceal his Dialectical Method?', in Bonefeld et al. (eds.) 1995.

Reichenbach, Hans 1951, *The Rise of Scientific Philosophy*, Berkeley: University of California Press.

Reuten, Geert 1993, 'The Difficult Labor of a Social Theory of Value', in *Marx's Method in 'Capital': A Reexamination*, edited by Fred Moseley, Atlantic Highlands, NJ: Humanities Press.

——— 1995, 'Conceptual Collapses: A Note on Value-Form Theory', *Review of Radical Political Economics*, 27, 3: 104–10.

———1997, 'The Notion of Tendency in Marx's 1894 Law of Profit', in *New Investigations of Marx's Method*, edited by Fred Moseley and Martha Campbell, Atlantic Highlands, NJ: Humanities Press.

——— 1998, 'The Status of Marx's Reproduction Schemes: Conventional or Dialectical Logic?', in *The Circulation of Capital: Essays on Volume Two of Marx's 'Capital'*, edited by Christopher J. Arthur and Geert Reuten, Basingstoke: McMillan.

——— 2000, 'The Interconnection of Systematic Dialectics and Historical Materialism', *Historical Materialism*, 7, 1: 137–65.

——— 2003, 'On "Becoming Necessary" in an Organic Systematic Dialectic: The Case of Creeping Inflation', in *New Dialectics and Political Economy*, edited by Robert Albritton and John Simoulidis, Basingstoke: Palgrave Macmillan.

——— 2005, 'Money as a Constituent of Value', in *Marx's Theory of Money: Modern Appraisals*, edited by Fred Moseley, Basingstoke: Palgrave Macmillan.

——— 2009, 'Marx's General Rate of Profit Transformation: Methodological and Theoretical Obstacles – an Appraisal based on the 1864–5 Manuscript of *Das Kapital III*', in *Re-reading Marx: New Perspectives after the Critical Edition*, edited by Riccardo Bellofiore and Roberto Fineschi, Basingstoke: Palgrave Macmillan.

Reuten, Geert, and Michael Williams 1989, *Value-Form and the State*, London: Routledge.

Ricardo, David 1951 [1817], *On the Principles of Political Economy and Taxation*, edited by Piero Sraffa with the collaboration of M.H. Dobb, Cambridge: Cambridge University Press.

Ritzer, George 2000, The *McDonaldization of Society*, Thousand Oaks: Pine Forge Press.

Robbins, Lionel 1994 [1935], *An Essay on the Nature and Significance of Economic Science*, in *The Philosophy of Economics*, second edition, edited by Daniel M. Hausman, Cambridge: Cambridge University Press.

Rosdolsky, Roman 1977 [1968], *The Making of Marx's 'Capital'*, translated by Pete Burgess, London: Pluto Press.

Rosenthal, J. 1998, *The Myth of Dialectics*, London: Macmillan.

Roth, Regina 2009, 'Karl Marx's Original Manuscripts in the Marx-Engels-Gesamtausgabe (MEGA): Another View on *Capital*', in *Re-reading Marx: New Perspectives after the Critical Edition*, edited by Riccardo Bellofiore and Roberto Fineschi, Basingstoke: Palgrave Macmillan.

Rubel, Maximilien 1981, *Rubel on Karl Marx: Five Essays*, edited by Joseph O'Malley and Keith Algozin, Cambridge: Cambridge University Press.

Rubin, Isaak Ilyich 1972 [1928], *Essays on Marx's Theory of Value*, translated by Milos Samardzija and Fredy Perlman, Detroit: Black & Red.

——— 1994 [1927], 'Abstract Labour and Value in Marx's System', in *Debates in Value Theory*, edited by Simon Mohun, Basingstoke: Macmillan.

Saad-Filho, Alfredo 2002, *The Value of Marx*, London: Routledge.

Sandel, Michael 1996, *Democracy's Discontent*, Cambridge, MA: Harvard University Press.

Sassen, Saskia 1998, *Globalization and Its Discontents*, New York: The New Press.

Sayer, Derek 1979, *Marx's Method*, Sussex: The Harvester Press.

——— 1987, *The Violence of Abstraction*, Oxford: Basil Blackwell.

Schiller, Friedrich 1967 [1795], *On the Aesthetic Education of Man: In a Series of Letters*, edited and translated by Elizabeth M. Wilkinson and L.A. Willoughby, Oxford: Oxford University Press.

Schor, Juliet B. 1992, *The Overworked American*, New York: Basic Books.

Schuler, Jeanne 1988–9, 'Back to Union Station', *Telos*, 88: 55–69.

Schweickart, David 2002, *After Capitalism*, Lanham, MD: Rowman & Littlefield.

Shortall, Felton 1994, *The Incomplete Marx*, Aldershot, Hampshire: Avebury.

——— 2000, 'Reply to Lebowitz', *Historical Materialism*, 6, 1: 115–24.

Simmel, Georg 1971 [1903], 'The Metropolis and Mental Life', in *On Individuality and Social Forms*, edited by Donald N. Levine, Chicago: University of Chicago Press.

——— 1997 [1903], 'The Metropolis and Modern Mental Life', in *Reflections on Commercial Life: An Anthology of Classic Texts from Plato to the Present*, edited by Patrick Murray, London: Routledge.

Smith, Adam 1979 [1776], *An Inquiry into the Nature and Causes of the Wealth of Nations*, edited by R.H. Campbell and A.S. Skinner, Oxford: Oxford University Press.

Smith, Tony 1990, *The Logic of Marx's 'Capital': Replies to Hegelian Criticisms*, Albany: State University of New York Press.

——— 1993, *Dialectical Social Theory and its Critics*, Albany: State University of New York Press.

——— 1994, 'Flexible Production and the Capital/Wage Labour Relation in Manufacturing', in *Capital & Class*, 18, 2: 39–64.

——— 1997, 'Marx's Theory of Social Forms and Lakatos's Methodology of Scientific Research Programs', in *New Investigations of Marx's Method*, edited by Fred Moseley and Martha Campbell, Atlantic Highlands, NJ: Humanities Press.

——— 1998, 'Value Theory and Dialectics', *Science & Society*, Special Issue: Dialectics: The New Frontier, edited by Bertell Ollman and Tony Smith, 62, 3: 460–70.

——— 1999a, 'Brenner and Crisis Theory: Issues in Systematic and Historical Dialectics', *Historical Materialism*, 5, 1: 145–78.

——— 1999b, 'The Relevance of Systematic Dialectics to Marxian Thought: A Reply to Rosenthal', *Historical Materialism*, 4, 1: 215–40.

——— 2000, *Technology and Capital in the Age of Lean Production*, Albany: State University of New York Press.

——— 2003, 'Systematic and Historical Dialectics: Towards a Marxian Theory of Globalization', in *New Dialectics and Political Economy*, edited by Robert Albritton and John Simoulidis, Basingstoke: Palgrave Macmillan.

——— 2006, *Globalisation: A Systematic Marxian Account*, Leiden/Boston: Brill.

Sohn-Rethel, Alfred 1978 [1970, 1972], *Intellectual and Manual Labor: A Critique of Epistemology*, translated by Martin Sohn-Rethel, London: Macmillan.

Starosta, Guido 2012, 'Cognitive Commodities and the Value-Form', *Science and Society*, 76, 3, 365–92.

Steedman, Ian 1977, *Marx After Sraffa*, London: New Left Books.

Steinbeck, John 1986 [1939], *The Grapes of Wrath*, New York: Viking.

Stroud, Barry 1993, '"Gilding and Staining" the World with "Sentiments" and "Phantasms"', *Hume Studies*, 19, 2: 253–72.

Sweezy, Paul 1942, *The Theory of Capitalist Development*, New York: Modern Reader Press.

Thompson, Edward Palmer 1967, 'Time, Work-Discipline and Industrial Capitalism', *Past and Present*, 38: 56–97.

Tomba, Massimiliano 2009, 'From History of Capital to History in Capital', in *Re-reading Marx: New Perspectives after the Critical Edition*, edited by Riccardo Bellofiore and Roberto Fineschi, Basingstoke: Palgrave Macmillan.

Torrens, Robert 1821, *Essay on the Production of Wealth*, London.

Tucker, Robert C. 1961, *Philosophy and Myth in Karl Marx*, Cambridge: Cambridge University Press.

Uchida, Hiroshi 1988, *Marx's* Grundrisse *and Hegel's* Logic, London: Routledge.

Veblen, Thorstein, 'Pecuniary Emulation', from *The Theory of the Leisure Class*, in *Reflections on Commercial Life: An Anthology of Classic Texts from Plato to the Present*, edited by Patrick Murray, London: Routledge.

Vercellone, Carlo 2007, 'From Formal Subsumption to General Intellect: Elements for a Marxist Reading of the Thesis of Cognitive Capitalism', *Historical Materialism*, 15, 1: 13–36.

Von Neumann, John and Oskar Morgenstern 1953 [1944], *Theory of Games and Economic Behavior*, 2nd ed., Princeton: Princeton University Press.

Waismann, Friedrich 1968 [1945], 'Verifiability', in *The Theory of Meaning*, edited by G.H.R. Parkinson, Oxford: Oxford University Press.

Weber, Max 1958 [1905], 'The Spirit of Capitalism', in *The Protestant Ethic and the Spirit of Capitalism*, translated by Talcott Parsons, New York: Charles Scribner's Sons.
——— 1997 [1905], 'The Spirit of Capitalism', in *Reflections on Commercial Life: An Anthology of Classic Texts from Plato to the Present*, edited by Patrick Murray, London: Routledge.
Welch, C. 1987, 'Utilitarianism', in *The New Palgrave: A Dictionary of Economics* in four volumes, edited by John Eatwell, Murray Milgate et al., London: Macmillan.
Wendling, Amy E. 2009, *Karl Marx on Technology and Alienation*, London: Palgrave Macmillan.
White, James D. 1994, 'Marx: From "The Critique of Political Economy" to *Capital*', *Studies in Marxism*, 1, 89–105.
Willet, Sabin 2002, *Present Value, A Novel*, New York: Villard Books.
Williams, Bernard 1972, *Morality*, Cambridge: Cambridge University Press.
——— 1973, 'A Critique of Utilitarianism', in *Utilitarianism For and Against*, edited by J.J.C. Smart and Bernard Williams, Cambridge: Cambridge University Press.
——— 1985, *Ethics and the Limits of Philosophy*, Cambridge: Harvard University Press.
Winfield, Richard Dien 1988, *The Just Economy*, New York and London: Routledge.
Wood, Allen W. 1981, *Karl Marx*, London: Routledge.
——— 1991, 'Editor's Introduction', in *Elements of the Philosophy of Right*, edited by Allen W. Wood, translated by H.B. Nisbet, Cambridge: Cambridge University Press.
——— 2004 [1981], *Karl Marx*, 2nd ed., London: Routledge.

Dissertations

Badeen, Dennis. 'A Marxist Account of the Ontological Foundations of Neoclassical Economics', Ph.D. diss., York University (Canada), 2011.
Schuler, Jeanne A. 'Logics of Theoretical and Practical reason in G.W.F. Hegel's *Phenomenology of Spirit*', Ph.D. diss., Washington University, 1983.

Index

www.ingramcontent.com/pod-product-compliance
Ingram Content Group UK Ltd.
Pitfield, Milton Keynes, MK11 3LW, UK
UKHW021853100926
8556IPUK00020B/1209

9 781608 468225